I dedicate this book to my family: Marsha, Andy, Miwako, Hilary, Bruce, Jason, May and Kai.

CONTENTS

Huddling or Clumping • Microhabitat Selection • Shivering Thermogenesis • Non-shivering Thermogenesis • Regional Heterothermy • Nightly Torpor • Hibernation • Combinations of adaptive traits • References

ACKNOWLEDGEMENTS

I thank all my colleagues at the University of Alaska Fairbanks for their insights and perspectives over the years. Many of them and their students performed the research upon which much of the book is based. Their studies are referenced in the chapter bibliographies. Special thanks go to Dave Murray, Fred Dean, Dave Klein, Brian Barnes, Joan Braddock, Bob Wheeler, Terry Chapin, Ed Murphy, Judy MacDonald and Robert Rausch, all of whom critically read parts of or all of the manuscript. Their comments were invaluable. However, any mistakes or misinterpretations are strictly my own.

My greatest encouragement, professionally, came from Dale Guthrie and Paul Matheus. I have profited from years of conversations with both. Parts of my education came while nailing shingles, spiking together house logs, wrestling roofing steel or while glassing caribou from a high tundra ridge. Special thanks to these two.

My gratitude goes to Sheryn Hara, Book Publishers Network, who has coordinated and managed the production of this book. Thanks also to Carolyn Acheson (indexing), Stephanie Martindale (layout), Laura Zugzda (cover design) and Laura Danforth (book distribution). Pamela Bruton edited the entire book and, as a result, it has been greatly improved. Thanks.

A debt of gratitude is owed to the illustrators. Mareca Guthrie and Mark Ross provided all but one of the illustrations that do so much to make this book a pleasure for me to see. George West kindly provided the drawing of the diving loon.

Finally, without the continued encouragement of my wife, Marsha, I couldn't have finished this book. She allowed me the time and space within busy schedules of house building, remodeling, participation in Fairbanks Summer Arts Festival and many other activities to actually complete it.

Ronald L. Smith
Fairbanks, Alaska
February, 2008

PREFACE

My first visit to Alaska was in the dead of winter in 1967. I flew up from Miami, Florida, to interview for a job in Fairbanks. Strolling across the tarmac toward the terminal in a light jacket at –30°F certainly gave me a perspective on life in the Far North. In August 1968, my father and I drove out of the scorching heat of the California desert to Alaska. I'd landed a job at the University of Alaska Fairbanks. Dad always referred to that trip as our "drive north into autumn," because the aspen leaves were turning yellow as we crossed into eastern Alaska. Since then I have learned (and forgotten) a lot about the plants, animals, climate, and landforms of Alaska from colleagues, friends, students, and my own personal observations and scientific research.

I wrote this book primarily to share some of those interesting things I've learned over the years. I designed it to appeal to a variety of readers, including both residents of and visitors to Alaska, both students and professional biologists. It is not intended to be exhaustive. Instead, I provide my take on some of the interesting processes, plants, and creatures of interior and northern Alaska. I try to point out interesting

or essential anatomical, physiological, or behavioral features that allow these species to survive in the Far North.

The first chapter deals with the landscapes, what they looked like in the past, what creatures were on the landscapes, and how some of those past landscapes still affect Alaska today. Northern Alaska had the highest latitude at which dinosaurs were known to have existed. A variety of mammals, plants, and other creatures were present over the Pleistocene epoch, roughly the last 2 million years. Fluctuations in climate in interior and northern Alaska caused progressions from periods of glaciation with nearby grassland floras and faunas to periods of glacial recession that led to the expansion of forests and forest-dwelling animals. Changes from glacial to interglacial episodes resulted in localized and, sometimes, more widespread extinctions.

Second, I deal with specific mechanisms that allow plants and animals to survive the (seasonally) cold, Far North. What are the advantages of migration versus permanent residency, of being cold-blooded versus warm-blooded, of tolerance to versus resistance to freezing? One aspect of migration is that the migrator connects habitats in Alaska with quite different habitats in the temperate, tropical, or Southern Hemisphere high-latitude zones. We need to think on a larger scale than just the local biological community to ensure healthy populations of "Alaskan" species.

The third and seventh chapters are about the plants and plant communities of the boreal forest and tundra, respectively. What species are present? How and why do plant communities change through time? How can slow-growing conifers ever compete with rapidly growing deciduous trees? Why don't trees grow on the tundra? What are the roles of complex chemical compounds produced by these plants? The chemicals influence competition among plant species and also limit browsing by some of their major herbivores.

Some of the terrestrial animals of interior and northern Alaska are treated in chapters four, five, six, and eight. For convenience, I divided the fauna into boreal forest and tundra faunas but that division is, to an extent, arbitrary. For example, caribou often spend winter in the boreal forest yet, most of the year, live on the tundra. Similarly, moose occur in tundra habitats but I've written about them in the Chapter 3. In spite of our penchant to neatly pigeonhole creatures, life is complex.

In Chapters 9 and 10, I discuss some aquatic birds and mammals. Is the muskrat an aquatic or a terrestrial animal? How do beavers modify the landscape and the plant communities in which they live? What are the anatomical and physiological features of these mammals that allow them to spend lots of time in and under water? I will describe the feeding mechanisms of birds associated with aquatic systems in Alaska.

Aquatic systems are included in this book because fish and other aquatic life are crucial to Alaska's economy, culture, and terrestrial biology. Salmon feed us humans as well as bears, bald eagles, and many other predators. Salmon fertilize the streams in which they die but also the surrounding forest and tundra. Their bodies and/or nutrients are transported some distance from streams by predators and scavengers. I will briefly describe some other fish species that occupy the lakes and streams of Alaska and interact with the salmon species.

The final chapter points out how we might expect Alaska to change in the near future. Certainly the message from the Pleistocene, from the last 10,000 years, and also from the last 50 years is that change is a part of earth history and a part of the natural history of Alaska. What species and plant and animal communities will most likely be impacted by changing climate, and by expanding resource extraction and human populations?

We already see evidence of the encroachment of shrubs into tundra systems. Storm surge along Alaska's northern and western coasts is an ever more visible problem. Sea level is rising, glaciers are retracting, and tree lines are moving upslope. The survival strategies of polar bear, arctic fox, white spruce, red squirrel, and caribou will be tested anew in the coming years. Perhaps some of those strategies will be found wanting; perhaps extinction of these and other Alaskan species looms. Stay tuned for breaking news.

Finally, if in reading this book you get half the enjoyment I got out of writing it, I will consider it to be a great success.

Ronald L. Smith
Fairbanks, Alaska
October, 2007

INTRODUCTION TO INTERIOR AND NORTHERN ALASKA

The land mass of interior and northern Alaska, for the purposes of this book, extends from the Uplands of south-central Alaska, through the Alaska Range, across the Yukon River drainages of the interior, past the Brooks Range, and onward to the coast of the Arctic Ocean's Beaufort Sea. I also include much of western Alaska because it consists largely of arctic tundra habitats similar to other tundra areas of the state.

The three major ecological systems present in this landmass are boreal forest, tundra and aquatic systems. I will describe details and interesting features of each of these major ecosystems and try to point out some of the variations in these systems and in the plants and animals that occupy them.

How can life exist in such a cold place?

This question is the subject of Chapter 3. First, the tundra and boreal forest of Alaska are not frigid places year-round. Second, cold is a relative term. We think of Alaska in winter as being harsh. It is certainly harsh to largely naked bipeds such as humans, who are much more comfortable in semitropical conditions. But Alaska's landscapes are, truly, harsh places to make a living, as evidenced by the very few species, relative to the tropics, that are able to exist there. There are physiological, anatomical, and behavioral mechanisms that allow plants and animals to survive in such a harsh environment. Which plants and animals survive by tolerating freezing of the body? Which can resist freezing and for how long? I will point out that a trait such as being warm-blooded is both a blessing and a curse since it allows animals to remain active all through the year but requires the animal to burn more energy than it would need if it were cold-blooded.

Hibernation, though an adaptation to the Far North, is also a constraint. The hibernator, during its active season, may establish and defend territory, reproduce, lay on fat reserves, and, perhaps, dig a new hibernation den. All these activities are contracted into a 3-5 month period. The rest of the year the hibernator is completely invisible on the landscape. Who are the hibernators, and what are the characteristics of hibernation?

In the context of adaptation to the Far North, I will describe three advantages of migratory behavior. These three are an energetic advantage, a reproductive advantage, and a feeding advantage. Seasonal migrators have limitations but also have tremendous advantages over animals that simply have to stay put and tough it out. In the boreal forest system, some migrators are temporary, seasonal or occasional members of the forest fauna. For example, moose occupy the boreal forest but have the strength, locomotory power, and the will to move above or beyond tree line for parts of the year. During those times moose could be considered part of the tundra fauna. Caribou, primarily inhabitants of treeless tundra, migrate down into forested habitats in the winter, primarily because it is easier to find food.

It is this topic, adaptations to life in the Far North, which will occupy our attention in Chapter 3. We will have a look at trees, frogs, insects, and intertidal invertebrates, as well as birds and mammals.

What is a boreal forest?

Since boreal forests occupy much of interior and northern Alaska, I need to define what a boreal forest is and to establish some limits or boundaries for boreal forests. Of all the forests in the world, boreal forests are those found at highest latitudes. These conifer-dominated forests stretch from eastern Canada all the way across the continent to interior and western Alaska (Figure 0.1). Similar plant communities, also boreal forests, pick up again across the Bering Sea and are found from eastern Asia all the way to Western Europe and the Scandinavian countries.

Figure 0.1: Extent of the boreal forest in North America. Compare this figure with Figure 0.2, showing permafrost zones in the northern hemisphere.

Cold air and soil temperatures strongly influence boreal forests. The northern boundary of boreal forests corresponds roughly with the southward extent of continuous **permafrost**. Soil that is permanently frozen is called permafrost. The latitudinal zone occupied by boreal forests is one in which permafrost is discontinuous (Figure 0.2). That is, the permafrost is patchy in distribution. In Alaska, continuous permafrost exists from the Seward Peninsula and the south slope of the Brooks Range to the arctic coast. Over the rest of the state permafrost is patchy or discontinuous. Southward, beyond the patchy permafrost, the boreal forest gives way to grasslands, prairies, and/or northern deciduous forests.[1] But, back to permafrost. Where did it come from and what signs of permafrost would we expect to see in Alaska's boreal forests?

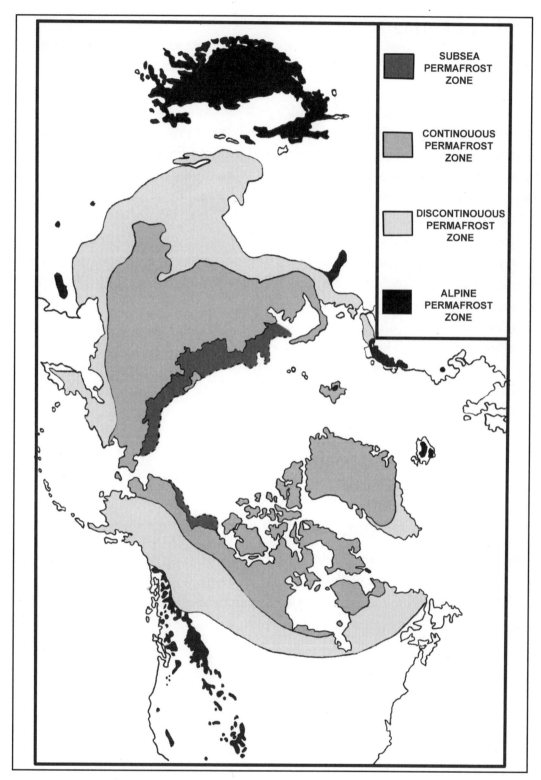

Figure 0.2: Permafrost in the Northern Hemisphere. Notice that the northern extent of boreal forest roughly matches the northern edge of discontinuous permafrost. Virtually all of Alaska is subject to permafrost soils. Redrawn from Bliss (2000).

More About Permafrost And Frozen Ground

Most permafrost in Alaska and elsewhere was formed during the last or earlier glacial episodes in the Pleistocene epoch. The Pleistocene roughly corresponds to the period in earth history, dominated by glaciation, extending from about 1.8 million years ago to about 10,000 years ago. Permafrost on the North Slope of Alaska may be as much as 600 m (1970 ft) thick (Figure 0.3); permafrost in Siberia reaches over 1400 m (4600 ft) in depth.[2]

Aside from permafrost of Pleistocene origin, Alaska has a wealth of sites at which frozen soils have formed more recently. The succession of plant communities in the boreal forest of the interior leads, eventually, to a black spruce forest with mosses covering the forest floor. The mosses are typically damp in the fall, then freeze and allow heat loss from the forest soil in the winter. In summer the mosses dry and provide insulation for the cold soil. Thus, the vegetation cover allows for the formation and continuation of permafrost.

The surface layer of Alaskan soils, permafrost or otherwise, thaws during summer and refreezes in winter. This upper layer is the **active layer**. The depth of the active layer varies across Alaska. In Anchorage the active layer may be 2-3 m, in Fairbanks 1-3 m, and in Barrow 0.5 m deep (Figure 0.3).

The depth of the active layer and the presence of permafrost are important determinants

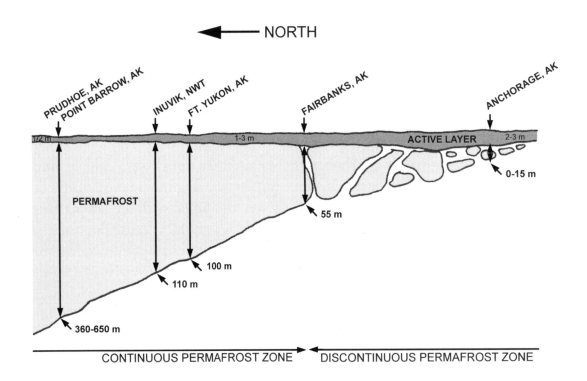

Figure 0.3: Diagram showing the depth of the active layer, the depth of permafrost and the difference between continuous and discontinuous permafrost along a transect from Anchorage northward to Point Barrow. Redrawn from Davis (2001).

of plant growth, animal burrows and human construction techniques. First, tree roots cannot penetrate permafrost. Areas with a very thin active layer may not allow trees to adequately anchor themselves with their root systems. Trees under these circumstances simply blow over in a strong wind. Second, animals such as ground squirrels, foxes, and marmots require burrows for hibernation, escape from predators, and raising offspring. Excavation of these burrows or dens can only be accomplished in the active layer; the permafrost is too hard for any but the strongest, most determined diggers such as grizzlies. Third, roads and houses built on permafrost are liable to damage if heat is transferred to the soil and it thaws. Thawed permafrost is typically waterlogged and unstable. It also occupies less volume than when in a frozen state due to the expansion of water upon freezing. Foundations and roadways may experience cracking and settling as a result of soil thawing.

Permafrost prevents percolation of rain and melt water into the soil. Consequently, much of the landscape of the interior and northern Alaska is covered in ponds and bogs even though the annual precipitation in Fairbanks is similar to that of parts of the Mojave Desert in California.

I mentioned the thawing of permafrost and the consequent reduction in soil volume. Permafrost thaws for any of several reasons. Climate change since the last glacial maximum, roughly 20,000 years ago, accounts for a loss of permafrost. Other processes that thaw frozen soils involve the removal of the insulative cover of vegetation. For example, land clearing for agriculture or commercial development or forest fires can result in the thawing and slumping of permafrost. The slumping produces pits or depressions often referred to as **thermokarst** pits or thermokarst topography. Trees and shrubs that ordinarily would be upright lean over in thermokarst areas, forming the drunken forests so common along the roads of interior Alaska and northern Canada. Thaw ponds can develop in a black spruce forest as a result of removal of insulation caused by moose tracks depressing the moss.

Frost heaving results from the freezing of a waterlogged active layer in the fall and winter. Frost heaves can uproot telephone poles, fence posts, and pilings. Annually, secondary roads around the interior of Alaska buckle due to frost heaving.

Ice wedges are a common feature in tundra or former tundra habitats. Exposures along the arctic coast and in interior Alaska often show massive ice wedges penetrating the sediments (Figure 0.4). The formation and expansion of ice wedges account for the presence of **polygonal ground,** or tundra polygons, in the Far North. How do ice wedges form? The wedges start as cracks in permafrost, which develop in two ways, either from severe cold or through drying. In winter, ground temperatures of -15°C or lower combined with air temperatures rapidly falling below -15°C cause the frozen ground to contract and crack. There are many reports of an audible, shot-like noise associated with the cracking. Desiccation, or drying, can also lead to cracking, much as mud cracks develop in dry lakes in deserts. Both cold and dry conditions were met during glacial periods. The spring after a crack formed, melt water flowed down into it and, in fall, froze. The freezing caused an expansion of the crack. In successive years the crack

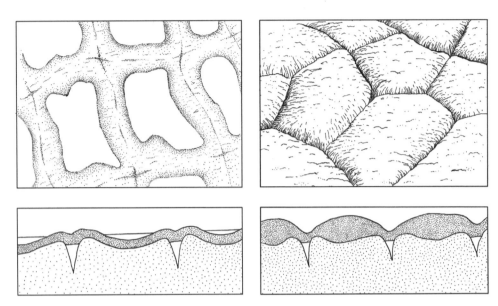

Figure 0.4: Low-centered (left panels) and high-centered (right panels) polygons in relation to the ice wedges that are thought to have formed them. Heavy stippling represents an organic layer and/or surface vegetation. Some low-centered polygons evolve into high-centered polygons by slowly filling in the depression with detritus. See text for explanation of these polygons. Redrawn from Pielou (1994).

thawed, refilled with water, and refroze, further expanding what was, initially, a narrow wedge. The ultimate size of the wedge was determined by local climatic conditions.

Polygonal ground is a result of the formation of ice wedges. Typically, the pattern of cracks formed is either six-sided (hexagonal) or four-sided (orthogonal). As the ice wedges grow, they push the adjacent soil away, forming ridges that surround lower ground. Thus are formed **low-center polygons** (Figure 0.4). Low-center polygons often fill with water and form small ponds. Eventually, sediment and plant debris collect in the low centers, creating **high-center polygons**. On sloping ground, water flowing down through a series of high-centered polygons forms beaded streams.

Polygonal ground is very characteristic of arctic and alpine tundra but can also be seen in the boreal forest. One of the more exciting runs on the University of Alaska Fairbanks ski trails takes you through the forest, alternating between high ground (the high centers of polygons), and low, short ditches (the outer boundaries of the same polygons). This polygonal ground is further evidence, in addition to the pollen records in ponds, that the interior of Alaska supported treeless vegetation and permafrost during glacial periods.

A landform feature related to the top, active layer of permafrost is the **solifluction lobe**. On slopes underlain by permafrost the thawed active layer in the summer slowly flows downslope over the frozen layer, carrying vegetation with it. Examples of solifluction lobes or ridges can be seen along the Denali Highway and Steese Highway above tree line (Figure 0.5). Since the bottom edge of the lobe is much steeper than the other parts, it constitutes a different micro-habitat in terms of moisture, slope, and vegetation compared to the rest of the lobe.

Extent of boreal forest in the northern hemisphere

The boreal forest of the northern hemisphere covers about 17% of the land surface of the earth. It is one of the greatest ecosystems on earth in terms of geographic extent, biomass of living plants, and **carbon reservoirs** (carbon locked up in vegetation). Roughly, the boreal forest extends from about 45°N latitude to the northern extent of tree line in both North America and Eurasia. In North America, the latitudinal extent of this system may be as much as 10°; in Asia it can extend as much as 20° of latitude. At high latitudes the boreal forest is the system that is found when climatic conditions combine cold and wet. The other possible combinations at high latitudes are cold and dry (producing tundra), warm and wet (producing the deciduous forests of the east and the coastal rainforests of the west) and, finally, warm and dry (producing prairies or grasslands). This delineation is somewhat oversimplified. For instance, experts on tundra vegetation differentiate between wet and dry tundra habitats. Nevertheless, this broad characterization is helpful in thinking about habitats. Boreal forest covers about 28% of the surface of North America north of Mexico.

Tree line

Why does continuous permafrost establish the northernmost extent of the boreal forest? Another way of asking this question: what is it that determines tree line as one moves northward and/or higher in altitude? Tree line is a theoretical line above (or beyond) which no trees grow. The northern edge of the boreal forest coincides fairly well with the southern boundary of continuous permafrost, as described earlier. In

Figure 0.5: Solifluction lobes on a tundra slope (background). These lobes result from down-slope movement of the active layer in summer. The caribou in the foreground is exhibiting an alarm display. See Chapter 8 for a description of caribou alarm displays.

the zone of continuous permafrost, the depth of the active layer is very shallow. Typically, the active layer is less than 50 cm (20 inches) deep in permafrost soils and 50 cm is not very much in which to anchor a tree. Further, air temperatures cold enough to maintain a continuous permafrost zone aren't warm enough for photosynthesis to proceed rapidly. Therefore, a tree in the Far North photosynthesizes slowly in the growing season but does not make enough organic material to add much wood. The nearer we get to tree line, the shorter the trees. Even if a lucky tree manages to put on a growth spurt and attain a height of 5 m (16 feet), it will likely blow over in a high-wind event. As we will see in the next chapter, air temperatures never get cold enough in the boreal forest to actually kill the trees growing there.

The geographic extent of boreal forests in North America has changed dramatically during and since the glacial episodes of the Pleistocene. At the heights of glaciation, forests were displaced far southward in Canada and the "lower 48," and totally eliminated from Alaska. At the warmest "moments" of the interglacial periods, forests reappeared in the Far North. In fact, during the Little Climatic Optimum (about 9,000 years ago), spruce trees were well established on the Seward Peninsula near Nome, on the North Slope of Alaska and northeast of the Mackenzie River delta in the Northwest Territories, points well beyond current tree line.

Thus, climate change in the last 1.8 million years has led to successive extinction and reestablishment of the boreal forest in Alaska. It is clear that the spread of trees northward is much slower than the northward spread of favorable climatic conditions. The lag in northward expansion is due to the limits on seed dispersal. Tree species having seeds that can be easily dispersed by winds, such as paper birch, poplar and aspen, repopulated Alaska long before tree species with seeds that don't blow quite so far on the wind (white spruce, black spruce). An example of this lag can be seen in the present distribution of lodgepole pine. Introduction of lodgepole pines as ornamentals in interior Alaska has resulted in their survival and growth. But, out on the landscape, lodgepole pines have not yet reached Alaska on their own. Based on pollen analyses of lake cores, this species reinvaded southern British Columbia about 12,500 years ago, reached central British Columbia about 5,000 years ago and arrived just east of the Alaska/Yukon border within the last 400 years.[3] It is probable that trees are still "marching" northward and westward, invading tundra habitat and expanding the boreal forests.

Similarly, tree line through time has pulsed up- and down-slope in the mountains of Alaska, responding sluggishly to climate changes of the last glacial age and subsequent climate oscillations. If you drive through the changing vegetation near and, finally, above tree line along the Steese Highway north of Fairbanks or the highway between Haines and Haines Junction you will see an occasional isolated tree, out in the middle of nowhere. Are these trees boldly advancing beyond the current limits of their fellows? Or, instead, are they remnants of a forest that occupied the location in warmer times? Since the Little Climatic Optimum the Far North has been in a general cooling trend. Therefore, chances are good that some of those loners are the last holdouts of what was once a forested slope.

The vegetation of the boreal forests of Alaska consists of trees, shrubs, herbaceous flowering plants, horsetails, mosses, and lichens. Some of the interesting biology of these critical elements of the forest will be described in the Chapter 3, including growth and reproductive characteristics, competitive interactions among plants, impacts of animals on these plants, impacts of plants on the animals, and the effects of soils on plant survival and distribution.

Animals of Alaska's boreal forest

In North America, the Alaskan boreal forest is at the northwestern geographic extreme. Just as the plant community is a simplified version of those found further to the east and south, so also is the animal community. Elk, white-tail deer and mule deer are missing from Alaska's interior forests as are several ground squirrel and chipmunk species. Only one bat species reaches interior Alaska; no hummingbird extends so far north.

If we compare the Alaskan fauna with that across the Bering Strait, the former lacks many Asian species. The raccoon dog, European beaver, and sable are all missing from North America. Unfortunately, neither do we have Siberian tigers in Alaska. These great cats would put a lot more excitement into berry picking in the fall or cross-country skiing in the winter!

Some of the fascinating aspects of the lives of the mammals, birds and insects of Alaska's northern forests are described in their respective chapters. Certainly, the mammals and birds are the charismatic animals upon which we tend to focus. However, in terms of in-your-face contact, mosquitoes, blackflies, and their nemesis, the dragonflies, may have

a larger, more immediate, and more constant impact on humanity. The insect pests of trees are also making their presence felt to the trees but also to human observers. Anyone in interior Alaska cannot help but have noticed the toll these insects are taking on aspen, white spruce, tamarack and birch.

The Tundra and its Vegetation

The treeless areas of the Far North generally correspond with the distribution of continuous permafrost (see Figure 0.2). The continuous permafrost zone, therefore, more or less defines the arctic tundra. Alpine tundra, however, is not necessarily underlain by permafrost. Alpine tundra is found from the equator all the way to the Brooks Range. As I mentioned above, the temperature and length of the growing season are determinants of tree line in Alaska and elsewhere.

There is a clear, inverse relationship between latitude and altitude at tree line. The higher the latitude, the lower the altitude at which tree line occurs. Some examples will illustrate this relationship. In Colorado, above Boulder, tree line occurs at about 3550 m (11,500 ft) elevation. In southern Idaho tree line is at about 3050 m (10,000 ft); in northern Idaho it is at approximately 2140 m (7,000 ft). In southeastern interior Alaska the highest tree line is at 1025 m (3350 ft) elevation. At Twelvemile Summit on the Steese Highway, northeast of Fairbanks, tree line is at 920 m (3000 ft) on the south side and 790 m (2600 ft) on the north side.

Though a simple concept, tree line is difficult to determine. How sparsely populated can the trees be and still qualify as forest rather than tundra? Are the few, widely scattered trees at the top of the ridge at Twelvemile Summit actually above tree line? I think so. As I mentioned above, those few trees could be the advance guard of the forest sweeping up the ridge or, instead, could be the remnants of a previous forest that has been replaced by tundra.

Temperature and tundra

There are many ways to express tundra temperatures. The extreme range is of interest but is not, perhaps, as biologically meaningful as some other measures. For example, the boreal forest of Alaska probably has a more extreme annual temperature range than either arctic or alpine tundra in the state. Also, wintertime temperature minimums for tundra are probably no lower than winter lows in the boreal forest. Are extremely low temperatures lethal to tundra plants? Based on the cooling and freezing experiments I will describe in Chapter 2, it seems unlikely that tundra shrubs are directly killed by low temperatures. Boreal forest trees can survive temperatures as low as -70°C (-94°F); tundra shrubs are probably at least as hardy.

Mean or average annual temperatures have been calculated for a variety of locales in the arctic, tundra realm of Alaska. Kotzebue, Alaska, with its maritime influence, has a mean annual temperature of -4.3°C, but Umiat, in the foothills of the Brooks Range, away from the ocean, has a mean annual temperature of -11.7°C. Two sites at higher latitude are Barter Island and Barrow, with mean temperatures of -11.6 and -12.1°C, respectively. July (generally the warmest month) average temperatures for these localities are 12.4, 11.7, 4.6 and 3.8°C

for Kotzebue, Umiat, Barter Island, and Barrow, respectively.

One way of expressing, in a general way, the extent of the warm, relative to winter, growing season is to calculate the number of degree-days above 0°C. For example, if a locale had only one day of +10°C and the remainder of the year at 0°C or below, the number of degree-days above 0°C would be 1x 10°, or 10 degree-days. The higher the degree-days, the better the growing conditions for plant life, we presume. The degree-days above 0°C for Kotzebue, Umiat, Barter Island, and Barrow are 1462, 993, 368, and 288, respectively.[5]

In terms of suitability for plant growth, the above sequence represents a decreasing scope for plant growth. Note that a premise underlying the degree-day concept is that only temperatures above 0°C are conducive to plant growth. That premise is untrue; some plants achieve growth at temperatures below 0°C. However, the concept is still useful for comparing different locales. At the present we lack enough detailed data on degree-days above 0°C and plant species distributions across tundra landscapes to determine the degree-day requirements of individual plant species. In addition, other factors, such as soil moisture, snow depths, and winds, are undoubtedly important for individual plant survival.

Chapter 7, on the tundra and its vegetation, will address issues of temperature, soil, wind, snow, and the adaptations of tundra plants. The companion chapter on tundra animals (Chapter 8) will describe some of the tundra animals and the special features that help them survive in this harsh environment.

Aquatic systems of interior and northern Alaska

A summer visitor to this great land might or might not notice peculiarities or differences in the freshwater environment of Alaska. Certainly, the annual cycles of life in lakes and streams are somewhat more severe than in upstate New York or in Minnesota and considerably more difficult for life than in Georgia or Florida. A chief factor is the presence of ice, its duration, and the effects it produces. The length of winters, the severity of air temperatures, and the lack of a thick, insulating snow cover often combine to produce very thick river and lake ice. In many streams of interior and northern Alaska, streams freeze to the bottom, eliminating fish habitat. Even when liquid water remains under the ice its suitability for fish may be compromised by **hypoxia** (low oxygen) or **anoxia** (absence of oxygen).

Glaciation and glacially produced sediments affect fishes in Alaska. First, glaciers occupy watersheds that could provide fish habitat were the glaciers not there. Second, glaciers, by abrading and scouring the underlying bedrock, produce fine sediments (glacial flour) that flow down glacial streams and make them turbid and, therefore, less desirable as fish habitat.

The fish and aquatic invertebrate faunas of interior and northern Alaska are impoverished in comparison to those at lower latitudes. The physical rigors of the environment have constrained many species that exist further south. Also, many species that could live in Alaska and, perhaps, did live in Alaska before the Pleistocene, may not have been able to disperse back into the Far North.

A visitor to Alaska might also notice or have read about the importance of salmon to the freshwaters of this land of the midnight sun. Arguably, salmon have greater significance to the human and natural economy of this state than in any other state of the U.S.A. or province of Canada. I address the life histories of the salmon and other freshwater fishes in Chapter 9. Chapter 10 includes accounts of some of the waterfowl that rely on freshwaters and accounts of several mammals that could just as easily have been put in the chapter on the mammals of the forest.

Ancient landscapes

Before I talk about modern Alaska, I want to briefly describe some of the ancient landscapes and some of the long-dead creatures that inhabited them. A discussion of those landscapes and those creatures is linked to cold and adaptations to cold. The presence, and survival of dinosaurs in Alaska leads me to think about three questions. One question is, "Was Alaska actually in the Far North during the time of the dinosaurs?" The second question is, "Was Alaska cold during the Cretaceous, when dinosaurs were about?" The third question is, "Did dinosaurs have adaptations to help them survive the cold?"

To answer the first question requires information about the drifting of continents and smaller bits of crust called terraines. The geological terraine corresponding to the North Slope of Alaska, where most of the dinosaur remains in Alaska have been found, was located at about 75°N latitude late in the dinosaur age. In other words, in the late Cretaceous epoch, northern

Alaska was as far north as it is today. For the answer to the other two questions you will need to read Chapter 1.

The history of the last 1.8 million years has been one of fluctuations between relatively cold periods, the glacial episodes, and warmer, interglacial episodes. This whole time period is referred to as the Pleistocene Epoch. Sometimes, the Pleistocene is simply called the "ice age" but that is an oversimplification. Clearly, plants and animals on the landscape during a glacial episode must have had a different set of adaptive characteristics than those that occupied interglacial Alaska. Therefore, the shift from glacial to interglacial, or *vice versa*, favored some existing plants and animals, put others at a severe competitive disadvantage, drove others to extinction, and served as the selective pressure that led to the evolution of new species. Of course, one important fact about the Pleistocene is that, even at the maximum extent of glaciation, there were vast tracts of landscape in interior and northern Alaska that were not covered with ice. We begin the natural history of interior and northern Alaska with these ancient landscapes in the next chapter.

REFERENCES

1 Johnson, D., Kershaw, L., MacKinnon, A. and Pojar, J. 1995. Plants of the western boreal forest and aspen parkland. Lone Pine Publishing, Edmonton.

2 Davis, N. 2001. Permafrost: a guide to frozen ground in transition. University of Alaska Press, Fairbanks.

3 Pielou, E.C. 1991. After the ice age: The return of life to glaciated North America. University of Chicago Press, Chicago and London.

1.

DINOSAURS, GLACIERS, MAMMOTHS, AND GIANT BEARS: ANCIENT LANDSCAPES AND SOME OF THEIR CREATURES

ALASKA IN THE MESOZOIC: THE DINOSAURS!

Insights into high-latitude dinosaurs

One of the most surprising aspects of the natural history of Alaska is the presence of dinosaur fossils. We often think of dinosaurs as cold-blooded, relatively slow moving creatures living in a tropical or semitropical environment. Which one of the above assumptions is incorrect if dinosaurs actually survived in Alaska in the Mesozoic era? Probably all three assumptions are wrong. But first, when and where were the dinosaurs?

The first discovery of dinosaurs in Alaska was made by R. L. Liscomb, a Shell Oil Company geologist, in 1961. He found a variety of bones in outcroppings on bluffs along the Colville River. To date, remains of twelve different dinosaur species have been identified from the Colville River deposits.

The Colville River dinosaurs date from the late Cretaceous, some 68-72 million years ago. Their presence in Alaska raises some interesting questions. First, what were conditions like in the Alaska of that time? Reconstructions of past continents and their locations indicates that the North Slope of Alaska was at 70-85°N latitude in the late Cretaceous, somewhat closer to the North Pole than today.[1] That means that winters included very short days and periods of several months in the dead of winter during which the sun stayed below the horizon. Although controversial, paleotemperatures are thought to have averaged 10-12°C (50-54°F) in the warmest months and down to 2-4°C (35-39°F) in the winter months.[2] These temperatures were warmer than at present but still cold enough to cause us to wonder about metabolism and sources of food in the cold season.

Several scenarios have been constructed to account for dinosaurs at such high latitudes.

One hypothesis focuses on dinosaur body temperatures. Some scientists now think that many dinosaurs were warm-bodied and maintained constant body temperatures. That is, they were homeotherms. This metabolic strategy is described for birds and mammals in Chapter 2 but what about dinosaurs? Some paleontologists argue that dinosaurs were actually warm-blooded like modern mammals.[3] If so, dinosaurs could have maintained activity in the cold winters of Cretaceous Alaska.

However, a warm body loses heat to its cool surroundings and, in winter, heat loss would have necessitated a continuing and high metabolic rate. Carnivores could have hunted something down for food in order to maintain their high metabolic rates. Herbivores probably went through some stress in winter but may have been able to survive on the aquatic vegetation, woody ground cover, and perhaps some evergreens known to have existed in the Far North in this time period.[4]

Several alternatives to staying warm and active during winter may have been employed by dinosaurs. Some scientists argue that, like modern migratory birds, dinosaurs may simply have headed south to warmer winter climates. To migrate from Alaska would have necessitated a round trip of thousands of kilometers, however. Another possibility, suggested by our knowledge of modern-day mammals, is hibernation. Hibernation is a state of lowered metabolic activity leading to lower body temperatures. Heat loss is proportional to the difference between body temperature and external temperature. Therefore, the colder the body, the lower the amount of energy required to maintain it. What would we consider as evidence that dinosaurs actually hibernated? Perhaps a fossilized mother and offspring in a fossilized cave would suffice but such a discovery is extremely unlikely.

Dinosaur fossils have been found elsewhere in Alaska. A set of 14 footprints of Jurassic (> 140 million years old) dinosaurs were found on the Alaska Peninsula near Black Lake. Additional footprints of seven species of mid-Cretaceous (ca. 100 million years old) dinosaurs were found on the North Slope. The Talkeetna Mountains, in central Alaska, yielded the skull of the nodosaur, *Edmontonia*.

Edmontosaurus

On the Colville, the most common dinosaur fossil is *Edmontosaurus*, a **hadrosaur** (duck-billed dinosaur) that, at full growth, stood about 3 m (10 ft) tall, weighed at least 2700 kg (3 tons) and reached lengths of 12 m (40 ft) (Figure 1.1). About 60% of the bones of the entire skeleton of this dinosaur have been found. The fossils include, mainly, juveniles and young adults. *Edmontosaurus*, unlike many other hadrosaurs, had no crest on top of the head. Its teeth were adapted for grinding plant material and its jaws were capable of chewing both front-to-back and side-to-side.[5] The efficiency of this grinding mechanism is thought to have made **gastroliths**, gizzard stones, unnecessary although such stones are found in association with four-legged plant-eating dinosaurs such as *Brachiosaurus*. A fossilized *Edmontosaurus* mummy, now at the American Museum of Natural History, apparently had material in its stomach that included conifer cones and needles plus some unidentified fruits and seeds.

Figure 1.1 *Edmontosaurus*, a duck-billed dinosaur present in northern Alaska during the Cretaceous. Note the bipedal locomotion, the use of forelimbs, and the flattened muzzle.

The same mummy yielded sandstone impressions of its skin. The skin of *Edmontosaurus* was composed of tubercles or plates that interlocked but did not overlap. On some parts of the body the tubercles were uniform in size but elsewhere there were small and larger plates mixed together. The plates weren't large enough or thick enough to afford much protection from the largest predatory dinosaurs. *Edmontosaurus*, like all other hadrosaurs, walked bipedally but could revert to quadrupedal locomotion.

Teeth and a few skull bones of two other hadrosaurs have been found: *Kritosaurus* (a non-crested species) and a lambeosaurid species. Lambeosaurid duckbills had a helmet-like crest that had a hollow, air-filled cavity connected to the nostrils. The space is thought to be a resonating chamber used to produce sounds. Such sounds were undoubtedly used in communication in the same ways as sounds are used in modern vertebrates.

Some, if not all, duck-billed species exhibited parental care. Vegetation-lined nests of eggs and baby hadrosaurs have been found in Montana. Shells in the nests were broken into tiny pieces, suggesting that the active babies stayed in the nest for some time. Remains of these young hadrosaurs had worn-down teeth, lending credence to the idea that their mothers periodically returned to the nest with food for their offspring. The Montana hadrosaur was *Maiasaura*, not *Edmontosaurus*, so we can't be sure that the Alaskan hadrosaur also exhibited parental care.

Pachyrhinosaurus

Two **ceratopsian,** or horned dinosaurs, lived in Alaska. These creatures walked on all fours and had frilled plates protecting the head. *Triceratops* is the familiar genus of ceratopsians, but it hasn't been found in Alaska. The Colville deposits have yielded parts of the skulls of two different ceratopsians, *Pachyrhinosaurus* and a species resembling *Anchiceratops*.

Perhaps atypical of ceratopsians, *Pachyrhinosaurus* is thought by many paleontologists to have had no horns on its snout or behind the eyes. This lack of horns encourages the question: what were the functions of frilled plates and horns in these beasts? Almost every dinosaur book has an illustration of *Triceratops* goring an attacking *Tyrannosaurus* with its horns. Certainly defense is one possible function of the horns but are there others? Skull variation within some ceratopsians suggests that males had larger, more ornate head frills (and, possibly, horns) than females. If this were true, an important function of the ornamentation might have been to aid males in establishing dominance. In other words, males secured their rank in the order of things by virtue of the size and effective use of their horns or frilled plates in display and/or combat with other males. I will describe this behavior more fully in the section on moose (Chapter 4).

The bones of some ceratopsian species, including *Pachyrhinosaurus*, are often found in dense accumulations with almost no other dinosaur species present. Paleontologists interpret this fact as indicating that some ceratopsians were herd-oriented in their behavior.

Pachycephalosaurus

Another bipedal herbivore on the Colville was a species of *Pachycephalosaurus*. Looking at the bulge on the top of the skull, one might think that this was a large-brained, highly intelligent dinosaur; in reality, *Pachycephalosaurus* had a tiny brain encased in a really thick, domed skull (Figure 1.2). The 0.6 m (2 ft) skull of this creature was topped with a bone layer 20 cm (8 inches) thick. No wonder these animals are called bonehead dinosaurs! Several ideas about the skulls are prevalent. One idea is that individuals butted heads in much the same way that Dall and bighorn sheep butt each other. This behavior in male sheep is useful in establishing dominance; maybe it performed the same function 70 million years ago. Domehead dinosaurs may have also attacked would-be predators and competitors by ramming them.[3] Another possibility is that the skull may have helped in heat dissipation on really hot days.

Tyrannosaurid dinosaurs

Where there are herbivores, there are bound to be carnivores also. Three members of the Tyrannosauridae family left teeth along the North Slope, one of them the famous *Tyrannosaurus rex*. The other two were smaller species: *Albertosaurus* and *Alectrosaurus*. Some features common to

Figure 1.2: *Pachycephalosaurus*, another herbivorous dinosaur of the Far North. The top of the skull was as much as 20 cm thick. *Pachycephalosaurus* probably butted heads much as modern-day Dall sheep do.

all three species include bipedal locomotion, huge jaws filled with long teeth, a short, powerful neck, and short forelegs with two toes each. Tyrannosaurids had special rods of bone, the **gastralia**, that supported and protected the visceral organs. These bones occupied the midventral (belly) line between the shoulder and hip bones.

Albertosaurus was first discovered in Alberta, Canada. Other fossils of this species are known from Montana and Baja California. From nose to tail, *Albertosaurus* spanned 8-9 m (26-30 ft), stood 3.3 m (11 ft) tall, and weighed 1800-2700 kg (2-3 tons). The forelimbs of *Albertosaurus* were short but better developed than those of

Tyrannosaurus. The nasal bones of the *Albertosaurus* skull were very rough in texture, which has been interpreted as possibly indicating the site of attachment of a horn.[6] A horn in front of the eyes, if present, might have been used as a display organ, much as antlers in deer and moose are used in establishing dominance.

Alectrosaurus remains have been found in Mongolia and Kazakhstan. A tooth characteristic of this species was found in the Colville River bone beds. This species is another smaller, lighter, and perhaps speedier relative of *Tyrannosaurus*.

Tyrannosaurus rex was, perhaps, the largest terrestrial carnivorous animal ever to exist. Individuals reached 15 m (50 ft) in length from snout to tail. Large specimens stood 5-6 m (18-20 ft) tall and weighed 5500 kg (6 tons). The head was 1.2 m (4 ft) long with 90 cm (3 ft) jaws. The 60 jaw teeth were 8-15 cm (3-6 inches) long. The snout of *Tyrannosaurus* was narrow, allowing the forward-pointing eyes to achieve binocular vision and depth perception. These features helped in locating an object precisely in the visual field and in determining distance. These huge predators were capable of ripping off and swallowing huge chunks of prey. The lower jaw of *Tyrannosaurus* was hinged in the middle to allow a slight expansion of the back of the throat: bolting

their food was probably an everyday occurrence. The head was the primary or, perhaps, the sole weapon for predation.

Front limbs were reduced to short, tiny "arms" that were shorter than a human arm (Figure 1.3). The paleontologist Bob Bakker contends that any normal human could have beaten *Tyrannosaurus* at arm wrestling and that the limbs were probably useless.[3] However, the forelimbs, with their two claws might have functioned in holding prey while the head killed it.[6] Either way, I wouldn't arm wrestle any tyrannosaur should I ever have the chance.

Figure 1.3: A 15 m long *Tyrannosaurus* attacks a nodosaur, *Edmontonia*, in northern Alaska 70 million years ago. *Tyrannosaurus'* use of the hind leg to overturn *Edmontonia* is speculative; the predator may simply have used its 1.2 m head to flip this prey onto its back.

Hind limbs were also simplified or stream-lined. For example, the claws and claw tendons are reduced in *Tyrannosaurus* in comparison to its earlier relatives. Bakker argues that hind limbs weren't weapons but, instead, were designed for speed and nimbleness. The fighting capability of both sets of limbs was sacrificed to maximize the power and effectiveness of the neck and head.

In spite of its ferocious appearance, there is some debate as to whether *Tyrannosaurus* was an active hunter or merely a scavenger. The debate is, perhaps, a non-issue since virtually all active predators also scavenge when opportunities arise.[7]

Dromeosaurids

Two cousins of the frightening *Velociraptor*, made famous in the movie *Jurassic Park* , were present in Alaska in the Cretaceous: *Dromeosaurus* and *Saurornitholestes*. Both of these fast, bipedal predators were about 1.2 m (4 ft) tall and weighed about 45 kg (100 lb). As is the case for *Velociraptor*, *Dromeosaurus* and *Saurornitholestes* are thought to have hunted in groups. Teeth and vertebrae of both species have been found. One interesting feature of these predators is the claw on the inner toe of each hind foot. In *Dromeosaurus* this raptorial claw was 8 cm (3 inches) long and undoubtedly functioned as a weapon and perhaps also to aid in ripping apart its kills. The claw was strongly hooked and had a sharp lower surface. During normal locomotion the claws were held off the ground. The tail of *Dromeosaurus* was stiff but not totally rigid due to a series of cable-like connections between adjacent vertebrae.[8]

Troodon

A *Troodon* species, less than 1.8 m (6 ft) tall, left behind teeth and skull fragments. *Troodon* had a large brain and very large eyes. The teeth were pointed with serrated edges. The orbits in the skull faced anterolaterally, possibly providing stereoscopic vision.

Based on the numbers of teeth left behind, *Troodon* was far more abundant than either *Dromeosaurus* or *Saurornitholestes*. Since all three were about the same size, what accounts for the dominance of *Troodon*? By virtue of its superior vision, *Troodon* may have been highly effective at hunting in the prolonged twilight and darkness of high-latitude winters in northern Alaska and also in the gloomy, forested landscapes during the summers.[9,10]

Edmontonia

This creature, related to ankylosaurs, was a heavily armored plant-eating dinosaur perhaps 1.8 m (6 ft) tall, 7 m (23 ft) long, and weighing 3600 kg (8,000 lb). The entire upper surface of *Edmontonia* was covered with a flexible pavement of small bony plates. A series of laterally projecting horns or spikes, increasing in length from back to front, provided additional protection (Figure 1.3). The shoulder spikes, pointing somewhat forward, would have been effective in countering attacks of *Tyrannosaurus* once the predator got close enough for a quick counter-charge by *Edmontonia*. Probably the predator's best chance was to flip *Edmontonia* on its back and attack its poorly defended belly.

Bob Bakker [3] put *Edmontonia* in the "low-level cropping brigade" of the Late Cretaceous.

He contrasts the late Jurassic herbivorous dinosaur fauna, dominated by multiple species of long-necked brontosaurs, with that of the late Cretaceous, dominated by horned dinosaurs, ankylosaurs, and duckbills. Only a single brontosaur, *Alamosaurus*, survived into late Cretaceous North America. Bakker and others have linked this change from high-level to low-level foraging to the rise of flowering plants and the reduction in numbers and dominance of cycads and coniferous trees. The nodosaurs, including *Edmontonia*, had the smallest teeth of all the dinosaurs, perhaps well adapted for herbaceous, flowering plants.

LANDFORMS OF ALASKA

Glaciers and Their Landforms

Glaciers are, quite literally, rivers of ice. Wherever they are located, glaciers flow inexorably down slope, eroding the containing basin as they move. Wherever glaciers occur or occurred in the past, they have effects on the landscape and on current-day plants and animals. Here are a few examples.

Sometimes a glacier excavates a **cirque,** a hollow in the mountain with steep sides and backwall. The cliffs of a cirque are often used as escape terrain by Dall sheep. As glaciers melt and recede they leave behind bare ground upon which plants gradually begin to grow. One set of plants gives way to another in a progression or succession that influences the animals present. Receding glaciers often leave ridges of soil and boulders previously carried along by the ice. These ridges are called moraines. **Terminal moraines** run perpendicular to the direction of glacier flow; **lateral moraines** run parallel to the glacial channel. These moraines may provide critical habitat. High, windswept moraines are used by caribou as calving areas. Melting glaciers left depressions called **kettles.** These kettles are sometimes filled with water, forming kettle ponds. Kettle ponds abound along the Richardson Highway near Donnelly Dome and along the Parks Highway near Cantwell. Such ponds are important tundra waterfowl habitat.

One final feature produced by glaciers is sand dunes. Sand-sized particles eroded by glacial scouring were blown by wind and formed dunes. Some of these dunes still exist today, such as the Kobuk Dunes in northwest Alaska. Other dunes have been overgrown by vegetation. Some of these fossil dunes can be seen in road cuts on the Parks Highway just south of Nenana.

Features of Floodplains

One of the most obvious features seen from an airplane flying into Fairbanks is the meandering Tanana and Chena Rivers. A characteristic of the lower reaches of rivers is **meanders,** that is, bends in the river. For meanders to occur, the grade, or steepness, is typically low. Over the last several million years the Tanana River has wandered across the Tanana floodplain, depositing sand and gravel on the insides of the bends and eroding the plain on the outsides of the bends. These meanders affect vegetation patterns on the floodplain. First, the newly deposited bars are new habitat upon which plants can grow. Second, the river has a large thermal mass. That is, the river holds heat, even when it is frozen over in the winter, and transfers this heat to the channel below the river and to the riverbanks.

Typically, riverbanks in interior and northern Alaska are underlain by thawed soils, allowing root penetration to greater depths than might be possible in permafrost soils.

As is the case elsewhere in the world, meandering streams and rivers change course as the meanders move back and forth across the floodplain. Occasionally, parts of the old river channel are isolated as the meander moves on across the floodplain. If the part remains filled with water, it forms an **oxbow**, or cut-off, lake. The oxbow pond or lake typically fills in with sediment and vegetation over the course of hundreds of years. In other words, over time the pond will exhibit a succession of forms ranging from the original pond to a meadow to a forest. This succession of plants is described more completely in Chapter 3.

A meandering stream with several channels is often referred to as a **braided stream**. Braided streams occur at all latitudes. However, a stream type that occurs only at high latitudes is the **beaded stream**. Beaded streams appear to zig-zag across the landscape from one puddle or bead to the next. Beaded streams are a result of water flowing down a series of high-centered polygons, a land feature characteristic of permafrost soils.

I mentioned the process of glaciers abrading the underlying bedrock. This grinding process produces, among other particles, a fine powder called glacial flour. This rock flour is the source of **loess** deposits. Loess is windblown, fine-grained sediment that was, during glacial episodes, deposited on the hills of the Tanana Uplands. Almost every road cut in the interior has a layer of loess overlying the bedrock. On Chena Ridge, west of Fairbanks, the loess may

vary from 1 to 10 m (3-33 ft) in thickness. One of the thickest deposits of loess in Alaska is the Gold Hill-Eva Creek deposit between Fairbanks and Ester. The entire deposit, down to gravel, is almost 32 m (105 ft) thick and spans over 2 million years. Except for two **unconformities**, places where a part of the sequence of loess has been eroded and is missing, this one deposit would contain a record of the entire Pleistocene. Included in the 32 m layer are **primary loess**, the windblown material, and **secondary loess**, material that was relocated by water. Secondary loess contains dead plant and animal (organic) material and is black. Fossils are typically found in the secondary loess layers rather than in the primary loess.

ALASKA AND THE PLEISTOCENE GLACIATIONS

The Pleistocene geologic epoch began about 1.8 million years ago and is typically characterized as the beginning of a significant worldwide cooling compared to the earlier Pliocene. The beginning of the Pleistocene was long thought of as the start of the ice age, but it is too simple to think of the Pleistocene as synonymous with glaciation. First, glaciers may have existed in Alaska's mountains for the past 10 million years. Second, Antarctica was at least partially glaciated at least 25 million years into the past.[11]

The classic view of the Pleistocene was of four major glacial episodes, or **stadials**, separated by **interstadial** (interglacial) periods in which glaciers were in retreat or disappeared completely. From the oldest to youngest these episodes were referred to as the Nebraskan, Kansan, Illinoian and Wisconsinan glaciations.

This terminology is now outdated: within each of these four major glaciations, climate variation resulted in ice advances and retreats such that at least 17 identifiable glacial stages have been distinguished. Nevertheless, some remnants of that terminology are still found in the recent literature. For example, the late Pleistocene began about 132,000 years ago with an interstadial (the Sagamon) lasting about 10,000 years, followed by the early, middle, and late Wisconsinan. The late Wisconsinan episode and, indeed, the Pleistocene ended 10,000 years ago.

Glacial episodes led to the formation or enlargement of five or six ice masses in North America). The **Cordilleran Ice Sheet** formed in the Canadian Rocky Mountains, Alaska Range, Aleutian Islands and northern Cascades and spread seaward to and beyond the current coastlines of Washington, British Columbia, and Alaska. At maximum extent, the Cordilleran Ice Sheet extended eastward almost to Calgary, Alberta. Most of eastern Canada and parts of the United States were covered by the **Laurentide Ice Sheet**.

During the **Last Glacial Maximum** (LGM), about 18,000-20,000 years ago, the Cordilleran and Laurentide Ice Sheets butted against each other along a line from south of Calgary northwest into the Yukon (see map on page 13). The **Greenland Ice Sheet** covered Greenland, and the **Innuitan Ice Sheet** covered the extreme northern islands of the Canadian High Arctic, including Ellesmere, Devon, Melville, and Axel Heiberg Islands. **Cordilleran mountain glaciers** occupied peaks in the Rocky Mountains, Sierra Nevada and Cascade Ranges south of the ice sheets. In Alaska, the **Brooks Range,** several points on the Seward Peninsula, and Mt.

Harper in the Tanana Uplands were also glaciated during the LGM.

Did all these ice sheets in North America advance in synchrony? It appears that the glacial advance of the early Wisconsinan period (79,000-66,000 years ago) occurred at the same time in the Laurentide and Cordilleran ice sheets in both Canada and the United States. The mountain glaciers of North America also advanced simultaneously. In contrast, during the LGM the Laurentide sheet peaked in geographic extent, but mountain glaciation had been declining for several thousand years. The Cordilleran ice sheet did not reach its maximum extent until perhaps 14,000 years ago, well after the LGM. Our modern view of the Pleistocene is much more dynamic than we had imagined even as recently as 30 years ago.

In the following sections I will discuss some of the effects that glacial advances and retreats had on the landscape, plants, and animals of Alaska, including dispersal, local and widespread extinctions, expansion and reduction of available habitats, and wholesale changes in the plant and animal communities in Alaska.

What caused the Pleistocene ice ages?

What were the conditions that led to Pleistocene glacial advances and retreats? The Pleistocene was merely the latest in a long series of glacial episodes in earth history. Nine separate ice age episodes occurred on planet Earth before the last, Pleistocene period. These non-Pleistocene glacial episodes are the subject of a great deal of current research but probably had little, if any, direct bearing on what we see on the Alaskan landscape.

We know that the surface of the earth in the Pleistocene was cooler than today during stadials and that temperatures moderated during interstadials. These temperature changes were more pronounced at high latitudes than near the equator. Scientists think that, for the most part, these temperature fluctuations were caused by changes in the amount of solar radiation reaching the earth's surface. Milutin Milankovitch, a Serbian mathematician, addressed this problem in the 1920s and calculated the earth's movements relative to the sun. He found three variables that potentially affected incident radiation. First, the shape of earth's orbit around the sun changes through time. At times the orbit is nearly circular; at other times it is much more elliptical. The cycle from circular to elliptical lasts about 105,000 years. Second, the tilt of the earth's axis relative to the plane of its orbit also changes and cycles every 41,000 years. The third variable is the precession of the equinoxes. Simply put, the date on which the earth's orbit is closest to the sun changes through time; that date shifts forward or later in the calendar year. For example, the near point in earth's orbit now occurs in Northern Hemisphere winter but, in the future, will occur in spring. The cycle of precession of equinoxes is 19,000-21,000 years long.

The net result of all three oscillations is a cycle of about 100,000 years, the **Milankovitch cycle**. This cycle produces small variations through time in the amount of radiation reaching the earth's surface. One of the ways this variation plays out in the natural world is in the contrast between summer and winter temperatures. At one extreme is a climate that produces warm summers and cold winters (elliptical orbit). At the other extreme is a regime (circular orbit) that yields cool summers and mild winters. The first extreme is associated with glacial retreats and the second with glacial advances. The rationale is that during cool summers not all of last winter's snowfall melts, leading to accumulation of ice in glaciers. There are other factors that contribute to the development of an ice age, including the positions of the continents, the directions of surface ocean currents, the patterns of deep ocean circulation, and atmospheric carbon dioxide levels.

Sea-level changes and the existence of Beringia

An enormous amount of ice accumulated in North America during the Last Glacial Maximum, about 18,000 years ago. The Laurentide and Cordilleran ice sheets were at least 3000 m (9800 ft) thick, covered 16 million km^2 (6.1 million miles^2), and had a volume of 32-38 million km^3 (7.6-9.0 million miles^3). All this ice in North America, plus the ice in Eurasia, Antarctica and elsewhere, amounted to a significant proportion of the world's water supply. From the standpoint of a global water budget, huge volumes of water were transferred from oceans to ice, enough to lower sea level about 120 m below its current level. Actually, a small portion of that 120 m can be accounted for by the reduced volume occupied by cooler seawater since average ocean temperatures were lower back then. Such a reduction in sea level meant that the landmasses of Alaska and Siberia were connected (Figure 1.4). This land connection is often referred to as the Bering Land Bridge but

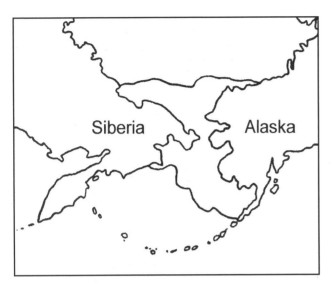

Figure 1.4: The land connection between Siberia and Alaska during the height of glaciation in the Pleistocene. The land bridge plus parts of Alaska and Siberia are referred to as Beringia. At least part of the Sea of Okhotsk, west of the Kamchatka Peninsula (extreme left of map) was also above sea level during glacial maxima.

the name conjures up an image of a narrow link. In fact, most of the Bering Sea was dry land; the Pribilofs, St. Matthews, St. Lawrence, Nunivak, and Wrangel Islands were merely high ground on a broad, undulating plain. This land area is called Beringia. Beringia is important to the fauna and flora of modern Alaska for two reasons. First, the broad land connection between eastern Asia and North America was a potential corridor for the dispersal of plants and animals, including humans. Second, almost all of Beringia, including interior and arctic coastal Alaska, was ice-free during glacial periods. Thus, Beringia served as a refuge for plants and animals that, as the glaciers receded, could disperse into or reoccupy deglaciated habitat. The Beringian Refuge is one of several that allowed survival of life forms in North America. The largest glacial refuge was the huge area south of the ice

sheets between the Rocky and Appalachian Mountains. This was the Mississippi Refuge. West of the Cascades was a Pacific Refuge; east of the Appalachians was the Atlantic Refuge. Additional areas are known or thought to have been safe havens for the survival of plants and animals during the worst of the glacial periods. Based on the mitochondrial DNA sequences in wolves and some plant species, it appears that parts of southeast Alaska also remained ice-free. This area has been named the Alexander Archipelago Refuge. Similarly, DNA studies of lemmings suggests an ice-free refuge in the high Canadian Arctic.

Recall that the Pleistocene was a series of alternating glacial and interglacial episodes. Therefore, as ice accumulated or receded, sea level fell or rose accordingly. In the context of Beringia, we have to imagine an alternation of land connection and disconnection and varying widths of the land contact between continents. Animals dispersing during a warm interstadial probably found their way blocked by the flooded landscape we now call the Bering Sea. Alternatively, direct connection of the continents during full glacials provided an avenue to disperse. Even when the land route between continents existed, the movement of terrestrial animals into middle North America was blocked by ice sheets. Species surviving the LGM might have been able to colonize the lower 48 states by dispersing down the **ice-free corridor** that developed as the Cordilleran and Laurentide ice sheets retreated and separated from each other. The ice-free corridor opened about 12,000 years ago (see Figure 1.5).

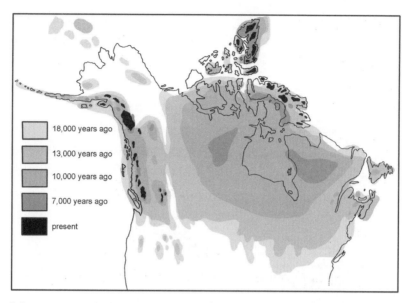

Figure 1.5: Map of the extent of glaciation in North America from the Last Glacial Maximum (LGM, about 18,000-20,000 years ago) to the present. Notice the ice-free corridor in western Canada developing around 12,000-13,000 years ago. This corridor was an avenue for dispersal of plants and animals, possibly including humans, during this time. At the heights of glacial episodes the coastlines of Alaska extended farther north and west, at times connecting with Siberia (see Figure 1.4). Redrawn from Pielou (1994).

The Flora of Pleistocene Alaska

We simply cannot identify a single assemblage of plants that is representative of the entire Pleistocene. During glacial maxima, forests virtually disappeared from the Alaskan landscape. During interstadials, forests were reestablished and at times were more widespread than they are today.

How do we know what plant communities were like over the last 20,000 years? Macroscopic plant structures such as leaves, cones, twigs and tree trunks occur only infrequently in the fossil record. Fortunately, the pollen grains of plants are usually well preserved in the bottoms of ponds and lakes. Pollen plus sediment accumulates, forming thick deposits that can be cored from a floating platform. Of course, the deepest material is the oldest and that on the surface is the most recent. The pollen grains of most species of flowering plants can be distinguished from each other. The pollen from the different levels of a core, representing different ages, are identified and counted. The result of looking at the entire column from a lake core is a series of pollen diagrams that give insight into the plants present around the lake at different times (see Figure 1.6).

There are some limitations to pollen diagrams. First, pollen from a large geographic area around the lake is deposited. Second, the bottom of the lake is reworked by larval insects that slightly disturb the pollen strata. Third, some species produce more pollen than others. Finally, plants that are pollinated by insects are underrepresented in lake cores because the insects gather much of the pollen. Nevertheless,

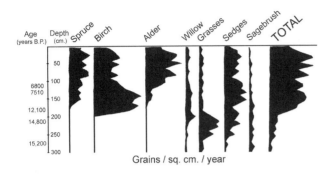

Figure 1.6: Pollen diagram. This diagram shows the abundance of pollen from different plants that were deposited in the upper 3 meters of sediment in a Yukon Territory lake. Several dates (years before present) are shown corresponding to sediment depths. Notice the transition at about 13,000 years ago. Tree pollen began to appear while grass pollen became less common. This diagram is clear evidence of vegetation changes in the last 15,000 years.

a pollen core analysis gives a general picture of what plants were in the area in the past.

What that picture shows for ice-free Beringia is that, at most locations, trees such as spruce, birch and alders weren't present from 20,000 to 12,000 years ago. During the same time period, grasses and sagebrush were more common than they are today.

During the LGM, much of unglaciated interior and northern Alaska was covered with grasses, sagebrush, juniper, and other plants adapted to aridity. This is an assemblage of plants that, currently, is most nearly matched on the high, arid **steppes** of central Asia. In modern-day Alaska, the nearest thing to the Pleistocene steppe is found on steep, well-drained, south-facing bluffs along interior rivers. These bluffs have grasses, juniper, and sagebrush but, unlike true steppes, may have an occasional white spruce, alder, or balsam poplar. There is no modern equivalent of the steppe in Alaska. Dale

Guthrie[12] coined the term "mammoth steppe" to describe this assemblage of plants and large mammals that extended from the Yukon, across interior and northern Alaska, and westward through central Asia to Spain and England during stadials in the Pleistocene. In the mammoth steppe concept, northern Alaska isn't just a part of the Beringian Refuge from which plants and animals disperse into the rest of North America after the glaciers recede. Rather, interior and northern Alaska and much of the Yukon constitute a geographic, faunal, and floral extension of the steppes of central and eastern Asia with connections to Pleistocene Europe.

In much of the interior of Alaska, steppe habitat was gradually replaced by plant species that eventually made up the assemblage we now know as the boreal forest. The dominant elements, at least visually, are the tree species, including black spruce, white spruce, larch, Alaska birch, quaking aspen, and balsam poplar. Depending on how we define "tree," we could also list several alder and several willow species.

Not all of Alaska was steppe during Pleistocene stadials. And not all of Alaska was transformed into boreal forest after the end of the Pleistocene. What we see in modern Alaska above tree line on mountains and north of tree line on the Arctic Coastal Plain differs from the steppe community in several ways. First, there is more moisture on the landscape, and second, the plant communities are adapted to that moisture. Among the modern plant communities of Alaska the treeless mountaintops and coastal areas are tundra. There are three types—alpine, moist, and wet—that differ in plant species composition but have many in common.[13] The critical point is that tundra is wetter than the steppe it replaced. Grasses, though present in modern tundra, do not dominate the landscape. The arid-adapted sagebrushes, *Artemesia*, of the Pleistocene steppe survive only in specialized habitats in the boreal forest. Willow species, and dwarf birch and resin birch shrubs found in modern tundra were not present during stadials of the Pleistocene.

The Fauna of Pleistocene Alaska

The *National Geographic* magazine published an article on the Pleistocene fauna of Alaska featuring a wonderful mural by Jay Maternus. The mural depicted a complete array of the large, charismatic mammals that are known to have existed in northern and interior Alaska over a period of some 300,000 years. If we could take a time machine back to a single date in the Pleistocene in Alaska, would we see all these animals? The answer, for several reasons, is no.

First, not all these species existed throughout the Pleistocene. For example, moose probably evolved within the last 60,000 years, reached Alaska by 12,500 years ago and the rest of North America about 9,000 years ago. So moose may have never coexisted with shrub-ox or short-faced bear on this continent since these two species disappeared from Alaska about 20,000 and 30,000 years ago, respectively.

Second, the climatic changes that accompanied or caused the successive glacial episodes and their intervening interglacial periods led to radical changes in vegetation upon which many of these mammals relied directly for food. Further, these alternating periods of relative warmth and cold led to alternating terrestrial connections and disconnections of the North American and Asian land masses. With these constraints in mind, I'll describe a few of the interesting mammals in Alaska during the Pleistocene.

EXTINCT PLEISTOCENE MAMMALS

Short-faced bear

As a youngster I had recurring nightmares about being dragged out of the family car by a large bear. Consequently, I've had a lifelong fascination with them; the bigger the bear, the more interesting I found them. The giant short-faced bear, *Arctodus simus*, is the epitome of the large bear. These long-legged bears of the Pleistocene, in height and weight, dwarfed even the largest brown and polar bears. Based on relationships between long bones and body weight in bears, the weights of large male *Arctodus* were 700-800 kg (1540-1760 lb) with exceptional individuals weighing perhaps 1000 kg (2200 lb).[14]

Based on skeletal material, height at the shoulder was about 1.7 m (5 ft 8 in) for *Arctodus* and about 1.5 m (4 ft 10 in) for the largest coastal brown bear or polar bear.[15] On its hind legs, the largest short-faced bear would have stood 3.7 m (12 ft) tall (Figure 1.7)! By one estimate, on its hind legs, *Arctodus* had a vertical reach of 4.3 m (14 ft). Defending the basket against Shaq would have been a cinch for any adult *Arctodus*. No wonder Nancy Sisinyak[16] referred to *Arctodus* as "mega bear." Of all the bears, living or extinct, *Arctodus* was the largest. Indeed, the short-faced bear was, perhaps, the largest mammalian carnivore to ever walk the earth.

Figure 1.7: A size comparison between a modern, large, coastal brown bear (represented by the bear in the University of Alaska Museum) and a large short-faced bear. The brown bear stands 2.6 m (8.5 ') tall; the short-faced bear stood 3.5 m (11.5') tall on its hind legs.

Any carnivore as large and as charismatic as the short-faced bear generates a host of questions among wildlife enthusiasts and paleontologists. Perhaps the first is: was this bear a carnivore? Based on energetics of such a large mammal and on similarities between *Arctodus* and its closest living relative, a few scientists contend that *Arctodus* was an omnivore with most of its diet consisting of plant material, but most of the experts conclude that the short-faced bear was primarily carnivorous.

Since the largest of extant brown bears rely heavily on salmon, one might next ask if *Arctodus* also relied on marine fish to attain their huge sizes. The measurement of stable isotope (^{13}C and ^{15}N) ratios from an animal's tissues is a technique that provides information about reliance on both plant material and marine organisms as food. Ratios from fossil *Arctodus*, fossil brown bears from Beringia and also modern brown bears from southwest and southeast Alaska showed that *Arctodus* was, indeed, a carnivore but didn't show any evidence of eating salmon. Brown bears from the Pleistocene showed a broad range of diets including plants but no salmon either.[17] *Arctodus* was strictly a meat-eater.

Did this immense bear actually pull down its own prey or, rather, did it simply scavenge already dead animals? This argument centers on the huge size, the relatively slender build of the legs, and skull morphology. Some argue that the long, slender legs of *Arctodus* were designed for high-speed running consistent with chasing down herbivores such as horses, bison, camels or small mammoths.[18] However, Paul Matheus presented an alternate and perhaps more realistic view based primarily on his exhaustive biomechanical analysis of the limbs and skull.[15] Paul argues that the legs weren't structured for rapid acceleration or for attacking really large prey such as adult mammoths. Rather, he suggests that *Arctodus* was primarily a scavenger that, by virtue of its long legs, could efficiently cover a very large home range seeking out large, dead animals. Some of those carcasses were due to natural mortality and others were killed by other predators such as brown bears, lions, saber-tooth cats or wolves. In Paul's view,

Arctodus' size allowed it to attack and drive off any other predator on the kill (Figure 1.8).

The skull of the short-faced bear has several features that bear (pun intended) upon the question of its feeding ecology. As its name suggests, the muzzle of *Arctodus* is short compared to other bears. The advantage is that the length of the lever closing the mouth is shortened, allowing more power to be applied to the jaws. **Carnasial** teeth allow shearing of tendons, muscle and ligaments. In *Arctodus*, however, the shearing carnasial teeth (upper fourth premolar [^{4}P] and the lower first molar [M^1]) are poorly developed; most skulls show flattened M^1 and ^{4}P teeth, better employed for crushing. Such crushing molars are found in sea otters, which crush clams, and hyenas, which crush bones. The marrow of long bones is an excellent source

of fat for those animals that have access to it; *Arctodus* undoubtedly had access.

Another feature of the skull is the width of its snout, similar to that of the polar bear. In fact, the width of the skull is about 80% of its length. Polar bears are known to use their noses to find seal lairs under the snow. It is likely that the wide snouts of polar bears and short-faced bears evolved to accomodate superb olfactory senses. *Arctodus* was probably a master at catching the scent of a dead animal at very long range and, then, rapidly reaching that potential meal with its mile-eating gait.

In Matheus' view, the short-faced bear covered vast areas with an efficient pacing gait, seeking out large mammal kills. Pacing involves swinging both limbs on one side of the body in unison, much as a modern day camel moves.

Figure 1.8: A giant short-faced bear driving a large, Pleistocene grizzly bear off its kill, a young woolly mammoth.

Once on the kill, the absolute size and power of *Arctodus* was more than a match for several lions, several brown bears or a pack of wolves. The specialization for carrion feeding may have been the downfall of the short-faced bear. The diversity and numbers of large mammals in North America during the Pleistocene glacials probably translated to a variety of large mammal deaths at all seasons of the year. *Arctodus* could sustain itself by moving from kill to kill.[15] However, at the end of the Pleistocene, large mammal extinctions led to a diminished fauna with most of the natural deaths occurring in late winter or early spring. Not only were there fewer types of prey mammals but also fewer large predators from which to steal prey. There simply may not have been enough carcasses to sustain these large bears through the winters.

It is thought that *Arctodus* didn't hibernate like brown and black bears. Their closest living relatives, spectacled bears, don't hibernate. Maintaining an active metabolism all winter would have been a tremendous additional drain on *Arctodus*. In contrast, brown bears hibernate, a huge energy savings, and can subsist on a variety of foods including carrion, prey such as moose and caribou, salmon in streams, and vegetation.

Woolly mammoth

In the mammalian history of North America there have been from three to possibly six mammoth species. The first was *Mammuthus meridionalis*, a species of forest mammoth that entered the New World about 1.5 million years ago and became extinct maybe 1 million years ago. Before it died out it gave rise to the Columbian mammoth, *Mammuthus columbi*, a

species adapted to open country and a diet of grassland species. Experts on fossil mammoths are still debating the variability of the Columbian mammoth. Some scientists recognize the imperial mammoth, *Mammuthus imperator*, as a separate species and others think that the Columbian mammoth gave rise to a more advanced species, *Mammuthus jeffersonii*. This Columbian mammoth complex was confined to central and southern North America ranging at various times from Florida to California and from southern Canada to northern Mexico. Remains of a dwarf mammoth have been found on the California Channel Islands. At some point, Columbian mammoths probably swam out to the islands. Modern elephants are excellent swimmers. Sea-level changes weren't great enough to directly connect the islands to the mainland, so swimming is the logical method used to occupy these habitats. Once established on the islands, dwarfing occurred as a result of forage quality and quantity. Island mammoths had to compete for a very limited resource and smaller individuals with lower overall metabolic requirements were favored. Lack of predators was probably another factor influencing dwarfing. Without predators there is no selective pressure to grow large. These island mammoths, designated *Mammuthus exilis*, died out about 12,000 years ago, about the same time their mainland cousins became extinct.

The mammoth of Pleistocene Alaska was the woolly mammoth, *Mammuthus primigenius* (Figure 1.9). The woolly mammoth was a grazer on grasses and other vegetation from treeless, steppe-tundra habitats. This species apparently evolved from the steppe mammoth, *Mammuthus trogontherii*, an inhabitant of the arid grasslands

Figure 1.9: Size and shape comparison of woolly mammoth (rear) and an American mastodon (middle). The woolly mammoth was about 3 m (10') tall at the shoulder. The mammoth in front is a pygmy form, full-grown, such as existed on Wrangel Island (Chukchi Sea) and the Pribilof Islands (Bering Sea).

of the Far North of Eurasia. The woolly mammoth came on the scene about 250,000 years ago and by 100,000 years ago was spread from the British Isles across northern Eurasia and into Alaska.[19]

Remains of the woolly mammoth have been found south of the continental ice sheets in North America. A natural sink hole at Hot Springs, South Dakota, has yielded many skeletons of Columbian mammoth and a few skulls of woolly mammoth. Did the range of these two mammoth species overlap? Over the entirety of the Pleistocene, yes, their ranges did overlap. However, it is most likely that the two species did not occur at the same locations simultaneously; woolly mammoths dispersed southward during glacials and Columbian mammoths dispersed northward during interglacials.

What we know about the size, appearance, anatomy, diet and geographic distribution of woolly mammoths has been derived from a variety of sources. Alaska has been a rich source of fossil bones of mammoths but also has contributed mummified remains. Several mammoth mummies have been found in Siberia. Mummies provided information on food in the stomach, color of the hair, configuration of the trunk, length of tail and other details. The ages of fossil mammoths have, in many cases, been established by [14]carbon dating, described later in this chapter. Here is a snapshot of woolly mammoths.

Adult woolly mammoths, at their largest, were 2.7- 3.4 m (9-11 ft) tall and weighed 4-6 tons, about the same size as modern African elephants. This generalization can be misleading; one might conclude that woolly mammoths everywhere they occurred and at all times during their existence achieved this stature on adulthood. That wasn't the case.

First, just as was the case with Columbian mammoths, a mammoth population became isolated on an island and suffered dwarfism. Wrangel Island, off the northeast coast of Siberia, was Uplands as a part of Beringia during glacials. At the end of the last glacial, sea level rose and, by 9,000 years ago, isolated a population of mammoths. Woolly mammoths survived for another 5,000 years on the island, disappearing about the time Egyptians were building pyramids to the pharaohs. The last of the mammoths were small in stature, not 9-11 ft tall.

A second factor that influenced adult body size is sex of the individual. At adulthood, as determined by complete eruption of molar teeth, mammoths exhibited a **size dimorphism**; that is, males were much larger than females. Third, mainland mammoth populations, as were those on islands, were also subject to the influence of forage quality and quantity. As stadial and interstadial climates alternated, so also did the vegetation of the Far North. Some of the plant communities were poor habitat for mammoths. Under poor nutrition mammoths and, indeed, most mammals, did not achieve maximum possible size. Fourth, due to dominance-hierarchy interactions, non-dominant individuals may not have had access to sufficient resources to achieve large body size. One interesting and puzzling point on body size: There is no indication that woolly mammoths were exhibiting stunting or dwarfing near their point of extinction in Alaska.

The trunk of the woolly mammoth was long and muscular as is characteristic of all elephants and mammoths. Based on mummified remains and cave paintings, we know the tip included the two nostrils and two finger-like projections, one long and one short. The fingers differ from both the Asian elephant (one finger) and African elephant (two equal fingers). The fingers were probably sufficiently dexterous to pluck flowers, buds and the short grasses that made up much of their food. The trunk, in cross-section, had lateral projections or wings that may have functioned to scoop snow into the mouth in winter. Proboscidians (elephant-like mammals) require lots of water because they lose lots of water in their feces. Water requirements would be critical in the dead of winter when lakes and rivers were frozen and a mammoth's forage would be dry. So the shape of the trunk was probably an adaptation to the cold, Far North.

What other features adapted these creatures to the frozen Arctic? First, woolly mammoths, as the name suggests, had dense coats of fur for insulation. Some of this fur was intact on a baby mammoth mummy discovered in 1977 in Siberia. The long hair is depicted in numerous paintings of mammoths inside European caves occupied by Paleolithic humans.

Two other external features tended to reduce heat loss in woolly mammoths: the tail and the ears. Mammoth tails were short, about 60 cm (24 inches); those on African elephants are over 160 cm (63 inches). The ear of an adult mammoth discovered in Siberia measured 33 cm (13 inches) in height; that of an adult African elephant measures about 183 cm (72 inches). The surface area of the elephant ear is about 15 times greater than that of the mammoth. A smaller surface translates to a smaller amount of heat lost from the ears. So, woolly mammoths had small ears that conserved heat. African elephants have very large ears, probably as a mechanism for promoting heat loss in a hot climate.

The teeth of mammoths included molars for processing vegetation and also large tusks. At birth, a mammoth calf had four molars no larger than adult human molars. As is the case with living elephants, mammoths produced six sets of molars during a complete lifetime. The first set lasted about 18 months but, by six months, a second set began erupting. Unlike human teeth, proboscidean molars erupt from behind the previous teeth. This process is a continuous conveyer belt system of tooth replacement.[19] Molars were constructed of up to 26 ridges of hard enamel separated by layers of dentine and cement (Figure 1.10). The enamel ridges of

Figure 1.10: Molars of American mastodon (top) and woolly mammoth (bottom). The pronounced cusps of the mastodon molar were suitable for crushing coarse material such as twigs, branches and leaves. The mastodon was a browser. The mammoth molar has a much broader grinding surface suitable for processing finer vegetation such as grasses; the mammoth was a grazer. The mammoth molar has many enamel ridges (lighter areas in illustration) for grinding food. They run perpendicular to the long axis of the molar. Chewing was forward-backward rather than side to side as in ungulates.

upper and lower molars ground past each other, crushing the tough grasses and sedges that made up much of their diet. Over time, the silica in grass stems and grit taken incidental to plant material wore down the enamel. The number of ridges on the molars is a general indication of diet; more ridges were required to deal with grasses as opposed to shrubs. The woolly mammoth, with more enamel ridges, was better adapted to a grassland diet than either Columbian or steppe mammoths. One last tidbit about molars: the enamel ridges run perpendicular to the jaw. For grinding of food to occur, chewing must be a forward and backward set of motions. This contrasts with the side-to-side chewing motion of bison, moose and caribou. In these latter species the enamel ridges run parallel to the jaw.

Two "milk" tusks, each about 5.2 cm (2 inches) long, erupted at about six months of age. The milk tusks were replaced after about a year with the permanent tusks that grew from 2.5-15 cm (1-6 inches) per year. Tusks grew in a spiral or corkscrew pattern with opposite tusks spiraling in opposite directions. Often the tusks overlapped in front of the head. The largest woolly mammoth tusk found to date measured 4.2 m (13 ft 7 in) and weighed 84 kg (185 lb). A typical male tusk weighed 45 kg (100 lb) and measured 2.4-2.7 m (8-9 ft). Female tusks were smaller, averaging 1.5-1.8 m (5-6 ft) and 9-11 kg (20-25 lb). By comparison, the largest Columbian mammoth tusk, from Post, Texas, is over 4.9 m (16 ft) long.

Several functions have been proposed for mammoth tusks. First, the difference in size suggests that males used tusks to compete for mates. That competition included pushing and shoving matches as indicated by two inter-locked skulls found in Nebraska. However, tusk size alone may have intimidated lesser males and established dominance. Further, females may have actively selected males with huge tusks. Tusks of many individuals were worn and flattened on the bottom surface, suggesting the possibilities that mammoths scraped snow to expose winter foods or simply rested their heads on the tusks.

Mastodon

The American mastodon, *Mammut america-num*, and its close relative from Eurasia, *M. borsoni*, differed in many respects from the woolly mammoth described above. Mastodons and mammoths were probably similar in body weight, with large males weighing 3600-5500 kg (4-6 tons), although a particularly large male discovered in 1936 in Hillsborough, New Brunswick, was estimated to have weighed 8300 kg (9 tons). Mastodons were shorter at the shoulder than woolly mammoths, 2-3 m as opposed to 2.8-3.4 m, and had longer bodies. Tusks were straighter and the tail was longer (see Figure 1.9). The tusks, composed of den-tine, exhibit annual growth increments, like the rings on trees. Thus, the age of the mastodon at the time of death can be estimated.

The molar teeth of mastodons can't be mis-taken for mammoth teeth. A typical molar, seen in Figure 1.10, has four sets of cone-shaped cusps of very thick enamel. This tooth structure was effective in chewing coarse, woody browse. Guts of well-preserved mastodons contain wood twigs, chewed wood, and resins and pollen from spruce, pine, and herbaceous plants. Molars were

replaced in the same way as in mammoths. Over the mastodon's lifetime, each jaw had two sets (one left and one right) of six successive molars, for a total of 24 molars—if the individual lived to a ripe old age. Life expectancy in woolly mam-moths was about 60 years and presumably was about the same in American mastodons.

At several periods of the Pleistocene, Ameri-can mastodon occurred in Alaska. They were present mainly during forested episodes, the interstadials, but mastodon remains have also been found in association with steppe grazers such as mammoths, horses, and bison. Did mastodons graze when the forests were gone? Probably not. It is more likely that mastodons subsisted by browsing on a landscape that was a mosaic of habitats including some stands of trees or shrubs. River bottoms in modern tundra habitats often support stands of spruce, willows, and poplar; the mammoth steppe may have had a few trees on the landscape as well.

Extinction of the American mastodon occurred about 9,000 years ago. Climate, as well as plant communities, had changed consider-ably. However, what we know of the mastodon's diet suggests that its major foods were still pres-ent. Mastodons were hunted by Paleo-Indians in North America. Kill sites have been found in Washington, Michigan and Missouri.

Steppe bison

The steppe bison, *Bison priscus*, was one of the most common large mammals in Pleistocene Alaska. The species is thought to have evolved 700,000 years ago and then spread over most of the Holarctic region. Steppe bison were pres-ent in England, Europe, the Asian steppes, and eastward to the Northwest Territories. With the glacial advance of the LGM, steppe bison were displaced south of the ice sheets and occupied middle North America as well as the Far North. They survived until 10,000-12,000 years ago in eastern Beringia and until about 8,000 years ago in middle North America.

The dates of extinction of *Bison priscus* are uncertain for two reasons. First, it probably gave rise, evolutionarily, to at least two other bison species in North America. An initial infusion of steppe bison into the Great Plains apparently led to the emergence of the giant bison, *Bison latifrons*. Large bulls may have weighed up to 1800 kg (4000 lb), with straight horns over 2.1 m (7 ft) long. Toward the end of the Pleistocene, *B. latifrons* body and horn size decreased and *Bison antiquus* was the result. Meanwhile, in Beringian isolation, *B. priscus* is thought to have evolved into the smaller bodied *Bison occidentalis*, which had the sweptback horns of *B. priscus*. But wait, the story isn't over. Once the ice-free corridor opened from Beringia to mid-continent, *B. occidentalis* moved south and intermixed with *B. antiquus*. It may be that they interbred, giving rise to the modern plains bison, *Bison bison* (Figure 1.11). Alternatively,

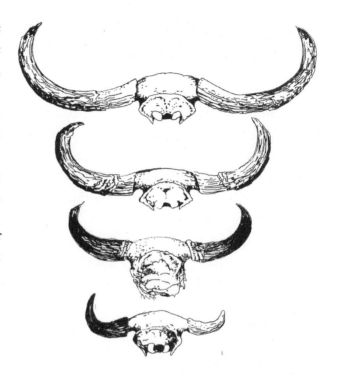

Figure 1.12: Horn size in steppe bison varied considerably; small horns such as those of Blue Babe in the University of Alaska Museum (second from bottom) were characteristic of interstadial (interglacial) periods. Third from bottom is a typical steppe bison. Largest horns were present on bison from glacial episodes (top). The horns of a large, modern plains bison (bottom) are shown for comparison. Redrawn from Guthrie (1990).

one or the other of the two may have evolved into the modern form.

There is considerable variation among the *Bison priscus* fossils from Alaska. In terms of horn size, interstadial animals had smaller horns than animals that lived during full glacial episodes (Figure 1.12). These fluctuations in horn size don't represent replacement of one bison species by another; they merely indicate that conditions were not always optimal for horn and, presumably, body growth. The best conditions seem to have been when the steppe/grassland vegetation of the stadials flourished. In other

Figure 1.11: Profiles of plains bison (left), wood bison (center) and steppe bison (right). The hump on steppe bison was farther back than on modern bison and the horns were longer. Color patterns on the three species differ. For complete pelage color details, see Guthrie (1990).

words, fossil steppe bison bones may, at some place and/or time, look like or be described as another species. Maybe the differences we see among *B. priscus, B. latifrons,* and *B occidentalis* are no more profound than those among Masai, NFL football players, and world-class Moroccan marathoners.

Perhaps the most fascinating aspect of the steppe bison is that modern humans have been able to deduce so much about it even though it is now extinct. Dale Guthrie filled most of a book on deductions about the steppe bison based on everything from 25,000-year-old cave paintings to tooth wear patterns to the struts and air-filled spaces in the frontal region of the skull.[21]

For instance, what did the steppe bison eat? Molars are a rough indicator of diet. The molar teeth of modern plains bison wear rapidly due to the silica content of the grasses they typically eat. In contrast, Wood Buffalo Park bison, because of a scarcity of grasses, graze primarily on sedges and show reduced wear and higher crowns on their molars. Steppe bison molars show a wear pattern typical of eating grasses, not sedges. More direct evidence comes from analysis of the material found in the stomachs of bison mummies. One such stomach from a Siberian mummy was found to be full of grass macrofossils.[22] A third line of evidence relies on the ability to examine the cuticle material from plant fragments and identify the kind of plant. Each plant species has a rather unique cuticle pattern. If we were studying an extant species we could either collect gut contents or droppings, have an expert examine them, and draw up a list of plants that appeared in the diet. The number of steppe bison stomachs and/or droppings available for analysis is near zero, how-

ever. But Guthrie found another way to get at the problem. Bison molars have highly folded enamel layers within the dentine. The enamel often surrounds an empty space or cavity, the infundibulum. As the bison grazed, it mashed plant fragments into the cavities. Guthrie teased out these fragments from the first molars of 44 steppe bison and had the cuticles analyzed. Grasses made up 80% of the fragments; woody browse contributed only 7%.

Of course some cautions are required to make deductions about bison food. First, minor items in the diet may have been grazed incidental to the main forage species simply because the plants were growing next to or among the dominant food. Second, in marginal habitat or in winter, bison may graze on plant species that they do not prefer. There are instances of moose and deer dying of malnutrition with guts full of indigestible plant material. We wouldn't want to conclude that the starved moose preferred what it was forced to eat out of desperation. Therefore, season of death is an important piece of information.

The large horns performed several functions in steppe bison. Males had much larger horns than females, which means that one of the primary uses was in establishing male dominance. Short of actual combat, a bull steppe bison displayed its size and strength, and the horns were an integral part of that display. Lateral displays were, undoubtedly, also important. Shoulder and neck manes depicted in cave art probably served to enhance status in the same way that neck ruffs on wolves and modern African lions do.[21] And, as is the case with moose, the size of the head weaponry often confers dominance without combat. Two evenly matched bulls probably engaged their horns and pushed. Once a bull was backing up, it ran the risk of turning its body and exposing its flanks to the forward-pointing, hooked horns of its opponent. A fossil steppe bison scapula shows the puncture wound that would have resulted from such combat.

In addition, hooked horns undoubtedly played a role in defense. The hook could have caught and ripped American lions, scimitar cats or other Pleistocene predators. Fossil lion and scimitar cat remains have been found with healed injuries perhaps inflicted by bison horns, the trunks and tusks of mammoths, or the hooves of horses.

Scimitar cat

Over the course of the Pleistocene there were several large cats with very long upper canines.

Perhaps the best known in North America is the saber-toothed cat, *Smilodon fatalis*. This species lived south of the ice sheets and is well represented in the fossil assemblage from Rancho La Brea tar pits in Los Angeles, California. Some 1200 individuals contributed bones to the pits! The saber-toothed cat was present from 800,000 years ago until about 8,000 years ago. Apparently, the species never reached Alaska. A South American version of the saber-toothed cat, *Smilodon populator*, was similar in build and in dentition. However, the South American species was much larger than the North American species, about the size of a lion.

The scimitar cat, *Homotherium serum*, was the long-toothed cat of Alaska's Pleistocene. The upper canines were up to 10 cm (4 inches) long (Figure 1.13), compared to 17 cm (7 inches) for the saber-toothed cat. Unlike those of the

Figure 1.13: Two scimitar cats subduing a juvenile woolly mammoth. The exact use of their 10 cm canine teeth is still being argued but the infliction of deep puncture wounds, depicted here, is one possibility.

saber-toothed cat, the canines of *Homotherium* were serrated along the back edge, making them well-adapted for cutting through hide. The exact function of these huge canines is still a matter of controversy among paleontologists. Almost all agree that the long upper canines were used to inflict wounds on prey animals. A common assumption is that *Homotherium* and *Smilodon* used their fangs to stab their prey and inflict a mortal wound. But these teeth may have been too fragile to withstand the shear forces generated by plunging them deep into a thrashing, active prey unless, perhaps, the bite was to the throat region.[23]

Instead, envision a more superficial bite, anchored by the lower canines, that either produced massive hemorrhaging or actually tore out a chunk of skin and flesh. The strategy would be to cause massive blood loss and, eventually, the death of the prey. In this scenario, the scimitar cat would have the patience to wait around until the prey animal dropped dead. This predatory style isn't far-fetched: modern wolves behave in this way when hunting moose.

Another notion about these long canines is that they were effective at slicing through hide. Analysis of adult canines from these cats shows too little wear to support this proposed function. Yet another misconception about these long-toothed cats is that they were "overevolved" in that they had such huge teeth that they couldn't open their mouths wide enough to actually use them effectively. Not true. Skulls of saber-tooths and scimitar cats differed from lion and tiger skulls in six ways that either increase the strength of the bite or increase the gape of the jaws or both.[23] Lions and tigers can achieve an

angle of 65-70° with their mouths wide open; scimitar cats could open to 90-95°.

Homotherium remains have been found in caves in both the Old and New Worlds. The presence of both cub and old adult skeletons in the same cave suggests that caves were occupied routinely, not just for natal den sites. Along with cat remains are the bones of juvenile mammoths, apparently killed and dragged to the caves by the cats. A similar *Homotherium* in Eurasia killed the young of mastodons and woolly rhinos as well as mammoths.

Homotherium is thought to have reached maximum weights of 280 kg (620 lb), heavier than the largest of modern African lions but smaller than Pleistocene lions. The front legs were longer than the hind legs, causing the back to slope downward toward the rear. In profile, the scimitar cat looked similar to modern hyenas. This form has been described as well adapted for a cantering gait and for covering long distances while hunting. Claws were nonretractable, a trait shared with modern cheetahs. Some paleontologists think that the scimitar cat, like the cheetah, was capable of rapid locomotion.

Horses

Horses originated in North America back in Eocene times, between 56 and 35 million years ago. Horse ^{14}C dates from eastern Beringia range from over 40,000 years down to 12,900 years ago[21] but the Yukon horse undoubtedly dates from about 200,000 years ago. The scattering of more recent (< 50,000 year old) dates indicates that horses survived during and through the LGM and into the final warming trend.

However, unlike mammoths, horses appear to have exhibited dwarfing after the LGM, an indication that habitat conditions were deteriorating.

A 26,000-year-old horse carcass was discovered on Last Chance Creek, near Dawson City, by placer miners. Part of the intestinal contents were intact and included grasses, sedges, poppies, mustards, buttercups, and members of the rose family.[24]

The Yukon horse was small, about 1.3 m (4 ft) tall at the withers (shoulders). The cheek teeth (molars) are typical of caballoid horses rather than of either asses or hemionids. Przewalski's horse, *Equus przewalskii*, an extant species from Mongolia, is the closest living relative to the Yukon horse. Indeed, some paleontologists consider the two as just a single species.

Other horses existed in North America during the Pleistocene. The most common horse found in the La Brea tar pits is the western horse, *Equus occidentalis*; the next most common is the Mexican horse, *Equus conversidens*. A single, huge, horse premolar from the Pleistocene of North America was described as the giant horse, *Equus giganteus*. The giant horse must have weighed about 525 kg (1150 lb) if its body weight/tooth size relationship was the same as for modern horses. Modern wild stallions weigh up to about 390 kg (860 lb).

Camels

Camels first showed up on the evolutionary scene about 40 million years ago in North America. About 5 million years ago camels dispersed into South America, giving rise to modern llamas and vicunas, and to Eurasia, where the modern dromedary and Bactrian camels originated.

In North America during the Pleistocene there were a variety of camels, at least two of which occurred in eastern Beringia.

The western camel, *Camelops hesternus*, was found throughout the western United States and north to the Yukon and Alaska. This camel is also called yesterday's camel. Its legs were about 20% longer than those of the dromedary. Like the dromedary, it had a hump. The western camel is thought to have reached Beringia from the south during a warm interstadial but was able to survive until at least 23,000 years ago, during the "run-up" to the LGM, when it was cooler than modern times.

Bones of a second, much larger camel have been found in the Old Crow River basin of the Yukon. This area was at the eastern extreme of Beringia during the Pleistocene. The shape and size of these bones are very similar to those of the Nebraska camel, *Titanotylopus nebraskensis*. It is likely that a population of the Nebraska camel existed in the Far North in early Pleistocene times. Elsewhere in North America the Nebraska camel became extinct around 1 million years ago, so these two camel species probably never coexisted in Alaska. The Nebraska camel would have dwarfed the western and the two modern camel species. Large males of this beast stood 3.5 m (12 ft) at the shoulder compared to 1.8-2.1 m (6-7 ft) for the dromedary. It is scary to imagine how far one of these monsters could spit.

Saiga

The saiga is an antelope species that today occupies the steppes and semideserts of central Asia. At their maximum geographic dispersal in the

Pleistocene, saigas were found from England in the west all the way to the western Yukon and Northwest Territory in Canada. This steppe species, unlike the woolly mammoth, bison, caribou, and muskox, never dispersed south of the ice sheets in North America. Based on dates of fossil finds it appears that saigas greatly expanded their geographic range during glacials and contracted it during interglacial periods when steppe habitat was replaced with boreal forest. In Alaska and Siberia saigas were most abundant just before and just after the LGM.

Saigas are about the size of pronghorn antelope, standing 60-70 cm (24-28 inches) tall and weighing 26-32 kg (57-70 lbs). Like pronghorns, saigas are fast afoot, capable of reaching speeds of 70 km per hour (40 mph). These antelopes are nonterritorial and can travel 80-120 km (50-70 miles) per day.

In summer, the coats of saigas are light buff; in winter they are almost white. The pelage is thick, offering good insulation against winds and temperatures ranging down to -40°C (-40°F) in winter. Males have horns; females do not. Both sexes have an inflatable, proboscis-like snout that is thought to be excellent in filtering dust out of the air they breathe. This filter mechanism would have been helpful during a glacial episode with its characteristic clouds of wind-blown loess coming off glacially fed rivers.

As climate warmed following the final (to date) glaciation, grasslands gave way either to tundra or boreal forests. Neither are suited to saigas and, thus, their range retracted back to the steppes of central Asia. Saiga became locally extinct in North America around 12,000 years BP.

Lion

The lions of the Pleistocene in Eurasia and the New World are designated as a subspecies (*Panthera leo atrox*) of modern African lions. Several differences have been discerned based on analysis of bones from fossil lions from North America and from examination of depictions of lions in Paleolithic cave art. First, based on the size of the long bones, American lions are thought to have been about 25% larger than modern lions. Males averaged about 235 kg (530 lb); females about 175 kg (385 lb).[25] Second, an engraving of a lion in a French cave shows stripes. So also does an ivory figurine attributed to Paleolithic Russia. In both representations the cat is long-tailed and, therefore, can't be either a scimitar or saber-toothed cat.

Lions reached Alaska during the Illinoian glaciation (187,000-129,000 years ago) and the rest of North America by about 128,000 years ago. With the final glacial advances of the Wisconsin (90,000-10,000 years ago) American lions would have been isolated in Beringia and south of the ice sheets. In Beringia lions are thought to have been more common than either scimitar cats or short-faced bears.

Capable of short bursts of speed to 48 km per hour (30 mph), lions hunted horses, bison and probably young mammoths in Beringia. The 36,000-year-old steppe bison on exhibit at the University Museum in Fairbanks, Blue Babe, was killed by lions. You can see the claw marks on his preserved hide.

Pleistocene lion males apparently didn't have the long, showy mane characteristic of modern African lions. In African lions the mane is a status symbol for males and helps them achieve dominance and control of the pride of females and young. The lack of a long mane hints that the social behavior of lions may have been different in the Pleistocene; perhaps there was no pride structure.

OTHER MODERN SPECIES PRESENT IN PLEISTOCENE ALASKA

Part of the fauna of Pleistocene Alaska is very familiar to us modern humans. Some of the ice age species are still present here. These animals include caribou, moose, muskox, red fox, wolf, brown bear, polar bear, hoary marmot, and parka squirrel. The lives of these species during the Pleistocene were, roughly, the same as they are in modern times. However, the changes associated with alternating stadials and interstadials must have resulted in changes in distribution and abundance.

The Pleistocene mammoth steppe was occupied by several grassland species now restricted to lower latitudes. The American badger, *Taxidea taxus*, is widely distributed today across grasslands and desert from the Great Lakes states through Missouri, all the states to the west, and in the prairie provinces of Canada. The black-footed ferret, another prairie species, was also present in the Far North. A specimen of this animal was found by placer miners on the Sixtymile River near the Yukon-Alaska border. The carcass was so well preserved that its fur was intact! These two members of the weasel family plus the saiga antelope are among the strongest pieces of evidence supporting the concept of the mammoth steppe. All three are grassland species in modern times. The inference we should draw from their pres-

ence in the Pleistocene Far North is that grasslands abounded. The alternative hypothesis is that all three species radically changed their habitat preferences since the end of the Pleistocene; this isn't a very plausible hypothesis.

The wapiti or elk, *Cervus elaphus*, was also present in interior Alaska during the ice age. Elk are highly adaptable and, as late as the 19th century, were primarily a plains species. Thousands were shot off grazing range by ranchers to reduce competition with domestic livestock. The remnants, in many areas, retreated to forested habitat. In many areas of the American West, elk still occupy open rangeland, including sagebrush prairie.

GIGANTISM IN THE PLEISTOCENE

Many of the large mammal species found in Alaska during the Pleistocene exhibited gigantism.[26] One indicator is indices of body size in Dall sheep, both recent and fossil. The lengths of 2nd and 3rd molars from recent trophy rams have been compared with lengths from sheep teeth found at the Dry Creek archeological site near Healy, Alaska. The Dry Creek fossils date from 11,000 years ago and are beyond the size range of modern rams. Similarly, plots of the diameters of horn cores from recent and fossil Alaskan Dall sheep shows that the fossil horns were generally much larger.

Bison horns from the Pleistocene and from recent specimens show the same trend in size reduction. After about 12,000 years ago, bison horn size rapidly declined to modern plains bison dimensions. Is it fair to compare horn sizes of the steppe bison, *Bison priscus*, with those of plains bison, *Bison bison*? As I indicated above, the differentiation of these two nominal species may be artificial. If it is true that *B. priscus* was in the direct lineage of *B. bison,* one could argue that the differences are simply a character gradient through time. Studies of mitochondrial DNA from Pleistocene steppe bison from across the mammoth steppe and DNA from modern plains bison suggest that eastern Beringian steppe bison were more closely related to North American plains bison than they were to the steppe bison of Europe and western Asia.[27] This finding supports the trend mentioned above in North American bison horn size.

Both elk (wapiti) in North America and red deer in England show a reduction in antler size since the Pleistocene. Some of the Alaska/Yukon elk were, judging by their antler bases, enormous.[28] One elk antler found in the Yukon has a base the diameter of a saucer. It is typical for Pleistocene elk to have an extra antler tine. Modern elk have three forward-pointing tines; Pleistocene elk had four. Based on comparisons of molars, both caribou and moose were notably larger during the late Pleistocene than they are now.

What accounts for this trend of reduced body size since the last glacial age? Another way of putting the question is: what was better about the Pleistocene? Several factors were involved. One possibility is that growing seasons were longer during the Pleistocene, producing more high-quality forage for these herbivores. Growth season for vegetation probably began earlier in the spring due to aridity. That is, the thin snow cover melted off earlier in the spring than it does currently. Early springs led to deeper thawing, more soil microbial activity, more nutrient

regeneration, and better plant growth. Second, populations of caribou, elk, moose, and bison were probably understocked back then because of high wintertime mortality.

EXTINCTIONS

Why did so many of the large mammals become extinct at the end of the Pleistocene? Gone are all the species of mammoths, both mastodon species, woolly rhino, helmeted muskox, saber-tooth cat, scimitar cat, both species of cave bears (European and Florida), both short-faced bears, stag-moose, several ground sloths, and several camel species. In North America, additional, localized extinctions occurred that eliminated American lions, horses, cheetahs, and saigas. While large mammals were falling by the dozens, the small-mammal fauna survived the Pleistocene-to-Holocene transition largely intact.

Two general hypotheses attempt to explain late Pleistocene extinctions of large mammals. The first and more plausible relies on our knowledge of changes in climate and vegetation at the end of the Pleistocene. The transition from the Pleistocene to the modern, or Holocene, period is marked by an increase in mean annual temperatures in the Far North and, perhaps more important, an increase in precipitation. Winter snowfall was deeper and covered grasses and other steppe vegetation, making them less available for the large mammals that relied on them. Gradually, the landscape shifted from arid to moist, leading, in part, to the expansion of boggy terrain and the replacement of arid-adapted plant species with moisture-loving species. This replacement further disadvantaged steppe species. Shrubs and trees gradually invaded Alaska. These woody plants favored browsing herbivores rather than grazers. Further, many of these woody species produce chemical defenses (discussed in Chapter 3) that effectively reduce the amount of their tissues that herbivores can eat. Steppe mammals simply weren't capable of switching from grazing to browsing, and generalists probably couldn't handle the chemicals. Extinctions elsewhere, mid-latitude North America for example, could have been caused by changes in climate and vegetation that led to changes in large-mammal competitive interactions.

These were the same kinds of changes required of the Alaskan fauna during transitions from glacials to interglacials, and some of those earlier transitions were also marked by large-mammal extinctions. However, the Pleistocene/Holocene transition may have been more dramatic in terms of temperature and vegetation, both in Alaska and elsewhere, than those earlier fluctuations.

The second idea used to explain these extinctions is often referred to as the prehistoric overkill hypothesis. Paul Martin is the chief proponent of this hypothesis.[29] In essence, the idea is that as humans expanded their range into North America at the end of the Pleistocene they hunted many of their prey species to extinction. The large-mammal species that succumbed were those species, camels and Columbian mammoths, for example, that had evolved in North America in the absence of human hunters. The survivor species, including moose, elk, bison, and caribou, were relatively recent immigrants from Asia, where they, presumably, were more experienced in avoiding human predators. One piece of evidence for

this hypothesis is that North American extinctions coincide pretty closely with the entry of humans into the continent. In Europe and Asia, where large mammals had a long history of contact with humans, extinctions were fewer and more gradual.

Several arguments have been raised against the overkill hypothesis. First, many scientists think that there were too few humans initially in North America to drive prey to extinction. Second, several large North American carnivores also became extinct. These included the Florida cave bear, giant short-faced bear, American lion, scimitar cat, saber-tooth cat and dire wolf. It seems unlikely that any (or all) of these carnivores were purposely hunted by early humans. However, there is a possibility that carnivores could have been affected by prey reductions due to human hunting.

ESTABLISHING THE AGE OF FOSSILS

How do scientists place fossil remains at their correct time in the past? Several methods are used. Perhaps the best known is the **radiocarbon dating** technique. This technique relies on the fact that there are three naturally occurring isotopes of carbon on earth. The two common isotopes are ^{12}C and ^{13}C; these aren't radioactive. A third isotope, ^{14}C, is produced by cosmic rays and, once formed, begins to decay to ^{14}N by emission of a beta particle. How fast does this change occur? If we could make a pound of ^{14}C today, half of it would have changed to nitrogen in 5570 years. So, its **half-life** is 5570 years. After 11,140 years we would only have a fourth of our original pound. All plants and animals incorporate small amounts of ^{14}C into their tissues, and the rate of incorporation is thought to be constant over geologic time. But, as soon as it is incorporated, it begins to decay. Therefore, dating a fossil bone entails determining how much of the original proportion of ^{14}C still remains in the bone. If only an eighth remains, three half-lives must have passed, about 16,710 years. There are definite limits to this technique: after about ten half-lives, the relative change in radioactivity due to an additional half-life is so slight that the method is useless. Therefore, beyond about 50,000 years before present other techniques must be used.

In addition to the limitation to 50,000 years, radiocarbon dating has other pitfalls. Great care must be taken to ensure that the sample analyzed for radiocarbon has not been contaminated by more recent material. For example, a fossil horse pelvis might have been deposited in soil in which plants took root, say, 2,000 years later. Let's assume the roots grew into the crevices of the pelvis, died, and began to decompose. Some of the plant material with its higher proportion of ^{14}C (younger age) may be imbedded in the pelvis. If we simply grind up the pelvis, we will get a radiocarbon age that is younger than the age of the fossil. One way around this difficulty is to remove a core from the bone and analyze only material from the center of the bone, assuming that the center is probably uncontaminated with more recent material.

Another dating method that relies on the decay of a radioactive element is potassium/argon dating. An isotope of potassium, ^{40}K, decays to argon gas with a half-life of 1.26 billion years. This decay process is useful for determining the age of materials in the 10,000-3 billion year age range.

A third technique relies on volcanic eruptions. When volcanoes erupt, ash layers are deposited in soils. Major eruptions leave deposits over large geographic areas. Each major eruption has its own unique combination of elements, its own signature, and these ash, or **tephra,** layers can be correlated across large geographic areas. If independent dating techniques, based on radioactive decay sequences with longer half-lives than ^{14}C are used, absolute dates for all the identical tephra layers can be established.

One other feature of sediments that is helpful in establishing the age of bones in those sediments relates to the presence of iron particles. As tiny iron particles are deposited in sediment, they tend to orient according to the earth's magnetic field, so all the particles will line up with their "south poles" pointing toward the earth's north magnetic pole. We know that the earth's magnetic field has reversed in the past; a record of the reversals is found in sedimentary and igneous layers containing these iron particles. The absolute ages of some of these reversals have been established by other means, so it only remains to correlate the specific reversal in the stratum of interest with the known, dated sequence. This is the field of **paleomagnetic** dating.

A recently developed technique for aging fossils is electron spin resonance (ESR) dating. This technique relies on the knowledge that a fossil bone gets a steady dose of radiation from the surrounding rocks and from cosmic rays. That radiation causes the formation of electrons inside the bone. Basically, the ESR dating procedure measures the amount of trapped electrons within the bone; the greater the age, the more electrons. The ESR technique can date material within the last 2 million years.

REFERENCES

1   Wilson, F.H. and Weber, F.R. 1994. Prehistoric Alaska: the land. Alaska Geographic 21(4): 6-23.

2   Wolfe, J.A. and Upchurch, G.R. Jr. 1986. Vegetation, climatic and floral changes at the Cretaceous-Tertiary boundary. Nature 324: 148-152.

3   Bakker, R.T. 1986. The dinosaur heresies: new theories unlocking the mystery of the dinosaurs and their extinction. Zebra Books, New York, 481 pp.

4   Brouwers, E.M., Clemens, W.A., Spicer, R.A., Ager, T.A., Carter, L.D. and Sliter, W.V. 1987. Dinosaurs on the north slope, Alaska: high latitude, latest Cretaceous environments. Science 237: 1608-1610.

5   Forster, C.A. 1997. Hadrosauridae, pp. 293-299 In: P.J. Currie and K. Padian, editors, Encyclopedia of dinosaurs. Academic Press, New York, 869 pp.

6   Carpenter, K. 1997. Tyrannosauridae, pp. 766-768 In: P.J. Currie and K. Padian, editors, Encyclopedia of dinosaurs. Academic Press, New York, 869 pp.

7   Currie, P.J. 1997. Theropoda, pp. 731-736 In: P.J. Currie and K. Padian, editors, Encyclopedia of dinosaurs. Academic Press, New York, 869 pp.

8   Currie, P.J. 1997. Dromeosauridae, pp. 194-195 In: P.J. Currie and K. Padian, editors, Encyclopedia of dinosaurs. Academic Press, New York, 869 pp.

9   Fiorillo, A.R. and Gangloff, R.A. 2000. Theropod teeth from the Prince Creek formation (Cretaceous) of northern Alaska, with speculations on arctic dinosaur paleoecology. Journal of Vertebrate Paleontology 20: 675-682.

10 Gangloff, R.A. 1998. Arctic dinosaurs with emphasis on the Cretaceous record of Alaska and the Eurasian-North American connection, pp. 211-220 In: S.G. Lucas, J.I. Kirkland and J.W. Estep, editors, Lower and middle Cretaceous terrestrial ecosystems. New Mexico Museum of Natural History and Science Bulletin No. 14.

11 Hambray, M.J. 1994. Glacial environments. UBC Press, Vancouver, Canada. 296 pp.

12 Guthrie, R.D. 1982. Mammals of the mammoth steppe as paleoenvironmental indicators, pp.307-329, In: D.M. Hopkins, editor, Paleoecology of Beringia. Academic Press, New York.

13 Viereck, L.A. and Little, E.L. 1972. Alaska trees and shrubs. Forest Service, United States Department of Agriculture, Agriculture Handbook No. 410, 265 pp.

14 Christiensen, P. 1999. What size were *Arctodus simus* and *Ursus spelaeus* (Carnivora: Ursidae)? Annales Zoologici Fennici 36: 93-102.

15 Matheus, P.E. 2003. Locomotor adaptations and ecomorphology of short-faced bears (*Arctodus simus*) in eastern Beringia. Paleontology Program, Government of the Yukon Occasional Papers in Earth Science No. 7: 1-126.

16 Greiner, N. 2000. Mega bear. Alaska Magazine 66: 24-28.

17 Matheus, P.E. 1995. Diet and co-ecology of Pleistocene short-faced bears and brown bears in eastern Beringia. Quaternary Research 44: 447-453.

18 Kurten, B. 1967. Pleistocene bears of North America 2. genus *Arctodus*, short-faced bears. Acta Zoologica Fennica 117: 1-60.

19 Lister, A. and Bahn, P. 1994. Mammoths. Macmillan USA, 168 pp.

20 Guthrie, R.D. 2004. Radiocarbon evidence of mid-Holocene mammoths stranded on an Alaskan Bering Sea island. Nature (London) 429 (6993): 746-749.

21 Guthrie, R.D. 1990. Frozen fauna of the mammoth steppe: the story of Blue Babe. University of Chicago Press, 323 pp.

22 Korobkov, A.A. and Filin. 1982. An analysis of the plant remains from the digestive tract of the bison that was found in the deposits of the late Pleistocene of the Krestovka River [Kolyma Basin]. Botanical Zhurnal 67: 1351-1361.

23 Turner, A. and Anton, M. 1997. The big cats and their fossil relatives. Columbia University Press, New York, 234 pp.

24 Harington, C.R. 2002. Yukon horse. Yukon Beringia Interpretive Center www.beringia.com.

25 Harington, C.R. 1996. American lion. Yukon Beringia Interpretive Center www.beringia.com.

26 Guthrie, R.D. 1984. Alaskan megabucks, megabulls and megarams: the issue of Pleistocene gigantism, pp. 482-510 In: H.H. Genoways and M.R. Dawson, editors, Contributions in Quaternary vertebrate paleontology: A volume in memorial to John E. Guilday. Carnegie Museum of Natural History Special Publication No. 8, Pittsburgh.

27 Shapiro, B. Drummond and Cooper, B. 2003. Late Pleistocene population dynamics of Beringian steppe bison (*Bison priscus*). Impacts of late Quaternary climate change on western arctic shelf-lands: insights from the terrestrial mammal record.

28 Guthrie, R.D. 1966. The extinct wapiti of Alaska and Yukon Territory. Canadian Journal of Zoology 44: 47-57.

29 Martin, P.S. 1984. Prehistoric overkill: the global model. pp. 354-403 In: P.S. Martin and R.G. Klein, editors, Quaternary Extinctions, University of Arizona Press, Tuscon.

2.
SHIVER, FREEZE, OR COOL YOUR KNEES: WAYS OF COPING WITH COLD

Before I describe some of the interesting ways that creatures in Alaska's boreal forest survive the cold, I want to dispel the notion that it is cold in Alaska's interior and northern regions year-round. It is a little amazing that many folks still think it is frigid in Fairbanks in the summer. At a high school reunion in southern California a former classmate asked me about my Fairbanks house. I replied that I lived in an igloo and, for a while, he believed me! As far as I know, the record temperatures for the interior (boreal forest) of Alaska are 37°F (99°F) and –55°C (–67°F). Thus, plants and animals contend with a 92C° (166F°) temperature range; no mean feat! From our human perspective, adapting to the bottom end of this temperature range seems to be far more difficult and interesting than coping with the upper end. And, indeed, from the broader perspective of the range of living organisms, it is more difficult to deal with these low temperatures. Simply count the total number of living species

in the Far North: There are far fewer than in either temperate or tropical climates.

Cold temperatures affect tundra plants and animals as well as those found in the boreal forest. So methods of coping with cold should be similar in tundra and boreal forest organisms. In this chapter I will draw examples from both the boreal forests and tundra to illustrate anatomical, physiological and behavioral mechanisms that help these organisms survive in the cold.

HEAT TRANSFER

There are four mechanisms of heat transfer, all of which influence living organisms. **Conduction** is heat gain or loss by direct contact. If you sit on a hot stove you gain heat by conduction; if you sit on a block of ice you lose heat by conduction. Animals, including humans, when standing in snow lose heat to the snow by conduction.

Radiation is heat gained or lost through space and, therefore, does not involve physical contact. Plants and animals can be warmed by radiation from the sun and achieve temperatures well above that of the surrounding air. Butterflies, dragonflies, and other insects orient themselves to maximize solar heat gain when they are cold.

Conversely, heat can be lost by organisms via radiation. Radiative heat loss depends on the temperature difference between the animal and its surroundings. A snowshoe hare resting in the open at night is radiating heat to the night sky, which is extremely cold. If, instead, it is resting beneath snow-covered spruce branches, it is losing far less heat via radiation because the boughs are much warmer than the night sky. So, even though hares do not dig burrows, they gain some thermal advantage by hiding from the night sky. Radiative heat loss from warm-blooded animals is in the infrared portion of the electromagnetic spectrum. The infrared is, for humans, just outside the visible range we see. But through the wonders of electronics, we can "see" animals radiating heat by looking through night-vision telescopes and binoculars. In the animal world there are creatures that see in the infrared region and others that see into the ultraviolet end of the spectrum where we cannot see. You can imagine what advantage might be gained by an animal with even limited infrared vision.

Convection is heat transfer due to moving air or water. Even in still air as we warm the air immediately around us, it begins to rise, carrying away some of our body heat. Cooler air moves in to replace the risen air and we tend to warm this cooler air, too. Heat loss in a wind is even greater than at the same air temperature on a calm day. Tables of wind-chill factors account for this convective heat loss at different temperature-wind combinations.

A fourth mechanism of heat transfer has to do with changing the state of water. In order for ice at 0°C to melt to liquid water at 0°C, a lot of heat energy is required (80 calories per gram of ice). This heat is referred to as the **latent heat of fusion.** When the human skin melts a hunk of snow, it spends almost twice the amount of energy it would take to warm that amount of liquid water at freezing to body temperature, from 0 to 37°C. Of course, the reverse process, freezing liquid water to ice, liberates heat energy rather than absorbing it. **Latent heat of evaporation** is the extra heat required to convert water from a liquid state to a gaseous state (540 cal/g). This latent heat is significant in evaporating sweat from your skin. In warm weather, evaporation of sweat cools the skin; evaporative cooling, in this context, is adaptive. However, in cold weather, sweating can lead to a dangerous level of heat loss. Latent heat of evaporation is also important in breathing in warm-bodied animals. Some water in the lungs is converted to water vapor, requiring extra heat energy. As we exhale, the heat energy we put into the conversion is lost with the exhaled water vapor.

Incidentally, this exhaled water vapor is an important component in water balance too. The nasal passages of caribou help conserve both heat and water by being long and convoluted. As water-saturated air is exhaled, it wends its way out and cools because the caribou's muzzle is cooler than deep-body temperature. Water condenses on the cool nasal lining, thus liberating heat and conserving water.

Some of the problems of the Far North have to do with heat loss from warm-blooded creatures. Humans unable to generate enough heat to match heat loss can develop **hypothermia,** in which the entire body cools below our thermostat *set point*. Without dramatic intervention, hypothermia can be fatal once body temperature has fallen to a critical level, about 86°F (30°C). When only the extremities are exposed to severe cold and insufficient heat is distributed to the periphery, **frostbite** can occur. Fingertips, toes, and ears can be lost. Humans are not the only susceptible animals out there in the winter. Mountain lions encroaching on the Far North typically lose their ears to frostbite. Muskrats in very severe winters have been observed with their tails frozen off.[1] Even when things don't go terribly wrong, cold weather means higher energy expenditures by warm-blooded animals to maintain relatively constant body temperatures. I will return to a discussion of **metabolic expenditures** later in this chapter.

Some other problems associated with cold weather can affect both warm- and cold-blooded animals. As soils freeze, they become hard to dig whether it is a vole or an insect doing the digging. Aquatic habitats, as they freeze in the late fall, are reduced in volume or eliminated. To avoid being trapped in ice, fish and invertebrates may need to relocate. Finally, the dramatic seasonal cycles in the Far North produce a profound seasonality of food quality and availability. Succulent, aboveground vegetation is completely unavailable for much of the year. Insects are available at very high biomasses in the summer but are difficult to find in any quantity in the winter. Herbivorous and insectivorous animals have to make seasonal adjustments to these realities.

MIGRATION

One adaptive strategy to beat the cold, short days and lack of food is migration. Whenever

I describe an adaptive strategy, whether in animals or plants, I am referring to a set of features such as behaviors, physiological mechanisms, or functional morphology that the species has evolved over the eons to cope with a problem it faces in the environment. I do not intend to suggest that an animal is employing a thought process to calculate, plan, or consciously prepare for the future. Instead, these adaptations have come about by means of natural selection. That is, they have evolved through time.

Migration is a directed movement of individuals that is repeated by those individuals or their offspring. Thus, migration is not to be confused with random wandering. Nor is migration the same as dispersal movements, which tend to be one-time-only events in the lives of the dispersers. There is a repeatability or predictability in migration movements that is lacking in either wandering or dispersal. In some species, such as the sandhill crane, the annual migration brings the same individuals back to locations (barley fields in Big Delta and Creamer's Wildlife Refuge in Fairbanks, for example) they have frequented for many years. In other cases, such as interior Alaska chum salmon, no individual ever repeats the migration.

What are the biological rationales or selective pressures that drive an animal to migrate? Another way of asking the question is: what are the advantages to migration? Biologists have identified three major driving factors in migration. First, some animals gain an **energetic** advantage by migrating. Second, some migrate to gain a **feeding** advantage. Third, some gain a **reproductive** advantage by migrating. Let us examine each of these briefly, but keep in mind that these three rationales, or "reasons" to migrate may all be operating together in a single species and its migratory behavior.

An energetic advantage can be gained by species that migrate out of interior Alaska in the fall to a warmer winter location. These migrators are reducing the metabolic expense of maintaining constant body temperatures. Since heat loss is proportional to the difference between body temperature and that of the surroundings, the migrator is reducing its heat loss by moving to warmer surroundings. The total energy savings over the winter must be greater than the energy expended in the migration or there is no advantage. The little brown bat, found in interior Alaska in the summer, is a species that undoubtedly migrates to achieve an energetic advantage. Hummingbirds reach south-central Alaska in the late spring but return to the south before the dead of winter, presumably for the same reason.

We should not constrain our thinking and assume that all migrators leave the Far North entirely. There are climate variables that trigger or synchronize migratory patterns within Alaska. Depth of snow cover in coastal areas varies considerably depending on season and weather systems. On Kodiak Island depth of snow is a major determinant of blacktail deer vertical movement. When the snow is deep on the ridges, deer move down to the shore, where they do not spend as much energy walking through snow. And it is undoubtedly easier to find food if the snow is absent! The annual cycle of migration in caribou is, in part, driven by winter winds crusting snow in the tundra. Caribou migrate down out of the tundra into the boreal forest where snow cover is not so crusted and, therefore, is easier to dig through for food.

In this case, the boreal forest is no warmer than the tundra; the energetic savings is in the ease of acquiring winter food. Do caribou migrate to gain a metabolic advantage or a food advantage? The answer is: both.

Clearly, food availability is a driving factor in the migration of many Alaskan species. Summer in interior and northern Alaska is characterized by strong pulses in the abundance of food organisms. Aerial insects, including mosquitoes, flies, moths, and butterflies, are extremely abundant and provide food for four swallow species, robins, and a host of other migratory songbirds as well as resident dragonflies and chickadees. In other words, the resident insectivores cannot possibly eat all these insects, and the excess is available for migratory birds and bats. One might ask: why don't resident species expand their populations to take advantage of all the excess food available? The answer, undoubtedly, is that the crunch would come in winter, when insect populations plummet and the enlarged chickadee population wouldn't find enough winter food to maintain itself.

Aside from swallows, there are several good examples of migrating populations driven by food availability. Migratory waterfowl feed on a variety of aquatic vegetation and invertebrates. Perhaps better examples are the Pacific salmon species that spawn in freshwaters, hatch out there, and eventually head to sea to grow, reach adulthood, mature sexually, and migrate back to their natal streams for spawning. In the case of salmon, the rich food resource is in the Gulf of Alaska. The plankton populations there are vast in comparison to those available in Alaskan streams, rivers, and lakes. If Pacific salmon weren't physiologically tied to development in freshwater, they probably would have given it up long ago in favor of a completely marine existence.

Gray whales migrate to Alaska for the rich feeding on bottom-dwelling amphipods in the Bering and Chukchi Seas off the west and north coasts of Alaska. Amphipods are so numerous that gray whales have adopted a feeding style in which they swim down to the bottom, roll on their sides and open one side of the mouth while expanding the oral cavity. This causes water laden with amphipods to be sucked into the mouth and trapped on the baleen filters.

Why don't gray whales just stay in Alaska all year? Gray whale calves are born without the insulative blubber layer of the adults. And, since they are so much smaller than the adults, they lose heat rapidly. So it is much better to give birth to the calves in warmer water, let them grow and accumulate some insulation, and then travel north for the rich summer harvest in Alaska. Is this migratory pattern driven by food availability or by the energetic advantage of calving in warm water? Both. Or, is it driven by a reproductive advantage?

Reproduction can be a driving factor in migration as well. One of the biological rationales is to reproduce where predator populations are low compared to elsewhere. Resident populations in Alaska are limited primarily by the amount of food they can find in winter. In winter, migratory species are gone and at least some of the locals are hibernating. That leaves predators looking for small winter-active prey or for winter-killed animals. So, dense breeding colonies of migratory birds, for example, usually produce more offspring than local predators can possibly eat. The predator population simply cannot respond fast enough reproductively to

take full advantage of the migratory prey. This "predator swamping" will be discussed later.

Earlier I mentioned caribou migrating to achieve an energetic advantage (easier food acquisition under soft snow in the forest) and a food advantage (more food acquired in the forest). It turns out that part of the annual migration cycle also yields a reproductive advantage. In the spring, pregnant females move to high, wind-swept ridges where their calves are born. Biologists think that the wind keeps biting insects off the newborn calves and adults and the high ridges provide good visibility, allowing females to spot approaching predators. Both these features probably increase survival of newborn calves. Therefore, caribou migration satisfies all three of the rationales I mentioned earlier.

Migration is not an unalloyed blessing. That is, there are some disadvantages that counter potential advantages. First, the energetic costs involved in the migration itself can be considerable. Individuals in poor condition may not survive the experience. Or, if they do survive, they may not have the physiological reserves to avoid predators on their newfound range. Another potential problem is that the northern environment is, to an extent, unpredictable. In most years, interior Alaska in April is sunny, promoting snow sublimation and snow melt. Temperatures gradually warm so that, by early May, the snow is nearly gone in the boreal forest, temperatures are warm (above freezing), and leaf-out occurs. In one recent year it snowed and rained all April, ponds remained frozen several weeks longer than usual, and leaf-out was two weeks late. Under these circumstances do migratory populations delay their arrival in Alaska, or do they arrive at the usual time?

Some species manage to delay their arrival. They face the potential problem of not having enough time in Alaska to successfully rear their young. There is a "drop-dead" date in the fall by which migratory birds need to be on their way south. Once the drop-dead date arrives (environmental cues are just right) the adults take off. If the young of the year have not fledged their flight feathers, they cannot fly and are left behind. These birds may be lost. On the other hand, having an inflexible arrival date has similar disadvantages. In short, flying north for the summer is still a little bit of a gamble.

Other aspects of the life history of migrators are the necessity for orientation and homing mechanisms. That is, how do migrating animals figure out where they are and where they are going? Mechanisms that are potentially available to migrators include sun-compass orientation, magnetic field detection and orientation, recognition of visual cues on the ground, and navigation by the stars. If an individual is deficient in the appropriate mechanism, it may be unable to find its way. On the other hand, it may simply be able to follow one of its fully functional fellows.

What is happening in the migrator's "other" habitat? While in the Far North, a tundra swan occupies tundra ponds and their surroundings. So far, there are vast tracts of tundra which have remained undisturbed and, therefore, provide uncompromised habitat for these birds. But when they fly south and occupy winter habitat in California, Utah, Nevada, Oregon, Washington, and Idaho, are those habitats also healthy and/or undisturbed? Many species that migrate to Alaska in our summer spend winters in Central and South America where

the pace of development and change is often much greater than is true of the Far North. In essence, these migratory species could be exposed to changing habitats on both ends of their migration routes.

MIGRATORY BIRDS

The Migrant-Resident Continuum

There is no clear-cut distinction between bird species that are resident and those that are migratory. Rather, birds exhibit a variety of patterns of movement that form a continuum between the two extremes. Resident populations may move from one local habitat to another on a regular basis. Willow ptarmigan near Eagle Summit on the Steese Highway occupy willow thickets at or above tree line in spring through fall. In winter, some birds move and concentrate in just a few drainages at tree line. Other birds fly down-slope into the spruce-aspen forests of the Chatanika River and Birch Creek valleys. Some birds leave the Tanana Uplands and winter in Goldstream Valley or in Fairbanks. Therefore, part of the population moves a few kilometers while another part moves 50 km or more. Are willow ptarmigan migratory? It depends on your definition.

Some species such as the boreal owl are considered resident within the boreal forest ecosystems of Canada and Alaska. But, when food resources get scarce, birds may move south in winter and show up in the prairie provinces of Canada and the prairie states of the U.S.A. These periodic movements, called irruptions, are not really the same as migrations because they are not regularly repeated.

Finally, there are bird populations some members of which are resident in the same general area all year and other members of which migrate great distances. The blackcap, a European warbler, exhibits such behavior. In Alaska, the red-breasted nuthatch may be similar. Nuthatches are supposed to leave in the fall, but we had several of these little birds visiting our feeder all through the winter of 2003.

Similarly, migratory waterfowl in interior Alaska leave behind individuals in areas where open water is produced by either natural hot springs or by the warm water effluents from power plants. The Chena River, with its power plant effluent in downtown Fairbanks, is such a location where mallards, red-breasted mergansers and several other ducks can linger all winter.

Physiology of Migration

The timing and physiological preparation of the bird for migration are driven by complex changes in hormonal levels. Hormones themselves are regulated by day length. One of the aspects of preparation involves an increase in appetite, causing the bird to eat more food. This **hyperphagia** leads to fat deposition that may, under ideal conditions, amount to a daily weight gain of 10%. This is the fat that will fuel the migration. Actual weight gains are usually less than 10% per day and depend on food availability, likelihood of food at stop-over points, distance migrated, and age of the bird. Often, as is the case with sandhill cranes, adults put on weight faster than juveniles. In some cases, a bird will double its body weight in added fat.

Fat storage for migration has several implications for migration itself. First, fat deposition should be centered on the bird's center of gravity to have the least impact on the actual mechanics of flight. Second, the added weight will require a higher wing beat frequency in flight. These relationships could affect migration altitudes. A heavily loaded bird needs more lift, best accomplished at low altitudes where air is denser. After exhaustion of some of the fat, less lift will be required and, presumably, the bird could fly higher.

Some birds fly at very high altitudes. Several crane species fly over the Himalayas on their annual migration. Tundra swans migrating from Iceland to Ireland have been observed at 8200 m (27,000 ft) elevation. Buntings and finches have been shown to have a high tolerance for hypoxia and, therefore, are adapted to survive and function at high altitudes such as they might experience in migration. Metabolism during flight may be as high as 14 times that measured at rest.

A Few Migrants and Their Routes

Arctic tern—The arctic tern, *Sterna paradisaea*, is the long distance record holder for migration. In Northern Hemisphere summer, birds nest in tundra pond habitats along the arctic coast, Aleutian Islands, southern Alaska, northern British Columbia and inland locales such as Great Slave Lake. Both autumn and spring migrations take birds far offshore. In the fall, birds depart on a 12,000-mile migration to Antarctica. An annual round trip amounts to 24,000-25,000 miles. Since day length is long in the arctic summer and, again, in Antarctica in austral summer, these birds get exposed to more daylight than any other animal species.

Sandhill crane—The sandhill crane, *Grus canadensis*, is perhaps Alaska's most spectacular migratory bird. I love hearing these birds in the fall as they aggregate in Fairbanks and, finally, head south in flocks of hundreds to thousands, all croaking excitedly.

The Creamer's Field Migratory Bird Refuge in Fairbanks is a wonderful place to watch and study sandhill cranes. The Alaska Department of Fish and Game attached satellite transmitters to the legs of four sandhill cranes on August 8, 2001, hoping to get a clear picture of the route these birds take moving to their wintering grounds. The birds remained in Fairbanks until September 5. They reached a resting area just south of Saskatoon, Saskatchewan, on September 10 and remained there nine days.

In these first five days the birds covered 500-800 km (300-500 miles) per day. Then they moved south to South Dakota for a few days and on to wintering habitat east and southeast of Lubbock, Texas. These four birds stayed in the Lubbock area from November 8 to March 14. By March 15, they were on the Platte River near Kearney, Grand Island and Elm Creek, Nebraska, along with about 500,000 other sandhills (see Figure 2.1).

The 2002 springtime return migration was almost an exact reverse of the fall migration. Birds flew northward, spent a short time resting in the same area of Saskatchewan they used in the fall, then onward to Fairbanks. During the summer of 2002 three of the four birds nested just across the Tanana River from Fair-

Figure 2.1: Sandhill crane migration recorded from an individual radiotagged in Fairbanks, Alaska, August 8, 2004. 1) August 8- September 5- Creamer's Field Waterfowl Refuge in Fairbanks. 2) September 6- in flight 10 miles east of Delta Junction. 3) September 7- In flight 175 miles northeast of Whitehorse, Yukon Territory. 4) September 8- In flight 10 miles east of Fort Nelson, British Columbia. 5) In flight in eastern Alberta. 6) September 10 to 14- Staging about 55 miles south of Saskatoon, Saskatchewan. 7) October 19- 5 miles northwest of Lacreek National Wildlife Refuge, South Dakota. 8) October 24 to November 3- Wintering about 90 miles east of Lubbock, Texas. 9) November 8 to 18- Wintering about 100 miles southeast of Lubbock. 10) Wintering about 150 miles southeast of Lubbock. 11) March 14 to April 13- Staging on the Platte River in southern Nebraska. 12) April 14- 50 miles north of Bismark, North Dakota. 13) April 19- 100 miles west of Regina, Saskatchewan. 14) April 24- 240 miles northwest of Regina. 15) 80 miles southeast of Dawson Creek, British Columbia. Data from Alaska Department of Fish and Game.

banks and the fourth nested near Minto, just west of Fairbanks.

Although the Fairbanks birds flew over Delta Junction, they apparently were not a part of the staging aggregations that can be seen there. John Wright, of the Alaska Department of Fish and Game, says the consensus is that the Delta Junction birds derive from populations that summer and nest in western Alaska and fly along the north edge of the Alaska Range to reach Delta Junction.

Sandhill cranes also breed west and north of Cook Inlet, south-central Alaska, the Copper River delta and at various locations in southeast Alaska. These birds take a coastal route to wintering grounds in the Portland, Oregon, area, and in the Central Valley, Imperial Valley and lower Colorado River Valley of California.

Tundra swan—Tundra swans, *Olor columbianus*, in Alaska include representatives of both the eastern and western North American populations. Birds that breed along arctic coastal habitats from Point Hope northward and eastward to eastern and southern Hudson Bay are part of the eastern wintering population. In the fall, these birds accumulate in staging areas on arctic river deltas and head south in late September. By early October they arrive in North Dakota and northern Minnesota. Their final wintering destinations, Chesapeake Bay and North Carolina, are reached by mid-November to mid-December.

The springtime return to the Far North begins in mid-March. Staging areas in southeast Pennsylvania, southern Ontario, and Minnesota and North Dakota are occupied successively as birds migrate northward. First arrival times on the Mackenzie and Anderson rivers in Northwest Territories are in the second and third weeks of May[2] and birds probably reach the North Slope of Alaska about the same time. There are upwards of 100,000 eastern tundra swans of which about 10,000 breed in Alaska.[3] Swans occupying breeding ponds and lakes from Kotzebue Sound, the Seward Peninsula, the Yukon-Kuskokwim delta, Bristol Bay, Alaska Peninsula and Aleutian Islands are all members of populations that winter in the western United States.

Swan habitats in Alaska seem to be in excellent if not totally pristine condition. Wintering habitats, however, have been altered in historic times by pollution and human impacts on wetlands. Preferred foods, submerged aquatic vegetation and benthic organisms, have been hit hard by these changes but swans have learned to feed in grain fields instead.[2]

A similar pattern of long-distance migration is exhibited by Alaska's other swan species, the trumpeter swan, *Olor buccinator*. Trumpeters breed in southern and interior Alaska, as well as Alberta, Saskatchewan, and a few northern-tier states. In interior Alaska boreal forests, these swans establish nests along lake margins, on islands, and on beaver lodges. In the fall, birds from the interior fly south to overwintering locations. One particulary popular destination is the Skagit River valley in northwest Washington State, where trumpeters congregate by the thousands.

Swallows—Five species of swallows reach the interior and/or northern Alaska during breeding season. They are the barn (*Hirundo rustica*), cliff (*Petrochelidon pyrrhonota*), violet-green (*Tachycineta thalassina*), tree (*Iridoprocne bicolor*), and bank (*Riparia riparia*) swallows. Swallows are excellent examples of species that have long migration paths and wintering habitats that may be subjected to increased human perturbation in the future.

The tree swallow is limited in the north by the presence of trees or nest boxes. Its winter habitat is primarily Florida and the Gulf states, but flocks regularly are seen along the Caribbean coast of South America. Tree swallows arrive in Alaska earlier than other swallows, perhaps because they must compete with non-swallows for nesting sites within hollows of trees. Tree swallows are able to feed on seeds and berries as well as insects, a useful ability that may allow them to arrive on breeding grounds before the strong seasonal pulse of insects has begun.[4]

The cliff swallow occurs in a few colonies north of tree line in Alaska. Otherwise, it is very widespread across North America, including Alaska, south of tree line. Cliff swallows establish breeding colonies and nest sites underneath both naturally occurring and human-built rock ledges. This species expanded its breeding range markedly in the twentieth century, apparently due to the construction of bridges, overpasses, and culverts associated with road building.[5] Birds spend the winter in southern Brazil, and south to central Argentina.

The bank swallow is a cosmopolitan species, occurring across most of Eurasia and North America in breeding season. In Alaska, bank swallows breed in most areas south of the Brooks Range. Typical nesting habitat consists of vertical banks along meandering streams and rivers and cliffs and bluffs along seacoasts. Elsewhere in North America, bank swallows nest in quarries and road cuts in addition to natural sites.[6] During winter these birds occur in southern Texas, Mexico, Chile, Ecuador, Peru, and the Caribbean Islands. They occupy a variety of winter habitats, including mangrove swamps, grasslands, savannas and agricultural fields.

Violet-green swallows are primarily birds of western North America. Summer finds them in coniferous and mixed forests: ponderosa, lodgepole, and Monterey pines in the lower 48, spruce and aspen in Alaska. They also occupy more open habitat in Washington, Arizona, and elsewhere. These swallows nest primarily in cliffs and holes in dirt banks. Winter is spent in Mexico, Guatemala, and El Salvador.

Snow bunting—The snow bunting, *Plectrophenax nivalis*, and the closely related McKay's bunting, *Plectrophenax hyperboreus*, exhibit a variety of migratory patterns. Let's start with McKay's bunting. This species is restricted in its breeding distribution to just two or three islands in the Bering Sea: St. Matthew, Hall Islands and, occasionally, St. Lawrence Island. These birds leave their breeding islands in October and fly east to the west coast of Alaska. From there they disperse both northward and southward along the coast, wintering in coastal marshes, beaches, and fields with exposed vegetation.

These western Alaska habitats are shared with their close relatives, snow buntings. Occasionally McKay's buntings occur in winter in south coastal Alaska and have been reported in Washington and Oregon. The dominant wintering migration is from west to east; the reverse is true for the breeding migration.

Snow buntings in North America breed in the high Canadian Arctic and southward in Canada to the limit of continuous permafrost, in Greenland, the coastal tundra of northern and western Alaska and the alpine tundra over most of Alaska.

In the fall snow buntings in northern Canada move south into a broad band of wintering habitat that extends from tree line in the north to the central great plains and New England in the south. Occasionally they are sighted as far south as Arizona, New Mexico, Arkansas, and northern Florida. Populations that breed in western Greenland overwinter in the United States; those breeding in eastern Greenland overwinter in Eurasia.[7]

What about Alaska? Populations breeding in western Alaska may not migrate any great distance. Birds that breed in the interior (alpine tundra) and northern Alaska (both alpine and arctic tundra) may fly either west to the Bering Sea coast or southeast into Canada in the fall; we really are not sure. We do know that arrival times in the spring are variable. Males show up first in mid-March, three to six weeks before the females. Arrival may be delayed up to a month by bad weather in the springtime staging areas south of interior Alaska.

Compasses and Maps

How do migrating birds sense direction? There are three likely mechanisms: sun compass, magnetic compass, and star compass. In addition, several other mechanisms have been proposed: polarized light compass, infrasound compass, and odor compass.

We do not really know how widespread the ability to orient by the sun's position is in birds. Only a dozen species have been shown convincingly to use this method of orientation. Most bird species simply have not been studied.

In theory, a magnetic compass would be the most reliable method because the earth's magnetic field doesn't change with season, time of day, or weather conditions. And it does not require a complicated time compensation mechanism, as is the case with sun compass orientation. Birds respond to magnetic field lines and their inclination in space. They do not respond to the earth's actual polarity, so the periodic (about every 100,000 years) reversals in earth's magnetic field shouldn't completely disorient migratory birds. All bird species studied so far, including both nocturnal and diurnal migrants, have been shown to orient using magnetic field lines.[8]

Many bird species migrate at night; these species probably do not use the sun to guide them on their way. Besides the magnetic field, the logical method is to use the stars to navigate. Birds with star compasses must be able to sense the axis of stellar rotation. That is, they must recognize the polar direction; they may learn constellations or other stellar configurations with reference to the North Star. Star compass navigation may be used by many bird species that migrate at night; we just do not know. However, some nocturnal migrants are unaffected by overcast skies.

Navigation requires more than simply a compass. Without map coordinates a migrating bird displaced from its course would simply resume its initial compass heading and arrive at an incorrect destination. In other words, it would have exhibited orientation but not navigation. What constitutes a map for birds? It appears that birds use **grid maps**, maps based on two or more gradients of physical substrate(s) that extend over large geographic areas. These physical gradients could include strength and/or orientation of the earth's magnetic field, wind fields, infrasound fields (generated by mountains, ocean, and winds), and perhaps odors.

Migration by route reversal may be the case in some migratory birds. However, at least in some birds, a repeated migratory route involves more than simple route reversal; that is, it involves the use of a map. Experiments have shown that many birds are born with an innate, preprogrammed compass orientation that is asserted at migration time. It is unclear if they have a preprogrammed destination. In social species, naive juveniles can learn the destination from adults. In the process of performing the first migration, these juvenile birds could learn their route and destination by imprinting or memorization.

MIGRATORY BATS

There is only a single species, the little brown bat, *Myotis lucifugus*, that makes it into interior Alaska. This species has a wide geographic range, occurring from tree line in the north to the mountains of southern Mexico. Little brown bats are missing from some of the prairie states east of the Rocky Mountains but occupy the far west, and the eastern United States south to north Florida.

Five other species of bats occur in Alaska but are restricted to southeast Alaska: California myotis (*Myotis californicus*), long-legged myotis (*Myotis volans*), Keen's myotis (*Myotis keenii*), silver-haired bat (*Lasionycteris noctivagans*), and big brown bat (*Eptesicus fuscus*).[9] Whereas all little brown bats of the interior are thought to fly south for the winter, some of the southeastern Alaska bats are suspected of overwintering in hibernation in old mines or limestone caves. Clearly, the severe cold in interior Alaska would be a huge metabolic drain on hibernating bats.

COLD-BLOODED VERSUS WARM-BLOODED ORGANISMS

The context in which cold-blooded animals are compared to warm-blooded animals is the cold environment. In the cold, creatures such as frogs and fish are cold-bodied and, hence, cold-blooded. What about these same creatures at high environmental temperatures? One would have to say they are warm-blooded in warm surroundings. So, cold-blooded and warm-blooded are not the most useful of terms. An alternative is to refer to cold-blooded animals as **ectotherms**. The bodies of ectotherms are warmed by heat from external sources, hence the name: ecto= outside; therm= heat. Ectotherms can gain heat by radiation through basking in the sun or by conduction through touching a warm object. The parallel term for warm-blooded animals is **endotherms**. Endotherms, as the name suggests, produce heat inside their bodies sufficient to reach and maintain temperatures well above their surroundings. The heat is generated by muscular activity and by the process of cellular metabolism.

There are two more terms I need to introduce. Animals that are warm-blooded all of the time, endotherms, are also referred to as **homeotherms**. Homeo- means constant and, therefore, homeotherms maintain constant and relatively high temperatures primarily by means of high metabolic rates. The corresponding term for cold-blooded animals is **poikilotherms**. The Greek prefix poikilo- means variable, and the sense of the term is that cold-blooded animals have variable temperatures.

I mentioned above that it is the high metabolic rates that allow homeotherms to maintain high and constant body temperatures.

2. SHIVER, FREEZE, OR COOL YOUR KNEES:
WAYS OF COPING WITH COLD

Metabolism is merely the heat generated by the sum total of all the chemical reactions in the body. Most chemical reactions generate a little waste heat as a byproduct of the reaction. It is the accumulated waste heat that warms the homeotherm body. We will return to metabolic rates later in this chapter.

Advantages and Disadvantages of Being Poikilothermic

As we will see shortly, homeotherms have to nurture and conserve the waste heat of metabolism to maintain a constant body temperature. No special, energy-demanding mechanisms for heat conservation are required in poikilotherms. Poikilotherms do not have to constantly fuel the metabolic fires, do not have to put on an insulative layer in the fall, and do not have to incur the expense of growing denser fur to keep warm.

Since poikilotherms allow their body temperatures to match those of the external environment, they save a great deal of metabolic expense. They do not have to find food in the winter, nor do they have to remain active.

One of the problems with being slowed down or stopped by low temperatures has to do with potential predators. Warm-blooded or homeothermic predators may remain active and continue to forage after poikilothermic prey have metabolically shut down for the winter. Mike Kirton studied overwintering in wood frogs in the Fairbanks area. He could locate his animals with a Geiger counter because he had inserted a thin radioactive wire into the space just beneath the skin on their backs. In spring, after emergence of surviving frogs, he exhumed the ones that hadn't crawled out of their hiber-

nacula. Most of these dead frogs were either emaciated or desiccated or both. They probably died because they ran out of energy during hibernation. One frog, however, was in good condition and not desiccated. Its chest and throat had been gnawed by a shrew and it had been pulled out of its hibernaculum and 12 cm (4 inches) down into a shrew tunnel. [10] The frog was at an obvious disadvantage in that it could not escape its predator because it was frozen and completely immobile.

Another potential disadvantage is that life cycles and life stages of poikilothermic animals (and plants) are advanced or delayed by unseasonably warm or cold weather. Delays in onset of spring and, therefore, poikilotherm activity may delay or prolong reproductive seasons and/or lengthen life cycles. Insects must grow through a number of larval stages or instars; growth is strongly influenced by temperature. If the required number of instars cannot be completed with this year's temperature regimes, maturation and reproduction may be delayed for a year or more. For example, tropical dragonflies typically complete a life cycle each year but dragonflies in Alaska require three to six years to produce adults. Perhaps the extreme example of this phenomenon of delayed or protracted life cycles is the moth *Gynaephora groenlandica*. This species occurs in Greenland, northern Canada and, possibly, northern Alaska. In the high Arctic, the combination of low temperatures, short summers, arid conditions and dramatic photoperiod changes dictate that growth and development of this moth occurs over a very short period each year. Typically, it requires 14 years for *Gynaephora groenlandica* to complete its life cycle. [11]

Advantages and Disadvantages of Being Warm-blooded

Warm-blooded predators seeking cold-blooded prey in the winter have their prey at a distinct disadvantage. Again, the prey cannot crawl away. Constant, warm body temperatures mean that temperature sensitive chemical reactions proceed at relatively constant rates. Also, the metabolic expense of synthesizing antifreeze chemicals (mentioned below) is not necessary.

As I mentioned earlier, the curse of warm-blooded creatures is winter. The metabolic expense of maintaining a body temperature warmer than cold surroundings can be staggering. Small mammals and birds must find food every day without fail. Most of the interesting stories about Alaskan birds and mammals center on how they overcome the problems of finding enough food, staying warm or reducing metabolic expenses.

SOME POIKILOTHERMIC (ECTOTHERMIC) POSSIBILITIES

Freezing Avoidance

For many insects and other ectotherms, survival through the winter depends on avoiding freezing. How is it possible for animals to keep from freezing when air temperatures often fall to -40°C? First, air temperatures may not be a good indication of temperatures in the exact locations of these animals. Part of the preparation for winter for these animals is behavioral. They move to sites where they will usually be protected from the coldest air temperatures. Overwintering may occur in the duff (leaf litter layer), in burrows within the soil or in decomposing tree stumps. Some insects, such as the whitespotted sawyer beetle, survive winter under the bark of dead or dying spruce trees. These sites often will be under the snow once some snow has accumulated. All these **subnivean** (under the snow) locations benefit from the insulative value of the snow itself.

From a human perspective, these overwintering locations hardly seem like habitats. Humans are on the upper end of the size spectrum of living organisms and we require a lot of space. Insect overwintering sites are just too small for us to use. Biologists refer to these tiny habitats as **microhabitats**. Part of winter survival depends on selection of an appropriate microhabitat. Do all insects select sites in which they are assured of survival? Not necessarily. Burrowing into the base of a tree stump virtually assures that insulative snow cover will protect the burrower. How about the same stump but 1 meter above ground level? Variation in snow accumulation from year to year might mean that in some years the above-ground location would lack insulative cover entirely.

Fresh snow has about the same thermal conductivity as glass wool and is 13 times better an insulator than old snow or wet peat. Thermal conductivity is inversely related to snow density and, therefore, we might deduce that old snow is denser than fresh snow. It is. In terms of maintaining a relatively constant subnivean temperature, the bottom line seems to be 40-50 cm of snow, irrespective of snow density.

Once the snow is on the ground, it can undergo several forms of metamorphosis including destructive, constructive and melt metamorphosis.[12] **Constructive metamorphosis** involves the loss of water vapor from the deepest, warmest snow depths. Near ground level, the snow consists of very small, loosely connected crystals, the so-called **depth hoar**. Depth hoar is easily tunneled through by animals that are still active under the snowpack.

In spite of microhabitat selection by poikilotherms, many individuals experience temperatures down to -20 to -25°C and some to −60°C. How is it that freezing can be avoided? One possibility is **supercooling**. Supercooling is a phenomenon in which the body reaches temperatures far below that at which the fluids would normally freeze but they do not freeze. Sounds like a paradox. Pure water held in a test tube and surrounded by refrigerant gets colder and colder, usually cooling well past its freezing point of 0°C. When the water finally freezes it crystallizes to ice and its temperature goes up.

Recall that water has a latent heat of fusion, so, when freezing occurs, heat is liberated. The latent heat of fusion accounts for the temperature increase, often called the **exotherm**. The freezing and exotherm both occur if you were to drop a tiny crystal of ice in the tube. The tiny crystal is an **ice nucleator**; it initiates ice crystal formation and growth. Body fluids from most living organisms exhibit at least a small amount of supercooling before ice crystallization. Moreover, living organisms have freezing points below 0°C (32°F) because the substances dissolved in the body fluids depress the freezing point. For terrestrial insects in summer, the freezing point depression, just based on the concentration of **solutes** (dissolved chemicals) in the body fluids, is about 2C°; that is, without supercooling, the fluids would freeze at -2°C and melt at -2°C.

But, as they say on television, "Wait, there's more!" The specific structure and nature of the chemicals in solution may have an additional effect on supercooling. Glycerol, ethylene glycol, mannitol or sugars such as trehalose, glucose or fructose are found in high concentrations in cold-adapted, freeze-intolerant insects. Ethylene glycol is the same chemical used as an antifreeze in car radiators: same chemical, same function.

These low molecular weight antifreezes, typically referred to as **cryoprotectants**, lower freezing points primarily by virtue of their high concentrations. There may be a separate inhibitory effect on ice crystal formation since cryoprotectants lower the supercooling point as well. Supercooling points for a variety of freeze-intolerant insects in winter typically range from -10 to -30°C.[13]

Antifreeze proteins are found in some insects and in arctic and antarctic fishes. These high-molecular weight antifreezes apparently adsorb onto tiny ice crystals and physically block further crystal growth. Thus, they, like the low molecular weight cryoprotectants, lower both the freezing point and the supercooling point.

Freeze tolerance

Another group of poikilotherms in the Far North adopt a different strategy; they undergo freezing in the winter. Many freeze-tolerant insects, like their freeze-intolerant relatives, synthesize cryoprotectants and exhibit supercooling. However, with a few exceptions, freeze-tolerant insects have supercooling points in the -5° to -10°C range, not as low as freeze-intolerant species. Ice nucleation is an important feature of freeze-tolerant insects. Many of these species produce special proteins that are released into the extracellular spaces and function as ice nucleators. These ice nucleating proteins cause the insect to freeze at relatively high temperatures, apparently to slow the rate of ice formation and to promote extracellular freezing instead of intracellular ice formation. A note on terminology: **intercellular** means between the cells; **extracellular** means outside the cells. Although not synonymous, these words are often used interchangeably. The other term, **intracellular**, means within cells. It is the freezing of cells, intracellular freezing, that destroys cell membranes and cellular organelles. Freezing also disrupts chemical reactions inside cells. All these effects result in cell death.

Ice nucleation is known to occur in the guts of insects at sub-zero temperatures. So, for freeze-tolerant insects, a last meal in the fall may be adaptive in that it triggers freezing. The same meal in a freeze-intolerant insect might really be its last! Several species of bacteria occurring in insect guts are known to have proteins that act as ice nucleators. These species or their close relatives have now been isolated from the guts of some insects caught in the field. It is unclear if these bacteria account for all the ice nucleation within guts of insects.

One other mechanism of ice nucleation, mentioned above, is contact with an ice crystal. This mechanism is called **inoculative nucleation**. This last mechanism is important in the freezing of aquatic insects as their external medium freezes in the autumn.

Do trees freeze? It is possible to assail boreal forest trees with experimental conditions or freak, unseasonable weather and cause them to die from the cold. However, if allowed to achieve their normal autumn cold hardiness, interior Alaskan trees are amazingly tough. Killing temperatures for white spruce, black spruce, quaking aspen and paper birch are below -80°C.[13] That is -112°F, much colder than any of these trees ever experience in the Far North! But do they freeze? Yes. Trees are freeze-tolerant in much the same way as the insects mentioned above. In cooling experiments, tree temperatures exhibit supercooling and an exotherm associated with the freezing of fluids in the spaces between cells, the intercellular fluid. If the experiment is continued and the tree cooled further, at some point a second exotherm may occur. The second exotherm corresponds to the freezing of the cells and to tree death. Based on the lethal temperatures of Alaskan trees listed above, tree death occurs at extremely low temperatures or due to unrealistically rapid cooling rates in the laboratory.

In the paragraphs above I mentioned the concept of cold hardiness, sometimes called cold hardening. Cold hardening or becoming cold hardy is a process of physiological adaptation to winter. We know that trees, insects and frogs are not cold hardy throughout the entire year. Expose them to freezing temperatures in the middle of summer and they die.

Cold hardening in trees is a two-stage process. In the first stage the trigger or triggers are decreasing day length and /or desiccation. Growth stops and some sort of chemical signal is translocated from the sensing structures, the leaves, to the rest of the tree. One chemical that appears in the leaves at this time, and may be the signal, is abscisic acid. Abscisic acid has an important role in initiating leaf-drop in deciduous plants. But there are other chemical changes going on in the leaves and one of these other chemicals may be the real signal. The result of the first stage of adaptation is a lowering of the lethal temperature to about -10°C.

The second stage is triggered by subfreezing temperatures and involves changes in the cell membranes of the tree. Cell membranes become more permeable to water and solutes. Water movement out of cells is critical to protecting them from freezing. First, water removed from the inside of the cell cannot freeze there. Second, as water leaves the cell, it causes the cell contents to become more concentrated, thus lowering freezing and supercooling temperatures. The lipids of cell membranes also become more unsaturated, lowering their crystallization temperatures. That means that membranes will remain more fluid, flexible and functional at colder temperatures.

The only amphibian of interior Alaska, the wood frog (*Rana sylvatica*), is also freeze-tolerant. In the fall, wood frogs dig down into the duff, where they remain until the following spring. Each frog has, over the summer, stored energy reserves in the liver as glycogen. Freezing or crystallization temperatures in wood frogs are in the -2 to -4°C range.[14] As tissues begin to freeze, liver glycogen is converted to glucose and it is released into the blood. The extent of freezing protection depends on the amount of glucose released into the circulation.[15] The glucose apparently serves several functions. First, it enters frog cells at high concentrations. Within cells it traps water, keeping proteins in solution and also interferes with ice crystal formation. This is the cryoprotectant function of glucose. Second, glucose serves as an energy-releasing substrate that helps meet the metabolic demands of the frog's tissues when the circulation is out of business. Just before total

freeze-up and immediately after thawing, blood glucose is very high; the frog has hyperglycemia. Several mechanisms operate to conserve as much glucose as possible. After thawing, blood glucose is removed by the liver and resynthesized into glycogen. Glucose filtered through the kidneys is recovered from the urinary bladder by an active reabsorption process.

There may be a lower temperature limit beyond which wood frogs cannot survive. In one lab study, frogs survived freezing at -5°C in the laboratory but not -7.5°C;[16] in another, frogs survived down to −18°C.[17] At overwintering sites of individual wood frogs in Fairbanks temperatures were recorded as low as -8°C at soil depths where frogs actually survived the winter.[10]

Recall in the discussion of supercooling, freeze-tolerant insects, that it was to the insect's advantage to freeze at relatively high sub-zero temperatures. The same is apparently true of wood frogs. Three different mechanisms insure freezing in these frogs. First, inoculative freezing is promoted by the moist, permeable skin. Ice crystals coming in contact with the frog cause it to freeze with 3-24 hours.[16] Second, the wood frog synthesizes a plasma protein that functions as an ice nucleator.[18] In case these mechanisms fail, wood frogs have at least three different species of ice-nucleating bacteria in their guts in winter.[19]

Some readers may remember dissecting frogs in high school biology. One of the unwelcome discoveries I made was a large parasitic fluke in one lung of my frog. In the context of frozen wood frogs, we might wonder what happens to frog parasites in winter. At least two parasites, one a lungworm (nematode) and the other a larval trematode, are freeze-tolerant, too.[20]

There are no marine animals in the boreal forest but discussion of their relationship to freezing fits in at this point. We wouldn't necessarily think about marine animals in the context of freezing. After all, they are down in the water, right? Which marine organisms are potentially subject to freezing? Intertidal invertebrates and algae are liable to be exposed to freezing temperatures in the Far North, especially if they are **sessile**, that is, firmly attached to the substratum. At low tide, barnacles attached to rocks in the **intertidal** (within the range of tides) can be exposed to subfreezing temperatures. Intertidal invertebrates in the subarctic and Arctic are freeze-tolerant and exhibit many of the characteristics I mentioned for freeze-tolerant insects.

For example, the salt marsh snail, *Melampus bidentatus*, goes through a period of cold-hardening in the fall and is freeze-tolerant in winter. This little snail is remarkably resistant to cold, even in the summer. Its lower lethal temperature is -5°C in summer and -13°C in winter. Actual freezing or crystallization temperatures for this species are -9°C in summer and -7°C in winter. So in the summer *Melampus* suffers lethal damage without freezing but can survive freezing in the winter.[21]

As in insects, freeze-tolerant intertidal invertebrates exhibit extracellular freezing. And, as in insects, freezing of extracellular fluids causes movement of water out of cells. This results in increasing solute concentrations inside cells, thus lowering their freezing points further. A key part of the system is the production of ice nucleating proteins in the fall. These proteins occur in the extracellular fluids.

Again, as in insects, freezing of intracellular fluids is potentially damaging to enzyme systems and to the membranes of cells. Cryoprotectant chemicals are produced by many intertidal marine invertebrates; these chemicals prevent denaturation of protein enzymes and also prevent membrane damage. Triggers for the production of ice nucleating proteins and cryoprotectant amino acids include low temperatures, high salinity and anaerobic (no oxygen) conditions.

SOME HOMEOTHERMIC (ENDOTHERMIC) POSSIBILITIES

Metabolic Rates

If we are to make any inferences about an animal's metabolism and compare its metabolism to that of other animals we need to have all of the animals at the same "standard" level. In humans we measure a **basal metabolic rate** the conditions for which are: prone, relaxed, motionless and fasted. Obviously, movement and excitement elevate metabolic rate above basal levels. The process of digesting food, referred to as **heat increment** or specific dynamic activity, raises metabolic rate by about 10% in humans and other animals. Some studies of animal metabolism report basal metabolic rates and others report **resting metabolic rates**; what is the difference? Essentially, we cannot be sure that basal conditions are ever really achieved during measurements on non-human animals. Measurement often requires that the animal be enclosed in a relatively confined space and we aren't sure that the confined animal achieves a calm, relaxed state, even if it isn't moving around or digesting food. Resting metabolic rate, as a concept, takes this uncertainty into account.

Back to the actual measurement: what do we measure? The chemical reaction that provides much of the energy and the heat within our bodies is the catabolism (breakdown) of glucose. In words, a glucose molecule is broken down into six molecules of carbon dioxide plus six molecules of water, using up six molecules of oxygen. The amount of energy used in the body, therefore, is usually directly proportional to the amount of oxygen consumed. So, one way of expressing and measuring metabolic rate is to measure the rate at which oxygen is consumed. Each ml of oxygen consumed equates to a specific amount of calories released. This **caloric equivalent of oxygen** differs depending on whether the animal is burning pure carbohydrate (5 calories per milliliter [cal/ ml] oxygen), fat (4.7 cal/ml), protein (4.5 cal/ml in mammals) or a mix of the three. We could also measure the rate at which carbon dioxide is produced but it is not as easy and is nearly impossible when working with aquatic animals because CO_2 dissolves so easily in water.

What does a careful measurement of resting metabolic rates (RMR) at different external temperatures tell us? First, in a poikilotherm such as a frog, RMR is directly proportional to temperature (Figure 2.2). RMR in a homeotherm with a constant body temperature is, within part of the range of external or ambient temperatures, constant (Figure 2.2). This temperature range is called the **thermal neutral zone**. At the high end of this zone, the upper critical temperature, metabolism increases due to energy-consuming mechanisms, such as panting, used to regulate body temperature. Below the low end of the thermal neutral zone, the lower critical temperature, internal temperature can be maintained constant only by increasing heat production, that is, by increasing metabolic rate.

What is the animal's response to changing temperature within the thermoneutral zone? At the higher end of the zone, cooling mechanisms are employed that require no additional energy. One of these is evaporative cooling by sweating. Another is shunting of blood to the extremities and dilation of peripheral blood vessels. This brings warm blood out to the skin, where heat can be lost to the external environment. Toward the lower end of the zone, erection or fluffing of the fur or feathers increases the insulative layer without raising metabolism.

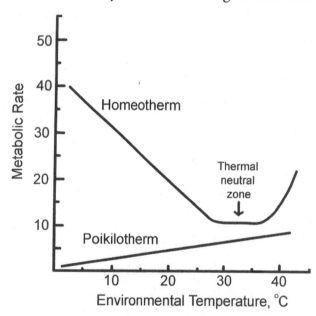

Figure 2.2: Relationship between metabolic rate (energy expended) and external temperature in a homeotherm (animal with constant body temperature) and a poikilotherm (animal with a variable body temperature). The thermal neutral zone is the temperature range in which the homeotherm passively adjusts insulation to cope with heat loss. At temperatures below the thermal neutral zone, the animal increases its heat production (metabolic rate) to counter increased heat loss to the surroundings.

Figure 2.3: Black-capped chickadees—fluffed and non-fluffed. Fluffing the feathers increases the thickness of the insulative layer, thereby reducing heat loss.

At the lower critical temperature, changes in insulation have been maximized and metabolic rate must increase to offset increasing heat loss. Metabolic rate increases in proportion to decreasing temperature.

All of the adaptive strategies employed by endothermic animals involve, in one way or another, reducing the metabolic energy cost incurred by being in the cold. One evolutionary approach is to maximize the temperature range of the thermoneutral zone by producing excellent insulative layers. Another involves behaviors such as selecting the warmest spot available or huddling with your neighbors. Several of these approaches, nightly torpor and hibernation, seem to violate the very concept of homeothermy. That is, in both hibernation and nightly torpor internal body temperature actually fluctuates rather dramatically. An essential requirement is that, eventually, internal temperature returns to its normal set point. Let's look at some of these adaptive strategies.

Pelage/Plumage Changes

Many animals of the Far North increase their insulation in the fall by undergoing a molt or, in the case of marine mammals, by laying on fat reserves. In the context of the temperature-metabolism graph (Figure 2.2), these animals are shifting their lower critical temperature downward. The coat of the red fox, has thicker underfur in winter; its lower critical temperature is 8°C in summer and -13°C in winter.[22] The redpoll, one of our resident songbirds, adds another 50% of feather weight in winter and, thereby, can reduce its heat conductance by 30-50% by fluffing its feathers.[23] Snowshoe hares have lower critical temperatures of 10°C and 0°C, respectively, during summer and winter.

Surprisingly, one of the worst animals at making the insulative adjustment to winter is the red squirrel. This animal is active all winter but has the same lower critical temperature year round, 20°C.[23] On the other extreme, the arctic fox develops such a thick, warm fur in the winter that it can withstand -40°C without revving up its metabolism.

We need to distinguish between the morphological adaptation of adding extra fur or feathers in the fall and the behavioral adaptation of fluffing the pelage or plumage (see Figure 2.3). It is certainly the case that birds at very low temperatures do not always have their feathers fully fluffed. Fluffed feathers would develop a great deal of air resistance in flight. The fluffing of fur or feathers is accomplished by the contraction of small muscles, the *erector pili* muscles, attached to the base of the hair or feather follicle. The muscle is obliquely oriented from the base of the hair to near the skin surface so, when it contracts, it causes the hair or feather to stand on end. This behavior is called **piloerection**. Piloerection, in humans, is responsible for our hair standing on end and also for "goose bumps" when we are frightened or cold. Fluffing is, recall, also involved in temperature regulation in the thermoneutral zone.

Body Size

Body size, by itself, is not necessarily an adaptive feature helping warm-blooded animals cope with the cold. It is more complicated than that. There is a large amount of information on the metabolic rates of homeotherms of different sizes and the overall relationship of size and metabolism. So, let's sort through some aspects of size and its relationship with heat loss, metabolism and the cold, Far North.

First, we need to think about the size of an animal, its volume and its surface area. The smaller the animal, generally, the larger the ratio of surface area to volume. Compare two hypothetical mammals, both shaped like cubes: one of them is 1" by 1" by 1" in dimension,

the other is 3" by 3" by 3" in size. Although their proportions are exactly the same, cubic, their surface to volume ratios are different. The smaller beast has an overall surface of 6 square inches and a volume of 1 cubic inch for a ratio of 6:1. The larger beast has a surface of 54 square inches and a volume of 27 cubic inches for a ratio of 2:1. How does this relate to the cold? Simply put, mammals generate heat in proportion to their volumes but lose heat in proportion to their surface areas. After all, heat is lost from the surface. Therefore, small mammals and birds lose heat faster than do larger mammals and birds and must generate heat faster in each of their units of volume to maintain constant temperature.

The metabolic rates of each of these body volumes (or weights) contribute to the total metabolism. So, biologists measure and calculate these rates in two ways. The whole animal's metabolism, **total metabolic rate**, can be estimated. If the total rate is divided by the weight in g or kg, a **specific metabolic rate** is the result. This latter term allows us to compare equal units of different sized animals. Comparing the (total) metabolic rates of a shrew and a horse, present here in the Pleistocene, the shrew consumes 0.0036 liters of oxygen per hour and the horse, 71.1 liters per hour. That horse, what an inefficient hay-burner, huh? Not necessarily. The specific metabolic rates of the two are: 7.4 liters of oxygen per kilogram per hour for the shrew and 0.11 liters of oxygen per kilogram per hour for the horse.[24] Each unit of the shrew's body is burning fuel 67 times faster than a comparable-sized unit in the horse. To maintain such a high specific metabolic rate, the shrew must eat, proportionally, a lot more food each day than a horse.

If these metabolic rate considerations were the only ones operating in Alaska, natural selection might well have produced Alaskan "Rodents of Unusual Size," (R.O.U.S.) similar to those depicted in the movie, *Princess Bride*. However, there are many other factors at work in evolution. Small size is not an unalloyed disadvantage. Recall that microhabitat selection by small animals can put them in a much warmer place than a large creature such as a moose could occupy. Could you imagine a moose tunneling under the snow? Is total, rather than specific, metabolic rate ever a significant factor in dealing with the cold? Yes. Shrews actually reduce body weight and even skull dimensions in the winter, apparently to reduce their overall metabolic expense.[25]

Huddling or Clumping

One way for an animal to effectively reduce the rate of heat loss to the environment is to increase body mass by huddling with others of its own kind. Huddling or group nesting has been reported in redback voles, meadow voles, tundra voles and yellow-cheeked (taiga) voles, all found in Alaska. Yellow-cheeked voles occur in black spruce forests around Fairbanks. Males are territorial in spring and summer but participate in communal nesting in winter. Communal groups average seven members and include females, males and several different age classes. In the fall the group members collectively construct an underground nest and food storage area. The two main foods stored for the winter are rhizomes of horsetails (*Equisetum*) and fireweed (*Epilobium*). The nest, 25-30 cm in diameter, consists of dried grass. Temperature measurements in air, ground and the nest indicate that the communal nest never fell to ground temperatures. Air temperatures at the study site were -5 to -23°C; those of the ground near the nests were -3 to -5°C, and inside the nest temperatures varied from +4 to +7°C.[26] The advantages of communal nesting include a relatively warm surrounding or microhabitat, reduced heat loss, reduced metabolic requirement, reduced food requirement and (until the food cache is exhausted) no necessity to leave the warm nest for foraging. Those individuals that leave the nest return to a warm nest. All of this amounts to both physiological and behavioral thermoregulation.

Another mammal that aggregates in winter is the northern flying squirrel. Nests of flying squirrels consist of either tree cavities or witch's brooms. The cavities are formed by insects, woodpeckers, decay and/or frost cracking and are enlarged by the squirrel. In Alaska, tree cavities are generally abandoned in the fall in favor of hollowed out witch's brooms. These brooms are actually the spruce tree's response to a fungal infection. The spruce broom rust causes the spruce to produce a dense cluster of extra branches that turn brown. Flying squirrels burrow into the broom, hollow out a chamber, and line it with insulation. This lined nest is the site of aggregation. A study focused on the winter metabolism of southern flying squirrels found that huddling in groups of either three or six reduced individual energy costs by 27 and 36%, respectively.[27] Southern flying squirrels are near cousins of our northern species and are known to form aggregations of up to 14 individuals in the same nest.

Microhabitat Selection

I mentioned microhabitat selection as an adaptive behavior enabling freeze-intolerant insects to avoid freezing. Similarly, homeotherms employ microhabitat selection to reduce heat loss. For example, part of a red squirrel's habitat is the tops of spruce trees, where cones are harvested for consumption or storage. However, during a winter bout of -40°C (also -40°F), a squirrel in the treetops would lose heat at a horrendous rate. If, instead, it spends this time in its below-ground midden under a layer of snow, its surroundings will be around 0°C and its heat loss will be about half what it would be in the treetops. This is microhabitat selection. Bears exhibit microhabitat selection when they enter a den for hibernation and so do humans when they enter a snow cave or a tent.

Shivering Thermogenesis

Let's return to the metabolism versus temperature relationship described in Figure 2.2. At temperatures lower than the lower critical temperature, additional metabolic heat must be produced to match increasing heat loss to the environment. Shivering generates heat; shivering bouts can be graded in both duration and intensity, resulting in different levels of heat output to match heat loss. Both birds and mammals use shivering as a means to produce heat, **shivering thermogenesis**.

Some species, such as the red-backed vole, adapt to winter by (among other things) increasing muscle myoglobin, used in oxygen transfer inside skeletal muscles. This allows the vole's muscles to shiver more efficiently and

generate more heat. The maximum metabolic rate achievable by red-backed voles in winter is about double its summer maximum. High metabolic rates are mediated by or triggered by release of the chemical norepinephrine, one of the sympathetic neurotransmitters and adrenal hormones. In winter, voles exhibit a much higher response to norepinephrine and also are able to naturally synthesize larger amounts of norepinephrine.[28] One additional adaptation relates to their ability to produce heat (in response to norepinephrine secretion) without increasing muscle activity, that is, to produce heat via non-shivering thermogenesis.

Non-shivering Thermogenesis

This method of heat production relies on the presence of a specialized tissue, brown fat. Brown fat differs from regular white fat deposits in several ways. It is brown due to the high degree of vascularization (presence of blood vessels) and to the presence of many mitochondria, the cellular inclusions that provide energy and heat. Also, brown fat is connected to the nervous system.

When a burst of heat production is needed, the sympathetic nervous system signals the brown fat tissue and the fat cells begin to burn fat rapidly, producing heat. The heat is carried away from the fat to the rest of the body by the blood vessels and by conduction.

Hibernating mammals have significant amounts of brown fat in the chest. These deposits and their heat production are partially responsible for the warming involved with periodic arousal exhibited by hibernators. The newborn young of non-hibernating mammals, including humans, also have brown fat. Birds, however, do not have the capability to produce brown fat. Physiologists are still studying and debating whether birds exhibit non-shivering thermogenesis and, if so, how they accomplish it.[29]

Regional Heterothermy

One of the more obvious features of warm-bodied animals in the cold is that not all parts of the body have the same temperature. The term heterothermy simply means different temperatures; **regional heterothermy**, then, means different temperatures in different regions of the body. Is regional heterothermy merely a characteristic of all homeotherms, or is it actually an adaptation that allows boreal animals to conserve heat? First, any homeotherm in an ambient temperature lower than its body temperature will exhibit a temperature gradient from deep body to the surface and from torso to the extremities. This makes sense because the surface of the fingers, for instance, is relatively great, its supply of blood is far removed from the warm, deep body and it is losing heat to a cooler environment by radiation, convection and conduction. So, regional heterothermy is normal; it is adaptive if the animal employs mechanisms to regulate the amount of heat lost from the extremities and/or has mechanisms that allow these extremities to function at low temperatures that, in other animals, would render the extremity useless.

Let us look at some of the dramatic temperature gradients first. Caribou standing in snow in winter at an air temperature of -31°C had a core (deep body) temperature of 38°C, a head temperature of 36° and a temperature of 20°C on the muzzle. Lower leg temperature was measured at 9°C, ankle, near the dew claws, was 12°C and hoof was 9°C (Figure 2.4).[22] Arctic

Figure 2.4: Regional heterothermy in a caribou at an air temperature of -31°C. Numbers are temperatures in degrees C. In the cold the caribou's extremities are much cooler than deep body temperature. The energy cost to keep lower legs at or near deep body temperature would be prohibitive. Redrawn from Irving (1972). This caribou is exhibiting a threat display; see Chapter 8.

sled dogs have very similar gradients at -30°C with muzzle, lower leg and ankle temperatures of 5, 14 and 8°C, respectively.

Even more impressive are some animals that immerse part or all their bodies in ice water. The glaucous-winged gull of the Far North spends at least part of the year standing or swimming in water at 0°C or snow at even lower temperatures. Its lower legs and feet are naked and, thus, are highly susceptible to cooling. A gull standing at an air temperature of -16°C had upper leg temperatures in the 38 to 15°C range, depending on proximity to the torso. Lower leg temperature was measured at 7 to 8°C and the web of the foot ranged from 4.9 to 0°C. Temperatures in the naked tails of muskrats and beavers fall to near 0°C in ice water.

The obvious question comes to mind: why don't the feet and tails freeze? The answer lies in the structure and functioning of the circulatory system of these extremities. Within the leg of the gull, blood vessels are anatomically positioned such that each artery is surrounded in close proximity by several veins. This arrangement causes the hot arterial blood to lose heat to the cold venous blood returning from the foot. Heat is conserved by these blood flows running in opposite directions but close together. The system of vessels is a **countercurrent heat exchange** mechanism. If all the heat were conserved, the foot (or tail) would actually freeze. But when the foot cools to 0°C or colder, a special circulatory mechanism takes over. The leg has another, alternative circulatory pathway for getting blood to the foot. This shunt or bypass system allows blood to bypass the countercurrent exchanger and go directly to the foot. The result of having these alternate pathways is that the foot temperature fluctuates around 0°C. Notice above that I mentioned the web of the gull's foot ranged from 4.9°C to 0°C. Clearly, the shunt was working during the higher measurement and the countercurrent exchanger was working during the 0°C measurement. Heat loss from one foot accounts for less than 5% of total heat loss when the bird is standing in cold water.[30] Countercurrent heat exchangers are known to function in the feet of wolves[31] the fins of whales and porpoises[32] and in warm-bodied fishes such as bluefin tuna[33] and Alaska's own salmon shark.[34]

What do we know about nerve conduction at low temperatures that are experienced by birds and mammals in Alaska? Certainly, as my hands approach freezing temperatures I cannot make the muscles contract, either because the muscles do not work at those temperatures and/or because the muscles simply are not getting the message from the motor nerves. Consider the naked tails of beavers and muskrats in icewater; temperatures approach freezing, but tails still slap or wag! Comparison of conduction velocities of nerves from the beaver chest (phrenic nerve), leg (tibial nerve) and tail (caudal nerve) found the caudal nerve least affected by cold. The temperature response in conduction velocity is linear, allowing extrapolation to a temperature at which, presumably, conduction stops altogether. The extinction (of conduction) temperatures for the phrenic, tibial, and caudal nerves, respectively, are 4.5, -0.7 and -5°C, suggesting that the caudal nerve really is adapted to function in the cold.[35] In the muskrat tail, extinction temperature is also about -3 to -5°C. In contrast, Alaska mammals with furred tails cannot make them work at temperatures much below +5°C.

Nightly Torpor

Nightly torpor is also known as **nocturnal hypothermia**. Hypo- means below; thermia means temperature. Hypothermia, then, refers to a lowering of the body temperature. Recall that, in humans, a body temperature of 30°C is one at which we are unable to rewarm without dramatic intervention and an external heat source.

The black-capped chickadee and the redpoll are two of the most common resident birds in interior Alaska in winter. The black-capped chickadee exhibits nightly torpor; the redpoll does not. Comparison of the energetics of these two similar-sized species at 0°C revealed the following. At dusk, the redpoll has a fat reserve equivalent to almost 12% of its body weight; the chickadee's fat reserve is only 7.5%. The redpoll maintains its body temperature at 39-40°C; the chickadee allows its temperature to fall to 31-34°C. Since heat loss is proportional to the difference in temperatures of the bird and its surroundings, the chickadee is losing less heat and, therefore, has to spend less metabolic energy. The metabolic rate of the chickadee, under these circumstances, is about half the redpoll's. Over the course of a 19-hour night, typical of the shortest days in winter, the overall energy expense of the chickadee is less than half that of the redpoll.[36] These energy expenditures would be considerably greater at lower temperatures. It is quite common for these small birds to experience -40°C temperatures in interior Alaska.

Black-capped chickadees become hypothermic by slowing the rate at which they shiver.

One might wonder if Alaskan black-capped chickadees differ in their ability to deal with cold when compared with their relatives at lower latitudes. Alaskan birds are able to use nocturnal hypothermia at any season of the year to cope with extremely or unseasonably cold temperatures.[37] Birds from the lower forty eight statees are not able to use nocturnal hypothermia in summer no matter what the ambient temperature is.[38]

I will mention one final point about nocturnal torpor. Since the body temperature changes over a 24 hour cycle, chickadees, by definition, are also exhibiting heterothermy. This circumstance could be referred to as temporal heterothermy rather than regional heterothermy.

Hibernation

The evolutionary rationale for hibernation is the same as that for nightly torpor, namely, a reduction in metabolic expense in cold or unpredictable environments. One way of looking at hibernation is that it is an exaggerated, prolonged nightly torpor.

Some characteristics of hibernation include reduced body temperatures, reduced heart rates, reduced metabolic rates, reduced ventilatory (breathing) rates, and periodic arousal. We will start with temperatures, look at the magnitude and duration of body temperature fluctuations and try to understand the enigmatic process of periodic arousal.

Perhaps the world champion of mammalian hibernators is the arctic ground squirrel, *Spermophilus undulatus*. This species spends from 5.5 to 6.5 months in hibernation in Alaska.

At the onset of fall, squirrels begin to exhibit nightly torpor with core temperatures varying from about 37°C during the day to 33-34°C at night. Gradually the minimum temperature in torpor falls to below 25°C. Hypothermic bouts occur in their nest within the burrow system. After a period of several weeks, squirrels exhibit multi-day torpor bouts with minimum internal temperatures falling with each successive bout until they reach lows in the dead of winter of -0.2 to -2.3°C.[39]

All these multi-day torpor bouts occur within the burrow. In other words, once multi-day events begin, the squirrel is confined to its burrow until spring. Individual bouts of torpor vary in length, gradually increasing in the fall and winter to 26-27 days and then decreasing in duration into spring. Between torpor bouts the squirrel undergoes **periodic arousals**. During periodic arousal the animal warms to about 35°C and its metabolic rate increases accordingly.[40] Ground squirrels do not get up and move around during periodic arousal; typically they spend most of the time sleeping and a little time exhibiting nesting behavior akin to humans fluffing the pillow and rearranging the bedcovers. In spring, squirrels end hibernation more precipitously than they entered it. The last one or two multi-day bouts are shorter than those in midwinter, and then hibernation is over without the protracted series of nightly torpor bouts.

Several questions arise from these hibernation details. First, how is it that the arctic ground squirrel can drop below 0°C and not freeze? They avoid freezing by supercooling. Actually, only parts of the squirrels are supercooled. Some parts of the squirrel (feet, skin and abdominal cavity) were below the actual freezing point of its blood and tissue fluids (-0.5°C) but head and chest temperatures were above freezing. So, in hibernation, arctic ground squirrels exhibit regional heterothermy as well as supercooling.

Second, what is the point of periodic arousal? After all, the evolutionary rationale for hibernation is energy savings at extremely low temperatures, yet the rewarming of periodic arousal is metabolically expensive. There are several hypotheses to explain this phenomenon. Two of these center on the idea that the hibernator, before entering hibernation, synthesizes a chemical that triggers or induces hibernation. Then, during deep hibernation, the chemical is slowly exhausted. In these hypotheses the function of periodic arousal is to bring the body up to a temperature at which more of the "hibernation chemical" can be synthesized.[41,42]

An alternative hypothesis is that the periodic arousal allows the hibernator to catch up on its sleep. Brain waves recorded after arousal are characteristic of sleep patterns; those during torpor/hibernation are not. Experimentally induced sleep deprivation during periodic arousal prolongs the arousal bouts.[43] This idea and that of the brain neurochemical, mentioned above, are not mutually exclusive.

How much energy is saved by hibernation? Richardson's ground squirrels, *Spermophilus richardsonii*, in Alberta hibernate 6-8 months and, during hibernation, use only 12% of the energy they would have if they had remained active in their burrows.[44] Minimum temperatures in Richardson's ground squirrel burrows, about -3°C, are not as severe as those of arctic ground squirrels, -12 to -26°C.[45] Presumably, these lower burrow temperatures require a greater metabolic output over the course of hibernation in arctic ground squirrels.

During torpor, arctic ground squirrels maintain very low and constant metabolic rates as surroundings drop from +16 to 0°C and core body temperatures fall. As burrow temperatures fall below 0°C, body temperature stabilizes but only because metabolic rates increase. For example, total metabolic rate at an ambient temperature of -16°C is 15-20 times higher than that at 0°C.[46]

Combinations of adaptive traits

My final thought on ways of coping in the Far North is to reiterate a point made earlier in the chapter. Namely, a plant species or, more especially, an animal species may employ a combination of the above-described features to successfully deal with the cold, winter environment of Alaska's boreal forests or tundra habitats. For example, a black-capped chickadee employs shivering thermogenesis, nightly torpor, regional heterothermy, microhabitat selection and changes in metabolic rate in order to get through one 24-hour day in the winter.

REFERENCES

1 Errington, P.L. 1963. Muskrat populations. Iowa State University Press, Ames, 665 pp.

2 Limpert, R.J. and Earnst, S.L. 1994. Tundra swan. The Birds of North America, No. 89, 19 pp.

3 Rosenberg, D. and Rothe, T. 1994. Swans. Wildlife Notebook Series. Alaska Department of Fish and Game, Juneau, Alaska.

4 Robertson, R.J., Stutchbury, B.J. and Cohen, R.R. 1992. Tree Swallow. The Birds of North America No. 11.

5 Brown, C.R. and Brown, M.B. 1995. Cliff swallow. The Birds of North America, No. 149, 23 pp.

6 Garrison, B.A. 1999. Bank Swallow. The Birds of North America No. 414.

7 Lyon, B. and Montgomerie, R. 1995. Snow bunting and McKay's bunting. The Birds of North America, No. 198-199, 27pp.

8 Berthold, P. 1996. Control of bird migration. Chapman and Hall, London, 355 pp.

9 Parker, D.I., Lawhead, B.E. and Cook, J.A. 1997. Distributional limits of bats in Alaska. Arctic 50: 256-265.

10 Kirton, M.P. 1974. Fall movements and hibernation of the wood frog, *Rana sylvatica*, in interior Alaska. MS Thesis, University of Alaska Fairbanks 57 pp.

11 Kukal, O. 1991. Behavioral and physiological adaptations to cold in a freeze-tolerant arctic insect. pp 276-300 In: R.E. Lee Jr. and D.L. Denlinger, editors, Insects at low temperature. Chapman and Hall, New York and London, 513 pp.

12 Marchand, P.J. 1991. Life in the cold: an introduction to winter ecology. University Press of New England, Hanover and London, 239 pp.

13 Lee, R.E. Jr. 1991. Principles of insect low temperature tolerance, pp. 17-46 In: R.E. Lee, Jr. and D.L. Denlinger, editors, Insects at Low Temperature. Chapman and Hall, New York and London, 513 pp.

14 Layne, J.R. Jr. 1995. Crystallization temperatures of frogs and their individual organs. Journal of Herpetology 29: 290-298.

15 Layne, J.R. Jr., Lee, R.E. Jr. and Cutwa, M.M. 1996. Post-hibernation excretion of glucose in urine of the freeze tolerant frog *Rana sylvatica*. Journal of Herpetology 30: 85-87.

16 Costanzo, J.P., Bayuk, J.M. and Lee, R.E. Jr. 1999. Inoculative freezing by environmental ice nuclei in the freeze-tolerant wood frog, *Rana sylvatica*. Journal of Experimental Zoology 284: 7-14.

17 Barnes, B. M. 2005 personal communication.

18 Storey, K.B., Baust, J.G. and Wolanczyk, J.P. 1992. Biochemical modification of plasma ice-nucleating activity in a freeze-tolerant frog. Cryobiology 29: 374-384.

19 Lee, M.R., Lee, R.E. Jr.,Strong-Gunderson, J.M. and Minges, S.R. 1995. Isolation of ice-nucleating active bacteria from the freeze-tolerant frog, *Rana sylvatica*. Cryobiology 32: 358-365.

20 Woodhams, D.C., Costanzo, J.P., Kelty, J.D. and Lee. R.E. Jr. 2000. Cold hardiness in two helminth parasites of the freeze-tolerant wood frog, *Rana sylvatica*. Canadian Journal of Zoology 78: 1085-1091.

21 Loomis, S.H. 1991. Comparative invertebrate cold hardiness, pp. 301-317 In: R.E. Lee, Jr. and D.L. Denlinger, editors, Insects at low temperature. Chapman and Hall, New York and London. 513 pp.

22 Irving, L. 1972. Arctic life of birds and mammals, including man. Springer-Verlag, Berlin.

23 Dawson, W.R. and Carey, C. 1976. Seasonal acclimatization to temperature in Cardueline finches. I. Insulative and metabolic adjustments. Journal of Comparative Physiology 112: 317-333.

24 Schmidt-Nielsen, K. 1997. Animal physiology: adaptation and environment. Fifth Edition, Cambridge University Press, Cambridge and New York, 607 pp.

25 Churchfield, S. 1991. The natural history of shrews. Cornell University Press, Ithaca, 178 pp.

26 Wolff, J.O. 1984. Overwintering behavioral strategies in taiga voles (*Microtus xanthognathus*). pp. 315-318 In: J.F. Merritt, editor, Winter ecology of small mammals. Special Publication of Carnegie Museum of Natural History, Pittsburgh. 380 pp.

27 Stapp, P., Pekins, P.J. and Mautz, W.W. 1991. Winter energy expenditure and the distribution of southern flying squirrels. Canadian Journal of Zoology 69: 2548-2555.

28 Feist, D.D. 1984. Metabolic and thermogenic adjustments in winter acclimatization of subarctic Alaskan red-backed voles, pp. 131-137 In: J.F. Merritt, editor, Winter ecology of small mammals. Special Publication of Carnegie Museum of Natural History, Pittsburgh, 380 pp.

29   Carey, C. 1993. Does Nonshivering thermogenesis exist in birds? pp. 527-528 In: C. Carey, G.L. Florant, B.A. Wunder and B. Horwitz, editors, Life in the cold: ecological physiological and molecular mechanisms. Westview Press, Boulder, 575 pp.

30   Steen, J. and Steen, J.B. 1965. The importance of the legs in the thermoregulation of birds. Acta Physiologia Scandanavica 63: 285-291.

31   Henshaw, R.E. and Folk, G.E. 1969. Peripheral circulation mediated resistance to freezing in arctic wolves. Federation Proceedings 29: 791.

32   Scholander, P.F. and Schevill, W.E. 1955. Counter-current vascular heat exchange in the fins of whales. Journal of Applied Physiology 8: 279-282.

33   Carey, F.G. and Teal, J.M. 1969. Regulation of body temperature by the bluefin tuna. Comparative Biochemistry and Physiology 28: 205-213.

34   Smith, R.L. and D. Rhodes. 1983. Body temperature of the salmon shark, *Lamna ditropis*. Journal of the Marine Biological Association, U.K. 63: 243-244.

35   Miller, L.K. 1970. Temperature-dependent characteristics of peripheral nerves exposed to different thermal conditions in the same animal. Canadian Journal of Zoology 48: 75-81.

36   Chaplin, S.B. 1974. Daily energetics of the black-capped chickadee, *Parus atricapillus*, in winter. Journal of Comparative Physiology 89: 321-330.

37   Sharbaugh, S.M. 2001. Seasonal acclimatization to extreme climatic conditions by black-capped chickadees (*Poecile atri-*

capilla) in interior Alaska (64°N). Physiological and Biochemical Zoology 74: 568-575.

38   Cooper, S.J. and Swanson, D.L. 1994. Seasonal acclimatization of thermoregulation in the black-capped chickadee. Condor 96: 638-646.

39   Barnes, B.M. 1989. Freeze avoidance in a mammal: body temperatures below 0°C in an arctic hibernator. Science 244: 1593-1595.

40   Barnes, B.M. and Ritter, D. 1993. Patterns of body temperature change in hibernating arctic ground squirrels. pp.119-130 In: C. Carey, G.L. Florant, B.A. Wunder and B. Horwitz, editors, Life in the cold: ecological physiological and molecular mechanisms. Westview Press, Boulder, 575 pp.

41   Wang, L,C.H. 1993. Neurochemical regulation of arousal from hibernation. pp. 559-561 In: C. Carey, G.L. Florant, B.A. Wunder and B. Horwitz, editors, Life in the cold: ecological physiological and molecular mechanisms. Westview Press, Boulder, 575 pp.

42   Martin, S.L., Srere, H.K., Belke, D., Wang, L.C.H. and Carey, H.V. 1993. Differential gene expression in the liver during hibernation in ground squirrels. pp. 443-453 pp. 559-561 In: C. Carey, G.L. Florant, B.A. Wunder and B. Horwitz, editors, Life in the cold: ecological physiological and molecular mechanisms. Westview Press, Boulder, 575 pp.

43   Barnes, B.M., Omtzigt, C. and Daan, S. 1993. Hibernators periodically arouse in order to sleep. pp. 555-558 In: C. Carey, G.L. Florant, B.A. Wunder and B. Hor-

witz, editors, Life in the cold: ecological physiological and molecular mechanisms. Westview Press, Boulder, 575 pp.

44   Wang, L.C.H. 1979. Time patterns and metabolic rates of natural torpor in the Richardson's ground squirrel. Canadian Journal of Zoology 57: 149-155.

45   Buck, C.L. and Barnes, B.M. 1999. Temperatures of hibernacula and changes in body composition of arctic ground squirrels over winter. Journal of Mammalogy 80: 1264-1276.

46   Barnes, B.M. and Buck, C.L. 2000. Hibernation in the extreme: burrow and body temperatures, metabolism, and limits to torpor bout length in arctic ground squirrels. pp.65-72 In: G. Heldmaier and M. Klingenspor, editors, Life in the cold: Eleventh international hibernation symposium. Springer, Berlin, 546 pp.

3.

A FEW TREES, SOME SHRUBS, AND PERENNIALS OF ALASKA'S BOREAL FOREST

An obvious characteristic of boreal forests everywhere and particularly in Alaska is the scarcity of species of both plants and animals. An important determinant of this scarcity is the set of environmental rigors that I discussed in the previous chapter. In this chapter I'll describe the plant communities we see on the forest landscape and discuss how and why they change through time.

I will examine growth strategies of plants and the relation between growth rates and the production of chemicals in plants that act as feeding deterrents. Then I will focus on the importance of fungi to boreal forest trees and shrubs. Finally, I will describe some interesting features of the biology or life histories of some of the trees, shrubs, herbaceous plants, and lichens of Alaska's boreal forest.

The boreal forest has a huge longitudinal range. It is no surprise that its composition in terms of tree and shrub species differs considerably across this range. The boreal forest of Alaska is impoverished, having fewer tree and shrub species than are found in central or eastern Canada. Tree species in the Alaskan interior boreal forests are restricted to just six: black spruce, white spruce, tamarack, quaking aspen, paper birch and balsam poplar. This list excludes green alder and the willows, some of which grow to the height of small trees. Delineation of small trees of 4-9 m (12-30 ft) in height from large shrubs of 2-6 m (6-20 ft) in height isn't very clean due to the overlap in heights.[1] An added complication is that some species reach tree heights in northern British Columbia and coastal Alaska but occur only as shrub-sized plants in the interior of Alaska.

Some additional tree species found in the boreal forests of central and western Canada include jack pine, lodgepole pine, balsam fir, burr oak, American elm, maple, box elder and green ash.[2] Similarly, the shrub flora of Alaska is depauperate in comparison with that of even northern British Columbia. For example, neither chokecherry nor pin cherry occur naturally in Alaska but both occur in British Columbia.

ECOLOGICAL (PLANT) SUCCESSION IN THE BOREAL FOREST

Anyone driving in interior Alaska has noticed some of the differences in vegetation when comparing south-facing and north-facing slopes. Flat ground, the floodplains, has a somewhat different assortment yet. If we were looking at a south-facing slope in the interior that hadn't been disturbed for hundreds of years we would probably see mature stands of white spruce trees with a few understory plants and mosses. In contrast to these sites, north-facing slopes tend to be dominated by black spruce and feather mosses. Floodplain vegetation, if left alone for hundreds of years, will be dominated by mature black spruce or mixed stands of black and white spruce. But even the most casual observer will notice stands of quaking aspen on south-facing slopes and, on floodplains, mixed stands of paper birch, balsam poplar, willows, alders and the two spruce species. Is there any sense to be made of these observations? All these plant communities fit together in a biological concept called ecological succession. The basic idea is that after some sort of disturbance to the habitat the plant assemblage in evidence will slowly change through time. This progression (succession) will eventually lead to a plant community that is dominated by the most competitive species for that particular habitat type.

A key concept in plant succession is **disturbance**. Disturbance is some event that partially or completely removes the vegetation that for-merly occupied the ground. If the disturbance results in bare ground we have the starting point for **primary succession**. Examples of disturbances that initiate primary succession are lava flows, landslides and deposition of sand and gravel by rivers. If some of the vegetation or organic soil layers remain after a disturbance event, the process of **secondary succession** ensues. Disturbance events can be either naturally caused or produced by humans. Two of the most important natural disturbances are fire (typically caused by lightning) and the meandering of rivers. Some other natural disturbances include landslides, volcanic eruptions, winds, insects, diseases, and even the tracks of moose in the muskeg. Some examples of human-induced disturbance include timber harvest and land clearing for agriculture or mining.

Succession on floodplains

Floodplains, as the term suggests, are areas formed by rivers. Floodplains are gently sloping, may have river-borne gravels underlying the soil and, in interior Alaska, typically have discontinuous permafrost. The rivers themselves strongly influence soil characteristics on floodplains, largely by heat transfer. The Tanana River, flowing past Fairbanks, is unfrozen underneath the ice in winter. The water transfers heat to the underlying sediments and bedrock and, over time, thaws adjacent permafrost. Typically, riverbanks have a deep active layer and no permafrost, conditions that promote the growth and eventual dominance of white spruce. In the summer, the Tanana and other interior rivers carry sediment and gravel and, as flows slow, drop them along the banks or river bottom.

These banks or deposits are new ground available for colonization by plants. In other words, the deposition of this alluvial material is a disturbance event. Eventually, the river will change its course, or meander, and leave its former channel behind. So the floodplain consists of a patchwork of recent deposits (nearest the current riverbed) and areas abandoned by the river hundreds or thousands of years ago. Also, some of the abandoned channels may exist as lakes cut off from the present river channel(s). These isolated lakes are called oxbow lakes.

Initially, bare or disturbed ground is colonized by plants that have seeds dispersed by wind or water and that have physiological tolerances to direct sun and wind. These colonist species include grasses, horsetails, fireweed, yarrow and willow species. This array of plants dominate for the first two to five years (Figure 3.1). Heavier seeds such as those of alder and spruce aren't distributed as widely and rapidly

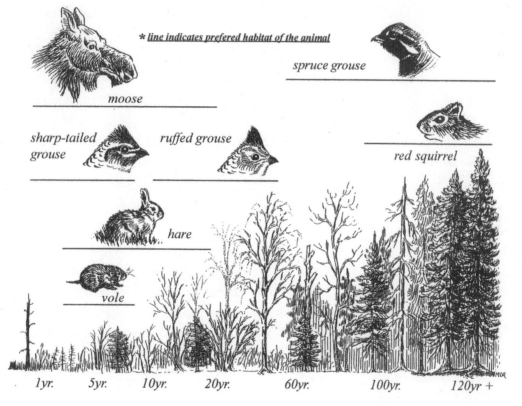

Figure 3.1: Succession of vegetation and fauna on an interior Alaska floodplain. At the left of the diagram is the immediate aftermath of a disturbance event, in this case, fire. Pioneer plant species including fireweed and grasses recruit into the burn in the first five years. Progressively, spruce, willows and poplar become established. The eventual dominant in well-drained soils, white spruce, is present early in succession but grows very slowly. If left undisturbed for hundreds of years the white spruce promote development of permafrost, which leads to replacement by black spruce. The cycle restarts at each new, major disturbance. The fauna changes as the plant community changes. Stages dominated by willows favor snowshoe hares, moose and sharp-tailed grouse. Pure stands of spruce favor red squirrels and spruce grouse.

as the lighter seeds mentioned above.[3] A closed (blocking light from falling on the forest floor) shrub community of willow and alder is reached in approximately five to ten years, but balsam poplar, birch and white spruce are already present. The young balsam poplars grow rapidly and reach dominance maybe twenty years into the successional sequence, with willows and alder persisting as a shrub layer under the canopy of poplars. During this stage soil temperatures are warm, productivity is high and some litter (dead leaves and branches, primarily) accumulates on the ground. Some of the litter is decomposed by fungi and bacteria in the soil, yielding inorganic nutrients that are, once again, available for the plants. Fairly rapid nutrient cycling is, therefore, characteristic of these early successional stages.

After about 100 years, the white spruce that established themselves very early in the sequence have grown large enough to begin to dominate the birch and balsam poplar; they are outcompeting these two deciduous tree species in large part by shading them. By 200 years into the sequence, the white spruce are mature and have replaced the poplar. Up to this stage in the succession, there has been a continual and significant accumulation of litter, primarily deciduous leaves. White spruce trees produce very little litter because they retain their needles year-round. Mosses don't do well on a deciduous forest floor because they are blanketed by the leaf litter. As spruce begins to dominate, mosses are finally able to establish a thick mat. The mat during summers is typically dry and insulates the soil from warming. In the fall the moss mat is dampened by early snowmelt and loses its insulative capacity. In winter, the forest floor cools, and in summer it doesn't rewarm. The result after 300

years or so is that a permafrost layer develops in the soil that, over the next 200-800 years, allows black spruce to outcompete and replace white spruce.[4] Another result is that cold soil temperatures slow decomposition of litter material and, therefore, slows nutrient cycling.

If the eventual dominant species is black spruce, why don't we see it everywhere in interior Alaska floodplains? The answer is: parts of the floodplain have been disturbed in the last 800 years. Fire is perhaps the most important form of disturbance. Portions of the floodplain vegetation burn every year and the burn sites quickly start the process of ecological succession over again. The result of these disturbance events, scattered in time and place, is a mosaic or patchwork of successional stages all thrown together. Fire intensity is another complicating factor. Hot fires burn above-ground vegetation but also consume the organic material in the soil including suckers and rhizomes of plants. These underground plant parts might be able, after less intense fires, to rapidly regenerate the parent plants. This regeneration is much faster than reestablishment of the same species by means of seed dispersal into the burn, followed by sprouting and subsequent growth.

The classic view of plant succession holds that competitive interactions among plant species and the changes brought about by colonizing species both affect the progression of species. This view is supported by studies of interior Alaskan floodplain succession. For example, willow is eliminated from alder-dominated midsuccessional floodplains, in part, because the alders shade willows and outcompete them. Another aspect of competition is longevity. In the boreal forest, balsam poplar replaces alder and, in turn, spruce replaces poplar primarily because, among the three, alder has the shortest lifespan and spruce has the longest.[4] Added to these effects are the often ignored effects of herbivores in plant communities. An example of herbivore-mediated progression in vegetation relates to moose in the boreal forest. Exclosure experiments have shown that, in the absence of moose, willows are more competitive with alders and tend to persist longer through succession than they do in the presence of moose.[5] In other words, willows are preferred, eaten selectively by moose, and the alders are left behind.

This floodplain successional scenario may be too simplistic. Mixed black and white spruce stands greater than 200 years old have been found. Black spruce should have completely dominated and replaced white spruce after that long. Subsurface geology may be more important than is now generally accepted.[6,7]

Let's go back to the oxbow lakes. Now that water no longer flows through these lakes, finer sediments, perhaps windblown, and litter from nearby vegetation can accumulate. The lake or pond develops aquatic vegetation that adds to the litter accumulation that eventually forms a peat layer on the bottom. Through time the

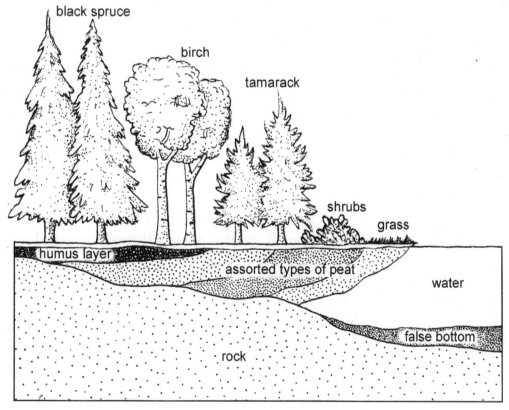

Figure 3.2: Succession from oxbow lake, on the right, to forest, on the left. Oxbow lakes, cut off from the river from which they are derived, slowly fill in with detritus generated by the surrounding vegetation and by aquatic vegetation in the lake. The false bottom is organic material generated by the lake. The layers of peat (also organic detritus) are the roots, twigs and shed leaves of the grasses, shrubs, and trees growing on the margin of the lake. Over time the lake will fill in with peat, become land, and support forest vegetation.

pond will fill in, the former pond will grow up in mosses, willows, alders, followed by tamarack and, finally, black spruce (Figure 3.2). This is a succession from an aquatic community to a terrestrial one. The sequence can be seen in all stages of succession along the Chena Hot Springs Road east of Fairbanks, the Chena Pump Road west of Fairbanks and along the Parks Highway or Alaska Highway.

A reversal of this pond-to-forest sequence is seen in the boreal forest. Muskeg underlain by permafrost can begin the thawing process due to a disturbance as slight as a moose walking through, leaving deep tracks. The muddy track can absorb more radiant heat than its surroundings and, thereby, promote melting of permafrost. Water accumulates in the track, absorbs more heat from the sun and continues the thawing. After many years a pond can develop from that initial moose track.

Succession on south-facing slopes (uplands)

A similar successional process occurs on well-drained, relatively dry south-facing slopes. The soils are primarily windblown loess. The soils are generally permafrost-free due to the dryness and to the warmer temperatures associated with southern exposures. Following fire, the first plants to invade are species with light, windborne seeds such as fireweed, bluejoint grass (*Calamagrostis canadensis*) and willows. Some species resprout from stumps or roots, including fireweed, prickly rose, highbush cranberry, alder, aspen and birch. Some species are able to develop from seeds that didn't burn.[4] These species may hold sway for the first 25 years. From

25-50 years post-burn, shrubs and deciduous tree saplings dominate. White spruce seedlings are already present but, because of their slow growth, aren't very obvious. Tree densities of 2000-3000 per hectare (800-1200 per acre) are sometimes seen, creating a canopy dense enough to shade out understory vegetation.

Mature or maturing deciduous trees dominate for the next 50-100 years; aspen on the steeper slopes, birch and poplar on the gentler slopes. As these stands mature, the canopy opens because tree density decreases to perhaps 700 trees per hectare for aspen, 300 trees per hectare for birch (280 and 120 trees per acre, respectively). About 100 years after a fire, white spruce finally becomes dominant.

The final stage of succession is a mature white spruce forest with an occasional aspen and/or paper birch. The spruce trees average about 30 cm (12 inches) diameter at breast height (d.b.h.) and 25-35 m (82-115 feet) tall. Tree densities vary from 500-1000 per hectare (200-400 per acre). About 200 years is required to reach this stage. Understory vegetation includes clumps of Siberian alder, prickly rose, highbush cranberry (*Viburnum edule*) and horsetail.

The south-facing bluffs along the Tanana River are steep and very dry. On these bluffs a sage/grass plant community persists long after moister, more gently sloping areas have succeeded to spruce forest. These bluff habitats may never be dominated by spruce. Indeed, one view of the bluff communities is that they have persisted, with some floral changes, since the last full-glacial episode.

Succession on north-facing slopes

North-facing slopes in interior Alaska, because of their lack of exposure to sunlight and their ice age thermal history (Chapter 1), are usually underlain by permafrost soils. Fire is perhaps more important in driving succession here than it is on floodplains or south-facing slopes. The susceptibility of plant communities on these slopes is due to the low branches of the black spruce, to the mosses and lichens in the understory, to frequent periods of drought and to lightning strikes.[4]

After a fire, sprouts of shrubs and herbs may be abundant within several weeks due, primarily, to sprouting from underground plant parts that survived the fire. Of course, the intensity of the fire will influence what, if any, rhizomes and roots survive. Mosses and liverworts recruit rapidly, as well as light-seeded herbaceous species such as fireweed. Black spruce seedlings also recruit to the burns.

A shrub stage develops from about six to 25 years after the burn, with alder and willows dominating. By 25-30 years after the fire, black spruce begins to dominate. Stands of black spruce 40-60 years old are very dense with up to 6000 trees per hectare (2430 per acre). In this time frame the forest floor is invaded by feathermosses (*Hylocomium splendens* and *Pleurozium schreberi*) and *Sphagnum*. These mosses lead to the rapid development of a thick, insulating organic layer. Further vegetation changes are subtle, leading to mature stands of black spruce about 100 years post-fire.

Some variation in the climax community can be seen. One variant is a closed black spruce community with the two feathermosses. Another is an open black spruce forest with understory of Labrador tea, bog blueberry, lowbush cranberry and either feathermoss or *Sphagnum*. Canopy coverage in the first community is about 60 % and 25 % or less in the second. The better sites on these north-facing slopes may produce black spruce up to 10 m (33 feet) tall and 15 cm (6 inch) d.b.h. Old black spruce on poorer sites may reach only 5 m (17 feet) tall and under 6 cm (2.5 inch) diameter.[4] In both types of stands there may be occasional alder and willow shrubs hanging on from earlier in the succession.

GROWTH STRATEGIES AND ALLELOCHEMICALS IN THE BOREAL FOREST

One way of looking at the plants of the boreal forest has to do with growth patterns. Some plant species grow rapidly, have relatively short lifespans, and tend to recycle nutrients rapidly. Another strategy is to grow slowly, live a long time, and, consequently, turn over nutrients slowly. Generally, deciduous trees and shrubs of the boreal forest exhibit the rapid-growth strategy, and evergreens, such as white and black spruce and juniper, exhibit the slow-growth strategy.

Clearly, deciduous trees build an entire set of new leaves each year while evergreens simply add to the existing complement of leaves. The annual production of new leaves in an aspen requires huge investments in nitrogen and phosphorus, the two inorganic elements that appear to limit growth in boreal forest plants.[8] The leaves also constitute an investment in carbon and energy. Although some of these elements are conserved by translocating them out of the leaves and back into the roots, not everything can be salvaged before the leaves fall in the autumn. Why put such a large investment into annually regenerated leaves? Apparently, the volume of photosynthetic machinery contained in the leaves allows for the rapid growth exhibited by these plants.

Evergreens retain their old leaves or needles and add to them each year. The advantages of this strategy are several. First, evergreens don't have to spend time and energy translocating materials out of the leaves in the fall to prevent losing them when the leaves drop off. Second, there isn't a significant energy loss from leaf fall at all. Third, the leaves or needles are available for photosynthesis whenever temperatures allow it. No need to quickly build leaves to start production. The disadvantage is simply the low volume of photosynthetic machinery in the needles and, consequently, their low productivity. Such slowly growing plants can't afford to suffer much browsing by herbivores because they can't make up the lost tissues with a spurt of compensatory growth. Therefore, part of the metabolic activity of evergreens is devoted to synthesizing chemicals that are noxious to herbivores.

These chemicals are often referred to as **secondary metabolites**. The inference is that these chemicals are not the primary ones needed for energy metabolism or direct regulation of plant production or growth. Secondary metabolites, in this context, could also be called **allelopathic** chemicals, chemicals produced by an organism that have a negative impact on another organism. The secondary metabolites of boreal forest evergreens can work in several ways. They may taste bad to the herbivore and thereby deter feeding. They may be toxic and adversely affect some aspect of the herbivore's metabolism. These effects are not mutually exclusive.

Deciduous and evergreen trees function in the context of nutrient availability, nutrient recycling, herbivory, and the changes in these features through succession. In boreal forest Uplands after a fire, nutrients (inorganic phosphate, ammonium, and nitrate) are moderately high in concentration. Colonizing plants establish themselves, grow rapidly, and produce a lot of litter. Some of the litter is decomposed, regenerating the inorganic nutrients needed to continue the growth of these species. As succession progresses, soil nutrient concentrations decline, favoring the growth of slower-growing trees with more modest nutrient requirements. The composition of the litter changes from deciduous leaves and twigs, high in nitrogen content, to those of evergreens with low nitrogen and high concentrations of allelopathic chemicals (tannins and terpenes).

Decomposing bacteria are also inhibited by allelopathic chemicals. Therefore, the **remineralization** (changing organic chemicals to inorganic) of allelopathic chemicals in the spruce needles is extremely slow. Nutrient cycling has slowed on the forest floor. These circumstances make the forest ever less favorable for the faster-growing, colonizing species that are being or have been replaced.[9] Of course, the preference for the less defended (early successional) plant species by herbivores is also a factor in the succession process. That is, herbivores selectively remove early successional species and leave behind the chemically defended, late successional species.

Faster growing trees and shrubs are not totally defenseless against herbivores. When snowshoe hares browse on new growth of willow and birch, they induce the production of feeding deterrents in the stems and twigs that remain. New shoots sprouting from browsed stumps are much more toxic to hares than were the original shoots. The effects of hare browsing on vegetation and the toxicity of boreal forest vegetation are thought by many to be the primary determinants of snowshoe hare population cycles.

Similarly, quaking aspen has a chemical defense mechanism for reducing browsing intensity of ruffed grouse. Aspen produce a toxic chemical, coniferyl benzoate, and store it in the flower buds. The grouse can sense the deterrent before they eat it and avoid buds with very high concentrations. Ruffed grouse fed diets containing high levels of this chemical lost weight, suffered a net loss of body nitrogen, and excreted more water.[10,11] Studies have shown that ruffed grouse reliance on aspen buds varies considerably from year to year. What we don't know is what accounts for the variability in prevalence of this allelopathic chemical from tree to tree and from year to year.

MYCORRHIZAS IN THE BOREAL FOREST

The term **mycorrhiza** derives from two Greek words: *myco* means fungus and *rhiza* refers to root. So, a mycorrhiza is an association between the roots of vascular plants and a fungus. Of course, there are plenty of fungi that are simply parasitic on plants or are decomposers of dead and dying plants. Mycorrhizas are gener-

ally thought to be mutually beneficial to the fungus and the host plant. The fungus benefits by absorbing organic carbon compounds (sugars and amino acids) from the roots of the plant. The plant benefits by gaining inorganic nutrients absorbed by the fungal network surrounding its roots but also ramifying through the adjacent soil. In other words, the host plant saves a considerable expense of building an even larger root system than it does.

Scientists recognize four different types of mycorrhizal associations; examples of all four occur in Alaska. The most widespread of the four is the **arbuscular mycorrhiza**. This association is found in perhaps two/thirds of all vascular plants. In this association the fungi are members of the Zygomycota, a group including the common bread mold. The fungus produces long, thin filaments of tissue, the **hyphae**, that infiltrate the soil. A network of hyphae is called a **mycelium**. The mycelium absorbs water, mineral nutrients the plant requires such as phosphate, and micronutrients such as copper and zinc. Since the mycelium closely invests the root hairs of the plant, transfer to the plant is straightforward. The fungus in this association is dependent on the plant for all its energy requirements.

The **ectomycorrhiza** is an association between a tree and a basidiomycete fungus. These fungi are, in their fruiting stages, recognizable as mushrooms. Unlike some of the arbuscular mycorrhizal fungi, the hyphae of ectomycorrhizal fungi do not actually penetrate into the root cells of the tree. This type of association involves less than 10 % of the plant world but is extensive in boreal forests. As discussed earlier, boreal forests are often nutrient-limited. Ectomycorrhizas are extremely important because of phosphate uptake and transfer but also because the fungi decompose organic material in the soil. This means that the energy cost of this association to the tree is less because the fungus comes up with part of its own energy requirement. But perhaps more importantly, decomposition converts the organic nitrogen to **ammonium**, an inorganic nitrogen source the tree requires, and delivers it directly to the tree. Normal remineralization of organic nitrogen involves decomposition by soil bacteria and releases nitrate or nitrite into the soil. Once in the soil, these nitrogen sources are subject to absorption by every plant root system in the community. Trees with ectomycorrhizas avoid the competition for inorganic nitrogen; it is simply never released to the soil. An example of an ectomycorrhiza is the association between tamarack and *Boletus elegans*, an edible bolete.

Ericoid mycorrhizas involve associations between species of cup-fungi, Ascomycetes, and members of the heather order, Ericales. As in the ectomycorrhizas, the fungi in **ericoid mycorrhizas** decompose organic detritus and provide ammonium to the plant. Heathers often grow in extreme, often acidic, soils. It is thought that the fungus in the association protects the heather from toxic metals sometimes prevalent in these acidic soils. Examples of ericaceous plants in the boreal forest include bog rosemary (*Andromeda polifolia*), Lapland rosebay (*Rhododendron lapponicum*), bog blueberry (*Vaccinium uliginosum*), Labrador tea (*Ledum groenlandicum*), moss heather (*Cassiope stelleriana*) and lowbush cranberry (*Vaccinium vitis-idaea*).

The **orchid mycorrhiza** is a fourth association. In this association there is no movement of carbohydrates (energy) from the orchid to the fungus; the orchid is a parasite. Fungi in orchid mycorrhizas are, typically, basidiomycetes (mushrooms). Sometimes the fungus is parasitic on another plant, making the orchid a parasite of a parasite. Orchids in the boreal forest that are involved in such associations include the calypso or fairyslipper (*Calypso bulbosa*) (Figure 3.3), northern green bog orchid (*Platanthera hyperborea*), round leaf orchid (*Orchis rotundifolia*) and yellow ladyslipper orchid (*Cypripedium calceolus*). One orchid species of our boreal forest, the pale coralfoot (*Corallorrhiza trifida*) is

(a)   (b)

Figure 3.3: Calypso orchid (a), and pasque flower (b). Both these flowers bloom early in the spring. The pasque flower is the first flower out in early May. The calypso orchid is a mid- to late May bloomer. It is also an example of a parasitic plant, subsisting on fungal tissues in the soil.

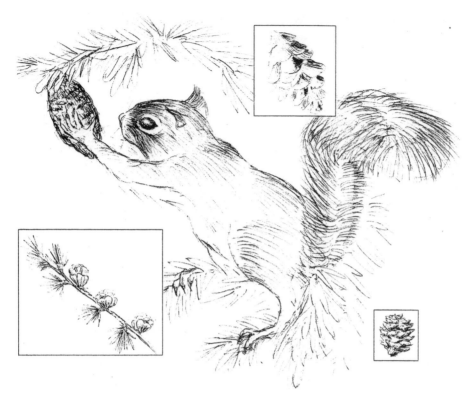

Figure 3.4: Cones of conifers in interior Alaska: tamarack cones (lower left); black spruce cone after opening and release of seeds (lower right); white spruce cone after seed release (upper); and red squirrel harvesting unopened white spruce cone.

a **saprophyte.**[2] Saprophytes obtain their nutrition from dead or decaying organic material. The pale coralfoot has very little chlorophyll for photosynthesis. Its close relative of the southern part of the North American boreal forest, the spotted coralfoot, (*Corallorrhiza maculata*) has no chlorophyll whatsoever. All fungi are considered saprophytes.

CONIFERS OF THE BOREAL FOREST

White spruce

In the boreal forest of interior Alaska, the white spruce, *Picea glauca*, is the most common tree along river banks and the dominant conifer of south-facing slopes. This tree species occurs extensively in the interior, north to the south slope of the Brooks Range, west to parts of the Seward Peninsula, southwest to Bristol Bay, in south-central but not in southeast Alaska. White spruce are found from Alaska eastward across Canada near the northern limit of trees to Hudson Bay, Labrador and Newfoundland but also in southern British Columbia. In the United States (lower 48) white spruce occur south into New York, Minnesota, Montana and, locally, in the Black Hills.

It can be distinguished most easily from its relative, the black spruce, by its cones. The cones of white spruce are elongated, almost cylindrical in shape and 3- 6 cm (1.25- 2.5 inches) long. These cones fall from the tree at maturity (Figure 3.4). The cones of black spruce are egg-shaped or nearly round and are 2.5 cm (1 inch) or less in diameter. Black spruce cones remain on the tree at maturity.

The white spruce is a large tree for interior Alaska, typically reaching heights of 12- 20 m (40- 70 feet) and 15- 45 cm (6- 18 inches) diameters. In the most favorable locations, it will reach heights of 25- 35 m (80- 115 feet) and diameters of 76 cm (30 inches). In contrast, the largest black spruce are 22 m (72 feet) in height.[1] Compared to black spruce and tamarack, white spruce grows relatively rapidly and, therefore, its growth rings are easily visible in cross-section. At tree line this species may appear as a shrub, blown flat by winds, or in several bizarre, distorted growth forms. In areas of steady winds white spruce may take the form of a **flag tree** with all the branches on the upwind side missing. An accumulation of these misshapen trees is often referred to as elfin woods. An alternative term for these elfin trees is **krumholtz** trees. In tundra areas of light snow and fierce winter winds, branches above snowline may be blasted away by blowing snow, leaving a **dumbbell tree** (see Figure 3.5). Typical ages for white spruce in mature stands at lower elevation range up to 200 years.

Seeds are about 10 mm long and occur two per cone scale. Each seed has a wing attached that aids in dispersal by wind. Wind is the primary means of seed dispersal; gusts can easily lift seeds higher than the parent cones and spread them great distances from the parent trees. Two enthusiastic Alaskan scientists chased seeds across a clearing outside Fairbanks and measured distances traveled and time air-borne. The parent tree was 18.5 m (60 feet) tall and had cones in the upper 3.1 m (10 feet); shortest time air-borne was 7 seconds, the longest was 125 seconds.[12] Average distance traveled was 33 m (109 feet) and 4% went further than 100 m

Figure 3.5: a) White and black spruce growth forms. The clubbing at the top is characteristic of black spruce. b) Black spruce clone. Small individuals derive vegetatively from an original parent tree by branch layering. Note the larger trees are dumbbell-shaped, a result of abrasion by blowing snow in winter.

(320 feet). Of course, winged seeds don't necessarily travel in a straight line. One seed was airborne for a total distance of 121 m (390 feet) but its path described a tight curve and it landed only 13 m (42 feet) from its parent tree.

Speaking of cones, white spruce cone production varies tremendously from year to year. Under optimal conditions, spruce set huge numbers of cones, turning the treetops brown. Such sporadic cone crops are a windfall for red squirrels and grosbeaks.

White spruce trees are attacked by a variety of insect pests, some of which damage and kill trees and destroy the commercial value of spruce forests. Significant insect pests of white spruce include the spruce budworm, the spruce beetle, whitespotted sawyer, and spruce seed moth.

One of the most serious insect pests is the spruce beetle, *Dendroctonus rufipennis*. An infestation of these beetles in south-central Alaska killed 29% of the white spruce, destroying 59% of the commercial value.[13] Beetles tend to attack slower-growing trees, and these are the larger trees of greater commercial value. Stands of immature trees and mixed stands of white spruce and other species are less susceptible to attack.[14,15]

Individual spruce beetles exhibit either a one- or a two-year life cycle depending on their location on the spruce tree. Optimal conditions, allowing growth to maturation in one year, occur when individuals are located on the south or top of fallen logs or on the south and east sides of standing trees. Locations on the north and west sides of standing trees or the north and undersides of fallen trees result in a two-year cycle. With warm spring and summer temperatures, even less favorable sites may allow a one-year cycle.[13]

Adult spruce beetles are dark, either brown or black, are about 5 mm long and 3 mm wide. Their activity in the spring begins in May with air temperatures of about 7°C. Emergence from the host tree and dispersal occur at air temperatures of 16°C and above. Females disperse first, find a favorable tree (usually a blowdown) and excavate an egg gallery under the bark. Males and additional females are attracted by sex and aggregating **pheromones**. Pheromones are produced by the beetles, are species-specific, and function as chemical attractants. After mating, the female deposits eggs in the gallery and plugs the opening with boring material. By August, eggs hatch into white, legless grubs that expand the galleries in the process of eating the wood. The grubs overwinter under the bark. Most larvae pupate the following summer, a process requiring 10-15 days. Newly emerged adults often migrate to the base of an infested tree to overwinter. The second spring, adults emerge and disperse for reproduction.

Spruce beetle overwintering is governed by the same three essential factors that govern human real estate...location, location and location! Lab studies found that neither larvae nor adults can tolerate actual freezing but can supercool down to -31°C in the winter. Temperature measurements under the bark of white spruce in the winter showed that, during a typical interior winter, only those individuals overwintering in sites beneath snowline would be expected to survive.[16] Therefore, snow depth, severity of winter and adult choice of attack location all influence overwinter survival of spruce beetles.

Another insect pest of white spruce is the spruce budworm, *Choristoneura fumiferana*. This "worm" is the caterpiller larva of a moth species. The adults are grey-brown with wing-spans of 22-28 mm.[15] Adult females lay egg masses on spruce needles in midsummer. Eggs hatch in about 12 days, producing larvae, about 32 mm long, with brown heads and bodies covered with white spots. Young larvae overwinter under the scales of bark wrapped in a silk cocoon. In spring, larvae emerge and begin to feed on spruce buds or old needles then moving on to the current year's needle crop. Caterpillers form pupae in late June or early July and emerge 12-18 days later. In addition to white spruce, the spruce budworm will also attack larch and black spruce in Alaska and alpine fir and lodge-pole pine in British Columbia.

Spruce budworm infestations may last for years. Defoliation can be extensive enough to kill the tops of trees but, apparently, rarely leads to tree mortality. Analysis of tree rings showed that mature white spruce infested by this pest lost 3-5 % of the growth they would normally have attained during a year. In addition, birch and aspen occurring in mixed stands with infested white spruce appear to put on extra growth, suggesting that defoliation of spruce allowed more sunlight to reach these competing trees.[17]

Another insect attacking dead and dying white and black spruce is the white spotted sawyer, *Monochamus scutellatus*. This beetle is also called the longhorned beetle because the antennae are often twice as long as the body. From a human perspective, these bugs are sometimes frightening, sometimes disgusting, primarily because they are so clumsy in flight. Sawyers flying through the woods or through your yard will, as often as not, blunder right into you. I have a friend who swears that they do it on purpose! Most of us in the interior who have built log cabins are familiar with sawyers. The adults are attracted to spruce sap, a chemical cue they use to find the injured trees on which they will lay their eggs. Freshly cut spruce logs, especially those being peeled by the do-it-yourself builder, are irresistible.

Adult sawyers emerge between early July and mid-August, find a mate, find an appropriate tree and deposit eggs under bark scales. These eggs hatch into white grubs that eventually grow to 50 mm in length, eating on the cambium and sapwood while they grow. The mandibles or jaws are dark brown, heavy and made out of chitin, a structural polysaccharide. Feeding activity is so boisterous that, if you stand near an infested woodpile, you can easily hear the larvae chewing. Pupation occurs in the second year of life, so, the larvae must overwinter twice. If the larvae attack a dying tree, I'm sure they help push it along toward mortality, damaging the cambium and introducing wood-rotting fungi. Adults feed to an extent on spruce foliage and branches. Sawyers are just one of the many species that bore into spruce. Others include the horntail (the larva of a wasp), ambrosia beetles, flat-headed wood borers and engraver beetles.

Several fungal diseases are prevalent in white spruce. Two of the more common diseases rely on the presence of another plant species to complete their life cycles. The spruce broom rust is caused by infection with the fungus *Chrysomyxa arctostaphyli*. On white and black spruce trees this fungus causes the proliferation of branches attacks the current year's needles, making the tips of branches turn orange when fruiting occurs.[15]

Some significant decay fungi of white spruce include: honey mushroom (*Armillaria* sp.), artist's conk (*Ganoderma applanatum*), quinine fungus (*Fomitopsis officinalis*), purple conk (*Hirschioporus abietinus*), red ring rot (*Phellinus pini*) and red belt fungus (*Fomitopsis pinicola*). Most of these species form a conk or bracket fungus on the trunk of the infected tree. Generally, decay fungi attack only dead trees or trees that have been injured (e.g., bark removal) or stressed (attacked by insect pests). Fungal attack on trees can lead to wind-breakage and windthrow by weakening the heart or base of the tree. However, two species, *Armillaria* and *Heterobasidion annosum*, can kill trees directly.[15]

Figure 3.6: Witch's broom investing a white spruce tree. Witch's brooms provide winter nesting habitat for flying squirrels. The flying squirrel in this illustration is being pursued by a boreal owl.

that we recognize as a **witch's broom** (Figure 3.6). Fruiting of the fungus causes the current year's spruce needles to turn yellowish and, then in the fall, to drop off. The growth of infected trees is inhibited and, sometimes, the trees are killed. Below, we will discuss the use of witch's brooms by birds and mammals of the boreal forest. The other host in the life cycle of this fungus is the kinnikkinnick, *Arctostaphylos uva-ursi*. So, this fungal disease only occurs in areas where both the conifers and this bearberry co-occur or overlap in distribution.

A second pathogenic fungus that attacks white and black spruce is the spruce needle rust, *Chrysomyxa ledicola*. This species alternates its life stages between the spruces and Labrador tea. Again, infections in spruce only occur in boggy areas where both host species occur. The rust appears on the leaves of Labrador tea as a series of raised orange bumps. On spruce, this fungus

Black spruce

Black spruce, *Picea maraina*, is less widespread in Alaska than white spruce. Both species reach Bristol Bay, Norton Sound and the Seward Peninsula but the black spruce has a more restricted distribution on the lower Yukon River. The species occurs across Canada near the limit of trees, southward into New Jersey, Minnesota, Manatoba and British Columbia.

It is clear from my earlier discussion of plant communities and succession in the boreal forest that black spruce does better in poorly drained soils. In fact, the seeds of black spruce and tamarack require wet, acidic soils to successfully germinate. Such conditions are not conducive to white spruce germination. Whereas white spruce requires a soil depth of about 50 cm (20 inches), black spruce can do well in soil depths of only 25 cm (10 inches). Therefore, black spruce in many areas competes well with white spruce in terms of advancing above and beyond both arctic and alpine tree lines.

At the limits of spruce survival, trees are unable to muster enough surplus energy to produce cones. Instead, they may reproduce vegetatively. That is, rooting occurs from the lower branches, a process called **layering**, and new individuals spring up around the base of the founder tree (Figure 3.5). You can easily spot these little clumps of trees, **clones**, near tree line on the Elliott, Steese, Parks and Richardson Highways. These tree line clones may be very ancient, 4000 to 5000 years old. Reproduction by layering is much more common in black spruce than in either white spruce or tamarack.[18] Near tree line, black spruce exhibits the dumbbell and other bizarre shapes mentioned above for white spruce. In addition, black spruce, characteristically, exhibit **clubbing**, especially in muskegs or bogs. Clubbing is the formation of a bulge of foliage at the apex of the tree. In contrast, white spruce simply taper to a point (Figure 3.5).

Recall that black spruce, when they do develop cones, retain them on the tree. The seeds are released over a period of years rather than all at once like in white spruce. This feature might make it easier to recruit black spruce back into suitable habitat after a fire or other disturbance. Even if the black spruce near the disturbed site couldn't produce cones that year they may have seeds left over from the last successful cone crop.

Earlier I discussed the advantage of evergreens being able to perform photosynthesis any day the air temperature is warm enough, summer or winter because the needles persist. One liability of retaining needles through the winter is that they can lose water by transpiration on a relatively warm winter day, yet the ground is frozen. In other words, evergreen needles can lead to water stress.

While deciduous leaves fall each autumn, black and white spruce needles have a lifespan of about 30 and 7 years, respectively. The new (1 year old) needles have the highest photosynthetic rates. Rates are almost as high through the fifth year and then slowly decline until by year 13, productivity is down to about 40 % of the maximum. Another contrast between deciduous and evergreen trees in the forest is in leaf-out. Birch and aspen leaves emerge from the leaf buds in early to mid-May; new needles of black and white spruce emerge from the leaf bud in mid-June. If a tree already has needles photosynthesizing, there is no rush to produce them in May.

Black spruce grow in the coldest, wettest sites occupied by trees in the boreal forest, and black spruce stands have the lowest productivity within the boreal forest.[19] Comparison with other forest types show that black spruce forests have the lowest **standing crop** (amount of mass present),about 6% of that found in white spruce forests, and the lowest annual **productivity** (accumulation of new material),56 g/m²/year, about 6% of that found in a balsam poplar stand.[20]

And if conditions weren't bad enough for black spruce, it has competitors for space, nutrients, and sunlight even in mature stands. Mosses on the forest floor compete vigorously for phosphorus, one of the two limiting nutrients for plant growth. While making up only 17 % of the above-ground pool of phosphorus, mosses were able to absorb 75 % of the available phosphorus.[21]

Tamarack

My father and I took the ferry to Haines and drove on to Fairbanks in the early fall of 1968. As we drove by muskegs, I kept noticing what looked like dying spruce trees. The needles were yellow and, at first glance, some of the branches appeared to be completely naked. Only months later did I figure out that we had been looking at tamarack trees. The tamarack or eastern larch (*Larix laricina*) is, among Alaskan conifers, unique. It sheds its needles in the fall. In other words, it is a deciduous conifer, not an evergreen. These trees can be mistaken for black spruce, but a close examination will easily allow you to distinguish between the two even in the summer when both have needles. First, if you look closely at the twigs of tamarack you will see that most of the needles are attached in clusters of 12-20 on short bumps projecting from the main twig. Only the current year's needles are attached as single needles directly to the twig. Second, the cones are attached to the top of the branch while both spruces have cones hanging down from the bottoms of the branches. Tamarack cones are almost spherical, 1-1.5 cm (3/8-5/8 inches) in diameter, and have only about 20 cone scales. The spruces have many more cone scales (see Figure 3.4).

The tamarack has the most restricted distribution in Alaska. It is locally abundant along the Tanana River but widely scattered along the Yukon and Kuskokwim Rivers. It does not occur in south-central or southeast Alaska. Aside from Alaska, tamarack is distributed from the Yukon Territory eastward along the northern limit of trees to Hudson Bay, Labrador, Newfoundland and south into New Jersey, Illinois, Minnesota and locally in Maryland and West Virginia.

Tamarack occurs in muskeg and other moist soils in association with black spruce, paper birch, willows and alder. It, along with black spruce, is able to germinate seeds in the acidic, peat soils common to floodplains and upland bogs. Growth of tamarack in these moist, boggy habitats is very slow, producing trees 9-18 m (30-60 ft) high and 10-25 cm (4-10 inches) in diameter.[1] Occasionally, tamarack is found in upland sites alongside white spruce. In these favorable conditions it grows rapidly, reaching 33 cm (13 inches) diameter in 100 years. In northern Wisconsin peatlands (and probably in Alaska) tamarack grows faster than black spruce in wetter soils with higher mineral content. Black spruce is more shade tolerant and becomes more abundant as plant succession progresses.

As is true of the other conifers, tamarack have their pests. Defoliation by insects has a significant impact on growth in tamarack. The larch sawfly, *Pristiphora erichsonii*, is a recurring problem in eastern North America, producing documented growth depressions of tamarack in Quebec stretching back over 200 years.[22] In Alaska, the larch bud moth is the principal defoliator. A fungal root rot, *Armillaria*, affects all the tree species in the boreal forest of Alaska. Tamarack and black spruce are more susceptible to this fungus than birch and white spruce.[23]

In Canada, tamarack is sometimes infested heavily by aphids, *Adelges lariciatus*. A sugary waste material, honeydew, is produced by actively feeding aphids. The honeydew is a food resource for one species of blackfly, *Simulium venustum*. In one study, 50 % of the blackflies swept from tamarack had actually fed on aphid honeydew.[24] So, if you are swarmed by blackflies in the Alaskan muskeg, you may be comforted by the knowledge that these pesky insects feed on the fluids of other species, too.

Common juniper

We live on an old bluff over the Tanana River, west of Fairbanks. The house is located in a mixed stand of aspen, balsam poplar and spruce. Downslope in the trees is a juniper bush. I imagine it is somehow hanging on in the shade, far past the glory days of the last, arid glacial episode in Fairbanks. Juniper in Alaska is scattered to rare in occurrence, showing up in rocky tundra, on sunny slopes, and, in forest openings. It is a low shrub, up to 0.6 m (2 feet) in height or spreading out as a prostrate clump up to 3 m (10 feet) in diameter; in New England and Europe this species may occasionally grow into small trees. The cliff at the east entrance to the University of Alaska in Fairbanks is a good place to see juniper. I've seen it elsewhere along the Tanana River and in the mining district around the town of Central.

Two researchers compared juniper biology in open areas and in forest to see which was better habitat. They found that junipers in open areas produced more flowers, more pollen and more cones than their relatives in the forest.[25] Juniper bloomed earlier in the year in open areas.

Common juniper, *Juniperus communis*, occurs across northern Europe and Asia, Alaska, Canada, Greenland and southward into the mountains of Georgia, Illinois, New Mexico and California.

It is the most widely distributed conifer in the world. In Alaska, populations occur in southeast, interior, north of the Brooks Range, Kenai and Seward Peninsulas and Bristol Bay.

A second juniper species, the creeping juniper (*Juniperus horizontalis*), although widespread across Canada and the lower 48 states, occurs only rarely in southeast interior and south-central Alaska. The two are easily distinguished by their leaves. Common juniper has leaves shaped like needles or awls; creeping juniper has scale-like leaves. Common juniper leaves have a shiny bronze (not green) lower surface; the upper surface bears a white line down the center of the needle. Needles (leaves) occur in whorls of three around the twig.

Juniper, being an evergreen, exhibits a conservative growth strategy. That means that it generates allelochemicals for its protection from browsing. The essential oil of juniper from Greece was shown to have 56 different organic chemical compounds, but primarily alpha pinene.[26] In Norway, the proportions of the three major chemicals (pinene, sabinene and limonene) were shown to vary among habitats. Pinene's proportion increased dramatically in plants from cold, weatherbeaten sites.[27] We don't know if this particular compound is more effective at preventing browsing, but it is tempting to speculate that plants growing in the least favorable habitat are the most heavily defended.

These allelochemicals are, in a real way, antibiotics. That is, they exhibit activity that inhibits other life forms. Are they of any potential use to human beings? The answer is yes. Chemical fractions from juniper berries have an inhibitory effect on herpes virus.[28]

The sexes are separate in juniper; some plants have seed-bearing cones while others have pollen-bearing cones. The juniper berry consists of three fleshy scales that have grown together. These cones (berries) require two years to reach maturity. A 1-year old berry is small and green; a 2-year old is larger and blue. Each berry contains from one to five seeds. The common juniper blooms in the late spring (May- June).

To my knowledge, no one has studied longevity of common juniper in Alaska. A study of this species in England showed that individuals reach about 100 years old in southern England on chalk substrata but can live to over 200 years in the north.[29] Trunk diameters are poor indicators of lifespan because age appears to be inversely correlated with growth rate. That is, short-lived individuals grow faster than long-lived.

FLOWERING TREES AND SHRUBS

Quaking aspen

When I was a child growing up in northeastern Arizona we occasionally drove up into the San Francisco Mountains around Flagstaff. I loved the mountains because of the large trees, much bigger than the pinon pine and creosote bush of most of the Colorado Plateau. The ponderosa pines were great, but I loved the aspens with their white bark and golden leaves in the fall. Moving to interior Alaska and the aspens of the boreal forest reminded me of my childhood. The golden leaves were the same as I remembered but the bark had a slightly green tint I hadn't noticed as a child. The green color is caused by chlorophyll in the bark. This chlorophyll makes it possible for aspens to fix carbon

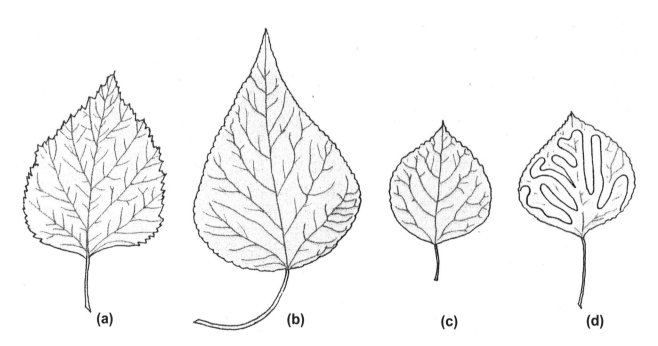

Figure 3.7: Leaves of: a) paper birch; b) balsam poplar; c) quaking aspen, and d) quaking aspen infested with aspen leaf miner.

(make carbohydrates) in the springtime even before leaf-out.

Quaking aspen, *Populus tremuloides*, is sometimes called trembling aspen, aspen or popple. It can be readily identified based on leaf size and shape (Figure 3.7) and on bark color and texture. Leaf blades range in length from 2.5 - 5 cm (1 - 2 inches), are rounded at the base but serrated (toothed) toward the apex. Aspen leaves are usually wider than they are long, shiny green on top but pale beneath. In a breeze, leaves flutter or tremble, making a characteristic sound. Bark is either white or greenish gray and smooth. Knots on the bark are black and the scars of old branches, also black, have a characteristic inverted chevron shape.

The quaking aspen is the most widely distributed tree species in North America. Aspen range from Alaska eastward across Canada to Labrador and Newfoundland, extending into northeastern United States and south to New Jersey and Virginia. In the west, aspen are found in the Rocky Mountains, into Texas, Mexico and California. In Alaska, aspen are found on the south slope of the Brooks Range, west to the Koyukuk and Kobuk Rivers, down the Yukon River to Holy Cross and on the Kuskokwim to Bethel. The species is common in south-central Alaska but in southeast only occurs in the northernmost corner around Haines and Skagway.[1]

As I suggested in the discussion of forest succession, aspens interact with other plant species in a dynamic way. In mixed stands of aspen and white spruce, the two species compete for nutrient absorption from the soil. The spruce is more efficient at this process, an important aspect leading to its eventual dominance. On the other hand, aspen prepare the way for spruce by establishing shade conditions and moister soil than would otherwise be available. Whereas white spruce are shade-tolerant and can even recruit into a closed canopy forest, aspen are shade-intolerant. That intolerance even affects (determines) the actual shape of the aspen tree. Mature aspen have lots of branches at the top of the tree but no living branches lower on the trunk. Those lower branches thrived when in direct sunlight but, with shading, withered away. The aspen shape is good for developing a closed canopy. Aspens grow rapidly, for Alaska, reaching maximum size and longevity after about 100 years. Large aspens may reach 24 m (80 feet) in height and 46 cm (18 inches) in diameter.

Flowering occurs in May in Alaska, before the leaves are completely developed. Male and female catkins occur on different trees. Seed capsules mature in catkins about 7-11 cm (3-4.5 inches) long from late May to June. Each catkin produces hundreds of tiny, cottony seeds. Once these capsules are mature, seeds or entire capsules drop from the tree. In a healthy stand of aspens, this event can be so dramatic as to appear like snowfall in June with the forest floor virtually buried in cottony catkins. Seeds, once they fall from the parent tree, have a very short span of viability. Typically, germination must occur within the first 2- 3 weeks.

Propagation from roots is common in aspen, constituting asexual reproduction. New saplings sprouted in this manner are usually still connected by their root systems to the "parent" tree. All the individual aspens derived by asexual propagation from a single parent tree are genetically identical to that parent. In other words, they are clones of the parent tree and, if still connected, could be considered a single individual organism. It is easy to see these clones on an Alaskan hillside in the fall when leaves are turning. All the individuals in a clone have the same genetic information for timing the yellowing and loss of leaves. Nearby, unrelated clones often have slightly different genetic instructions for leaf yellowing. In September, you can see clumps of yellow adjacent to clumps of green or yellow-green leaves. Each clump represents a separate clone. In the spring, clones may have slightly different leaf-out dates, again, driven in part by different genetic controls.

In interior Alaska quaking aspen are browsed by the caterpillar of the large aspen tortrix (*Choristoneura conflictana*), a species of moth. Outbreaks of these insect pests occur every 10 to 15 years and last for two to four years. Adult moths emerge from pupae in late June or July. Adults are grey with brownish markings on the forewings. They deposit eggs on the upper leaf surfaces with first instar larvae (caterpillars) hatching in July. These larvae feed actively until mid-August, then migrate to a protected site, spin a shelter, molt and overwinter. The following May, the caterpillar becomes active, boring into leaf buds and may completely destroy leaves before they open. In addition, 2nd to 5th instar caterpillars spin a web between two or more adjacent leaves and, within the relative safety of the web, feed on the leaves. After completion of growth and maturation of the 5th instar, the caterpillar pupates in a rolled leaf on the aspen or in the understory, emerging as an adult the next spring.[15]

An infestation of tortrix larvae can lead to 80-100 % defoliation of aspen trees. One might expect that, if unchecked, these insects could wipe out the aspens in an entire area. However, there are several mechanisms at work in the forest to actually check these outbreaks. First, if the larvae completely defoliate a tree before they complete the 5th and final instar, they may starve to death. Defoliated aspen can develop new leaves but the two weeks required is too long for the tortrix larvae to go without food. Switching to other foods may result in improper nutrition for complete development. Third, tortrix larvae are parasitized by at least one species of fly which lays its egg on the larva. Upon hatching, the fly maggot feeds on the larva.

Further, quaking aspens have some means of defense. The leaves of aspen contain several phenolic compounds that, in feeding experiments, are known to be toxic to the aspen tortrix. Crushing the leaves causes a rapid translocation of these compounds from adjacent twigs. The two major chemical components, salicortin and tremulacin, are converted in the caterpillar's gut into other toxic byproducts, thereby increasing the toxicity.[30] Tortrix larvae fed high concentrations of these phenolics exhibit reduced growth. This response to insect herbivory is an example of a short-term induced defense (STID). How does this defense mechanism help the aspen? Presumably, poorly defended leaves on an aspen can increase levels of toxicity to subsequent attacks by large aspen tortrix. Also, one assumes that, eventually, the growth, survival and reproduction of this insect pest are retarded sufficiently to end the outbreak.

Another moth that plagues aspen trees is the aspen leaf miner, *Phyllocnistis populiella*. For the last three summers, the canopy of the forest around my house, instead of looking its normal green, looks silvery instead. A close examination of the aspen leaves shows that almost all of them have a pattern as if someone had drawn a maze on them with white-out (Figure 3.7). The pattern is produced by tiny white larvae (5 mm in length) tunneling through the leaf between the upper and lower epidermal layers. After the larvae go through the fourth larval stage or instar, they pupate inside the leaf.

Emergence of the adult from the leaf occurs in the autumn, sometimes before the leaf falls, sometimes after. The very small adult spends the winter tucked under the loose bark of spruce or birch trees. Since the larvae reduce the amount of photosynthesis in the leaves there is a significant metabolic drain on the tree. Repeated or heavy infestations can reduce growth or kill the tree. It appears that climate warming in the Far North favors or promotes leaf miner outbreaks.

Balsam poplar

The balsam poplar, *Populus balsamifera*, is often referred to as cottonwood in Alaska. This leads to its confusion with the closely related black cottonwood, *Populus trichocarpa*. Geographic ranges of these two species overlap in south-central, Kodiak Island and near Haines in southeast Alaska. Basically, balsam poplar is an interior, boreal forest species; black cottonwood is a tree of coastal forests.

The balsam poplar is Alaska's most northern of deciduous trees. It occurs on the south slope of the Brooks Range and, in isolated stands, north of the Range along many of the streams and rivers flowing into the Arctic Ocean. Balsam poplar is common in the interior, western Alaska and the Alaska, Seward and Kenai Peninsulas,

Kodiak Island and two locations in southeast Alaska (Haines-Skagway area, Taku Inlet near Juneau). Outside of Alaska, the balsam poplar occurs from Alaska eastward across Canada to Labrador and Newfoundland and southward into West Virginia, Indiana, Iowa and, in western mountains, as far south as Colorado.

Balsam poplar establishes itself on floodplains where few or no competitors exist. Since mature seeds have a short lifespan, the availability of bare ground must coincide with seed maturity. Due to more rapid growth by herbaceous colonizers and by willows, balsam poplar doesn't really dominate until mid-succession. Poplar trees tolerate moist soils better than aspen, which may account for poplar occupying locations farther north and at higher elevations than aspen and white spruce. Balsam poplar can be seen in isolated clumps north of tree line and also above tree line further south. Examples of these isolated stands can be seen in the Donnelly Dome area south of Delta Junction, in the Tangle Lakes area along the Denali Highway and in similar locations.

"It is thought that this species was one of the earlier colonizer trees after the Pleistocene glaciation.[31] Interpretations of pollen records are somewhat confounded by the fragile nature of poplar pollen; it simply doesn't preserve as well as some other species.

Typically, balsam poplars reach 9-15 m (30-50 feet) in height with an occasional large tree of 24-30 m (80-100 feet) tall. These largest trees reach 60 cm (2 feet) in diameter. Both poplar species in Alaska differ in leaf shape and size from quaking aspen. The poplars have large (6-13 cm in length) leaves that are longer than they are wide. Balsam poplar leaves are shiny dark green above, pale green and rusty brown underneath. Black cottonwood have leaves that are whitish underneath, often with rusty specks. Saplings of balsam poplar in the interior occasionally have huge leaves. I measured a 28 cm (11 inches) leaf on a 2 m (6.5 feet) tall balsam poplar in my front yard.

Not surprisingly, the poplar suffers most of the same diseases and decay fungi as its relative, the quaking aspen. Poplars in the interior are affected by leaf rust, *Melampsora* sp., shephard's crook disease, *Venturia populina*, three different canker species and the decay fungus, honey mushroom (*Armillaria*). Poplar are also attacked by insect pests including defoliators such as the aspen leaf miner (*Phyllocnistis populiella*), blotch miner (*Phyllonorcyter ontario*) and leaf beetles (*Chrysomela* sp.).

Paper birch

For years I have carried a little fire-starting kit in my daypack for hikes, cross-country skiing, and snowshoeing. That kit consists of waterproof matches and/or a butane lighter plus several sheets of paper birch bark inside a sealable sandwich bag. I intend to be able to start a fire and dry out if I ever go through the river ice, get lost or become hypothermic. Fortunately, I haven't had a real emergency (since I put the kit together) that required building a fire but I'm quite confident I can. Birch bark can be made to burn even if it is wet! This fact leads one to ask, what is the point of a birch tree having bark that burns so easily? It turns out that the bark fuels fires that tend to destroy the evergreens (white and black spruce) that shade birch.[18] Therefore, even though an individual paper birch tree may

be consumed by the fire, it will be contributing to the continuation of birch stands. These stands may include some of its own offspring. In addition, paper birch often sprouts from cut or burned stumps. Paper birch, like aspen, is shade-intolerant.

Paper birch has growth characteristics and longevity that are similar to the two poplars (balsam poplar and quaking aspen). Trees reach 6-24 m (20-80 feet) in height and 10-61 cm (4-24 inches) in diameter. Birch develops best on warm slopes with moist soils, habitat it shares with white spruce and aspen. But, paper birch is also common on cold, north-facing slopes and on poorly drained floodplains.[20] One clear difference between birch and aspen is that birch do not sprout from suckers. Consequently, there are no paper birch clones in the boreal forest; each tree must stand on its own!

There are three species of paper birch in Alaska. Western paper birch (*B. papyrifera*) is an uncommon tree of southeast Alaska, occurring along river drainages and around lakes. This tree doesn't occur in interior boreal forests. The dominant form through the interior, the Alaska paper birch (*Betula neoalaskana*), can be distinguished mainly by its bark. The bark is white or pinkish white, sometimes grayish white or yellowish white. For many years the Alaska paper birch was considered a subspecies of the western paper birch under the name *Betula papyrifera* variety *commutata*. The bark of the other tree species in the interior, the Kenai birch (*Betula kenaica*), is usually dark brown, often blackish or reddish brown. Paper birches are the most widespread birches on the continent. They are distributed from northwest Alaska across Canada to Labrador and Newfoundland. Alaska paper birch appears to hybridize with two shrubby birches in Alaska, the resin birch and the dwarf birch. The former hybrid is often referred to as the Yukon birch; the latter hybrid is called Horne birch.

Let's briefly consider some other birch species in the boreal forest. Several birch species of eastern North America simply don't occur in Alaska. These species include the gray birch of New England and the maritime provinces of Canada and the water birch, ranging from Manitoba westward into British Columbia. Two others that occur in the interior were mentioned above: the dwarf birch and the resin birch. Dwarf birch, *Betula nana*, is a low shrub of up to 1 m in height that is found in muskegs, bog, alpine slopes, and tundra. Leaf blades are rounded and are often broader than they are long (0.5-1.6 cm wide; 0.5-1.2 cm long). Dwarf birch is an important species of the forest/tundra **ecotone** (transition zone). It is also one of my favorite plants because of the variety of colors of fall leaves, ranging from yellow to orange to purple.

Resin birch, *Betula glandulosa*, is also called shrub birch. As the common name suggests, it is intermediate in size between dwarf birch and paper birch. Resin birch can reach heights of 1-2.5 m (3-8 feet). Leaves of the resin birch are larger than those of dwarf birch (1-2 cm long), are longer than they are wide but have rounded tips (unlike paper birch). Further adding to the confusion is the potential for hybridization of dwarf and resin birches. Some authors consider resin and dwarf birches to be variants of the same species.

Birches are wind-pollinated like spruces, alders, and poplars. The pollen grains from dwarf, resin and paper birches exhibit overlapping size distributions. That means, from a paleoecological standpoint, that it is very difficult or impossible to distinguish these species in lake cores. So the sequence and timing of arrivals of the different birch species after the major glacial episodes of the Pleistocene is, at best, tenuous. Also, due to the tremendous pollen output per tree, birch pollen is probably over-represented in the pollen record.

There are many uses of paper birch. Birch are tapped for the collection of sap for syrup. Sap from springtime flow is clear and sweet; later, the sap turns milky and bitter. The bark has been used for birchbark canoes, birch baskets and, when shaped into cones, for moose calls. The wood has been used for firewood, pulpwood, veneers, children's tops, toothpicks and ice cream sticks. There is at least one business in Fairbanks that turns bowls from birchwood on a lathe.

Paper birch are attacked by a variety of insect pests. Defoliators include leaf rollers(*Clepsis* sp., *Epinotia solandriana*), leaf beetles (*Chrysomela* sp.) and spear-marked black moth (*Rheumaptera hastata*). The birch aphid, *Euceraphis betulae*, sucks birch sap. Birch wood is bored by Ambrosia beetles, *Trypodendron betulae*, and by bronze birch borers, *Agrilis anxius*.

Alders

There are three alder species in the boreal forests of interior Alaska. The Siberian alder, *Alnus fruticosa*, is found in all of Alaska except parts of the North Slope, Alaska Peninsula and southeast. Beyond Alaska, this alder is found across Canada to Labrador, Newfoundland and Greenland. It occurs south to the mountains of New York, North Carolina, Michigan, and Oregon. Siberian alder also occurs across northern Asia. The thinleaf alder, *Alnus tenuifolia*, is found in the Tanana and Yukon River drainages and on the Koyukuk River. It also occurs in coastal habitats in northern southeast Alaska, south-central and in Bristol Bay. Outside Alaska, the thinleaf alder ranges through southwestern Saskatchewan and southward, in mountains, to New Mexico and California. Sitka alder, *Alnus sinuata*, is found in southeast, south-central and western Alaska as well as interior Alaska south of the Yukon River.

Siberian alder grows 1-4 m (3-13 feet) tall, often taking the form of a spreading shrub. Thinleaf alder grows to heights of 4.5-9 m (15-30 feet). Both form thickets, along with willows, early in succession of interior floodplains. Both species develop root nodules containing bacteria of the genus *Frankia*. These bacteria convert atmospheric nitrogen to ammonium ion, an important nutrient for plants. Part of the competitive advantage of alders is related to their ability to "self-fertilize" using these bacteria. This process of **nitrogen fixation** will be revisited below in the discussion of legumes.

Alders do not get the respect they probably deserve from Alaskan outdoors persons. I have heard more than a few cuss words directed at alder thickets by hunters trying to traverse them with heavy loads. The problem is that the thickets are really thick, with not only upright trunks you have to push aside but also almost recumbent stems that you have to step over. Once, my father and I had to make our way through a sizable alder patch to complete a stalk on a caribou bull. We got so tangled up in that thicket that the caribou was long gone when we

finally got clear. Several years later I gave Dad a wooden spoon carved from alder. He was very pleased knowing that somebody chopped down an alder tree to make that spoon.

Willow species

There are 33 different species of willows in Alaska, eight of which reach the size of small trees.[1] Twenty four of the 33 species occur in the boreal forest. Most are characterized by short-stalked leaves that are long and narrow with smooth or finely toothed edges. Willows produce yellowish or greenish male and female flowers (pussy willows) in the spring, often before leafout. Sexes are separate in willows; some plants are male, others female. The female catkins bear small seed capsules that split open in spring and summer, liberating tiny, cottony seeds. Individual species of willows will be mentioned relevant to the feeding habits of animals in the boreal forest. Willows are particularly important as food for moose, snowshoe hares and willow ptarmigan.

Prickly rose

The prickly rose, *Rosa acicularis* occurs throughout the interior, south-central, Seward Peninsula, parts of the Alaska Peninsula and in several areas on the North Slope. The prickly rose is widespread across Eurasia, interior Alaska and eastward to Labrador. Its range extends southward into West Virginia, Minnesota, New Mexico, Idaho and British Columbia.

Leaflets of this rose are pale green and slightly hairy; the flowers are about 5 cm (2 inches) across and light pink to rose colored.

Some prickly rose flowers are almost pure white. As the name suggests, the prickly rose is loaded with spines.

Rose hips (Figure 3.8) are one of the fruits collected in interior Alaska in the late summer. These are the fleshy red or orange seed pods of the prickly rose. Hips are boiled and the flesh and juice is strained through a collander or cheesecloth and used for jams, jellies and syrups. The large, hairy seeds are left behind. Fruit-eating creatures may swallow the seeds and pass them later, presumably at some distance from the parent rose.

Germination of seeds requires two years. First, the mature seed, inside the hip or on the ground, has to experience a warm period, the summer after maturity. Then it must also experience a cold period, the following winter.[32] These periods are called **warm stratification** and **cold stratification**, respectively. So, if you collect rose seeds for planting in your garden, be sure to expose these seeds to the appropri-ate temperature regimes before you plant them. Aside from reproduction or regeneration from seed, prickly rose can spread and, if chopped out of the garden, regrow from rhizomes.

Prickly rose is subject to parasitization by a number of species of wasps (Hymenoptera: Cynipidae). These wasps are gallers; they are responsible for the formation of **galls** on the stems, roots, leaves or buds of roses. The female wasp deposits eggs under the epidermis of the stem or leaf. The egg initiates or induces a tissue response in the rose. Cells beneath the egg begin to break down, forming a cavity in which the egg and hatched larva will subsist. The lining of the cavity develops, enlarges, produces nutritive tissues upon which the larva feeds. This swollen area is the gall. One gall wasp found in Alaska is *Diplolepis polita*. This species produces spiny galls on the upper surfaces of rose leaflets.[33] Eggs are deposited in early spring, hatching in about 5 days. The larvae inhabit their galls through

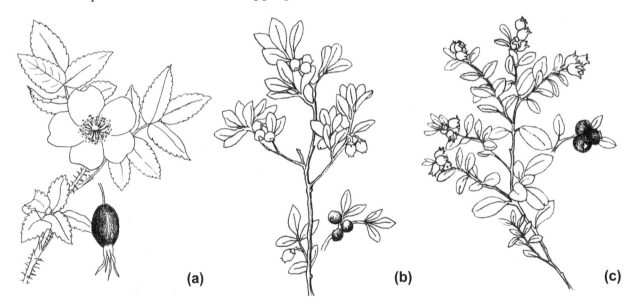

Figure 3.8: a) Prickly rose shrub with flower and rose hip. Flowers appear in late May to early June; rose hips (seed pods) mature and turn red from July to August. b) Bog blueberry. c) Lowbush cranberry.

the summer and following winter. Pupation and emergence of the adult wasp occur the following May.

Another leaf galler of prickly rose is *Diplolepis rosaefolii*. An interesting aspect of the life of this galler is that the larvae inside the gall are subject to predation and parasitization by other wasps. First, wasps of the genus *Periclistus* use the ovipositor to lay their own eggs within the gall cavity. Then the female uses the stilleto-like ovipositor to kill the larva.[34] Its own eggs hatch and feed on the gall larvae. These predatory larvae are **inquilines**, living within the same gall as the gall larvae. In addition, parasitic wasps of seven different genera actually deposit their eggs directly into the gall larva. So, even parasites have their parasites.

Highbush cranberry

One of the most pungent reminders of fall in the boreal forest is the "old gym socks" odor in the woods. This is the smell that reminds us to pick our last berries, get after the moose and, otherwise, prepare for winter. The odor derives from the ripe (some say overripe) fruits of the highbush cranberry. Berries are picked for jelly, juice and catsup. Aside from the olfactory delight in the fall is the visual delight. The leaves (Figure 3.9) turn a brilliant red, often with a hint of violet, making an interesting contrast with the yellow leaves of the aspen or birch canopy.

The highbush cranberry, *Viburnum edule*, is also called mooseberry and squashberry. In Canada this species is called lowbush cranberry, and the term "highbush cranberry" is reserved for *Viburnum opulus*, a very similar species. In

Figure 3.9: Highbush cranberry shrub with berries. Highbush cranberries are a staple food of spruce grouse in the fall.

Alaska, the term lowbush cranberry refers to *Vaccinium vitis-idaea* (see below).

This species is widely distributed in the interior, south-central, southeast, Kodiak Island, eastern Alaska Peninsula, Seward Peninsula around Nome, Noatak River and the Arctic National Wildlife Refuge. Its range extends eastward to Hudson Bay, Ungava Bay and Newfoundland, north to the mouth of the Mackenzie River, south to Pennsylvania, Michigan, Minnesota, Colorado and Oregon.

Lowbush cranberry

Multiple common names are applied to this berry, *Vaccinium vitis-idaea*. Other names in use include mountain cranberry, lingonberry, lingberry, partridgeberry and cowberry. To add to the confusion, a closely related species, the bog cranberry (*Vaccinium oxycoccos*), occurs in some of the same boggy, moist habitats. The bog cranberry is also called swamp cranberry and small cranberry. The two species can be distinguished by the flower shape. The lowbush cranberry has flowers shaped like little pink bells (see Figure 3.8); bog cranberry flowers have red or pink petals that bend backwards, making the flower resemble a tiny shootingstar. In both species, flowering occurs from mid-June into July with berries ripening in August. Bog cranberry is seldom abundant, and the plants are so small as to generally be unnoticed. If you find good quantities of cranberries, they are, most likely, lowbush cranberries.

Both of these species are evergreen; the blueberries mentioned below are all deciduous. Both species are important sources of food for grouse, ptarmigan and bears. Cranberry vegetation is eaten by caribou. Humans enjoy making jams, jellies, relishes and beverages out of lowbush cranberries. The berries are sour, so add plenty of sugar. Bog blueberries are sweeter and are used in pies and for the same purposes as lowbush cranberries.

Lowbush cranberry is a highly adaptable species. It is common is spruce and birch stands but also in bogs and muskeg of the forest. In these wetter settings it forms a mat in association with mosses. In addition, it does well in both alpine and arctic tundra, where it forms dense mats on dry, rocky slopes.

Lowbush cranberry is found all over Alaska from southeast to the Arctic Coastal Plain to the tip of the Aleutian chain. Its geographic distribution extends eastward to Baffin Island and Greenland. It occurs south to Massachusetts and the Great Lakes region. It also occurs on Vancouver Island, British Columbia. In the old world this species is spread across northern Europe and Asia where the berries and foliage grow larger than in Alaskan plants.

Bog blueberry

The only blueberry species that occurs in interior and northern Alaska is the bog blueberry, *Vaccinium uliginosum* (Figure 3.8). It is found virtually everywhere in the state where suitable habitat occurs. Only a portion of the Arctic Coastal Plain is excluded from its distribution. Beyond Alaska, bog blueberry is distributed across Canada to Labrador and Greenland. Its range reaches southward to the New England states, New York, and Minnesota. It also occurs across Asia and Europe. Blueberries are used widely in Alaska for jams, jellies, pies and syrup. Many bird and mammal species eat these berries.

Labrador tea

There are two species of Labrador tea in Alaska, and they are very similar. So similar, in fact, that some authors consider them as subspecies of a single species. The narrow-leaf Labrador tea (*Ledum decumbens*) is a shrub 30-60 cm (1 -2 ft) tall, with small (8 -15 mm long, 1.5 -3 mm wide), evergreen leaves. The leaves are rolled under at the edges, are shiny green on the upper surface and have reddish-brown woolly hairs on the under surface. Flowers are white, have five petals and ten stamens and are clustered at the tips of stalks. Each flower is about 12 mm (0.5 inch) in diameter.

The narrow-leaf species is common on the tundra (arctic and alpine) in sedge meadows and in wet depressions. It is also found in the boreal forest in muskeg habitats. Narrow-leaf Labrador tea occurs throughout Alaska eastward to Labrador and Greenland, south to Hudson Bay and Lake Athabaska. This species is also found in Europe and Asia.

Labrador tea, *Ledum groenlandicum*, is taller (to 1 m), has larger leaves (25 -50 mm long, 5 -12 mm wide) and the upper leaf surface is roughened. The flowers are larger (15 mm diameter), with five petals and usually eight stamens. Labrador tea is common in black spruce and birch forests and, near tree line, in open white spruce forests. The geographic range of Labrador tea extends from western-interior Alaska eastward across Canada to Newfoundland and Greenland, south to New Jersey, Ohio, Minnesota and Washington.[1] Labrador tea is replaced along the Pacific coast, in Idaho and Wyoming by trapper's tea, *L. glandulosum*.

Labrador tea blooms in June in Alaska, producing its white to pinkish flowers. Seed capsules develop that dry through the summer and open in September. The seeds are very small and are dispersed by wind. The seeds apparently almost never germinate in the fall. Germination experiments indicate that short day length and low temperatures (5-10°C), both of which we have in the fall, combine to inhibit germination success. At long day lengths characteristic of springtime in Alaska, germination rates are much higher, even at low temperatures.[35] Exposure to cold is beneficial to germination.

In addition to reproduction by means of seed production and dispersal (sexual reproduction), Labrador tea can also revegetate in burned forest by resprouting from roots. Of course, if the fire is hot enough to burn the entire organic soil layer, the roots don't survive.

A feature common to both varieties of Labrador tea is the aromatic leaves. Pick off a leaf and roll it between your fingers. Then smell the result. The leaves contain a number of chemical compounds including an oil called ledol, narcotic substances, andromedotoxin and some other phenolic compounds.[2] Ledol causes cramps and, in high doses, paralysis. Andromedotoxin causes headaches, cramps and indigestion. In spite of the potential for a "bad brew," Labrador tea is and has been used by Crees, Chipewyans and other native North Americans for medicinal purposes. The leaves, either brewed as a tea or ground, have been used to treat insomnia, headaches, fevers, burns, sores, chapped skin and diaper rash. In Europe, the leaves were used to repel mice, rats, fleas and clothes moths and to kill lice. Obviously, these chemicals perform some useful functions for Labrador tea itself. They serve as deterrents to feeding in some herbivores and may help Labrador tea compete against other plant species in the boreal forest.

Where Labrador tea is present in black spruce forests, black spruce exhibit an inhibition of growth. A study comparing black spruce growth in adjacent plots, one with *Ledum* and one without, showed that growth (annual stem height, basal diameter, growth ring width and cumulative wood volume) was inhibited for the first seven years after planting on the plot with *Ledum* present.[36] The mechanism of inhibition of spruce is still unknown, however. One possibility is that the *Ledum* phenolics are inhibiting spruce growth. It is also possible that *Ledum* is simply competing with spruce for nutrients.

The other outcome of the presence of exotic chemicals in Labrador tea is the deterrence of feeding. Field observations in Alberta showed that Labrador tea has a very low palatability for snowshoe hares.[37] Feeding trials in which hares are given a choice of twigs from Labrador tea, white spruce, black spruce, dwarf birch and three species of willows result in hares almost never eating Labrador tea. Chemical extraction of the leaves and twigs of Labrador tea led to the purification of a complex sesquiterpene, germacrone.[38] Germacrone applied to oatmeal deterred feeding in snowshoe hares.

Three arctic rodents (brown and collared lemmings and tundra voles) do poorly and have lower survival when fed extracts from narrow-leaf Labrador tea.[39] The chemicals are a defense mechanism to insure that little of the Labrador tea is browsed. The deterrance goes beyond simple unpalatability; growth rates of the rodents are slowed.

Aside from nasty tasting chemicals, evergreen shrubs such as Labrador tea exhibit other traits characteristic of a conservative growth strategy. Comparisons of the two dominant understory shrubs in black spruce forests, bog blueberry (deciduous), and Labrador tea (evergreen), indicates that Labrador tea puts less effort into above-ground growth.[40] In early spring, narrow-leaf Labrador tea has already developed a new network of fine roots, undoubtedly because its photosynthetic machinery is up and running as soon as temperatures are suitable. Dwarf birch (deciduous) has no new fine roots early in spring but surpasses the Labrador tea by early summer.[41,42] Both dwarf birch and bog blueberry grow more aggressively and are less well defended than Labrador tea.

Fringed and Alaska sagebrushes

There are 20 Alaskan sagebrush species, but only two of these members of the family Astera-ceae take on a shrub form. These sages are both primarily herbaceous, but the basal stems and twigs are woody. Both occur on south-facing slopes and bluffs, preferring warm, very dry sites. These sites are often too steep, dry or unstable for trees to take hold. Sagebrushes can be seen along bluffs of the Tanana, Yukon, Copper, Matanuska, Colville and other rivers in Alaska. Both species are perennial, spreading shrubs reaching 30-60 cm (12-24 inches) in height with silvery foliage. Both have the strongly aromatic odor of...you guessed it, sage.

If you stop your car on the Richardson Highway along the Tanana River bluffs between Delta Junction and Fairbanks you can find both species growing on the same slopes. Together the two are easily distinguished based on their leaves. The fringed sagebrush, *Artemisia frigida*, has leaves divided into 2-3 linear segments about 1 mm wide and 6-12 mm long. Alaska sagebrush, *Artemisia alaskana*, has leaves divided into 3-5 segments and each of the segments is very narrow and only about 2 mm long. The latter species looks frillier due to the more finely divided leaves. Both bear yellow flowers on narrow, erect, leafy branches. Flowers bloom in July and August with seeds maturing in August and September.

The fringed sagebrush occurs in two locations north of the Brooks Range, throughout the interior and in south-central Alaska. Elsewhere, this species is found across Canada to Minnesota and southward to Texas and Arizona. Across the Bering Strait, *A. frigida* occurs in Asia.

Alaska sagebrush has a very limited distribution. It occurs in interior Alaska north to the North Slope and in one location on the Seward Peninsula near Nome. The species occurs only in the Yukon Territory around Kluane Lake and in the headwaters of the Yukon and Tanana Rivers. The Asian *A. krushiana* is closely related.

In modern times these two arid-habitat shrubs are only very sparsely distributed across the Alaskan landscape. However, during the glacial episodes of the Pleistocene epoch in Alaska both species were widespread. Under full glacial conditions, unglaciated terrain consisted of almost all of interior Alaska, a much expanded Arctic Coastal Plain and a land connection to Asia, the Bering Land Bridge. All or virtually all of this unglaciated landscape was an arid grassland across which these two sage species were widely dispersed.

HERBACEOUS PLANTS OF THE BOREAL FOREST

Fireweed

In Alaska there are two species in the evening primrose family that bear pink to red-violet flowers. The more common and more widespread geographically is *Epilobium angustifolium*, referred to as fireweed, red fireweed, or blooming Sally. The other is *Epilobium latifolium*, known as dwarf fireweed, river beauty, or broad-leaved willowherb. Dwarf fireweed is shorter (15-70 cm) and has fewer (1-7) but larger (2-6 cm diameter) flowers than fireweed. Fireweed grows to heights of 2 m or taller, has more than 15 flowers per stem, and has flowers that are smaller (1.5-3.5 cm) than those of dwarf fireweed. Dwarf fireweed occurs on river bars and floodplains and, generally, could be considered a tundra plant.

Fireweed is found over a huge area of the northern hemisphere. Its geographic distribution stretches from Greenland and Labrador in the east, westward across North America and Eurasia to the British Isles. This species occurs in moist habitat in the Pacific Coast states, where it can reach heights of 2.2-2.8 m (7-9 ft).

In Alaska and elsewhere, fireweed is a pioneer species. That is, it is typically one of the first species to colonize habitats disturbed by fire, avalanche, timber harvest and changes in stream and river channels. Fireweed takes over abandoned agricultural land in the Far North. One of the reasons that fireweed is so successful in colonizing new, unoccupied ground is its production of seeds that are dispersed by wind. Alaskans are quite familiar with the cottony seeds blowing in the early autumn wind, like snow blowing on a warm, sunny day. In a Swedish study, fireweed seeds were collected from a tall tower. From 20 to 50% of dispersing seeds were collected more than 100 m (330 ft) above the ground.[43] If seeds reach these heights, they probably disperse 100-300 km (60-180 miles) downwind, falling at times on ground appropriate for fireweed colonization.

Fireweed commonly occurs in recently burned-over forest. An experimental burn was conducted in a black spruce forest near Fairbanks to study soil nutrients and patterns of revegetation.[44] In some parts of the forest there was considerable fuel in the form of fallen trees, organic material in the soil layers, and standing trees. Other areas had less combustible fuel. The burn resulted in a mosaic of lightly burned (less fuel) and heavily burned (more fuel) areas. Since fuels amount to inorganic nutrients (phosphate and nitrate) locked up in organic form, it shouldn't be surprising that both the lightly and heavily burned areas exhibited increased levels of available phosphorus (fourfold and sixteen-fold increases, respectively). Heavily burned patches were quickly dominated by fireweed, firemoss, and greentongue liverwort, all invading species by virtue of wind-borne seeds and spores. Lightly burned patches were dominated by species previously present in the forest that had root systems that survived the burn. These species, including bog blueberry, Labrador tea, and bluejoint grass as well as fireweed, simply resprouted from unburned roots or rhizomes. Thus, revegetation resulted in a patchwork or mosaic of species.

In the context of reforestation, foresters are interested in the interactions of pioneer species and tree seedlings. Do some of these early dominants such as fireweed or bluejoint grass negatively affect tree seedling growth? A study in northern Alberta specifically compared fireweed and bluejoint effects on soil temperatures. Fireweed produces dark litter that absorbs heat, decomposes readily, and, therefore, doesn't form a persistent litter layer. In contrast, bluejoint produces a persistent litter layer. Its light-colored shoots reflect light and heat, resulting in colder soils that are less favorable to spruce seedling growth than fireweed-dominated soils. Thus, bluejoint exerts a noncompetitive inhibition on spruce seedling growth by affecting its physical environment. There may be competitive effects of these pioneer vegetation types too.[45]

Flower development in fireweed is followed with more than casual interest in interior Alaska. There is a recurring "old spouse's tale" stating that "when the last fireweed flower blooms at the top of the stalk, summer is over." So those

Figure 3.10: Fireweed in bloom. Blooming progresses from bottom to top. Young flowers function as males and old flowers function as females even though each flower has both male and female parts.

of us in interior Alaska who are jealous of our all-too-short summers really pay attention to fireweed. Of course, the initiation of and completion of flowering, even in a single locality, encompasses a spread of dates. Flowering times depend on the accumulation of thermal "units" over the course of the growing season. But the amount of heat reaching an individual fireweed stalk depends on this summer's weather (temperature, cloud cover), the slope and aspect of the plant's location, its altitude, and shading by members of its own and other species. In short, they don't all bloom at exactly the same time.

Each fireweed stalk has an inflorescence of 15-30 or so individual flowers (Figure 3.10).

Blooming begins from the bottom of the stalk and progresses upward. Complete flowering, from bottom to top, takes 15-35 days. Each flower is **protandrous**; that is, it is first a male flower and then becomes a female flower. The male stage, lasting about one day, has closed stigmas and releases pollen. The female phase follows and lasts 2-3 days or longer, depending on temperature (flowers last 2-3 d at 32°C and 5-6 d at 14°C).[46] Initially, the styles (pollen receptors) are parallel to and physically far from the petals. But with further flower maturation, the styles curl backward and come to lie much closer to the nectar reservoir (see Figure 3.13).

The significance is that more-mature female flowers are more likely to be pollinated by bees collecting nectar. Fireweed is visited by several species of bumblebees and a variety of solitary bees and other flying insects. Bumblebees typically alight near the base of the inflorescence and work their way up the stalk in a more or less spiral pattern. Thus, the bees are visiting female flowers first and males last. This reduces the likelihood that pollinators will self-fertilize fireweed. You can see if a flower has been pollinated by looking for bright green pollen grains on the white stigmas.

Nectar production is an important feature affecting the activity of bees and, therefore, pollination. Nectar is almost entirely sugar water. Each flower produces a small volume of nectar amounting to 0.7 to 4.1 mg sugar per day. Temperature is important. A flower at 14°C produces about 5.2 mg over its entire life; a flower at 24°C produces about 8.7 mg.[46] Obviously, nectar is made by the flower, evolutionarily speaking, to attract pollinating insects such as bumblebees.

So temperature and light will influence how much "reward" is available for these insects.

Assuming that pollination has occurred, the next event in fireweed reproduction is the maturation of the seeds. Seed capsule formation and maturation proceeds from the base of the stalk upwards, in the same way the flowering progresses. At capsule maturation the capsule splits open lengthwise along the pod and the seeds are exposed. As the capsule dries, the openings enlarge and the seeds are held more and more loosely until the wind pulls them out and carries them away.

Even without insect pollinators, fireweed can successfully reproduce. First, some cross-pollination between adjacent plants is accomplished by the wind. Perhaps more important is vegetative or **asexual reproduction**. Fireweed develops an extensive root system that produces buds in late summer, lies dormant over the winter, and produces new shoots from the buds the following spring. A single root system can eventually produce an entire colony of fireweed stems. The colony derived from one root system consists of individual plants that are all identical genetically. Such a colony is another example of a clone. The roots are often referred to as **pseudorhizomes**.

Fireweed watching is something of a sport in Alaska, not only because of its supposed connection with the onset of fall but also because most Alaskans enjoy the bright colors of summer in contrast to the monotonous dark green and white of the long winters. There is also practical value to watching the progress of flowering in fireweed. Foresters looking to collect mature seeds from important tree species need some indication of when those seeds actually mature.

In white spruce, the seeds mature about two weeks before the cone opens. Of course, if one waits until the cones open, most of the seeds are scattered and lost. In a particular location, spruce seeds are mature at the same time that the seed capsules burst at the base of the fireweed inflorescence.[47] Therefore, fireweed can tell foresters when to collect spruce seeds. This is an example of how careful observations in nature can lead to useful predictions. It is important to point out that fireweed acts as a meteorological station integrating weather effects at each potential source of spruce seeds. In other words, don't look at fireweed on the north side of a ridge as an indicator of spruce seed maturation on the south side of the ridge.

Aside from affecting the physical environment of forest plant species, fireweed might be potentially detrimental if it serves as a reservoir of pathogens of commercially valuable species. Fireweed can be infested with a root-rotting fungus (*Armillaria*) that attacks both lodgepole pine and quaking aspen.[48] At this geologic moment, the commercially valuable and important lodgepole pine is not an Alaskan resident. It will probably arrive in eastern Alaska within 100 years. Perhaps of more immediate concern to potato farmers of interior and south-central Alaska is that *Rhizoctonia solani*, a fungus pathogenic to potatoes, has been shown to develop an epiphytic relationship with fireweed.[49] Fireweed and other weeds could contribute to the survival of pathogens and their infestation of potatoes.

Yarrow

The common yarrow, *Achillea millefolium*, is an early successional herbaceous plant native to Eurasia and the British Isles that was introduced into eastern temperate North America. It is a composite, related to daisies, asters, and dandelions. There are, apparently, two more almost identical species of *Achillea* in Alaska, *A. borealis* and *A. lanulosa*. These three plus additional *Achillea* species form a species complex that constitute a taxonomic nightmare. The evolution of this group has been by the mechanism of **polyploidy**. Polyploidy results from a mistake in the partitioning of chromosomes into gamete cells during the process of meiosis. This infrequent event produces gametes with multiples of the "correct" number of chromosomes. In most plants and animals, a set of chromosomes is inherited from each parent, yielding pairs of the appropriate number of chromosomes. The normal condition is for each offspring to have two complete sets, the diploid condition. In Europe, *Achillea* includes species showing the diploid (2n = 18), tetraploid (2n = 36), hexaploid (2n = 54) and octaploid (2n = 72) conditions. *A. millefolium* is a hexaploid, *A. lanulosa* is tetraploid.[50] It isn't clear if *millefolium* has reached Alaska but much of the scientific literature of Alaska boreal forests refers to *A. millefolium*. Based on the similarities in appearance and habitat, I will treat them as a single species.

Yarrow is a perennial reaching 30-70 cm (12-28 inches) in height with fern-like leaves alternating up the stalk. It blooms in July and August, with 10-30 white (rarely pink or reddish) flowers arranged in a flat-topped cluster (Figure 3.11). This species is common in disturbed ground such as clearings, forest breaks, roadsides and open meadows.

The pollination of yarrow is accomplished by flies as well as by bees. When pollinators visit

Figure 3.11: Yarrow and sharp-tailed grouse. Both species occupy open, early-succession habitat. Yarrow is one of this grouse's foods.

flowers, they do so to feed on nectar supplied by the host plant. Specialized flies such as flesh flies and blow flies may visit flowers if there is a sufficient reward. Analysis of the nectar of yarrow found, in addition to sugars, an array of ten different amino acids. Amino acids are the precursors of proteins; proteins are required by female flesh flies before they can successfully lay their eggs. In an experiment in which flesh flies were deprived of protein, they selected nectar containing amino acids over nectar containing only sugars.[51] After a meal of liver, their preference for yarrow nectar disappeared. Of the ten amino acids in yarrow nectar, six are known to be essential for insects. Those six are also amino acids that stimulate the sugar receptors of flies. So, yarrow nectar tastes sweeter than sugar-only nectars because the flies get an "extra dose" of sweet taste. The flies are getting a nutritional benefit, amino acids, that may help them meet their reproductive needs in the absence of suitable flesh.

We have no clear conception of how long flowering plants have been used as either ornamentation or as medicine. Ralph Solecki, dig-

ging in Shanidar Cave, Iraq, discovered a Neandertal burial site at least 50,000 years old. Samples from the burial soil contained huge numbers of flower pollens of seven different species, including yarrow and a species of groundsel or fleabane.[52] Did Neandertals attach medicinal significance to yarrow and fleabane, or did they simply place flowers in a grave for sentimental reasons? We will never know. We are pretty sure that *A. millefolium* was used at least as early as the Trojan War. The story of Achilles binding the wounds of his comrades with the leaves of this species ultimately led Linnaeus to name the plant *Achillea*. The leaves have been used down through the ages to stop bleeding. This characteristic, probably due to the alkaloid achilleine, accounts for some of the common names applied to this species: knight's milfoil, staunchweed, woundwort and nosebleed. This last name points to the plant's ability to stop nosebleeds rather than to start them. Yarrow contains a volatile oil that kills mosquito larvae and *Staphylococcus*, *Bacillus* and *Escherichia coli* bacteria. European starlings line their nests with yarrow, apparently to discourage parasitic insects. The oil contains sagebrush ketone and sagebrush alcohol.[53]

How will yarrow fare in the changed climate of the near future in Alaska? Certainly one element of that new climate might be higher soil nutrient levels due to warmer soils and, therefore, more rapid remineralization. In an experimental fertilization study involving boreal forest species, yarrow responded to added soil nitrogen. With fertilization, *Achillea* increased stalk density but not size. Yarrow increased the number of flowering stalks and the average leaf size with increasing nitrogen levels.[54] So yarrow growth would, apparently, be stimulated by warmer soils.

The other likely change is elevated carbon dioxide. Greenhouse experiments show that high carbon dioxide led to increased plant size; yarrow also formed flower buds earlier than normal. Flower opening was advanced under the high CO_2 regime.[55] Apparently, yarrow will do well in the increasingly altered atmosphere resulting from the continuing burning of fossil fuels.

Wild legumes

There are more than a dozen members of the bean family, Fabaceae, in Alaska. This group includes wild sweet pea (*Hedysarum mackenzii*), Eskimo potato (*Hedysarum alpinum*), arctic lupine (*Lupinus arcticus*), purple oxytrope (*Oxytropis nigrescens*), beach pea (*Lathyrus maritimus*), yellow oxytrope (*Oxytropis campestris*), hairy milk vetch (*Astragalus umbellatus*), alpine milk vetch (*Astragalus alpinus*), American milk vetch (*Astragalus americanus*), showy locoweed (*Oxytropis splendens*), reflexed locoweed (*Oxytropis deflexa*), yellow sweet clover (*Melilotus officinalis*) and the introduced alsike clover (*Trifolium hybridum*).

Virtually all of these legumes are early successional species colonizing roadsides, riverbanks and forest openings. Most members of this family have a symbiotic relationship with bacteria called **rhizobia**.[56] The roots of the sweet pea plant forms nodules that house the bacteria. These bacteria are able to convert atmospheric nitrogen to ammonium, a form that the sweet pea can use for synthesis of amino acids, proteins and other nitrogen-containing compounds. I mentioned this process in the section on alder,

above. The process is called nitrogen fixation. This association helps explain why legumes are so often able to colonize nutrient-poor habitats such as disturbed slopes and gravel bars along a river. Simply put, the legumes, by virtue of their cooperating bacteria, are able to make their own nitrogen fertilizer. Legumes not only do well in nitrogen-deficient soils but also, by their very presence, enrich the soil. This phenomenon is well known to farmers who practice crop rotation, alternating a legume such as alfalfa with another crop such as corn.

With such a powerful advantage, why don't legumes such as wild sweet pea dominate boreal forests? First, legumes add to the organic content of the soil when their roots die and when they drop leaves in the fall. This organic material can be decomposed by other plants, often through their mycorrhizas. Legumes are essentially preparing the soil for their competitors, species requiring a higher nitrogen content in the soil. Those competitors take root, grow, and compete with legumes for sunlight. Legumes don't do well in the shade, apparently because there is a high cost associated with maintaining the nitrogen-fixing bacteria. About 10% of the energy acquired by the legume goes to the bacteria. Therefore, if photosynthetic production of sugars and other energy-containing chemicals is seriously curtailed because of shading, the legumes begin to lose out in the competition.

Two of the most noticeable legumes are the **wild sweet pea** and the **eskimo potato**. These species are very similar. Both have pinnately compound leaves but the sweet pea has thicker, narrower leaves. The leaves of eskimo potato have prominent veins on the lower surface that don't show up on the leaves of wild sweet pea.

The flowers of both species are pink to reddish-purple; sweet pea flowers are a somewhat deeper purple and are 2.5-3 cm long. Eskimo potato flowers are only about 1-1.5 cm long. Both flowers bloom in June and July in Alaska. Transplanting either of these species to your garden is very difficult because both are perennials that send down woody taproots. If you try to dig them up, you will, invariably, break the taproot and the plant will lose a lot of its fine root system.

The eskimo potato, *Hedysarum alpinum* , is also called alpine sweet vetch and alpine hedysarum. The common name derives from the fact that Alaskan natives eat the taproots. These roots can be eaten either raw or cooked and apparently taste a little like carrots. Please note that the taproot of wild sweet pea is reported to be **poisonous**. Eskimo potato grows on rocky alpine slopes, open forests, and along roads in most of Alaska. It occupies tundra habitat along the arctic coast but not in the southeast or on the Aleutian chain.

The legumes produce a variety of secondary metabolites that may have allelopathic effects on herbivores. Several species of locoweed, *Oxytropis* spp., occur in Alaska and elsewhere. Interior Alaska species include showy locoweed (*O. splendens*), reflexed locoweed (*O. deflexa*) and viscid locoweed (*O. viscida*). When grazed by livestock, these plants may be poisonous due to the presence of an alkaloid, locoine. Uptake of selenium from the soil may either increase or induce toxicity in locoweed.[2]

Introduced legumes

Alfalfa—There are four alfalfa species in Alaska, all introduced. *Medicago sativa* is a purple-flowered species along the lower Tanana River, downstream of Fairbanks. Two yellow-flowered alfalfa species occur near Fairbanks, *M. falcata* and *M. lupulina*. The fourth species, *M. hispida*, is confined to southeast Alaska.

Vetch—Vetches, in the genus *Vicia*, are represented by five species in Alaska. Three of these species are found in southeast Alaska (*V. angustifolia, V. gigantea, V. americana*). *Vicia villosa* is an introduced species found in the Anchorage area. The vetch of interior Alaska is *Vicia cracca*, another introduced weed from Europe. This vetch got its start near the university campus and has since slowly spread into the greater Fairbanks community. It can now be seen growing on Chena Ridge, along the Chena River, Farmer's Loop and Goldstream Valley, where it serves as forage for moose. Vetches are found along roadsides and in open fields.

Clover—Clovers are in the genus *Trifolium*. There are ten species in the state, of which six occur in interior, western, or northern Alaska. All ten are introduced. Several of these have escaped from cultivation. It is now common practice to include clover seed in the "hydro-seeding" that follows road construction or improvements. So, we can expect to see more clover along roadsides throughout Alaska. Two introduced species of sweet clover, genus *Melilotus*, occur in Anchorage and Fairbanks; both are introduced.

Dandelions

Dandelions in the genus *Taraxacum* are extremely widespread in the northern hemisphere. At least ten species have been recognized in Alaska, but the identification of individual species is very difficult. Several species occupy meadows in the boreal forest (*T. lacerum, T. ceratophorum*); others inhabit tundra and alpine scree slopes (*T. arcticum, T. alaskanum, T. carneocoloratum*). *Taraxacum officinale* is the most ubiquitous of the dandelions found in Alaska. It occurs across almost all of North America south of the continuous permafrost boundary and throughout much of Eurasia. One additional dandelion species, the autumn dandelion, *Leontodon autumnalis*, is an introduced weed from Europe.

Horsetails

Horsetails, family Equisetidae, are among the first plants emerging as new growth in the springtime of interior Alaska. These are non-woody vascular plants that reproduce by spores rather than seeds. All are perennials with vertically grooved, jointed stems containing silica. This last feature makes horsetails harsh on your hands if you pull them while weeding your garden. On the other hand, several species have been used for sanding woodwork, polishing pewter, or scouring pots on camping trips. The common scouring-rush, *Equisetum hyemale*, is sold in music stores for shaping the reeds of clarinets and oboes.[2]

This is a really old plant family, dating back at least 400 million years to the Paleozoic Era. In those ancient times some horsetail species formed forests with trees reaching 1 m in diameter and 25 m in height. Presumably, they were outcompeted in most habitats when flowering plants evolved and diversified.

All horsetails have stems growing from an underground rhizome. In the three scouring-rush species the stems are perennial, evergreen, and, typically, unbranched. The three are the common scouring-rush, *E. hyemale*, dwarf scouring-rush, *E. scirpoides*, and the variegated scouring-rush, *E. variegatum*. The other five species, the horsetails, produce new above-ground stems annually from perennial rhizomes. The Alaskan horsetails include woodland horsetail, *E. sylvaticum*, swamp horsetail, *E. fluviatile*, marsh horsetail, *E. palustre*, common horsetail, *E. arvense* and meadow horsetail, *E. pratense*.

All horsetails and scouring-rushes exhibit two very different stem types. Fertile stems appear in the spring and are brown. Infertile stems are green and don't develop cones. The cone matures quickly and falls off, releasing its spores. Branches emerge from the joints of both fertile and sterile stems.

Horsetails contain an enzyme called thiaminase that destroys thiamine (vitamin B_1). Thiaminase is a problem for livestock that happen to eat a lot of horsetails and can also be toxic to humans. Cooking inactivates the enzyme but there are reports of other toxic effects following human ingestion.[2]

Wild iris

The wild iris of Alaska is *Iris setosa*. It occurs in bogs, meadows and along the shores of lakes over much of Alaska except the northeast and north of the Brooks Range. Two forms are recognized: the subspecies *Iris setosa setosa* is more coastal in distribution, extending from southeast Alaska to the Bering Sea and Aleutians. *Iris setosa interior* is the subspecies found in interior and northern Alaska. While visiting my son Andy in Japan, I enjoyed silk screens, woodblock prints, and ceramics with irises as a prominent theme. It was only while preparing this chapter that I realized that the Japanese iris is *Iris setosa*.

Pasque flower

The pasque flower, *Pulsatilla patens,* is one of the earliest blooming plants in our area. By the second week in May, this species is showing purple to blue flowers. The five to eight sepals (not actually petals) are pointed and covered with silky hairs on the back side. Each flower is large, about 10 cm (4 inches) in diameter. When this plant first blooms its stems are short and there are no basal leaves (Figure 3.3). The leaves grow after the flower is fully developed. As the flower matures its stalk elongates and the flower droops.

Seed dispersal is by the wind. Technically, the seeds are **achenes** with feathery styles. After the seed lands, the style coils and uncoils depending on humidity. This twisting is thought to aid the seed in working its way into the soil.

Pasque flowers are found primarily on dry, south-facing slopes and open forests in interior Alaska. However, there are several records of this species from north of the Brooks Range and it also occurs in the Mackenzie River valley and eastward along the arctic coast in Northwest Territories.[59] Elsewhere, pasque flowers are common in prairie habitats in Canada and the United States. It is the official flower of the state of South Dakota and the Province of Manitoba. The same species is found across Asia to Eastern Europe.

LICHENS

Lichens are an important component of boreal forest and tundra ecosystems. Each lichen consists of a **symbiotic** association between a fungal species and a single-celled photosynthetic partner species. The fungal partner is referred to as the **mycobiont**; the photosynthetic species as the **photobiont**. Photobionts may be either algae or cyanobacteria. A lichen "species" is defined as an association of a fungus and a photosynthetic symbiont resulting in a stable **thallus** (body) of specific structure. Each lichen species has a unique fungus but its photosynthetic partner species may occur in a variety of lichen species and even, occasionally, occur as a free-living species. Lichens always bear the name of the fungal partner.

What is to be gained by the relationship? Fungi, by themselves, lack chlorophyll and cannot photosynthesize. Normally, fungi rely on dead organic matter or the living juices of plants to sustain themselves. A lichenized fungus has photosynthetic organisms, the photobionts, imprisoned within its own physical structures. In short, the fungus gets its carbohydrates from its symbionts. If the photobiont is a nitrogen-fixing cyanobacterium, the fungus also gets amino acids. What does the photobiont get out of the association? First, algae and cyanobacteria are usually confined to an aquatic or very moist habitat. By themselves they could never colonize a bare rock. The fungal structure provides a suitable microhabitat for the alga. The structure also screens the alga from direct sunlight.

The thallus consists of at least three layers: an upper layer called the **cortex**, an **algal** (middle) **layer,** and a lower **medulla**. Lichens occur in three major forms. The **crustose** lichens, as the name suggests, are closely attached to the substratum forming a crust on rock or tree trunk. Leaf-shaped lichens (**foliose** forms) are attached more loosely and usually have a fourth layer, the lower cortex. Some lichens are radially symmetrical and more or less round in cross section. These are the **fruticose** lichens. Fruticose lichens are sometimes further divided into club, shrub, and hairlike forms.

Growth rates

Lichens are able to colonize most habitats on earth. They are numerous in the tropics and warm temperate regions, where they may grow more than 1 cm per year. In more severe habitats such as the boreal forest or alpine and arctic tundra, lichens grow more slowly, perhaps far less than 1 mm per year. These northern lichens may live for several hundred years.

Tombstones and burial sites have been very useful in allowing us to estimate growth rates of lichens. For example, *Xanthoria elegans* growing on the headstone of one of the members of the Franklin Expedition to the Arctic grew to a diameter of 4.4 cm in 102 years. This works out to 0.4 mm per year.

Metabolites

Lichens, as other photosynthetic organisms, produce a variety of organic chemical compounds. These can be divided into primary (functioning inside cells) and secondary (functioning extra-cellularly) metabolites. The primary metabolites include amino acids, proteins, polyols, polysaccharides, carotenoids, and vitamins. Some of these chemicals are synthesized by the alga and some by the fungus. Secondary metabolites, apparently, are all produced by the fungal partner. Hundreds of different metabolites have been identified from lichens; the majority are unique to lichens.

What are the functions of all these secondary compounds? One probable function of some secondary metabolites is as light screens. In lichens growing on surfaces exposed to direct sunlight, several light-absorbing compounds are found in the upper cortex. They serve to regulate solar radiation reaching the algal layer. Many algae and higher plants have been shown to exhibit inhibition of photosynthesis at high light intensities; light screens are undoubtedly helping to maximize lichen photosynthesis. These same compounds may also protect the lichen thallus from ultraviolet radiation damage.

Lichens have been investigated for the potential pharmacological use of their secondary metabolites. Lichens have long been used in folk and Chinese herbal medicines. As an example, the usnic acids, derived from the beard lichens (*Usnea*) have antihistamine, antiviral, and antiseptic properties. They are active against gram-positive bacteria and streptomycetes and are used in several commercially available antiseptics. Usnic acid exhibits low-level activity against lung carcinoma and a strong inhibitory effect on the mold *Neurospora crassa*.

Several lichen metabolites are toxic to higher vertebrates. Vulpinic acid is the active ingredient of the European lichen *Letharia vulpina*. This lichen has been used for centuries as a poison for foxes and wolves. The compound is toxic to all meat eaters, to insects, and to molluscs but not to herbivorous mammals such as mice and rabbits. Another group of lichen metabolites, the secalonic acid derivatives, are highly poisonous to grazing herbivores and thus protect lichens from some herbivores.

Exposure of forestry workers in North America to a variety of lichen compounds may result in a severe skin rash, contact dermatitis. The phenomenon is known as woodcutter's eczema or cedar poisoning. Lichen spores brought home on the woodcutter's clothing can cause skin reactions in their families.

Lichen secondary metabolites are put to several nonmedicinal uses. Two European species, oak moss (*Evernia prunastri*) and tree moss (*Pseudevernia furfuracea*), are important in the perfume industry. Finally, lichens have been and still are used in dying fabrics. A common lichen on rocks in the Mediterranean area, *Roccella montagnei*, after treatment with ammonia, produces red and purple dyes for wool and silk. These dyes date back at least to the time of the ancient Greeks but are of little significance today. Harris tweeds were originally dyed with lichen dyes and some still are down to the present.

Lichens and Pollution

Lichens have no roots. Minerals, nutrients, and water are readily absorbed by the outer (upper) cortex since it is not protected or made impermeable by a waxy cuticle. Consequently, lichens absorb materials directly from the air or from the surface of the cortex. In a pristine world,

only natural, presumably benign, materials would fall on lichens. In reality, lichens are exposed to many anthropogenic chemicals and elements. That is, human activity has changed the local environment of lichens. Some of these chemicals have detrimental effects on lichens while others may have no effects at all.

In the nineteenth century, observers in England, Paris, and Munich reported the disappearance of lichens from cities. This "city effect" was widely blamed on coal soot. At one point lichens were eliminated over most of southeast England. Mapping the distribution of lichen species revealed that some species were extremely sensitive and some were more resistant to bad city air. Changes in distribution over time can indicate worsening or improving levels of airborne pollutants.

Aside from mapping, two other methods are routinely used to determine lichen sensitivity to pollutants. In the **transplant method,** lichens attached to a substratum such as a board are moved from a pristine area to a polluted area. In the **fumigation method,** lichens are experimentally exposed to various levels of air-borne pollutants. After exposure, lichens are monitored for accumulation of heavy metals and for changes in their physiological functions.

A major problem for lichens is sulfur dioxide, SO_2, released during the combustion of fossil fuels containing sulfur and also released during volcanic eruptions. Burning fossil fuels has been a "problem" only since the beginning of the industrial revolution but is now known to be responsible for the "city effect" noted above and for a number of specific detrimental effects on lichens. Some of the effects recorded include reduction in rates of nitrogen fixation, reduction in photosynthetic rates, degradation of chlorophyll, loss of potassium and other electrolytes, reduction in thallus size, detachment of thallus from the substratum, and the reduction and/or absence of fruiting bodies.[58] A fumigation experiment conducted at Anaktuvuk Pass, Alaska, showed that several lichen species important to caribou (*Cladina stellaris*, *C. rangiferina*) had reduced photosynthetic rates on exposure to less than 0.25 parts per million of SO_2.[59] Acid rain, which contains SO_2 and other toxic components also adversely affects a variety of lichens, including *Cladina stellaris*, *C. rangiferina* and *C. mitis*. Therefore, pollution can have negative effects on caribou by reducing some of their important food resources.

Heavy metals may or may not have direct effects on lichens. Much depends on the lichen species, the specific metal, and the concentration of the metal. Some heavy-metal effects on lichens that have been reported include reduced nitrogen fixation, reduced photosynthesis, and altered membrane permeabilities.

A variety of other agents have been found to be harmful to lichens. Nitrogen dioxide (NO_2), another by-product of burning fossil fuels and a constituent of acid rain, inhibits lichen photosynthesis at low concentrations. Ozone, O_3, has several harmful effects on lichens and is lethal at concentrations found in severe Southern California smog. Another component of smog affecting lichens is peroxacetyl nitrate (PAN). PAN forms from nitrous oxide and ozone in the presence of hydrocarbons and sunlight. Closer to home, crude oil from Prudhoe Bay either kills lichens or severely inhibits their NO_2 and CO_2 fixation.[60] Oil-spill dispersants, should they be used to clean up an oil spill in Alaska, will inhibit photosynthesis or directly kill lichens.[61] Not surprisingly, road dust in northern Alaska decreases the number of lichens inhabiting soils and tree bark near the roads.[62]

SOME LICHENS OF THE BOREAL FOREST

Powdery beard

Usnea lapponica is a shrub or hair lichen found on the bark and branches of trees (Figure 3.12). The tufts are pale yellowish green due to the presence of usnic acid. This lichen is one of the species consumed by caribou in winter. A common species in the boreal forest, powdery beard is also one of the important winter foods of flying squirrels in interior Alaska. There are a variety of *Usnea* species across North America and Eurasia. The common powdery beard species of southeast Alaska, the Pacific northwest and northern California is *U. longissima*.

The distribution of *Usnea* in Britain has been tracked for several hundred years. By 1800 *Usnea* had disappeared over one third of Britain. Due to improvements in air quality, powdery beards, starting about 1970, began to reinvade areas in which they had been locally extinct.[63]

Elegant orange lichen

I walk our golden retriever along the frozen Tanana River in the wintertime. We often start at the wayside on Chena Pump Road and walk downriver past several bluffs overlooking the river. Ravens have a traditional nesting site on a particularly inaccessible spot on the first bluff. Below the nest is a bright orange crust on the rock that, if we could examine it more closely, would prove to be the lichen *Xanthoria elegans*. This species grows relatively flat against the rock and has a leaf-like growth form (Figure 3.12). I have also seen this lichen on large boulders above tree line in the White Mountains, north of Fairbanks, and it has been reported in the Himalayas at altitudes of 7000 m (23,000 ft).[64] The common denominator for the occurrence of *Xanthoria* in these two locations is birds. Bird nesting and roosting sites are places where birds deposit urine and feces that are rich in nitrogen. Specifically, birds excrete uric acid, usually with a consistency similar to toothpaste. The uric acid breaks down to ammonia, a form of nitrogen that can be used readily by *Xanthoria*. It is one of the most colorful lichen species.

Another *Xanthoria* grows on the trunks of aspen and poplar in the Fairbanks area. This is the pincushion orange, *Xanthoria polycarpa*; it is the same bright orange as *X. elegans* but the shape of the thallus is more rounded and less leaflike. A third species of this genus, the powdered orange lichen, *X. fallax*, is bright yellow to yellow-orange and also grows on deciduous trees. This yellow lichen doesn't (yet) occur in Alaska but reaches as Far North as southern British Columbia and southern Northwest Territories.[65]

True reindeer lichen

Cladina rangiferina, the gray or true reindeer lichen, is the species most frequestly grazed by caribou and reindeer in winter (Figure 3.12). It, along with the green reindeer lichen, constitutes an important ground cover over much of the boreal forest. Reindeer lichens, like several other species, are highly resistant to drying. After desiccation to 50% of its original water content, gray reindeer lichen continues metabolizing at 80% of its original rate. This species is sometimes erroneously referred to as reindeer moss. It is not a moss.

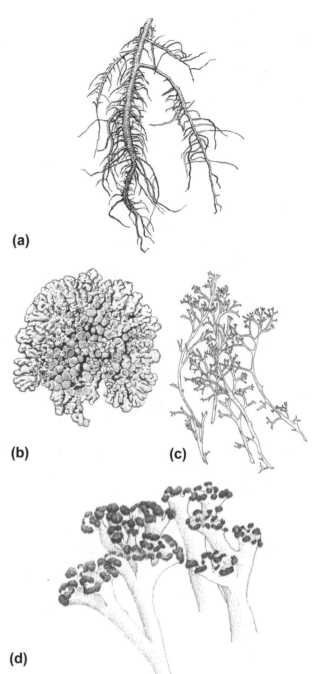

Figure 3.12: a) Powdery beard lichen, a common epiphyte of spruce trees in Alaska. b) Elegant orange lichen, often found in association with bird roosting sites. c) Reindeer lichen, a winter staple of caribou. d) Red pixie cup, *Cladonia cristatella*, one of several "British Soldiers" in Alaska. The dark reproductive structures in the illustration are bright red in life.

Green reindeer lichen

This species, *Cladina mitis,* is also called the yellow reindeer lichen. The stalks are yellow-green to yellow-gray. The entire plant may grow to 10 cm (4 inches) tall. This species is common in open forests of white and black spruce in Alaska and those of lodgepole pine and jack pine in Canada and more southerly locations. Both these reindeer lichens are often placed in the genus *Cladonia.*

Red pixie cup

Pixie cups are club-shaped lichens in the genus *Cladonia.* Red pixie cups have bright red fruiting bodies on the tops of the clubs. These red-fruited lichens are often called British soldiers because the red tops are reminiscent of the red-coated British soldiers of the colonial period in North America. One of the most common red pixie cup in interior Alaska is *Cladonia cristatella* (Figure 3.12). This species occurs on acid soils and on decaying spruce logs. Two other British soldiers in North America are *C. pleurota and C. borealis.* Another red pixie cup, *C. floerkeana,* occurs in Great Britain.

Ring lichen

The ring lichen, *Arctoparmalia centrifuga,* grows very close to its substratum, acidic rocks. As the lichen grows, the central part of the thallus dies, leaving behind a ring. Further growth produces concentric rings. This species is common on outcroppings in subalpine boreal forest but also occurs on talus slopes in tundra habitats. My first encounter with the ring lichen was in the saddle of Eagle Summit, Mile 104 on the Steese Highway. The rings were attached to a horizontal rock slab at the base of a talus slope. As I worked my way up the slope, I found other ring lichens on vertical surfaces as well.

Now we've seen some plants; what about the animals?

This chapter has introduced some of the plants and their individual characteristics. I talked about some aspects of how these species are distributed in space and time and the idea of plant succession on the landscape. In the next several chapters, we turn to the animals that live in, on, under, and around these plants. What animal species exist in Alaska's boreal forests? What are some of the adaptations and behaviors of these animals? How do the abundances and distributions of these animals respond to the succession of plant communities? What are the interactions among these species? I will begin by looking at some of the mammals of Alaska's boreal forests.

REFERENCES

1 Viereck, L.A., and Little, E.L. 1972. Alaska trees and shrubs. Forest Service, United States Department of Agriculture Agriculture Handbook No. 410. 265 pp.

2 Johnson, D., Kershaw, L., MacKinnon, A and Pojar, J. 1995. Plants of the western boreal forest and aspen parkland. Lone Pine Publishing, Edmonton. 392 pp.

3 Walker, L.W., Zasada, J.C. and Chapin, F.S.III. 1986. The role of life history processes in primary succession on an Alaskan floodplain. Ecology 67: 1243-1253.

4 Viereck, L.A., Van Cleve, K. and Dyrness, C.T. 1986. Forest ecosystem distribrion in the taiga environment, pp.22-43 In: Van Cleve, K., Chapin, F.S. III, Flanagan, P. W., Viereck, L.A. and Dyrness, C.T. Forest ecosystems in the Alaskan taiga. Springer-Verlag, New York and Berlin, 230 pp.

5 Kielland, K. and Bryant, J. 1998. Moose herbivory in taiga: effects on biogeochemistry and vegetation dynamics in primary succession. Oikos 82: 377-383.

6 Mann, D.H., Fastie, C.L., Rowland, E.L. and Bigelow, N.H. 1995. Spruce succession, disturbance, and geomorphology on the Tanana River floodplain, Alaska. Ecoscience 2: 184-199.

7 Timoney, K.P., Peterson, G. and Wein, R. 1997. Vegetation development of boreal riparian plant communities after flooding, fire and logging, Peace River, Canada. Forest Ecology and Management 93: 101-120.

8 Chapin, F.S.III and Kedrowski, R.A. 1983. Seasonal changes in nitrogen and phosphorus fractions and autumn translocation in evergreen and deciduous taiga trees. Ecology 64: 376-391.

9 Bryant, J.P. and Chapin, F.S.III. 1986. Browsing-woody plant interactions during boreal forest plant succession, pp 213-225 In: K. VanCleve, F.S. Chapin III, P.W. Flanagan, L.A. Viereck and C.T. Dyrness (editors). Forest ecosystems in the Alaska taiga. Springer-Verlag, New York and Berlin.230 pp.

10 Jakubas, W. J., Karasov, W. H. and Guglielmo, C. G. 1993. Coniferyl benzoate in quaking aspen (*Populus tremuloides*): its effect on energy and nitrogen digestion and retention in ruffed grouse (*Bonasa umbellus*). Physiological Zoology 66: 580-601.

11 Jakubas, W. J., Wentworth, B. C. and Karasov, W. H. 1993. Physiological and behavioral effects of coniferyl benzoate on avian reproduction. Journal of Chemical Ecology 19: 2353-2377.

12 Zasada, J.C. and Lovig, D. 1983. Observations on primary dispersal of white spruce, *Picea glauca*, seed. Canadian Field-Naturalist 97: 104-105.

13 Werner, R.A. and Holsten, E.H. 1985. Factors influencing generation times of spruce beetles in Alaska. Canadian Journal of Forest Research 15: 438-443.

14 Hard, J.S. 1985. Spruce beetles attack slowly growing spruce. Forest Science 31: 839-850.

15 Holsten, E.H., Hennon, P.E. and Werner, R. A. 1985. Insects and Diseases of Alaskan Forests. USDA, Forest Service, Alaska Region Report Number 181, U.S. Government Printing Office, 217 pp.

16 Miller, L.K. and Werner, R.A. 1987. Cold-hardiness of adult and larval spruce beetles *Dendroctonus rufipennis* (Kirby) in interior Alaska. Canadian Journal of Zoology 65: 2927-2930.

17 Shore, T.L. and Alfaro, R.I. 1986. The spruce budworm, *Choristoneura fumiferana* (Lepidoptera: Tortricidae), in British Columbia. Journal of the Entomological Society of British Columbia 83: 31-38.

18 Pielou, E.C. 1988. The world of northern evergreens. Comstock Publishing, Ithaca and London, 174 pp.

19 Van Cleve, K., Dyrness, CT., Viereck, L.A., Fox, J., Chapin, F.S.III and Oechel, W. 1983. Taiga ecosystems in interior Alaska. Bioscience 33: 39-44.

20 Viereck, L.A., Dyrness, C.T., Van Cleve, K. and Foote, M.J. 1983. Vegetation, soils, and forest productivity in selected forest types in interior Alaska. Canadian Journal of Forest Research 13: 703-720.

21 Chapin, F.S. III, Oechel, W.C., van Cleve, K. and Lawrence, W. 1987. The role of mosses in the phosphorus cycling of an Alaskan black spruce forest. Oecologia 74: 310- 315.

22 Jardon, Y.,Filion, L. and Cloutier, C. 1994. Long-term impact of insect defoliation on growth and mortality of eastern larch in boreal Quebec. Ecoscience 1: 231-238.

23 Gerlach, J.P., Reich, P.B., Puettmann, K. and Baker, T. 1997. Species diversity and density affect tree seedling mortality from *Armillaria* root rot. Canadian Journal of Forest Research 27: 1509- 1512.

24 Burgin, S.G. and Hunter, F.F. 1997. Evidence of honeydew feeding in black flies (Diptera: Simuliidae). The Canadian Entomologist 129: 859-869.

25 Raatikainen, M. and Tanska, T. 1993. Cone and seed yields of the juniper (*Juniperus communis*) in southern and central Finland. Acta Botanica Fennica 149: 27-39.

26 Chatzopoulou, P.S. and Katsiotis, S.T. 1993. Chemical investigation of the leaf oil of *Juniperus communis* L. Journal of Essential Oil Research 5: 603-607.

27 Looman, A., Baerheim Svendsen, A. 1992. The needle essential oil of Norwegian mountain juniper, *Juniperus communis* L. var. *saxatilis* Pall. Flavour and Fragrance Journal 7: 23-26.

28 Markkanen, T., Maekinen, M.L., Nikoskelainen, J., Nieminen, K., Jokinen, P. Raunio, R. and Hirvonen, T. 1981. Anti-herpetic agent from juniper tree (*Juniperus communis*), its purification, identification and testing in primary human amnion cell cultures. Drugs under Experimental and Clinical Research 7: 691-697.

29 Ward, L.K. 1982. The conservation of juniper: longevity and old age. Journal of Applied Ecology 19: 917-928.

30 Clausen, T. P., Reichardt, P. B., Bryant, J. P., Werner, R. A., Post, K. and Frisby, K. 1989. Chemical model for short-term induction in quaking aspen (*Populus tremuloides*) foliage against herbivores. Journal of Chemical Ecology 15: 2335-2346.

31 Murray, D.F. 1980. Balsam poplar in arctic Alaska. Canadian Journal of Anthropology 1: 29-32.

32 Densmore, R. and Zasada, J.C. 1977. Germination requirements of Alaskan *Rosa*

acicularis. Canadian Field-Naturalist 91: 58-62.

33 Shorthouse, J.D. 1986. Significance of nutritive cells in insect galls. Proceedings of the Entomological Society of Washington 88: 368-375.

34 Shorthouse, J.D. and Brooks, S.E. 1998. Biology of the galler *Diplolepis rosaefolii* (Hymenoptera: Cynipidae), its associated component community, and host shift to the shrub rose. Canadian Entomologist 130: 357-366.

35 Densmore, R. 1997. Effect of day length on germination of seeds collected in Alaska. American Journal of Botany 84: 274-278.

36 Inderjit and Mallik, A.U. 1997. Effects of *Ledum groenlandicum* amendments on soil characteristics and black spruce seedling growth. Plant Ecology 133: 29-36.

37 Keith, L.B., Cary, J.R., Rongstad, O.J. and Brittingham, M.C. 1984. Demography and ecology of a declining snowshoe hare population. Wildlife Monographs 90: 1-43.

38 Reichardt, P.B., Bryant, J. P., Anderson, B.J., Phillips, D., Clausen, T.P., Meyer, M. and Frisby, K. 1990. Germacrone defends Labrador tea from browsing by snowshoe hares. Journal of Chemical Ecology 16: 1961-1970.

39 Jung, H.-J.G. and Batzli, G.O. 1981. Nutritional ecology of microtine rodents: effects of plant extracts on the growth of arctic microtines. Journal of Mammalogy 62: 286-292.

40 Chapin, F.S.III. 1983. Nitrogen and phosphorus nutrition and nutrient cycling by evergreen and deciduous understory shrubs in an Alaskan black spruce forest. Canadian Journal of Forest Research 13: 773-781.

41 Kummerow, J., Ellis, B.A., Kummerow, S. and Chapin, F.S.III. 1983. Spring growth of shoots and roots in shrubs of an Alaskan muskeg. American Journal of Botany 70: 1509-1515.

42 Chapin, F.S.III and Tryon, P.R. 1982. Phosphate absorption and root respiration of different plant growth forms from northern Alaska. Holarctic Ecology 5: 164-171.

43 Solbreck, C. and Andersson, D. 1987. Vertical distribution of fireweed, *Epilobium angustifolium*, seeds in the air. Canadian Journal of Botany 65: 2177-2178.

44 Dyrness, C.T. and Norum, R.A. 1983. The effects of experimental fires on black spruce forest floors in interior Alaska. Canadian Journal of Forest Research 13: 879-893.

45 Hogg, E.H. and Leiffers, V.J. 1991. The effects of *Calamagrostis canadensis* on soil thermal regimes after logging in northern Alberta. Canadian Journal of Forest Research 21: 387-394.

46 Michaud, J.P. 1990. Observations on nectar secretion in fireweed, *Epilobium angustifolium* L. (Onagraceae). Journal of Apicultural Research 29: 132-137.

47 Mercier, S. and Langlois, C.-G. 1993. Relationships between *Epilobium angustifolium* phenology and *Picea glauca* seed maturation. Forest Ecology and Management 59: 115-125.

48 Klein-Gebbinck, H.W., Blenis, P.V. and Hiratsuka, Y. 1993. Fireweed (*Epilobium angustifolium*) as a possible inoculum

reservoir for root-rotting *Armillaria* species. Plant Pathology 42: 132-136.

49 Carling, D.E., Kebler, K.M. and Leiner, R.H. 1986. Interactions between *Rhizoctonia solani* AG-3 and 27 plant species. Plant Disease 70: 577-578.

50 Chandler, R.F., Hooper, S.N. and Harvey, M.J. 1982. Ethnobotany and phytochemistry of yarrow, *Achillea millefolium*, Compositae. Economic Botany 36: 203-223.

51 Rathman, E. S., Lanza, J. and Wilson, J. 1990. Feeding preferences of flesh flies (*Sarcophaga bullata*) for sugar-only vs. sugar-amino acid nectars. American Midland Naturalist 124: 379-389.

52 Solecki, R. S. 1971. Shanidar: The First Flower People. Alfred A. Knopf, New York, 290 pp.

53 de la Puerta, R., Saenz, M. T. and Garcia, M. D. 1996. Antibacterial activity and composition of the volatile oil from *Achillea ageratum* L. Phytotherapy Research 10: 248-250.

54 Nams, V.O.,Folkard, N.F.G. and Smith, J.N.M. 1993. Effects of nitrogen fertilization on several woody and nonwoody boreal forest species. Canadian Journal of Botany 71: 93-97.

55 Reekie, J. Y. C., Hicklenton, P. R. and Reekie, E. G. 1994. Effects of elevated CO_2 on time of flowering in four short-day and four long-day species. Canadian Journal of Botany 72: 533-538.

56 Fitter, A. 1997. Nutrient acquisition, pp.51-72 In: M.J. Crawley (editor) Plant Ecology. Blackwell Science, London. 717 pp.

57 Hulten, E. 1968. Flora of Alaska and neighboring territories. Stanford University Press, Stanford,1008 pp.

58 Ahmadjian, V. 1993. The lichen symbiosis. John Wiley & Sons, Inc. New York, 250 pp.

59 Moser, T.J., Nash, T.H. and Clark, W.D. 1980. Effects of long-term field sulfur dioxide fumigation on arctic caribou forage lichens. Canadian Journal of Botany 58: 2235-2242.

60 Walker, D.A., Webber, P.J., Everett, K.R. and Brown, J. 1978. Effects of crude and diesel oil spills on plant communities at Prudhoe Bay, Alaska, and the derivation of oil spill sensitivity maps. Arctic 31: 242-259.

61 Goudey, J.S., Dale, M. and Hoddinott, J. 1986. The effects of oil spill chemicals on CO_2 assimilation by the fruticose lichen *Cladonia mitis*. Environmental Pollution Series A 42: 23-35.

62 Walker, D.A. and Everett , J.R. 1987. Road dust and its environmental impact on Alaskan taiga and tundra. Arctic and Alpine Research 19: 479-489.

63 Purvis, W. 2000. Lichens. Smithsonian Institution Press, Washington, D.C. 112 pp.

64 Vitt, D.H., Marsh, J.E. and Bovey, R.B. 1988. Mosses lichens and ferns of northwest North America. Lone Pine Publishing, Edmonton. 296 pp.

4.
FROM MIGHTY MOOSE TO
MIGHTY SMALL BATS:
SOME MAMMALS OF THE BOREAL FOREST

It is difficult to briefly summarize the life styles and adaptations of the various mammals of the boreal forest. They are simply too diverse. In Chapter 2 I described some of the physiological, anatomical and behavioral mechanisms that allow animals to survive in the Far North. Although all the mammals in Alaska are warm-blooded (homeotherms), some species hibernate, and others do not. Some migrate dozens of kilometers while others spend their entire lives in a very small area. Only one mammal travels hundreds to thousands of kilometers: the little brown bat. Virtually all of Alaska's boreal forest mammals molt and put on thicker coats for the winter. Several (snowshoe hare, short-tailed weasel) even undergo a coat color change from brown to white in the fall. It is really impossible to generalize.

What follows is an account of some of the behaviors, interesting anatomical features, and relationships of Alaska's forest creatures. Not every single species found there is included;

space simply does not allow it. The discussion of wolves and grizzlies, two charismatic species that occur in boreal and coastal forests and also in tundra habitats, has been placed in the chapter on tundra animals.

Moose

The moose, *Alces alces*, is the largest member of the deer family, Cervidae. Indeed, on the North American continent, large moose are only outweighed by the largest bison and the largest of the great bears. Adult females weigh 360-600 kg (800-1300 pounds); males weigh 550-725 kg (1200-1600 pounds). A large bull will stand over 2 m (7 feet) at the shoulder. If you are road-hunting moose in Alaska or elsewhere, don't plan on loading your trophy onto your vehicle's fender or hood intact unless you are willing to pay for a lot of auto body work. The long legs of moose pose a unique driving hazard to motorists in Alaska. When the average sedan hits a moose on the road, it usually knocks the legs out from under the moose, causing it to fall on top of the car. Serious injuries and some human fatalities have resulted from these accidents.

Based primarily on antler characteristics such as maximum spread, beam length, palm size, and brow palm size, North American moose have been divided into four different subspecies. The Alaska-Yukon subspecies, *Alces alces gigas*, as the name suggests, is the largest of the four. The smallest is *A. a. shirasi* of Colorado, Utah, and Wyoming. The other two are *A. a. andersoni* in the upper Midwest and into Canada and *A. a. americana* of New England and Quebec. Until very recently, the explanation for these subspecific differences and the current distribution of the subspecies was couched in a discussion of moose surviving the late-Pleistocene glaciation in refugia (Beringia and south of the ice sheets; see Chapter 1). However, there are no fossil remains of moose south of the ice sheets older than about 11,000 years before the present.

Another idea, based on the lack of genetic diversity in North American moose, is that moose arrived in North America in the last 10,000-11,000 years, dispersed southward through the ice-free corridor mentioned previously, and rapidly moved eastward.[1] Then, as the ice sheets melted back, they dispersed northward to their present areas of distribution. The oldest fossil moose remains from Alaska are dated at 12,500 ybp.[2]

To hunters and outdoors persons, perhaps the most fascinating and amusing aspect of moose biology is their reproductive cycle. Certainly, the sights, sounds and odors of moose in the rut are intrinsically interesting and are of practical value. Rut begins in early September in Alaska and lasts for 3-4 weeks. Typically, males are ready for and interested in breeding before the females are. Females generally mature by 28 months after birth; a few mature at 16 months. The estrous cycle in moose lasts from 25 to 30 days. During this time they are receptive to males and they ovulate. In Alaska, about 85% of females are bred from late September to mid-October. Unbred females typically come into estrus again in early to mid-November. Overall, pregnancy rates in populations in Alaska vary between 70% and 90%. There are a few exceptional records of cow moose breeding in December, January, or even into February.

If it were not for their sets of bony antlers up to 2.05 m (80 inches) wide and weighing up to 40 kg (88 pounds) and body weights up to 725 kg (1600 pounds), the antics of moose during the rut might be quite comical. To begin with, both sexes vocalize during the rut. I was moose hunting on a ridge at tree line one mid-September evening and heard what I, at the time, thought was a very unhappy, drunken woman moaning very loudly. Within seconds a cow and a calf moose emerged from a big willow patch, followed a few seconds later by a young bull, maybe three years old. The cow was interested in feeding; the bull was interested in the cow. I began to do my crude imitation of a bull grunt. The cow drifted away and the bull started after her but stopped and turned back every time I grunted. He did not vocalize, perhaps because I did not give him enough time to really get into it. But, on another September evening I had a bull respond to a combination of cow and bull calls by grunting, brush thrashing, and approaching.

There are two interpretations of the "unhappy woman" moan of the female. Some think it is an announcement that the cow is responsive and looking for a mate. The other idea is that the cow is upset with the bull and the call is actually one of irritation, not passion. In either hypothesis, the moan will likely attract another and perhaps larger bull. It is to the cow's advantage to breed with the healthiest, most dominant bull available; her offspring will inherit some of these desirable traits. Over the years I have managed to come up with a reasonable cow moan. My bull vocalizations, however, are not up to par. A mature bull has a very deep grunt and smaller bulls have higher pitched grunts. My speaking voice isn't a booming bass and my bull grunts sound about like a 2-year-old bull, hardly challenging.

Actually, bulls have at least two different vocalizations. One is a challenge grunt, issued just before (or to avoid) combat. This is a one-syllable grunt, a deep-pitched "wah." The other sound bulls make is a two-syllable grunt, "oo-wah," used apparently to herd or move females. Just as in human courtship, bulls (or humans imitating bulls) can say the wrong thing at the right time. A challenge grunt issued to a bull that already has a cow may cause the bull to herd his cow away.

If either you or the real bull issues a convincing challenge the other bull may respond with challenge grunts of his own and/or begin thrashing shrubs and trees with his antlers. This thrashing can be quite violent, breaking saplings and completely uprooting small trees. Sometimes moose hunters imitate this thrashing sound as part of their hunting repertoire. At other times, hikers may accidentally imitate

these thrashing sounds. One sunny day in early October a friend and I set out to hike across an old burn on Murphy Dome, west of Fairbanks. Most of the burned trees had fallen down over the years, so we had to step across logs of all sizes. It was impossible to move silently because we were constantly stepping on (and breaking) branches. After an hour of this, we heard someone coming upslope in our direction making at least as much noise as we were. It turned out to be a large bull moose in rut. He must have thought we were another bull thrashing the countryside. He chased us around a standing tree for an hour with his head down, wagging his antlers and pawing the ground. Hollering at him did no good whatsoever.

Odors are an integral part of the moose rut. When females go into estrus, their urine takes on a characteristic odor that can be sensed by the male. A bull standing with his head high and his upper lip curled up and away from his teeth is checking for the scent of a cow in heat (Figure 4.1). The sensory area being used is a specialized chemoreceptor called the vomeronasal organ, or Jacobson's organ. This structure is located on the anterior part of the palate; it is well developed in bulls but poorly developed in cows. This organ is used to detect air-borne droplets or aerosols containing female pheromones that are not volatile enough to be reliably sensed by the bull's nasal chemoreceptors.[3]

Bulls produce highly scented urine during the rut also. To increase the signal value of the urine, bulls urinate on their hind legs and/or urinate on the ground and then wallow in the urine. These guys really smell bad...to a human. What is the point? There is undoubtedly an intimidation value to having very

Figure 4.1: Bull moose exhibiting lip curl. The lip is curled to expose the vomeronasal organ that detects a chemical emanating from a female ready to breed.

stinky urine. Several times I have called bull moose into close proximity with grunts, and every time the bull starts to circle downwind. They seem to be trying to assess how big and "bad" the other bull is.

The other possible use of stinky male urine is as an attractant for females. Dale Guthrie informally tested that hypothesis one fall. After helping me butcher a big bull in mid-September, we collected urine from an intact bladder. He took the urine home and poured some of it on a bale of hay in his yard. Over the next several days, several cow moose came in to the bale, rubbed and butted the bale to pieces. The urine apparently attracted cow moose.

Further, the pheromone in male urine is thought to "prime" or trigger estrus in females.[4] Several chemicals probably account for the odor and for the behavioral significance of the odor. Butyrolactone was found only in adult males. P-cresol occurred in the urine of all males but in much higher concentrations in rutting males. This latter compound is a byproduct of the metabolic breakdown of energy reserves that keep the rutting bull going even though he isn't feeding. So, in a very real sense, the scent of p-cresol is an indicator to the female of how "into it" the bull is.[5]

Both males and females scent-mark trees. First, the moose selects an appropriately sized white spruce or willow. Then he/she rubs forehead, behind the ears, and/or, face on this bare area. Moose faces have suborbital scent glands below the eyes, but no one has yet reported scent glands behind the ears. Marking by females occurs at the peak of the rut and probably advertises their readiness to breed. Male scent-marking of trees occurs late in rut (mid-October to November) and probably attracts females that haven't already been bred.[6]

Moose in North America exhibit two different kinds of breeding associations. In the lower 48 and southern Canada, males exhibit a **tending bond.** That is, a male will find a cow in estrus and stay with her until she is bred and out of estrus. Then, he goes out and finds another cow and starts over.

In Alaska and the Yukon, males attempt to form a **harem** (group of females) and defend the harem from other males. Obviously, it is the largest, most powerful bulls, usually with the largest antlers, that are successful at assembling and maintaining harems. Challengers to the dominant bull approach while vocalizing, and, typically, both bulls will wag their heads, first dipping one antler and then the other. Head wagging is a way of displaying antler size. If the two bulls are unevenly matched, the one with the smaller antlers typically retires or is chased off without having to endure combat. Evenly matched bulls do fight, however, and these battles inspire awe. The bulls engage their antlers and begin to push and, believe me, it isn't a dainty, faint-hearted push. The contest may result in broken antler points, puncture wounds to either or both contestants and leave even the victor exhausted.

Fatalities are often the outcome of these matches, especially if the antlers actually lock together. Two moose skulls with antlers locked together hang in the lobby of the Alaska Department of Fish and Game office in Fairbanks. Someone found them in that configuration in the woods.

As a result of these vigorous and dangerous conflicts, large bulls dominate matings. In interior Alaska, 88% of all copulations are performed by these large, dominant bulls.[7] What about the other 12%? Most harems have, in addition to the dominant bull, a lesser bull hanging around the periphery, a **satellite bull**. Once in a great while the dominant bull is too busy struggling with a "worthy" opponent to prevent a satellite bull from successfully copulating with one of his cows.

Back to the business of harems in Alaska: why are Alaska and the Yukon Territory different? Alaskan and Yukon moose habitat is much more open terrain than in Maine. Moose tend to form larger groups in Alaska, perhaps as better protection from predators and perhaps in response to patchy distribution of forage plants. One cost incurred by these larger groups is a lower foraging efficiency.

Gestation in moose is about eight months. Since breeding occurs mainly in September and October, 85% of calves are born in late May. The remaining 15% are born later, mostly in June. There is a supposed advantage to being born with most of the others: predators of moose calves may not be able to catch and eat all of them, and successful predators may even become satiated. This phenomenon is called **predator swamping,** and, in mammals, was originally proposed as the explanation for wildebeest birth synchrony.[8] However, an Alaskan study found no evidence to support the notion that calves born at the end of the rather short calving period had lower mortality rate than those born earlier.[9] Climate constraints rather than predator swamping might drive birth synchrony in moose. Late May corresponds to the first appearance of high-quality moose forage; preferred food plants are leafing out. Because there is only a short summer season for newborn moose to grow and store energy reserves for the coming winter, moose have their calves as early as possible to coordinate with the appearance of appropriate foods. If climate changes, the timing of moose calving may also change.

Let's return to the subject of moose antlers. Clearly, of all living deer species, moose have the largest antlers. Every fall the *Fairbanks Daily News-Miner* runs a column on the "over 60 club." The article describes some of the new inductees, hunters that have harvested moose with racks over 60 inches in spread. The variability in spread, number of points, and size of the brow palms of moose antlers is fascinating, and some of these antlers are truly immense! Several in the 2 m (80 inch) range have been harvested recently.

Bear in mind that antlers are produced each year. Growth begins in late April or early May and is complete by late August. In four months a bull has to find sufficient energy reserves and sufficient calcium to construct these antlers. During the later phases of antler development, growth is so rapid that growth bands, perhaps corresponding to daily growth increments, are laid down on the antler. These bands look like the growth rings on a tree stump. Once the antlers reach final size, the bull will thrash brush and knock off the velvet layer covering them.

Male calves at the end of the first summer have bumps on their heads where antlers will grow the following year. Yearling bulls typically develop small paddles on each side, each projecting 10-20 cm (4-8 inches) out from the skull. Occasionally in Alaska, a yearling will, instead,

grow either a spike or a forked antler on one or both sides. Research has shown that these yearlings will never produce huge antlers; they have a defective gene for antler development. If the Alaska Department of Fish and Game wants to manage for trophy quality, especially in areas where bulls are heavily harvested, it may wish to eliminate these "inferior" bulls from the gene pool and otherwise restrict harvest so bulls can reach mature size. This is the essence of the "spike, fork-50 inch" regulation in many game management units in Alaska.

Each fall or winter, sometime between November and January, bulls shed their antlers. Each successive year through about age 11, the bull will grow larger antlers if it has sufficient food resources. After 11, bulls begin to senesce, producing smaller, often misshapen antlers. Maximum longevity in moose is about 16 years. Moose antlers are not as dense as caribou antlers. During dominance struggles, points are often broken off moose antlers, but such breaks are extremely rare in caribou.

Food intake in moose is truly prodigious; up to 20 kg (44 pounds) of food may be consumed each day.[10] During the summertime moose feed on a wide variety of plant material, including willow leaves and twigs, grasses, sedges, fireweed, and submerged vegetation. In winter, moose subsist on willow twigs, dwarf birch, aspen, poplar, and paper birch but not spruce. In interior Alaska, four willow species (feltleaf [*Salix alaxensis*], diamondleaf [*S. planifolia*], littletree [*S. arbusculoides*] and grayleaf [*S. glauca*] willows) account for 94% of the biomass of winter food consumed.[11] In Canada and the lower 48, winter food can include some of the less chemically defended conifers such as balsam hemlock and Douglas fir.

I discussed plant succession in the boreal forest in Chapter 3 and suggested that the early stages, those with plentiful supplies of willows, were better for moose. The implication was that plant succession to a very real extent influences the population dynamics of moose.

There is also evidence that moose, by virtue of their selective feeding and other activities, affect the progress of plant and animal succession. I mentioned moose selecting willows while leaving alders alone, thus promoting progression to an alder canopy.[12] Moose may also promote or accelerate the succession from mixed aspen-spruce forests to the last stage, the coniferous forest. In late winter and early spring, moose may strip the bark from aspens, balsam poplars, and willows if sufficient browse isn't available. Spruce trees are not stripped. If the deciduous trees are partially or completely girdled, translocation of nutrients and water up and down the stem is interrupted. The greater the bark stripping, the higher the mortality of these shrubs and trees.[13] Bark stripping favors the survival of spruce while partially eliminating its deciduous competitors. This is a long-term process.

On shorter time scales, moose have an impact on the chemistry of the willows they browse. Previously browsed feltleaf willow has higher leaf nitrogen concentrations and higher digestibility than unbrowsed willows. When this material is added to the forest litter layer, it decomposes faster than that of unbrowsed plants. In addition, moose urine and fecal material left behind in the willow patches amounts to about a third of the total nitrogen input. So, in the short term, moose browsing speeds up soil organic matter turnover.[14] Similar changes in leaf nitrogen concentrations in previously browsed paper birch have been reported. These leaves are processed in interior streams at higher rates than leaves from unbrowsed birch. This suggests that stream productivity for insects and other invertebrates may well be higher if moose have been browsing birch nearby.[15]

Moose, other members of the Cervidae, cattle, sheep, and antelopes are all **ruminants**. That is, they have specialized, four-chambered stomachs that act as large fermentation vats (Figure 4.2). In sequence from anterior to posterior, these chambers are rumen, reticulum, omasum, and abomasum. The **rumen** is the first stop for

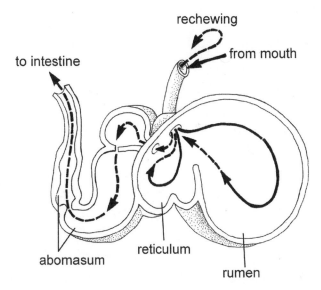

Figure 4.2: Four-chambered stomach of a ruminant such as a moose. Arrows indicate flow of material through the stomach. The rumen and reticulum function to culture bacteria and protozoa that ferment cellulose and other plant material converting it into more bacteria and protozoa. The omasum, or third chamber, captures solid particles, returning them to the reticulum for further digestion. The abomasum is the acid-secreting chamber that kills microorganisms and begins their digestion.

food ingested by the moose. The walls of the rumen secrete juices that, along with a huge production of saliva, keep the fluid volume of the chamber constant. The chamber is a large incubation vat for bacteria and protozoa, single-celled creatures that digest the plant material. One of the chief structural materials of woody plants is the polysaccharide cellulose. Mammals are not capable of synthesizing an enzyme that will digest cellulose, but the bacteria and protozoans in the moose rumen can digest cellulose. To mix the rumen contents thoroughly and to help mechanically break down the plant material, moose, as do cows and sheep, occasionally regurgitate rumen contents to chew their cud.

Bacterial and protozoan metabolism in the rumen is anaerobic. That is, there is no oxygen available to completely metabolize the sugars liberated from cellulose. So, instead of producing water and carbon dioxide as end-products, these microorganisms make short-chain fatty acids, sometimes called **volatile fatty acids,** or VFAs. Moose will use VFAs for energy metabolism. Inside the rumen, microbes digest cellulose, reproduce themselves, and produce VFAs and also B vitamins (and methane, a greenhouse gas) as byproducts.

The second chamber is the **reticulum**. As the name suggests, the inner surface has a network, or reticulum, of raised ridges. The functions of this chamber are to continue the fermentation (anaerobic digestion) and to absorb some of the VFAs produced in the rumen. This is the chamber that, in cows, is sold as tripe. The third chamber is the **omasum.** Its function is to filter or trap particles that are too large and to send them back to the reticulum. The inside of the omasum is highly folded. The folds are called omasal leaves;

the leaves are the strainer or filter that traps the particles. The fourth chamber, the **abomasum**, is the equivalent of our stomach. It is the chamber that produces the acid and enzyme secretions that typically begin the process of digesting proteins and fats. The acid secretion actually kills the protozoa and bacteria that enter this chamber. Now begins the process of digesting and absorbing the proteins these microorganisms have made out of the food ingested by the moose. The small intestine of the moose completes the digestion and absorption of the dead microbial bodies, VFAs and B vitamins.

One other aspect of moose digestion should be mentioned. The plant material moose eat is low in protein but the microorganisms in the stomach are high in protein. How is that accomplished? Ruminants are very efficient in recycling nitrogen. Instead of simply flushing their nitrogen-containing waste product, urea, out with the urine, moose reabsorb it from the bladder, send it back around the circulatory system and, when it reaches the wall of the rumen, secrete it into the rumen chamber. The bacteria break down the urea and convert it to amino acids, the building blocks of their own proteins.

A final thought related to feeding: Moose use mineral licks. Mineral licks have been identified in Alaska and are an important source of sodium in the spring and early summer. There are several reasons moose require sodium. First, they may have become mineral depleted over the winter. Second, spring foliage is rich in potassium and they need sodium to balance the potassium. Third, the processes of molting, lactation and antler growth all require mineral intake.[16] Males use these licks more than females. Some have proposed that summertime use of aquatic vegetation by moose is a response to sodium hunger. But ponds produce more vegetation than adjacent terrestrial habitats, it is more digestible, and it can be harvested with a relaxed vigilance for predators.[17]

Moose are an important source of food for subsistence and sport hunters across North America. A mature bull will yield about 500 pounds of boneless meat. The total moose population of North America is estimated at 0.8-1.2 million animals, and the annual harvest is around 90,000. Alaska contributes about 10,000 animals to that annual harvest.

It is interesting to note that in Scandinavia, with a land area smaller than Alaska, some 100,000 moose are harvested annually. Moose there are subjected to intensive hunting: landowners attempt to shoot all barren cows, one of every pair of twin calves, very young bulls and very old bulls. Such hunting-induced mortality undoubtedly contributes greatly to the quality of habitat available for the remaining moose and also increases the rate at which twin calves are produced. The moose of Isle Royale, Michigan, increased their rate of twinning significantly after the introduction of wolves on the island.

Aside from human hunters, moose fall prey to black bears, brown bears and wolves. Adolph Murie spent years observing grizzly bears and wolves interacting with moose in McKinley Park, Alaska. Calf moose are much more susceptible to grizzly predation than are adults, especially newborns. He found that the size of the bear significantly influenced the outcome of a grizzly attempting to take a moose calf. Grizzlies 1-3 years old were chased by female moose, whereas larger bears caused the female to retreat rather than defend her calf.[18] Try as they might,

mothers are unable to protect all their young. Grizzlies account for 79% of moose calf mortalities in south-central Alaska.[19]

The occurrence of animal remains in the scats (feces) of wolves in McKinley Park have been examined. Based on examining 1,174 wolf scats, moose was the sixth most frequent food.[20] However, in some areas wolves have become moose hunting specialists. Moose-wolf interactions have been studied in great detail on Isle Royale, Michigan, where moose is the only prey available to wolves.[21] Wolves don't always make a kill; their success rate on Isle Royale is about 5%. Wolves are often injured and sometimes killed in attacks on moose. Finally, alternative prey, when available, may be much easier to obtain.

Only a few parasites and diseases pose significant threats to moose populations in North America. They include meningeal worm (*Parelaphostrongylus tenuis*) in eastern North America, winter ticks (*Dermacentor albipictis*), brucellosis, and, in some populations in western North America, arterial worm (*Elaeophora schneideri*).[22] The meningeal worm is a roundworm (nematode) whose usual host is white-tailed deer. These worms, as adults, are found on and around the brain membranes (meninges). Completion of the worm life cycle involves brief stints in the deer (or moose) lungs, esophagus, stomach, and intestine, in vegetation or forest soil, and in an intermediate host, any of a half-dozen snail species. In discussions of parasite life cycles, the term **intermediate host** refers to a species in which the parasite exists as a juvenile or in which it reproduces asexually. The parasites accomplish sexual reproduction, as adults, in a different species, the **definitive host**. Symptoms of meningeal disease include weakness of the hindquarters, lethargy, circling behavior, and turning the head and neck to one side. This disease can be lethal to moose but is rarely so devastating to white-tailed deer. Fortunately for Alaska, this disease doesn't occur here.

Brucellosis is a disease caused by bacteria of the genus *Brucella*. *Brucella abortus*, principally associated with domestic cattle, has been isolated from dead and dying moose in Minnesota, Alberta, and Montana but not in Alaska. Moose are probably a poor natural reservoir for this bacterium because infected animals die quickly, before they can pass it on to other moose. This bacterium can be passed to humans and, in humans causes undulent fever. A variant of *Brucella suis*, a pathogen in domestic swine, occurs in caribou, but its potential significance in moose is unknown. Brucellosis is transmitted to humans through cuts and scratches in the skin or through the eyes, nose, or mouth. Bacteria can also be transmitted from improperly cooked, infected meat.[23]

Cystic hydatid disease is caused by a tapeworm, *Echinococcus granulosus*. The life cycle includes a herbivore, either moose or caribou in Alaska, as the intermediate host. Larval tapeworms are deposited in vegetation with the feces of wolves or domestic dogs. Moose ingest the larvae, which burrow their way out of the gut and finally lodge in the lungs or, occasionally, in other organs. Each larva forms a cyst that could develop into several adult worms. This is the hydatid or alveolar cyst. If cysts are not very abundant, infected moose can remain in good condition. If, however, infections are heavy or if cysts form in kidney or brain, moose could be crippled or killed.[24] If the moose is pulled down by a predator which eats its viscera, the cysts are ingested, the walls of the cysts are dissolved and the larvae are released. The worms are passed into the small intestine where they mature and sexually reproduce. Eggs, embryos really, are released from the adult worm, are shed with the feces and the life cycle starts over.

The adults of *Echinococcus* are among the smallest of all tapeworms. Those of *E. granulosus* are only 2-6 mm (0.25 inches or less) long and are only rarely pathogenic to wolves. How do humans pick up this parasite? The typical route is through domestic dogs. Dogs fed uncooked viscera from butchered moose can develop adult *Echinococcus*. The eggs can be transmitted to humans by handling dog feces (or wolf feces) or can even be inhaled. An infected dog can transmit this parasite by licking your face. In such a case, we become unwitting and unintended intermediate hosts; our dogs become the definitive hosts. Human infections in Alaska and northern Canada tend to be relatively benign and may be treated either with medication or surgery. A close relative of this worm, *Echinococcus multilocularis*, is found in red foxes.

The curious hunter who dissects the entrails of moose should brace her/himself. Intestinal tapeworm, *Monezia expansa*, adults reach lengths of 3 m (10 feet) or more! Even the uncurious may see some moose parasites; many of us have seen muscle tapeworm cysts while cutting and wrapping moose meat. These cysts are whitish, 1-2 mm in diameter and are killed by thorough cooking.[23] Hunters take heart and don't throw away that meat!

Black bear

It was a sunny, warm, mid-August afternoon west of Fairbanks, not a cloud in the sky. The bear lay on his back in the blueberry bushes. Every now and then he would leisurely pull down a stem and rake the berries off with his teeth (Figure 4.3). I was reminded of a Roman emperor reclining on a couch eating grapes. However, the feasting I was watching was not nearly as dainty. He was taking in berries, leaves, twigs and all! Black bears, *Ursus americanus*, in interior Alaska rely heavily on blueberries and other berries as fall food. In fact, they digest so many blueberries that the blueberry pigment released in the process dyes the abdominal body fat; the fat is actually bluish purple. The easiest way to see black bears in the interior is to use your binoculars to glass slopes at tree line where berries are abundant and where you have good visibility.

Back to the business of eating leaves and twigs: how would you know the bear was eating twigs and leaves? This is a rephrasing of a more general question. Namely, how do we know what animals eat? There are three methods commonly used to determine the diet of an animal. First, you watch and see what they put in their mouths. Was I actually close enough to the bear to see the leaves and twigs in his mouth? Yes. But if I hadn't been close enough, I still would have strongly suspected as much. The second method is to see what comes out the back end of the bear. This is the method that, over the years, had given overwhelming evidence that bears, both black and grizzly, eat leaves and twigs with their berries. Bear scats in the fall are purple from the blueberries and they have

Figure 4.3: black bear feeding on bog blueberries in the autumn. Bears eat berries, leaves and twigs.

blueberry twigs and leaves in them. If you look closely, you can even see many intact blueberries. Of course, the third way to find out what they eat is to examine the stomach contents. This method is not always a lethal proposition in biology. There are really good techniques for pumping the stomachs of fish to determine their diets. But, I would much rather hold a sedated grayling during a stomach pumping than a black bear, sedated or otherwise! In addition to blueberries, bears also eat the berries of prickly rose, lowbush cranberry, highbush cranberry, crowberry (*Empetrum nigrum*), alpine bearberry (*Arctostaphylos alpina*), kinnikinnick (common bearberry; *Arctostaphylos uva-ursi*) and wild red currant (*Ribes triste*).

Berries aren't available during the entire feeding season; black bears make do with other foods. In the springtime, after emergence from their dens, bears spend most of their time in lowlands feeding on vegetation, especially horsetails (genus *Equisetum*). Other green vegetation includes material from grasses, wild rhubarb (*Polygonium*), arctic lupine, Labrador tea, resin birch, quaking aspen and willows.

Of all members of the mammalian order Carnivora, bears are the most highly modified evolutionarily for eating plant material. Their molars are flattened for crushing and grinding, similar to our own molars. Most other carnivores, such as wolves and foxes, have the shearing molars, called carnassials, which can cut through tendons and animal hide. **Omnivorous** (eating both plant and animal material) bears have intestines over twice as long as those of carnivorous wolves.[25] Even so, the undigested leaves and berries in bear scats indicate that bears still aren't completely adapted to a plant diet. In one study, only about 15% of black bear diets in the interior consisted of animal matter, and most of that was insects. A listing of mammal prey includes bog lemming, red-backed vole, beaver, moose, and Dall sheep. Nests of waterfowl are, on occasion, "cleaned up" by these bears. Bears have been reported to systematically work the edges of lakes, living for a time almost exclusively on duck eggs.

Black bears on the Kenai National Wildlife Refuge eat 15 different kinds of fruits and berries; lowbush cranberries are the most important. Among animal remains, insects occurred most frequently, followed by moose and snowshoe hare.[26]

Are black bears actively hunting moose and snowshoe hares or are they simply feeding on the carrion of winterkills? The answer is: they are definitely predators. On the Kenai National Wildlife Refuge over half of the non-winter moose calf mortality is due to predation by black bears. The Kenai, as is characteristic of much of the boreal forest, is subjected to frequent wildfires, mostly ignited by lightning strikes. The burned areas form a mosaic of habitats. The more recently burned patches are excellent moose and bear habitat; older burns

aren't as good. Bear predation on moose was compared in two different habitats, one a 12-year old burn (early succession), the other a 32-year old burn (mid-succession). There were more moose calves on the more recent burn and also more moose calves killed by black bears. Bears were larger on the more recent burn and, on the average, females reached maturity over a year earlier on the recent burn.[27] These are all indicators that both moose and black bears do well in early succession forest.

Overwintering is a critical behavior for bears in the cold, Far North. On the Tanana River floodplain, interior Alaska, black bears enter hibernation, on average, October 1 and emerge the following spring, on average, on April 21. This amounts to a 205 day denning duration.[28] Females initiate denning earlier than males. Of the dens occupied, about 83% are actually excavated by the bear, and an additional 5% take advantage of an existing, natural structure such as a blow-down or an undercut stream channel. The remainder (12%) are surface dens consisting of huge piles of grasses and sedges that the bear heaps up. There are significantly more dens that open to the north than would be expected.

The average length of hibernation or denning in interior Alaska (205 days), southwestern Washington (127 days)[29] and central California (104 days)[30] conforms to our expectation that climate is more severe and time available for foraging more restricted in Alaska near the limit of the black bear's latitudinal range. In the Sierras of California, over a third of the black bears are active all winter. As one might expect, most of these winter-active bears were males.

To purists, the term "hibernation" isn't quite appropriate for black or grizzly bears. As we discussed in an earlier chapter, bears in the winter do not exhibit the radical declines in body temperature and metabolic rate characteristic of true hibernators. Winter dormancy in black bears is characterized by body temperatures of about 35°C (95°F), a lowered metabolic rate and periodic arousal from the dormant state. Unlike mammals in true hibernation, black bears spend a lot of their time sleeping. They may urinate and/or defecate during the winter, probably during one of the periods of arousal from the dormant state. The bear may actually come out of the den during some of these periods, especially if its energy resources have been exhausted. Such bears can be dangerous in the winter because they are desperate for food. Several encounters between bears and dog mushers have occurred in the past several winters in northern and interior Alaska.

Female black bears come into heat (estrus) in the spring and remain in heat until bred, typically in June or July in Alaska. Copulation with a male causes the ovary to release one or more ova. This phenomenon is called **induced ovulation**. The gestation period is about seven months. However, during almost half that time no embryonic development occurs. Bears exhibit **delayed implantation**; the fertilized ovum (embryo) doesn't implant in the wall of the uterus immediately like it does in humans. Implantation takes place around the first of December in some areas[10] but probably occurs earlier in Alaska. Effectively, these fetuses have a 3-3.5 month nurturing period *in utero*.

At birth, black bear cubs weigh about 250 g (8-10 ounces), are naked and have their eyes closed. This birth weight, as a proportion of adult weight, is the lowest among all placental mammals. This is a good example of **altricial** young, born incompletely developed and requiring a lot of parental care. The opposite condition, in which young are born fully furred with eyes open and capable of coordinated movement, is seen in snowshoe hares. Their young are said to be **precocial**. Each female black bear may give birth to 1-4 cubs but most frequently have two. By emergence in the spring, cubs weigh about 2.3 kg (5 pounds).

After emergence, cubs stay with their mother for the first year or, in the interior, the first two years. Thus, the cubs enter the den with their mother after their first summer and sometimes after their second summer as well. Weaning usually occurs at the end of the first summer. Suckling appears to prevent females from coming into heat, so females breed every second or third year.

All this reproductive biology helps us understand why males will try to kill cubs when they find them. Since bears are so solitary except for breeding, it is likely that a male encountering cubs is not the father of those cubs. Yet, to achieve reproductive success, the male must find a female in heat. If the cubs are killed, the female quickly comes into heat. In the meantime, the male hangs around and, typically, is able to breed the female. Because of delayed implantation, the timing of breeding isn't as critical as in some other species, so these "late breedings" are not really a problem. One final sidelight on black bear reproduction: if a female is in poor nutritional status after breeding, she may not implant the embryos at all. It is better for the bear to lose those potential offspring and live through the winter than to try to have a cub and die during the winter because of the additional energy demands on her body.

Black bears come in more different colors than any other carnivore. The most common color variant in the boreal forest of Alaska (and also in eastern North America) is black. No matter what color phase, however, the muzzle is brown and the outline of the back is straight, not humped at the shoulder as is the case for grizzlies. I've seen several brown phase black bears in interior Alaska. The brown, cinnamon and blond color variants are more common in the open forests of western North America. The Pacific Northwest has two fascinating color morphs of *Ursus americanus*. One is the Kermode bear, a creamy white bear found on a few islands in northern British Columbia. The other is the glacier bear, a bluish-gray color variant whose center of abundance is Yakutat. If you are used to glassing for those jet-black bears of interior Alaska, the glacier bear will really look odd.

Body sizes of adult bears vary considerably. Over their entire range, adult males vary in size from 1.4-2.0 m in length and 47-409 kg weight. An average weight for males is 120 kg (264 pounds), but the 409 kg maximum weight corresponds to 900 pounds, far larger than many grizzlies. Females are 1.2-1.6 m long and 39-236 kg, averaging 80 kg (176 pounds) in weight. Bear weights are highly variable over their entire range and also within Alaska, primarily due to differences in the quantity and quality of food available, the severity of climate and, of course, the age of the bear. In general, bears are somewhat larger in the northern half of their range than in the southern half. [31] However, black bears in the interior average consid-

erably smaller than bears found to the south along the coast in south-central and southeast Alaska. This fact is mainly due to the greater access to high-quality food in coastal habitats. The big difference is the greater availability of salmon in rivers and spawning streams near the coast. Pink salmon, the most abundant of the salmon species in Alaska, run up short rivers and streams to spawn and don't reach the interior of Alaska at all. The salmon species that do reach the interior are dispersed in streams over a vast geographic area and are simply not as abundant as populations in more coastal locations.

Adult bears exhibit seasonal changes in body weight. Upon emergence from hibernation, bears are extremely lean, having exhausted all of the body fat reserves stored the previous year. Over the active feeding season, a bear's weight may increase by 20% or more.

Population densities of bears are difficult to assess. Intensive live-trapping and tagging of black bears in Prince William Sound, south-central Alaska, resulted in a one bear per 2 km^2 density estimate.[32] Population densities in the interior are undoubtedly lower.

Aside from humans, black bears have very few predators. Instances of grizzly bears killing black bears in their dens have been reported in interior Alaska[33] and western Alberta.[34] In the Alberta incident, a sow grizzly with two yearlings came upon the tracks in the snow of a black bear with two cubs of the year. The grizzlies followed, found the den and, at the least, killed and ate the two cubs. The black bear denned a week later than most of its kind. Perhaps denning after snowfall leaves too obvious a trail to the den. However, the incident in Alaska involved an adult black bear that denned before snowfall. In this latter case, the den was discovered by a grizzly that, in its attempts to flush out the occupant, dug an entirely new entrance to the den! Apparently, the black bear emerged, fought the grizzly, was killed and eaten. Since the ranges of black and grizzly bears overlap considerably, there must be many encounters between these two species when both are active. Undoubtedly, some of these encounters result in predation on the black bear. The outcome of such an encounter is far from certain, however. There are several reports of black bears with cubs successfully defending themselves against larger grizzlies.[35]

Wolves and black bears don't necessarily get along either. In northern Minnesota a pack of six wolves attacked a female black bear with two cubs in a shallow den consisting of downed trees. The site offered no protection for the bears on two sides. The wolves drove her out of the den, killed the cubs and, eventually, killed the female as well.[36] Again, the outcome of these species interactions isn't always the same. One incident of a black bear killing a wolf has been reported; the wolf was a female near her den. Some other predators of cubs and sub-adult black bears include eagles, mountain lions, bobcats and coyotes.

Population size for black bears in North America is 600,000 or greater, about 12 times more abundant than grizzly/brown bears. This figure is down considerably from Ernest Thompson Seton's estimate of 2 million black bears in North America before Columbus arrived on our shores. Black bears are found in at least 30 of the 49 continental states of the USA and in all of the Canadian Provinces and Territories. Washington has about 30,000 bears,

Maine about 20,000, perhaps 6,300 in Pennsylvania and 4,100 in New York.[31] I haven't seen a firm estimate on the number of black bears in Alaska but the consensus is that the statewide population is very healthy at, perhaps, 30,000 to 100,000.[37]

Home ranges have been estimated for black bears from several locations in North America. A home range is the area in which an individual animal normally restricts its movements in search of food and mates. This concept is valid for black bears but doesn't apply to species that aggregate and/or migrate such as caribou. In bear studies males always have much larger home ranges than females. Male home range estimates include 70-100 km^2 (Prince William Sound), 98 km^2 (Kenai Peninsula) and 234 km^2 (upper Susitna River). This last estimate is from an upland habitat far from the ocean.[32]

Black bears are hunted in Alaska for their hides and meat. In my opinion, an interior black bear, harvested in the fall, makes some of the best wild game eating in Alaska. The meat should be cooked well done, just as pork is cooked. Bears and pigs share similar parasites, trichina worms. The nematode, *Trichinella spiralis*, affects pigs; *Trichinella nativa* is the worm found in bears and other wild carnivores.

Briefly, the life cycle of *Trichinella* goes like this: The infective stage is a juvenile worm that has bored into the skeletal muscle of the host animal and formed a small cyst. If the host muscle is eaten by another animal, its digestive tract dissolves the cyst but not the worm. The larval worms grow, mature and then reproduce within the small intestine. Female worms give birth to larval offspring in the small intestine; these new larvae enter the bloodstream eventually boring into the muscle tissues of skeletal muscles, tongue, masseters (jaw muscles) and diaphragm. The immune system of the host animal, a black bear in this case, responds by building cysts around these tissue invaders. The boring process causes inflammation and tissue damage. Once encysted, the worms cause no further problems for the host but can remain viable for years. Infection rates vary widely among carnivores in Alaska.[24] Aside from black bears, the following are also known to harbor *Trichinella*: polar bear, brown bear, domestic dogs in rural Alaska, wolf, red fox, arctic fox, wolverine, ermine and lynx.

Surprising is the occurrence of this parasite in some herbivores. Snowshoe hares, arctic ground squirrels, red squirrels, beaver, brown lemmings, red-back voles and muskrats all have low incidences of *Trichinella* infection. These worms cause damage to the host in two ways. First, as larval worms leave the small intestine, they bore small holes in the lining. These holes result in hemorrhages and blood loss. If the infection is severe (large numbers of larvae), blood loss can be fatal. Second, as the worms bore into skeletal muscle they cause inflammation, pain, lesions, muscle, degeneration and, in severe cases, death. Epidemics resembling trichinosis were first described by the Carthaginians in 427 B.C. Outbreaks in humans have been attributed to ingestion of belukha whale, walrus, black bear and brown bear.

Another parasite of black bears in Alaska is a tapeworm, *Diphyllobothrium ursi*. This tapeworm parasitizes three different hosts to complete its life cycle. The first intermediate host is an aquatic copepod (crustacean) and the second intermediate host is a salmon species. Both sockeye and coho salmon have been identified as hosts. The definitive host is the bear. Once a bear eats the infected salmon, development of adult tapeworms from the encysted larvae may be very rapid. A black bear experimentally infected with larvae was found, after only 10 days, to have mature tapeworms almost 1 m (3.3 feet) long.

Snowshoe hare

The snowshoe hare, *Lepus americanus*, is a common resident of the boreal forest from Alaska across Canada. Populations also occur southward in the spruce and fir forests of the Rocky Mountains, Cascades and Sierra Nevadas in the west, hardwood-coniferous forests of the lake states and hardwood forests of the New England states and Appalachia. One of its most obvious physical characteristics is its huge hind feet. In an adult, each foot is about 12 cm (5 inches) in length, allowing these hares to stay up on top of snow rather than sinking in; hence, the common name, snowshoe hare.

The other familiar and obvious feature is the change in coat color over the course of the year. In summer, these hares are brown and grayish with only the tail and nostrils white. In midwinter, the same animal is all white except for the black-tipped ears and the yellowish-white forepaws. Fall molt is drawn-out with ears and paws turning white first, followed by the body. In spring, the ears and paws are the last to change. Within a local population, some hares can be almost pure white in late fall while other individuals have only the white ears; molting isn't completely synchronized within a local population.

In Alaska, the snowshoe hare is often referred to as "low-bush moose." Certainly both moose and hares are browsing herbivores, sometimes feeding on the same plant species. While skiing or snowshoeing in the winter one can often see willow, aspen, birch and even an occasional alder or spruce that has been browsed or girdled by these hares. When deep snow melts away these girdle horizons are sometimes 1-2 m off the forest floor. Several times I have pointed out these browse lines to summer visitors and commented that the very long legs of hares allowed them to reach such heights while standing on the ground! Almost everyone realizes, eventually, that I am pulling his/her leg.

Though snowshoe hares are browsers like moose, they have very different digestive systems for handling vegetation. Hares and rabbits have a simple, one-chambered stomach similar in design and function to our own; none of the complicated, four-chambered affair I described for moose.

Hares have a way to metabolize the structural carbohydrates of woody browse but, unlike the adaptation of moose, the specialized structure is downstream from the stomach. Similar to most mammals, the hare gut is separated into stomach, small intestine, and large intestine. At the junction of the two intestines, hares and their relatives have a large, blind sac corresponding to the human appendix but much larger. This sac is the **cecum**; the cecum (sometimes spelled caecum) is the hare's fermentation vat (Figure 4.4). It contains a community of bacteria and protozoa that function to anaerobically digest some of the fibrous structural material eaten by the hare. As in moose, this assemblage of microscopic creatures extracts some of the stored energy, producing bacterial and protozoan bodies, volatile fatty acids (VFAs) and B vitamins. Structurally, the cecum is almost identical to the large intestine. It can absorb VFAs but it can't absorb B vitamins nor can it digest the microorganisms.

For the hare to gain full benefit from its foraging behavior and its investment in plumbing, it must re-ingest some of the material it defecates. Hares produce two different kinds of pellets. The hard, fibrous droppings you see in the woods, **fecal pellets**, are the remnants of material high in fiber content that passed directly from the small intestine through the

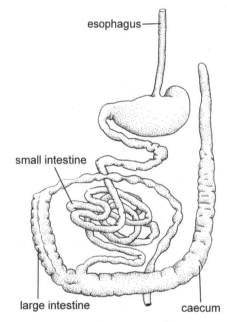

esophagus

small intestine

large intestine

caecum

Figure 4.4: Hare digestive tract. The stomach is very similar to other non-ruminants including humans. The small intestine joins the large intestine and, attached to that junction is a large, blind sac, the cecum. The cecum is a fermentation chamber in which bacteria and protozoa digest some of the plant fiber. In order to harvest the bacteria, the hare has to reingest the material produced in the cecum and pass it through the stomach and small intestine. Therefore, hares and their relatives eat cecal pellets.

large intestine and out. Material of lower fiber content moves from the small intestine into the cecum for processing and, later, continues down the large intestine and exits the gastrointestinal tract as softer, mushy, **cecal pellets**. The hare can sense the difference in consistency of these two different pellets; it has an educated anal sphincter. The fecal pellets are voided; the cecal pellets never even hit the ground. The hare eats the cecal pellets and its stomach digests the microorganisms. The small intestine absorbs the B vitamins and other nutrients released from digested microbes.

Therefore, hares have a different set of anatomical, physiological and behavioral adaptations to accomplish approximately the same thing that moose and other ungulates do. I say "approximately" because the cecal digestive system is not as refined as the ruminant system. It requires higher quality plant material. That is, hares do not do well on extremely high fiber material or on material with very low protein content.

In general, snowshoe hares tend to feed on herbaceous plants in the summer and, in the fall, switch over to woody browse as herbaceous plants become harder to find or disappear. Because woody foods have high fiber, snowshoe hares will work hard for herbaceous material in winter. Winter feeding certainly includes browsing above snow level but also consists of digging craters in the snow to get down to herbaceous plants. Hares crater for arctic lupine, *Dryas* and wild sweet pea, among other plants.[38] Craters average 580 cm² (90 in²) but some are up to 2600 cm² (400 in²). The digging is done by the forepaws and the snow is swept between the hind-legs. As snow depth increases, hares dig smaller craters, a response that is opposite to how caribou respond to snow depth.

What other foods do hares eat in winter? John Bryant and Peggy Kuropat looked at this problem but did not use any of the three methods for examining an animal's diet that I mentioned above. The three were: watch what they eat, see what is in the stomach or see what comes out the back end. Instead, they performed feeding trials. Hares were kept in an enclosure and provided with weighed amounts of a variety of woody species for forage. After several days the piles were reweighed to see how much of each forage species was eaten. In this method they didn't have to watch the hares eat.

Seven plant species were used in the trial. From the most highly preferred to the least preferred, the species were: willow, aspen, larch, dwarf birch, white spruce, black spruce, alder.[39] Each of these species synthesize secondary metabolites. These chemicals deter feeding to an extent and, for snowshoe hares, willow offers the least deterrent and alder the most. Earlier, I mentioned that, at least initially, the new growth of willows is quite palatable to hares, but after browsing, the remaining twigs or newly sprouted twigs become highly unpalatable. These twigs are synthesizing lots of secondary metabolites to fend off further browsing. Branches higher up, out of the hare's reach, remain palatable, as demonstrated in additional feeding trials. These higher branches simply have lower concentrations of the feeding deterrents.

There are several interesting twists to feeding deterrence in snowshoe hares. First, the juvenile twigs of high latitude (Maine) paper birch and quaking aspen are more strongly rejected than are those of the same species from lower latitude (Connecticut).[40] The higher latitude twigs are more highly defended, perhaps because they have longer dormant periods and cannot afford to lose critical growth to herbivores. Also, longer winters mean longer reliance on woody browse because herbaceous plants are not available. Second, juvenile twigs of the same species in Alaska are even more repulsive than those from Maine.[41] Twigs from Alaskan paper birch contained more than three orders of magnitude more defensive chemicals than those from eastern North America. Why? It is most likely that the greater incidence and severity of wildfires in Alaska, as opposed to eastern North America since the Pleistocene, has been the driving force. With more frequent fires, woody plant species have evolved to put a premium on rapid growth to maturity and simply can't afford to lose all of last year's growth to herbivores.

One of the most fascinating aspects of snowshoe hare biology is their population cycles. In interior Alaska, the lake states of Minnesota, Wisconsin and Michigan and throughout Canada except for southern British Columbia, these hares exhibit an eight to eleven-year cycle of abundance. At low points in the population cycle, it wouldn't be worth your time to hunt them. During population highs, hunting hares for meat would be more efficient than hunting moose with hare population densities of over 600 hares per 100 hectares (2.4 per acre) in Alaska and 1100/100 hectares (4.5 per acre) in Alberta.[42]

What drives these population cycles? One possibility is that predators control and synchronize the cycle. Fur records from the Hudson's Bay Trading Company in the 19th century show

that receipts of snowshoe hare pelts from trappers exhibited approximately a ten-year cycle of abundance and scarcity. Abundance of lynx pelts received at the trading posts also showed the same cycle but often offset by a year or two (Figure 4.5). One supposition is that lynx regulate hare numbers by increasing their litter sizes and, therefore, increasing their predation on hares as hares became abundant. There is little doubt that lynx and other predators hit hares hard at population highs and on the downswing and probably influence the lows to which hare populations dive.

However, several lines of evidence indicate that predators aren't actually driving the cycle. First, there is the introduction of snowshoe hares to Newfoundland in the 1860s. Before introduction, Newfoundland had populations of lynx, red foxes and arctic hare, all with relatively stable populations. Snowshoes increased, stabilized at high population densities for

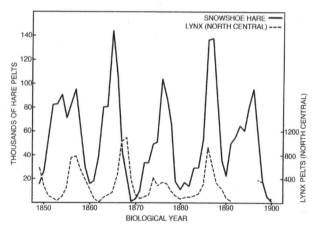

Figure 4.5: Population cycles of snowshoe hare and Canada lynx as recorded from numbers of furs purchased by the Hudson's Bay Trading Company in north-central Canada. Note that hare abundance peaks about every ten years. Lynx reach peak abundance with or a year after peaks in hare abundance.

Figure 4.6: Great horned owl capturing a snowshoe hare.

several decades and then began to cycle at about ten-year intervals. If predators drive the cycle, one wonders why tundra hares didn't exhibit cycles too. After snowshoe hares began cycling so, too, did lynx. Second, snowshoe hares were also introduced to an island in the Gulf of St. Lawrence on which no lynx or other mammalian predators existed. After awhile, the hare's numbers began to cycle! Therefore, predators don't seem to drive hare cycles.

The most likely scenario for snowshoe hare cycles involves the chemical defenses of their woody browse species. At low population levels, snowshoe hares browse relatively few of the potentially available willows and aspens. Instead of continuing to browse the same few plants, they move on to previously unbrowsed material. Thus, they rarely encounter the high levels of secondary metabolites induced by their previous browsing. These hares are in good condition with low parasite loads. At high population densities, preferred foods are scarce, have already been browsed and have high concentrations of feeding deterrent chemicals. Other potential foods, especially in winter, are even lower in preference and even more heavily defended chemically. During highs, hares are in poorer

physiological condition, have higher parasite loads and may be spending most of their time defending territories instead of feeding and mating. After a population crash, willows, aspen and birch have six or seven years of respite to grow rapidly without investing, metabolically, in chemical defense.

I mentioned lynx as a major predator of snowshoe hares. There are many more. Some avian predators are great horned owl (Figure 4.6), barred owl, goshawk, red-tailed hawk and gray jay. Other mammalian predators include short-tailed weasel, long-tail weasel, mink, red fox, coyote, wolf, bobcat (outside Alaska), Arctic ground squirrel and red squirrel.

These last two species may be a bit of a surprise since almost everyone would classify them as herbivores. In a study of newborn snowshoe hares in western Yukon, 254 newborns (**leverets**) were radio-tagged and followed through the summer. A total of 170 mortalities occurred the first month. Of these, 20% were found cached in red squirrel middens; another 27% were found cached in spruce trees, probably victims of red squirrels. Another 11% of the mortalities were found in the burrows of ground squirrels.[43] Of all newborns studied, 70% died in the first five days of life.

Reproductive potential in snowshoe hares must be impressive to make up for such losses. First mating of the year occurs around mid-April; gestation takes 36 days. The litter of three to five leverets are highly precocial, born fully furred, mobile and with eyes open within the first hour. These newborns differ markedly from newborn rabbits (genus *Sylvilagus*), which are hairless, immobile and blind (altrical). Littermates huddle together and remain motionless all day for the first 3-5 days. The mother visits only once each 24 hours, near midnight, to nurse the young.

Parental care by the mother is variable. The natal sites of five different litters were observed in the Yukon. Mothers were never observed at three of the sites. At the other two, females remained within 30 m and vigorously chased red squirrels and ground squirrels from the area.[44]

Immediately after dropping the litter, the female ovulates and breeds again. In many years females have three litters. Leverets weigh 40-60 g (2 ounces) at birth and at weaning 28 days later, weigh 425-480 g (9 ounces). Hares begin feeding on vegetation 7 days after birth.[45]

Tularemia is an important disease of snowshoe hares and one that can be transmitted to humans. The pathogen is a bacterium, *Francisella tularensis*. Other animals known to contract tularemia include muskrats, voles, red and arctic foxes, coyotes, beavers, bobcats, dogs, cats, sheep, horses, mule deer and bears. The presence of this bacterium in natural waters undoubtedly accounts for its occurrence in muskrats, beaver and, perhaps, other species as well. Probably a more typical means of transmission is by biting insects such as deer flies, rabbit lice and ticks.

Humans contract the disease by insect bite, drinking contaminated water or by handling infected carcasses or eating improperly cooked meat of those carcasses. Trappers of muskrats and hunters of snowshoe hares should, ideally, skin and clean these animals while wearing rubber gloves. Getting contaminated blood in cuts on your hands will, likely, transmit the disease. Symptoms in humans include weakness, headache, vomiting and ulcerated raised areas of the skin at the point of infection. These symptoms

may progress to pneumonia or fatal septicemia if left untreated with antibiotics. Ticks are present on hares only from May through September; the disease disappears from hares from October through April.[23]

Lynx

The Canada lynx, *Lynx canadensis*, is the only wild cat native to Alaska. Once in a while there are sightings of mountain lions in eastern Alaska, the Yukon, and Northwest Territories, but these cats are in their juvenile dispersal phase and may not live very long in the Far North. A mountain lion spotted on the Mackenzie River delta on the Beaufort Sea appeared to have its ears frozen off. Lynx are slightly larger than their bobcat cousins, have shorter tails, larger paws, and ears with black tufts on the tips.

Lynx occur widely in Alaska except for the Aleutians, the Kodiak Island group, and some of the islands in southeastern and south-central Alaska. In North America, these cats are found all across the boreal forest from Alaska to Newfoundland. The northern tier of states in the U.S.A. (Maine, New York, Michigan, Minnesota, Wisconsin) have lynx especially during population highs. Parts of the Rocky Mountain states are also lynx country. In Eurasia, *Lynx lynx*, a closely related species, occurs from eastern Siberia across the boreal forests to the Baltic Sea and Scandinavia. Populations of the Eurasian lynx also are found in the Pyrenees, Alps, Turkey, China, and Sakhalin Island.

Adult lynx are solitary except that females are usually accompanied by their young of the year through most of the winter. Home ranges, 11-300 km² (4.2-116 mi²), vary depending on prey abundance. Adults scent-mark areas they habituate with urine and feces deposited in prominent places such as rocks or logs. Kittens bury their urine and feces if possible. Mating in Alaska takes place from March into April; gestation takes 60-70 days. One to five kittens are born in a den under a tangle of roots or logs, in a tree stump or other protected location. Their eyes open after 30 days, and they are weaned after two to three months. Kittens have a pattern of dark stripes running along the back and sides, in contrast to the indistinctly spotted pelage of the adults.

As I mentioned in the previous section, lynx populations cycle along with the cycles of their principal prey, snowshoe hares. Actually, lynx populations usually peak a year after the hare peak. Abundance of hares allows lynx to successfully rear many offspring in the year of the hare high, and these animals are still around the next year when hares start their crash. When faced with a shortage of their favorite prey, lynx do not stubbornly stick only to hares as their prey. Although they have the flexibility to switch to alternative prey, many of them still starve. A classic example of prey switching involves lynx in Newfoundland. Before humans introduced snowshoe hares onto the island of Newfoundland, lynx preyed principally on arctic hare, a non-cycling prey. Lynx populations were relatively stable. Once snowshoe hare populations were well established, lynx targeted them. However, unlike arctic hares, snowshoe hares exhibited population cycles. What happened during a hare low? The "excess" lynx got hungry and went looking for alternative prey. They began to target newborn caribou calves, a prey they had never exploited before. So the overall result of introduction of

snowshoe hares was that the previously stable lynx population began to exhibit cycles, and so did the caribou.[46] This sort of evidence plus the increased incidence of grouse in lynx diets during hare lows fuels the scientific debate about whether hare cycles cause grouse cycles.

Alaskan lynx also seem to be adept at capturing and killing both caribou calves (young of the year) and adults. Bob Stephenson describes 12 incidents of lynx predation on caribou, including several in which the observer actually saw the lynx riding on the back of the caribou. All these successful attacks occurred from November through March when caribou generally occupy boreal forest habitat rather than open tundra.[47]

Lynx employ several hunting strategies. Their mobile strategy consists of moving across the landscape until prey flushes, then pursuing. A stationary strategy involves sitting or lying in one place for long periods until prey is spotted. An intermediate approach, moving slowly through the country and stopping often to look for prey, has also been reported.[48] A listing of lynx prey from the Kenai Peninsula includes snowshoe hare, grouse, red squirrel, vole, shrew, mallard, gull, salmon, porcupine and ermine. Road-killed carcasses of moose provide sustenance for lynx, and many have been observed feeding on carcasses in spite of heavy traffic. Domestic rabbits, chickens, ducks, and turkeys have been taken from Kenai Peninsula yards, but most of these incidents could have been prevented by proper animal husbandry. A lynx seized a house cat in Kasilof, but the family dog gave chase and the lynx dropped the cat. In another incident a lynx grabbed a domestic duck, but the property owner pulled the duck out of the lynx's mouth.

There are several reports of lynx traveling and hunting together. Three lynx, two adults and a juvenile about a third of adult body size, were observed on a talus slope in Glacier Park, Montana. While one adult and the juvenile remained still and partially concealed at the bottom of the slope, the other circled above and then trotted down the slope in plain view of hoary marmots and ground squirrels. The "solo" lynx chased a squirrel and it darted toward and was captured by the other adult. All three shared the ground squirrel.[49]

An interesting twist to lynx life history in the Far North is the recent rapid expansion in geographic range of coyotes in North America. The first (recent) record of coyotes in southeast Alaska dates from 1889; coyotes arrived in south-central Alaska in the 1920s. By 1925 coyotes were established on the Kenai Peninsula. Thus, coyotes and lynx probably have a very short history of co-occurrence in boreal forests and may at times compete for limited resources.

The most obvious potentially limiting resource is snowshoe hare prey during a hare population low. It is clear that lynx rely heavily on snowshoe hares as prey; their population numbers rise and fall depending, ultimately, on hare availability. What about coyotes? How much do they depend on snowshoe hares? Coyotes were studied in Alberta during a hare population low and hares made up about 3% of the diet. Carrion was the "big ticket" item, accounting for about half the total intake, with small rodents making up about 20%.[50] Coyote studies in Missouri and Utah found coyotes responding to increased hare density by taking more hares.

Other studies of coyote and lynx feeding in the sub-arctic indicate that both species prey significantly upon hares and, therefore, may compete for prey. Lynx and coyotes on the Kenai Peninsula, south-central Alaska, have a significant diet overlap although there are some differences in what areas these two predators use.[48]

Lynx and coyotes are similar in size (8-18 kg for lynx, 10-15 kg for coyotes) but lynx have much larger feet. Lynx exhibit lower foot-loading and, therefore, are able to walk on snow without sinking in as deep as coyotes do. This difference seems to explain why lynx favor areas of higher elevation and deeper and softer snow. Coyotes are found at lower elevation, tend to walk on trails and prefer areas with shallower snow. Both predators hunt mainly snowshoe hares; coyotes tend to ambush them, but lynx are also equipped to chase them.[51]

Lynx and red fox occur together across most, if not all, of lynx range in North America. The two species share a list of common prey including snowshoe hares, grouse, voles, and red squirrels. Some differences in preferred habitat may allow these two species to coexist: foxes tend to hunt more open meadows and river banks while lynx seem to hunt more in the forest. In Alaska, lynx kill and eat red foxes, especially when hares are scarce.[47]

Red fox

The red fox, *Vulpes vulpes*, is arguably the most successful small mammal predator on the planet. Certainly, it has the largest geographic range of all members of the carnivore order. Red foxes occur all across Eurasia from eastern Siberia to Scandinavia and England. In North

America they occur from Florida to the high arctic islands of Canada. In Alaska, red foxes are found in the boreal forest, alpine and arctic tundra and in some parts of southeast. It is native to Kodiak Island but its presence on many other islands in Alaska is the result of introductions.

What is the place of the red fox in the ecological grand scheme of things? There are three basic life styles in the Canidae (dog family). Wolves are a large (about 45 kg or 100 pounds), social predator that, although it may occasionally hunt alone, typically hunts in a pack. Their cooperative efforts allow them to pull down prey that may outweigh them, individually, 20 to 1. Foxes, about 7 kg (15 pounds), are small, solitary, highly specialized predators of small prey. The largest prey red foxes tackle are jackrabbits, which weigh only about 60-70% of the fox's weight. Coyotes represent the third canid life style in North America. They are intermediate in size, about 11-22 kg (25-50 pounds), and can take down large prey up to four times their individual body weights by hunting cooperatively. They aren't as proficient at large game as are wolves. Coyotes have the behavioral flexibility to hunt individually for small prey including some of the same species relied upon by red foxes. But, again, coyotes aren't as proficient at vole hunting as are red foxes.

One of the trademarks of red fox behavior is the pounce or lunge. Our golden retriever, Murphy, is exactly the same color as a red fox and loves to pounce to retrieve a ball thrown in the snow. His individual pounces cover maybe 3 m (10 feet) but he has to have a run at it. Coyotes pounce on mice and voles, covering up to 2.5 m (8 feet) from a standing start. Red foxes, however, are the masters. A red fox was observed to pounce, from a standing start, a horizontal distance of 5.2 m (17 feet) and land on the mouse![52] How is it possible for foxes to make such prodigious leaps? That is, what governs the distance a projectile (in this case the fox) travels? The variables are: angle of the launch, weight of the projectile, force applied to the projectile, length of time the force is applied, and, of course, gravity. The maximum distance traveled is achieved with a launch angle of 45°.

Analysis of video recordings of very long pounces and calculation of the launch angles used by the foxes showed that foxes launch at an angle of 40±6°, very close to the theoretical optimum (Figure 4.7). [53] For shorter leaps a lower angle is typically used. However, if the fox is pouncing in crusted snow, it uses a high angle of launch, achieves a lot of height, and is able to break through the crust to get at the prey. In winter, foxes successfully capture voles in snow depths of at least 0.6 m (2 feet) by pouncing.

What about the weight of the fox projectile? The red fox exhibits several adaptations that reduce weight. It isn't simply a matter of small stature. What about general build? Large red foxes (males from England) and small coyotes (females from the American Southwest) are almost exactly the same length. The coyotes weigh 12±1.4 kg (26.5±3.1 pounds); the foxes weigh 6.9±0.2 kg (15.2±0.4 pounds). How do foxes achieve this weight reduction as compared to coyotes? For one, stomach sizes differ. The maximum meal size eaten by a predator is a rough measure of stomach size. Foxes can eat up to 10% of their body weight at a sitting; wolves can eat 20% of their body weight. That means a fox stomach is proportionally smaller than a wolf stomach; coyotes are undoubtedly

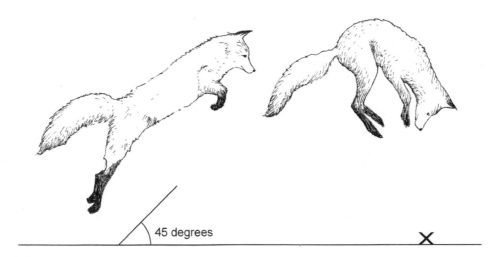

45 degrees

X

Figure 4.7: Red fox pounce. The launch (left) angle that achieves the greatest distance is approximately 45°. As the fox nears its landing (right), it aims all four feet at the target represented here by an X. Redrawn from Henry (1996).

in between. The bones of foxes are slender and weigh 30% less than predicted for an animal its weight, while those of the coyote weigh about what they should according to the equations for body scaling.

Red foxes prey on a wide variety of mammals, birds and insects. Small mammals including voles, mice, shrews, snowshoe hares, muskrats, red squirrels, ground squirrels, porcupines, marmots, pikas and beavers fall prey to foxes in Alaska. Bird prey include ruffed grouse, spruce grouse, ptarmigan, snow bunting, black-capped and boreal chickadees, common snipe, white-crowned sparrow, gray jay, goshawk, mallard, scaup and magpie. Of course, the complete list is much longer and would ultimately include prey from the red fox's entire geographic range. I watched a red fox capture a Pacific staghorn sculpin from the surf along the southeastern Bering Sea coast, run up the beach and cache it in a sand dune. Add this fish to the list.

In years of high snowshoe hare population density, hares dominate fox diets in inte-

rior Alaska. During population lows, voles are extremely important. Since snowshoe hares rarely occur above tree line, red foxes from alpine tundra habitats in Alaska rely on alternative prey, including significant amounts of arctic ground squirrel. In the upper Susitna River drainage of south-central Alaska, an area of subalpine forest and alpine tundra, foxes prey on arctic ground squirrels, red-backed voles, meadow voles, tundra voles, singing voles and bog lemmings. Remains of hoary marmot, porcupine, beaver, pika and goshawk were also found at den sites.

There are clear indications that foxes have serious effects on the abundance of their prey. Introduced foxes have extirpated seabird breeding colonies on many islands in Alaska and elsewhere (see below). Natural reductions of red fox populations in Norway were paralleled by increases in willow ptarmigan, black grouse, mountain hare, and capercaillie (another grouse species).[55]

When a fox approaches a hare across open country with short vegetation, the hare will stand on its hind legs and face the fox as if to say, "I see you!" Clearly, the element of surprise is gone. European hares can easily outrun red foxes and could just as easily have taken off running at first sight of the fox. This behavioral signaling saves both the hare and the fox the wasted energy of the chase and the escape.[56] Perhaps the same is true for snowshoe hare-fox interactions.

Since foxes have small stomachs, they cache, or hoard, excess food when hunting is good. In the animal world there are two kinds of hoarding. In **scatter hoarding**, the animal caches small amounts of food in locations dispersed over a large area. **Larder hoarding** is the storing of many prey or food items in one or a few locations. In some species of birds and mammals, only a single type of hoarding is used. Red foxes typically exhibit scatter hoarding.

At the start of the day's hunting, a fox may consume the first several mice or voles, become satiated, but keep hunting. Prey captured after satiation are cached. Typically, a fox will scatter hoard additional prey as he/she continues to hunt. Scatter hoards are usually used within a week of the hoarding activity. The fox may remember the exact location, but, just in case, he/she doesn't bury the hoard so deep that it can't be found by scent. The trick is to hide it deep enough to protect it from other scavengers but not so deep as to lose track of it. The caching is stereotyped behavior. The fox digs a narrow hole about 10 cm (4 inches) deep, deposits the meat, covers it with dirt, tamps the dirt with its nose, and covers the dirt with twigs and leaves. Burial is necessary to reduce losses to other mammal scavengers; camouflaging is essential to reduce losses to bird scavengers such as magpies, gray jays, and ravens.[52]

There must be times when the hunting is just fabulous and the prey are so localized that scattering caches would use up valuable hunting time. For example, red foxes living on islands with seabird colonies have easy hunting and a superabundance of food, at least seasonally. The menu includes adults on roosts or in burrows, eggs, and chicks. Instead of digging hundreds of individual cache holes, why not just dig one or a few? Under these special circumstances, red foxes exhibit larder hoarding. Eleven larder hoards of red foxes were unearthed on a seabird island in Newfoundland. The average number of dead birds per larder hoard was 94; several had as few as six birds but one contained 320 and another 396. Some hoards contained five different prey species.[57] The large number of prey in larder hoards is, in my mind, exactly analogous to humans filling freezers for the winter. The conditions that allow red foxes to larder hoard are undoubtedly pretty specialized. I imagine competing mammalian scavengers must be at low population densities for this technique to work. But red foxes have the behavioral flexibility to employ both types of hoarding.

Males establish territories within which one to four females reside. There seems to be little, if any, overlap of adjacent male territories. The male patrols his territory, looking and listening for intruders. Advertising the territory includes scent marking with feces, urine and, possibly, secretions from glands between the toes. Advertising also involves vocalizations.[58]

The dens of red foxes are typically oriented with the opening facing from southeast to west. North-facing dens are not common. In tundra habitat dens may be developed from ground squirrel dens by additional excavation. Some of these fox den sites may be lost to wolves who convert them to their own use.[59] The dens of both red and arctic foxes typically have multiple entrances. In the upper Susitna, active dens have an average of 19 openings each and one den had 53 separate openings.[54] Each year the resident female undoubtedly contributes to the effort. Large dens with dozens of openings are thought to be hundreds of years old.

The denning season in red foxes can be divided into three phases. First is a **pre-emergence** period during which pups are present but remain in the den. Second is a **confined use** period in which pups are active above-ground but stay close to the den. Third is a **dispersed use** period in which pups may range far from the den and may even use several dens. In the Susitna River study, the pre-emergence period lasted from early May, when pups are born, to mid-June; confined use lasted from mid-June to mid-August; dispersed use lasted from mid-August to early October. Whelping of pups in low-altitude boreal forest near Fairbanks and Delta Junction occurs in early April.

After pups are born, mothers (vixens) remain in or near the natal den for 7-10 days and nights. After that, the female begins to make short forays away from the den that initially last for less than an hour. By three weeks after birth, the female will spend as much time out of the den as within, often lounging or sunning nearby. At four weeks the pups begin to eat meat and the vixen forages most of the day, returning with food frequently at night. After the pups are out of the den, foxes continue to use them. Based on locating radio-collared foxes and observing tracks in the snow around dens, we know that foxes use dens occasionally through the winter, especially during bouts of bad weather.

No discussion of red foxes would be complete without some mention of rabies. The red fox is responsible for the continuation and spread of rabies in northern and eastern North America, northern Asia, and Europe. The gray fox is also involved in rabies. In the Arctic, the arctic fox is the reservoir species.

The causative agent of rabies is a rhabdovirus; the disease is usually transmitted by bite. The virus doesn't normally penetrate intact skin but, apparently, can occasionally pass mucous membranes. Infection by ingestion is also possible. Air-borne infection only occurs under exceptional conditions such as inside a cave filled with rabid bats. After a bite, viral replication occurs in the muscle cells surrounding the point of entry. From there, viruses move into the peripheral nervous system and are transported to the central nervous system. Because they are within the neurons, the viruses do not trigger the animal's normal immune responses. Infection of spinal nerves and brain is quickly followed by spread of the virus back to the peripheral nerves. In late stages of infection, virus can be found in a variety of organs, including the salivary glands.[60]

It is via salivary secretions into a bite wound that rabies is passed on. After infection, a fox will start to show symptoms within 4-181 days. With such variation in incubation period, it is no wonder that the disease has been so hard to study and control. Once symptoms are exhibited, the fox only has from 1 to 17 days to live. Symptoms include loss of appetite, sudden aggressiveness, hyperactivity, and tremor.

Convulsions and paralysis are common late in the disease.

Rabies is almost always fatal to foxes. As I write this (February 2002), a rabies epidemic is under way in northern Alaska. In the last five months the state virology laboratory has verified 81 positive tests for rabies in rural Alaska: 15 human exposures, 44 rabid arctic foxes, 18 red foxes and four dogs. According to Don Ritter, state epidemiologist, epidemics occur every three to five years and correspond to fox population highs.

Sometimes our view on the benefits and/or harms of a particular species introduction change over time or as new information becomes available. The introduction of foxes into Alaskan islands is a good example. Starting in 1750, Russians introduced arctic foxes onto islands in the Aleutian chain including Attu, Atka, and the Rat Islands. The objective was to enhance the production of furs from their far eastern territories. After the purchase of Alaska by the United States, fox introductions continued. Foxes were introduced to islands near Kodiak in 1867 and the Shumigan Islands in 1880. The Semidi Islands and many islands in Prince William Sound were stocked, as well as many islands in Southeast Alaska. The U.S. Government began leasing Alaskan islands for fur farming in 1882. Of course, the impetus for all these introductions was the production of furs for the fur trade. Foxes, either arctic or red, were introduced to a total of 455 islands in Alaska that we know of. Foxes are still present on 46 of those islands.

The history of fur farming in Alaska has been one of boom and bust and of havoc to island bird populations. At its inception, fox introductions were viewed almost solely in the context of economic development. In that view, indigenous breeding colonies of seabirds were considered "feed" for the foxes. In case the local feed might prove inadequate to keep the foxes well fed, forage species were introduced along with the foxes. Norway rats, house mice, European hares, snowshoe hares, arctic hares, hoary marmots, voles, and arctic ground squirrels were all introduced, usually to provide food for introduced foxes. But foxes, Norway rats and ground squirrels all prey on birds. As early as 1811, Aleuts began complaining to the Russians that the foxes were depleting the bird populations they relied upon for skins and feathers for clothing. Burrow or surface nesting birds including tufted puffins, gulls and ducks were hard hit, but even cliff nesting birds are, to an extent, vulnerable. Local populations of birds, including Cassin's auklet, ancient murrelet, storm-petrel, northern fulmar, whiskered auklet and crested auklet were eliminated by introduced foxes. Rock ptarmigan were eliminated from six islands after fox introductions.[61]

What happened to the foxes on all those islands? First, the bottom fell out of the fox fur market in the Great Depression; most fur farmers gave up. Once foxes on islands in southeast Alaska weren't being actively fed by the farmers, they simply couldn't find enough to eat in the forest and eventually died out. Brown bears and river otters may have outcompeted or actually killed off foxes on many of the islands. On some islands, foxes ate all the available food (seabirds) and starved. A tsunami in 1946 reportedly swept away all the foxes on several small islands in the eastern Aleutians. Finally, the U.S. Fish and Wildlife Service has conducted an eradication program on several islands that now constitute National Wildlife Refuges. The first target was Amchitka Island, where Aleutian Island Canada geese once sustained breeding colonies. In 1949, when eradication began, the Aleutian subspecies was endangered and bred on only a single small island, Buldir Island.

So far, foxes have been eradicated from 21 islands. Trapping was the main method used but a biological control agent, the red fox itself, was used to eliminate arctic foxes on two Aleutian islands. The U.S. Fish and Wildlife Service introduced two sterilized red foxes on one island and within several years, the arctic foxes were gone.[62] Eventually, the red foxes will die of old age and the islands should remain fox-free. In a later chapter I will return to the competitive interactions between red and arctic foxes.

Red squirrel

Tree squirrels appear to have evolved in North America and later spread to Eurasia, South America, and Africa. These specialized rodents have long, bushy tails used for balance, steering during leaps, thermoregulation and behavioral signaling. The eyes are large, wide-set on the head and capable of range finding.

Tree squirrels have both rod and cone receptor cells in their retinas but studies of the spectral absorbance of these cone cells and behavioral discrimination tests indicate that there are only two types of cones, unlike the human situation of three cone types, each with its own spectral sensitivity. What this means is that tree squirrels, probably including the red squirrel, have the retinal mechanisms for at least limited color vision.[63] If their retinas were in humans we

would refer to those humans as deficient with respect to color vision. In other words, our best guess is that tree squirrels are probably partially color blind in a way similar to human red-green color blindness. Until we can get squirrels to tell us what number they see on the Ishihara color blindness charts, we won't be certain.

The red squirrel, *Tamiasciurus hudsonicus*, has a huge geographic range in North America. Its northern limit is the maximum northern extent of tree line across Alaska and Canada. To the south, it occurs in the Rocky Mountain states south to Arizona and New Mexico, the Appalachains south to North Carolina and Tennessee and the Great Lakes states. In the west, red squirrels are found on Vancouver Island and the eastern side of the Cascades in British Columbia, Washington and Oregon. The primary habitat across its range is coniferous forest, but in the southeastern states it occupies mixed deciduous and coniferous forests.

A very closely related species, the Douglas squirrel, occurs on the western slopes of the Cascades. Douglas squirrels and red squirrels have similar calls, territorial behaviors, and caching behavior. *Tamiasciurus douglasii* differs in having an orange or yellow eye ring and an orange underbelly instead of white as in the red squirrel. Red squirrels are larger, have larger jaw muscles, better muscle attachment to the skull (saggital crest on top of skull) and have jaws that exert more force in chewing than Douglas squirrels.

These latter three features in red squirrels make them better adapted at opening the hard cones of conifers that are fire-adapted.[64] Lodgepole pine east of the Cascades have **serotinous** cones that remain closed and retain their seeds until after a fire. In Alaska, black spruce cones are similar. Fire is not a common feature of the western Cascades because of the rainfall. Consequently, conifers there, including lodgepole pine, do not have the tough cone structure and don't require as much effort to open them.

Red squirrels are highly territorial and defend their territories from adjacent males and females without regard to gender. Territories are roughly circular with no overlap between adjacent territories. The resident squirrel announces his/her ownership with a chatter call. A bark call is an aggressive call used against intruders, even humans.

Red squirrels in the interior depend mainly on spruce cones as a source of food (Figure 3.4). Every summer they harvest cones and store them in caches for future use. These caches or hoards are usually at traditional feeding sites. As squirrels open spruce cones, discard the cone bracts and eat the seeds, they slowly build a pile of debris, a **midden**. Squirrel middens on the forest floor often amount to a mound heaped over several entrances to an underground storage area. Middens of 1 m diameter are common in the interior.

Red squirrels exhibit larder hoarding. Hoards beneath middens in the Bonanza Creek Experimental Forest near Fairbanks contain thousands of stored cones. It's been estimated that red squirrels normally harvest 12,000-16,000 cones a year.[65] The Bonanza Creek study was conducted in a two-year period of cone production failure. In the first year of a failure, many of the stored cones from the previous year are eaten, but squirrels maintained on old cones rapidly lose weight. After the first winter following the cone crop failure, the study population was reduced by 67%. In the absence of new cones, squirrels eat mainly mushrooms in the summer and switch to spruce buds in the winter. Squirrels cache mushrooms in the branches of white spruce in the summer for use in winter. Squirrels occasionally eat *Amanita muscaria*; apparently red squirrels can handle the toxins in *Amanita,* at least in small amounts.

In the spring and early summer, red squirrels add animals to their diets as they can. I earlier described red squirrel predation on the young of snowshoe hares. In addition, they take bird eggs, chicks from their nests and are able to capture grouse chicks that are following their mother through the woods.

Reproductive season begins with courtship behavior and, in interior Alaska, starts around mid-April. Males leave their territories and enter those of females. This is the time you can see squirrels chasing each other over the forest floor, up trees and across roads. In these sprints it is hard to tell who is in the lead and who is doing the chasing. Since the female is receptive to the male for only a single day, a one-day estrus, it is likely that she is doing most of the chasing, trying to repulse the male. Sometimes there are two males in pursuit of (or being pursued by) the same female.

Once mating occurs, males return to their own territories. Gestation takes about 35 days, after which a litter of 1-7 young are born. Each of the altrical young weighs about 7.5 g (0.3 oz.); their eyes do not open for 27-35 days after birth. Juveniles emerge from the nest after 50 days, weighing about 90 g (3 oz).

In the late summer juveniles disperse away from their natal territory, looking to establish their own. In a study in Alberta, most successful juveniles were able to acquire a territory adjacent to their natal territory; a few actually took control of their natal territory.[66] Unlike the situation in many ground-dwelling squirrels, both male and female juvenile red squirrels disperse, and they tend to travel about equal distances from the natal territory to establish their own "digs." It is essential for a juvenile to establish or occupy a territory. Vacant territories typically have a hoard and midden already in place. Without the hoard the new occupant has little or no chance of surviving the winter.

Nests of red squirrels are of two types. Aerial nests are built in trees either in a cavity lined with vegetation or in the form of more exposed spherical nests of twigs, lichens, and other vegetation. In interior Alaska, underground nests are common; squirrels spend time underground during periods of severe cold. These underground nests are contiguous with their hoards.

Red squirrel densities are highly variable depending on the habitat. Populations of 7-8/ hectare (17-20/ acre) have been reported, but 1-2/ hectare is more typical of interior Alaska. Obviously, cone crops are important determinants of population densities. So also are forestry practices. Clear-cutting eliminates red squirrel territories; thinning of spruce stands reduces red squirrel populations and results in larger territory sizes for those that remain.[67] Another factor that may affect population density is prey switching associated with the snowshoe hare cycle. In Alberta, simultaneous declines in numbers of red squirrels, flying squirrels and Franklin ground squirrels two years after a hare population crash were attributed to predator switching.[68]

Northern flying squirrel

Many people are quite surprised to learn that the northern flying squirrel, *Glaucomys sabrinus*, is present in Alaska. Actually, it is probably as common as the red squirrel. The red squirrel is a diurnally active species, and the flying squirrel is nocturnal. So, if you don't spend much time in the woods at dusk and dawn, you may not have noticed these interesting creatures. Most observations of flying squirrels in the interior are made around bird feeders next to homes in the woods.

Some features of flying squirrels that suit them to their life style include huge eyes, lateral skin folds and dense, flat tails. The eyes are well adapted for night vision. Behind the retina is a reflective layer, the **tapetum lucidum**. This is the feature that is responsible for eye shine in many nocturnal animals. When photons of light pass through the retina without stimulating a receptor cell, the *tapetum* gives those photons one more chance to score a hit on a rod or cone receptor cell and, thereby, generate a signal to the optic nerve and brain. Therefore, the tapetum makes the eyes more sensitive at low light intensity. I haven't found a study of the visual receptor cells and visual pigments of flying squirrels, but it would be a safe guess that the retina is composed almost entirely of rod-receptor cells because they are more sensitive at low light intensity. In other words, this creature probably has no color vision.

One other feature of the eyes of flying squirrels is their lateral position on the head. Human eyes are on the front of the head, pointing in the same direction. We are able, through binocular vision, to achieve depth perception. Surely binocular vision would be a great asset to a species that hurls itself off the top of a tree, glides for considerable distances, and performs braking behavior just before it lands in the target tree. Flying squirrels don't have binocular vision, but they do have behaviors that allow them to compensate and judge distances. A flying squirrel in the top of a tree, preparing to launch on an unfamiliar glide, looks at its target and moves its head from side to side and up and down. By repositioning the head, it is comparing two slightly offset images, thereby generating a three-dimensional picture from two slightly different two-dimensional images. This was the same technique used by photographers to produce pictures for stereoscopes in the early 20th Century. After several leaps to the same target tree, the squirrel doesn't need to triangulate, it simply leaps.

The lateral skin folds, or **patagia**, are gliding membranes connecting the front and hind legs on each side (see Figure 3.6). To better support the outside (distal) edge of the patagium, flying squirrels have evolved an additional wrist bone, the **styliform process**. This extra bone articulates with the fifth metacarpal (pinkie finger) and two wrist bones. So, by moving the limbs and contracting muscles in the flaps themselves, flying squirrels adjust the speed of the glide, the billow of the patagia, and the glide ratio.[69]

The densely furred, flat tail differs remarkably in appearance from the red squirrel tail. Flying squirrels use the tail for achieving stabilization, lift, drag, attitude adjustments and turning during the glide. The tail accounts for 20-30% of the entire gliding surface. The resulting wing loading is two to three times greater than that found in bats.

In Alaska, flying squirrels glide an average of 19.8 m (62 feet) per glide. A maximum glide distance of over 90 m (294 feet) was reported for a flying squirrel gliding down a mountain slope. Once in flight, a flying squirrel can maneuver around obstacles it can see and has been observed changing direction completely. Maximum glide ratios are about 3:1; these squirrels can move 3 feet horizontally for every foot they drop vertically. Flying squirrels apparently try to avoid gliding in high winds, fog or heavy rain.

One other aspect about the glide is the landing. I mentioned above that, just before touchdown, a flying squirrel performs a braking maneuver. It is highly beneficial for the squirrel to not slam into the target tree headlong. To avoid this, the squirrel, at the last instant, bends its body to bring the hind feet forward and raises its head and tail. These adjustments cause the patagia to form a parachute and cause all four feet to hit the tree almost simultaneously. It also gets the head away from the onrushing tree. Immediately after landing the flying squirrel scampers to the opposite side of the tree trunk.

The point of this very last maneuver, moving to the other side of the tree, has to do with predation. Some of the flying squirrel's most significant predators are aerial. A variety of hawks and owls manage to capture flying squirrels, probably during the glide. The scamper to the other side of the tree is, undoubtedly, to avoid the talons of a pursuing raptorial bird. In the Pacific Northwest, flying squirrels are the principal prey of northern spotted owls, a controversial endangered species of old-growth forests. A pair of spotted owls takes as many as 500 flying squirrels a year. It appears that powered flight has significant advantages over gliding in this owl-eat-squirrel world.

Flying squirrels also fall prey to terrestrial predators. The list includes marten, weasel, lynx, and red fox. A friend, Nancy, made some interesting observations at her bird feeder related to flying squirrel habituation and predator recognition. She and her two golden retrievers often watched a flying squirrel come to her bird feeder at night. She kept the deck light on, and neither the light not the presence of two large dogs less than 2 feet away detered its feeding. One night she decided to see if the squirrel would react to a novel stimulus behind the glass patio door. She slowly raised her trapper's hat made of the fur from a lynx head, complete with fake eyes, to see what the flying squirrel would do. The poor thing leaped 3 feet straight up in the air and, as soon as it came down, immediately launched off the deck. The next night the squirrel was back. So much for short-term memory in flying squirrels.

Nests are of two types: those inside tree cavities and those outside. Cavity nests consist of naturally occurring holes in rotting trees or of cavities excavated by woodpeckers. One nesting tree in British Columbia, a dead hemlock, had a vertical section some 20 feet long that was hollow. In the hollow space was evidence of at least 14 nests constructed one on top of the other. Nesting material was made of finely shredded cedar bark with some 'fluff' made of wool scavenged from a nearby cabin.[70]

Outside nests are roughly spherical in shape, 20-38 cm (8-15 inches) in diameter and composed of twigs, leaves, moss, lichens and are typically lined with shredded bark. There are several reports of females raising their young in these outside nests. It has been supposed that outside nests were not suitable, nor warm enough for these squirrels to use in the winter. However, flying squirrels in Alaska move from cavity nests to outside nests in the fall.[71] These outside nests are often constructed in witch's brooms resulting from conifers infected with spruce broom rust.

My initial notion about the diet of flying squirrels was that it must be about the same as that of red squirrels. That isn't the case at all. Whereas red squirrels can be maintained quite well on a straight diet of white spruce cones, flying squirrels on the same diet rapidly lose weight.[72] Mushrooms and other fungi probably constitute the bulk of the diet in summer; lichens, including *Usnea* and *Alectoria*, are the chief winter food. Although caching of food for the winter hasn't been reported in Alaska, flying squirrels elsewhere cache food. Flying squirrels are thought to raid the mushroom caches of red squirrels. In the spring and early summer, flying squirrels, like red squirrels, take bird eggs and nestlings as well as insects. Berries contribute later in the summer and into fall. Although there is some overlap in the diets of red and flying squirrels, their major foods are different.

After ingestion of fungi, flying squirrels and other rodents digest away the fleshy, spore-bearing part. The spores themselves are usually highly resistant to digestion and pass through the digestive tract intact and viable. Flying squirrel feces contain spores and perhaps nitrogen-fixing bacteria that are spread wherever the squirrel goes (pun intended). When conditions are favorable, these spores germinate and either establish a new fungal colony or fuse with an existing one of the same species. New colonies are, thus, available for mycorrhizal association with the very tree species the flying squirrels require.[73]

In Alaska, northern flying squirrels breed sometime between late March and May. The variability in breeding dates suggests that this species does not synchronize its reproduction strictly to photoperiod. A cold spring can, apparently, put these squirrels off their rhythm. Gestation requires 37-42 days, after which a litter of 1-6 (usually 2-4) young are born. Newborns weigh 5-6 g (1.8-2.1 oz), measure 70 mm (2.7") in length and are completely hairless and unpigmented. Their eyes and ears are shut and their toes are fused together, but they already have the patagia as thin, transparent membranes. After 18 days they can crawl about awkwardly; eyes open on day 32. Young begin to appear outside the nest on day 40 and are weaned by day 60. During this early period the female may make occasional forays away from the nest.

A fascinating story about maternal care in flying squirrels was reported by J. W. Stack.[74] A college forestry class was out trimming trees along a river. One student sawed off a dead limb, revealing a flying squirrel nest with mother and four tiny young. The mother ran up the tree, glided across the river and began searching furiously for an alternative nest site. The student lifted the nest out of the tree trunk and the others gathered around. Then the mother glided back, landed near the students, ran up the pant leg of the student holding the nest, picked up one pup, climbed the nearest tree and launched. After depositing the little one in its new nest, she returned three more times to retrieve all her offspring. In her panic, she climbed the wrong pant leg once but quickly corrected her mistake.

Flying squirrels, like red squirrels, are active all winter; they do not hibernate. Unlike red squirrels, flying squirrels do not defend territories, they tolerate the presence of other flying squirrels and, in winter, huddle in small groups in a single nest. The thermoregulatory advantages to communal nesting were described in Chapter 2.

Forest management with a view to maintaining flying squirrel populations should take into account: 1) squirrel use of spruce trees with witch's brooms for outside nests, 2) the important role flying squirrels play in propagating fungi critical to tree health and 3) the role these squirrels play in the diet of other endangered or economically important (furbearing) species.

Mustelids

The Mustelidae is the weasel family. There are eleven species in North America, and seven of these occur in Alaska. Of these seven, six are found in the boreal forests of the interior. Mustelids are a diverse group of carnivores, but all members have a pair of musk glands, the anal glands, near the base of the tail. In addition, some species have a ventral gland as well. These anal glands produce a musky, stinky, oily secretion similar to but not as powerful as the secretions of skunks.

In interior and northern Alaska there are three species of *Mustela*: the least weasel (*Mustela nivalis*), the ermine (short-tailed weasel; *Mustela erminea*) and the mink (*Mustela vison*). One of the two North American *Martes* occurs in Alaska, the marten, *Martes americana*. The largest terrestrial mustelid in Alaska is the wolverine (*Gulo gulo*), treated in Chapter 8. The other two members of the family are the northern river otter and the sea otter.

Several other mustelids either should be part of the Alaskan fauna or, in fact, once were part of the fauna. The fisher, *Martes pennanti*, is common in the boreal forests of Canada and Siberia but doesn't occur in interior Alaska. This species may still be expanding its range northward since the last glacial retreat. More likely, the fisher simply doesn't have the prey it needs, larger squirrels, to subsist in the Alaskan boreal forest. The badger was undoubtedly present in Alaska during periods in which grasslands or steppe tundra covered much of the interior. Fossil remains of badgers have been found in Pleistocene deposits near Dawson City in the Yukon, just across the Alaskan border. But, currently, it occurs only as Far North as northern British Columbia.

Carolyn King[75], in her excellent book on weasels, contends that "the origin of northern weasels as Pleistocene rodent specialists is the key to understanding everything about them." Their anatomy, ecology and behavior all fine-tune them to take advantage of unstable populations of rodents in a harsh environment. Some of their adaptations include flexibility, long necks, head and visual modifications.

Weasels are extremely flexible; a weasel can turn around in a burrow and stick its head out before the tail is all the way in! They accomplish this by walking back over their own hind end. The skull is the widest part of the skeleton; if it can go down the burrow, the rest of the body can follow. The neck is long enough to allow weasels to carry prey in the mouth without tripping the animal. Weasels are incredibly strong,

able to carry (and run with) prey twice their own weight.[75]

Weasel ears fit their life style well. External ears lie flat on the head. Huge tympanic cavities in the middle ear help make their hearing among the best in the mammalian world. Eyes are well adapted for vision at low light intensity. As was the case for flying squirrels, weasels have a *tapetum*. During the day, weasels protect the sensitive retina by constricting the iris.

Humans have circular irises. A more efficient design, one that closes tighter, is an iris forming a slit pupil. Weasels have slit pupils similar to those in cats. However, in weasels the slit is horizontal while in cats it is vertical.

As I mentioned, the weasel's body is long and slender, well designed for moving through rodent burrows and ice tunnels. The down side to this shape is that the surface area to volume ratio is high and, therefore, heat loss is high. Consequently, weasels have very high metabolic rates and have huge appetites. The food consumption of captive weasels has been measured. Ermine eat 14-22% of their body weight per day; least weasels eat up to 40% of their body weight per day. In their natural environments food intake is likely to be even higher. They aren't likely to put on much fat under natural conditions. Even if they could, the extra girth would impair their ability to move through prey tunnels.

Although weasels usually hunt alone, cooperative hunting is sometimes exhibited by a female and its young before they disperse. King suggests that a family of weasels on the move would "give the impression of great energy and alarming predatory power." She reports an incident in England of a man being chased by a pack of eleven weasels. The gentleman ran for it, lost his hat and the weasels got the hat.[75]

Another technique to potentially reduce the danger of attacking prey larger than the weasel is psychological warfare. King mentions that stoats are believed to be able to mesmerize rabbits. Some think that a state of near paralysis can be induced either by the weasel's behavior and/or the musky scent of a weasel excited by the hunt. There are reports of "stoated rabbits" that, even in the absence of injuries, escape the weasel only to drop dead later.

No matter how they locate prey, weasels launch their final attack based on visual cues. If the prey "freezes," the weasel may not be able to recognize it as prey. Once the vole, mole or mouse moves, the weasel bounds after it, and delivers a killing bite to the back of the head and neck. Weasels usually attack larger prey by leaping onto the back to get at the back of the neck.

If there is an excess of prey, weasels may cache the surplus. Weasels' killing mechanisms are **innate behavior** patterns, that is, they are on automatic. In a chicken coop or a communal nest of yellow-cheeked voles, a weasel will probably keep killing individuals until there is nothing left moving. Then it may settle down to eat one individual or parts (usually brains first) of several individuals. The rest goes into a food cache. There are many reports of weasel caches of 30-50 individual prey organisms including mice, voles, moles, frogs, lizards and songbirds. Caching occurs in ermine, least weasels, martens and wolverines.

Ermine; *Mustela erminea*—The ermine goes by several common names including short-tailed weasel and stoat. This species has one of the largest geographic distributions of any North American mammal. On this continent ermine are found throughout Alaska and Canada, even into the high arctic islands. They occur in New England southward to Virginia and, in the west, as far south as California and New Mexico. In Eurasia, ermine occur all the way from northern Portugal, Spain, the British Isles and Scandinavia to eastern Siberia, China and the Japanese islands. It is intermediate in both size and tail length between the least weasel and the more temperate long-tailed weasel. Maximum body weights of male ermine, least and long-tailed weasels are 116 g, 55 g and 450 g, respectively. Tail length as a percentage of body length is 30-45%, <25% and 40-70%, respectively. Because of their presence in both alpine and arctic tundra habitats, ermine could be discussed in the section on fauna of the Alaskan tundra. This is one more species that cannot be neatly pigeonholed into a single habitat.

Ermine in the Far North go through a molt in autumn in which brown hair is replaced with white (Figure 4.8). The black tail tip is retained all year and is thought by some to be helpful in avoiding predation. One idea about this is that predators most easily see the black tip and, therefore, focus their attack on the tail. The ermine may lose part of its tail but not its life. Individuals from more temperate, southern populations also go through a fall molt but do not turn white. Of course, it is adaptive for weasels living in snow country to turn white and for those that rarely ever experience snow to remain brown, but how is this all worked out? Are we sure that southern weasels molt at all in the fall? What cues the molting process, temperature or day length?

Figure 4.8: Annual molt cycle in the ermine. See text for discussion of timing of the molt. Redrawn from Feder (1990).

Some of these questions were answered by comparing ermine, some of which were captured in the Fairbanks area and some of which were trapped in coastal Oregon and flown to Alaska. The Oregon ermine remain brown all winter. During shortening days both Alaska and Oregon ermine molted. However, our local ermine molted to white and the Oregon individuals molted to brown. Even weasels held at indoor temperatures molted.[76] Therefore, photoperiod triggers molting and cold temperatures aren't necessary to initiate molting. Neither is temperature, itself, responsible for coat color after the molt.

The molt is influenced by temperature. Studies have shown that warmer temperatures in the spring cause ermine to initiate molting earlier than in cooler temperatures.[77] Also, the fall molt seems to be completed faster in cold temperatures than in warm.[78] Comparing Alaska and Minnesota ermine in their natural locations suggests that Alaskan animals initiate molting at longer day lengths in the fall than those in Minnesota and complete the molt faster, typically in

1-2 weeks.[76] The spring molt is not simply the reverse of the fall molt. In the fall, each weasel gradually becomes paler over the whole body. In spring, a distinct brown patch begins on the head and spreads to the neck, back, and then downward on the body.

My last encounter with an ermine occurred this fall. My friend Alex and I had climbed down from a tree stand just before twilight. An ermine ran out of a brush pile and darted up to us. It scampered off, only to return and jump up on my boot The look in its eyes as it gazed at me seemed to say, "If I could pull this off, I'd eat like a king!"

Mice, voles and lemmings are the preferred items on the menu of Alaskan ermine. When rodents are scarce ermine may also capture and eat shrews, pikas, birds, snowshoe hares, fish and insects. The diet of ermine in New York consists of about 75% rodents and 25% lagomorphs (hares and rabbits).

Several interesting features of weasel reproduction need to be mentioned. First, males have one more bone in the body than females. The

baculum is a bone that stiffens the penis during copulation. Young males have the baculum, but it grows longer and thicker with age. The baculum in an adult male ermine is typically about 23mm (0.9 inches) long. The weight of the baculum increases steadily with age. When not in use, the baculum and associated penis are completely hidden inside the body. This bone occurs in all members of the mammalian order Carnivora including the families of cats, dogs, bears and pinnipeds (seals and sea lions).

A second feature, common in ermine and long-tailed weasels, is delayed implantation, mentioned in the discussion of black bears. After copulation and fertilization (mid- to late summer in Alaska), the embryos develop for about two weeks, at which time they are **blastocysts**, hollow balls of cells, and have entered the uterus. Further development is arrested until the following spring. Once implantation occurs, gestation is completed in 27-28 days. Young are born in May or June in Alaska.[79] Molting can be used as a predictor of birth of offspring in ermine from the Far North. Young are born 22-25 days after the first brown hairs begin to appear on the female's nose!

Least weasel; *Mustela nivalis*- The least weasel has a circumboreal distribution but does not occur as Far North as ermine. In North America least weasels do not occupy the High Canadian Arctic islands but extend into the American Midwest to Nebraska, Iowa, and Arkansas. In the east, they occur in the Appalachians as far south as North Carolina. Least weasels occupy the Mediterranean countries, the Middle East, and eastward to the Korean peninsula.

Least weasels also turn white after an autumn molt. This molt includes the tip of the tail; a winter least weasel is all white. Unlike ermine, least weasels don't exhibit delayed implantation.

Though the smallest of the mammalian order Carnivora, the least weasel is a ferocious hunter. They are adept at climbing trees and will attack birds as large as pigeons, water hens, and grouse. Not all of these encounters turn out well for the weasel. In England a water hen was observed flying with a least weasel hanging on to its throat. The water hen finally dove into a lake, taking the weasel with it.

In the tundra around Barrow, least weasels subsist entirely on lemmings and voles when these rodents are abundant. In years of lemming scarcity, however, weasels diversify their diets if they can. In summers of scarcity, weasels switch to the eggs of sandpipers and Lapland longspurs. Once these birds leave in the autumn, weasels have to fall back on what few lemmings and voles remain. Since lemming populations cycle in the Far North, it is no surprise that least weasel populations do too.

American mink; *Mustela vison*- Mink in Alaska are larger than the weasels and about the same size as marten. The males of both mink and marten reach lengths of 550-700 mm (21.5-27.5 in) and weights of 500-1250 g (1.1-2.8 lb). Females weigh about a third less than males. Mink are essentially large weasels that are closely associated with bodies of water. Unlike short-tailed and least weasels, mink have dark brown fur with only a few blotches of white on the chin, throat, or chest. And unlike the two weasels, mink do not turn white in the winter.

The movement of mink in summertime Alaska follows watercourses closely. These mustelids travel overland from slough to slough only if the distance between sloughs is very short.

During winter, air temperatures seem to govern movement above snow. At temperatures lower than -18°C (0°F) mink tracks are rarely seen in the snow. Above 0°, mink tracks become far more prevalent. However, tracks don't tell the whole story on the wanderings of mink in the winter. Stream flows decline in winter, and surface ice forms on ponds and sloughs. Typically, water levels drop under the surface ice, leaving enclosed spaces under ice and snow, subnivean spaces, through which mink travel.[80]

With warming temperatures and crusted snow in the spring, and the approach of breeding season, above-snow activity increases. Males occupy home ranges that may stretch a mile or more along a waterway and typically encompass several female home ranges. Males may breed with more than one female. In Alaska, breeding probably occurs in mid- to late April. A gestation period of 51 days includes only 30-32 days during which embryos are actually implanted in the female uterus. In the interior of Alaska, pups are born in mid-June and remain in the natal den until the first part of August. Litters of 2-3 young are typical in Alaska, but litters of up to six are produced in more temperate parts of the mink's geographic range. Den sites include inactive beaver houses, muskrat bank dens, drift and/or brush piles and red squirrel middens.

In general, mink reproduction occurs later at higher latitude; mating occurs in late autumn in Florida, February to early March in southern Britain, and March in Sweden. In an exceptional population of mink in southeast Alaska, breeding is in May with females giving birth in mid- to late July. Everywhere else in the mink world, latitude and day length probably cue reproduction. Why is this population out of step? Riv-

erine and coastal mink in southeast Alaska rely heavily on salmon carcasses during summer and fall, when salmon have migrated upstream. Mink carry salmon carcasses away from stream banks and deposit them in the root cavities of spruce trees and under rock overhangs. Reproduction is timed so that lactation in females coincides with the availability of salmon carcasses.[81]

Typically, rodents are the main items in mink diets in Alaska and elsewhere. Rodent prey includes meadow voles, red-backed voles, tundra voles, northern bog lemmings, brown lemmings, red squirrels, and muskrats. Snowshoe hares are an important food resource when they are abundant. Fish, birds, insects, and snails also are eaten in the interior, plus the leaves and berries of cloudberry and leatherleaf. Food remains at natal den sites include waterfowl, passerine birds, grayling, pike, burbot, chum salmon, muskrat, and hare.[80]

Mink can swim, dive, and forage underwater. Muskrats are pursued and often captured underwater (Figure 4.9). Even so, mink are not

Figure 4.9: Mink pursuing muskrat underwater. Both are excellent swimmers. Note the flattened, hairless tail on the muskrat. See Chapter 10 for a discussion of muskrat biology.

well adapted to diving. Their elongated shape enhances heat loss while in water. Their feet have small surface areas for propulsion. They have little oxygen storage for use in a dive and, consequently, their dives are of short duration (5-20 sec) and shallow.

Some of the sensory capabilities mink use on land are not very efficient underwater. Olfactory cues are probably useless underwater since mink don't pass water through their nostrils during a dive. Visual acuity underwater is worse than in air.[82] Mink typically locate their aquatic prey from an aerial vantage point, and then plunge in after it. If they lose sight of the fish or other prey while underwater, they emerge to relocate it. In spite of these deficiencies, mink are able to capture fish and muskrats underwater.

The aquatic realm is really the domain of another, larger mustelid, the northern river otter. Do these two species compete with each other for resources since they both occupy some of the same habitat? The coexistence of mink and river otter was studied in Idaho. Otters always seem to forage from the water on aquatic prey. Any terrestrial prey is either scavenged or captured when it falls into the water. Though both mink and otter rely heavily on fish in Idaho, otters took more and larger fish than mink. In terms of diet overlap, both species rely on some of the same fish species but mink to a much lesser extent than otter and on smaller fishes than otters. In addition, mink capture a variety of mammals, birds, and invertebrates that otters do not use.[83]

The mink is widespread in its distribution, occurring from Alaska across most of Canada and south into Oregon, through the Midwest down into Louisiana, Mississippi, Alabama, and Florida. Even though the mink is a North American species, it has been introduced into England and Europe. These introductions were accidental releases from fur farms. In both England and Sweden mink population increases have been associated with population declines of the European otter (*Lutra lutra*). The European otter is smaller than the American northern river otter, that is, closer to the mink in body size. Studies of the diets of mink and European otter indicate that in England the average dietary overlap is about 40%[84] and, in Sweden, as high as 60-70%.[85] So, the jury is still out on the question of an exotic species, the mink, negatively impacting a native species, the European otter.

Marten; *Martes americana-* Slightly larger than mink, marten are more constrained geographically. Marten are found associated with the boreal forest from Alaska across Canada, into Minnesota, Michigan, Maine, and New York. They are also found in the Rocky Mountains, California, and Oregon.

Although marten can swim and dive underwater, they much prefer to be in or near trees. When traveling across somewhat open terrain, a marten will walk under every available tree. Obviously, trees serve as both escape terrain and as locations of potential food sources. Cleared fields and large meadows are almost completely avoided by marten. This avoidance is important in understanding how marten might respond to forest practices such as clear-cutting. Leaving isolated patches of forested habitat in large clear cut areas may completely eliminate those patches as marten habitat because marten will not cross large stretches of open country.[86] Connecting patches of forest with corridors of uncut forest allows marten to move from one patch to another. On a larger scale, this marten behavior explains why some mountain ranges with appropriate habitat in the lower 48 which have lost their marten simply don't get them back.

The most important foods of martens in interior Alaska are meadow and red-backed voles followed by berries, small birds, eggs and vegetation.[87] Red squirrels are occasionally eaten but they are not a major food source. However, in south-central Alaska (upper Susitna River drainage) red squirrels make up 9% of the total volume of prey and, next to microtine rodents, are second in importance as prey.[88] Among the microtines, the red-backed vole is the most important prey when small rodents are scarce. When small rodents are abundant, meadow voles and tundra voles are the principal prey probably due to their clumped distributions. These latter two voles occupy meadows and other early successional habitats, while red-backed voles are scattered across most habitat types. Thus, optimal conditions for marten require a variety of habitats including white spruce woodlands, meadows and transitional habitats.

In the upper Susitna, almost half the small mammals captured by martens are shrews, yet shrews make up only about 1% of the volume of scats. Shrews must taste really awful. Remains of arctic ground squirrels appear in marten scats in months when the ground squirrels are hibernating. Therefore, either martens are caching ground squirrels in the summer for use later or they are digging ground squirrels out of their hibernation chambers. Berries, about 6% of all the scat material examined, include rosehips, bog blueberry, lowbush cranberry, crowberry, and wild raspberry.

Red squirrel midden holes provide martens with resting places in the winter out of the reach of most larger predators. Some red squirrel middens are used repeatedly by marten as indicated by the presence of marten scats layered down through the snow near midden entrances. Frequently when martens are occupying a squirrel midden, a resident squirrel can be heard vocalizing or can be seen nearby.[89] It isn't clear whether martens and squirrels coexist in the middens at the same time or if martens kill or evict the squirrels. It is clear that these subnivean spaces are warmer than the outside, wintertime air and that these elongated predators are gaining an energetic advantage by using them.

Porcupine

A friend worked several summers at the BLM Visitor's Center at Coldfoot, on the Dalton Highway. One afternoon a lady walked in and asked her where she might be able to view the porcupine herd. Nancy explained that the caribou she would likely see from the Dalton Highway were undoubtedly members of the Central Arctic Herd. The lady very patiently explained that she wasn't interested in caribou; she wanted to see the herd of porcupines. Except for courtship and reproduction time, porcupines are solitary creatures, not given to form herds. Chalk it up to another interesting day at the Visitor's Center.

The North American porcupine, *Erethizon dorsatum*, is the only New World porcupine to occur in North America; all the rest inhabit Central and South America. Actually, our porcupine also originated in South America and migrated north after the most recent land connection formed between North and South America.

New World porcupines (3-10 kg; 6.6-22 lb) are all arborial and feed primarily on parts of trees including bark, leaves and fruit. Old World porcupines are larger (up to 30 kg; 66 lb), live on the ground and eat either fallen fruit or foods they dig up. The North American porcupine is highly adaptable. It occupies northern forests and tundra habitats in our area as well as deserts in the American southwest.

Of course, the most widely known feature of porcupines is their defensive structure, the quill. Many dog owners in interior Alaska have experienced porcupine quills vicariously through their dogs. Our black lab came home one evening with about 80 quills in his nose and mouth; fortunately he had the patience to sit still while I pulled each one out with pliers. That was his only encounter; he "got the point" the first time.

The quill shafts are white against a black fur background. Rows of quills on each side of the black tail make it noticeable even on a pretty dark night. More shafts are conspicuous on the head and across the hindquarters. Why black-on-white? Porcupines are nocturnally active and, therefore, most vulnerable to predation at night. Predatory birds and mammals that are active at night have eyes adapted to low light intensity, and that means black-and-white, as opposed to color, vision. Therefore, the white-on-black pattern is the most visible at night.

Porcupines have two other warning mechanisms: First, they clatter their teeth together when it appears that an encounter is imminent. The incisors chatter, then the molars. Second, porcupines under duress emit a powerful odor

that makes most people's eyes water and noses run. In a confined space this odor could be a powerful deterrent.[90]

If the three previously mentioned mechanisms fail, the porcupine still has over 30,000 quills covering all parts of the body except muzzle, ears and belly. The tail is often used in a very fast slapping motion that can imbed hundreds of quills in the attacker. Sometimes a quill will be completely buried in the flesh of the victim. One scientist got swatted on the inside of the upper arm by the tail of a porcupine. One of the quills was buried in his biceps muscle. After five hours it had worked its way to his elbow, and two days later it emerged from his forearm. He thought it amazing that the quill pathway through his arm remained completely free from infection.[90]

Chemical separations and analysis show that quills are coated with fatty acids, primarily palmitic acid. These fatty acids have an antibiotic effect on gram-positive bacteria. Aside from humans, porcupines seem to be the only mammals with antibiotic skin secretions. The adaptive value to the porcupine may have to do with falling out of trees. When porcupines fall out of trees, they frequently impale themselves on their own quills. The antibiotic offers them the chance of the quills working through the body without causing infections.

How does a predator attack a well-armed porcupine? The fisher is a serious predator further south. Its method relies on circling the porcupine and dexterously darting in to bite the unprotected face. Many bites may be necessary to finally stun or kill the victim. Once the porcupine is down, the fisher eats the head and/or starts working on the underside. Occasional predators of porcupines include lynx, wolf, coyote, wolverine, red fox, and great horned owl.

Porcupines eat a variety of foods over the course of a year. In springtime they select the buds and very young leaves of birch, aspen and willow.[91] Shortly after leaf-out these plants begin to pump tannins into the leaves and, consequently, they become unpalatable and toxic to porcupines for the remainder of the spring. In summer Olaus Murie observed Alaskan porcupines feeding on grass and herbaceous plants up in the tundra. Porcupines return to aspen leaves in mid-summer and fall and I wonder if tannin levels are reduced by that time of year. Ground-feeding occurs in northern forests with porcupines taking grasses, clover, and other succulent vegetation. Raspberry leaves are a favorite of porcupines in New York. Presumably, wild raspberries in Alaska would be equally tempting.

Winter diets consist mainly of tree barks that generally contain about 0.5% protein. In Alaska the tree of choice in winter is spruce but aspen and alders will suffice if that is all that is available. This fall we hunted in an old white spruce forest along the Wood River and found patches of white spruce that had been hit hard by porcupines. A number of trees had been completely girdled and killed.

The amount of protein available in winter is insufficient to allow porcupines to maintain body weight and, thus, they lose weight. The cecum in porcupines, with its fermenting capabilities, is probably most important in winter when the porcupine's diet is lowest in quality. The cecum with its contents amounts to about 6% (3-10%) of the body weight, somewhat less than in rabbits and hares (7.8% of body weight). In snowshoe hares, and, pre-sumably in porcupines, the cecum functions as a fermentation vat in which bacteria convert woody material containing mostly cellulose to volatile fatty acids.

Salt drive is a behavior associated with the shift to spring and early summer diets. This is the same drive that causes Dall sheep to frequent mineral licks, moose to congregate along the salted portion of the Richardson Highway near Donnelly Dome, and snowshoe hares to eat dirt along roadsides near Anderson and elsewhere in Alaska. I described the problem in discussing moose biology. Again, the problem is the high potassium content relative to sodium in vegetation eaten by herbivores. Animals have a much higher requirement for sodium than do plants because their excitable tissues, the nerves and muscles, require sodium for their activation. In the spring herbivores are typically shifting to new growth vegetation that has higher potassium/sodium ratios than their winter foods. Therefore, in the spring porcupines with a yen for sodium may walk into your yard and gnaw the sweat-impregnated wooden handle off your favorite axe or the salty glue holding together the plywood on your outhouse.

Gnawing trials were conducted to see if wooden pegs impregnated with high salt concentrations were more attractive to porcupines than those with low concentrations. Porcupines favored the higher concentrations. They did not gnaw pegs soaked with other ions such as magnesium, aluminum, potassium or calcium. They could also detect pegs with a high sodium/potassium ratio. Females were much more likely to exhibit salt drive than males because the hormones of pregnancy trip off a craving for sodium and because pregnant and lactating female mammals incur a significant sodium loss.[90] The salt drive may explain observations of porcupines eating mud along an interior Alaskan river in early June.[91]

Breeding season is September through November. Several males may be attracted to a single female; they find her by olfaction. A female in a tree urinates and, as the urine falls through the canopy of leaves and branches, it produces an odor cloud that drifts downwind. The exact location of the female is determined by sniffing around the bases of trees until the correct one is found. Males will fight each other for access to the female in heat. Combat probably occurs primarily on the ground but, on occasion, may continue in the trees. Bites and swats with quill-studded tails are the main techniques. After a dominance battle between males hundreds of quills and many large tufts of hair lie on the forest floor. Many of the quills are bent or broken, indicating they were pulled out by one of the combatants. If one male quits the contest and flees up a nearby tree, the other will follow and climb out on the same branch. This guarding behavior keeps the subordinate male isolated from the female.

Eventually, one male is the winner. He has access to the female. No matter how eager, he must wait for the 8-12 hour period of heat when the female is receptive. She is simply too well armed to press the point. In one of the last behavioral moves in courtship, the male stands on his hindlegs facing the female and drenches her with high-pressure jets of urine. If she is not quite ready for copulation, she shakes it off and moves away. If she is ready, she tolerates this outrageous (from our viewpoint) behavior, and copulation follows shortly. The male, at this point, is a "urine cannon!"

Porcupines have a very long gestation of 210 days. Some time between April and June the female gives birth to a single precocial offspring. The eyes are open, teeth are erupted and the quills are in place at birth, hardening in a few hours.

Bison

Ken and I were hunkered down in a thin strip of poplar and birch adjacent to a barley field east of Delta Junction. The snow was coming in horizontally, making it tough to assess the size and sex of the 35 bison milling around in the barley stubble. The object was to find a bull that wasn't either directly in front of or directly behind another animal. Several minutes after we sneaked up to this bunch, they began to feed. One old cow started bashing the snow with her muzzle in a side-to-side motion that was so comical that we both laughed out loud. Both of us were used to watching caribou feed in the winter by pawing through the snow (cratering), so this "head thing" took us by surprise.

Bison bison, a grassland species, would seem to be a misfit in the boreal forest. Until perhaps as recently as 450-500 years ago, however, bison roamed interior Alaska. There are reports of bison in the oral tradition of Athabascans of the middle Yukon River basin. Therefore, the introduction of 23 Montana bison near Delta Junction in 1928 could really be considered a reintroduction. Currently, the Alaska Department of Fish and Game is trying to introduce bison onto the Yukon River floodplain near Fort Yukon. The rationale is to restore a population that could have considerable importance as a subsistence and cultural resource to interior peoples. Portions of the target area for introduction are within the Yukon-Charley National Park and Preserve; another portion is managed by the U.S. Fish and Wildlife Service. The U.S. Bureau of Land Management controls other lands upon which these bison might roam. These federal agencies have taken the view that the bison is an exotic species and its introduction could cause major and, as yet, unspecified perturbations to the natural landscape of the Yukon River valley. Times have changed since the three other introductions of Delta herd bison to other locations in the state.

In 1950, seventeen bison were moved from Delta Junction to the upper Copper River near Slana. The current status of this Copper River herd is uncertain but there are very few animals, if any. In 1962 an additional 39 bison were removed from the Delta herd and released on the Chitina River, in another part of the Copper River basin. The Chitina River herd has, apparently, stabilized at over 50 animals. In 1965 and 1968 a total of 38 animals were relocated to the Farewell Lake area of the Kuskokwim River, west of the Alaska Range. This population fluctuates between 100 and over 300 animals. The Farewell burn in 1977 covered some 1400 km² and enhanced winter range for this herd. Its population increased considerably in response to the vegetation changes that followed the burn.

Of these populations, the Delta herd is the most accessible for viewing. Summer range consists of the early successional floodplain of the Delta River from Black Rapids to the Tanana River and mid-successional grass meadows on the west side of the Delta River, opposite Don-

nelly Dome. These early successional stages are maintained by the braiding and meandering of the river itself, by wind scouring, sediment deposition in the area, and by fires. Winter range consists of sedge meadows along the Tanana and Clearwater Rivers sometimes including the shores of Healy Lake and the Gerstle River to the east.[92] The Delta Junction Bison Range was established in 1979 as a fall and winter foraging area for bison. The rationale was to provide an alternative to feeding in the Delta Agricultural Project. The Bison Range is south of the Alaska Highway and west of the Gerstle River; the Delta Junction Agriculture Project is north of the Alaska Highway. Generally, bison can forage on the Bison Range until crops are harvested in the Agriculture Project. At least, that was the idea.

In winter, after the harvest, the stubble fields of the farms are available and are used by bison. Increasingly, Delta barley farmers are fencing their acreage, presumably, to discourage incursions by trespassing humans and bison. In the case of the bison, the fences are ineffective. The top strand, at 1.5 m (5 feet) high, can be jumped by a bison from a standing start, and there is a report of a big bull jumping a 2.2 m (7 feet) log fence from a standing start. [93] Bison run right through some fences when spooked. I heard the result of a hunter spooking a band of bison toward a barbed-wire fence. As the three strands broke, they sounded like a three-note ascending scale being played on a guitar. It would have been a very loud guitar; I heard it from 100 m away.

American bison are the largest land mammals on the continent. Mature bulls may reach weights of 900 kg (1980 pounds); females about 550 kg (1200 pounds). A big bull will stand 1.8

m (6 feet) at the shoulder. The hump on a bison (see Figure 1.11) is due to long neural spines on the thoracic vertebrae. These spines are 25-30 cm (10-12 inches) long on a big bull.

A summer food list in the Delta area includes 14 different species of grasses, three sedge species, four willow species, and eight species of herbaceous plants including fireweed, wild sweet pea, Eskimo potato, field oxytrope, burnet, goldenrod, valerian, and death camas. The remains of other species, such as birch, silverberry, horsetails, and black currant, show up in bison feces. The entire list of plants eaten by bison is a long one.[94]

Two other things about bison foraging are noteworthy. First, the Delta herd bison influence the vegetation in their habitat. Exclosure studies show that bison impact their habitat by reducing the biomass of legumes and grasses. Recently, these bison are changing their foraging pattern, devoting more attention to wet sedge meadows. These meadows may be better able to withstand the grazing pressure than the more arid, nutrient-limited river bars. Second, bison urine and feces are sources of nitrogen for plants in bison habitat. One summer, my father and I spent several days on the Chitina River looking for bison and looking at bison "pies." It was obvious that most of the pies had flowers growing out of them. Dad coined the term "enriched flower" on this trip to emphasize our supposition that the plants were, indeed, being fertilized. As an aside, we gave in to the temptation to test bison chips as firewood substitute. Those pies put up the awfulest stench I ever experienced. No insect or any other creature would get near us after we sat around a chip fire one evening.

Woodchuck

I had a habit of jogging a 4.5 mile loop from my office on the University of Alaska campus in Fairbanks, around the University Experimental Farm, and back to my office. One summer day I ran off the Parks Highway onto Geist Road and saw a reddish-brown lump of fur in the fast lane. It was a young of the year male woodchuck that wasn't fast enough to make it across four lanes of traffic. I was feeling lucky, so I ran out to the center median and retrieved the woodchuck. I stashed the carcass alongside the road and came back for him later. He made a fine dissection that fall in biology lab. People from further south are often surprised to find woodchucks, *Marmota monax*, in interior Alaska. Woodchuck distribution extends from Alaska and the Yukon, south into British Columbia and Washington, eastward through the boreal forest of Canada and through most of the eastern United States.

Peak activity of woodchucks occurs early in the morning and late in the afternoon although they may leave their burrows at any time of the day. Very infrequently woodchucks venture out at night. In areas of heavy human use, such as urban parks, woodchucks may modify their typical behavior and spend time foraging after dark.[95] Other marmot species spend time each day basking in the sun; woodchucks are no exception. I have seen both juvenile and adult woodchucks sunning themselves along the shoulder of the Parks Highway west of Fairbanks.

The alarm call of woodchucks is very similar to that of the hoary marmot, a loud whistle. Typical escape behavior involves running toward and, finally, entering the burrow. Woodchucks exhibit flexibility in this behavior, however. The nearer the woodchuck is to its burrow, the closer it will allow a potential predator to approach before it flees.[96] At great distances from their burrows, woodchucks may have to exhibit alternate behaviors when confronted with trouble. Most instances of tree climbing involve woodchucks greater than 50 m from their burrows. These ground-dwelling squirrels haven't completely forgotten their ancestry; they climb to heights of 1.8-5.5 m (5.9-18 feet). In one instance tree climbing appeared to be for sunning. Occasionally, woodchucks also climb fence posts, presumably, to sun themselves.

The woodchuck, *Marmota monax*, is one of six species of *Marmota* in North America and the only one that could be considered a true forest (as opposed to alpine) dweller. This ground-dwelling squirrel digs burrows up to 9 m (30 feet) long in the loess of the boreal forest. Burrows are typically constructed under rocks, stumps, or some other protection. Burrows are used for sleeping, escaping inclement weather and predators, and for hibernating in the winter. Compared to the hoary marmot, woodchucks have very thick, tough skin, perhaps to protect them in encounters with bears and badgers. A woodchuck in a burrow in loess, even a deep burrow, may not be as protected from encounters with predators as a marmot burrowing in a boulder field.

Foods of woodchucks include bark and buds of trees in spring before there is an abundance of herbaceous plants. Herbs in the diet include dandelion, sorrel, grains, chickweed, clover, alfalfa, grasses, and legumes. [10] Many studies have verified that woodchucks, by virtue of their feeding, change the vegetation surrounding their burrows. In hayfields in Connecticut,

woodchucks reduce the amount of alfalfa and increase the amount of orchard grass; woodchucks prefer alfalfa.[97] Orchard grass near the burrows is lusher and has higher protein levels than the same grass further away. Apparently, woodchuck feces fertilizes the grass. On old fields and abandoned farmland, woodchucks reduce plant species numbers immediately around their burrows and reduce total plant cover near burrows.[98] No studies of woodchucks and their possible effects on natural forest vegetation have been conducted in Alaska. Presumably, cropping of plants near burrows could open up space for less palatable, opportunistic plants. The result might be a mosaic of plant associations such as are produced in old fields and croplands.

Springtime is breeding time. Copulations occur in March and April further south but probably in May in Alaska. The gestation period is 30 days; two to seven young are born in a single litter for the year. Weaning occurs about six weeks after birth. The young, such as the roadkill mentioned above, begin to disperse away from the natal burrow about four weeks after emergence from burrows.[99]

Adult woodchucks grow to about 51 cm (20 inches) long and weights of 0.4 to2.7 kg (2-6 pounds). Maximum weights for the year are reached in late summer; animals should have lots of body fat to get them through the rigors of winter hibernation. Unlike most other marmot species, the woodchuck is a solitary hibernator. At the onset of winter, a woodchuck enters the burrow and plugs the tunnel leading to the hibernation chamber with a mixture of dirt, vegetation and feces.[100] This plug freezes into a solid mass.

Woodchucks are true hibernators. During hibernation, they exhibit slowed heart rates, slowed metabolic rates and body temperatures that may drop to 4°C (39°F). Even with reduced metabolism, woodchucks lose about 40% of their body weight in hibernation.[101] Woodchucks, as do other hibernators, experience bouts of periodic arousal in which transient increases in temperature, heart rate and metabolism occur. It appears that in the fall woodchucks begin to synthesize a peptide (short protein) that acts as a trigger to hibernation. In a rare example of common sense, scientists labeled this material "hibernation trigger." It is an opium-like peptide that is not found in the bloodstream of summer woodchucks.[102] This peptide, when infused into the brain of a summer woodchuck or a monkey, causes hypothermia, heart slowing, cessation of feeding and reduced kidney function. These are all characteristics of hibernation. Monkeys don't hibernate, but humans would like to be able to hibernate so that we could successfully complete long voyages in space. Perhaps woodchucks hold the key to suspended animation in humans.

Of all marmot species only the woodchuck is capable of reaching maturity after only a single hibernation. All the other species require an additional summer to reach sufficient size and development to successfully disperse and reproduce. Only two species of marmots are known to regularly reproduce each year, the woodchuck and the yellow-bellied marmot. These traits, rapid growth and annual reproduction, require access to sufficient nutrition. We could infer that woodchucks generally have access to better food resources than their alpine tundra relatives. However, there

is no guarantee that juvenile woodchucks survive to reproduce. My wife, Marsha, and I watched a young woodchuck dig a burrow in a loess bank along Rosie Creek Road, west of Fairbanks, one late summer. The burrow went undisturbed all winter, but the woodchuck did not emerge in the spring. Certainly at the extreme northern extent of their distribution, woodchucks may be reaching the limits of their adaptability.

One other consequence of woodchuck growth and maturation rates is that they are solitary animals. Other marmot species not only delay maturity but also delay dispersal from the natal area.[103] Because of these traits, woodchucks are thought to have the most rudimentary social systems among marmots.

There are five other *Marmota* species in North America. The Olympic marmot, *Marmota olympus*, is restricted to the Olympic Peninsula in Washington; the Vancouver marmot, *Marmota vancouverensis*, is restricted to a small area on Vancouver Island, British Columbia. The yellow-bellied marmot, *Marmota flaviventris*, is found in the mountains of the western United States. The two other Alaskan species are tundra species. The Alaska marmot, *Marmota broweri*, is confined to the Brooks Range in northern Alaska. The hoary marmot, *Marmota caligata*, is found over much of Alaska, Yukon Territory, British Columbia and into northern Washington, Idaho, and Montana.

Voles

Voles (subfamily Microtinae) are small rodents having short tails, short legs, short muzzles, and stout bodies. Their skulls have prominent ridges for the attachment of jaw muscles. They are related to the more familiar mice and rats of North America (subfamily Cricetinae), members of which have longer tails and legs and have skulls with no prominent ridges. An interesting feature of microtines has to do with the long incisors these herbivores use for nipping off vegetation. The incisors tend to wear and, therefore, grow continuously throughout life. The incisors of *Microtus* are rooted behind the molars in the condylar process of the mandible.

Winter is a harsh time for these rodents because of low ambient temperatures, the vole's small body size, and the fact that voles do not hibernate. The cold air temperatures of wintertime Alaska are, to a great extent, avoided by small mammals that stay in the snow layer. Subnivean spaces are insulated, experience lower fluctuations in temperature, and provide some protection from predators. The layers of snow themselves may provide some of the food needed by voles to survive the winter. There is an intermittent rain of birch seeds through the winter that, as new snow falls, is buried but is still available to voles burrowing through the snow.[104]

Scents play significant roles in the lives of voles. Voles mark the boundaries of their territories with urine and feces, mark their own runways with urine, and may use scents to advertise their status to other voles. There is a definite down side to leaving these urine samples all over the surroundings. Kestrels are able to visually detect the urine markings while flying overhead. Apparently vole urine strongly absorbs ultraviolet wavelengths that kestrels can detect. Hence, these predators can concentrate their hunting in areas of high vole density.[105]

Voles and their cousins the lemmings are very important in the ecology of the living systems of the Far North. Ecologists might refer to the important role of these rodents as **trophic intermediaries** in these systems. The term simply means that voles and lemmings eat plant material, temporarily store some of the plant nutrients and energy in their bodies and then, as they are eaten, pass them on to their predators. Plants are on the first (bottom-most) trophic level, herbivores such as voles are on the second level, and predators of voles are on the third level. Of course, nature is never that simple. Animals in the wild do what they do without regard to what humans are thinking about them. For instance, some voles and grouse chicks eat insects in the spring and early summer. Insects are an excellent source of protein for rapidly growing young grouse and voles. Similarly, we saw that red squirrels are significant predators of newborn snowshoe hares.

Do these facts mean that grouse, voles and red squirrels are not primarily herbivores? No. It just means they cannot be easily pigeonholed by humans. However, back to the point: because of their abundance, sometimes a fluctuating abundance, these rodents may drive population fluctuations in their predators much as hare fluctuations tend to drive lynx abundance.

As I discussed in the moose section, predators and prey often both play host to parasites. This is certainly the situation with voles and their predators. One parasite worth mentioning is the tapeworm, *Echinococcus multilocularis*, which infects voles and lemmings (intermediate hosts) and arctic foxes, red foxes and occasionally domestic dogs (definitive hosts). Very infrequently this parasite can be accidentally spread to humans. Infected dogs that lick their owners on the face could spread the worm to humans.

Unlike the juveniles of *Echinococcus granulosis*, those of this worm continue to grow. Typically, the liver is the target but other organs (lungs, brain) may also be invaded. 70% of untreated cases in humans are fatal.[24] The other source of human infection is by careless handling of fox furs by trappers.

There are eight species of voles plus three lemmings in Alaska. Several including the southern red-backed vole and long-tailed vole occur primarily in southeast Alaska in coastal forests. Two others, the singing vole and tundra vole, though they both occur in some forest habitats, are primarily tundra species and are discussed as members of the tundra fauna.

Northern red-backed vole—The northern red-backed vole, *Cleithrionomys rutilus*, inhabits most of Alaska and northwestern Canada east to the western shore of Hudson's Bay, occupying both boreal forest and dry tundra habitats. This species is also found across northern Eurasia but occurs only in boreal forests. In areas of overlap in distribution between northern and southern red-backed vole, the former appears to occupy more arid habitats, the latter more moist including bogs, sedge marshes, and muskeg.

The northern red-backed vole is, like other voles, a very short-lived species. Maximum life span in captivity is two years. Breeding begins in late winter, under the snow, and continues through autumn. Females are capable of having up to four litters per year of 2-11 young per litter. Young of the year overwinter as subadults, maturing the following spring.

Feeding habits of the northern red-backed vole vary depending on the season, the habitat and the presence of other small rodents. Populations in forested habitats feed on seeds, berries, leaves and some insects in the summer and fall. During winter, diet shifts toward lichens and mosses but tree seeds layered into the snow are an important food resource. In tundra habitats tree seeds are not available and are replaced by leaves. In Canada, where the northern red-backed vole range overlaps with mice of the genus *Peromyscus*, it functions more as a grazer; when it overlaps with *Microtus* it functions more as a seed eater.[105]

Around Fairbanks these rodents are found in spruce forests (north-facing and south-facing), birch, poplar and alder associations, bogs, and creek beds. This vole has even been seen in trees. If you find a mouse in your house in interior Alaska, it is, more than likely, a red-backed vole.

Red-backed voles are more abundant in undisturbed boreal forest habitat than in areas recently dredged[107] or burned.[108] In other words, disturbance reduces populations of *C. rutilus*. The very early successional stages of recovery from a very hot fire in a black spruce forest have low population densities of red-backed voles. Fire negatively impacts these voles in several ways. First, their normal seed, berry, and leaf supplies (summer foods) are severely diminished by the burn. Second, the insulative moss layer needed for overwintering is often burned off. Third, winter foods, such as lichens and mosses, are also reduced by the burn. Finally, without the vegetative cover, red-backed voles are more susceptible to predation, especially by avian predators.

Meadow vole—The meadow vole, *Microtus pennsylvanicus*, has the largest geographic distribution of any North American vole. In the north it is absent beyond the extreme limit of tree line;

it is missing from the North Slope, Seward Peninsula, and most of the Alaska Peninsula. In Canada it appears to be limited by the line of continuous permafrost but extends southward into the American Midwest, the Carolinas, and the Rocky Mountain states including Arizona and New Mexico. There is a relict population of meadow voles in Chihuahua, Mexico.

Mating behavior in meadow voles has a few interesting twists. Females are very picky about mates. When a female is sexually receptive and meets a male, she beats him up. If he is deemed acceptable as a mate, she will nudge him in the ribs with her nose while he is recovering from the attack. This is an inducement for the male to mate with her...if he is still interested. Over the several days during which she is receptive, she may accept several males. Therefore, there may be multiple fathers of the individuals in her litter.

What makes a male acceptable to a female? Male meadow voles were maintained in captivity on different levels of dietary protein. The higher the dietary protein, the more attractive the male's scent was to females.[109] In the natural world, high protein vegetation is very patchy in its distribution, so males with high-protein scents are individuals that have successfully found the patches. They, presumably, have qualities that would increase the fitness of the female's offspring.

Yellow-cheeked vole—This vole, *Microtus xanthognathus*, is sometimes called the taiga vole. **Taiga** is another term that refers to the boreal forest. This species can be distinguished from other voles by its size and by its yellow-orange nose. Its geographic distribution is limited compared to red-backed and tundra voles,

being found in Alaska only in the interior and northeast corner of the state. In Canada it occurs in the MacKenzie River drainages and eastward to the southwest corner of Hudson's Bay.

Yellow-cheeked voles are the largest of North America's voles. They occur in a variety of habitats in Alaska including stream and riverbanks, burned spruce forests, deciduous forests, marshes, and bogs. Population densities vary widely in these habitats but seem to be higher in floodplain white spruce than in either floodplain black spruce or upland black spruce habitats.[110]

Yellow-cheeked voles feed primarily on horsetails, bog blueberry, lowbush cranberry, and fireweed. Where horsetails are not abundant, voles will eat jointgrass. Berries and green vegetation are favored in the summer, but by fall the rhizomes of both horsetails and fireweed dominate the diet.

During summer, these voles may be active at any hour. They maintain runways both above and below ground. Nests are built of grass and maintained 15-20 cm (6-8 inches) down in the moss layer. Yellow-cheeked voles are active all winter, living communally in groups of 5-10, subsisting off cached rhizomes that they collectively stored.[111] Underground nests in winter are 25-30 cm (9-12 inches) below ground. These rodents occupy a space under the moss and under the snow, both of which provide insulation from extreme temperatures. In addition, they huddle, sharing body warmth and reducing their individual metabolic costs.

Soil conditions are undoubtedly important for yellow-cheeked voles. Burrowing in cold, wet soil is more energy-consuming; dry, warm soils are preferred. Recently burned areas typically have warmer soil temperatures, deeper summertime thawed layers and are drier. These characteristics must play an important role in the abundance of this vole species. These preferred habitat characteristics last only about 10 years, leading to ephemeral populations.[10]

Potential predators of yellow-cheeked voles include red fox, black bear, least weasel, mink, red-tailed hawk, great horned owl, and pine marten. Both great gray owls and northern hawk-owls capture these voles. Marten use of burn habitat in the interior is probably highly correlated with presence of yellow-cheeked voles.[112]

Shrews

Cat owners in interior Alaska are undoubtedly aware of the existence of shrews in the Far North. Back in the mid-70s we owned two cats that spent parts of the days outdoors around the cabin. Invariably, our pets would bring home shrews, uneaten, and present them to us on our doorstep or living room rug. Our cats quickly consumed any voles and red squirrels they caught but they did not like eating shrews. I mentioned earlier that martens also have an aversion to shrews. The inference drawn by biologists is that shrews taste bad. Shrews have a variety of scent glands including flank, caudal, anal, chin, throat, and belly glands; some species have scent glands behind their ears. Shrews are, indeed, eaten by foxes, weasels and bobcats but make up only a small proportion of the total diet of these predators. Shrews are really hit hard by avian predators; some 23 species of birds have been found to prey on shrews. Birds have relatively poor senses of smell and, apparently, are not deterred by shrew odors. Aside from any predator deterrence, odors in

shrews may serve in species identification, may help one shrew determine the sex of another and undoubtedly function to mark the boundaries of territories. In some species, females in breeding condition lack flank gland secretions. Therefore, the absence of some of these scents also has signal value.

If scents have signal value in shrews, so too do sounds. There are four categories of sounds produced by shrews based on usage: 1) calls made during courtship, 2) calls of alarm, defense or aggression, 3) sounds made during mother/young interactions and 4) sounds produced during exploration and foraging. Twelve different types of vocalizations are made by shrews and each has its own context. For instance, when young fall out of the nest, they produce a series of clicks or a bark that causes the mother to search for and retrieve the young. The different sounds are apparently produced in three different ways. Some sounds such as hisses are made by inhalations and/or exhalations through the nose. Clicks may be produced by clicking the tongue. The rest of the vocal repertoire is produced by the larynx, including barks, chirps, shrieks, and very high-pitched ultrasounds.[113]

Evidence is growing that these ultrasonic pitches are used in echolocation. First, these sounds are in the 30,000-60,000 cycles per second frequency range, similar to those of echo locating bats. Second, shrews emit these ultrasonic pulses when placed in a novel location, or when foraging. Their snouts move rapidly during these ultrasonic pulses, as do the snouts of echo locating bats. Third, owls, with excellent hearing capability, have been reported to prey on shrews far more than would be expected based on their abundance. The inference is that owls hear the high-pitched pulses of foraging shrews. Finally, several investigators have trained shrews, in total darkness, to find a platform and jump down to it.[114] Those shrews emitted high-frequency pulses while searching for the platform. When the investigators plugged the shrew's ears with wax, they couldn't find the platform. Shrews in dark cages can successfully avoid obstructions while running at full speed and can distinguish between open and closed tubes. Hunting at night by means of echolocation seems well within their capabilities.

Although shrews are, at first glance, similar in appearance to voles and mice they are not rodents. Shrews are in a different mammal order, the Insectivora. It is important to note that this order is defined and recognized based on the anatomical features of its members and not on the basis of the diets of its members. It is true that many if not all members of the Insectivore order do, indeed, eat insects. However, there are other insect-eating mammals (and non-mammals) that, due to their diet, are called insectivores but do not belong in this order. The same confusion surrounds the mammalian class Carnivora; there are plenty of carnivores in the world, based on diet, that don't belong in the mammalian order Carnivora.

An interesting feature of shrews is that the milk teeth (baby teeth) are shed while the embryos are still developing. This means that shrews are born with their permanent teeth. The molars and premolars are cusped and pointed, unlike those of rodents. It is assumed that these cusps facilitate breaking and tearing the hard cuticles of the beetles and other insects shrews eat. Shrews in the subfamily Soricinae (the red-toothed shrews) have pigmentation on the tips of the teeth. The pigmentation is often red but sometimes dark purple or yellow or anything in between. The pigment is iron deposited in the outer layer of enamel and, presumably, hardens the teeth.[115] Unlike in most rodents, the teeth of shrews do not grow throughout life; hardening prevents tooth wear in teeth in which the worn portion cannot be replaced.

Population densities of shrews are highly variable. Generally, shrews are abundant in summer when young of the year are present and less abundant in winter. Shrew populations also fluctuate from year to year.

Shrews may be rather pragmatic about defending territories. At times of high resource availability, shrews don't seem to defend territories. However, during winter when food availability is much lower, territories may be marked and defended.

I need to briefly consider thermoregulation and winter for shrews in Alaska. Many shrews go into winter weighing 5 g or less. Such small mammals have very high surface-to-volume ratios and, thus, tend to lose heat rapidly. How do shrews counter this potential heat loss problem? First, shrews have very high specific metabolic rates; no surprise. However, since they are so tiny their total metabolic requirements are small. Shrews of the Far North do not hibernate, do not exhibit daily torpor with its accompanying lowering of body temperature, and do not appear to clump together to share body heat and create a smaller surface to volume ratio. They cache food to help tide them over the winter. They also do something totally unexpected; they get smaller. Reductions in body weight, skull, and skeleton in shrews are mechanisms to reduce total metabolic requirement during the season when food availability is lowest.[116]

Thirty-three species occur in North America, and at least eight occur in Alaska. One of these is confined to the Arctic, the barren ground shrew. The tundra shrew can be found in tundra, boreal forest and coastal habitats. Other boreal forest shrew species are the pygmy shrew, masked shrew, montane (dusky) shrew, and water shrew. Two are endemic to their respective islands: the St. Lawrence Island shrew and the Pribilof Island shrew (St. Paul Island). At high latitudes in North America, shrews are an important part of the fauna, making up more than 25% of the small mammals.

Water shrew—My only experience with the water shrew, *Sorex palustris*, relates to minnow traps. One summer in the mid-1970s, I was using minnow traps in Goldstream valley, north of Fairbanks, to capture Alaska blackfish. I sank my traps to the bottom of the outlet stream below a beaver dam and checked them daily. One afternoon I pulled up the line, about 90 cm of it, to retrieve the trap and there was a furry creature inside, quite drowned.

Water shrews have to paddle vigorously to swim to the bottom of a creek or pond. They have a lot of floatation in the form of trapped air bubbles in their fur that hinders their diving but aids their thermoregulation. To their advantage they are among the larger shrews (8-18 g; the largest Alaskan shrew) and, therefore, are somewhat better able to tolerate heat loss than other shrews.

Water shrews have fringes of short (1 mm) stiff hairs projecting from the sides of their toes and feet. These hairs expand the surface area of the feet, making them more effective in swim-ming. They are, apparently, also used for grooming after the shrew emerges from the water. [113] In addition, the tail has a row of stiff hairs on its ventral surface, making it a more effective paddling structure.

Water shrews enter the water to escape potential predators and to feed. Aquatic prey include a variety of insects (caddisfly larvae, damselfly larvae, dragonfly larvae, and trichopteran larvae), adult aquatic invertebrates, and small fish. Terrestrial foods include snails and terrestrial insects. Water shrews in Alaska probably prey on wood frogs either as tadpoles or as they emerge from their natal ponds.

Pygmy shrew—The pygmy shrew of North America, *Sorex hoyi*, is one of the smallest North American shrews, especially in the southern part of its range. In Alaska and elsewhere in the Far North, individuals are much larger, often three times the weight of their southern cousins. Pygmy shrews are most abundant in boreal forests, occurring from Alaska eastward to eastern Canada and the New England states. Two disjunct, relict populations exist in the lower 48 states; one is found in Colorado and Wyoming, the other in east-central United States including Georgia, Tennessee, Kentucky, Virginia, southern Illinois, and Indiana. Litter size ranges from 2 to 8 and second litters may be produced in very favorable habitats.

Masked shrew—This shrew, *Sorex cinereus*, has a very broad geographic distribution, being found all around the world at high latitude except for Greenland. Zoologists have identified a *cinereus* **species complex**, that is, a group of very closely related species thought to have common ancestry. Currently, there are at least nine shrews in this species complex.[117]

The masked shrew is one of the most common small mammals in the forests of southwestern Alaska. Disturbed (including previously mined) sites have fewer individuals and fewer species of small mammals than undisturbed sites. This shrew prefers dense vegetation (less likely to be found at disturbed sites) presumably because its food is typically found in the litter layer under such vegetation. However, alder thickets, in spite of an overstory, have few shrews. Since shrews often supplement their diets with berries and seeds and these items don't occur in alder thickets, shrews may avoid them.[107]

Montane shrew—*Sorex monticolus*, the montane or dusky shrew, has one of the widest latitudinal distributions in North America, occurring from the Sierra Madre Occidental of central Mexico to the MacKenzie River delta. In Alaska, this species is found everywhere except north of the Brooks Range and most of the Seward Peninsula.

Molting in the montane shrew occurs in September or October, when the brownish fur is replaced by a darker, longer winter coat. In tundra and forest habitats this shrew is typically found in willow and alder thickets along streams. When found in assemblages of other shrews, the montane shrew is usually the most abundant.

During breeding season, male montane shrews maintain home ranges that encompass up to five female home ranges. Females usually first breed after their first winter, producing 2-9 young. Few reach the ripe old age of 2 years.

Tundra shrew—*Sorex tundrensis*, is, perhaps, inappropriately named because it occurs throughout the state with the exception of south-central Alaska. It prefers dense vegetation consisting of grasses, dwarf birch, and dwarf willow growing on hillsides and other well-drained habitats. The species occurs in the boreal forest, coastal locations, and tundra habitats.

Little brown bat

I mentioned the annual migration of little brown bats previously. Little brown bats roost in trees and other foliage, hollows, caves, mine tunnels, and abandoned buildings during the day. Near dusk, they launch out to forage on insects. A colony of 500 bats can consume a half million mosquitoes in an evening.[118] Fortunately for the bats (and unfortunately for humans) there are plenty of mosquitoes in the boreal forest to support a large population of little brown bats. In addition, these bats feed on caddis flies, mayflies, and midges.

During flight, little brown bats continuously emit a string of high-pitched calls used for echolocation. While cruising, the calls are about 20 per second with 50 milliseconds between calls. When actively pursuing prey, the frequency of calls goes up to 200 per second with 5 milliseconds between calls. Calls are in the 40 to 80 kilohertz frequency range, that is, 40,000-80,000 cycles per second. The huge ears are an adaptation to receive these high-pitched sounds. Bats are able to calculate distance to objects by measuring or sensing the time it takes for their own calls to return from, or bounce off, the object.

Breeding occurs in the fall but, in little brown bats, embryonic development does not begin until the following May. During the winter, male sperm are stored in the female uteri. Finally, in the spring, ovulation and fertilization occur and gestation begins. A single, occasionally two, young is born in June or July. Each pup weighs about

25% of the body weight of the mother. While the mother forages, offspring are either left roosting with other young of the year in maternity colonies or are carried on the abdomen. Within a month the young are pretty independent. Most, if not all, of these maternity colonies in Alaska are thought to be associated with human-made structures that are heated. Recently, however, a maternity colony was found in southeast Alaska located under beach boulders.[119] This colony is geothermally heated.

Forest mammals on a changing landscape

I have indicated in several species accounts that the change of seasons affects the behavior, activity levels and location of mammals in Alaska's boreal forests. Moose, red squirrels, black bears and woodchucks behave differently in spring as opposed to fall. They are often located in different habitats in spring and in fall.

Similarly, the longer-term changes associated with ecological or plant succession have effects on the abundance of moose, red squirrels and bears at particular locations or geographic areas. Early to mid-succession forests tend to have more moose, more black bears and fewer squirrels than will be found at the very same location after it has progressed to late succession.

Birds of the boreal forest are affected in similar ways by the changing seasons and the progression of plant communities known as succession. In addition, migratory birds have to contend with disturbance events and succession in their winter habitats, often far removed from the boreal forests of Alaska. Now we turn to a few of these birds of the boreal forests.

REFERENCES

1   Hundertmark, K.J., Shields, G.F., Udina, I.G., Bowyer, R.T., Danilkin, A.A. and Schwartz, C.C. 2002. Mitochondrial phylogeography of moose (*Alces alces*): late Pleistocene divergence and population expansion. Molecular Phylogenetics and Evolution 22: 375-387.

2   Guthrie, R.D. 2006. New carbon dates link climatic change with human colonization. Nature 441: 207-209.

3   Bubenik, A.B. 1998. Evolution, taxonomy and morphophysiology, pp. 77-124 In: A.W. Franzmann, C.C. Schwartz and R.E. McCabe, editors, Ecology and management of the North American moose. Smithsonian Institution Press, Washington and London, 733 pp.

4   Miquelle, D.G. 1991. Are moose mice? The function of scent urination in moose. American Naturalist 138: 460-477.

5   Whittle, C.L., Bowyer, R.T., Clausen, T.P. and Duffy, L.K. 2000. Putative pheromones in urine of rutting moose (*Alces alces*): evolution of honest advertisement? Journal of Chemical Ecology 26: 2747-2762.

6   Bowyer, R.T., Van Ballenberghe, V. and Rock, K.R. 1994. Scent marking by Alaskan moose: characteristics and spatial distribution of rubbed trees. Canadian Journal of Zoology 72: 2186-2192.

7   Van Ballenberghe, V. and Miquelle, D.G. 1993. Mating in moose: timing, behavior, and male access patterns. Canadian Journal of Zoology 71: 1687-1690.

8   Estes, R.D. 1976. The significance of breeding synchrony in the wildebeest. East African Wildlife Journal 14: 135-152.

9   Bowyer, R.T., Van Ballenberghe, V. and Kie, J.G. 1998. Timing and synchrony of parturition in Alaskan moose: long-term versus proximal effects of climate. Journal of Mammalogy 79: 1332-1344.

10 Wilson, D.E. and Ruff, S. (editors) 1999. The Smithsonian book of North American mammals. Smithsonian Institution Press, Washington and London. 750 pp.

11 Risenhoover, K.L. 1989. Composition and quality of moose winter diets in interior Alaska. Journal of Wildlife Management 53: 568-577.

12 Kielland, K. and Bryant, J. 1998.Moose herbivory in taiga: effects of biogeochemistry and vegetation dynamics in primary succession. Oikos 82: 377-383.

13 Miquelle, D.G. and Van Ballenberghe, V. 1989. Impact of bark stripping by moose on aspen-spruce communities. Journal of Wildlife Management 53: 577-586.

14 Kielland, K., Bryant, J.P. and Ruess, R.W. 1997. Moose herbivory and carbon turnover of early successional stands in interior Alaska. Oikos 80: 25-30.

15 Irons, J.G.III, Bryant, J.P. and Oswood, M.W. 1991. Effects of moose browsing on decomposition rates of birch leaf litter in a subarctic stream. Canadian Journal of Fisheries and Aquatic Sciences 48: 442-444.

16 Tankersley, N.G. and Gasaway, W.C. 1983. Mineral lick use by moose in Alaska. Canadian Journal of Zoology 61: 2242-2249.

17 MacCracken, J.G., Van Ballenberghe, V. and Peek, J.M. 1993. Use of aquatic plants by moose: sodium hunger or foraging efficiency? Canadian Journal of Zoology 71: 2345-2351.

18 Murie, A. 1981. The grizzlies of Mt. McKinley. University of Washington Press, Seattle, 251 pp.

19 Ballard, W.B., Spraker, T.H. and Taylor, K.P. 1981. Causes of neonatal moose calf mortality in south central Alaska. Journal of Wildlife Management 45: 335-342.

20 Murie, A. 1944. The wolves of Mt. McKinley. University of Washington Press, Seattle, 238 pp.

21 Mech, L.D. 1970. The wolf: the ecology and behavior of an endangered species. Natural History Press, Garden City, 384 pp.

22 Lankester, M.W. and Samuel, W.M. 1997. Pests, parasites and diseases, pp. 479-518 In: A.W. Franzmann and C.C. Schwartz, editors, Ecology and management of the North American moose. Smithsonian Institution Press, Washington and London, 733 pp.

23 Elkin, B. and Zarnke, R.L. 2001. Common wildlife diseases and parasites in Alaska. Alaska Department of Fish and Game, Anchorage, 58 pp.

24 Dieterich, R.A. 1981. Alaskan wildlife diseases. University of Alaska, Fairbanks, 524 pp.

25 Hatler, D.F. 1967. Some aspects in the ecology of the black bear (*Ursus americanus*) in interior Alaska. MS Thesis, University of Alaska Fairbanks. 111 pp.

26 Smith, P.A. 1984. Kenai black bears and cranberries: bear food habits and densities. MS Thesis, University of Alaska Fairbanks, Alaska. 144 pp.

27 Schwartz, C.C. and Franzmann, A.W. 1991. Interrelationship of black bears to moose and forest succession in the northern coniferous forest. Wildlife Monographs 113: 1-58.

28 Smith, M.E., Hechtel, J.L. and Follmann, E.H. 1994. Black bear denning ecology in interior Alaska. International Conference on Bear Research and Management 9: 513-522.

29 Lindzey, F.G. 1976. Black bear population ecology. PhD Thesis, Oregon State University, Corvallis. 105 pp.

30 Graber, D.M. 1990. Winter behavior of black bears in the Sierra Navada, California. International Conference on Bear Research and Management 8: 269-272.

31 Bauer, E. and Bauer, P. 1996. Bears: behavior ecology and conservation. Swan Hill Press, Shrewsbury, England. 159 pp.

32 Modafferi, R.D. 1982. Black bear movements and home range study. Alaska Department of Fish and Game Final Report (Job 17.2R), Federal Aid in Wildlife Restoration. Juneau, 73 pp.

33 Smith, M.E. and Follmann, E.H. 1993. Grizzly bear, *Ursus arctos*, predation of a denned adult black bear, *U. americanus*. The Canadian Field-Naturalist 107: 97-99.

34 Ross, P.I., Hornbeck, G.E. and Horejsi, B.L. 1988. Late denning black bears killed by grizzly bear. Journal of Mammalogy 69:818-820.

35 Miller, S.D. 1985. An observation of inter- and intra-specific aggression involving brown bear, black bear and moose in south-central Alaska. Journal of Mammalogy 66: 805-806.

36 Rogers, L.L. and Mech, L.D. 1981. Interactions of wolves and black bears in northeastern Minnesota. Journal of Mammalogy 62: 434-436.

37 Sherwonit, B. 1998. Alaska's bears. Alaska Northwest Books, Anchorage and Seattle. 94 pp.

38 Gilbert, B.S. 1989. Use of winter feeding craters by snowshoe hares. Canadian Journal of Zoology 68: 1600-1602.

39 Bryant, J.P. and Kuropat, P.J. 1980. Selection of winter forage by subarctic browsing vertebrates: the role of plant chemistry. Annual Reviews of Ecology and Systematics 11: 261-285.

40 Swihart, R.K., Bryant, J.P. and Newton, L. 1994. Latitudinal patterns in consumption of woody plants by snowshoe hares in the eastern United States. Oikos 70: 427-434.

41 Bryant, J.P., Swihart, R.K., Reichardt, P.B. and Newton, L. 1994. Biogeography of woody plant chemical defense against snowshoe hare browsing: comparison of Alaska and eastern North America. Oikos 70: 385-395.

42 Keith, L.B. 1990. Dynamics of snowshoe hare populations, pp. 119-195 In: H.H. Genoways, editor, Current Mammology, volume 2. Plenum Press, New York and London

43 O'Donoghue, M. 1994. Early survival of juvenile snowshoe hares. Ecology 75: 1582-1592.

44 O'Donoghue, M. and Bergman, C.M. 1992. Early movements and dispersal of juvenile snowshoe hares. Canadian Journal of Zoology 70: 1787-1791.

45 Graf, R.P. and Sinclair, A.R.E. 1987. Parental care and adult aggression toward juvenile snowshoe hares. Arctic 40: 175-178.

46 Bergerud, A.T. 1983. Prey switching in a simple ecosystem. Scientific American 249: 130-138.

47 Stephenson, R.O., Grangaard, D.V. and Burch, J. 1991. Lynx, *Felis lynx*, predation on red foxes, *Vulpes vulpes*, caribou, *Rangifer tarandus*, and Dall sheep, *Ovis dalli*, in Alaska. Canadian Field-Naturalist 105: 255-262.

48 Staples, III, W. R. 1995. Lynx and coyote diet and habitat relationships during a low hare population on the Kenai Peninsula, Alaska. MS Thesis, Fairbanks, 150 pp.

49 Barash, D.P, 1971. Cooperative hunting in the lynx. Journal of Mammalogy 52: 480.

50 Nellis, C.H. and Keith, L.B. 1976. Population dynamics of coyotes in central Alberta, 1964-68. Journal of Wildlife Management 40: 389-399.

51 Murray, D.L. and Boutin, S. 1991. The influence of snow on lynx and coyote movements: does morphology affect behavior? Oecologia 88: 463-469.

52 Henry, J.D. 1996. Foxes: living on the edge. Northword Press, Inc., Minocqua, WI, 143 pp.

53 Henry, J.D. 1996. Red fox: the catlike canine. Smithsonian Institution Press, Washington, D.C., 174 pp.

54 Hobgood, T.W. 1984. Ecology of the red fox (*Vulpes vulpes*) in the Upper Susitna Basin, Alaska. MS Thesis, University of Alaska Fairbanks, 163 pp.

55 Smedshaug, C.A., Selas, V., Lund, S.E. and Sonerud, G.A. 1999. The effect of a natural reduction of red fox *Vulpes vulpes* on small game hunting bags in Norway. Wildlife Biology 5: 157-166.

56 Holley, T. 1994. No hide, no seek. Natural History 103: 42-45.

57 Sklepkovych, B.O. and Montevecchi, W.A. 1996. Food availability and food hoarding behaviour by red and arctic foxes. Arctic 49: 228-234.

58 Niewold, F.J.J. 1980. Aspects of the social structure of red fox populations: a summary. Biogeographica 18: 185-193.

59 Lawhead, B.E. 1983. Wolf den site characteristics in the Nelchina Basin, Alaska. MS Thesis, University of Alaska Fairbanks, 80 pp.

60 Wandeler, A.I. 1980. Epidemiology of fox rabies. Biogeographica 18: 237-249.

61 Bailey, E.P. 1993. Introduction of foxes to Aleutian islands—history, effects on avifauna and eradication. U.S. Fish and Wildlife Service Resource Publication 193, Washington, D.D., 53 pp.

62 Bailey, E.P. 1992. Red foxes, *Vulpes vulpes*, as biological control agents for introduced arctic foxes, *Alopex lagopus*, on Alaskan islands. Canadian Field-Naturalist 106: 200-205.

63 Jacobs, G.H. 1981. Comparative color vision. Academic Press, New York and Londin, 209 pp.

64 Smith, C.C. 1981. The indivisible niche of *Tamiasciurus*: an example of nonpartitioning of resources. Ecological Monographs 51: 343-363.

65 Smith, M.C. 1968. Red squirrel response to spruce cone failures in interior Alaska. Journal of Wildlife Management 32: 305-317.

66 Larsen, K.W. and Boutin, S. 1998. Sex-unbiased philopatry in the North American red squirrel: (*Tamiasciurus hudsonicus*). pp. 21-32 In: M.A. Steele, J.F. Merrit and D.A. Zegers, editors, Ecology and evolutionary biology of tree squirrels. Special Publication, Virginia Museum of Natural History, 320 pp.

67 Wolff, J.O. and Zasada, J.C. 1975. Red squirrel response to clearcut and shelterwood systems in interior Alaska. USDA Forest Service Research Note PNW-255, 7 pp.

68 Keith, L.B. and Cary, J.R. 1991. Mustelid, squirrel, and porcupine population trends during a snowshoe hare cycle. Journal of Mammalogy 72: 373-378.

69 Wells-Gosling, N. and Heaney, L.R. 1984. *Glaucomys sabrinus*. Mammalian Species No. 229: 1-8.

70 Cowan, I. McT. 1936. Nesting habits of the flying squirrel, *Glaucomys sabrinus*. Journal of Mammalogy 17: 58-60.

71 Mowrey, R.A. and Zasada, J.C. 1985. Den tree use and movements of northern flying squirrels in interior Alaska and implications for forest management. In: W.R. Meehan, T.R. Merrell, Jr. and T.A. Hanley, editors, Fish and wildlife relationships in old-growth forests: proceedings of a symposium (April 1982, Juneau, Alaska). Bookmasters, Ashland, Ohio.

72 Brink, C.H. and Dean, F.C. 1966. Spruce seed as food of red squirrels and flying squirrels in interior Alaska. Journal of Wildlife Management 30: 503-512.

73 Maser, Z., Maser, C. and Trappe, J.M. 1985. Food habits of the northern flying squirrel (*Glaucomys sabrinus*) in Oregon. Canadian Journal of Zoology 63: 1084-1088.

74 Stack, J.W. 1925. Courage shown by flying squirrel, *Glaucomys volans*. Journal of Mammalogy 6: 128-129.

75 King, C. 1989. The natural history of weasels and stoats. Cornell University Press, Ithaca, 253 pp.

76 Feder, S. 1990. Determinants of seasonal coat color change in weasels (*Mustela erminea*) from two populations. MS Thesis, University of Alaska Fairbanks, 155 pp.

77 Rust, C. 1962. Temperature as a modifying factor in the spring pelage change of short-tailed weasels. Journal of Mammalogy 43: 323-328.

78 Rothschild, M. 1942. Change of pelage in the stoat *Mustela erminea* L. Nature 149: 78.

79 Lieb, J. 1994. Weasels. Alaska Department of Fish and Game Wildlife Notebook Series, 3 pp.

80 Harbo, S.J.Jr. 1958. An investigation of mink in interior and southeastern Alaska. MS Thesis, University of Alaska Fairbanks, 108 pp.

81 Ben-David, M., Flynn, R.W. and Schell, D.M. 1997. Annual and seasonal changes in diets of martens: evidence from stable isotope analysis. Oecologia 111: 280-291.

82 Sinclair, W., Dunstone, N. and Poole, T.B. 1974. Aerial and underwater visial acuity in the mink (*Mustela vison* Schreber). Animal Behaviour 22: 965-974.

83 Melquist, W.E., Whitman, J.S. and Hornocker, M.G. 1980. Resource partitioning and coexistence of sympatric mink and river otter populations, pp. 187-220

In: J.A. Chapman, and D. Pursley, editors, Worldwide furbearer conference Proceedings, Volume I

84 Wise, M.H., Linn, I.J. and Kennedy, C.R. 1981. A comparison of the feeding biology of mink *Mustela vison* and otter *Lutra lutra*. Journal of Zoology, London 195: 181-213.

85 Erlinge, S. 1969. Food habits of the otter (*Lutra lutra* L.) and the mink (*Mustela vison* Schreber) in a trout water in southern Sweden. Oikos 20: 1-7.

86 Buskirk, S.W. and Powell, R.A. 1994. Habitat ecology of fishers and American martens, pp. 283-296 In: S.W. Buskirk, A.S. Harestad, M.G. Raphael and R.A. Powell, editors, Martens, sables, and fishers: biology and conservation. Cornell University Press, Ithaca and London, 484 pp.

87 Shepherd, P. and Melchior, H. 1994. Marten. ADF&G Wildlife Notebook Series.

88 Buskirk, S.W. and MacDonald, S.O. 1984. Seasonal food habits of marten in south-central Alaska. Canadian Journal of Zoology 62: 944-950.

89 Buskirk, S.W. 1984. Seasonal use of resting sites by marten in south-central Alaska. Journal of Wildlife Management 48: 950-953.

90 Roze, U. 1989. The North American porcupine. Smithsonian Institution Press, Washington D.C. and London. 261 pp.

91 Murie, O.J. 1926. The porcupine in northern Alaska. Journal of Mammalogy 7: 109-113.

92 Fancy, S.G. 1980. Spring studies of bison along the northwest Alaskan pipeline route.

LGL Alaska Research Associates, Inc. Final Report, 6 pp. + 5 maps.

93 Griffin, B. and Johnson, D,M, 1994. American bison. Wildlife Notebook Series, Alaska Department of Fish and Game, 2 pp.

94 Berger, M. 1996. Summer habitat relationships and foraging ecology of the Delta bison herd. MS Thesis, University of Alaska Fairbanks, 113 pp.

95 Koprowski, J.L. 1987. Nocturnal activity of the woodchuck, *Marmota monax*, in an urban park in Ohio. Canadian Field-Naturalist 101: 606-607.

96 Bonenfant, M. and Kramer, D.L. 1996. The influence of distance to burrow on flight initiation distance in the woodchuck, *Marmota monax*. Behavioral Ecology 7: 299-303.

97 Swihart, R.K. 1991. Influence of *Marmota monax* on vegetation in hayfields. Journal of Mammalogy 72: 791-795.

98 English, E.L. and Bowers, M.A. 1994. Vegetational gradients and proximity to woodchuck (*Marmota monax*) burrows in an old field. Journal of Mammalogy 75: 775-780.

99 Holecamp, K.E. 1984. Dispersal in ground-dwelling squirrels, pp. 297-320 In: J.O. Murie and G.R. Michener, editors, The biology of ground-dwelling squirrels. University of Nebraska Press, Lincoln.

100 Curby, C. 1994. Marmot. Wildlife Notebook Series, Alaska Department of Fish and Game, 2 pp.

101 Ferron, J. 1996. How do woodchucks (*Marmota monax*) cope with harsh winter conditions? Journal of Mammalogy 77: 412-416.

102 Spurrier, W.A., Oeltgen, P.R. and Myers, R.D. 1987. Hibernation 'trigger' from hibernating woodchucks (*Marmota monax*) induces physiological alterations and opiate-like responses in the primate (*Macacca mulatta*). Journal of Thermoregulatory Biology 12: 139-142.

103 Armitage, K.B. 1999. Evolution of sociality in marmots. Journal of Mammalogy 80: 1-10.

104 Pruitt, W.O.Jr. 1967. Wild harmony: animals of the north. Harper and Row, New York, 180 pp.

105 Viitala, J., Korpimaki, E., Palokangas, P. and Koivula, M. 1995. Attraction of kestrels to vole scent marks visible in ultraviolet light. Nature 373: 425-427.

106 Whitney, P.H. 1973. Population biology and energetics of three species of small mammals in the taiga of interior Alaska. MS Thesis, University of Alaska Fairbanks, 254 pp.

107 Durst, J.D. 1984. Small mammals in relation to natural revegetation of gold dredge tailings at Nyac, Alaska. MS Thesis, University of Alaska Fairbanks, 105pp.

108 West, S.D. 1974. Post-burn population response of the northern red-backed vole, *Cleithrionomys rutilus*, in interior Alaska. MS Thesis, University of Alaska Fairbanks, 66 pp.

109 Ferkin, M.H., Sorokin, E.S., Johnston, R.E. and Lee, C.J. 1997. Attractiveness of scents varies with protein content of the diet in meadow voles. Animal Behaviour 53: 133-141.

110 Lehmkuhl, K.L. 2000. Population dynamics and ecology of yellow-cheeked voles (*Microtus xanthognathus*) in early post-fire seres of interior Alaska. MS Thesis, University of Alaska Fairbanks, 106 pp.

111 Wolff, J.O. and Lidicker, W.Z. Jr. 1981. Communal winter nesting and food sharing in taiga voles. Behavioral Ecology and Sociobiology 9: 237-240.

112 Johnson, W.N., Paragai, T.F. and Katnik, D.D. 1995. The relationship of wildland fire to lynx and marten populations and habitat in interior Alaska. Final Report, U.S. Fish and Wildlife Service, Galena, Alaska.

113 Churchfield, S. 1991. The natural history of shrews. Cornell University Press, Ithaca, 178 pp.

114 Buchler, E.R. 1976. The use of echolocation by the wandering shrew (*Sorex vagrans*). Animal Behaviour 24: 858-873.

115 Dotsch, C. and Koenigswald, W.V. 1978. Zur Rotfarbung von Soricidenzahnen. Zeitschrift Saugetierk. 43: 65-70.

116 McNab, B.K. 1991. The energy expenditure of shrews, pp. 35-45 In: J.S. Findley and T.L. Yates, editors. The biology of the Soricidae. The Museum of Southwestern Biology, University of New Mexico, Albuquerque, 91 pp.

117 Demboski, J.R. and Cook, J.A. 2003. Phylogenetic diversification within the *Sorex cinereus* group (Soricidae). Journal of Mammalogy 84: 144-158.

118 Whitman, J. 1994. Bats. Alaska Department of Fish and Game Wildlife Notebook Series, 2 pp.

119 West, E.W. and Swain, U. 1999. Surface activity and structure of a hydrothermally-heated maternity colony of the little brown bat, *Myotis lucifugus*, in Alaska. Canadian Field-Naturalist 113: 425-429.

5.

VEGETARIANS, MEAT-EATERS, AND JACKS-OF-ALL-TRADES: A FEW BIRDS OF THE BOREAL FOREST

Grouses

Seven species of grouse are found in Alaska. Three of those—ruffed grouse, spruce grouse and sharp-tailed grouse—occupy the boreal forests. Three others, the ptarmigans, turn white in an autumn molt and are usually thought of as tundra species. These three are willow ptarmigan, rock ptarmigan and white-tailed ptarmigan. The ptarmigan species are discussed in Chapter 8, although, in winter these birds often migrate down into the boreal forests. The seventh species is the blue grouse of the coastal rain forests.

The habitat preferences of the three forest grouse species are fairly distinct in summertime and through most of the winter. The sharp-tailed grouse is a bird of prairie, steppe and brushland. In the interior these habitats are associated with disturbance. Hence, sharp-tailed grouse are linked with early plant succession and can be found around the Delta barley fields, river bars and burns dominated by grasses and fireweed. The spruce grouse lives mainly in dense conifer-

ous forests and, therefore, is a late successional animal. Ruffed grouse live in hardwood and mixed hardwood/coniferous forests. That is, ruffed grouse are mid-successional birds.

Each of these species is unique but all share some common characteristics. All male grouse and ptarmigan have inflatable, brightly colored **combs** over the eyes, especially during breeding season (see Figure 8.7). Several species have air sacs in their necks as well. These air sacs can be expanded revealing, in some species, a patch of brightly colored skin called the **cervical** (neck) **apterium** (no feathers). The bare skin is a display mechanism used by males in dominance-hierarchy and courtship behaviors.

Another feature common to these species is the presence of feathers on the legs, at least to the base of the toes. The insulative value of these feathers is obvious. The three ptarmigan species add feathers to the toes in the fall for even better insulation and for increased foot surface area for walking on snow. In lieu of feathers, the other four grouse species develop small projections from the toes, like little scales, that increase the surface area of the feet and aid in walking on snow. These toes, with their scales, are called **pectinate toes** (Figure 5.1).

Unlike many birds of the Far North, grouse have feathers over their nostrils. It is likely they function in water conservation by causing exhaled water vapor to condense before it completely leaves the body.

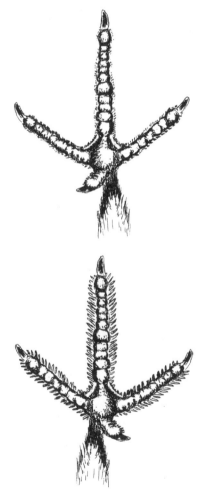

Figure 5.1: Comparison of a grouse foot in summer (top) and in winter (bottom). Note that the tarsus (lower leg bone) is covered with feathers. In winter, each of the three front toes has small lateral projections called pectinations. These projections give the bird better floatation in the snow.

The digestive tracts of all the grouse species are similar though they have somewhat different diets (Figure 5.2). Like other birds that eat seeds and other fibrous material, grouse have a two-part stomach that includes a grinding **gizzard** and an acid-producing chamber, the **proventriculus**. Ground up material leaving the stomach enters a small intestine, where digestion of proteins, and readily metabolized carbohydrates proceeds. The structural carbohydrates of woody buds is cellulose, the same material that requires such complicated plumbing in ruminants and hares. How do grouse handle cellulose? Structurally and physiologically, grouse are more similar to hares than to moose. At the junction of small and large intestines in the grouse species there are two ceca (pleural of cecum) that receive part of the partially digested food material. As in lagomorphs, these ceca support bacterial populations that digest cellulose and produce energy-rich volatile fatty acids. The VFAs are absorbed through the walls of the caeca, along with B-vitamins released by the bacteria. Some of the bacteria may be digested in the large intestine. Grouse seem to be better adapted to a diet of vegetation than ducks and geese. The caeca of grouse are five times longer than those of waterfowl, perhaps due to the energetic costs waterfowl would incur if they carried the extra weight on long-distance migrations.[1]

For decades, biology students at the University of Alaska Fairbanks were greeted at the lab door by what appeared to be the spruce grouse from hell. The bird was mounted in a threat display with eye combs fully inflated, wings spread and tail feathers erect. The wingspan was almost three feet. It was a specimen of the capercaillie, a native of Eurasian pine forests and the world's

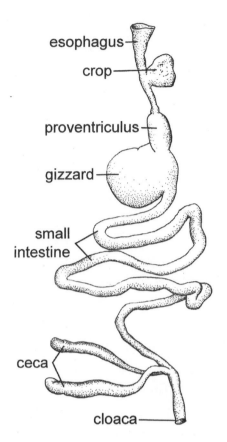

Figure 5.2: Digestive tract of a grouse. The stomach consists of two parts, the proventriculus and the gizzard. The proventriculus is the acid-secreting part; the gizzard is the grinding part. Near the posterior end of the intestine are a pair of ceca that function much as the cecum in hares. Unlike hares, grouse do not reingest cecal material.

largest grouse. Male capercaillie may weigh up to 6.5 kg (14 pounds).

The largest of the North American grouse is the sage grouse, with males sometimes exceeding 3 kg (6.6 pounds) in weight. The blue grouse is the largest grouse in Alaska, followed by the sharp-tailed grouse. The smallest is the white-tailed ptarmigan with males only about a third the weight of male sharp-tails. The other five species all weigh about the same, almost double that of the white-tailed ptarmigan.

Spruce grouse—In Alaska, spruce grouse (*Canachites canadensis*) are widespread but missing from the North Slope, Seward Peninsula, Alaska Peninsula and parts of southeast Alaska. Its range extends eastward through the boreal coniferous forest to eastern Canada. In the west, populations occur in the northern Cascades and parts of the northern Rockies including Idaho, western Montana and northwestern Wyoming. Elsewhere in the U.S., spruce grouse are found in Wisconsin, Minnesota, Michigan, Vermont, Maine and New York.

As the name suggests, there is a strong relationship between spruce grouse and spruce trees. In interior Alaska, preferred habitats are 1) white spruce-birch communities with an understory of grasses, blueberries and cranberries and, 2) black spruce communities with blueberry, cranberry and lichen understory.[2] A critical factor seems to be the presence of concealing cover at ground level. In Michigan, other conifers such as balsam fir and jack pine contribute to spruce grouse habitat. Balsam firs are often frequented by grouse, and jack pines are a critical source of winter food.

The diet of spruce grouse varies considerably over the course of the year in Alaska. In summer, berries predominate (cranberries, crowberries and blueberries) with horsetail stems and tips and blueberry leaves also contributing (Figure 3.9). In the fall, berries are supplemented with spruce needles; by early November the diet is almost entirely spruce needles.[3] In the spring, snowmelt exposes last year's cranberries and unripe crowberries, both of which are added to the diet. Young chicks through their first summer subsist largely on insects.

One wonders about the nutritional value of spruce needles to these grouse. First, recall our discussion of the toxic resins in the needles of spruce. Surely these compounds must have some effect on grouse. In addition, analyses show that these needles have only 8-9% protein, far less than the berries of summer. Though spruce grouse eat more food in the winter (daily intake of up to 30% of body weight in spruce needles), they lose weight.[4] One functional response to this increase in fiber and resin intake is to increase the size of the caeca in winter.

In the spring (late April), adult males establish breeding territories in fairly dense stands of spruce or spruce and birch with open understory. The male employs several behaviors to entice females to breed. Strutting is performed with tail feathers erect and fanned, neck fairly erect, eyecombs engorged (inflated), neck feathers fluffed (erected), throat feathers lowered and wings drooped slightly. During the actual strut or deliberate walk, the male fans the tail feathers on the side opposite the foot being lifted. So alternate sides of the tail are fanned as the male alternates feet in the walk. This feather movement produces a rustling sound. Some other courtship behaviors include vertical head bobbing, wing flicking, neck jerk display and head-on rush.[5]

Males also produce aerial displays that often consist of short, vertical flights during which wings make a drumming sound, followed by fluttering back to the ground. In some cases this downward fluttering seems to be concluded by one or two loud sounds produced by clapping the wings together.

Females in Alaska lay about 7.5 eggs per clutch but, elsewhere in this bird's range, clutch size may differ (average of 5.8 eggs in Nova Scotia, 4.9 in Alberta, 4.7 in Minnesota). Hatching takes from 22-25 days with a hatching success of over 80%. During incubation, females spend about 90% of the daylight hours sitting on the nest.

Spruce grouse fall victim to a variety of predators including red foxes, coyotes, weasels, barred owls and great horned owls. Red squirrels are nest predators, eating the eggs before they hatch.[6] One wonders if red squirrels take the hatchlings as well in light of their predation on newborn hares.

Aside from direct observation of a predatory act, how would we identify predators of spruce grouse? Finding spruce grouse feathers in the woods can provide clues. If the shafts or bases of the feathers are broken, the predator was probably a mammal. Foxes and coyotes chew the feathers. Predatory birds typically pluck the large feathers, leaving them intact. Feathers outside the dens of foxes are an obvious indicator of who did the deed. Weasels leave leftovers of grouse meals under nearby logs. Finally, spruce grouse toes show up in regurgitated owl pellets.

Ruffed grouse—Ruffed grouse (*Bonasa umbellus*) can be recognized by several morphological characters. Both males and females are crested (separating them from spruce grouse) and both have rounded tails (separating them from sharp-tailed grouse). Both sexes have a ruff of dark neck feathers that, in males, is erected during courtship and aggressive displays. Ruffed grouse have a broad black band across the tail with narrow gray bands on both sides. In females and some immature males the black band is incomplete or interrupted in the center of the tail. In contrast, the tails of spruce grouse have, at the tip, a broad brown band. Ruffed grouse, across much of their range, occur in two color phases, gray and reddish-brown.

The geographic range of the ruffed grouse includes the boreal forest of North America plus southward extensions to south-central Alaska, British Columbia, Washington and Oregon. The Cascades, northern Rockies, Appalachians and the New England states are part of the range of this species. Isolated populations occur in Indiana, Illinois, Missouri, North and South Dakota and central Montana.

Ruffed grouse occupy a variety of habitats from mixed conifer-deciduous woodlands to deciduous forests and forest edges. Usually the habitat includes aspen and birch. Habitat improvement for ruffed grouse amounts to turning back the succession clock. Logging can have a beneficial effect; cutting mature aspen stands in interior Alaska leads to increases in ruffed grouse population densities. Part of the post-fire ecology of the boreal forest, therefore, includes a succession from sharp-tailed to ruffed to spruce grouse as the early, open stages, give way to mid-succession aspen woods and, ultimately, to mature spruce forests.

In terms of feeding, aspen and poplars are critical and birch is important. Winter foods are, mainly, buds, twigs and catkins of trees, especially aspen, and buds of willow. In spring and summer, birch catkins, strawberry and other herbaceous leaves and berries sustain ruffed grouse. Insects are eaten, to an extent, by adults but chicks feed heavily on insects. In the first two weeks of life, 70% of the diet is insects. The percentage falls to 30% in weeks 3-4 and 5% by late summer.

Ruffed grouse exhibit population fluctuations typically approximating a 10-year cycle.

In peak years bird densities of 69 per km^2 (180 per mile^2; Michigan) and 136 per km^2 (353 per mile^2; Minnesota) have been estimated. These are about 8-15 times higher than population densities at their lowest. Several explanations have been offered for this cycling: 1) there appears to be some cycling in aspen seed crop which may affect grouse cycles, 2) cycles may be driven by predators switching to alternate prey when snowshoe hare populations are low and, 3) ruffed grouse may regulate their own populations by adjusting breeding territory size according to population size. This last possibility is based, primarily, on research on willow ptarmigan.

In ptarmigan populations at high population densities, males establish huge breeding territories, forcing lots of birds onto marginal habitat, where they fall prey to an array of predators. This high predation brings the population down. At low population density, males establish smaller territories and, thus, a larger proportion of males can establish territories where their survival is higher. Under these latter conditions, the population increases.[7] We don't know if these relationships apply to ruffed grouse.

Adult ruffed grouse are relatively sedentary, rarely moving a mile from their familiar haunts. Young of the year disperse from their broodmates in early fall. Dispersal of perhaps 1.6 km (1 mile) from the female's home range is the norm but some birds disperse up to 12 km (7.5 miles). Adult males, especially, exhibit a high fidelity to their home range.

Perhaps the most spectacular behavior of ruffed grouse is the spring drumming of territorial males. Drumming can be heard from long distances by grouse and by humans. A male finds a suitable log in relatively dense forest cover, braces itself with its tail and digs its claws into the wood. Then it begins flapping its wings in a series of powerful upstrokes and downstrokes (Figure 5.3). Each individual male tends to use the same number of wing beats with every drumming episode. The drumming or throbbing sound is a result of the air compression caused by the wing beats. A range of 44-51 beats per drumming episode has been reported; each episode takes 8-11 seconds. The drumming serves to attract females and announce the male's territory to other males.

After copulation the female finds a suitable nest site, typically near a clone of aspen trees. She establishes a nest at the base of a tree with open undergrowth and a relatively open canopy. She lays two eggs every three days, so an average clutch of 11 eggs takes 17 days. Incubation doesn't start until all eggs are laid. This insures that all the eggs will hatch in a 1-2 day period.

Figure 5.3: Ruffed grouse drumming behavior. The drumming noise results from the rapid displacement of air by the wings. Redrawn from Johnsgard (1983).

Incubation to hatching takes 23-24 days; the female is on the nest 95% of the day, taking short breaks to feed in nearby aspens.

Females actually defend their nests with a "broken wing" stunt involving an erratic, fluttering flight that lures potential predators away from the nest. After the chicks hatch, she will, at the approach of predators, spread her tail, hiss and squeal. As an added protection, chicks scatter in response to vocal signals from their mother.

Predators of ruffed grouse may focus on the nest with its relatively defenseless eggs and/or chicks. Nest predators include both birds and small mammals. Corvids (ravens, crows and magpies) work the edge of the forest or throughout a small patch of trees. Weasels, mink and red foxes take eggs and, occasionally, chicks and adult birds. Predatory birds that occasionally prey on ruffed grouse include great horned owl, gyrfalcon, northern hawk owl and long-eared owl.[8]

Sharp-tailed grouse—Alex and I were wading through 18 inches of snow, working our way up an abandoned road near Donnelly Dome, south of Delta Junction. Our eyes were focused in the alder patches on either side of the road because we were hunting snowshoe hares. Without warning the snow erupted beneath our feet and off flew a sharp-tailed grouse! This was an exciting demonstration of the grouse's subnivean roosting, an energy-conserving behavior. The air temperature that winter day was -18°C (0°F); the temperature down in the snow was -6°C (20°F). Until we disturbed it, the bird was enjoying a 12C° advantage. The lower the air temperature, the greater the advantage. Ruffed grouse and the three ptarmigan species also rest under the snow.

The sharp-tailed grouse (*Pedioecetes phasianellus)*, as the name suggests, has central tail feathers that are longer than the rest. The pointed tail is especially obvious during male courtship displays but can be seen during other activities. The sharp-tailed is the only grouse of interior and northern Alaska with yellowish eye combs; all the others have red combs. Also, the male sharp-tailed is the only one in the area that displays a cervical apterium during courtship. The naked skin of these inflatable air sacs is pinkish to pale violet. Blue grouse, in coastal Alaska, have yellow eye combs, but yellowish cervical apteria, and their tails are not pointed.

This grouse occupies prairie, steppe, brushy, and muskeg habitats across the northern part of North America. Its geographic distribution extends southward through the great plains of the Canadian provinces and northern states with isolated populations as far south as southern Colorado and southwest Nebraska. Formerly, sharp-tailed grouse were even more widespread. Hunting and habitat alteration led to its extirpation from Kansas, Illinois, California, Oklahoma, Iowa, Nevada, New Mexico, and Oregon. Attempts to reintroduce this species are ongoing.

Summer habitat is characterized by relatively dense herbaceous cover interspersed with shrubs. In Alaska, these habitats are either early successional stages on floodplains and Uplands or muskeg habitat. Ground that was cleared for agriculture and abandoned is prime habitat for sharp-tails. Alternatively, burns that have progressed to a mixture of grasses, fireweed and shrubs also support these birds. The 1983 Rosie Creek burn, west of Fairbanks, is moving through plant succession that has been favorable for sharp-tails but is rapidly becoming better ruffed grouse habitat. At this point in the history of Alaska, the distribution of sharp-tailed grouse is scattered and ephemeral. However, we might imagine that during glacial episodes in the Pleistocene when the grass-dominated steppes were widespread, this grouse was probably also widespread.

In winter the open areas occupied during the summer are often subjected to winds that put a hard crust on snow. This crust may cut the birds off from regular forage species and make it impossible for them to roost under the snow. Sharp-tails are known to exhibit seasonal movements from more open terrain in the summer to more protected, more forested habitats in winter. In Alaska, these movements might be tens of km in distance. In the Saint James Bay area of eastern Canada a migration southward from the muskeg in fall may amount to 180 km (110 miles) or more.

During the snow-free period, foods include clover, dandelion, goldenrod, yarrow and members of the buckwheat family (dock, bistort, and smartweed). Cultivated grains, where available, contribute significantly to the diet. Barley and hay fields in the interior are visited regularly by sharp-tails. Insects such as ants, beetles, moths, crickets, and grasshoppers contribute to the diet and are especially important for rapidly growing young of the year. In Alaska, winter foods include the buds and catkins of paper birch and dwarf birch, aspen buds, rose hips, buffaloberry and tamarack leaf buds. In the summer, birds forage most actively near dawn and dusk. In winter, birds forage all day long. In winter Alaska day length is not very long.

Are these winter foods enough to sustain sharp-tailed grouse? The answer probably depends on the severity of the winter and accessibility of foods of highest nutritional value. In the aspen parklands of Canada males suffer the greatest weight losses during the spring, presumably due to territorial defense and courtship behaviors. Females lose nearly 1% of body weight per day while incubating eggs in the spring.[9] In interior Alaska, where energy demands in winter may be higher, these birds may exhibit greater weight losses in winter than in spring.

At the onset of breeding season in the spring males congregate in habitat suitable for displaying to prospective mates. Dominant males establish and defend small territories within which they strut their stuff for the females. An assembly area with its array of territories is referred to as a **lek** breeding system. The leks are typically located on relatively open, dry, and elevated ground. Few leks are found in depressions. These breeding sites are probably reused until vegetation changes render them unsuitable. In other words, leks are probably established on grounds exhibiting a specific stage in plant succession.

In the lek breeding system, some males establish territories and some don't. The non-territorial males have no chance to mate. One would assume that all the territorial males have some breeding success; however, that is not the case. A study in southern Manitoba tracked 47 established (territorial) males over a breeding season. Of those 47, 23 were not observed to breed at all. Nine of the 47 males accounted for 75% of the observed copulations.[10] So, even on breeding territories, breeding success is variable.

One would assume that birds in the center of the lek would be most successful and those out on the periphery less successful. These centrally located birds are heavier, in better condition and, presumably, able to stay on territory longer and compete more successfully for females.[11]

A male defends his territory from intruding males by rushing forward while making cackling and whining vocalizations. If these behaviors do not work, the resident male dances. With head low, tail erect, combs inflated, air sacs expanded, and wings outstretched, the male rapidly stamps his feet. This behavior is followed by an attack including pecking, feather pulling, and wing-beating. Often both males will flutter into the air up to 1 m high while scratching and wing beating.

Receptive females allow copulation and then leave the area. That is, the breeding territory has only one habitat requirement for the female: the dominant male. Nest sites average 0.4-1.8 km away from the nearest lek and are typically located in thicker cover than found on the lek. Nests are often located under trees or shrubs. One to three days after copulation the female begins laying eggs at a rate of an egg every 1-2 days. Each female lays an average of 9-11 eggs and begins to incubate them after the last egg is laid. Hatching begins after 21-23 days incubation.

Breeding male sharp-tailed grouse appear to be much more sensible in terms of time management than bull moose in the rut. Bulls, once they have accumulated a harem, are constantly vigilant lest a satellite bull or another worthy bull sneak in for a copulation. Among sharp-tails, males arrive on the territory before dawn, display and hang out for 2 to 4 hours and then

Figure 5.4: A size comparison of six owls of interior and northern Alaska. The snowy owl is primarily a tundra dweller but occasionally is seen in forested or grassland habitats.

move to foraging areas for much of the rest of the day. They return to the territory in the evening and then roost for the night. Thus, breeding behaviors are strongly tied to a daily clock and also to day length.

It is interesting that males display on territories in the fall, when days are the same length as during breeding in the spring. Fortunately for the species, females are not similarly stimulated; they are not interested in the males. If a female were to be attracted and also reproductively ready, she might end up laying a clutch of eggs that would hatch in early winter with virtually no chance for survival. Fall reproductive effort in females would be totally wasted. So, females are definitely more "sensible," in an adaptive sense, than are males.

The eggs of these grouse are taken by ground squirrels, magpies, ravens, and several mustelids. Chicks and adults fall prey to an array of terrestrial and aerial predators. Coyotes, mink, weasels and red foxes all take a toll. Aerial predators include red-tailed hawk, northern goshawk, peregrine falcon, gyrfalcon, great horned owl and northern harrier.[12] Raptorial birds often capture grouse in flight but also take them on the ground.

Owls

Ten owl species regularly occur in Alaska. The barred owl, northern pygmy owl, northern saw-whet owl, and western screech owl are (in Alaska) restricted to the coastal forests of Southeast Alaska. The snowy owl is primarily a tundra resident. The other five species are residents of the boreal forest. They include the boreal owl, great gray owl, great horned owl, northern hawk-owl and the short-eared owl (Figure 5.4). Of the five, three are primarily **diurnal**, that is, active in daylight hours. The other two (boreal and great horned) are **nocturnal**.

Hunting at night requires heightened senses. The eyes of owls are large and specialized for vision at low light intensity. The weight of an owl's eyes makes up 1-5% of its body weight. That would be equivalent to a 100-pound woman having a 0.5 to 2.5 pound eye in each socket. Instead of being spherical, owl eyes are tubular and are surrounded by bony plates called **sclerotic rings**. With this configuration, the eye doesn't move around in the socket as it does in humans; the extrinsic eye muscles are almost nonexistent. Therefore, an owl cannot track the movement of an object in the visual field by moving its eyes. Instead, it has to move its head. Owls have great head mobility; they are able to swivel their heads 270° to each side. This rotation allows them to look behind them without turning around. For comparison, the field of view of an owl (without swiveling its head) is 110° of which the center 70° is binocular vision. In humans the field of view is 180°; binocular vision covers 140°.

Most owls are normally focused on distant objects, as are we, but can focus on objects as close as about 1 m (39 inches). Smaller species of owls are able to focus on objects less than 1 m away, a handy capability for predators of smaller prey. The **near point of vision,** the distance beyond which the eye can focus, for great horned owls is 0.85 m (2.8 feet); in barn owls it is 0.1 m (4 inches). How fast can owls change their focus? Hawk-owls have been reported to focus through 100 diopters per second. At that rate I'd get really dizzy and throw up!

What about night vision? Many owls have the eyeshine that indicates a *tapetum* behind the retina. A sacrifice made by many nocturnal animals is **acuity**. Visual acuity is the ability to accurately place an object in the visual field. It appears that the densely packed rod receptors are wired to relatively few interneurons, a condition called **sensory convergence**. The dense pack of rods ensures that a signal will be generated by a photon of light but the wiring ensures that the owl will not be quite sure exactly where the light came from. Errors in acuity are small errors, usually not large enough to cause an owl to miss a vole. Many owls are able to fine-tune their nighttime hunting skills by using their highly evolved sense of hearing.

Most studies of owl hearing have focused on barn owls. Barn owls and probably other owls can locate and capture mice scurrying along in total darkness. Owl hearing depends on several anatomical adaptations, the most obvious of which is the **facial disk**. When you look at an owl's face you see, around each eye, a pattern of facial feathers that makes a pair of parabolic dishes. These dishes collect and amplify sounds and direct them toward the external ear. In some owls there is an additional feature, the ear flaps (beneath the eyes), that may further accentuate hearing. By the way, the ear tufts of owls, the horns of the great horned owl, for instance, have nothing to do with hearing.

Yet another feature that enhances hearing is an asymmetry of the skull itself. In many owls the external openings to the ear canals are shaped differently and are positioned differently on each side of the head. The opening is high on the right side and low on the left side (Figure 5.5). To understand why, we will have to think about how animals use hearing to localize sounds.

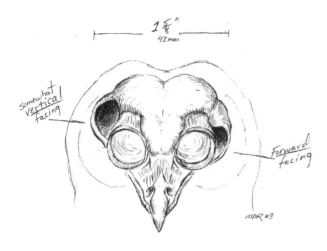

Figure 5.5: Frontal view of a boreal owl skull. Notice that the external ear openings on the sides of the skull differ in their positions; that on the right is higher than the one on the left. This skull asymmetry allows for more precise prey location (see text).

First, let us locate a sound source in the horizontal plane. There are two possible ways we can decide whether the sound is coming from the left or the right. First, our brains can register differences in arrival times at the two ears. If the sound arrives at the left ear first, it must have originated to our left. How much was the difference? That will determine how far to the left. Humans can detect differences of 570 microseconds; barn owls can detect differences of as little as 10 microseconds. The other possibility is to detect differences in the strength of the sound arriving in the two different ears. Stronger in the right ear? The source of the sound must be to the right.

What about the vertical plane? Owls with asymmetrical skulls are able to detect differences in arrival times of sounds from above or below the plane of the skull if the source is directly in front of them. When attempting to locate prey making sounds, an owl typically moves its head side to side until it is pointing directly at the sound. It then can get a reading on the vertical aspect of the sound source as well.

All birds of prey regurgitate indigestible bits of their prey. The digestive efficiency of owls seems to be less than that of hawks; they tend to include more bone in their regurgitated pellets than do hawks. One way to study what owls eat is to examine what they throw up. Often, investigators carefully search the ground underneath roosting sites and pick up the pellets. The teeth and sometimes the jaws of rodents, shrews, and even hares remain intact and can be identified as to genus or species. Of course, knowledge of food habits can be also gained from direct observations of kills or of prey returned to the nest during breeding season. Large owls cough up large pellets, and small owls make small pellets. It is impossible to identify the species of owl by examining the pellet, so some care is required to make sure you have matched the right pellet to the right owl.

Great horned owl—A number of summers ago the local *Fairbanks Daily News-Miner* reported on a retired couple driving through interior Alaska in a recreational vehicle. They had driven up from the lower 48 with their pet dog, Spiffy, a Pomeranian. One evening east of Tok they pulled over to "air" Spiffy. While Spiffy was out doing his business, a great horned owl swooped down, picked up the little dog, and carried him away. The incident definitively answered the question: will a great horned owl prey on house pets? Every year a number of domestic cats go missing in Alaska, and I doubt if they got lost.

Generally, great horned owls (*Bubo virginianus*) are resident in Alaska all year. However, if food becomes scarce in winter, these birds may fly south. We have a pair of these owls living in our rural-residential area west of Fairbanks. A mid-winter treat is to be outdoors in the evening and hear one of the pair hooting and the other responding. Male and female calls can be distinguished: the male's call is a *bu-bubu booh booh*; that of the female is *bu-bububu booh*. These calls look similar on paper, but the rhythms of the two are quite different. These duets are really a part of courtship. Nesting sites include old nests, hollows in trees, protected crevices on cliffs and ground under trees and between rocks.

Among western hemisphere owls, it is the great horned owl that has the largest geographic distribution. This species occurs from the tip of South America to the northernmost reaches of the boreal forest. The great horned owl occurs over an incredible range of habitats, elevations and latitudes. Minimum requirements include a nesting site, a roosting site and an area to hunt. Roosting sites are used during the day and must offer concealment. Conifers are preferred over deciduous trees but, in their absence, trees that tend to retain clusters of dead leaves through the winter may be used.[13]

Great horned owls hunt by perching in trees or on poles in the evening and waiting to detect prey. Once prey is detected, the owl flys out on silent wings and attempts to capture it. In North America the range of prey taken by these owls is huge. Insects, scorpions and small rodents are on the small end of the size spectrum; domestic cats, woodchucks, herons and geese are on the large end.

Great gray owl—This owl is found over much of forested Alaska from interior Alaska south to the Kenai Peninsula, southeast Alaska and eastward to Ontario, Canada. It occurs all the way across Eurasia. Great gray owls (*Strix nebulosa*) occasionally exhibit **irruptive** movements. That is, great numbers may appear in areas where they don't normally occur. One explanation of these winter invasions is that the owls have reached a high population level in previous years but this year their normal habitat can't support their numbers. The underlying problem might be a prey population decline or a weather event such as very deep snow or ice crusting the surface of the snow. Other owls exhibit irruptive dispersal; it is most obvious in snowy owls perhaps because they are white and are generally in open habitat.

In Alaska great gray owls do not usually migrate during the winter but may move considerable distances if their food supply is short. During years of food shortage, these owls may skip breeding. Clutch size is generally related to food availability. The greater the food supply, the more eggs are laid, up to a point. Nesting usually occurs in mature stands of poplar and aspen near muskegs or other open habitat.

Great gray owls hunt and capture prey using both vision and hearing and hunt prey both day and night. An owl was observed flying 200 m (650 ft) to capture a small mammal on top of the snow. Presumably the prey was located visually. These owls exhibit a technique called **snow plunging** that is mediated by their acute sense of hearing (Figure 5.5). The owl perches on a listening post, localizes prey under the snow, flies to it and plunges into the snow to capture it. The bird may hover momentarily before plunging vertically, often landing in the snow headfirst.[14] Legs and talons are extended

Figure 5.6: Snow plunging in the great gray owl. Just before impact with the snow, the owl brings its feet forward

either just before or immediately after hitting the snow. Great gray owls can capture prey as deep as 45 cm (18 inches) under the snow. This form of prey capture is occasionally exhibited by hawk-owls and boreal owls.

In spite of their large size, great gray owls concentrate on small mammals as prey. A study in Finland found that 94% of prey items were rodents. Another study in Alaska found that the yellow-cheeked vole made up 66% with other microtines adding another 28%.

Northern hawk-owl—The northern hawk-owl (*Surnia ulula*) is a **circumboreal** (found around the world at high latitude) species occu-

pying conifer forests in Alaska and Canada. It is only occasionally seen in the lower 48, having been sighted in Oregon, Colorado, Iowa, Ohio, Pennsylvania and a few other states. It is a medium-sized owl that, in many ways, resembles a hawk. First, when perching the hawk-owl does not sit upright like other owls. Rather, it leans forward like a kestrel. Also like a kestrel, it twitches its tail while perching. Third, it flies and hunts by day rather than at night. Fourth, the tail is long and the wings are pointed, adaptations for fast and maneuverable hunting. Finally, hawk-owls lack the assymetrical ears characteristic of owls that hunt primarily by hearing.

In Finland and Scandinavia hawk-owls feed almost exclusively on voles and lemmings that undergo a marked 3-4 year population cycle. These owls move from locale to locale, finding temporarily high densities of their prey and then moving on as vole populations decline. In North America, microtine rodents do not cycle so dramatically but snowshoe hares exhibit a pronounced, approximately 10-year cycle. Near Kluane Lake, Yukon Territory, snowshoe hares contribute 40-50% of the biomass of hawk-owl food during a hare population high; voles contribute 20-30% during the same period. Based on the availability of prey, voles are strongly preferred over hares. Even during a hare high, 73-79% of the individual prey of hawk-owls is voles.

The vast majority of voles in the study area are red-backed voles, *Cleithrionomys*, but hawk-owls take *Microtus* almost exclusively.[15] Remember, hawk-owls are visual predators and like to hunt over open, grassy fields; this is *Microtus* habitat. Red-backed voles are found in mature forest under cover of shrubs. In terms of preference, hawk-owls use voles about 15 times more than juvenile hares, about 25 times more than squirrels and about 40 times more than adult hares.

Adult hares? Hawk-owls weigh 300-400 g (9-14 ounces); snowshoe hares weigh 1300-1800 g (3-4 pounds). These little owls were actually observed attacking and, in most cases, successfully killing adult hares. Of eight observed winter-kills three were hares, three were red squirrels, one was a spruce grouse and another was a vole. Since voles are harder to see in the winter, it isn't surprising that winter-kills tend to be larger animals.

Red-backed voles are occasionally taken abundantly by hawk-owls. In both Scandinavia, and Denali Park, *Cleithrionomys* is the major prey in early spring when red-backs were active above snow cover.[16,17] As snow melts the red-backed proportion of the diet declines.[16]

The hawk-owl appears to be a generalist that feeds on voles when abundant and accessible but falls back on birds as prey in winter when voles aren't so readily available. A generalist would, perhaps, evolve toward preying on hares that are periodically abundant. Evidence of this evolution may be that North American hawk-owls are about 6% larger than their old world relatives. Added size would help in dealing with snowshoe hares.

These owls nest well off the ground (3.1-7.4 m above ground at Kluane Lake; 1.6-13 m above ground elsewhere[17]) in hollow cavities in the tops of spruce trees. Clutches of 2-5 eggs are initiated in the last week of April near Kluane Lake. Six nests in Denali Park had an average of 5.5 eggs each. After egg laying, the female does the incubating and the male brings her food. Hatchlings gain weight more rapidly than similarly sized owls, probably due to males hunting in the very long daylight hours at these latitudes and to the food caching behavior of the males.[17]

Boreal owl—The boreal owl (*Aegolius funereus*) is the smallest owl in the Alaskan boreal forest. The boreal owl is also found across northern Eurasia, where it is typically referred to as Tengmalm's owl. In Alaska, the boreal owl is common in the interior and is found as far west as King Salmon. It occurs on Kodiak Island, Prince William Sound and, occasionally, in southeast Alaska.

Over much of its range in North America it is **sympatric** (occurs together) with the saw-whet owl, which is even smaller. When together, boreal owls tend to feed on voles; saw-whets prey on the smaller mice (*Peromyscus*) and shrews. Boreal owls occupy a variety of habitats including coniferous, deciduous and mixed forests. In Colorado, roosting trees are conifers and average about 14 m (45 feet) high. The owls perch close to the bole, about 7 m off the ground. Typically, these roosts offer concealment from above but good visibility below.

Of all owls, boreal owls have the most noticable asymmetry of the skull (see Figure 5.6). One presumes that its abilities to locate prey using sounds is highly refined. These owls hunt for prey from low (< 2 m) perches and make relatively short flights (average 17 m) to make their captures. Once an owl sees (or hears) a prey, it turns toward the prey and orients its facial disk directly toward the prey. Sometimes it makes vertical or lateral head movements before taking off. These head movements undoubtedly fix the position of the prey accurately. The owl takes off using shallow wing beats, then glides on the final approach. Just before the strike both wings and tail are spread (braking), the feet are brought forward and extended, talons are extended, and the eyes are closed. There is no point in damaging the eyes if it can be avoided. Once the prey is seized, the owl grasps the head or neck with its beak, the *coup de grace*.[18]

Boreal owls exhibit a **size dimorphism**, that is, the sexes are different sizes. Females average 43% heavier than males. One of the supposed advantages to this size difference is that the two sexes tend to select different-sized prey, lessening competition for food. Female boreal owls tend to take relatively heavy, slow-moving prey such as voles while males take more agile prey such as birds, and, possibly flying squirrels (Figure 3.6). Similar dimorphisms are seen in other owls and hawks.

During incubation, the female tends the nest diligently and the male hunts and brings food to the female. Eggs hatch after 25-32 days and, in good years, all the chicks may survive to fledging. In low food years only the first-born chicks survive. They simply outcompete their nestmates for the little food available.

Short-eared owl—Unlike most other owls, the short-eared owl (*Asio flammeus*) nests on the ground in a depression that may be lined by the female with twigs and leaves. Egg laying occurs later in the spring for more northern populations: in Alaska and arctic Canada, from June 10-30. Clutch size averages 5.6 in North America with larger clutches at higher latitudes. Eggs are laid once every day or two, incubation begins with the first egg and continues 24-29 days. After hatching, chicks develop very rapidly. In 10 days they are often 10 times larger than at hatching. Although they do not fledge until 24-27 days post-hatching, they may leave the nest as early as the tenth day. This rapid developmental rate is thought to relate to the high vulnerability of these ground-dwelling chicks to predation.

An interesting part of the male courtship behavior is a clapping of wings under the body while in flight. The sound is similar to a flag snapping in a stiff breeze. Wing clapping increases in frequency as courtship progresses. It is thought that the clapping advertises the male's territory to potential mates and may serve to synchronize or prime the female's reproductive system.

Breeding habitats in North America include tundra, prairies, and other grassy areas. In winter, these birds are found near meadows, pastures, marshes, and other early successional plant assemblages. Prey, over the whole of North America, is about 95% mammals and 5% birds. Of the mammals, *Microtus* makes up the majority. Birds preyed upon include marsh and/or open-country species such as sandpipers, killdeer, meadowlarks, and red-winged blackbirds.

One behavior exhibited by short-eared owls is upside-down peering. That is, the owl swivels its head almost completely upside-down. In owl eyes, the part of the retina that forms the clearest image, the **temporal fovea**, lies above the middle of the retina. This arrangement works well when discriminating the shapes of prey that are below the head. If an object appears above the level of the head, such as a bird flying over, the best way to get a clear image of that object is to turn the head over so the image will fall on the temporal fovea.

The geographic distribution of this owl is pretty impressive. In addition to occurring all over Alaska, most of Canada, and the northern half of the lower 48, it is found in Hawaii, the Galapagos Islands, South American Andes, Brazil, Argentina, Chile, the Falkland Islands, and the Caribbean islands of Cuba, Hispaniola, and Puerto Rico. It occurs across northern Eurasia from Chukotka westward to France, England and Iceland.

Raven

The common raven, *Corvus corax*, is a member of the family Corvidae the family of crows with 41 members. Also included in the Corvidae are the jays, magpies and nutcracker. The raven differs from the American crow in several ways. First, it is a bigger bird, weighing four times the average American (common) crow; wingspan in ravens approaches 1.2 m (4 ft). Ravens have a wedge-shaped tail; crows have a square tail.

The common raven is probably the most widespread naturally occurring bird on the planet. It is present over much of North America, Europe, Asia and North Africa. The species is found in every major biome except the tropical rain forest.[19] Although ravens look pretty similar wherever you find them, the species has been divided into supposedly discrete subspecies: four in North America and an additional six in Eurasia.

One summer day I was driving along Rosie Creek Road at the base of some loess bluffs occupied by nesting violet-green swallows. Two ravens flew past me heading straight for the bluff. When they got within 1 m of the cliff, swallows literally erupted from their holes in the cliff. The ravens caught and ate several of the swallows. Other birds that are attacked, killed and eaten include rock dove, eider, northern flicker and black-legged kittiwake. Nests of a variety of species are raided by ravens. About 14% of sandhill crane nests in Oregon are depredated by ravens. Breeding colonies of herring gulls and ring-billed gulls have been hit so hard by ravens and American crows that the entire colonies experience reproductive failure. The synchrony of nesting in common murres at Bluff, Alaska, is thought to be an example of predator (raven) swamping.[20]

Direct observations have served to elucidate the feeding habits of ravens, but there are other ways of knowing what these highly intelligent birds eat. Stomach analyses and examinations of regurgitated pellets show that mammals, insects, grains and birds are each important at various seasons and at various locations. However, one needs to remember that remains in pellets are indigestible and, therefore, don't necessarily adequately represent the contribution of these different organisms to the nutrition of the birds. For example, the muscle protein of large mammal carcasses is highly digestible; none of it would be regurgitated. Therefore in Alaska, where ravens feed on the carcasses of caribou and moose, an analysis of pellets would suggest incorrectly that ravens don't forage on either species. In the Far North ravens have been observed to kill and consume newborn reindeer calves. Typically these calves have been abandoned by their mothers, but raven pairs have been seen to attempt to separate mother from calf.[21]

Some of the most interesting behaviors of ravens are exhibited on or near carcasses. Some ravens on a carcass make loud, raucous noises, called the "juvenile yell," that seem to bring in other ravens from as far away as 2 km. Why do ravens actively disclose to strangers of their species the valuable and rare food bonanzas that one of them is lucky enough to find? The seeming paradox is that the birds, by attracting others to the site of a kill, might end up with less food for themselves. It turns out that adult pairs who find a bonanza within their territory do not call. They keep the find to themselves. Only nonterritorial juveniles call others to the carcass. One reason for doing so is to assemble enough juveniles to overwhelm the adults in whose territory the bonanza rests and, thereby, gain access to a portion of the food. A second benefit is that

the recruiter usually emerges from the scuffles around the carcass as a dominant bird (for a juvenile) and can probably attract a high-quality mate with which to pair.

Caching behavior begins in raven chicks almost as soon as they get out of the nest. Young birds will pick up both food and nonfood objects, walk up to 1 m away from the nest and shove the object into a crack or crevice. In adult birds caches are established mainly on the ground and are covered with twigs and vegetation. If a raven and its mate are the sole occupants of a carcass, they will cache extra meat close to it. As more ravens aggregate on a carcass, birds will fly off to make their caches in secret. As the number of birds increases, the distance they fly to make their caches increases.

Memory of the locations of its own and other ravens' caches is excellent and lasts at least several months. The birds of Denali (Mt. McKinley) have discovered that mountain climbers leave food caches marked by green bamboo stakes with red flags tied to them. Ravens have excavated through almost 1 m (3.2 ft) of snow to retrieve this human food. Ravens that cache murre eggs can locate their egg caches up to three months later. The eggs are an important source of nutrition in the fall and retain 87% of their energy content for several months.[22] To summarize raven diets, ravens will eat all the dead animals they can find, all the live animals they can kill, and fruit and grain when they are available.[21]

Nest building or refurbishment begins between late January and early April. Nest sites include treetops, power poles and, occasionally, church steeples. A pair of nesting ravens live about 2 km from our house, occupying a cliff over the Tanana River. They and their offspring delight and entertain tourists on the Riverboat Discovery early each summer. Egg laying occurs 3-7 days after nest completion; incubation takes 20-25 days. Chicks hatch out more or less naked and sightless. By two weeks, the young are covered with down; their eyes are usually open. At three weeks old, the young still can't stand up but by five weeks they are fully feathered, flapping their wings and almost ready to leave the nest. Body weight reaches a plateau by week four. Once out of the nest, young birds begin to explore, examine and manipulate just about everything they encounter. This fascination with novel objects has been termed neophilia.[21] Unless they turn out to be edible, items that become familiar are soon ignored in favor of other, newer items. This exploratory play persists in wild birds for 4-5 months, then gradually fades out.

By fall of their first year young birds disperse away from their natal territory. Individuals may move >200 km (>120 miles) in search of a territory of their own. Typically, these juvenile birds hang out with birds of similar age and form roosting aggregations at night. Roosts may contain several hundred birds, and there is some evidence that cold weather promotes larger aggregations. Each morning at dawn birds leave the roost in small groups to explore for forage opportunities. Or, if a bonanza was discovered the previous day, the entire aggregation may fly off for a noisy, energetic bout of feeding and revelry.

Other birds of Alaska's boreal forests

Elsewhere is this book I have mentioned, in more or less detail, the lives of some of the other birds of Alaska's northern forests. Black-capped chickadees and common redpolls were described in Chapter 2. So also were some migratory species including the swallows, tundra and trumpeter swans, snow buntings and sandhill cranes. Woodpeckers and their effects on some insect pests of the boreal forests are mentioned in the following chapter. Birds are an obvious and interesting part of the animals of treeless landscapes (Chapter 8). In Chapter 10 I talk about waterfowl in relation to their aquatic habitats.

Not described are many species of migratory songbirds. These birds are no less interesting or important for having been left out. In fact, some of these songbirds may be the "canaries in the coal mine." That is, they may be indicators of habitat degradation either on Alaska's landscapes or in their alternative (winter) habitats.

Ravens, some owls and all Alaska's grouse species rely to an extent on insects in their diets. Insects are especially important to young of the year grouse. Their fast-growing bodies require more protein than can be readily obtained from a diet of seeds and berries alone. The next chapter treats some of the insects of boreal forests in terms of their importance as prey, their importance as human pests, and because they are intrinsically interesting.

REFERENCES

1   Sedinger, J.S. 1997. Adaptations to and consequences of an herbivorous diet in grouse and waterfowl. Condor 99: 314-326.

2   Ellison, L.N. 1968. Movements and behavior of Alaskan spruce grouse during the breeding season. Transactions of the meeting of the California-Nevada section of the Wildlife Society.

3   Ellison, L.N. 1966. Seasonal foods and chemical analysis of winter diet of Alaskan spruce grouse. Journal of Wildlife Management 30: 729-735.

4   Ellison, L.N. and Weeden, R.B. 1979. Seasonal and local weights of Alaskan spruce grouse. Journal of Wildlife Management 43: 176-183.

5   Johnsgard, P.A. 1983. The grouse of the world. University of Nebraska Press, Lincoln, 413 pp.

6   Robinson, W.L. 1980. Fool hen: the spruce grouse on the Yellow Dog Plains. University of Wisconsin Press, Madison, 221 pp.

7   Watson, A. and Moss, R. 1979. Population cycles in the Tetraonidae. Ornis Fennica 56: 87-109.

8   Bent, A.C. 1938. Life histories of North American birds of prey. Pt. 2. U.S. National Museum Bulletin 170: 1-482.

9   Caldwell, P.J. 1976. Energetic and population considerations of Sharp-tailed Grouse in aspen parklands of Canada. PhD dissertation, Kansas State University, Manhattan.

10   Gratson, M.W., Gratson, G.K. and Bergerud, A.T. 1991. Male dominance and copulation disruption do not explain variance in male mating success on Sharp-tailed Grouse (*Tympanuchus phasianellus*) leks. Behaviour 118: 187-213.

11   Tsuji, L.J.S., Kozlovic, D.R., Sokolowski, M.B. and Hansell, R.I.C. 1994. Relationship of body size of male Sharp-tailed Grouse to location of individual territories on leks. Wilson Bulletin 106: 329-337.

12   Connelly, J.W., Gratson, M.W. and Reese, K.P. 1998. Sharp-tailed Grouse. The Birds of North America No. 354, 19 pp.

13   Johnsgard, P.A. 1988. North American owls. Smithsonian Institution Press, Washington and London, 295 pp.

14   Mikkola, H. 1983. Owls of Europe. Buteo Books, Vermillion, South Dakota.

15   Rohner, C., Smith, J.N.M., Stroman, J., Joyce, M., Doyle, F.I. and Boonstra, R. 1995. Northern hawk-owls in the palearctic boreal forest: prey selection and population consequences of multiple prey cycles. The Condor 97: 208-220.

16   Nybo, J.O. and Sonerud, G.A. 1990. Seasonal changes in diet of hawk owls *Surnia ulula*: importance of snow cover. Ornis Fennica 67: 45-51.

17   Kertell, K. 1986. Reproductive biology of hawk owls *Surnia ulula* in Denali National Park, Alaska. Raptor Research 20: 91-101.

18   Norberg, A. 1970. Hunting technique of Tengmalm's owl *Aegolius funereus* (L.). Ornis Scandia 1: 49-64.

19   Boarman, W.I. and Heinrich, B. 1999. Common raven. The Birds of North America No. 476.

20   Murphy, E.C. and Schauer, J.H. 1996. Synchrony in egg-laying and reproductive success of neighboring Common Murres,

Uria aalge. Behavioural and Ecological Sociobiology 39: 245-258.

21   Heinrich, B. 1989. Ravens in winter. Summit Books, New York, 379 pp.

22   Rossow, P.D. 1999. The caching behavior of common ravens (*Corvus corax*) at Bluff, Alaska. MS Thesis, University of Alaska Fairbanks, 40 pp.

6.
THE FLIGHT OF THE DRAGONFLY, THE WHINE OF THE MOSQUITO: SOME INSECTS OF THE BOREAL FOREST

The ecological roles of insects in Alaska's boreal forests

Many insects of the boreal forest are herbivorous. That is, they consume parts of trees, shrubs or herbaceous plants. In Chapter 3 I described a few insect pests of aspen, birch and white spruce. These herbivorous insects fall into six distinct feeding strategies.

There are at least 15 species of **defoliators**. These insects eat the leaves of trees. Among the defoliators are the spruce budworm, aspen tortrix, leaf rollers, various loopers, and several leaf miners, all moth species. Several sawflies and beetles also defoliate trees in Alaska.

A variety of **sap-sucking insects** attack Alaskan trees. At least six species of aphids affect trees. Several gall insects affect poplar and willow. These sap-suckers deplete the nutrient supplies that allow for tree growth, reproduction, and survival.

Bark beetles live almost their entire lives within the inner bark, bark and conducting layers of trees. Interruption of water transport eventually kills the tree. Devastating outbreaks of bark beetles have occurred on the Kenai Peninsula, western Cook Inlet, and the Tanana Valley of the interior.

Wood borers excavate chambers in freshly cut, dying, or injured trees. Most of the wood borers are species of beetles but several are wasps. The damage to timber is mainly done by larval stages.

Cone and seed insects reduce the reproductive output of trees. These insects, including moth and fly species, probably have little impact on interior Alaska forests. Of much greater consequence are the **bud and shoot insects.** The spruce bud midge and spruce budworm are both responsible for loss of the new year's production of spruce needles. Since white spruce retain needles, on average, for three years, repeated infestations by budworms can be devastating by reducing the photosynthetic capabilities of these trees.

Many insects of the forest rely on other insects and invertebrates for food or on the blood of birds and mammals. The first group could be called insectivores; the second group consists of **hematophagous** (blood-eating) insects. Perhaps the most obvious examples of insectivorous insects are the damselflies and dragonflies. I discuss these beneficial (from the human perspective) insects below. Also treated in this chapter are mosquitoes, maybe our least favorite group of hematophagous insects.

Finally, insects are a food resource. They are the prey relied on by a host of bird and mammal species in Alaskan boreal forests. Swallows, woodpeckers and flickers, specifically target insects. The grouse species, especially young of the year birds, feed on insects in late spring. Shrews, red squirrels and black bears all add insects to their diets. The wood frog, the lone amphibian in interior forests, is an insectivore. As we will see in the next chapter, insects are important prey for fish also.

Mosquitoes

One of the seasons of the interior, familiar to all Alaskans, is the biting season. Depending on the timing of breakup and warmer spring weather, biting season can begin as early as mid-April. The peak of biting season in Alaskan boreal forests occurs in July as mosquito species that emerge in the spring have matured. By mid- to late July adult *Aedes* mosquitoes, with an adult life span of about 8 weeks, are dying of old age and the biting slackens off...thankfully! Every summer many of us have the emotional conflict of wanting the summer to last forever but wanting to get past the biting season.

What factors influence the abundance and activity of Alaskan mosquitoes? Abundance is favored by above-normal precipitation in the current year plus the two previous years.[1] Interior Alaska has a great variety of temporary and permanent ponds and sloughs, appropriate habitats for the aquatic larval stages of mosquitoes. In general, climatic conditions that favor maintenance, prolongation, or expansion of temporary and semi-permanent ponds should promote mosquito populations. The effects of higher than normal rain or snowfalls are, to an extent, offset by early breakups followed by prolonged warmer than usual temperatures. Almost all Alaskan mosquito species exhibit a crepuscular activity pattern. That is, peak activity is around dawn and dusk. In the summer, dusk may last three hours and mosquitoes are usually busy throughout this period. Temperature is also important, with most activity occurring between 7°C and 27°C (45°F and 80°F) with an optimum around 16°C (60°F).

One modification of this crepuscular pattern is seen in tundra mosquitoes at high latitude. Peak activity of two high Arctic (latitude 81°N) mosquitoes also found in Alaska is around noon with only minor activity peaks at dawn and dusk. Mosquitoes at the northern extreme of their ranges are apparently governed more by temperature as related to height of the sun in the sky.[2]

In addition to temperature, wind also affects mosquito flight activity. In the boreal forest, mosquitoes reduce flight activity at wind speeds of 2 miles per hour and stop flying altogether at 5 miles per hour. Tundra mosquitoes are made of tougher stuff; their flying isn't curtailed until wind speeds reach 7 miles per hour, and some stubbornly continue to fly at 10 miles per hour. Of course, a human walking through the forest or tundra in a wind generates a slipstream with some calm air on the downwind side. Mosquitoes sense this and can land on you and pester you even if there is some wind blowing.

Most mosquitoes (genus *Aedes*) overwinter in the fertilized egg stage. Eggs are deposited by the female in the late summer or early fall in water and the eggs simply don't hatch until the following spring. At least one species (*Culiseta morsitans*) may overwinter in the larval or pupal stages. Four species of *Culiseta*, *Culex territans* and *Anopheles earlei* all overwinter as adults. In the fall, the female finds a place to hide, either under loose bark on a tree, underneath leaves in the litter layer on the ground or in a dead tree stump. These are the first mosquitoes you see in the spring in the interior. They emerge from mid- to late April. Fortunately, these are the big, slow mosquitoes that are pretty easy to avoid.

Since tundra habitats don't have an abundance of trees, tree stumps or leaf litter, these six species aren't common in tundra habitats. A common feature of all these life histories is that there is only a single generation each year. Unless interrupted, a female may only take a single blood meal in her adult life. We don't know about the potential for Alaskan mosquito species to harbor agents of human disease. However, there seems to be little chance of them acting as significant disease vectors since they typically only bite once.

Experiments to determine biting rates in interior Alaska have been done using both shaved rabbits and human volunteers as bait. A "stan-dard" 357 cm^2 (54 inch^2) patch of bare human forearm got bitten 54-70 times per 15 minutes.[3] According to my friend, Marsha Sousa, a human anatomy and physiology expert, that area corresponds to about 2% of the surface area of the entire body. So an entirely naked human might get 10,000-14,000 bites per hour. Observations made using a "mosquito tower" indicate that "bait" placed 42 feet above ground level attracted about 7% of the numbers of mosquitoes attracted at ground level. A naked human could climb 42 feet up a spruce tree and suffer only 700-1000 bites per hour. Of course, the injuries suffered climbing the tree while totally naked might be worse than the bites suffered by staying on the ground.

If we are lucky, we get advance warning of an impending mosquito bite. That warning, for those with unimpaired hearing, is the high-pitched whine of mosquito wings. The rapid beating of mosquito wings generates the whine, a complex series of harmonics. The lowest pitch, the **fundamental** or **first harmonic**, corresponds to the actual frequency at which the wings beat. **Overtones**, or higher harmonics, are produced by the deformation of the wings. Overtones are always multiples of the fundamental, which in most female mosquitoes ranges from 200 to 600 cycles (wing beats) per second (200-600 Hz). If the first harmonic is 400 Hz, the second harmonic is 800 Hz, the third, 1200 Hz. How many overtones do mosquitoes generate? In *Culiseta inornata* from Canada and Alaska, fifteen have been detected. A few variables that affect wing beat frequency are 1) temperature (higher temperatures= higher frequencies), 2) size (larger mosquitoes = lower frequencies) and feeding (increased wing loading requires slightly higher frequencies).

Except for physicists and musicians, all this talk of frequencies and overtones may be too esoteric. However, there is one aspect to flight tones that is of practical importance to the mosquitoes themselves. Within a mosquito species, the wing beat frequencies (and the flight tones) of males and females are different. Males have higher frequencies than females and there is, typically, no overlap in frequencies. This means that a male can identify a female by her flight tone. For example, *Aedes communis* males have frequencies of 555±14 Hz; females have frequencies of 350±9 Hz. Other cues assist males in search for a mate but this sound cue is, at risk of making a pun, fundamental.

One more thing about mosquito wings: they only have two. Most winged insect groups have two pairs of wings, but all members of the insect order Diptera, including flies and mosquitoes, have only one pair. The name *diptera* literally means two (di-) wings (ptera). Dipterans evolved from insects with the normal allotment of four wings. There is still evidence of the other two (hind) wings on flies and mosquitoes; these vestigal wings are called **haltares** or balancers. The haltares are little knobs, located behind the flight wings, that can be moved. Essentially, the haltares function as gyroscopic stabilizers, allowing mosquitoes to make subtle adjustments of attitude and flight direction. No wonder flies and mosquitoes are so agile in flight!

What cues do mosquitoes use to home in on their hosts? Chemical cues are important and can come from the breath, skin or urine of the host species. Flatus (passing gas) also attracts mosquitoes.[4] So that you will be less attractive to mosquitoes, do not take chili on your next camping trip in summertime Alaska. The breath provides at least two different stimuli, carbon dioxide and water vapor. There are many organic compounds in breath, for example, lactic acid in all humans and ketones in fasting humans and other mammals. Emanations from the skin that may attract mosquitoes include lactic acid, and other organic acids and alcohols. Of the 27 different organic compounds found in human sweat *Anopheles* mosquitoes exhibit a positive chemosensory response to ten. Human urine contains three aromatic organic compounds that attract some mosquito species, and at least one mosquito responds to microgram amounts of hormones present in the urine of pregnant women.

Once the mosquito begins blood feeding, it alternates bouts of engorging (sucking) with bouts of salivating. Salivation occurs about five times per second. Aside from the blood loss, which can be considerable, the other problems associated with mosquito bites are immune responses in the host to salivary (foreign) proteins and the potential for disease transmission by species in which females take more than a single blood meal.

Dragonflies

Dragonflies and damselflies are among my favorite insects. Who in Alaska, pestered by mosquitos and blackflies every summer, wouldn't smile at these aerial insect killers? In the summer, I watch dragonflies capturing insects on the wing and marvel at their maneuverability; I grieve a little for every dragonfly I see dead along the road, victim of hit-and-run. Dragonflies and their close cousins the damselflies both belong to the insect order Odonata. Both have chewing mouth parts, strong wings, and huge compound eyes, and both are predatory on other insects. Both groups live through their **nymph** (larval) stages in ponds and lakes. Insects that go through immature or larval stages that bear little resemblance to the adult are said to exhibit indirect development (Figure 6.1). The other alternative is direct development, such as is exhibited by grasshoppers.

Figure 6.1: Aquatic nymphs of dragonfly (lower left) and damselfly (upper right). Both nymphs have protruded mouthparts attempting to seize the other nymph. Damselfly nymphs have leaf-shaped respiratory structures on the end of the abdomen; dragonfly nymphs do not.

From here on I'll refer to both dragonflies and damselflies as dragonflies unless there are specific differences in the two groups. Here is a brief description of the life of a dragonfly. After copulation, the female deposits fertilized eggs in one of three different ways. Eggs may be dropped in water, inserted into plant tissue, or attached to plants. After hatching, the larva, highly car-nivorous, grows and periodically molts to the next larger stage, or **instar**. Actually, growth in length is not continuous. Since these creatures have an external skeleton, they must shed it to grow in external dimensions. Growth in length is really a stairstep process with each successive instar being longer than the preceding one. These larvae are well adapted to an aquatic existence and, in the Far North, to the rigors of low temperature, **hypoxia** (low oxygen) and ice they must face.

After 9-14 instars the final instar crawls out of the water, reorganizes itself internally (undergoes metamorphosis) and emerges as an adult. This emergence is the creature's final molt. Once the adult's wings are fully inflated and dried, it flies away, leaving its larval skin behind. After a period of feeding and maturation, dragonflies court, mate and the cycle begins again.

There are two modes of feeding in adult dragonflies: capture of prey on a substrate and capture of flying prey. In both modes, prey are captured with the legs (Figure 6.2) and transferred to the mouth. This requires legs that are forward on the thorax and directed forward, a feat accomplished millions of years ago by evolving thoracic segments that tilt obliquely instead of being oriented vertically.

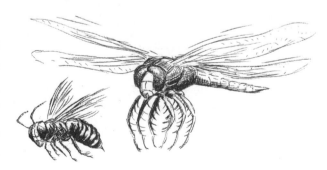

Figure 6.2: Dragonfly about to capture a yellow jacket with its legs.

Prey are located visually. The large compound eye typically has smaller facets (individual ommatidia) on the lower surface and this area is thought to be used for shape recognition of prey resting on a substrate. Aphids, moths, beetle larvae and spiders are picked off plants. Observers have seen dragonflies pick tsetse flies and eye gnats off human skin. There are reports of dragonflies capturing and eating small frogs.[5]

The upper surface of the compound eye is thought to be important in tracking prey that are in flight. This is probably the more common feeding mode. Dragonflies approach air-borne prey from below, whether they are primarily perchers or primarily fliers. Perchers spot prey while perching, then take off and pursue. Fliers course through the air searching for prey. Apparently, prey can be spotted up to 13 m (42 feet) away and other dragonflies up to 37 m (122 feet) away.

Feeding flights and mating flights are typically performed in different habitats and at different times of the day. Mating flights are over ponds, involve lots of hovering and involve interactions with other dragonflies. Feeding flights usually occur away from ponds, don't involve aggressive bouts with other dragonflies and usually involve rapid changes in direction or erratic flight. The erratic flying is due to pursuit of prey insects that are, presumably, taking evasive action.

Swarm feeding has been widely observed. This involves dragonflies dancing around inside a swarm of mosquitoes, midges, sandflies, stable flies or other prey insects, picking them off one by one. In this behavior, dragonflies are far superior to either swallows or bats because they don't have to fly through the swarm, turn around and come back.

As aquatic larvae, dragonflies often eat each other. Damselfly larvae comprise a large portion of the diet of dragonfly larvae in Alberta and dragonfly larvae also contribute. Elsewhere, the larvae of one species may consume those of other species or larger larvae may simply eat smaller larvae of their own or other species.[6] The larvae fall prey to a variety of other predators including pike, sculpins, perch (in Russia), frogs (Illinois and Florida) and 20 species of birds in the U.S.A. including gulls, herons, kingfishers, ducks, grebes and sandpipers.

In North America, there are 24 species of dragonflies found at or above the Arctic Circle; in Eurasia the number is 28 species. Only a few individuals of one or two species occasionally breed north of tree line in the Arctic.[7] Dragonflies in the Far North overwinter as larvae, often embedded in ice for four to five months. There is evidence that in some species of northern Odonata, the length of time spent in ice, is a determinant of survival; the longer in ice the lower the survival. In other species the important factor is the temperature to which the ice cools. Once the ice thaws, the larvae go about their business of feeding, occasionally molting and avoiding predators.

Other than a presumed resistance to death by freezing, what other life history traits do dragonflies of the Far North have that their more temperate and tropical relatives might not? First, all tropical dragonflies complete their larval life within one to nine months after the egg hatches. Some temperate species have similar durations of larval life, and some are able to produce more than one generation in a single year. But, species found in the Far North tend to have larvae requiring one to six years to complete growth and development. For species with populations at mid and high latitudes, there is a strong correlation between latitude and time required to complete the life cycle.[8] Exceptionally, in some damselflies and small dragonflies of the Yukon, larval development may be completed and adults emerge in the same summer in which they began life as fertilized eggs.[7]

In common with their more temperate relatives, Alaskan dragonflies are able to thermoregulate. Behavioral thermoregulation is accomplished in several ways. First, they can regulate temperature to an extent by perching or flying in either shady or sunny sites depending on whether they are above or below their preferred temperatures. This really amounts to microhabitat selection. Second, they can adopt postures that will either maximize heat uptake or mininize it, again, depending on whether they are below or above their preferred temperatures. Dragonflies above preferred temperatures adopt an "obelisk" posture with the abdomen pointing straight at the sun (Figure 6.3). This

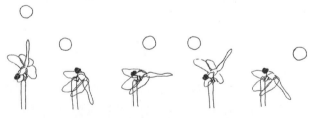

Figure 6.3: Dragonfly thermoregulatory postures. The obelisk posture with abdomen pointed either directly at or away from the sun (the two left-hand images) are cooling postures. In these positions almost no radiant energy is received from the sun. Basking postures in which the body and wings are held perpendicular to the sun's rays (right three images), maximize radiant heat gain. Redrawn from Corbet (1983).

minimizes the amount of heat absorbed from the sun. A similar result is obtained by pointing the abdomen directly away from the sun. The reverse, orienting so that the abdomen receives maximum solar radiation, can also be accomplished by postures. The dragonfly sits with abdomen at right angles to the sun, exposing the largest surface area to the sun's rays (Figure 6.3). Similar behaviors (pointing abdomen at or at right angle to the sun) have been observed in flying dragonflies, presumably, for the same functional effect. Wings can play a role in behavioral thermoregulation. Wings can be held so as to reflect sunlight toward or away from the abdomen. In cool dragonflies perched on a rock, the wings may reduce convective heat loss by trapping warm air between the rock and the thorax and abdomen.

Another behavioral, or ectothermic, thermoregulatory mechanism involves body coloration and color changes. Some species have the ability to change color in response to temperature. Male *Aeshna caerulea* have been shown experimentally to absorb more heat when in their dark color phase than when in their light, iridescent blue color phase. Four minutes after turning on an infrared lamp, blue-phase males had abdominal temperatures 2-3°C above ambient air temperature, but dark males were 10° above ambient.[9] A male could be dark until it reaches operating temperature and then turn blue to avoid further warming. Males of this species are more active during the heat of the day than are the darker females. This evolutionary strategy is carried to an extreme in dragonflies that have translucent windows in the dorsal, abdominal cuticle that allow sunlight down into the body until masked by dispersing pigments in the cuticle. The translucent windows are open during warming and closed when preferred temperature is reached.

Endothermy, as we saw early in the book, is the regulation of body temperature by means of metabolic heat output. In dragonflies, the metabolic heat is generated in the thorax by the flight muscles. On a cool summer morning in Fairbanks, a dragonfly's thoracic temperature is probably below that needed to actually take off and fly. To get up to temperature the dragonfly performs a **wing whirring** maneuver. This is equivalent to shivering in mammals. Wing whirring is more prolonged the colder the ambient temperature. What is the minimum thoracic temperature for flight? That depends. We don't know if Far Northern species have normal or low minimum temperatures but, elsewhere, crepuscular or forest species have lower minimum temperatures than do species of open fields or midday-active species.[10] It appears that large dragonflies have a higher minimum temperature than do small ones. Flight itself is a powerful heat generator for dragonflies.

Aside from postures and microhabitat selection, do dragonflies have cooling mechanisms? Experiments suggest that overly warm dragonflies shunt or circulate lots of blood (called hemolymph in insects) from the thorax, where heat is generated, to the abdomen, where it is dissipated. Another cooling mechanism is to increase the time spent gliding rather than active flying. This reduces flight muscle activity and, therefore, reduces heat production. Finally, there are many reports of adult dragonflies touching or even landing in ponds only to fly off. These incidents are unrelated to egg laying and are thought to be examples of cooling by either conduction to the water or by evaporative cooling. Dragonflies also drink water in nature, suggesting the possibility that water may be used normally for evaporative cooling.

Blackflies

There are 76 species of blackflies (Simuliidae) in Alaska, the Yukon and westernmost Northwest Territories.[11] Most of these species have been reported from Alaska, and about 40% of the total also occur in Eurasia.

Aside from swarming around your face, the most objectionable characteristic of blackflies is that they bite. That is, many of them bite. More specifically, females bite. Males, "...unable to bite and not needing blood for any physiological end, lead a blameless life: molesting neither man nor beast."[12] Among females, some species have mouthparts adapted for cutting the skin of vertebrates. The females of these species are **hematophagous**, that is, they feed on blood. Among these, some apparently prefer to feed on the blood of birds. These **ornithophilic** species have an accessory tooth at the base of the tarsal claw that is thought to aid the fly in hanging on to feathers. Some birds in our area that are known to be pestered by blackflies include pintail, blue-winged teal, mallard, red-tailed hawk, ruffed grouse, sandhill crane, common loon, raven and robin. **Mammalophilic** species lack the accessory tooth on the tarsal claw. Some North American mammals harrassed by blackfly females include moose (attacked by at least nine different species of blackflies), caribou, mule deer, northern otter, black bear, brown bear, beaver, woodchuck and ground squirrel. Are there "cross-over" biters?

That is, do ornithophilic species ever bite mammals and vice-versa? Yes.

Blood provides the proteins necessary to develop and mature the eggs in the female body. The male, with relatively little energetic contribution to those eggs, can make do without resorting to blood meals. Both males and females of hematophagous species also rely on plant nectar to supply them with the carbohydrates needed to meet the energy demand of flight. These flower nectars provide all the nutrients needed for metabolism and reproduction in non-biting blackfly species. In northwestern North America, 25% of the blackfly species are non-biting, 34% prefer birds and 40% prefer mammals.[11]

When camping in the summer and early fall in Alaska, it is impossible to get in the tent without letting in blackflies. I used to wonder if they come down from the tent walls in the dead of night to bite me. I now know that it is highly unlikely that they do; blackflies bite during the day and in the open.[12] They rarely, if ever, bite inside a building or a vehicle. Generally, biting activity is governed by the same factors that govern flight. That is, if they don't fly, they don't bite. Temperatures below 10°C inhibit both flight and bite. Strong or gusty winds and heavy rain inhibit biting and there is evidence that biters of large mammals prefer biting on the shady, rather than the sunny, side of the beast.

The mouthparts of blackflies are not piercing as in mosquitoes but are designed to cut a small wound. As blood wells into the wound, the fly sucks it up. Blackflies are pool-feeders. To get maximum benefit, the wound should continue to bleed. To accomplish this, the fly's saliva has **anticoagulants** to prevent clotting. The saliva also contains an **agglutinating** chemical, which causes clumping of red blood cells, but this chemical doesn't take effect until the blood meal is in the fly's stomach.

In New York state and elsewhere in North America, blackfly fever is a syndrome characterized by headache, nausea, sweating, swelling, tenderness of the lymph glands, aching joints and lassitude. The culprit is the blackfly *Simulium venustum*. Similar afflictions have been described in Japan (*S. aokii*), Europe (*S. erythrocephalum*) and England (*S. posticatum*).[12]

Filarial nematodes, spread by blackflies, have been shown to parasitize bears and ducks in Canada and deer in the U.S.A. The vector for bears, *Simulium venustum*, and one of the vectors for ducks, *Simulium rugglesi*, occur in the Yukon and Alaska.

Finally, two blackfly species are significant livestock-biting pests in Alberta and Saskatchewan. Some cattle die from toxicosis associated with the bites; others panic, stampede and trample other cattle. One of the two blackflies, *Simulium arcticum*, also occurs in Alaska. At the present time, cattle ranching is not an important Alaskan industry, but in the future it could be. Only time will tell if blackflies will make depradations on Alaskan cattle or wildlife species.

Dragonflies are predators of adult blackflies but, unfortunately, are thought to have a negligible impact on blackfly populations. The same is probably true of several families of predatory flies. Wasps often capture simuliids for their larval offspring. Fish, such as trouts, minnows and grayling, may be effective predators on emerging adult blackflies and on females laying eggs. Undoubtedly, swallows occasionally take adults, but blackflies are pretty small to attract a lot of attention. Many blackflies in the Far North emerge before the arrival of northward migrating swallows. So these birds can't target concentrations such as are evident at emergence.

Yet another group of biting flies is often mistakenly included with blackflies. The punkies or no-see-ums, are obnoxious blood-feeders like blackflies but belong in a different family, the Heleidae. The bites and bloodfeeding of no-see-ums and blackflies are similar.

Yellowjackets

At age 9, my older son, Andy, stepped on a ground nest of yellowjackets near our house. In a matter of seconds, he received 23 stings. Not only was he miserable and swollen, but he got very lethargic. Every parent's nightmare is that his/her child will be stung and slip into anaphylactic shock. Fortunately, it didn't happen that time. Although our main concern is with stings, these bugs bite too! Several summers ago a bunch of us were helping a friend put the roof on her cabin. It was a hot, dry summer and we had a bumper crop of yellowjackets. We had hundreds of yellowjackets flying around us; occasionally one would land on a patch of bare skin and bite off a chunk. It was the most hollering I ever heard on a roofing job.

One of the yellowjackets common to the interior of Alaska and the Yukon is *Vespula vulgaris.* This species occurs across the continent from Alaska to North Carolina and south to California and Mexico. It constructs nests either in the ground or on trees and shrubs. Nests hanging from branches are made of chewed wood or paper. Pregnant queens overwinter in underground nests and restart colonies in the spring.[13] Vespids are predatory on a wide range of insects.[14] They are strikingly colored with black and yellow, an advertisement for their potent defensive mechanism, the sting. The sting is thought to deter mammalian predators, but birds seem to be unaffected by the sting. Social vespids kill their prey with their mandibles.

Carpenter ants

In all, there are at least 18 species of ants in Alaska. Probably the largest and most noticable is the carpenter ant. Carpenter ants are large, black ants that burrow into wood. Those in interior Alaska are *Camponotus herculeanus,* a species found across Eurasia and North America in boreal forests (Figure 6.4). Unlike termites, carpenter ants do not eat the wood. Instead, they are merely excavating it for their places of habitation. Typically, these large ants attack logs and house timbers that are moist and, sometimes, the living heartwood of trees. They burrow through the softer spring growth

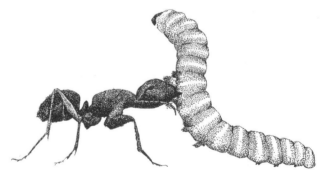

Figure 6.4: Carpenter ant carrying a spruce budworm in its mandibles. This prey is not a common item in carpenter ant diets. Other insects, and aphid honeydew are eaten; wood is not. Mature budworm larvae reach lengths of 3.2 cm, ant workers are up to 1 cm long.

in annual rings and, across their range, prefer the conifers such as spruces, balsam fir and eastern white cedar.[15]

If carpenter ants do not eat wood, what do they eat? One food consumed in western North America is the spruce budworm (Figure 6.4). Recall that the spruce budworm is a moth larva that damages spruce trees in the boreal forest. In its role as a predator of budworms, carpenter ants may be beneficial to humans. There is some question as to how effective these predators are. Most of the spruce budworms are up in the spruce trees; most of the budworms eaten are picked off the forest floor, mainly, worms that fell off the trees. It seems unlikely that *Camponotus* would be able to make much of a dent in spruce budworm populations during an outbreak.

The main food of carpenter ants is probably the honeydew from aphids. In many locales, there are underground colonies of aphids on spruce roots. These colonies are easily accessed by carpenter ants with their proclivity to burrow through not only wood but leaf litter and soil. Another food may be fungal mycelia encountered while digging.

Winged carpenter ants are seen in May or June. Males are physically restrained from flying for a time by workers but finally break free. As they take flight, they exude a pheromone from their mandibular glands that triggers the mass take-off of winged females.[16] The male secretion is pungent enough to be smelled by humans. After the nuptial flight, during which copulation and fertilization occur, the males quickly die. A fertilized female (queen) either goes back to the colony from which she came or establishes a new colony. In some cases, two or more queens will

return to their home colony. Typically, they fight and, to the extent possible, distance themselves within the colony. Rarely, two queens will produce viable offspring in the same colony.

Once eggs are laid, development to hatching requires about 24 days or less. Larval life takes about 21 days and the pupal stage lasts another 21 days. In the first year, new colonies have perhaps 10-20 workers plus some developing young. If the colony persists over the years it may reach a population of 2,000 or more. The queen may live for 15 years.[17] Workers, all sterile females, are 8-11 mm (0.3-0.43 inches); males are about 11 mm (0.43 inches) and winged females are 15-20 mm (0.6-0.8 inches) long.

By fall, a queen will have produced workers, males and virgin queens. The males receive and give food to their nest mates, acting very much like workers. In the winter, the individuals hibernate. In the spring, males burn off the "baby fat" they accumulated the previous summer, lightening their bodies for flight. At the same time, they transfer mature sperm to their seminal vesicles and are now ready for the nuptial flight. Males of this species are the longest-lived males in the entire ant world.[16]

Carpenter ants are the prey of a variety of birds in the north woods. Probably all woodpeckers in the boreal forest eat carpenter ants. In Alaska, that includes the hairy, downy, three-toed and black-backed three-toed woodpeckers and the yellow-shafted flicker. Resident woodpeckers in winter delve into old stumps, fallen logs and living trees for carpenter ants and other tree-dwelling insects. Inferences based on studies in Norway indicate that snow depth affects the ability of woodpeckers to feed on carpenter ants. If there is little accumulated snow, woodpeckers can forage on downed wood and short stumps as well as on upright, standing trees. With snow depths of 1 m or more, they focus on the trunks of standing trees and switch to the more abundant bark beetles.[18]

Insects as aquatic animals

In describing the biology of mosquitoes, black-flies and dragonflies, I mentioned that eggs are laid in bodies of water and that larval stages are passed in the aquatic environment. In a very real sense, these insect groups could be considered as aquatic organisms. In fact, dragonflies in the Far North spend most of their lives as nymphs in ponds and lakes. Only the last few months of perhaps a seven-year lifespan is spent in flight, snagging mosquitoes in midair and banging into our automobile grills.

It is only our human, terrestrial, bias that might cause us to place dragonflies in the terrestrial category instead of the aquatic. Reality is untidy. It keeps humans from neatly and completely organizing the world. As you read Chapters 9 and 10 about the aquatic habitats and creatures of the Far North, bear in mind that the aquatic life stages of terrestrial and aerial insects are underrepresented in the discussion. Also realize that muskrats, beavers and waterfowl do, indeed, walk on or fly over solid ground. Therefore, they, also, could have been addressed in previous chapters.

But, before we delve into aquatic habitats and organisms, I want to describe the treeless landscapes of Alaska and some of their plants and animals. These are the subjects of the next two chapters.

References

1   Gjullin, C.M., Sailer, R.I., Stone, A. and Travis, B.V. 1961. The mosquitoes of Alaska. Agriculture Handbook No. 182, U.S. Department of Agriculture, Washington, D.C., 98 pp.

2   Corbet, P.S. 1966. Diel patterns of mosquito activity in a high arctic locality: Hazen Camp, Ellesmere Island, N.W.T. Canadian Entomologist 98: 1238-1252.

3   Hopla, C.E. 1964-65. The feeding habits of Alaskan mosquitoes. Bulletin of the Brooklyn Entomological Society 59/60: 88-127.

4   Clements, A.N. 1999. The biology of mosquitoes Volume 2: Sensory reception and behavior. CABI Publishing, Wallingford and New York, 740 pp.

5   Corbet, P.S. 1983. A biology of dragonflies. E.W. Classey, Ltd., Farington, 247 pp.

6   Corbet, P.S. 1999. Dragonflies: behavior and ecology of Odonata. Comstock Publishing, Ithaca, 829 pp.

7   Cannings, S.G. and Cannings, R.A. 1997. Dragonflies (Odonata) of the Yukon. pp. 169-200, In: H.V. Danks and J.A. Downes, editors, Insects of the Yukon, Biological Survey of Canada (Terrestrial Arthropods), Ottawa, 1034 pp

8   Thompson, D.J. 1978. Towards a realistic predator-prey model: the effect of temperature on the functional response and life history of larvae of the damselfly, *Ischnura elegans*. Journal of Animal Ecology 47: 757-767.

9   Sternberg, K. 1996. Colours, colour change, colour patterns and 'cuticular windows' as light traps- their thermoregulatoric and ecological significance in some *Aeshna* species (Odonata: Aeshnidae). Zoologischer Anzeiger 235: 77-88.

10 May, M.L. 1991. Thermal adaptations of dragonflies, revisited. Advances in Odonatology 5: 71-88.

11 Currie, D.C. 1997. Black flies (Diptera: Simuliidae) of the Yukon, with reference to the black fly fauna of northwestern North America. pp.563-614, In: H.V. Danks and J.A. Downes, editors, Insects of the Yukon, Biological Survey of Canada (Terrestrial Arthropods), Ottawa, 1034 pp.

12 Crosskey, R.W. 1990. The natural history of blackflies. John Wiley and Sons, Chichister and New York, 711 pp.

13 Barnes, B.M., Barger, J.L., Seares, J., Tacquard, P.C. and Zuercher, G.L. 1996. Overwintering in yellowjacket queens (*Vespus vulgaris*) and green stinkbugs (*Elasmostethus interstinctus*) in subarctic Alaska. Physiological Zoology 69: 1469-1480.

14 Finnamore, A.T. 1997. Aculeate wasps of the Yukon, pp. 867-900 In: H.V. Danks and J.A. Downes, editors, Insects of the Yukon, Biological Survey of Canada (Terrestrial Arthropods), Ottawa, 1034 pp.

15 Sanders, C.J. and Pang, A. 1992. Carpenter ants as predators of spruce budworm in the boreal forest of northwestern Ontario. Canadian Entomologist 124: 1093-1100.

16 Holldobler, B. and Wilson, E.O. 1990. The ants. Harvard University Press, Cambridge MA, 732 pp.

17 Holsten, E.H., Hennon, P.E. and Werner, R.A. 1985. Insects and diseases of Alaskan forests. USDA Forest Service Alaska Region Report No. 181, 217 pp.

18 Rolstad, J. and Rolstad, E. 2000. Influence of large snow depths on black woodpecker *Dryocopus martius* foraging behavior. Ornis Fennica 77: 65-70.

7.
TREELESS LANDSCAPES, SUN-TRACKING FLOWERS AND STUBBY SHRUBS

THE PHYSICAL ENVIRONMENT

Temperature

The general relationships of soil and air temperatures to plant growth and the determination of tree line were described in the introduction. In short, the limitations of permafrost, the shallow active layer, and low air temperatures dictate limits to the geographic and altitudinal distributions of trees. In the absence of trees, the landscape is vegetated by a variety of plants of low stature and by plant communities of low diversity.

Soils

If a prairie state farmer took a look at soils from alpine and arctic tundra, he/she might well remark, "We're not in Kansas, Toto." Compared to typical temperate soils, tundra soils have nothing that resembles topsoil. Loam (a mixture of clay, sand and silt-sized particles) is found only rarely. The humus layer (partially decomposed organic material) found in temperate soils is nonexistent in some tundra soils and in others is replaced by a thick peat layer.

Recall, peat consists of dead plant material that has not decomposed. As such, peat is a storehouse of carbon, a biogeochemical **carbon sink**. The vast peat deposits of Alaska and the rest of the circumpolar region are warming as soil temperatures rise. Because of the climate-warming trend that began in the 1970s, these peat deposits in Alaska are now decomposing faster than they are accumulating.[1] In other words, climate change has turned a carbon sink into a **carbon source**, adding carbon dioxide to the atmosphere rather than reducing it.

In general, soil formation is a very slow process in the Far North. Peat accumulates and decomposes slowly and, therefore, nutrient cycling also creeps along. That is, the inorganic nutrients such as nitrogen and phosphorus are locked away in an organic form for hundreds or thousands of years. The weathering or erosion of bedrock to soil-sized particles certainly proceeded rapidly during the Pleistocene glacial episodes as glaciers scoured bedrock and ground it to silt and clay-sized particles (loess) as well as pebble, sand and boulder-sized pieces. Annual freeze-thaw cycles also weather rock, as do rivers and winds.

The relationship between peat thickness and glaciation was studied at three sites near Toolik Lake in the foothills of the Brooks Range. The sites were deglaciated 11.5, 60 and 125 thousand years ago. The older the deglaciation, the more acidic the soil and the thicker the organic layer.[2,3] At the risk of oversimplification, there is a gradual evolution of soils in the tundra landscape from non-acidic soils with little or no organic layer to acidic, peaty soils. The former soils have a lower biomass of vegetation, an active layer that is thicker, slower nutrient turnover, and fewer shrubs than the acidic soils.

Thus, it appears that the wet, acidic soils characteristic of *Sphagnum*-heath bogs and polygonal ground on the North Slope of Alaska may have taken over 100,000 years to evolve. I am not suggesting that the plant communities seen on these acidic soils are late stages in a succession from dry, non-acidic soil communities of 100,000 years ago. We know that glacial epoch plant communities from the North Slope and interior Alaska differed from all modern communities in these locales. Rather, it appears that the accumulation of the organic layer from whatever plant species existed at these sites may have taken 100,000 years.

The mechanism in this transition is called **paludification**. *Sphagnum* moss plays an impor-

tant role in this process. The gradual appearance of *Sphagnum* on dry soil results in waterlogging of the soil, the accumulation of organic detritus, and its acidification due to incomplete decomposition. Moss tends to dry and insulate the soil in summer but gets soggy in the winter. In winter, heat is conducted out of the soil. Under these conditions permafrost gets closer to the surface and the active layer gets thinner. Paludification is also at work in the boreal forest, converting white spruce communities to bogs or black spruce forests.

The increased biomass and productivity of acidic soils probably relates to nutrients being trapped in the very shallow active layer. These nutrients, though in low concentrations, are accessible to tundra plants. In contrast, nutrients that form in non-acidic soils may percolate down much deeper in the active layer and be out of reach of many tundra plants. Also, there is evidence that in non-acidic soils the nitrogen and phosphorus may become chemically attached to calcium and, therefore, unavailable to plants.

The model described above was developed on a deglaciated arctic landscape. But we see acidic and non-acidic soils in alpine tundra that did not experience glaciation at any time during the Pleistocene. Does this scheme apply to the Tanana Uplands, for example? And if it does, why doesn't the entire Tanana Uplands have acidic, waterlogged soil with its associated plant communities?

Part of the answer to the last question has to do with disturbance. At least three forms of disturbance either slow or prevent the evolution from dry, non-acidic to wet, acidic soils. First, streams and rivers deposit new sediments that bury old soils and serve as a starting point for the development of a new soil surface. Second, **eolian** (windblown) deposition of loess provides a fine-grained soil component that allows germination of the seeds of cotton-grass, a competitor of *Sphagnum*. Third, **cryoturbation** (disturbance due to cold characterized by the vertical movement of rocks through the soil) prevent the development of continuous plant cover, a peat layer and *Sphagnum* moss.

Wind

Wind is a highly variable factor on the tundra. An average annual wind speed of 19.3 km per hour (12 mph) at Barrow, Alaska, and 29.6 km per hour (18.5 mph) at Niwot Ridge, Colorado (elevation 3749 m) have been calculated.[4] Alpine tundra in Alaska occurs at lower elevations, but winds may be similar. Of course, on some (rare) days in either habitat the wind might not blow at all. Conversely, one fine fall day in the Alaska Range, I was hiking a tundra ridge when a gust of wind lifted me and my backpack off the ground and deposited me 3 m (10 feet) away. Unfortunately, I wasn't carrying a wind gauge.

Winds can affect tundra vegetation in at least three different ways. First, in winter, winds carry snow and ice particles across the surface of the landscape, scouring everything just above the snow or bare ground. The abrasive effects of blowing ice can be seen on the dumbbell spruce trees near tree line on windy ridges (see Chapter 3).

Second, wind can remove snow from ridges, leaving them bare, while depositing lots of snow in leeward depressions. The bare ridges will have little soil moisture to support tundra plants the following summer. On the other hand, late melting snow banks produce plenty of moisture but bury vegetation for much of the growing season.

Third, winds tend to desiccate plants that are exposed to them, especially in winter. Many tundra plants have evergreen leaves that can lose water by **evapotranspiration** (water loss through leaves and stems). Wind promotes such water loss, but in winter, soil moisture is frozen and unavailable to replace the lost water.

Habitat Variability

Clearly, the wind effects on tundra vegetation suggest that ridges, slight depressions, and valley bottoms present different sets of environmental variables to plants. Add to these the differences in precipitation, slope, aspect, and soil composition, and it is no wonder that one piece of tundra might not look like the next. For example, on solifluction lobes the differences in slope and moisture from the vertical face or toe to the flattened "stair tread" above the toe allow for tall shrubs to grow at the toe but only low heath and cushion species on the stair tread.

This variability in microhabitat and vegetation strongly influences the distribution and behavior of tundra animals. In Chapter 6 I mention the habitat preferences of several lemming species; two prefer wet tundra, and one prefers dry. Dall sheep, in the snow-free season, prefer to forage on new growth, which is high in nutrients and protein. In spring and early summer new growth is generally concentrated on south-facing slopes. But, as the sun climbs higher in the sky and the last snows melt out of depressions, new growth (stems, leaves, flowers) becomes more abundant in gullies and on north-facing slopes. Consequently, sheep move from one side of the mountain to the other and spend time exploring for late pockets of new growth.

Plant ecologists have described six different plant communities for the low arctic tundra and several more for the high Arctic. What constitutes low Arctic as opposed to high Arctic? Two differences are the length of the growing season (3-4 months vs. 1.5-2.5 months) and summer soil temperatures. Mean July soil temperatures at 10 cm (4 inches) depth are 5° to 8°C and 2° to 5°C for the low and high Arctic, respectively. In Alaska, only a small portion of the Arctic Coastal Plain near Barrow is considered high Arctic, so in this book I will ignore the high arctic tundra.

PLANT ADAPTATIONS TO ARCTIC CONDITIONS

Growth Form

Among herbaceous plants of the tundra, typical growth forms are squat, low, and cushion-shaped. Are these forms adaptive or, rather, responses to stress? Stated another way, are these plants small because they simply cannot grow any larger, or are they small because it is advantageous to be small? Some experiments with bitter cress, *Cardamine bellidifolia*, shed light on this question. Seeds collected from alpine areas of Alaska and the Yukon were grown under temperate conditions and resulted in taller-than-normal plants. Thus, these populations exhibit **phenotypic plasticity**: their growth form responds to environmental conditions. So small bitter cress plants on the Alaskan tundra are probably environmen-

tally stunted. However, seeds collected in the High Canadian Arctic from the same species and also grown under temperate conditions produced only dwarf plants. These high arctic plants are limited in their growth form by genetic as well as environmental factors.[5] It is no accident that the average heights of these arctic plants correspond, roughly, to the average depth of snow cover in winter.[1] By not extending higher than the snow cover, they protect themselves from drying winds and from snow ablation.

Wintergreen leaves

In discussing boreal forest trees, I distinguished between deciduous and evergreen leaves and their relative advantages and disadvantages. The same relationships hold true for tundra shrubs and herbaceous species. As in the forest, evergreen leaves have the advantage of being capable of photosynthesizing when winter temperatures and light intensities are adequate. However, the chief disadvantage is that these leaves are subject to desiccation because water loss by transpiration continues while soil water remains frozen and inaccessible.

An added wrinkle on the tundra is the occurrence of **wintergreen** leaves. These leaves last a year or two but die well before the plant itself dies. For example, individual leaves of cottongrass live more than a year, but the entire tussock may survive for more than 100 years. Leaves of *Dryas integrifolia* are functional for two years while the plant itself may last over 100 years. In *Dryas*, the dead leaves remain attached to the plant and decompose while still attached.

Perennial versus
Annual Life Histories

The annual life history is almost nonexistent in tundra plants. The only example I can find is *Koenigia islandica*, a diminutive species in the buckwheat family. The plant is red with short stems (a few millimeters in the Arctic) and small, three or four-petaled flowers. *Koenigia* occurs on the North Slope, Seward Peninsula, the Alaska Range, southwestern Alaska, some of the Aleutians and the Pribilofs. Where it occurs, it is found in wet habitat. Such sites have more stable night temperatures and may allow this fragile species to maintain more steady metabolic rates during the growing season. Clearly, the disadvantage of the annual life history is that the entire life cycle must be completed in one growing season from seed germination through root and shoot growth, flowering and seed development.

The vast majority of tundra plants are long-lived perennials. Deciduous species typically form leaf buds and, in many cases, flower buds in the fall. In most herbs and deciduous shrubs growth of above-ground structures is fast and occurs early in the growing season. Growth of roots, especially lateral roots, occurs later in the summer. Deepening and warming of the active layer are important in promoting root growth. Root growth in cotton-grass, *Eriophorum angustifolium*, and the sedge *Carex aquatilus* is sensitive to day length, at least at warm soil temperatures. In cotton-grass at soil temperatures of 14-16°C, root growth is zero at 15 hr day length but 4.7 mm per day at 18 hr and 7.5 mm per day at 24 hr.[6] Graminoids (grasslike species) continue to grow until cold temperatures retard them, whereas other arctic species may have a preprogrammed growing season. For example, the rush *Luzula confusa* exhibits leaf senescence after 45-50 days and, even in the lab under favorable growth conditions, stops growing in 55 days.[7]

Lichens are the ultimate long-lived perennials. A species of *Rhizocarpon* has been found to live up to 1300 years in the Alps and up to 4500 years in Greenland.[4] Lichens can remain dormant a long time and still return to normal function. Experiments have been conducted in which *Cladonia alcicornis* was frozen at -15°C for over two years and then thawed. Its photosynthetic rates after thawing were typical of its normal rates.

Several advantages accrue to the lichen lifestyle. First, lichens do not have to grow specialized reproductive structures such as flowers. Second, in the growing season they enjoy the warmest microclimate in the tundra: directly on the surface. Third, their photosynthetic systems are well-adapted to low temperatures. Optimum photosynthesis occurs at about 5°C in several species studied, with positive net photosynthesis continuing below 0°C. Fourth, lichens can withstand a greater degree of desiccation than can vascular plants. Finally, since lichens and mosses do not rely on roots, they do not have to wait until the ground thaws to rehydrate. They can simply absorb liquid water that forms on or adjacent to their tissues. One other advantage to lack of roots is that downslope movement of soil such as occurs in solifluction lobes has no effect. Rooted plants, especially those species with long-lived root systems, are, undoubtedly, affected to some extent.

Gaining a Thermal Advantage

Some tundra plants have physiological adaptations which allow them to function well at low temperatures during the growth season. However, vegetative growth, production of flowers, and development of seeds must occur in the short period when soil moisture is thawed. The warmer the plant, the faster these critical processes may proceed. Tundra plants have a variety of traits that may help to make their thermal environment more advantageous for their survival, growth, and reproduction. These include pubescence (hairiness), hollow stems, sun-tracking flowers, and growth form. I described above some of the reasons for prostrate arctic plants including gaining a thermal advantage.

Pubescence—We don't think of plants as being hairy but a number of tundra plants are! Dense layers of hairs on stems, leaves, or flowers help trap heat. Each hair absorbs some of the sunlight energy that strikes it. Each one also reflects a portion of that energy and, often, the reflected light strikes another hair or another part of the same plant.

The flower clusters of mastodon flowers, *Senecio congestus*, are pubescent; plants from the arctic coast are shorter than elsewhere in Alaska and are downright woolly. The mastodon flower stem is hollow and also hairy. All louseworts are hairy. The most extreme is the woolly lousewort, *Pedicularis kanei*, an inhabitant of dry, rocky alpine slopes and tundra. The flower stalk and buds are covered with fine hairs that help warm the reproductive parts. Most of the species of pussy toes, composites in the genus *Antennaria*, have either hairy stems, hairy leaves, or both. The one-flowered cinquefoil, *Potentilla uniflora*, a low (10-20 cm) plant of rocky and exposed tundra ridges, exhibits hairy undersides on its leaves, undoubtedly for retention of warm air in the cushion or clump.

Growth form—Prostrate, and cushion plants have a thermal advantage over tall, gangly plants during the growth season. Temperatures close to the ground are generally much higher than even 20 cm (8 inches) above ground level. Many of these species have a dense cluster of leaves at the base that traps warm air; sometimes temperatures inside the cushion are 15°C higher than outside. Also, dark stems and leaves absorb heat faster than light-colored leaves.

Hollow stem—I mentioned the hollow stem of mastodon flowers. Hollow stems warm more rapidly than solid stems, allowing the interior to warm to as much as 20°C above the surrounding air temperature.

Sun tracking—Several flowers on the tundra actually track the sun, a phenomenon called **heliotropism**. That is, as the day progresses, the flower turns so that it is always facing the sun (Figure 7.1). This is a thermoregulatory mechanism exhibited by poppies and two of the three

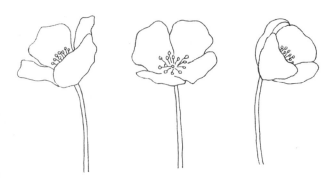

Figure 7.1: Heliotropism (sun tracking) in an Alaskan poppy. In this sequence, the sun is, successively, at the left, directly overhead, and to the right viewing the illustration from left to right.

species of *Dryas*. The thermal advantage is that the parabolic flower shape concentrates a little solar energy and warms the flower parts. By pulling petals off arctic poppies, we can determine their contribution to reproduction. The petals add about 3°C to the surface temperature of the ovaries. Intact flowers tend to produce more and larger seeds than petal-less flowers.[8] Similar results have been reported for eight-petaled dryas.[9] Does this mean that the heliotropism is responsible for improving the reproductive potential of these flowers, or is it just the presence of petals? Experiments were conducted on alpine buttercups in which some were tethered so they couldn't track the sun. These individuals produced fewer and smaller seeds than normal, sun-tracking flowers.[10] Also, insects, primarily flies, upon which these plants depend for pollination are able to maintain higher activity levels by periodically resting or basking inside the blooms of these species.

Since plants do not exhibit behaviors like animals do, how is it that the flowers are able to track the sun? One answer involves growth hormones. During the summer, growth of the flower stalk is stimulated by a growth hormone produced in the stalk itself. However, synthesis of the hormone is somewhat inhibited by sunlight. The result is that the fastest growth in the flower stem is always directly away from the sun. As the sun moves across the sky, flower stalk growth always keeps the flower pointing at the sun. Species with flowers that do not track the sun simply do not have this finely tuned, hormonally driven system.

A second answer involves the **turgor pressure** inside cells in the stem of the flower. Plant cells exhibit a turgor pressure due to the fluid contents of the cell pushing outward on the somewhat rigid cell wall. Fully hydrated cells push outward on the cell wall and the cell has a slightly larger volume. When dehydrated, the cell occupies a smaller volume. Thus, the cells on the side of the stem away from the sun are larger and, hence, taller. Those on the sunny side are shorter. The stem leans toward the sun and, therefore, the flower points at the sun.

Vegetative Reproduction

Before delving briefly into the sexual reproduction of tundra plants by means of seeds and seedlings, let's take a look at vegetative (nonsexual) reproduction. The advantage of vegetative reproduction, recall, is that a new plant can be generated using the resources of an individual that is already established. For instance, a new dwarf fireweed shoot can emanate from an existing rhizome of a healthy, mature dwarf fireweed individual. We could argue the semantics of the word "individual." If the new shoot is still actually attached to the parent plant, it could be considered to be part of the parent. Cut the rhizome connecting the two and, clearly, the result would be two individual plants. If we define "individual" as the above-ground stem, leaves and flowers, then a new shoot, even if it were still connected to its parent, would be considered a separate individual organism. We would have exactly the same difficulty, standing in the boreal forest, deciding whether a clone of thirty aspen trees, still connected by runners, represents a single or thirty individuals.

The disadvantage of asexual reproduction is that offspring are genetically identical to parents.

This means that all such individuals are equally susceptible to drought, low temperatures, ultraviolet radiation damage, and other environmental variables. Drought conditions that kill one individual, therefore, are likely to kill them all, leaving no survivors. The variability that results from genetic recombination in sexual reproduction means that not all individuals have the same susceptibility to a variable and, therefore, some may survive a really extreme fluctuation in the environment that kills others.

Several mechanisms of vegetative reproduction are in evidence among tundra plants. Reproduction by **tillers** is exhibited by cottongrass (*Eriophorum)* and other sedges (*Carex*). Tillers are shoots that form at the base of or in the axil of a leaf on an existing plant. **Rhizomes** are subterranean plant stems that occasionally give rise to above-ground shoots and below-ground roots. Rhizomes differ from true roots in having buds, nodes, and scalelike leaves. **Branch layering**, as described in Chapter 3, is a third way that tundra plants reproduce vegetatively. Tundra plants that reproduce by means of branch layering include dwarf birch (*Betula nana)*, crowberry (*Empetrum nigrum*), lowbush cranberry, blueberry (*Vaccinium* spp.), and willows (*Salix* spp).

A fourth mechanism is **viviparity**, which means "live birth." In the animal world this term is used in contrast to egg-laying, or oviparity. In plants the term applies to species that bypass the formation of seeds. In several species the flower structure is replaced with a small vegetative structure called a **bulbil** or **bulblet**, which can take root and produce a new plant that is genetically identical to the parent, that is, a clone. Species that form bulbils include

arctic red fescue (*Festuca rubra)*, alpine bistort (*Polygonum viviparum*), and nodding saxifrage, (*Saxifraga cernua*). The bulbils of alpine bistort sprout leaves and roots before they fall from the adult plant.

Finally, a variety of arctic and alpine species exhibit **apomixis**. In apomixis, seeds that have two complete sets of chromosomes are produced without the fusion of egg and sperm nuclei. Normally, the haploid egg cell is fertilized by the haploid sperm cell from the pollen, but in apomixis the seed develops from diploid cells in the ovule. Seeds produced in this way develop clones of the parent plant. The most common or well known of apomictic plants are the dandelions, genus *Taraxacum*. Some species of cinquefoils in the genus *Potentilla* and composites in the genus *Arnica* exhibit apomixis. Arctic representatives of the grasses (genus *Poa*) and hawkweeds (genus *Hieracium*) are also apomictic.

These mechanisms are not unique to tundra plants. However, the ability of tundra plants to reproduce themselves without necessarily producing seeds, successfully germinating those seeds, and producing viable seedlings means that they may persist for many years under conditions that may be too severe for sexual reproduction.

Tundra Seeds and Seedlings

In flowering plants sexual reproduction involves one gamete from the male part of the flower being carried in a pollen grain to the female part of the flower, the pistil. When pollination occurs, the pollen tube grows down the pistil to the ovary. Then the gametes fuse and produce a viable seed that can grow into a new plant. A benefit of sexual reproduction is the creation of a new combination of genes from the two parent organisms. Quite literally, a sexually produced individual may have a combination of traits never seen before on this planet.

Recall that some flowers are **perfect**, having both male and female parts on the same bloom. Others are **imperfect**, having either the male parts, stamens and anthers, or the female parts, stigma, style and ovary. Plants with perfect flowers are capable, theoretically, of self-fertilization but such an event produces offspring with reduced variability in comparison to those produced by cross-fertilization. In the tropic and temperate zones plants typically have mechanisms to prevent self-fertilization; some Alaskan plants do too. However, many arctic plants are self-fertile while maintaining the ability to cross-fertilize.

Two conditions may help explain why arctic plants emphasize self-fertility. First, insect pollinators (flies, butterflies and bumblebees), while present in the Arctic, are not as diverse or as abundant as at lower latitudes. Second, survival to reproductive maturity at the environmental extremes for a species depends on either good luck or a combination of traits that work well at these extremes. Self-fertilizing plants in extreme environments produce offspring that are similar genetically and, therefore, likely to survive to reproduce themselves.

In Chapter 3 I mentioned the seed bank: the collection of seeds from a variety of species within the soil. The greater the number of seeds in the bank, the greater the number of plants that might sprout and become established as seedlings. The seed bank is one source of potential colonists in disturbed areas in which some of the soil remains. Many estimates of seed bank size have been made for tundra communities. Cotton-grass tundra near Eagle Summit has about 3000 seeds per m^2. In contrast, 100 seeds per m^2 would be about right for a *Dryas* field in the interior.[11]

Seeds produced from flowers that bloom during one summer mature late in that summer or in the following spring. The growing season is so short that winter arrives before suitable conditions for germination of newly produced seeds are likely to occur. Therefore, virtually all seeds produced in one summer that escape seed-eating animals are deposited in the seed bank awaiting favorable conditions the following year. The seeds from some species could, if given favorable conditions, germinate and sprout almost immediately. Others, such as sedges and willows, must lie dormant for a time. Many cases of seed **dormancy** are due to seed coat inhibition. That is, the seed coats are so hard that they have to be scratched or cracked in order for the seed to germinate. Overwintering in icy soil can often accomplish the scratching. If undisturbed, how long can tundra plant seeds lie dormant? Arctic lupine seeds have apparently lain dormant for 10,000 –15,000 years after which they successfully germinated and produced seedlings.

This extreme example of seed dormancy (see arctic lupine below) leads to an interesting possibility related to the vegetation changes associated with cycling between glacial and interglacial periods in the Pleistocene and Holocene. It has been assumed that, for example, the reforestation of interior Alaska required the "migration" of trees northward or eastward from refugia in which they survived full glacial periods. That is, the pace of recolonization was thought to be dependent on dispersal of seeds into vacant habitat. Perhaps some of the plant species that were "missing" during full glacial periods in unglaciated Alaska were actually lying dormant, in seed form, waiting for appropriate germination conditions.

Germination of tundra seeds is usually in early summer of the year following seed production. Optimal temperatures for germination in most species are 15-30°C, similar to those of temperate and tropical plant species. Lab experiments suggest that no arctic or alpine species germinate at constant air temperatures of 10°C or lower. However, fluctuating temperatures, such as are seen in the field, can cause germination in mountain sorrel, *Oxyria,* even when average temperature falls below 10°C. These are air temperatures; soil temperatures are undoubtedly more important. It appears that most germination occurs when soil temperatures reach 10-15°C.[4] Moisture is also important; the drying of the soil in late summer probably prevents germination.

Seedling development on the tundra is slow. After germination, the shoot appears above ground in several days to a week. In some species several small leaves develop the first summer; in others true leaves don't appear until the second year. Most of the energy and growth activity is directed at the roots. Below-ground growth is critical so that reliable water supplies can be secured for survival. Also, winter frost heaving can affect seedlings with very shallow root systems, making them more susceptible to drought the following summer.

One might imagine that seedlings would establish themselves more effectively on bare ground than on vegetated ground. In the tropic and temperate zones, above-ground (for sun-light) and below-ground (for nutrients and water) competition among plants is intense, and bare ground might be a great place for a seedling to start. On the tundra that competition is balanced or offset by an advantage: soil stability due to established plants with extensive and deep root systems.

Physiological Adaptations

Several aspects of the physiology of arctic plants have been studied in relation to the harsh environment in which they live. Photosynthesis, the process of making carbohydrates from carbon dioxide, water and sunlight energy is one aspect. Maximum photosynthetic rates of arctic plants have been measured and are similar to those of comparable plants in temperate climates. The ideal temperature for photosynthesis in arctic plants tends to be at the low end of the range seen in temperate species. Many arctic species can maintain a positive carbon accumulation (photosynthetic gain > respiratory loss) over broad temperature ranges including, in some plants, down to -2° to -4°C.

Absorption of nutrients from the soil is essential. This process in arctic plants, as in plants elsewhere, works best at temperatures around 40°C (104°F). However, the process in plants of the Far North is relatively insensitive to temperature in comparison to temperate species, allowing arctic plants to absorb nutrients faster at low soil temperatures.

Nutrient absorption speeds up as soil nutrient concentrations increase. This means that, as tundra soils first thaw in spring, the initially high nutrient concentrations from snowmelt and thawing soils can be rapidly absorbed and put to use. Nutrient requirements for new growth differ among tundra plants; deciduous herbs and shrubs require more than grasslike species, which in turn, require more than evergreen shrubs. It is likely that the ability to acquire nutrients shows the same kind of variation in these groups of plants.

The classic conception of nutrient cycling came out of studies of temperate forests and grasslands. In that scheme organic nitrogen in the form of plant and animal proteins and nucleic acids is remineralized through decay and chemical conversion by bacteria and fungi. Part of this process occurs on top of the ground and part in the soil. Proteins are degraded to amino acids, then to ammonia (ammonium ion), and the ammonia is converted to nitrite and nitrate. These last two are the inorganic minerals that serve as nutrients for new plant growth.

Decomposition and remineralization are very slow processes in the Far North due to air and soil temperatures. One indication of these slow rates is the development of peat layers. Peat is the accumulation of plant detritus that hasn't decomposed. One way that tundra plants cope with this long, drawn-out nitrogen cycle is to take a short cut. Rather than waiting for the final nitrification step, many tundra plants preferentially absorb nitrogen in the ammonium and amino acid forms rather than the nitrate.[12] Plant species with ectomycorrhizal root associations have a greater absorption preference for amino acids than do plant species with no root symbionts.[13] The emerging view is that ectomycorrhizae and arbuscular micorrhizae for woody and herbaceous plant species, respectively, are widespread in the low Arctic and are important for nutrient uptake.

SOME PLANT COMMUNITIES

As I indicated earlier in this chapter, environmental variables such as snow accumulation, wind exposure and soil drainage vary considerably from one locale to another. It is no surprise that one set of habitat conditions gives rise to one plant community while a different set produces a different community. In areas of high relief, these plant communities may change over a scale of meters; elsewhere a community might cover kilometers of terrain. Here are some generalizations about plant communities of arctic tundra and polar desert.[11]

Arctic Semidesert: Cushion Plants and Cryptogams

Windswept ridges and slopes accumulate little or no snow in winter and tend to have relatively dry soils in the snow-free period. Also, exposure to winds, both summer and winter, can cause plant desiccation, hence, the term "semidesert." In such locales low, mat-forming or cushion plants dominate. For example, in the Brooks Range and northward along exposed ridges in the foothills, arctic dryad and eight-petaled avens make up about 85% of the vascular-plant cover. *Dryas* mats on these exposed sites may reach 1 m (3.3 ft) in diameter and only 5 cm (2 inches) in height. Other prostrate and cushion species in this community include moss campion, windflower, alpine bistort, several sedges, mountain saxifrage, and prickly saxifrage. The nonvascular plants (cryptogams) likely to be present include a moss and at least four lichen species.

Forest Tundra

The forest tundra community includes the typical members of the low-shrub community plus some tree species. Black spruce is the dominant tree and in most areas the only tree in the forest tundra. However, white spruce, balsam poplar and quaking aspen can be present.

The forest tundra is really a transition zone, or **ecotone,** between the boreal forest and arctic or alpine tundra. On a mountainside this community might occupy a band of 10 m (33 ft) width or less. On the flat Barren Grounds of Canada forest tundra can occupy a 10-50 km (6-30 mile) wide stretch.

Tall-Shrub Tundra

The tall shrubs of this community consist of willow and birch species and alder. In arctic Alaska the dominant species is the feltleaf willow, but other willows such as littletree willow, grayleaf willow, and diamondleaf willow can be important. The birch species are the shrub and dwarf birches.

This community is primarily associated with tundra rivers. Sandbars, gravel bars and islands tend to be well drained and have higher nutrients in the soil. These soils are warmer and have a deeper active layer (1-1.5 m) than other arctic soils. These conditions often promote an understory flora of herbaceous plants, including arctic lupine, wild sweet pea, wheatgrass and *Deschampsia* grasses.

Low-Shrub Tundra

This plant community is dominated by shrubs of lower stature, perhaps 40-60 cm (16-24 inches) tall. The most important of these are dwarf birch, grayleaf willow, plainleaf willow and Richardson willow. The ground cover species include several sedges, cotton-grass, crowberry, blueberry, low-bush cranberry, narrow leaf Labrador tea, alpine and red bearberries, cloudberry and at least three different mosses. At least five species of fruticose lichens are present, including two reindeer mosses. This low-shrub community is common in rolling Uplands in Alaska and northwestern Canada, beyond forest tundra. Much of the Uplands in the Brooks Range is low-shrub tundra.

Dwarf-Shrub Heath Tundra

Heath-dominated tundra occurs in small patches of hundreds of square meters rather than the square kilometer size range of other communities. These communities occupy well-drained soils where snow depths are a minimum of 20-30 cm (8-12 inches). These locales include river terraces, slopes and Uplands.

A heath plant is a member of the family Ericaceae. Tundra heaths include Labrador tea, mountain heather, the bearberry species, low-bush cranberry, bog blueberry, alpine azalea, and Lapland rosebay. Some experts include two other families, the Empetraceae and Diapensiaceae. This broader definition of heath would add crowberry and Lapland diapensia to the dwarf shrub community.

Cotton-grass and Dwarf-Shrub Heath Tundra

A plant community dominated by cotton-grass and including dwarf shrubs, lichens, and mosses occurs over broad areas of upland north of the Brooks Range but above the wet coastal plain. This community is also found scattered in small patches through the alpine tundra of the Tanana Uplands and the Alaska Range.

Sometimes this community is called cotton-grass tussock tundra. However, the standing stock (biomass) and net annual production of organic carbon of the heath and low shrubs equal or exceed those of the cotton-grass itself.

The low shrubs include dwarf birch and diamondleaf willow. Dominant heath species are low-bush cranberry, bog blueberry, Labrador tea and crowberry. At least seven species of mosses are present, as well as an abundance of lichen species.

Graminoid-Moss Tundra

In northern and western Alaska wetland meadows dominate the coastal plains and foothills but are not important in mountain valleys. Graminoid-moss is the community of tundra polygons. In this community the ground is almost completely covered by at least seven species of mosses. The graminoids include four grasses and at least seven sedge species.

The flora of lakes and ponds is included in this community. Pond edges have an abundance of sedges. Shallow depths of 20-30 cm (8-12 inches) are dominated by marsh cinquefoil and mare's tail. The flora of deeper water (40-50 cm; 20-24 inches) consists of bog bean, horsetail, and pendant grass.

TUNDRA SUCCESSION

Primary succession

Plant succession occurs in the arctic even though it is not the obvious process that I described for the boreal forest. Primary succession from bare ground occurs after fires, massive erosion, retreat of glaciers, or human-induced disturbance. In comparison to boreal forest plant communities, tundra floras have fewer species and very few pioneer species.

A fairly typical succession occurs along rivers in the low Arctic. An assemblage of herbaceous species including grasses, legumes and composites establishes itself on gravel bars. As these seedlings prosper, they trap fine sediments transported by wind and water and generate conditions appropriate for recruitment of feltleaf willow. In time, other willow species and alder become established. The shade provided by these shrubs promotes development of a moss layer and reduction of herbaceous species numbers. Eventually, an organic layer develops, insulating the soil and reducing the depth of the active layer.

On the Arctic Coastal Plain of Alaska a cyclic pattern of succession involves the formation and eventual drainage of thaw ponds. The cycle starts after the water of a lake or pond drains away. The lake bottom is the primary habitat upon which succession plays out. First, a series of high-center polygons develop with the boundaries established by the ice wedges that form in the mud cracks of the lake bottom. The troughs are occupied by mosses and a cotton-grass species. Over time, maybe several hundred years, aquatic sedge and Alaska cotton take over. Over the next thousand years a more diverse moss-grass community develops. During this time the centers of polygons thaw, sink, and become small ponds. Still later, these mini-ponds begin to fuse into what will become a large pond or lake. If drainage of this lake occurs due to erosion or seismic activity, the succession starts over again.[11]

Secondary succession

Secondary succession occurs as a result of fires or of human disturbance that doesn't reach down to mineral soils. After fire and some human disturbance, some or all vegetation is removed, nutrients are released (remineralized), peat layers are exposed, the remaining soil surface warms, and the active layer thickness increases. After fire, shrubs that haven't been completely killed resprout. Native grasses are established from seed, either from the soil seed bank or from seeds blown onto the site. These grasses, for a while, are much more abundant than normal. Two sedge species also recruit to these disturbed sites: *Eriophorum vaginatum* (a cotton grass species) and *Carex bigelowii*, a sedge of relatively dry slopes. Recovery by other heath, moss and lichen species may be quite slow.

Expansion of shrubs on tundra systems

A careful comparison of aerial photos of arctic Alaska taken from 1948-1950 with similar photos taken in 1999-2000 showed that at a major-ity of sites examined, shrubs had increased in height and diameter. Shrubs had expanded into previously shrub-free areas.[12] In the context of the communities described above, the tall-shrub and low-shrub communities have expanded at the expense of several other communities. Sub-sequent studies showed that the shrubs are alder, willows and dwarf birch. There is evidence that a similar expansion of shrubs has occurred in Canada, Scandinavia and parts of Russia.[13]

The inference, based on our understand-ing of the expansion of shrubs and trees into the Arctic at the end of the Pleistocene, is that climate warming is responsible for this more recent expansion. One can imagine that tree species might follow the shrubs as they did since the Pleistocene-Holocene transition. If this happens, tundra habitats will contract as boreal forests expand out into the tundra. The expan-sion of shrubs may lead to a positive feedback in which the stems and branches above snowline in spring absorb sunlight energy faster than the snow alone. Snowmelt may proceed faster, lead-ing to warmer temperatures, causing further shrub growth. I will return to these changes in Chapter 11.

SOME TUNDRA PLANTS

Cotton-grass

There are, perhaps, eight different species of the genus *Eriophorum* in Alaska.[16] All are referred to as cotton-grass or Alaska cotton. In fact, none of them are grasses. Members of the grass fam-ily, Gramineae, all have round stems. All mem-bers of the sedge family, Cyperaceae, including cotton-grasses, have triangular stems. You can demonstrate this to yourself by picking a stem of cotton grass and rolling it between two fingers.

Eriophorum vaginatum is a tussock-forming cotton-grass living in well-drained, aerobic soils (Figure 7.2). Tussocks are lumps of highly organic soil; the tussock can reach a height of 70 cm (28 inches). Aside from an alder patch there is no more formidable terrain to hike across than an extensive tussock bog. Many a hunter has reevaluated the wisdom of shooting a moose or caribou in the middle of a tussock bog.

About 75% of the annual production of plant material in this species is in the roots. Indeed, the entire root system is replaced each year. Most of the roots are in the warmer, elevated and nutritionally richer soil. Part of the roots penetrate down into the mineral soil and grow close to (< 1 cm) the permafrost level, where temperatures are near 0°C. Nutrient absorption from the soil is relatively slow because graminoids lack symbiotic mycorrhizae.

Eriophorum leaves usually live longer than a year. At the end of the growth season, the leaves translocate nutrients down into the rhizomes.[17] Thus, these nutrients are readily available in an accessible form the following growing season without having to be remineralized from dead leaves. New leaves and roots both emanate from an underground rhizome. An individual tussock may live from 120 to almost 200 years.[18]

Experiments have been conducted in which *Eriophorum vaginatum* was flooded, as might occur with increased snowfall associated with climate change. Initially, growth rates increased after flooding, probably associated with increased accessibility to nutrients. However, as soil nitrogen declined, growth stalled.

Figure 7.2: Two species of Alaska cotton. a) *Eriophorum vaginatum*, a tussock-forming species; b) *Eriophorum angustifolium*, a species of wet, flooded tundra. *E. angustifolium* has multiple flower heads per stem; *E. vaginatum* has only one.

Long-term survival of *E. vaginatum* in flooded ground is reduced.[19]

The other common cotton-grass is tall cotton-grass, *Eriophorum angustifolium* (Figure 7.2). This species occupies permanently flooded, wet tundra. Tall cotton-grass is a favorite food of several groups of arctic animals. Lesser snow geese congregate on the Arctic Coastal Plain in the autumn. While on these premigratory staging grounds, they feed primarily on the underground rhizomes of tall cotton-grass and the aerial shoots of scouring rush.[20]

Muskoxen in the Far North graze intensively on tall cotton-grass and several *Carex* sedges. In grazed areas cotton-grass biomass is lower than in ungrazed areas. No cotton-grass seedlings are found, and surviving individual *Eriophorum* tend to flower and set seed earlier than in ungrazed areas.[21]

The tundra vole, brown lemming and collared lemming all feed on tall cotton-grass. An interesting hypothesis explaining the population cycles of lemmings relates to their dietary intake of *Eriophorum*. Wounding of tall cotton-grass and *Carex bigelowii* similar to that caused by grazing stimulates these two sedges to produce **trypsin inhibitor**. Trypsin is a pancreatic enzyme critical to digesting dietary proteins; trypsin inhibitor blocks the digestive activity of trypsin. Trypsin inhibitor is high during lemming population highs and when the population is declining; it is low during population lows and increasing populations. Lemmings during population declines have lots of undigested proteins in their guts.

The lemming's inability to digest dietary proteins results from the chemical response of tall cotton-grass to grazing. This is another example of a plant producing an antiherbivory chemical in response to high grazing rates. The trypsin inhibitor is, therefore, an allelochemical. These relationships explain the adverse characteristics of the declining phase of a lemming population cycle: retarded growth, shortened breeding season, delayed maturation and low survival rates.[22] Lemming bites cotton-grass; cotton-grass bites lemming.

Arctic poppy

There are eight species of poppies in Alaska. Two of the species, *Papaver rhoeas*, the corn poppy, and *P. nudicaule*, the Icelandic poppy,

are introduced. The Icelandic poppy is a regular component of the seed mix used in reseeding roadside habitats following road improvements. Several other species have very limited distributions: *Papaver walpolei* is found only on the Seward Peninsula and easternmost Chukotka; *Papaver alboroseum* occurs on the Kenai Peninsula and Kamchatka.

The arctic poppy, *Papaver lapponicum*, is widespread across the circumpolar north; there may be several distinct species in an arctic poppy complex. The arctic poppy typically bears yellow flowers consisting of four petals, many stamens and a pear-shaped seed capsule. In areas of frequent or perpetual clouds and fog, the arctic poppy's flowers are often white. Apparently the metabolic cost of making the yellow pigment is higher than any metabolic benefit gained in absorbing sunlight energy since the sunlight is so indirect through the fog.[23] The arctic poppy is one of the flowering plants favored by high arctic caribou.

The Alaska poppy, *Papaver alaskanum*, is found over much of Alaska. The seed capsule is almost round. Unlike the arctic poppy, the Alaska poppy retains many dead leaves and stems around its base.

Both these poppy species have sun-tracking flowers. The flower has a parabolic shape that focuses the sun's radiant energy toward the very center of the flower. At the center are the female reproductive parts including the developing seed pod. So the center of the flower is well above air temperature, favoring faster development of seeds and also favoring flies that bask in the flowers. These flies have an important role in pollinating arctic and alpine flowers.

Arctic willow

The arctic willow, *Salix arctica*, is one of the few **dioecious** plant species in the arctic. Dioecious species are those that have separate male and female plants. The sex ratio is biased in favor of females, with almost twice as many individuals as males (1.9:1). Females are six times as abundant in habitats that are wet, cold and nutrient-rich. Males are more abundant (1.5:1 ratio) in drier, warmer, low-nutrient habitats.

Arctic willow is a long-lived species. On Greenland, many arctic willow plants were found to be over 60 years old, a few over 100 years old, and one plant was 236 years old.[24] These plants exhibit irregular growth patterns, adding little or no growth in some years. Arctic willow can produce woody growth on only one side of the stem.

Dryas

There are three different *Dryas* species in Alaska. Two of the three occur only in North America, while the third, *Dryas octopetala*, is also found across northern Eurasia and in Iceland and eastern Greenland. This species is an alpine and arctic tundra species. The other two species, *Dryas integrifolia* and *Dryas drummondii*, also tundra species, occasionally occur in lowland, forested, or river bar habitats.

A common feature of these three species is the arrangement of the seed cluster as the seeds mature. Initially, the seed head consists of a spirally twisted mass of seeds with a feathery thread attached to each. At full maturity the threads are spread out like a feather duster (Figure 7.3). Dispersal of seeds is by wind.

Yellow dryas—*Dryas drummondii* bears yellow flowers that, in contrast to the other two species, droop or nod rather than standing erect. Yellow dryas is the more restricted in its geographic range in North America, occurring continuously from the Alaska Range, through British Columbia with isolated populations in the Great Slave Lake area, northeastern Alaska, Ontario, Oregon, and Labrador.

Eight-petaled avens—*Dryas octopetala*, as the name suggests, has eight petals. It typically has creamy white petals although, rarely, yellow flowers are seen. The leaves have a strongly incised or indented margin; the leaves of *Dryas drummondii* are coarsely toothed, those of *D. intergifolia*, if toothed at all, are only so near the base of the leaf.

This species inhabits both exposed tundra ridges and late-melting snowbeds. I mentioned earlier that these two different habitats present

Figure 7.3: Eight-petaled avens growing near a pika and its hay pile. The leaves of this species have an indented margin. Mature seed clusters look like tiny feather dusters. See Chapter 8 for a discussion of pikas and their haymaking.

different challenges to the plants that occupy them. Overall, the snowbed allows *Dryas* to grow larger, produce higher leaf areas and flower more often.[25]

Arctic dryad—*Dryas integrifolia* is one of the hardiest of the arctic cushion plants. It occupies windswept sites with limited snow cover in the winter and limited soil moisture in the summer. Leaves remain two years and stay attached to the plant for years after wilting. The root system is located primarily at the base of the clump or cushion to conserve and recycle the limited nutrients available in this harsh habitat. In contrast to cotton-grasses, *Dryas* has more above-ground biomass than root biomass and has lower root and shoot growth rates. Individuals may live 100-150 years.

Arctic dryad is pretty specific in its nitrogen requirements. I mentioned earlier that tundra plants are able to absorb organic forms of nitrogen (amino acids, ammonium) and, therefore, don't have to rely so much on the complete remineralization of nitrogen. *Dryas integrifolia* and arctic willow are so specialized that they are unable to absorb and use the nitrate form of nitrogen.[26] They must rely totally on the organic forms of nitrogen.

The North American distribution of *Dryas integrifolia* suggests that it survived glacial episodes in several refugia. Analysis of DNA strands from chloroplasts confirms that there are at least two **haplotypes** (unique sequences of nucleic acids), one centered in Beringia and another in the high Arctic. Additional DNA variation suggests the possibility of two other refugia, one southeast of the ice sheets and another in a coastal area of the eastern Arctic.[27]

Arctic dryad is an excellent example of a cushion species occupying and, in part, creating a warm microhabitat on a typically cold landscape. On a sunny midday, the temperature underneath the cushion might be 18°C (64°F) and at the surface of the cushion 42°C (108°F). At the same time, air temperature 120 cm above ground might be 15°C (59°F); that at 5 cm above ground, 21°C (70°F) and the inside of a flower 5 cm above ground, 29°C (84°F).[28] Thus, both photosynthesis and flower maturation are proceeding at rates much faster than if the leaves and flowers were at the temperature 5 cm above ground. The number of insects on the flowers was high during warmest periods and insects were absent at low temperatures.

Arctic lupine

Arctic lupine, *Lupinus arcticus*, is a member of the pea family, Fabaceae. The leaves are **palmately compound**. That is, the 6-8 leaflets are arranged like the fingers on the palm of a hand. As in other tundra plants, the leaves are close to the ground. The flowers are borne on stalks, in 4-14 cm (1.5-5.5 inch) clusters, each an individual blue and white pea bloom. The pods that develop are yellow, hairy, 2-4 cm (0.8-1.6 inches) long and contain 5-8 seeds. Although the seeds look very much like small domestic peas, they are highly poisonous. The arctic lupine occurs on both damp and dry slopes, gravel bars, along roadsides, and in solifluction soils. It is not restricted to tundra habitat, occurring in lowland, disturbed sites.

There are five species of lupine in Alaska. The arctic lupine is the only species common to the interior and northern Alaska. The lupine typically seen along roadsides in south-central Alaska such as along Turnagain Arm and the Kenai Peninsula is the Nootka lupine, *Lupinus nootkatensis*. The Nootka lupine occurs in British Columbia, southeast and south-central Alaska, the Aleutians and Japan. The arctic lupine seems to be restricted to northwest North America.

Arctic lupine seeds can remain dormant for a long time. Seeds taken from an ancient lemming burrow in the Yukon were radiocarbon-dated at 10,000-15,000 years old. A number of the seeds were planted; six germinated within 48 hours. A year later, one of the plants flowered and produced seeds.[29]

Crowberry

The crowberry, *Empetrum nigrum*, is a low, mat-forming shrub with short (3-8 mm), narrow, needle-like evergreen leaves (Figure 7.4). Inconspicuous flowers bloom in May to early June, often before snow has completely melted. The blooms are maroon or purple and are located near the tips of branches in the axils of leaves.

In Alaska, crowberries occur in two different forms or subspecies. In southeastern, south-central coastal and the Aleutians, *Empetrum nigrum nigrum* is dioecious (separate male and female plants). Elsewhere in Alaska (interior, northern and western), *E. nigrum hermaphroditum* is a **monoecious** form, having flowers with both male and female flower parts on the same plant. In both forms the female flower part develops into a black berry containing 6-9 white nutlets or seeds.

Crowberries are edible but virtually tasteless. Humans harvest the berries and make syrups, jellies and even wine from them. Other mammals including voles, lemmings, arctic ground squirrels, grizzlies and polar bears also eat crowberries. Birds including jaegers, gulls and geese feed on these berries. Once at Izembek Lagoon in southwestern Alaska I crawled through the tundra trying to get photos of Canada geese feeding on crowberries. To my amazement, when they spooked there were so many birds,

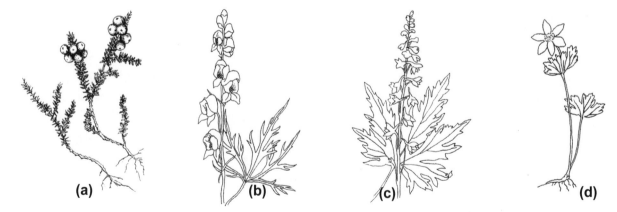

Figure 7.4: Some shrubs and flowers of the Alaska tundra. a) crowberry; b) monkshood; c) larkspur; d) Drummond's anemone. The variety of monkshood most commonly seen on the tundra has only a single flower per plant. Boreal forest monkshood has several flowers per plant. Similarly, larkspur from the boreal forest has broader leaves and is taller than tundra forms.

maybe 25,000, that they literally blackened the sky. That was a real testimony to the virtues of crowberries. The small, white seeds pass through the bird's or mammal's digestive system intact and, presumably, are deposited in scats at some distance from the plant from which they originated. In other words, birds and mammals are the agents by which crowberry plants disperse their seeds.

Moss Campion

Moss campion, *Silene acaulis*, is in many respects the archetypical tundra plant. It grows low to the ground, producing a dense mat of vegetation. The mat is springy to the touch, similar to moss. This growth form keeps the entire plant down near the ground in the warmest possible tundra habitat in the snow-free season. In winter, moss campion is at times snow-covered, sparing it from snow blasting and drying winds.

The pink flowers are about 1.2 cm (0.5 inches) in diameter and are not raised above the level of the mat. Each bloom has a tubular base with five petals that flatten out from the base. Moss campion blooms in June and July, producing an aroma likened to that of lilacs. The leaves are short, flat and covered with stiff hairs.

The habitat of moss campion is dry, typically sandy ridges. It occupies both alpine and arctic tundras. It is an arctic species in Scandanavia, European Russia, Greenland, Iceland and northern Alaska. It is found in the alpine tundra of south-central Alaska, Kodiak Island, British Columbia, Yukon, the Alps, Pyrenees and northern Britain.

Forget-Me-Not

The forget-me-not, *Myosotis alpestris*, is the state flower of Alaska. It reaches 15-38 cm (6-15 inches) in height with blue-green leaves that decrease in size up the stem. Flowers occur in clusters and each has five rounded, blue (rarely white) petals joined at the base with a yellow "eye." Each flower is 0.6-0.9 cm (0.25-0.38 inches) across. On south-facing slopes this species may begin blooming in late May. In areas with a northern exposure or persistent snow beds, blooming may be delayed until early August.

Forget-me-nots grow in alpine and subalpine meadows across much of Alaska out onto the arctic tundra but seem to be missing in the Yukon River drainage. Elsewhere, this species is found in the mountains of western North America, in Siberia, and scattered through the mountains of central Asia, Scandinavia, Spain and Scotland.

The arctic forget-me-not, *Eritrichium aretioides*, has flowers that are almost identical to the other forget-me-not in Alaska. The rest of the plant is, however, noticably different and much shorter in stature. Aside from the actual flower stem, the rest of the plant is a cushion close to the ground. That cushion includes withered leaves, probably leaves that senesced but remained attached. These dried, dead leaves undoubtedly contribute to heat retention at the base of the plant. The leaves of *Eritrichium* are small, densely covered with straight hairs and, because of these hairs, look pale gray instead of blue-green.

Harebells

Three species of the genus *Campanula* are referred to as harebells in Alaska. Other common names sometimes applied to them are bluebell or bluebells of Scotland. However, in Alaska, the term bluebell is usually applied to *Mertensia paniculata*, a forest species in the Borage family.

The mountain harebell or western harebell, *Campanula lasiocarpa*, is found on rocky slopes above tree line across much of Alaska, and throughout the Aleutians, on the Kamchatka Peninsula, and in extreme eastern Siberia.

Mountain harebells are small plants, usually reaching 5-10 cm (2-4 inches) in length. Almost a third of the total length consists of the large, blue-violet, upright bloom (Figure 7.5). In this species there is only one flower per stem. These hardy flowers are commonly found in rocky, disturbed tundra habitats, including the edges of roads and boulder fields. The leaves are

Figure 7.5: Mountain harebell in the foreground, hoary marmot in the background.

toothed or notched along the edges; the farther up the stem, the smaller and more slender the leaves. Mountain harebells transplant readily but are easily choked out by taller garden plants. Vegetative growth and reproduction are from a thin, branching rhizome.

The common harebell or bluebells of Scotland, *Campanula rotundifolia*, has a much broader geographic distribution, occurring across much of northern Eurasia, Greenland, the northern boreal forest of Canada and the Pacific coast states and British Columbia to coastal Alaska. There are isolated occurrences in the interior, near Nome and near Dawson City. The northern Alaska populations may have been introduced from other locations.[16]

Common harebells are taller plants, reaching heights of 20-35 cm (8-14 inches). There are often multiple blooms per stem. Basal leaves are often quite rounded in contrast to those of mountain harebell. However, these basal leaves often wither before flowers appear. Leaves higher up on the stem are very slender. Rather than the erect flowers of the mountain harebell, those of the common harebell nod or hang down.

These flowers are found along stream banks, open hillsides and meadows. Common harebell, should be considered as primarily a forest plant although it occurs in Iceland and on both coasts of Greenland where few, if any, trees grow.

A third species, *Campanula uniflora*, is the arctic harebell. It is a diminutive species, reaching total lengths of 5-7.5 cm (2-3 inches). This tundra species has small, slender, nodding flowers. Each plant bears a thick taproot. It occurs in the Alaska Range, Brooks Range, North Slope, Seward Peninsula and part of the Aleutians. Elsewhere, the arctic harebell is found in the Canadian arctic, Greenland, Iceland, Scandanavia and at various locations in the Rocky Mountains and Sierra Nevadas.

Characteristic of all three species is a blue, tubular or bell-shaped flower. One other *Campanula* can be found in the interior and northeastern Alaska but it doesn't have a tubular flower. *Campanula aurita*, instead, has five blue petals that are almost completely separated down to the base of the flower. This species is found in rock crevices.

Kinnikinnick

Three different members of the genus *Arctostaphylos* occur in Alaska. Two of the species are called bearberries and the other is the kinnikinnick. All are consumed by bears. The official name of kinnikinnick, *Arctostaphylos uvi-ursi*, is an excellent example of scientific redundancy because in Latin *ursa* is bear and *uva* is grape while in Greek *arctos* is bear and *staphyle* is a bunch of grapes.

The kinnikinnick is an evergreen shrub occurring in sandy, well-drained habitats both above and below tree line. The leaves are leathery, spoon-shaped, somewhat shiny on top and duller underneath. The first time I saw kinnikinnick leaves, I thought they looked almost identical to the leaves of the manzanita bushes I knew from my adolescence in southern California. That similarity is no accident; the manzanitas are also *Arctostaphylos* species. Another similarity is the reddish-brown bark that peels. The flowers are small, pinkish-white and shaped like an urn. Blooms appear in drooping clusters from mid-May to mid-June in Alaska. The berries of kinnikinnick are red-orange, dull, dry

and mealy. Their taste and texture have been compared to a mouthful of lint.[30] Each berry, actually a drupe, is 6-10 mm (0.25-0.38 inches) in diameter.

Growth form is a sprawling or trailing shrub 7.5-10 cm (3-4 inches) tall. The shrub forms mats with branches that may reach 1 m in length. These branches send down roots at intervals, and each shrub develops a tap root.

The geographic range of this species includes the tundra and boreal forest of North America extending south into the Appalachians, California and the mountain west. Elsewhere, kinnikinnick occurs in west Greenland, Iceland, northern Britain, Spain, France, eastern Europe, Scandanavia and the boreal forest of Siberia. In North America the kinnikinnick has, by far, the most extensive range of these three *Arctostaphylos* species.

The name "kinnikinnick" derives from an eastern Algonquin word meaning "admixture." Native Americans mixed the leaves with tobacco to make it go farther. The leaves have been used for tea, but prolonged use can lead to problems with the stomach and liver. The berries are prepared for consumption in a variety of ways by the Cree, Chippewyan and Athabascan peoples.

Alpine and Red Bearberry

The alpine bearberry, *Arctostaphylos alpina*, is my favorite tundra plant. The leaves turn brilliant scarlet in the fall, adding lots of color to the landscape. The alpine and red bearberries are both deciduous shrubs with tear-drop shaped leaves. In both species the leaves are conspicuously veined, the veins forming a network or reticulum with raised bumps between the veins.

The leaves of the alpine bearberry have hairs around the margin; those of the red bearberry do not.

In North America the distribution of alpine bearberry is disjunct with the Alaska, Yukon, and Northwest Territories population and with two other populations: one east of Hudson Bay and the other in the western barren grounds (tundra west of Hudson Bay) of Canada. In addition, at least three isolated relict populations exist in the mountains of the eastern United States. Asian populations occur from the Chukotsk and Kamchatka Peninsulas across the northern tundra to the Scandanavian Peninsula and across northern China into mountainous central Russia. Isolated populations exist in central Japan, the mountains of Europe, northern British Isles, and both coasts of Greenland.

Alpine bearberry is a prostrate (10 cm height or less), branching shrub of dry habitats of heaths, mountains and tundra. White, urn-shaped flowers bloom from mid-May to early June and produce large, dull black berries. The berries are juicy but have little flavor.

Red bearberry, *Arctostaphylos rubra*, is similar in appearance to alpine bearberry but has somewhat larger, nonhairy leaves with less texture. The ripe berries are red and translucent. Of the three *Arctostaphylos* shrubs in Alaska, the red bearberry has the most restricted geographic range in both North America and Asia. In northeastern Asia, the red occurs in an area devoid of alpine bearberry. This species is completely absent from Europe, Iceland and Greenland.

Mountain Sorrel

Oxyria digyna, or mountain sorrel, has the most northerly distribution of any flowering plant. The species is present across virtually the entire Arctic. In alpine tundra *Oxyria* occurs in Alaska south to the Colorado Rockies, the Cascades and the Sierra Nevada of California. It is found in the mountains of central Asia, eastern Siberia, Kamchatka, the northern Japanese islands, the Alps, Pyrenees and the middle east.

Mountain sorrel is a member of the buckwheat family. The leaves are kidney-shaped and have very long **petioles** (leaf stems) that attach to the base of the plant. The flower-bearing stem may occasionally reach heights of 35 cm (14 inches). Flowers are tiny and have four sepals but no petals. A fruit forms from each flower in the cluster and consists of a seed surrounded by a red, circular wing. The wing is a seed-dispersal mechanism.

The light and temperature requirements for flowering in mountain sorrel have been studied in the greenhouse. Alpine plants from mid-latitude (40°N) were compared with arctic plants. Alpine populations need at least a 15 hour photoperiod to flower, but arctic populations require even longer day lengths. The alpine populations are adapted to somewhat shorter photoperiods and higher temperatures than arctic populations.

Monkshood

Two species of monkshood occur in Alaska. One of these, *Aconitum maximum*, is confined to the western Alaska Peninsula, Aleutians, Komandorski and Kurile islands. The other species, *Aconitum delphinifolium*, is widespread over almost the entire state (Figure 7.4).

This second monkshood occurs in three forms, often recognized as subspecies. The standard form is found in meadows, thickets, along creeks and in mountains up to 1700 m (5600 feet) elevation. This monkshood has stems up to 70 cm (27 inches) in height with few leaves and bears a few dark blue flowers. The coastal form has longer stems (up to 1.2 m; 3.9 feet), many flowers per stem, and leaves with much broader lobes. This form is found from British Columbia through southeastern Alaska, into south-central, the Aleutians and the Alaska Peninsula. The alpine form is shorter than the standard form, usually bearing only a single flower per plant. This monkshood occupies rocky slopes and alpine tundra.

The leaves of all these forms are deeply notched into five lobes. Each of these lobes is subdivided into two or three segments. As the species name *delphinifolium* suggests, these leaves resemble those of the wild *Delphinium* or larkspur. Larkspurs and monkshoods are poisonous plants and no part should be eaten. The tubers of monkshood are highly toxic, containing an ester alkaloid called **aconitin**. Aconitin paralyzes nerves and lowers both body temperature and blood pressure.

Larkspurs

Two species of larkspur occur in Alaska. *Delphinium glaucum* is a tall species with stems up to 2 m (6.6 feet) in height and dark violet to purple flowers. This is a species of wet meadows and thickets. It is common in the boreal forest but also occurs in the treeless tundra of the Yukon delta, Seward Peninsula and the mouth of the Mackenzie River.

Delphinium brachycentrum is the tundra species. It is found on rocky slopes, meadows along tundra rivers and on solifluction lobes. Stems are shorter (up to 60 cm; 23 inches) and bear fewer flowers (Figure 7.4). The flowers are blue or creamy white mixed with blue.

Anemones

Five species of anemones are found in Alaska, and all occur on dry slopes, meadows, open woods and rocky areas. One of the five, *Anemone richardsonii*, also occurs in thickets in the boreal forest. These plants tend to have several basal leaves very close to the ground and upright flower stems, each bearing a single flower. The flower stem has a single, modified leaf that wraps entirely around the stem (Figure 7.4).

Richardson's anemone, *Anemone richardsonii*, is the only one of the five with yellow flowers. Each flower bears 5-8 pointed sepals (anemones don't have actual petals) that are brownish on the underside. The narcissus-flowered anemone, *Anemone narcissiflora*, has 4-10 white sepals that are slightly bluish underneath. The windflower, *Anemone parviflora*, has white blooms that are very bluish underneath. The cut-leaf anemone, *Anemone multifida*, flowers are creamy white, yellowish-white or gray on top and rosy or lavender on the bottom. Drummond's anemone, *Anemone drummondii*, has blue flowers or white tinged with blue. Most of these species bloom from June through August. However, the windflower, like its cousin the pasque flower, is an early bloomer. When the snow is gone, this species blooms.

Daisies

Flowers in the composite family Asteraceae are often given the generic name of daisies. In daisies, each flower head consists of two types of small flower components. The central disk is made up of numerous minute flowers called florets. The central disk is surrounded by rays, each of which is a flower with one strap-shaped petal. So each ray represents a separate flower and each floret in the disk is a separate flower. Hence, the entire bloom is a composite of many individual flowers.

Daisies with yellow rays or "petals" include the arnicas, groundsels and goldenrods. The arnicas of interior and northern Alaska include the alpine, frigid and Lessing's. The alpine arnica, *Arnica alpina*, is found on dry alpine slopes from southern British Columbia northward to interior and northern Alaska, eastern and central Siberia. These arnicas grow from a scaly rhizome, producing flowers that bloom in June and July. The plant reaches 18-31 cm (7-12 inches) tall and the leaves are narrow and pointed. Flower stems have one to three sets of leaves opposite each other.

Frigid arnica, *Arnica frigida*, is similar but has broader leaves almost all of which are basal. Frigid arnicas almost always have nodding flowers, whereas, in alpine arnicas, some flowers nod, some are upright and some are in between. This species is widespread on dry slopes in Alaska. Elsewhere, this species is found in extreme eastern Siberia, the northern Rocky Mountains and in extreme eastern Canada.

Both the above arnicas can be distinguished from Lessing's arnica, *Arnica lessingii*, by looking at the **anthers** (stalks bearing pollen) of the composite flower. In Lessing's arnica the anthers are purple; in the other two they are yellow. In Lessing's arnica the flowers nod; almost all the leaves are basal.

The goldenrods, *Solidago,* also bear yellow flowers. Three species occur in interior and northern Alaska: *Solidago multiradiata, Solidago canadensis* and *Solidago decumbens*. In Alaska, the most widespread of the goldenrods is the northern goldenrod, *Solidago multiradiata*. Stems sprout from a woody rhizome and bear leaves at the base and along the stem. This species is found in rocky woodland and alpine areas and, unlike the other two species, has a flower cluster confined to a roughly hemispherical shape.

Solidago canadensis is a species of meadows in moist woods. Although common throughout the boreal forest, it is not really a tundra species. In Alaska, this species is restricted to a few localities on the middle Yukon and Tanana Rivers. Elsewhere, this goldenrod occurs from the Pacific coast to the Atlantic coast of Canada, southward into the Great Plains and the Rocky Mountains.

The third species, *Solidago decumbens*, has spatulate basal leaves and flowers spread out along the flower stem. This is a mountain species extending from the Rocky Mountains of Colorado into central Canada and east-central Alaska.

The groundsels, ragworts and fleabanes are yellow daisies in the genus *Senecio*. There are ten species of *Senecio* from interior and northern Alaska. Of these, the most recognizable is the mastodon flower or marsh fleabane, *Senecio congestus.* This species grows on the margins of lakes, and in wetlands and marshes throughout Alaska, arctic Canada, Siberia and wet habitats across Asia to Europe. The stem is thick but hollow and bears toothed leaves that appear woolly. This tall (0.8-1.5 m; 2.5-5 feet) plant bears clusters of yellow, woolly, dense flowers that bloom in July to early August. Arctic representatives are shorter and woollier than individuals found elsewhere.

A daisy with light lavender or purplish ray flowers is the Siberian aster, *Aster sibericus*. This species is extremely widespread in Alaska, occupying river flats, meadows, stony slopes and mountains. It is missing only in southeast and the western Aleutians. Alpine specimens are short with a single flower head and almost smooth-margined leaves; lowland, interior specimens are tall, branched with multiple flower heads per stem and with fine, saw-toothed edges to the leaves. Siberian asters spread vegetatively from underground rhizomes, similarly to fireweed. And, similar to dandelions, mature, cottony seeds of Siberian aster are dispersed by winds. Speaking of dandelions, the native dandelions (*Taraxacum* spp.) and hawk's beards (*Crepis* spp.) are examples of composites that have strap-shaped (ray) petals only.

TUNDRA VEGETATION IN TRANSITION

Recall that the plant assemblages we see on modern treeless habitats in the Far North bear little resemblance to the steppe community of glacial episodes of the Pleistocene. Grass species dominated that earlier landscape, finally giving way to a wetter landscape with less grass, less sagebrush, and more woody shrubs. The transition or succession to the new plant communities may have taken hundreds or, perhaps, thousands of years.

Evidence is accumulating that tundra is now undergoing a change or succession leading to tall shrub community. The transition appears to be a succession in response to warming temperatures. This transition is probably similar to that that occurred at the very end of the Pleistocene, when shrubs and trees reinvaded previously glaciated landscapes. We know that tundra habitat meets forest on mountainsides in interior Alaska. The ecological transition, or ecotone, involves a blending of species from the two ecosystems. As the Alaskan climate warms, this ecotone will move up the mountain. In essence, forests are invading tundra communities in many locations.

Changes in tundra landscapes will undoubtedly affect the animal species now resident on the tundra, some of which are described in the next chapter. Some species such as caribou and muskoxen were present during glacial times and, therefore, have already survived a major ecological succession. Only time will tell how long these species (and humans as well) avoid extinction.

REFERENCES

1 Ostercamp, T.E. and Romanovsky, V.E. 1999. Evidence for warming and thawing of discontinuous permafrost in Alaska. Permafrost and Periglacial Pocesses 10: 17-37.

2 Walker, D.A., Auerbach, N.A. and Shippert, M.M. 1995. NDVI, biomass, and landscape evolution of glaciated terrain in northern Alaska. Polar Record 31: 169-178.

3 Hobbie, S.E., Miley, T.A. and Weiss, M.S. 2002. Carbon and nitrogen cycling in soils from acidic and nonacidic tundra with different glacial histories in northern Alaska. Ecosystems 5: 761-774.

4 Billings, W.D. and Mooney, H.A. 1968. The ecology of arctic and alpine plants. Biological Reviews 43: 481-529.

5 Sage, B. 1986. The Arctic and its wildlife. Facts on File Publications, New York, 190 pp.

6 Shaver, G.R. and Billings, W.D. 1977. Effects of daylength and temperature on root elongation in tundra graminoids. Oecologia 28: 57-65.

7 Addison, P.A. and Bliss, L.C. 1984. Adaptations of *Luzula confusa* to the polar semi-desert environment. Arctic 37: 21-132.

8 Corbett, A.L., Krannitz, P.G. and Aarsson, L.W. 1992. The influence of petals on reproductive success in the arctic poppy (*Papaver radicatum*). Canadian Journal of Botany 70: 200-204.

9 Kjellburg, B., Karlsson, S. and Kerstensson, I. 1982. Effects of heliotropic movements of flowers of *Dryas octopetala* L. on gynoecium temperature and seed development. Oecologia 54: 10-13.

10 Stanton, M.I. and Galen, C. 1989. Consequences of flower heliotropism for reproduction in an alpine buttercup (*Ranunculus adoneus*). Oecologia 78: 477-485.

11 Bliss, L.C. 2000. Arctic tundra and polar desert biome, pp. 1-40 In: M.G. Barbour and W.D. Billings, editors, North American terrestrial vegetation, Second Edition. Cambridge University Press, Cambridge, 708 pp.

12 Sturm, M., Racine, C. and Tape, K. 2001. Increased shrub abundance in the Arctic. Nature 441: 546-547.

13 Tape, K., Sturm, M. and Racine, C. 2006. The evidence for shrub expansion in Northern Alaska and the Pan-Arctic. Global Change Biology 12(4): 686-702.

14 Chapin, F.S. III, Moilanen, L. and Kielland, K. 1992. Preferential use of organic nitrogen for growth by a nonmycorrhizal arctic sedge. Nature 631: 150-153.

15 Kielland, K. 1994. Amino acid absorption by arctic plants: implications for plant nutrition and nitrogen cycling. Ecology 75: 2373-2383.

16 Hulten, E. 1968. Flora of Alaska and neighboring territories: a manual of the vascular plants. Stanford University Press, Stanford, 1008 pp.

17 DeFoliart, L.S. 1986. Regulation of growth, nitrogen and phosphorus storage and carbon uptake in *Eriophorum vaginatum*, an arctic sedge. MS Thesis, University of Alaska Fairbanks, 67 pp.

18 Mark, A.F., Fetcher, N., Shaver, G.R. and Chapin, F.S.III 1985. Estimated ages of

mature tussocks of *Eriophorum vaginatum* along a latitudinal gradient in central Alaska. U.S.A. Arctic and Alpine Research 17: 1-5

19 Gebauer, R.L.E., Reynolds, J.F. and Tenhunen, J.D. 1995. Growth and allocation of the arctic sedges *Eriophorum angustifolium* and *E. vaginatum*: effects of variable soil oxygen and nutrient availability. Oecologia 104: 330-339.

20 Brackney, A.W. and Hupp, J.W. 1993. Autumn diet of lesser snow geese staging in northeastern Alaska. Journal of Wildlife Management 57: 55-61.

21 Tolvanen, A. and Henry, G.H.R. 2000. Population structure of three dominant sedges under muskox herbivory in the high arctic. Arctic, Antarctic and Alpine Research 32: 449-455.

22 Seldal, T., Andersen, K.-J. and Hoegstedt, G. 1994. Grazing-induced protease inhibitors: a possible cause for lemming population cycles. Oikos 70: 3-11.

23 Pielou, E.C. 1994. A naturalist's guide to the Arctic. University of Chicago Press, Chicago, 327 pp.

24 Raup, H.M. 1965. The structure and development of turf hummocks in the Mesters Vig District, northeast Greenland. Meddelelser om. Gronland 166: 1-112.

25 McGraw, J.B. and Antonovics, J. 1983. Experimental ecology of *Dryas octopetala* ecotypes. Journal of Ecology 71: 899-912.

26 Atkin, O.K., Villar, R. and Cummins, W.R. 1993. The ability of several high arctic plant species to utilize nitrate nitrogen under field conditions. Oecologia 96: 239-245.

27 Tremblay, O.N. and Schoen, J.D. 1999. Molecular phylogeography of *Dryas integrifolia*: glacial refugia and postglacial recolonization. Molecular Ecology 8: 1187-1198.

28 Philipp, M., Bocher, J., Mattsson, O. and Woodell, S.R.J. 1990. A quantitative approach to the sexual reproductive biology and population structure in some arctic flowering plants: *Dryas integrifolia, Silene acaulis* and *Ranunculus nivalis*. Meddelelser om Gronland, Bioscience: 34: 1-60.

29 Johnson, D., Kershaw, L., MacKinnon, A. and Pojar, J. 1995. Plants of the western boreal forest and aspen parkland. Lone Pine Publishing, Edmonton, 391 pp.

30 Pratt, V.E. 1989. Field guide to Alaskan wildflowers. Alaskakrafts Publishers, Anchorage, 136 pp.

8.
WHITE SHEEP, WHITE BIRDS, GRIZZLIES AND GROUND SQUIRRELS: SOME TUNDRA ANIMALS

TUNDRA POPULATION CYCLES AND FLUCTUATIONS

One of the dominant features of tundra ecosystems is the tendency for animal populations to fluctuate dramatically in size. Earlier I discussed snowshoe hare population cycles in North America, indicating that those cycles, in turn, caused the regular cycling of other species in the boreal forest. Lynx is a good example of a species that is directly tied to hares and whose own population densities are largely dependent on hare abundance. I also mentioned that in eastern Canada, lynx population cycles result in the cycling of local populations of caribou, a tundra species. Therefore hare cycles have impacts far beyond the bounds of the boreal forest, especially for highly mobile species such as golden eagles.

Population cycles are also quite evident in lemmings. Brown lemmings and collared lemmings both exhibit regular population cycling for reasons we still don't fully understand. At high population densities these rodents consti-

tute a convenient and plentiful food resource for a range of tundra predators, including arctic fox, short-tailed weasel, snowy owl, long-tailed jaeger, and parasitic jaeger. However, when these prey species are at low points in their population cycles, predators are affected in terms of physiological condition, reproductive success, and, ultimately, mortality rates.

Population cycles in lemmings also affect non-predator populations. First, lemmings may compete with other mammals or birds for some of the food resources in the tundra. Any competitive interaction will be intensified during lemming population highs. Second, when lemming populations crash or are at very low levels, predators tend to switch to alternative prey. Predator switching may help explain population fluctuations in ptarmigan species, snow buntings, and a variety of waterfowl species that nest in tundra habitats.

PATTERNS OF MOVEMENT OF TUNDRA ANIMALS

Many bird species of tundra habitats are present only in the summer, or clement, months. Most of these are long distance migrators. Some populations winter along the western or southern coast of Alaska. Others fly to the prairie provinces or states or even farther south to the western coastal states. Some go as far as Chesapeake Bay or Central America.

Several species of birds and mammals move from boreal forest to tundra on an annual cycle. Caribou , *Rangifer tarandus*, spend winter in the boreal forest and summer on the tundra. The movement patterns of moose in many areas of the state include either regular or irregular excursions into the tundra from the boreal forest. Willow ptarmigan often migrate down from the tundra into the boreal forest in winter.

Many tundra species exhibit dispersal movements. These movements are usually undertaken by juveniles of highly territorial species in areas where all the best territories are already taken. Arctic ground squirrels and marmots exhibit dispersal movements.

Many movements by tundra animals are related to food availability. Dall sheep forage on low-lying herbs and shrubs, preferring new growth that is typically high in nutritional value. This results in sheep moving around the mountain, from spring through late summer. Dall sheep change their locations in the mountains not at random but in response to the change in availability of nutritious, new growth. On a smaller scale, snow buntings feed at the edges of snowmelt because this is where the seeds upon which they survive for three seasons of the year are most exposed. The daily movements of snow buntings involve bouts of seeking out areas of new snowmelt during feeding hours interspersed with bouts of roosting.

Many species restrict their movements within a territory or home range. The size of a territory depends on the species, its population density, and the availability of food resources. Territories of long-tailed jaegers on their nesting grounds average about 0.6 km^2 during lemming highs and about 1.8 km^2 at moderate lemming abundances. Home ranges—areas of customary use—may be quite large in tundra species. One Alaskan wolverine in tundra habitat was observed to have a home range of 637 km^2 (250 miles^2).

MAMMALS OF THE TUNDRA

Caribou

My son, Jason, and I were hiking along a tundra ridge high above Beaver Creek. A group of nine caribou was heading our way, and we decided to lie down in the tussocks and see how close they would come before they spotted us. The young bull in the lead didn't notice anything unusual until he was within thirty feet of us. Suddenly, he reared up on his hind feet and jumped almost straight up. When he came down, he and the rest of the band ran clear out of sight. We laughed, off and on, for the rest of the day.

What is the significance of this comical behavior? Biologists call it the **excitation jump**, a dramatic startle response that is surely noticed by most of the caribou in the vicinity (Figure 8.1). During the jump, all the caribou's weight bears down on the back feet, squeezing a gland positioned between the hooves of each foot.

Figure 8.1: Caribou excitation jump. See text for discussion of this extreme alarm response.

The speculation, still untested, is that the gland leaves a secretion on the ground that other caribou can smell. Thus, a fright response, the excitation jump, may alert caribou to a dangerous location even if they didn't see the jump.

One might ask how likely it is for other, unrelated caribou to pass by the exact same spot that our young bull may have marked. Actually, caribou exhibit a strong tendency to travel single file, forming deep ruts in the tundra that may result from centuries of use. Caribou spend most of the year walking through snow. Their ankles and feet are particularly well adapted to travel across snow and wet tundra. The hooves splay widely on soft ground and snow, increasing

the effective surface area, and resulting in a relatively low **foot loading** (the ratio of weight to foot surface area, expressed in pounds per square inch or kilograms per square centimeter).

Dewclaws are long and add support in soft substrata. Typically, caribou can traverse wind-packed snow without punching through the crust. But soft snow will not support the weight of a caribou. Walking single file through soft snow is beneficial to caribou for the same reason it is for humans: the lead animal is breaking trail for those to come. The group achieves a metabolic savings by making a single trail through the snow. We can only presume that caribou occasionally trade off the lead so that a single animal doesn't incur all the metabolic drain of breaking trail. Metabolic studies of caribou locomotory effort have shown that moving across wet tundra takes almost twice the energy required to walk along a gravel road. We would expect walking in snow conditions to be even more demanding. Although trails probably save energy, they often may cross terrain suitable for ambush by predators. A scent warning in the trail would alert caribou to a recent, startling event such as the presence of predators.

How do caribou follow each other, single-file, in the dark? Several friends and I were sheep hunting years ago in the Wrangel Mountains. We set up our tent on a hogback ridge; the only flat spot was right next to a game trail. In the middle of the night we were awakened by the click-click-click of the ankles of a passing band of caribou. The ankle bones are connected by a ligament that, during ankle flexion, snaps across another ankle bone. The snap can be heard, and this noise could easily serve as the signal allowing the followers to follow the leader even in the darkness.

Another caribou behavior commonly seen is the alarm pose. This pose is an exaggeration of the urination posture in which a hind leg is thrust out laterally and planted on the ground (see Figure 0.5). When one member of a caribou band strikes the alarm pose, all the other caribou go on alert to see what develops. In some cases the alarm pose is immediately followed by flight: they run away. In many instances, however, caribou will cautiously approach the object of their curiosity. The near point of the approach is, in my experience, about 20-25 yards, still far enough away to turn and outrun any of their natural predators. Caribou do not blindly and automatically exhibit this approach behavior after being hunted by humans. Caribou bands that have experienced human predation less frequently approach humans; more often they turn and run at the sight of humans.

Antlers are one of the most interesting and obvious features of caribou. Unlike all their other deer relatives, both sexes of caribou sport antlers. Other than this fact, the processes of antler growth and development are much like those in other cervids. Antlers are shed and regrown each year; they are made of bone. As is true in other deer species, antlers are mainly social organs, used to establish and/or maintain dominance. Occasionally a caribou may fend off a predator using its antlers, but this is a rare event. In other words, antlers are not a predator defense mechanism.

Antlers originate from two flat spots on the skull, the **pedicels**. The pedicels contain special cells, the osteoblasts, that initiate bone formation. These cells organize and direct antler growth by extracting minerals from the bloodstream of the overlying skin. As the minerals, primarily calcium phosphate, are deposited, the antler grows and the overlying skin, the velvet, grows with it. The metabolic demand for calcium during antler formation is enormous; a mature bull caribou may sport antlers weighing 18 kg (40 pounds). To marshal the required calcium, caribou must eat foods rich in calcium and often chew last year's shed antlers.

Antler growth begins in early spring and is complete by late August or early September. In early fall, males do a lot of brush thrashing with their antlers. Thrashing serves several functions. First, thrashing removes the velvet layer, allowing the outer surface of the antler to harden. Caribou actually polish their antlers on the brush, adding plant material to the surface of the antler. Second, thrashing is practice for the combat that often occurs between bulls during the rut. Well after the October rut, usually mid-December to January, bulls drop their antlers. The shedding process involves dissolving the bone connection between the base of the antler and the pedicel. This process is very similar to that exhibited by deciduous trees that drop their leaves in the fall.

But what about females? Why, of all members of the deer family, do female caribou alone grow antlers? The most likely explanation has to do with wintertime feeding. During winter, caribou use their forelegs to dig through the snow to find food. This cratering behavior is metabolically expensive but is especially important for pregnant females. Males, based on body size alone, could probably dominate females and expropriate female craters. However, through much of the winter females have antlers and males do not, and females are able to maintain control of their feeding craters by using their antlers. The males, quite literally, get the point. Near calving time females finally drop their antlers. The mineral demands of birthing and lactation are undoubtedly met, in part, by chewing the antlers they have just shed.

The antlers of mature bulls are often very ornate, with many points, and are, as a proportion of body size, the largest in the deer family. Only the extinct Irish elk had proportionally larger antlers. Why are caribou antlers so large? Certainly, it requires a greater investment of nutrients and energy to build large, as opposed to small, antlers. Work on the comparative biology of the deer family has yielded a connection between mature male antler size and growth potential in newborns. Here is the connection. Caribou have their young on the tundra, out in the open. Hiding those young from predators doesn't work; there is no place to hide. So caribou calves, if they are to survive, must be born large, grow fast, and be highly mobile from the start. Birth weight, as a proportion of final adult weight, is highest in caribou. Caribou milk has the highest fat content among cervids, and fat content translates into growth. Calves typically stand in the first hour after birth and can outrun a human within the first 24 hours of life.

How does all this relate to antlers? The physiological factors that combine to allow energy and nutrient mobilization to produce large calves and rich milk are probably the same factors needed to produce very large antlers. So, dominant bulls with huge antlers presumably have the genetic programming to produce offspring with a high degree of survivability.[1] Of course, actual antler size is a result of nutritional status and age of the male, as well as genetic makeup. A bull may not always reach his potential due to limitations of forage quality and/or quantity.

One other aspect of caribou antlers is of anthropological interest. Human hunters in the late Pleistocene fashioned projectile points out of antler tips. In some cases the point was fastened to a spear shaft without modification except for straightening. Another possibility was the "microblade" technology prevalent in the Far North in the Paleolithic. Microblades were flaked from obsidian, flint or chert and resembled the narrow blades in a twin-bladed shaving razor. Several microblades were set in grooves cut into the antler point, parallel to antler direction. Caribou antlers were the antlers of choice because they were the most dense antlers. Near the tips, caribou antler is entirely dense bone with no spongy bone in the center.

Caribou exhibit an annual cycle of movement. The Nelchina herd, in its annual cycle, crosses the Richardson Highway between Paxson and Sourdough in November and in March. This is one of about 25 more or less distinct herds in Alaska. In the summer, this herd occupies tundra habitats on the south side of the Alaska Range, and sometimes members can be seen along the Denali Highway. Individuals and small bands are spread out over an immense area.

During the summer large bulls are found in small aggregations separated from the cows, calves, and yearlings. During September, bulls rejoin the cows in anticipation of the rut. By late September or early October, females are coming into estrus and males are vying for their attentions. A dominant bull in the band is determined through behavioral interactions in which body size, antler size, and aggressive behavior all play a role. Most of the ranking in the dominance hierarchy is established without having to resort to actual combat. Displays of antler size in which one male turns broadside to a potential competitor allow males to, literally, size up their competition. Threat or chasing behavior by males involves holding the head level with the body, antlers back, and approaching the competitor (see Figure 2.4).

During and after the rut, Nelchina caribou form aggregations of several dozen to several hundred animals and move eastward to winter range, east of the Richardson Highway. Caribou in this herd traditionally overwinter in the boreal forest of the Copper River basin and the Mentasta area. In the early spring these same caribou will begin a westward movement back toward higher ground. By April, females will be on windblown tundra ridges ready to drop their calves. After calving, these animals undergo a general dispersal over the entire summer range. For this herd, the annual cycle of movement carries them generally in an east-west direction in the spring and the reverse in the fall. Similar annual migrations occur in other caribou herds in Alaska such as the Porcupine and Forty Mile herds.

One important factor driving the cycle may be access to favorable overwintering habitat. Caribou are able to paw through loosely packed snow much more easily than crusted snow and will avoid cratering activity in very hard, dense snow.[2] Another factor driving the annual cycle of movement is access to suitable calving grounds. Windswept ridges for calving offers several advantages. First, the incidence of annoying insects is lower on these ridges. Second, we presume that these areas allow the mothers to scan the surroundings for predators.

In a particular herd, almost all the females come into estrus within a few days of each other. Bulls have a lot of work to do in breeding season and have no time to feed. They rely on fat stored in a thick layer on the tops of their hindquarters. Not all females come into estrus each year. It appears that poor nutritional status can result in cows remaining barren for a year. This phenomenon is called a **reproductive pause.**[3] Body weights of females that do not become pregnant at breeding time are significantly lower than weights of females that will become pregnant.[4] Gestation in caribou is 215-230 days and since impregnation is synchronized, so is calving. About 90% of calves born into a herd arrive within a ten-day period. One evolutionary advantage to synchronized calving is predator swamping as described in Chapter 4. Pregnancy rates vary among herds but typically range from 75-90%. Birth weights average about 5.9 kg (13 lb) and calves double their birth weight in 15 days.[5]

Calf/cow ratios are often estimated as an indication of health of a herd. Immediately after calving, ratios may be 85-90%, but these ratios decline through the summer and through the first year of life. Typical ratios in early spring before calving are 10-25%. Of course, these declines are due, in part to predation mortality. While caribou calves can usually outrun grizzlies after about a week, they are still susceptible to poor nutrition, unseasonable weather and other predators. In spite of popular opinion, loss of one's mother apparently doesn't significantly reduce survivability in weaned young.[6]

Herds in Alaska go through periodic increases and declines in population size that aren't completely understood. Predator numbers[7,8] and food availability[9] definitely have an impact. We know that their favorite winter foods, lichens, are very slow growing. Since caribou can and do deplete lichens on parts of their range, this depletion may account for the changes in migration routes and summer ranges of some herds in Alaska. In the 1950s the Mulchatna herd, which summers near Lake Iliamna and winters west of Lake Clark in the Mulchatna River drainage, numbered about 15,000. By 1996, the herd had grown to about 250,000 and not surprisingly, parts of the Mulchatna River habitat were showing signs of overgrazing. In 2005 the Alaska Department of Fish and Game estimated the size of this population at about 80,000.

Another example of change in population size and shifts in the pattern of seasonal movement is the Steese-Forty Mile herd, which occupys the Tanana Uplands, north and east of Fairbanks. In the 1940s the population numbered about 50,000, and many animals overwintered in and around the Chatanika River drainage, within easy access of Fairbanks hunters. In 1948 about 5,000, of these caribou emigrated from the Tanana Uplands, crossed the Tanana River flats and joined the Delta herd on the North Slope of the Alaska Range. By the 1970s, the Steese-Forty Mile population was estimated at about 9,000 and, except for a few stragglers, didn't use the summer habitat near the Steese Highway, northeast of Fairbanks. In the early twenty-first century, the Forty Mile herd has increased to 25,000 animals.

And if predators weren't bad enough, caribou have a number of aggravating and debilitating parasites with which to contend. A variety of insects bedevil both caribou and caribou hunters, but the caribou have the worst of it. Both humans and caribou are pestered by blackflies, biting horseflies, and mosquitoes. Blood loss to these insects can be significant. A study of reindeer in Siberia estimated that as many as 6,000-10,000 mosquitoes might bite a reindeer simultaneously[10] and an individual might lose up to 2 kg (4.4 pounds) of blood in a season.

When insect pests are particularly troublesome, caribou often panic and run to find hiding places. Since insects are cold-blooded, caribou will seek out snow patches that are cool enough to slow down the insects and give the caribou a respite. I spent two hot days in mid-August one year looking for bull caribou in the Alaska Range, fighting insects every minute. Finally, I found a band of seven big bulls huddled together on a snow patch, all that was left of the previous winter's snow. The presence of mosquitoes and flies causes caribou to spend less time feeding, more time standing and more energy in general.[11]

Many hunters have skinned caribou and seen on the hide a mottled pattern, almost like a paisley print, on the back. These marks are scars made by the larvae of the warble fly, *Hypoderma tarandi*. Adult female warble flies lay 500-700 eggs on the legs, rump, or back of caribou. When the larvae hatch out, they immediately burrow under the skin and begin to migrate upward, toward the top of the back or rump. Once there, they make a breathing hole through the skin and form a cyst in which they can feed on connective tissue. The larval growth phase lasts almost a year, from summer to the following late spring. At a critical size, about an inch long, the larva digs its way out through the skin and drops off onto the ground. Each larva builds a cocoon in which it pupates, and metamorphoses to its adult body form. On emergence from the pupa case, the adults are reproductively mature. No further growth or feeding is required by the adults; they mate, the female lays her eggs, and the cycle starts over again. We have no way of knowing how irritating these larvae are to the caribou. Each larva is about the size of the end of a human adult's little finger.

A parasite that definitely annoys caribou is the nasal bot fly, *Cephenemyia trompe*. The adult female bot fly lays as many as 100 small larvae on or inside the nostrils of caribou. The larvae crawl deeper into the nasal cavity and occupy the mucous lining of the pharynx and/or larynx. During the winter the larvae feed on the mucus and outer lining of the nasal cavity, growing into large maggots about an inch in length but thinner than warble fly larvae. By late spring to early summer, the caribou sneezes the maggots out, allowing the larvae to pupate on the ground and reach their adult form. If the maggots are sneezed out early in the summer, they may mature to adults in the same summer. If their escape is made later in the summer, the individuals may overwinter as pupae. You can imagine that a bunch of large maggots in the pharynx could restrict breathing, especially during strenuous exercise.

The foods of caribou vary over the course of the year. While they occupy tundra habitat, caribou consume tundra vegetation. The mix of forage species changes over the summer as new plant parts become available. For instance, caribou on the North Slope feed on lupine flowers in June and early July, when lupines are in bloom, and don't eat lupine leaves until mid-August. Dwarf fireweed flowers and leaves are available more

continuously and are eaten by caribou through the months of June, July, and August. Cottongrass flowers are a major food in June; leaf parts in June through August.[12] The leaves of five species of willow and dwarf birch are important summer foods on the North Slope and, presumably, elsewhere in Alaska. So caribou are not confined to grazing but browse as well. In winter, caribou are in the boreal forest; lichens make up a large part of the winter diet.

How sensitive are caribou populations to human disturbance? We need to think about disturbance to both tundra and forest habitats and their effects. First, let us consider the boreal forest and the potential effect of natural and human-induced fires. In the short run, forest fires burn lichens and other forage species and, therefore, the forage available is reduced. Also, fire-felled trees can, at times, form an impassable obstacle to migration. However, as we saw in an earlier chapter, fire releases minerals necessary to stimulate plant productivity and resets the forest succession clock to an earlier stage.

The newest vegetation to grow after a burn may or may not be suitable food for caribou. Typically, the best foods are present in mid- to later stages of forest succession but not in the very oldest, most mature forest. Some longer-term possibilities include (1) replacement of forest with grasslands in repeatedly burned forests; (2) replacement of tree-line forests with tundra; (3) rejuvenation of lichen productivity in old forest; and (4) maintaining a diversity of succession stages and vegetation types in burned patches of different age. The first two possibilities could be detrimental to caribou populations; the latter two would probably be beneficial.[13]

Recall from chapter 3 that air pollution may play an important role in lichen well-being. One metal-smelting facility in central Siberia has, by virtue of its air pollution emissions, eliminated lichens from 300,000 hectares (almost 1200 square miles) of the surrounding countryside and dramatically reduced lichens in an area twice as large.[14]

Caribou populations are also affected by mineral and oil exploration and development. Caribou females with calves tend to avoid pipelines, roads, and other oil field structures.[14] Therefore, part of the traditional habitat is unavailable to them. Maternal caribou during calving appear to be particularly sensitive; their abundance is positively correlated to distance from roads.[15] Over the course of a ten-year study, pregnant female use of calving habitat near roads was consistently low.[16] In other words, they do not habituate to this type of disturbance. Males, however, seem to habituate to these features. As activities relating to pipeline construction and oil field development on the Arctic Coastal Plain continue, these effects may begin to exert a recognizable influence on the populations of the Central Arctic and Porcupine herds.

Pika

If you are walking in the tundra, mid- to late summer, skirting talus slopes, and happen onto a pile of hay, neatly stacked on a rock, you are looking at the winter food supply of a pika (see Figure 7.3). Pikas go by several different common names, including coney, rock rabbit, and haymaker. They come by the latter name honestly because these industrious little fellows spend a lot of time in late summer gathering the

food they will subsist on all winter. The term rock rabbit is, actually, pretty appropriate. The closest relatives to pikas are hares and rabbits. All are members of the mammal order Lagomorpha. Like other lagomorphs, pikas have a second set of incisor teeth behind the first, prominent set. Unlike hares, pikas have shorter, rounded ears and no tail. Pikas have caudal vertebrae, but they are imbedded under the skin.

Pikas share many anatomical, physiological, and behavioral features with their hare cousins. First, they have the same kind of postgastric, cecal digestion that hares have. Hence, pikas have a very enlarged cecum in which bacteria ferment plant material, extract its energy and convert it to volatile fatty acids, bacterial protein, and vitamins. To get full advantage of these nutrients, pikas reingest the cecal pellets, just as snowshoe hares do. In other words, they are **coprophages**.

Second, pikas, like hares, do not hibernate. While arctic ground squirrels and hoary marmots are safely tucked away hibernating for the winter, pikas remain active, feeding on the dried hay they stored the previous summer and fall.

Many experts lump all pikas in North America into a single species, *Ochotona princeps*. However, the form found in Alaska, Yukon Territory, and northern British Columbia has been assigned by some scientists to a separate species, *Ochotona collaris*, the collared pika, because of a light-colored ring of fur around its shoulders. If there are two distinct species, they must have differentiated during a Pleistocene episode in which the northern (Alaskan) population was isolated from the more southerly populations (Rocky Mountains, southern British Columbia). At present, there is still a break in the geographic distribution of North American pikas, a stretch of over 500 miles in central British Columbia.[18]

Pikas in North America are tied to talus slopes and boulder fields, occupying burrows down in among the rocks. Several Asian species of pikas, however, dig burrows in open fields well away from rocks.[19] The burrow and the hay pile that is built near it are the focal points of pika activity. Each individual adult ranges out from the burrow to feed, interact with its nearest pika neighbors and gather hay. Those activities cover about 0.5 acre and constitute the home range of the pika.

Within each home range is a smaller area that is defended from other pikas. The defended area is the territory. Pikas mark their territories by rubbing their cheeks on rocks or other projections along the boundaries. Their cheek glands produce odors that can be smelled by pikas. Pikas have been shown, experimentally, to be able to distinguish between familiar and unfamiliar odors and, possibly, may be able to identify individuals by their cheek-gland odors.[20]

A territory is also maintained through vocalizations. Pikas emit a short call that nearby pikas can recognize as their familiar next-door neighbor. Experiments have shown that pikas react differently to familiar, as opposed to unfamiliar, calls.[21] A pika calls often to let its neighbors know that it is still there, on the territory. One pika observed near Savage River in Mt. McKinley Park called 217 times in 13 hours and, about half the time, was answered by another pika.[22] We know these calls discourage intrusions by nearby pikas. Experimental removal of pikas from their territories results in a definite increase in the rate of intrusions, but if the territorial individual is replaced by a recording of its own call, no increase occurs.[23] These territorial boundaries are somewhat relaxed during breeding season but are vigorously enforced during haying season. If neither scent nor vocalizations discourage an intruder, the resident pika will chase away the intruder. How large is the defended area? One pika in the Savage River area had a home range of 0.25 hectares (0.62 acres) and a territory within it of (0.18 hectares (0.45 acres), 73% of the total home range. Only about half of the acreage within that territory was actually used for harvesting vegetation.

Pikas have an effect on the distribution of vegetation in their habitat. Foraging activity, whether for feeding or haying, is concentrated closest to the burrow and hay pile. This results in an intense cropping of vegetation near the burrow (talus pile) and a gradation of less cropping outward, away from the talus. Experiments have been conducted in which pikas are excluded from areas next to talus piles. Both the amount of vegetation present and the number of plant species present were greater inside the exclosure than outside.[24] In other words, the exclosure resulted in a pattern of vegetation very similar to that found outside the pika's feeding area. The same pattern of vegetational gradients have been found around marmot burrows.[25] Undoubtedly, risk of predation is an important factor in limiting pika foraging excursions into the surrounding habitat. Inexperienced, recently emerged juveniles stay close to the burrow and expand their foraging area only after several weeks. Lactating females range out further than nonlactating individuals, we presume because their higher metabolic demand leads them to take greater risks for greater rewards.[26]

Haying begins in late summer to early fall, July through September in Colorado, mid-July through late August in Alaska.[22] Pikas select a different assortment of plants when haying as opposed to simply grazing. When grazing, grasses dominate the diet. When haying, pikas are primarily selecting forbs (non-woody, non-grass, herbaceous plants).[27] In several hay piles from the Talkeetna Mountains, dwarf fireweed made up most of the material, with horsetails, low-bush cranberry (leaves and berries), crowberry, Labrador tea, willow leaves, ferns, dwarf birch (leaves and twigs), and other herbaceous species. Hay pile composition depends on what is available as well as what is nutritious. Also, pikas tend to harvest the entire plant when haying but not when grazing. Individuals will go farther afield to crop plants for the hay pile than they would go to graze.

Basically, the pika scurries out into its home range, clips vegetation and returns when it has a mouthful. The hay is laid on a rock and successive loads are typically stacked on top of the previous load, although, occasionally, an individual will build two piles. These industrious little creatures can accumulate huge piles, some measuring 19 inches high and 22 inches wide. In areas of high winds, such as the ridge near the Savage River bridge in Denali Park, hay piles are tucked in under overhanging rocks. Otherwise, they may be constructed right out in the open.

Territorial behavior intensifies during the haying season because the haypiles themselves are a valuable resource worth defending. Incidents of pikas stealing hay from their neighbors have been observed. And hay piles made by scientists in unoccupied pika territory are quickly commandeered by nearby pikas.[28] Such thievery is referred to as **kleptoparasitism**.

One interesting component of hay piles is the scats of marmots. In Colorado, pikas are known to gather the scats of yellowbellied marmots and put them in their hay piles. An experiment on captive pikas showed that pikas eat the scats, require less vegetation when they do so, and maintain condition as well as pikas fed just plain hay.[29] In Alaska, we could expect to find scats of hoary marmot in haypiles where marmots and pikas occur together. Weasel scats have also been found in Alaskan hay piles.[30]

Pikas have a lifespan of about three years and reproduce for the first time as yearlings. Breeding season begins in May; gestation takes 30 days. The average litter size is three and a female may be able to produce another litter in the same summer. Newborns reach adult body weight in three months. Females choose mates from the two or three nearest suitors, those occupying adjacent home ranges. Males do not actively assist in rearing the young but are friendly to juveniles after they emerge from the burrow. The male, due to its vigilance, acts as a sentinel and warns of impending danger by voicing alarm calls. In this way, a father indirectly aids in caring for his young.

Populations of pikas are relatively stable, especially in comparison to their lagomorph cousins the snowshoe hares. Young of the year tend to disperse late in the summer due to aggressive interactions with their siblings and also their parents. The probability of these dispersing juveniles surviving the first winter is low. First, all the good territories are already occupied and, second, these juveniles don't have as much time to gather hay for the winter. At low population densities, juvenile males tend to remain in or near the father's territory and juvenile females still tend to disperse.[31]

Predators of pikas include short-tailed weasels (ermine), ravens, coyotes, golden eagles, and other raptorial birds. Wolves probably take an occasional pika although Murie found no pika remains in wolf scats from Mt. McKinley Park. Weasels, with their long, slender, flexible bodies, are well-equipped to hunt pikas. This is the body design to successfully insinuate through the underground passages that must exist in every pika burrow. Several scientists have observed weasels carrying dead pikas. One important determinant in mate selection by female pikas is the type of den available. Dens with multiple entrances are poor choices because weasels are more likely to find an entrance (probably by scent), enter the den and kill the female and/or the young.[32]

When pikas sense weasels in the neighborhood, they remain silent, presumably to avoid attracting the predator's attention. This behavior contrasts with their alarm call response to aerial and larger terrestrial predators. Ravens have been observed to pick off pikas crossing roads.[22] In Colorado, the yellowbellied marmot has been observed to kill (and probably eat) pikas,[33] and so we might expect an occasional occurrence of hoary marmot predation on pikas in Alaska. Grizzlies do not seem to be able to move enough boulders to unearth pikas.

Lemmings

There are three species of lemmings in Alaska: the brown lemming (*Lemmus sibericus*), the collared lemming (*Dicrostonyx groenlandicus*) and the northern bog lemming (*Synaptomys borealis*).

Lemmings are small, vole-like rodents adapted to boreal/arctic conditions. They are separable from voles based on several differences in the structure and arrangement of teeth.

Two of the most interesting aspects of lemming biology are the dramatic population fluctuations and the supposed incidents of lemmings commiting mass suicide by jumping off cliffs and leaping into the ocean. These two features are related to each other and both are the subject of Chitty's book: *Do Lemmings Commit Suicide?*[34] Let's start with population cycles.

Both brown and collared lemmings in many parts of their range exhibit marked fluctuations in population density. For example, around Barrow, brown lemming populations peaked in 1949, 1953, 1956, 1960, 1965, and 1971, suggesting a 5-6 year cycle. Elsewhere in Alaska, brown lemming populations cycle in inland coastal tundra and foothills tundra. The collared lemming may cycle at some locations in coastal and foothills tundra but not as dramatically as the brown lemming. Though they are not present on the coastal plain near Barrow, both the singing and tundra voles occur in the foothills of the Brooks Range and, in some locations, also exhibit population cycles.

Back to brown lemmings: populations along the North Slope do not necessarily cycle in synchrony. Where lemmings are found with tundra-dwelling voles, the cycles of the different species, if there are cycles, are not synchronized with each other.

Among the extrinsic factors influencing or driving population density cycles in lemmings are air and surface temperatures, precipitation, snowpack, vegetation quantity and quality, and predation rates. Recall (Chapter 7) that cotton-grass and *Carex* apparently respond to grazing by producing allelochemicals that interfere with lemming metabolism, growth and survival. These two species are major items in the diet of brown lemmings. Hence, brown lemming cycles might be controlled by their forage species. Intrinsic factors include reproductive rates, survival rates, population size, dispersal rates, and nutritional state.

In addition to interannual variation, lemming populations vary significantly through a single year. Collared lemmings can breed in both winter and summer. Population density is probably highest during the late winter/early spring while snow cover is still providing protection from above-ground predators. Once the snow is gone, predators depress lemming populations. But predation may not be the most important regulator. In one study of collared lemming populations, the two most important determinants of population growth were autumn temperatures and insulative value of winter snow.[35]

The second aspect of lemming biology mentioned above was whether they commit suicide. Of course, the question stems from some exaggerated, secondhand observations reported in books and magazines and also from the Walt Disney movie *White Wilderness*. In that film lemmings are seen rushing down a steep incline to the sea, seemingly plunging into the water in a self-destructive frenzy. Let's deal with the film first. There are several problems with the film which allegedly describes lemming biology along the coast near Barrow. First, the more common species occupying the coastal plain in Alaska is the brown lemming; the species in the film, is the collared lemming. Second, the population of lemmings was very high, owing to the

fact that local children were paid to collect live lemmings for the footage. Third, the plunge to their doom was actually filmed in the Disney Studios in California. Fourth, brown lemmings, common at Barrow, haven't been observed to commit mass suicide.

What, then, is the basis for observations of lots of lemmings moving over the surface of the earth? As described above, lemmings exhibit population cycles or fluctuations. At very high population densities lemmings experience food shortages because they and their fellows have eaten most of the available food. They also experience far more lemming-lemming behavioral interactions than they do during population lows. Third, even at moderate population levels lemming juveniles tend to disperse away from their natal territories. Further, disappearance of snow in early summer coupled with lack of vegetation cover exposes lemmings to view. The natural tendency to disperse away from natal territories is exaggerated during food shortages and high levels of behavioral interactions.

Rather than viewing these dispersal movements as the result of lemming insanity, it seems more likely that the movements are adaptive in that they give the individual some chance of finding a location with more space and more food. But, you might argue, lemmings have been observed out on ice flows, far from land. Certainly, dispersal movements that landed those particular lemmings on sea ice were not beneficial to those particular lemmings. But there are no guarantees in life. Any adaptive behavior is, occasionally, thwarted by circumstances.

There is still the question of seasonal or periodic mass migrations. Let's assume for a moment that lemming population cycles are out of synchrony in relatively close locations, say 50 km (31 miles) apart. One year there is a population high here and, next year, there is a high 50 km away. You could jump to the incorrect conclusion that the lemmings walked from here to there even if you didn't actually see them walk there. It is more likely that North American lemming species disperse only short distances (< 1km).

In summary, lemming populations fluctuate everywhere they are found. In some locations lemmings exhibit a regular cycle of abundance. Lemming abundance is of critical importance to predatory birds and mammals in the Far North.

Northern collared lemming—Of all rodents, the collared lemming is probably the best adapted to the rigors of the Arctic. It is the only rodent that molts to a white winter coat. It is distributed to the farthest north extent of land in North America, farther north than brown lemmings, tundra voles, singing voles or arctic ground squirrels. The soles of the feet are furred to reduce heat loss; the ears are short and completely hidden by the body fur. It has specialized double claws that develop on the third and fourth front digits in winter to aid it in digging through crusted snow. On these digits the normal claw is augmented by the development of hard, enlarged pads of the toes that grow and attach to the claw. As winter progresses and collared lemmings employ these claws, the hardened pad sometimes separates from the normal claw giving the appearance of a forked claw.

Unlike brown lemmings, collared lemmings tunnel their way to the surface of the snow in winter and move about. As an individual digs upward, the newly excavated snow falls down and fills the tunnel behind it. Thus, as the lemming emerges, only a slight depression is left at the surface. After its above-snow excursion, it digs downward through the snow layer, leaving some at the surface and compacting snow sideways further down in the tunnel. The result is an obvious, intact tunnel. This structural, visual difference between upward- and downward-directed tunneling has given rise to the legend that white collared lemmings fall out of the sky with the new snow. The depression (remnant of the upward-directed tunnel) is where the lemming landed and the only visible (downward-directed) tunnel is where it found its home.

Northern collared lemmings occur across Eurasia, Greenland, the high Canadian Arctic, and in tundra habitats of northern and western Alaska. There are populations on several Aleutian Islands, St. Lawrence Island and the Alaska Peninsula. Two other collared lemming species are recognized in North America based on differences in coat color, complexity of the molars, and chromosomal differences. Richardson's collared lemming is found on the western shore of Hudson Bay, including parts of northeastern Manitoba and Northwest Territories. Richardson's and northern collared lemmings occur together along the northern edge of Richardson's distribution. In the area of overlap there is no sign of hybrid forms and, indeed, laboratory crosses resulted in sterile hybrids. [36]

The third species is the Ungava collared lemming, sometimes called the Hudson Bay collared lemming. This species is found east of Hudson Bay on the Ungava Peninsula of Quebec and Labrador. It is geographically separated from the other two collared lemming species. There is one more *Dicrostonyx*, *D. torquatus*, occurring across the Russian Far North. Some scientists think that this Asian species is the same as the North American northern collared lemming, *D. groenlandicus*.

Studies of mitochondrial DNA in different populations of northern collared lemming support the idea that, during the Pleistocene, populations survived glacial episodes in the Canadian Arctic as well as eastern Beringia (northern Alaska).[37] Indeed, the other North American *Dicrostonyx* undoubtedly derive from *D. groenlandicus* that were isolated during a glacial maximum, survived and, in the process, underwent evolutionary change and differentiation.

Collared lemmings respond to changing photoperiod as do other small mammals. However, unlike other microtine rodents, these lemmings increase their body mass and maintain their reproductive organs in a fully active state in winter.[38] Their winter weight gain is not simply the result of loading on fat. They increase muscle and bone, too. Another response to short day length, either natural or experimentally produced, is molting to the dense, white winter pelt. The combination of better insulation and larger size (lower surface to mass ratio) probably accounts for the lower resting metabolic rates of lemmings exposed to short day lengths as opposed to long day lengths.

Brown lemming—The brown lemming, *Lemmus sibericus*, occurs across the Canadian Arctic, much of British Columbia, Yukon, Alaska, and across Eurasia to western Russia. The lemming of the Scandanavian Peninsula is the Norway lemming, *Lemmus lemmus*. Some scientists call the North American brown lemming *Lemmus trimucronatus*; that is, they consider it distinct from the Eurasian brown lemming. Along the southern parts of their ranges, both the brown and collared lemmings occur in alpine tundra. They are primarily inhabitants of arctic tundra. In contrast to collared lemmings, brown lemmings occupy more moist tundra habitats such as wet lowlands and polygonal ground.

In the summer, foods of brown lemmings consist of almost equal measures of mosses, sedges and grasses with minor amounts of dicot flowers (saxifrage, whitlow grass, starwort, and lichens).[39] In winter, brown lemmings remain under the snow, dwelling just at ground level. Winter feeding is confined to grazing the live material in this area, including moss shoots and the basal leaf sheaths of grasses and sedges.

Nests are constructed both summer and winter. In summer, lemmings burrow through the moss layer and establish nests within the burrow system by adding dried plants. In winter nests consist of shredded vegetation shaped into a hollow ball up to 25 cm (10 inches) in diameter. Winter nests are placed at ground level, that is, at the base of the snow.

The reproductive potential of brown lemmings is prodigious. Females can breed right after having a litter. Since gestation is three weeks, new litters can appear every three weeks. Young, about eight per litter in summer, are sexually mature by 5-6 weeks of age. In favorable winters brown lemmings breed; in early and late winter 4-5 young are produced and average litters of three offspring are born in midwinter.

Northern bog lemming—Adult bog lemmings, *Synaptomys borealis*, weigh 27-35 g and have a total length of 110-140 mm. The fur is coarse, gray to brown on the back and pale gray on the belly. The tail is brown on top and whitish on the underside.

The geographic range of the northern bog lemming extends from Labrador and New Brunswick, across boreal Canada, over most of Northwest Territories and Alaska south of the Brooks Range. During the Pleistocene glacial advances, northern bog lemmings were found as far south as Tennessee and Kansas. At the end of the last glacial maximum this species retreated northward as the glaciers receded or simply died out in the south.

The habitat types occupied by this species are extremely varied. Important habitat features include high moisture levels and the presence of grasses and sedges to provide food and cover. Clearly, the word "bog" defines the species far better than the word "tundra," although bog lemmings are found in alpine tundra habitats. These adaptable rodents occur in interior Alaska in wet meadows, sphagnum bogs, sub-alpine meadows, riparian (streamside) zones in spruce forests, and in grasslands associated with recent burns.

Like other lemmings, northern bog lemmings are active all winter. They make nests of grasses, mosses and sedges under the snow, at ground level. In some cases, vegetation is stored inside burrow entrances, presumably, for use during the winter. In the snow-free months, underground burrows are excavated.

Breeding season extends from May to August; females bear 4-5 young per litter. Under favorable conditions, up to three litters are possible. In spite of this high reproductive potential, northern bog lemmings appear to be infrequent and unpredictable in occurrence over most of their range.

Singing vole

The singing vole, *Microtus miurus*, is restricted to Alaska, and parts of the Yukon Territory, Northwest Territory, and northern British Columbia. Primarily a tundra species, the singing vole also occupies sub-alpine habitats. Its closest living relative is the insular vole, found only on two islands in the Bering Sea.

Singing voles and pikas share the habit of gathering vegetation in late summer and making hay piles. This habit has given rise to the other common name for this species: Alaska hay mouse. Piles vary in size from 1-30 liters. There is controversy about whether each hay pile is built by a single vole or if cooperative hay-piling occurs. The pile is positioned where drainage is good, either well-drained slopes or off the ground in the base of a shrub. This pile is a major part of the vole's winter food supply.

Plant species found in hay piles include willow shoots, *Equisetum*, fireweed, willowherb, Jacob's ladder, lupine, aster, Eskimo potato and mountain avens. Other species in the diets of singing voles include bearberry, bistort and coltsfoot. These forage species tend to be the most abundant plants in the drier habitats favored by singing voles.

Populations of both singing and tundra voles fluctuate strongly. Abundance of the singing vole on the North Slope (Toolik Lake) vary from 5-50 per hectare (2-20 per acre) over a four year cycle. The cycles of both voles are synchronized at Toolik Lake. Since the two don't compete for food, their cycles are probably governed by other environmental factors. At low population densities, singing voles are negatively affected by the experimental removal of tundra voles. This effect may be the result of increased predation on singing voles when tundra voles aren't available.[40]

The common name of the singing vole derives from the fact that these rodents make a metallic, churring sound. These sounds are made most frequently in the late summer while the vole sits in the open. Why do these voles sing? One idea is that, since late summer is when the hay piles are constructed, the vole is singing to defend its hay pile and territory. The other idea is that these voles sing to warn other voles of the presence of predators. Predators of singing voles include grizzlies, wolves, wolverines, weasels, foxes, and jaegers.

Tundra vole

The tundra vole, *Microtus oeconomus*, has much the same geographic distribution as the northern red-backed vole, occurring in both the new and old worlds. However, in northwestern Canada it is much more restricted in its distribution than the red-backed vole. And, unlike the red-backed vole, the tundra vole occurs on the North Slope of Alaska, north of the Brooks Range. This species occurs in moist meadows, along streams and around lakes and marshes in arctic tundra but also is found in meadows of the boreal forest and several islands in the Gulf of Alaska.

Tundra voles occur in some of the same areas as collared lemmings but prefer somewhat different habitats. In summer, tundra voles prefer wet sedge meadows, where they are protected by vegetation. Collared lemmings preferentially occupy drier upland tundra, where vegetation is much sparser. Study of their diets in Northwest

Territories showed that the voles preferred primarily sedges, including cotton-grass while lemmings utilized mainly mountain avens, *Dryas*.[41] On the coastal plain of Alaska, *Dryas* is rare and collared lemmings don't have access to it. Willows, in part, replace *Dryas* in collared lemming diets on the North Slope. In the field, tundra vole abundance is so highly correlated with the presence of cotton-grass that it can be viewed as an indicator of tundra vole habitat.[40] Because of its penchant to cache rhizomes of grasses and sedges for use during the winter, the tundra vole is sometimes called the root vole. Root vole is the name used across Eurasia.

Tundra voles are important prey for aerial predators including snowy owl, short-eared owl, rough-legged hawk, peregrine falcon, gyrfalcon, jaegers, gulls and shrikes. Mammalian predators include weasels, arctic fox and wolverine. A study of arctic foxes on the Yukon-Kuskokwim Delta, western Alaska, found that tundra voles accounted for 95% of the diet in winter and spring[42] and the tundra vole is the primary prey of arctic foxes on St. Lawrence Island.[43]

Social organization during the summer breeding season involves mature females establishing territories. Each adult male occupies a home range that overlaps with several female territories. The size of the male's domain is positively correlated with his body size. Larger males have access to more females than do smaller males. In Northwest Territories and presumably Alaska male home ranges don't overlap and a mature male has breeding access to all the females within his home range.[44]

Neither tundra voles nor singing voles typically reproduce during winter. In tundra voles, breeding season lasts from May to September.

Two to three litters are born, each having 4-8 young. Gestation is 20-21 days. The singing vole has a similar breeding season and gestation period and has litters of 4-12 young.

Wolverine

The wolverine is a weasel on steroids. Or, for those cabin owners who have run afoul of the wolverine, it is the mustelid from hell! Wolverines are the largest terrestrial members of the weasel family; adult male wolverines weigh 9-20 kg (20-45 lb); females weigh 7-14 kg (14-30 lb). Wolverines occupy forested areas of Alaska as well as tundra.

My only encounter with a wolverine occurred at Izembek Lagoon on the Bering Sea coast. My vehicle broke down one evening and I had to walk back to Cold Bay by the light of a waning moon. Along the way a wolverine came out onto the road and walked beside me for about 30 minutes. It never made a sound and, except for my feet, I didn't either. Considering the wolverine's reputation, I was happy for a quiet and uneventful encounter.

Wolverines are generally thought of as scavengers. They certainly are not as agile or as swift as canid and felid predators but they do function as predators. Their locomotion, like that of the marten, is **plantigrade** (flatfooted), slow in comparison to wolves and lynx. Their skulls and teeth are better adapted for gnawing and breaking bones than those of wolves. They are, essentially, the nearest thing in North America to the hyena.

In northwest Alaska, summer foods consist of ground squirrels, caribou, ptarmigan, marmot and other small mammals. Ground squirrels are most of the prey in August, a time when juvenile squirrels are dispersing, digging their own burrows and, consequently, particularly vulnerable. Wolverines in both northwest and south-central Alaska prey on ground squirrels through the winter. Since ground squirrels hibernate from September through at least early March, wolverines must be either excavating them or caching them in the early fall for later use. One instance of an apparent excavation of a hibernating ground squirrel has been reported.[45] Ground squirrels become more accessible in mid-March, when the males emerge from hibernation, establish and defend territories. During territorial disputes, males are particularly vulnerable to predation.

Moose, when they occur in the diet, are carrion from winter starvation mortality or the kills of other predators. However, there have been observations of wolverines pulling down and killing caribou calves that are crippled and killing a yearling caribou. Other food items include snowshoe hare, porcupine, beaver, muskrat, red fox, berries, and insects.

How much area does a wolverine cover? In the upper Susitna River basin (south-central Alaska), a radio-collared male monitored for an entire year had a home range of 637 km^2 (246 miles^2) for the year, comparable to estimates from Montana. Summer home ranges of four individuals ranged from 92 to 451 km^2 (average: 385 km^2 or 148 miles^2); five winter home ranges were 69-515 km^2 (average 353 km^2 or 136 miles^2).[46] Food availability affects the size of the home range in wolverines. In comparison to south-central Alaska, home ranges are larger in northwest Alaska, where there is no predictable supply of large mammals.

There is some overlap in the home ranges of wolverines in Alaska and elsewhere. Chance meetings of two individuals within one's home range are likely to be distinctly unfriendly. Remains of a wolverine have been found in another wolverine's cache. In northwestern Alaska, adult females appear to maintain home ranges exclusive of other females except for their own offspring. Thus, relatedness may play a significant role in tolerance of other wolverines within a home range.

We just don't know enough about wolverines to be sure they establish and defend territories, but they do scent mark the areas they frequent. Scent-marking is accomplished by urinating on prominent objects in the landscape. In addition, wolverines have both ventral glands and anal sacs that play a role in scent-marking. When marking with these glands, a wolverine will straddle a tussock and rock side-to-side or, at times, back and forth, rubbing its ventral surface on the projection. They also exhibit a dragging behavior in which a wolverine briefly drags its ventral surface across the substrate after urination.[45] This behavior may be a variant of scent marking with these glands.

Dall sheep

A friend, John, and I had hiked 40 miles across ridge tops and tussock bogs to reach our sheep-hunting destination, Mt. Prindle. Mt. Prindle is north of Fairbanks in the Tanana Uplands, has rough, jagged escape terrain, and has Dall sheep. At least, we thought it had sheep. Finally, we were lying on a ridge immediately to the south of the mountain. To our surprise, we saw not a single sheep on Prindle. Instead, there were fif-teen white dots on some low-relief solifluction ridges about five miles north of Prindle. They were far from escape terrain and, for a while, we couldn't figure out why they were out there. Then, a helicopter flew low over our ridge and landed on the west flank of the mountain. There it disgorged several people who, as it turned out, were in the mineral exploration industry. They had set up a small drill rig, looking for ores. The operation of that equipment had scared off the sheep. They were on their way to the next nearest jagged country, about ten miles further north. This anecdote points out several things about Dall sheep. First, Dall sheep can be upset by human activity. Second, sheep normally are never very far from habitat that they, and almost nothing else, can climb. Oh well, we had a nice, long walk.

What would possess a human to walk 50 miles, including the shortcut back to the Steese Highway, to try to bag a Dall sheep? I won't even attempt to explain the mentality of sheep hunters, but their quest has to do with an intense interest in the biological structures on the heads of rams: the horns.

First, they are true horns. I know it is quite common for hunters and non-hunters alike to refer to the head bones of moose and caribou as horns. Those head bones are not horns; they are antlers. Horns are permanent structures that grow through the lifetime of the sheep. That is, unlike the antlers of deer, caribou, elk and moose, they are not shed annually. Horns are composed of two parts, an inner **horn core** and an outer **horn sheath** (Figure 8.2). The horn core is made of bone and is a permanent part of the skull. The horn sheath surrounds the horn core and is composed of **keratin**, a

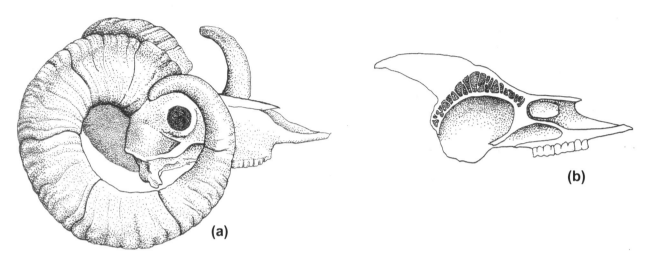

Figure 8.2: Dall sheep skull: a) Horn sheath showing growth rings (shallow grooves) and annual rings (deeper grooves). This ram was eight years old when it died. The first year's growth on the horn amounts to the very tip of the horn, barely visible. b) Sagittal section through a Dall sheep skull showing the air-filled spaces surrounded by bony struts that help absorb the shock of head-butting impacts. The bony horn core is also evident.

protein. Keratin is the same material that makes up mammalian hair, hooves, fingernails and claws. As the sheep grows, it adds material to both the horn core and sheath.

How much material is added depends on forage quality and quantity and the sex of the sheep. First, rams are programmed to add a lot more horn growth each year than ewes. Second, rams on high-quality forage grow larger horns than rams on poor forage. Third, seasonal fluctuations in food availability translate to significant horn growth in spring, summer, and fall and no growth in winter. Small, discrete growth increments are added all summer, leaving a series of shallow grooves around the horn. The end of each year's growth is marked by a deep groove, the annual ring, or **annulus** (Figure 8.2). The age of a Dall sheep can be estimated by counting the annual rings. Since ram horns are large, their annual rings are pretty obvious, and can be counted with confidence. The age of a ram can be determined easily unless he has broken

or **broomed** (worn off) horn tips. The ages of ewes can also be estimated, but the ages of old ewes are consistently underestimated when horn annuli are counted due to very slow growth of mature ewe horns.[47]

One aspect of the biology of sheep horns that should be considered is how much these structures contribute to heat loss. The horn core is live, vascularized bone. Warm blood flows over the horn cores and, at low air temperatures, heat from that blood is conducted through the horn sheaths. How warm are Dall sheep horns, and how much heat is lost? We don't know, but similar questions have been asked of Barbary sheep. Horn temperatures of a male and a female Barbary sheep held outdoors were measured. Both individuals maintained horn base temperatures around 3°C (37°F) down to air temperatures of -19°C (-2°F). At an air temperature of -10°C (14°F), the male exhibited a horn to air difference of 17C° (31F°) the female's gradient was 21C° (38F°). The heat loss associated with these warm horns amounts to 20% and 29%, respectively, of the female's and male's resting metabolic rates.[48] Males lose proportionally more heat because their horns are so much bigger than those of the females.

How would Dall sheep compare? The male Barbary sheep was a little larger than the largest Dall ram, about 116 kg versus 110 kg (255 vs. 242 pounds). The horn surface of the Barbary ram was estimated at 2971 cm[2]. Using the same estimation technique on a 38-inch (97 cm) curl Dall ram horn out in my garage resulted in a horn surface of 3392 cm[2]. The horn core in a Dall sheep is smaller than in a Barbary sheep but the vascularized surfaces of the horn cores are probably similar. Therefore, the horns of the Dall sheep probably lose as much heat as those of the Barbary sheep at similar air temperatures. However, air temperatures in Alaska fall far below the -10°C used in the Barbary sheep, study, and the metabolic cost of horn heat loss may be considerably higher.

Dall's sheep or Dall sheep, *Ovis dalli*, is one of two wild sheep species in North America. The other species is the bighorn sheep, *Ovis canadensis*. Populations of bighorn sheep are scattered through alpine habitats in the Rocky, Sierra Nevada and Cascade mountain ranges and isolated desert mountains across the western states. Two subspecies of bighorns are recognized, the Rocky Mountain bighorn and the desert bighorn, but that is another story.

Since there are only two wild sheep on this continent, one would assume that they are closely related. Based on chromosomal studies, they are, indeed, closely related. Wild sheep probably populated North America during a full glacial episode. During one of the glacial

maxima, a population of this species was isolated in the Far North, giving rise to our present-day Dall sheep. We don't know which North American sheep actually evolved first, but the Dall sheep may be the older of the two North American species. At one time, Dall sheep were probably distributed across Beringia into alpine habitats on the Kamchatka Peninsula. Isolation in one or another interglacial period sent the Kamchatka population on to its different evolutionary end point, the Siberian snow sheep, *Ovis nivicola*.

Let's return to horn thickness and length. Measurement of the circumference at the base of the horn of the largest bighorn and Dall rams yields 47 cm and 38 cm (18 and 15 inches), respectively. Length, measured around the outside of the curl, gives large Dall rams a slight edge (124-130 cm; 48-51 inches) over bighorns (124 cm; 48 inches).[49] Though bighorns have more massive horns, Dall horns, at their best, have a much wider lateral spread or flare. Maximum lateral flare is 88 cm in Dall rams, 66 cm in bighorns (34 and 26 inches, respectively). The Siberian snow sheep has thin horns that are smaller than those of Dall rams (36 cm [14 inch] bases, 111 cm [43 inch] length of curl, about 88 cm [34 inch] lateral spread from tip to tip). In Dall sheep, half, three-quarters, and full curls take about 2-3, 4-5, and 7-8 years, respectively, but horn growth differs among populations.

I've mentioned only two wild sheep in North America, but almost every hunter and many people who have driven the Alcan Highway have heard of the Stone sheep of British Columbia and southern Yukon. This sheep is a subspecies or color phase of Dall sheep. Stone sheep are silver to dark gray with black tail and white legs, muzzle, and rump patch. The other Dall sheep are entirely off-white with very few exceptions. The exceptions are color intergradations between the Dall and the Stone morphs. Intergrades are white with black tails and gray saddles across their backs. These individuals are often referred to as Fannin morphs or Fannin sheep. They occur occasionally in areas close to Stone sheep range and, more infrequently, in the Nebesna Range and the Tanana Uplands.[50]

As a child I spent a lot of time thinking about animals and asked my parents questions, often in the form of "Which one would win, a lion or a tiger?" Applying this approach might lead one to ask, "Which one would win, a Dall sheep or a bighorn?" Of course, body and horn size would strongly favor the bighorn. But if we standardized body size, which one would win? This is a silly notion, similar to the idea put forth in *Star Trek-Deep Space Nine* that a Farengi male would compete with a male "humaan" for a Beta Zoid woman.

Comparing skulls suggests that bighorns are even better adapted to surviving terrific impact than are Dall rams. Two adaptations are seen in most, if not all, head-banging mammals. First, the top of the skull, around the horns or antlers has air spaces surrounded by thick, bony struts. Wild sheep, bison and elephants all have these **pneumations**. Second, the **sutures** holding the skull bones together are highly convoluted in head-bangers, far more so than in species such as humans that try to intimidate and compete for dominance with facial expressions and hand gestures rather than head butts.

Experiments in which heavy weights were bashed into (nonliving) sheep skulls showed that, when struck in the front, the front of the skull stretches and the rear compresses. The sutures allow movement of the skull bones, giving the skull flexibility that helps dampen the impact of the weight or the head butt. But what about Dall versus bighorn? Simply put, bighorns have larger and more pneumations and more highly convoluted sutures than Dall rams.

Studies on bighorns indicate they can withstand an impact 60 times greater than that required to fracture a human skull. I got butted in the shoulder by a four-year-old captive Dall ram while I was trying to wrestle him down for an antibiotic injection. The impact knocked me backward hard enough to cause me to somersault and land face down in the sheep droppings! My advice is to leave the butting to professionals...the sheep.

I mentioned intimidation and dominance above. Clearly, the function of large horns in rams is to achieve dominance within the ram's immediate population. With dominance comes almost exclusive access to sexually receptive females. On good range, rams reach sexual maturity by about 18 months of age, females by 30 months. However, males must bide their time, grow, sharpen their competitive skills, and perhaps achieve dominance by their fifth to seventh (stone sheep) or seventh to ninth (Dall sheep) year.[49]

Dominance-hierarchy interactions do not always involve head butting. Rams perform lateral displays called **low stretches** that allow competing males to evaluate both horn and body size. **Frontal displays** with head and horns held at an angle to the body axis, accomplish the same thing. Only evenly matched rams end up actually fighting.

Actual dominance battles involve jump-kicks, butts and pushes to the side of the opponent as well as head butting (Figure 8.3). These contests typically are won by older, larger, more experienced rams. But injuries and senescence take their toll and, eventually, younger rams come to the fore.

Population dynamics includes the age structure of a population and how it might change through time. The Dall sheep population in the Sheep Mountain area of Kluane National Park in the Yukon is an unexploited population, which means it is not hunted, and other forms of disturbance such as mineral exploration and flightseeing are kept to a minimum. Over a 12-year study, the population averaged 226 sheep: 14% were lambs, 11% were yearlings, 5% were 2-year-old females, 5% were 2-year-old males, 36% were females 3 or more years old, and 30% were males 3 or more years old. Maximum longevity in that population was 12-13 years: each age class from 3 to 13 years had, on average, six rams and seven ewes. Similar to the human population of the preindustrial world, this sheep population is heavily weighted with young animals. There are very few very old sheep. Mortality rates of rams in years 3 - 7 were below 10% per year. Mortalities in years 8, 9, 10, 11, 12 and 13 were 14%, 23%, 34%, 70% and 100%, respectively.[51]

These population sizes, age structures and mortalities change over time. Productivity of ewes and lamb survival through the first year both vary. Although the average lamb contribution to the Sheep Mountain population was 14%, lambs made up 20% of the population in 1978 and only 4% in 1975. What are the causes of these fluctuations? First, the forage available on winter range probably sets the upper limit on sheep populations. Forage quality translates to nutritional input to pregnant ewes. The better the forage, the higher the lambing rate the following spring. Survival of lambs through the first winter also depends on forage quality. Negative impacts on winter range include lack of rainfall, burial of plants under deep snow, and lack of wind to expose vegetation. These same features must affect old rams and their ability to sustain themselves after years of battling the elements and, perhaps, suffering injuries in premating skirmishes with other rams. Adult ewes

Figure 8.3: Dall sheep rams butting heads. The impact generates a force dozens of times greater than required to fracture a human skull.

lose about 18% of their body mass over winter and rams may lose even more.[52] In other words, a bad winter with severe cold could tip these old boys over.

I mentioned disturbance by aircraft. Helicopters frighten animals worse than fixed-wing aircraft[53] but neither do the sheep any good. Sheep run away, burning up valuable energy reserves, and possibly incurring injuries. The social fabric of the band may be disrupted; group size could be reduced, and lambs could be separated from their mothers.

Predation is a significant cause of mortality in Dall sheep in spite of their tendency to always have escape terrain near at hand. Predators of sheep include coyotes, wolves, grizzly bears, lynx , golden eagles, and red fox. A friend reported an incident in which a single lynx chased an adult ram down an icy creek bottom, leaped on its back, and killed it with a bite to the neck.[54]

Wolves prey on both young and adult sheep. In three of seven wolf-sheep interactions documented at Kluane Lake, the wolf was successful. Two of the three incidents involved sheep getting too far away from escape terrain combined with inadequate vigilance. In one case, a ewe lost her 1-day-old lamb to a wolf that somehow managed to climb up into very rugged escape terrain.[55]

Of course, escape terrain isn't a meaningful concept with aerial predators such as golden eagles. Eagles swoop down toward lambs or perch above a lamb and wait for an opening. Ewes typically stand over their lambs when aerial predators are in view. In spite of this behavior, once in a while the eagle scores.

Mortality due to predation, then, is an ever-present feature of sheep population dynamics.

Predation pressure on Dall sheep is variable and depends, in part, on the availability of alternate prey for predators. There was a high frequency of wolves on Sheep Mountain, Yukon, in 1982. That year produced a very severe winter, leaving sheep in poor condition. Also, snowshoe hare, ptarmigan, and arctic ground squirrel populations were all very low. Wolves were switching to Dall sheep.[55]

A serious predator of adult rams is the sheep hunter. Cropping of old, mature rams obviously affects the age structure by removing many of these old boys. Are there other consequences? Since most or all the breeding is done by a dominant, large male, one could argue that the largest ram left in a hunted population will effectively maintain lamb productivity. We know that sub-legal, three-quarter to seven-eighth curl rams are sexually mature; these animals constitute a pool of candidates for title to "dominant ram" status.

Muskox

The muskox is a woolly, short, and stocky hoofed animal of the tundra. Adult males stand 1.2-1.5 m (3.9-4.9 feet) at the shoulder and reach overall lengths of 2.44 m (females) to 2.65 m (males) [7.9 and 8 feet, respectively]. Really large bulls weigh 410 kg; females reach weights of 190 kg (900 and 420 pounds, respectively). Although it looks like some sort of wild cow, it is actually more closely related to sheep and goats. The genus name, *Ovibos*, is a combination of *Ovis*, the genus for sheep, and *Bos*, the genus for cows.

Perhaps the most obvious feature of muskoxen is the pelage. The outer hair is very long and very coarse. In winter the underfur is thick and very fine, providing an excellent insulative layer. The wool of the underfur is called qiviut. It is collected from domestic herds in Alaska and from the natural range of wild herds. The wool is spun into yarn and used for knitting scarves and hats. The overall color on the animal is dark brown with off-white on the forehead, lower legs, and saddle (middle of back, behind the hump).

In the early 20th century, the muskox, *Ovibos moschatus*, was well on its way to extinction. The species had been completely extirpated from Europe and Asia perhaps 2000 years ago and Alaska's population was wiped out by overhunting in the mid-1800s. Remnant populations survived in east Greenland and in the Canadian High Arctic but well into the 20th century these stocks were being hunted hard. Alaska's current stocks date from a transplant of 34 animals captured in Greenland and brought to Fairbanks in 1930. These animals were released on Nunivak Island in 1935 and 1936. Extant popula-

tions on Nelson Island, Seward Peninsula, Cape Thompson, and the Arctic National Wildlife Refuge were all derived by further transplants from the Nunivak Island herd. Some of these animals were also transplanted to Wrangel Island and the Taimyr Peninsula in Russia.

The muskox is another head-banger. Both sexes have horns but those of the bulls are much larger (Figure 8.4). As bulls grow, the individual horn sheaths, or bosses, enlarge and nearly touch in the middle of the head. Beneath the 10 cm (4 inch) thick bosses is 9 cm (3 inches) of skull bone filled with pneumations. When two big bulls ram each other, the impact is equivalent to driving your car into a concrete wall at 27 km per hour (17 mph). Bulls during the rut back off as much as 40-45 m (50 yards), charge at top speed, and meet head-on. After the impact, each bull backs away shaking its head side to side. Then the process repeats (up to 20 impacts) until one bull has had enough and runs away. Muskox calves, especially males,

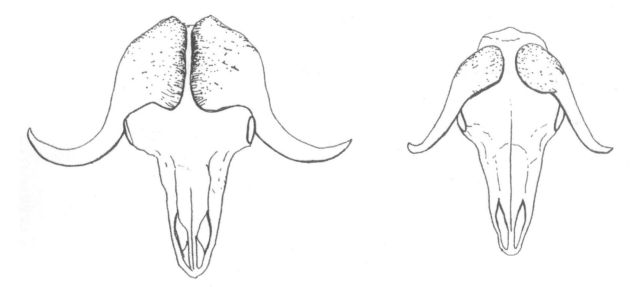

Figure 8.4: A comparison of mature male (left) and female (right) muskox skulls. These individuals were about five years old. Males are involved in far more head-butting than females. The bosses on the male are larger and have almost grown together.

begin butting early in life. Bob White, a muskox research scientist, once got down on his hands and knees to inspect a week-old male calf. Bob's head proved to be irresistible; the calf butted him and completely bowled him over.

Head butting is just one of the uses for horns in muskoxen. In the winter, mixed-sex herds of 75 or more individuals occupy a relatively compact range. To protect calves and, indeed, all members of the group, muskoxen respond to predators by forming a defensive line facing a single predator or a ring or circle to confront multiple predators. If the predator is persistent, single adults, usually bulls, will occasionally charge out of the ring, trying to hook the predator with a horn and then return to their original position. The principal predators of muskoxen, aside from humans, are wolves and grizzlies. A pair of adult grizzlies was observed killing five muskox calves out of a single herd in Northwest Territories.[56]

The defensive response is also elicited by helicopter overflights.[57] First, muskoxen run or gallop towards each other, form the defensive circle and then hold their position for, on average, 5 minutes after the helicopter passes overhead. The implication is that lots of helicopter overflights, such as could occur in mineral or petroleum exploration and development, would cause muskoxen to spend more energy running and less time feeding.

As with other tundra mammals, muskoxen vary their foods seasonally. In Canada, in spring, while animals were still on their winter range, muskoxen fed on the windward slopes and hills with a snow depth of only 6-10 cm (2-3 inches). Snow is cleared away with the front hooves. The preferred forage species are Labrador tea, crowberry, lowbush cranberry, bog blueberry and shrub birch. Small amounts of lichens and mosses are eaten incidental to feeding on other species.[58]

On the North Slope, preferred items in late spring include mountain avens (*Dryas integrifolia*), cotton-grass flower heads and new leaves of diamondleaf willow. In early summer the top three choices are a yellow oxytrope, wooly lousewort, and alpine milkvetch. All three of these have peak nitrogen contents in summer. By late summer, the preferred items are the leaves and flowers of wild sweet pea, yellow paintbrush, and feltleaf willow.[59] Access to food in winter can be critical to muskoxen. Conditions such as deep, crusted snow or surface ice from freezing rain prevent these animals from getting sufficient forage and can reduce calving rates or kill animals due to starvation. It appears that there is little diet overlap with caribou and, therefore, little competition for food, even though in some areas they select the same sorts of conditions for cratering and feeding. Reindeer and muskoxen on Seward Peninsula pick the same areas of windblown or soft snow cover for feeding in winter. Reindeer take mostly lichens; muskoxen concentrate mainly on sedges.[60]

Reproductive season begins in late summer with dominant bulls taking control of harems of multiple females. Actual mating occurs from August through October. Gestation takes 34 weeks; calves weighing 10-14 kg (22-31 lb) are born in late April and May. Females first reproduce as two-year olds.

Modern muskoxen evolved in Asia and dispersed to Europe, reaching the British Isles 500,000 years ago and surviving there, off and on, until 18,000 years ago. Their first appearance in North America dates to 150,000-250,000 years ago based on a skull found near Nome and remains found at gold mining operations around Fairbanks. Incursion of muskoxen into the middle of the continent occurred during the interglacial period, 129,000 -187,000 years ago, following the Illinoian glacial advance; dispersal southward was, undoubtedly, along an ice-free corridor between retreating Laurentide and Cordilleran ice masses. During this or some other interglacial period, muskoxen also dispersed eastward through the Canadian High Arctic to Greenland.

Marmots

As I explained in Chapter 4, there are actually three *Marmota* species in Alaska: the woodchuck, hoary marmot and Alaska marmot. The woodchuck is a forest dweller that reaches its extreme northwestern limit of distribution somewhere west of Fairbanks. The Alaska marmot is endemic to the Brooks Range in Alaska and, thus, has a very limited geographic range. The hoary marmot (see Figure 7.5) occurs in alpine tundra in the Rocky Mountains of Idaho and Montana and the Cascade Ranges of Washington and southern British Columbia and northward through northwest Canada and most of Alaska. Isolated populations of hoary marmots exist at Glacier Bay and on Montague Island. The Montague Island population undoubtedly was isolated by rising sea level at the end of the last glacial maximum. The Glacier Bay marmots may have survived through most of the Pleistocene in a local coastal refugium. In the state of Washington, hoary and yellow-bellied marmots occur on the same mountains. In these areas the hoary marmot is found in alpine and subalpine

meadows; the yellow-bellied marmot occupies meadows at lower elevations.

Hoary marmot—A. J. Paul and I have trapped quite a few hoary marmots over the years. A. J. grew up in upstate New York hunting gray squirrels and I spent part of my childhood plinking Albert squirrels along the Mogollon Rim in Arizona. Since marmots are nothing more than biggie-sized, ground-dwelling squirrels, we figured we had a gold mine of tasty meat as a by-product of our quest for fur. Initially, we pan-fried marmot, producing an object about the consistency of my rubber vapor-barrier boot. Then we tried stewing in a crock-pot and pressure cooking the meat. The outcome was chewable but, due to the very strong flavor, only marginally edible. Marmot meat, even when soaked for 24 hr in vinegar and brine, makes springtime bear and muskrats seem mild and tasty by comparison. I gave up, but A.J. kept at it, trying to mask the flavor with barbeque sauce, chili and many other spices.

Although Dave Klein reports that young marmots are more tender and less flavorful, we finally decided that we had enough marmot hides to last us through a lifetime of skin-sewing projects. The point is this: humans don't seriously compete with natural predators of marmots.

Those predators include, across the entire range of hoary marmots, golden eagles, coyotes, wolves, bears, bobcats, and red foxes. The grizzly only very rarely captures and eats marmots. Successful predation would depend on a bear catching a marmot far away from a refuge den or burrow. Such instances might happen during dispersal of juveniles into unfamiliar habitat adjacent to its natal territory. In 19 years of observations in McKinley Park, not a single case of a grizzly preying on hoary marmot was recorded.[61] The marmot's habit of digging burrows under boulders or in deep talus piles undoubtedly protects it from being dug out by these powerful bears.

Social organization in hoary marmots centers around a family unit. Unlike woodchucks, hoary marmots interact with each other in family units over much of the summer, above-ground part of their lives. In other words, the woodchuck is solitary and the hoary marmot is social or colonial. A hoary marmot colony in Washington or Idaho in early summer consists of one adult male, one, two, or more adult females, 2-year-olds, yearlings, and young of the year. The adult male may occupy a burrow of its own or may join the female and her offspring.

Reproductive maturity in females is typically reached at age three and dispersal from the home colony occurs at age two. Reproductively mature females have litters every other year. Colonies, undoubtedly, occasionally supply a female or two to adjacent colonies as 2-year-old females disperse away from their natal areas. The adult male guards his mature female(s) from other males to ensure that his females' offspring are indeed his. In addition, in early spring, males may occasionally make forays well away from the home burrow. This phenomenon has been referred to as **gallivanting**.[62] The most likely explanation is that the male is in search of copulation opportunities with other females.

In Alaska the social organization of a hoary marmot colony (family group) differs from the above. First, there is only a single mature female per family; males are monogamous. The association of a reproductively mature male with his partner lasts up to four years. Because there is only a single reproductively active female and because she breeds only every 2 or 3 years, a family unit has only a single age-class of juveniles, either young of the year or yearlings. Why are Alaskan hoary marmots different? Hibernation sites are so far apart that a male couldn't possibly control two of them during the summer. Second, there simply isn't enough vegetation around each hibernation burrow to support two females and all their offspring.[63]

All marmots communicate with each other vocally. Seven distinct vocalizations have been described for the hoary marmot.[64] Anyone who has hiked in marmot country has undoubtedly heard the **long call**. A high-pitched whistle, each long call lasts about 0.75 sec and is repeated about every 15 sec. The long call is usually a response to potential predators, including grizzlies, coyotes, and bobcats. Other members of the colony are immediately on the alert and look around. A second alarm call has been described, the **descending call**. During each vocalization the frequency of the call drops. Each call lasts about 0.5 sec and is repeated every 3 sec. The descending call is elicited by the sudden appearance of an aerial predator nearby. Instead of standing around alertly, marmots immediately dash for their burrows. A third warning, the **ascending call,** lasts about 0.25 sec and features an increase in sound frequency from about 2,000 to 3,200 hertz (cycles per sec) and is repeated every 1-3 sec.

Isn't the caller exposing itself to increased predation risk by calling attention to itself? Biologists are still studying this possibility of self-sacrifice for the common good. Such **altruistic** behavior has been a puzzlement to scientists because by warning others, the caller may lose its life and, therefore, end its (genetic) contribution to future generations. There are two questions to be answered. First, is the caller actually exposed to more risk? A definitive answer to this question would require lots of field observations. Seven years of observations (3017 hr) yielded 55 instances of alarm calling in response to a potential predator. In none of those 55 cases was the caller actually captured by the predator. In eight cases in which a predator successfully killed a marmot, none of those cases was preceded by an alarm call. Second, even under higher risk of predation, is there a potential reproductive payoff for the caller? Based on the social organization of the colony, described above, the answer is yes. The marmots most likely to hear and respond appropriately to the alarm call are members of the colony, that is, the family unit. Even adjacent colonies that might benefit from the warning are likely to include relatives of the caller that have dispersed to nearby locations. In other words, even if the caller were picked off by the predator, it would have protected its nearest relatives so that they might continue to live, reproduce and pass at least a portion of the caller's genes to future generations. This is a special case of natural selection referred to as **kin selection.**[65]

Hoary marmots feed on a variety of herbaceous plants of the alpine tundra. All their feeding is compacted into late spring, summer and early fall. That sounds like a long time to someone from temperate climates; in Alaska, that amounts to less than four months. Favored foods on the Kenai Peninsula include vetches (*Astragalus* and *Oxytropis*), fleabane, sedges and fescue grasses.[66] Commonly eaten plants in British Columbia include anemone, paintbrush, avalanche lily and lupine. Marmots are selective in what they eat; dominant plants in the study area on the Kenai were mountain avens (*Dryas*), bearberry and lowbush cranberry, three schrubby species that were hardly touched by marmots. However, some other herbaceous species such as fireweed and wild geranium were avoided. Marmots in south-central Alaska fed primarily on sedges with alpine arnica and fescue grass in second and third place. As is the case with pikas, marmot feeding activity near their burrows reduces plant biomass, especially of preferred items in the diet. Patches of vegetation farther from burrows, though they contain better and more forage, expose marmots to higher predation risk. Marmots, like Dall sheep, increase their vigilance as they get farther from safety. Vigilance is relaxed somewhat by the presence of other colony members; these other marmots help watch for predators. Thus, foraging patterns are due to quality and quantity of preferred foods, distance from burrow, and number of individuals feeding.[67]

The adult male emerges from hibernation in spring before the other members of his family group so that he can maintain his territory against other males. Mating occurs in May, gestation is about 10 weeks, and pups appear above ground in late July. During the summer, territorial or colony boundaries are maintained by scent marking. A marmot marks a rock by rubbing his/her cheek across it in an upward motion. Marmots appear to be capable of recognizing individuals by the specific odors of the scent marks.[68]

Hibernation begins by September and continues for about nine months. Each adult female, in the company of her offspring, occupys a single hibernation chamber or burrow, sometimes accompanied by the male. Hibernation is similar to that in arctic ground squirrels except that body temperatures do not drop below 0°C. Episodes of periodic arousal involve warming the body to near euthermic (active) temperatures. Since ambient temperatures in the burrow are lower than body temperatures and since marmots don't eat during hibernation, they all lose weight. One advantage to group hibernation is the decrease in effective surface area when huddling. This results in a metabolic savings as compared to the expense of hibernating alone. Young of the year would benefit most by group hibernation since they are smaller and, therefore, have higher specific metabolic rates. Also, they have less fat stored to carry them through hibernation. The advantage of group hibernation in harsh alpine habitats has driven the evolution of sociality in marmots.[69]

If humans didn't shoot or trap marmots, would we have any negative impact on them? Swiss scientists have looked at this question in relation to the alpine marmot (*Marmota marmota*) and hikers. They found that if hikers stay to recognized trails, there is little response by the marmots. However, leaving the trails, walking past marmot burrows and walking a dog all increasingly affected marmots. The typical response was to run to the burrow and hide. The length of time in the burrow increased as hikers got near the dens and, especially, in the presence of dogs.[70] The dogs didn't actually catch any marmots so, no harm done, right? Wrong. Overwinter survival of marmots depends on accumulating enough fat reserves to meet metabolic demands of 5-7 months in hibernation. Frequent interruptions of foraging may prevent a marmot from meeting its fat quota for the coming winter and lead to the winter death of the animal. These relationships probably apply

to hoary marmots. If so, marmots will be negatively impacted by increasing off-trail activities by humans and their dogs.

Alaska marmot—The Alaska marmot, *Marmota broweri*, is similar to the hoary marmot. Its range is restricted to the Brooks Range of northern Alaska and occupies the same alpine habitats as occupied by the hoary marmot elsewhere. It establishes burrows under boulders or rock outcroppings and forages in nearby meadows. The Alaska marmot, long thought to be a subspecies of the hoary, differs in coloration and behavior. The head and nose of the Alaska marmot are solid black. Male Alaska marmots weigh 3-4 kg; male hoary marmots weigh 5-6 kg. Alaska marmots, like their close cousins, are more active above ground on cloudy, windy days. Warm, calm, sunny days bring out the mosquitoes; marmots tend to stay in their burrows.

Hibernation in Alaska marmots lasts about nine months with the male occupying the same hibernation burrow as the female and young. Unlike the hoary marmot, the Alaska marmot completes mating behavior before emerging from the hibernaculum. Benefits from group hibernation would be even greater than those enjoyed by hoary marmots if there were more individuals in one hibernaculum. The Alaska marmot and the Siberian black-capped marmot are the most northerly distributed marmots in the world.

Grizzly bear

The grizzly is one of the glamor species of interior and northern Alaska. In all of the United States, Alaska is the prime location to see and/or hunt grizzlies. We need to clarify that grizzlies and brown bears are one and the same species, *Ursus arctos*. In some field guides the grizzly is still listed as *Ursus horribilis* and the brown bear as *Ursus middendorffi*. By popular convention, the common name grizzly is used to refer to populations in the interior and North Slope of Alaska and the rest of the interior of North America. Brown bear is the designation for coastal bears in North America and all populations in Eurasia. Brown and grizzly bears are fully interfertile. Before humans began to thin the grizzly's ranks, this species was endemic to northern Mexico, Nebraska, Oklahoma, the Dakotas, Rocky Mountain States, Pacific Northwest, and the American Southwest. On the other end of its distribution, brown bears were once found in the Atlas Mountains of North Africa.

Where do we draw the line between grizzly and brown bears in Alaska? In judging big-game trophies, the Boone and Crockett Club established a line 81 km (50 miles) inland from the coast of Alaska (or Canada) as the demarcation between brown and grizzly populations. The line is based on the notion that coastal food resources, especially salmon migrating up streams, are the single most important determinant of brown bear size. The relationship of bear size and access to salmon resources is real. However, large salmon populations migrate farther than 50 miles up many Alaskan rivers. The result is that there are some very large grizzlies farther than 50 miles from the coast.

The richness of food resources affects population density of brown/grizzly bears as well as average body size. Therefore, coastal brown bears are larger bodied and are more concentrated per km^2 than bears in the Alaska Range. Similarly, Alaska Range bears are larger, on average, and exhibit

higher population densities than grizzlies in the Brooks Range or Arctic Coastal Plain. Estimates of brown/grizzly densities are: high (Admiralty Island, southeast Alaska)- 1 bear per 2.6 km^2 (1 per mile^2); medium (Alaska Range)- 1 bear per 39-60 km^2 (1 per 15-23 mile^2); low (north slope) 1 bear per 780 km^2 (1 per 300 mile^2).

Clearly, grizzlies are highly adaptable and occupy a variety of habitats. They were once quite common on North American prairies and still occur commonly in coastal, interior forested, and tundra habitats. The inclusion of grizzlies in this chapter is merely a matter of convenience. People in the Fairbanks/North Pole area have been reminded repeatedly in the last several years of the grizzly's forest-dwelling habits. Sows with cubs have fed on dog food intended for musher's dogs in the Chena Hot Springs Road and Chena Lakes areas. A huge grizzly was shot in Goldstream Valley last fall. And every several years, an early spring fisherman fishing the confluence of the Chena and Tanana rivers is run off by a grizzly. This is an area about 10 km (6.2 miles) from downtown Fairbanks.

Grizzly bears, like humans, are **omnivores**. That is, they eat a variety of both plant and animal foods. Let's start with the plant material. Berries make up a substantial part of the diet in the Alaska Range. Blueberry is eaten in July and August; soapberry (*Shepherdia canadensis*) in August and September. Crowberries ripen in August and bears eat them then. But, since crowberries and lowbush cranberries make it through the winter in good condition, grizzlies feed on them in early spring too. Roots are a major food in May and June. The principal root taken in McKinley Park is the Eskimo potato. Other roots show up in the diet when grizzlies dig out tundra voles and their caches of vegetation. Grizzlies eat both the vole and the cache.

Carrion, already dead animals, is a welcome item at any time; the degree of putrefaction seems to matter little to the bear. Some of these animals died the previous winter; others were killed by other predators. Grizzlies often have no compunctions about taking prey away from other predators, including humans, if they can.

If the carcass is too large to finish at one sitting, the remainder is cached. Caching behavior involves burying the carcass under vegetation and soil. The grizzly will often sleep atop or near the cache. In one incident a grizzly attacked an Athabascan man in the Yukon. After a bit of a mauling the man decided to play dead. The grizzly promptly buried him under a heap of branches and other vegetation. The man waited a while, and then pushed himself up out of the heap. Unfortunately, the grizzly was still there and attacked him again. Again, the man played dead, a task that was getting easier with each mauling. After losing consciousness several times he dug himself out again and, this time, the bear was gone.[71]

Grizzlies are a major factor in moose calf mortality is some areas of Alaska. Sometimes a female is able to protect her calf and sometimes she is unsuccessful; a lot depends on the size of the bear and the experience of the mother. Female moose move away from large grizzlies but will ignore or even chase younger, smaller bears.

Caribou calves are also susceptible to predation by grizzlies, especially in the first several days of life. About two weeks after calving, grizzlies give up chasing bands of caribou. The weak have already been picked off and the surviving calves can outrun the bears. Of course, an occasional adult is pulled down. Most, but not all, of these adults are either injured or sick.

In the Alaska Range and elsewhere ground squirrels contribute to the diet in early summer but are most important from July to September. Late summer finds juvenile ground squirrels dispersing away from their natal home ranges and establishing burrows of their own. Many of these juvenile burrows are temporary excavations and, therefore, are easier to dig up. Also, the ground is easier to dig because it has thawed to an extent. A ground squirrel must be a delicacy because a grizzly will move enormous amounts of dirt, rock and vegetation to get at it. This is the one food that a mother grizzly won't share with her cubs.

One technique grizzlies employ to capture ground squirrels has been referred to as **jarring the sod**. In this behavior a grizzly locates a squirrel in a burrow. Then it rears back on its hind legs and, with all its weight behind them, slams its forepaws down on the ground (Figure 8.5). The impact sends tremors through the ground and, occasionally, panics the squirrel into fleeing the burrow. This gives the bear a chance to run down the squirrel without having to exert itself with all the digging.[61]

Since many ground squirrel burrow systems have multiple entrances, sometimes a squirrel will slip away unobserved by the bear. The bear will stop digging or jarring, apparently able to discern that the squirrel's scent is no longer as strong as it was. Their acute sense of smell is also important in finding caribou calves and in identifying family members.

Grizzlies interact with black bears and most, but not all, of those encounters turn out badly for the black bear. Several incidents have been

Figure 8.5: Grizzly "jarring the sod." As the bear slams its forepaws into the ground, the vibrations are transferred through the soil, sometimes frightening a ground squirrel into leaving its burrow.

documented of grizzlies digging black bears out of hibernation dens, killing and eating them. In areas where black and grizzly bears co-occur, black bears may be able to escape predation by climbing trees. A few incidents in which a black bear was able to successfully defend itself from a grizzly have been reported in the scientific and popular literature.

Grizzlies exhibit cannibalism. Large males occasionally chase, kill and sometimes consume other grizzlies. Mostly these incidents involve large males killing cubs for the same reason that black bears do. Namely, the large male may be able to successfully breed the sow when she comes into estrus after losing her cub. In addition, such behavior may constitute a mechanism for regulating bear population size in areas where resources may be limited. By killing other

bears, the perpetrator not only gets a meal but also eliminates some of the competition.

Typically, young bears leave their mothers in May or June as two- or three-year-olds. Breeding season for interior grizzlies extends from mid-May to mid-July. Females accompanied by young do not go into estrus and, therefore, breed only every three to six years.

Grizzlies, like black bears, exhibit delayed implantation: fertilization of ova and the formation of embryos occur from May through July, but the embryos don't implant in the uterus until November. A few other details of interior Alaska grizzly reproduction include: birth dates are late January to early February; emergence from dens occurs late April to early May; litter size is 1-3; female age at maturity is usually 6.5 to 8.5 years; male age at maturity is 5-7 years.

Wolf

One of the reasons wolves, *Canis lupus*, are so appealing to humanity is that they are so similar to dogs. Indeed, humans probably domesticated wolves for the first time back in the Pleistocene. Occasionally, humans still obtain wolf pups and domesticate them. The genetic similarity is evidenced by the fact that dog-wolf hybrids are fully fertile and can crossbreed with either wolves or dogs.

Behavioral similarities abound. Both species have a variety of facial expressions that, depending on the situation and individual, can signal dominance, anxiety, suspicion or threat. The tail can be equally expressive, with positions that connote self-confidence, threat, neutral attitude, or submission.

A few scientific authorities consider wolves and dogs as representing a single species. However, there are some consistent differences between dogs and wolves. A feature of the skull is the **orbital angle**, the angle formed by drawing a line across the top of the skull and another line from the upper to the lower edge of the eye socket. In wolves the angle is 40-45°; in dogs it is 53-60°. Another skull difference is the shape of the **tympanic bullae**. The tympanic bullae are located on the ventral surface of the skull behind the sockets for the lower jaws. In wolves the tympanic bullae are almost spherical; in dogs they are smaller, compressed, and crumpled. In addition, the wolf has a gland at the base of the tail, the **precaudal gland**, that dogs don't have. Finally, in wolves, the chest is about the same width as the pelvis, causing its hind legs to swing in the same line as the front legs. In dogs the chest is wider than the hips and, therefore, the tracks of its hind legs are between the tracks of its front legs.

With so many behavioral and genetic similarities one might expect wolves and domestic dogs to get along well. In spite of an occasional hybridization between the two, dogs and wolves don't really get on that well. In times of low prey availability, dogs turn into wolf food. Such was the case around Fairbanks in the early to mid-1970s, when wolf packs came into the outskirts of town and ate dogs right off their yard chains.

Vocalizations by wolves are fascinating and consist of four basic types: the whimper (friendly, submissive), the growl (aggressive), the bark (alarm or challenge) and the howl. Howling, one of the most exciting sounds one can hear in Alaska, is a pretty variable and complex vocalization. The howl lasts from a half to 11 seconds and has a fundamental frequency plus up to 12 overtones or harmonics. The pitch can remain constant or can smoothly slide from one frequency to another. Typically, an individual wolf howls for about 35 seconds. If joined by others, they chime in after the first or second howl but come in at different pitches (or notes) from the instigator. Each individual starts off with long, low howls and works up to shorter, higher pitched howls. On average a "group howl" lasts about 85 seconds but may be repeated.[72] Wolves can howl at any time of day, and any time of year.

What is the function of howling? One function that seems clear-cut is as an assembly call. Often during a hunt, members of the pack get separated. If one individual begins to howl, other members of its pack move to it. The howl is probably not a hunting call. David Mech watched part of a wolf pack chase and finally hold a moose at bay.[72] The rest of the pack wandered around awhile before they found the moose. If the howl were a hunting call, the individuals nearest the moose would have called the other pack members. Finally, howls are probably used by a pack to help delineate its territorial boundaries.

Aside from howling, wolves advertise the boundaries of their territories by scent-marking. Scent-marking is accomplished in one of several ways. The more obvious way is to urinate on the ground or, preferably, on a vertical object. Scent-marked posts or trees delineate the individual or pack boundary. There is some controversy as to whether only the alpha male scent-marks or if the task is shared among the pack members. One wonders how big a bladder an alpha male would need to effectively mark scent posts every 100 meters along kilometers of boundaries. A second method of scent-marking is body rubbing. Our golden retriever, Murphy, and I walk to the top of our driveway and up the road about 50 meters to get the daily paper. He invariably stops at the top of the driveway, drops onto his front knees and rubs his head side to side on the ground. He follows this by rolling or wallowing, typically ending up by writhing on his back. He is marking boundaries by depositing scent from his neck and head on the driveway and road. Dogs and wolves rolling in really stinky stuff is behavior derived from scent-marking.

Several other dominant behaviors include the "standing across," "riding up," mounting and staring behaviors and raising the hair of rump and mane. Subordinate behaviors include lying down with abdomen exposed, pawing movements, tail wagging and face licking. The face licking maneuver is also used by pups to beg for food. Parents and sometimes other pack adults respond to face-licking by vomiting partially digested food that the pups eat. And all this time you haven't been responding appropriately to your dog's face-licking behavior! All the above behaviors are incorporated into the social organization of a wolf pack. The dominance-hierarchy posturing and struggles eventually lead to the establishment of and reinforcement of a dominant or **alpha** male and an alpha female.

What does dominance mean to the pack? The pack is organized around the alpha pair. The alpha pair are the only members of the pack to mate. Other, subordinate individuals in the pack are either offspring of the alpha male and female or are individuals that have dispersed from another pack and been accepted by

the new pack. One of the jobs of the alpha male is to suppress mating behavior of other males. Similarly, the alpha female keeps the other females in line and, usually, celibate. The alpha male is the leader of the pack and gets first crack at prey. Usually the pack functions smoothly and mounts cooperative efforts in hunting and in feeding the pups. Fighting within the pack is held to a minimum by employing the ritualized behaviors that establish and enforce the dominance hierarchy. Fights to the death do occur but probably only rarely. Circumstances leading to fierce fighting might include very low food availability or the introduction of a high-status wolf from another pack.

Mating occurs from late February to late April in Alaska. The pregnant female digs a new den or reoccupies an existing den. The den is a 1.9-4.6 m (6-14 feet) tunnel dug into the earth with an enlarged chamber at the end for the pups. The den is completed well in advance of birth of the pups and may include several openings. Since gestation takes 62-63 days, whelping occurs from late April into June. Pups remain at the den for 8-10 weeks. It is this 8 to10 week period that, to an extent, ties the pack to its home range. Pack members can range out only so far and still bring back food for the pups.

Wolf pack territories vary considerably in size depending on the number of wolves in the pack and on the availability of prey animals. Territory sizes in Denali Park range from 88 to 2500 km^2 (34 to 980 miles^2). Undoubtedly, territory sizes of adjacent packs change dynamically as the fortunes (and sizes) of these packs wax and wane.

Some but not all wolves born into a pack leave at some point. Dispersal from the natal pack most commonly occurs in April and May, near the time new pups are born. Most dispersers are 1 to 3 year olds but four- and six-year-old individuals have been seen to leave their home packs.[73] Other than joining an existing pack living outside its natal pack's home range, a dispersing wolf may start its own pack. It must find another individual of the opposite sex and an area that is not occupied by other, existing packs. Though most wolves only travel a short distance (0-100 km), some have been tracked 890 km (550 miles) from their natal pack's location. A female radio-collared in Denali Park in 1987 was shot by an Inupiat hunter four years later on the Arctic Coastal Plain, a distance of 700 km (435 miles).

The fact that only the alpha pair mate in the wild has led to a nonlethal wolf control technique. If the alpha male can be sterilized, then no offspring will be born since he, presumably, prevents other pack males from copulating with the alpha female. To be extra sure, both alpha male and alpha female can be sterilized. For the present, this technique at least partially addresses the sensibilities of those who don't want to see wolves harmed or killed and the sensibilities of those who want wolf populations limited.

Play behavior is an important aspect of the biology of predators such as dogs and wolves. Our dog always pounced on moving objects such as balls and even blowing leaves. Obviously, pouncing is useful in capturing small prey. If you own a dog, I'm sure you have at some point played tug of war. Both you and your dog dug in heals and your dog tried to back up, low to the ground. This is exactly the tugging behavior exhibited by a wolf that has gotten a grip on the nose of a moose, muskox, or caribou. The

behavior functions to weaken the prey, to hold it while other wolves attack it, to promote blood loss, or to suffocate the prey (Figure 8.6).

A lot of attention has been focused in Alaska on the actual and/or potential impact of wolves on their prey populations. Of course, the prey populations of highest concern to Alaskans are moose, caribou and Dall sheep. These three species are extremely important to subsistence and meat hunters. Because of nonresident, sport hunting, these three are also an important component of Alaska's tourism industry. Further, wolf viewing may become another aspect of our tourism because wolves can be seen more easily in Alaska than in the Lower 48. Finally, wolves are an important element of the trapping scene in Alaska.

Let's begin by considering wolves as predators, that is, potential competitors of human hunters. First, wolves prey on a wide variety of animals, some of which can be considered human food only with a real stretch of the imagination. For example, wolves in Denali National Park and elsewhere eat, among other foods, voles and marmots. Voles aren't human food, in spite of the nutty wildlife biologist's behavior in the movie *Never Cry Wolf*. Hoary marmots are occasionally eaten by marmot trappers but, for reasons I explained earlier, humans and wolves are not in competition for marmots as food.

The really serious competition with humans relates to wolves taking moose and caribou. Understanding the predator-prey relationships and conveying this understanding is the job of wildlife biologists. Ultimately, decisions about controlling wolves and other predators in order to increase huntable populations of moose and caribou require more information than just the

Figure 8.6: Wolf tugging on a moose nose. The lead wolf is slowing down the moose so that other members of the pack can inflict injuries to the moose's flanks and belly.

scientific information. There are political, cultural, economic, and even emotional issues that relate to wildlife management. The point is this: science does not make value judgments. To an unbiased scientist, it isn't better or worse to control predators to increase prey populations. It is the scientist's responsibility to describe or elucidate the possible outcomes of particular courses of action, not to decide what is the "best" management scheme.

Getting back to biology: how effective are wolves at predation on big game species? Two extreme possibilities are that wolves are totally effective and kill every time they hunt, or that wolves kill off only the diseased and otherwise unfit members of the prey population. The truth is somewhere between these two.

Quite a bit is now known about wolves and their prey based on studies conducted in Alaska

and elsewhere. One of the most interesting and informative was conducted at Isle Royale National Park, Michigan. Isle Royale is a 540 km² (210 mile²) island 24 km (15 miles) out in Lake Superior. Moose colonized the island by walking across ice in a particularly cold winter early in the 20th century. Population size fluctuated through boom and bust cycles, reaching 3000 animals in the early 1930s only to drastically decline due to disease and starvation.

In the winter of 1949 wolves occupied Isle Royale. Aside from a few hares, birds, and an occasional beaver, the only prey available was moose. The Isle Royale wolves quickly became moose specialists. Wolf numbers on the island since 1959 have ranged from 18 to 40 individuals. During the same period, the moose population ranged from 600 to 2400.[74] Several interesting conclusions can be drawn from this long-term study. First, moose were not extirpated by the wolves. In fact, moose were able to increase population size pretty dramatically in spite of the presence of wolves. Factors other than predation affect moose populations. Second, wolves are not able to kill moose on every attempt.

Here is a summary of the results based on careful documentation of 131 separate moose-wolf encounters. First, the location of prey by wolves is primarily by scent. Once moose were detected from downwind or from a scent trail, wolves began the stalk. Individuals pointed upwind, touched noses, wagged their tails, and moved out in single file. Once the wolves actually encountered a moose, the most important factor was the moose's behavior. That is, did the moose run or stand at bay? In 36 of the 131 interactions (27%), the moose stood its ground and the wolves eventually left. In 89 instances (68%) the moose was chased but outdistanced the wolves. All of the remaining 7 (5%) were attacked, and 6 of those were killed. The other moose was wounded but, at least initially, escaped.[72]

It appears that wolves evaluate the strength or vulnerability of moose in several ways. Fight or flight is the first criterion. A confident, pugnacious moose has a chilling effect on the wolves. The chase provides the second clue. If the moose isn't caught quickly, chases tend to fizzle out. Short pursuits are most common but chases can go on for miles.

The actual attack almost always involves several wolves. Individuals take turns trying to wound the moose, primarily by biting the legs and hindquarters. The throat and nose are also targets once the moose has been slowed down. Contrary to expectation, wolves do not attempt to hamstring moose. That would require lung-ing at the trailing edge of the hind legs, the most lethal weapons a moose has at its disposal. This is simply far too dangerous a target. A technique I mentioned earlier is for a wolf to latch onto the moose's nose, sink in its teeth, and hang on. A moose is seriously inconvenienced with a 55 kg (120 lb) weight attached to its head, especially if that weight is promoting blood loss! The other members of the pack exploit this opportunity to inflict additional damage until the moose is down or shakes off its attackers. In one incident a wolf leaped and sank its teeth into the nose of a fleeing moose. The moose shook its head side to side as it ran, swinging the attached wolf through a wide arc. On one swing the wolf slammed into a large tree, lost its grip, and fell off. This incident notwithstanding, I'd bet that most moose that end up with a wolf attached to their faces don't survive the encounter.

Finally, wolves don't necessarily complete the kill immediately. Often, the moose was seriously wounded and the pack broke off the attack to rest and let the injuries take effect. Sometimes the pack left entirely only to return the following day to finish off the victim. From an anthropocentric point of view, this seems like vicious, heartless, evil behavior, but in reality it is simply a more efficient, safer way of bringing down large prey. From a scientific viewpoint, there is no such thing as vicious, heartless, or evil behavior.

Several studies have now eliminated the possibility that wolves are capable of killing every time they hunt. What about the other prospect, that wolves only kill the sick and weak? Assessment of age and condition of actual prey has been used to study this issue. The Isle Royale study assessed the age of as many moose that fell prey to wolves as possible. The same sort of analysis of Dall sheep kills in Mt. McKinley (Denali) National Park was also made.[75]

Due to the remoteness of Isle Royale and to the thoroughness with which wolves and scavengers clean up moose kills, it was impossible in that study to completely assess the condition of all moose killed by wolves. Ages of the moose killed by wolves consisted of calves and 4- to 9-year-olds; the very young and mature to elderly individuals. There were no 1- to 3-year-olds among the victims. Second, a sketchy comparison was made of the degree of parasitic infestation of wolf-killed moose versus moose that died of other causes. The incidence of hydatid cysts in the lungs of the dead moose was the indicator.

Recall that the tapeworm *Echinococcus granulosus* passes its juvenile life stage in slowly growing cysts in the lungs of moose and caribou. Through time, heavily infested hosts are undoubtedly slowed down due to less efficient lung function and to the extra metabolic expense of feeding its parasites. The lungs of four moose killed by wolves had an average of 41 golf-ball-sized hydatid cysts each. The lungs from four moose dead of other causes had an average of 3.5 cysts per individual. Collectively, this is evidence that wolves are probably having a bigger impact on the young, aged, and sickly than they are on the healthy individuals in their prime.[72] This evidence does not mean that wolves never kill individuals in their prime. There are always chance events that lead to an otherwise impressive, healthy bull caribou or moose getting picked off by wolves.

In Alaska several studies have evaluated the condition of prey animals successfully brought down by wolves. In south-central Alaska, bone marrow fat analysis suggests that wolf-killed moose are in about the same condition as the average (unkilled) moose.[76] According to the same evidence, in northwest Alaska wolves pull down healthy caribou in the winter but kill moose that tend to be in poor condition.[77]

Murie's analysis of age structure of Dall sheep mortalities in Denali Park suggests that wolves prey primarily on "weak" sheep. Two different collections of dead sheep were examined for age distribution. Lambs and yearlings are potentially vulnerable because of their inexperience, and 11- and 14-year-olds are the Geritol® crowd among Dall sheep. Sheep 2-8 years old were designated as "in their prime." In one collection, 95% of the mortalities were from among the inexperienced and old sheep; 5% were in their prime. The other collection yielded 88% "weak" sheep and 12% in their prime. Notice that age, by itself, doesn't mean the sheep was really in good physiological condition. Of course, even if these data "proved" that wolves hardly ever get prime animals (and they don't prove it), some Alaskans would still worry about wolf predation. As I mentioned above, sheep hunters go after the largest rams they can find. From their point of view, a trophy is the old-timer that is probably past its prime and pretty vulnerable to wolf predation. So, in a real sense, wolves compete with sheep hunters for trophy rams.

Caribou were the main prey of wolves in the Mt. McKinley Park study, but caribou are not available year-round. Calves are important in spring and summer where caribou movements brought them near wolves. Similarly, predation on adults mainly occurs in fall and winter when caribou pass back through the pack's home range. Here is perhaps another surprising feature of wolf biology: wolves don't simply follow caribou relentlessly throughout the year, pulling them down as needed. Instead, wolf packs, because of their denning requirements, have definite home ranges and, in most cases, have to make do with the prey resources within that home range for at least a portion of the year. Caribou dominates the diets of wolves in both south-central[76] and northwest Alaska[77] and Gates of the Arctic National Park.[76, 77,78] Caribou seem to be the preferred prey even though moose and Dall sheep are more abundant in Gates of the Arctic than are caribou.

Actual hunting techniques for caribou differ somewhat from those employed for moose. Three methods are ambushing, relay running, and chasing bands and then concentrating on animals that stumble or fall behind.[79] Ambushing at times involves one individual wolf, the killer, setting up ahead of the band while the other members of the pack flush or drive the caribou to the ambush. Relay running involves several members of the pack chasing caribou while other pack members rest. If the caribou should happen to turn back or run in a large circle, the rested members take up the chase.

The third technique, chasing a band until a "likely suspect" is revealed, is the technique that fits so nicely with the concept of wolves picking off the injured, weak, or sick. Pursuit of caribou by wolves rarely lasts longer than about 500 meters. If no weakling has fallen back by then, wolves break off the chase. The actual attack is usually focused on the front shoulders, neck, and head of the caribou. The wolf pulls alongside and tries to bite the flank, shoulder, or throat. This behavior differs from that employed in attacking moose, in which the rump is the primary focus.

How big an impact do wolves have on their principal prey, caribou and moose, in Alaska? Several studies have addressed this question. I cited a study of wolf-moose interactions on Isle Royale, above, to give some indication of hunting effectiveness but that ecosystem isn't the same as anywhere in Alaska. In Alaska, moose, caribou and sheep are susceptible to predation by black and grizzly bears in addition to wolves. Further, severe winter weather can stress prey animals physiologically, and deep, crusted snows can make them more susceptible than usual to depredations by wolves. Wolves within the range of the Western Arctic caribou herd account for 6-7% of the caribou population per year and 11-14% of the moose. The real question about the wolf's effect on prey populations is this: does wolf predation mortality add to other causes of mortality, or do wolves simply kill animals that would have died anyway due to harsh winters and human hunters?

The uncertainty lies in the fact that we cannot control nature and all the variables that influence mortality in prey populations. However, thirty years of information about interior Alaska moose and caribou populations tell an interesting story. The data show that wolf control was followed by population increases in both moose and caribou and that calf and yearling survival increased two- to fourfold. In severe winters (1973-1975) wolves removed from 13 to 34% of the moose population, values well above the percentages added to the population by calf births in the following years. It appears that severe winters, hunting, and predation are additive and that wolves can maintain a prey population at low levels even if they are not responsible for initiating the lows. It is highly likely that prey populations, moose and caribou, are held to levels below carrying capacity by predation in all its forms.[7]

What about the other prey of wolves? In McKinley Park, caribou and Dall sheep are the most frequent prey. Minor players are ground squirrel, marmot, porcupine, ptarmigan, beaver, snowshoe hare and red fox. In the Far North, muskoxen occasionally fall prey to wolves. In one documented encounter a single wolf managed to kill a lone muskox bull. The battle lasted about 70 minutes and involved the wolf provoking repeated charges by the muskox. Mostly, the wolf attacked head-on and seized the face of the muskox at least three different times.[80]

Wolves encounter and, at times, fight with bears, wolverines, coyotes, and foxes. One wolf-bear encounter involved a large grizzly that approached a wolf den. All five wolves attacked the bear, darting in to nip at its heels, jumping out of reach, and darting in again while the bear was distracted by another pack member. The grizzly finally gave up and fled. In this encounter, several of the wolves barely escaped the reach of the grizzly's paws. Sometimes they don't. In Ontario, a female wolf was found dead near her den with 11 broken ribs and two broken neck vertebrae. Hair around the den and carcass belonged to the perpetrator, a black bear.[81] Wolverines are chased and sometimes killed by wolves. Wolverines have been known to climb trees or attempt to do so when trying to get away from wolves. Foxes and coyotes are occasionally killed by wolves.

Coyote

The coyote, the wolf's smaller cousin. first showed up in southeastern Alaska in 1899. By 1915 they had moved into interior and south-central Alaska. Although a recent immigrant with respect to historical times, the coyote has had a presence here through much of the Pleistocene and, perhaps, even earlier. By the mid-Pleistocene, 500,000 years ago, the coyote had evolved to its present configuration more or less. Fossil remains of over 200 coyotes have been found in the Rancho La Brea tar pits in Los Angeles and several more in similarly aged deposits in Alaska. These coyotes differ from their modern-day descendants only in size; it seems like everything was larger back in the Pleistocene.

How does the coyote differ from the wolf? The most obvious differences have to do with size. Large male wolves weigh about 50 kg (110 lbs) with exceptional individuals in the 80 kg (175 lb) range. Coyotes, *Canis latrans*, average about a third the size of wolves, so a large male might weigh 16-17 kg (35-37 lb). A coyote stands 0.6 m (2 ft) at the shoulder and is about 1.2 m (4 ft) long, including the tail. A wolf stands about 0.8 m (2.5 ft) at the shoulder and is about 1.8 m (6 ft) long (Figure 8.7). Most dogs of comparable height to coyotes are more heavily built.

The skulls of coyotes are narrower, in proportion, than those of wolves and have much smaller sagittal crests. Their molar teeth are more deeply sculptured and have cusps and cones that the molars of wolves do not have. These differences are consistent with coyotes relying on vegetation as well as meat in their diets. The coyote cannot open its mouth as wide as a wolf and, therefore,

Figure 8.7: Size comparison of wolf, coyote, red fox, and the smallest canid in Alaska, the Arctic fox.

is not as capable as the wolf at attacking large animals. Picture in your mind trying to bite into a moose ham as the moose runs. The wider the gape of the jaws, the better the chance of inflicting a significant injury on the moose.

Along with its expansion into Alaska early in the 20th century, within the last hundred years coyotes have spread from the West and Midwest through southern Canada, into the Great Lakes region, and from there to New Brunswick and the northeastern United States. In addition, they have habituated to human civilization, as evidenced by many reports of them coming into the suburbs of large cities and eating food out of pet dishes in the backyards of residences. This canid has been able to expand its geographic range so remarkably, first, because wolves were extirpated from the eastern United States in the 1800s, and the canid predator niche was left unfilled. Second, coyotes are highly adaptable, in part because of their intelligence and in part because of their dentition.

What is the relationship between wolves and coyotes? First, the only wolf-coyote hybrids known to exist were conceived in captivity. In the wild, these two species probably never or only very rarely hybridize. Typically, when wolves encounter coyotes, they chase the coyotes and, if they catch them, kill them. Coyotes benefit from

the presence of wolves by feeding on the carrion of animals pulled down by wolves. In areas where wolves prey on elk and moose, coyotes scavenge the remains. Only on very rare occasions are coyotes able to successfully prey on live elk or moose and these are either calves or very weakened adults. Although wolves occasionally kill coyotes, coyotes follow wolves in order to scavenge.

The benefits to the coyotes outweigh the risks. On the Kenai Peninsula, coyotes prey mainly on snowshoe hares, porcupines, and other small mammals while wolves rely mainly on moose and secondarily on snowshoe hares, beavers, and small mammals.[82] Wolves and coyotes partition the food resources and avoid **exploitation competition** (competing for the same foods). However, there is evidence that wolves at times kill coyotes on the Kenai; this amounts to **interference competition**.

These wolf-coyote interrelationships led me to ask whether coyotes and red foxes compete. In boreal forest habitat in southwest Yukon, both species relied primarily on snowshoe hares as prey during hare population highs and lows. However, during hare population lows foxes switch to alternate prey such as ground squirrels and voles; coyotes do not. The habitat is partitioned: coyotes hunt open ground and the edges between brushy and open ground while foxes stick to brushy habitat.[83] Both fox and coyote populations fluctuate along with fluctuations of hares. In Alberta, 20-40-fold changes in hare populations resulted in 3-6-fold changes in coyote populations.[84]

Is there interference competition between coyotes and foxes? A study in Ontario, Canada, suggests that red foxes and coyotes establish adjacent home ranges and that foxes place their den sites as far away from coyotes as they can. In other words, foxes avoid coyotes.[85] In central Alberta, coyotes chase red foxes and foxes dig dens close to human habitation, probably to avoid coyotes.[86]

Arctic fox

DNA studies suggest that as recently as 150,000 years ago the arctic fox, *Alopex lagopus*, evolved from a stock of swift foxes in North America.[87] The swift fox, *Vulpes velox*, is a grassland species now restricted to the Great Plains (southern Canada to northern Mexico) and desert habitats of the Southwest. Back in an interglacial period of the Pleistocene a population of swift foxes may have existed in ice-free Beringia. Isolation in Alaska during a full glacial period would have produced strong selective pressures to adapt to an environment of ice, cold, and dramatically fluctuating prey numbers. Rapid evolution of this fox would be favored by large litter sizes, high mortalities, and short generations. Since its appearance on the scene, the arctic fox radiated across northern Canada, reached Greenland and Iceland, and crossed the Bering land bridge. It is now circumpolar in distribution.

The arctic fox is smaller than its cousin the red fox (Figure 8.7): it is lighter in weight (2.7-4.5 kg versus 2.7-6.8 kg for red foxes) and shorter (110 cm versus 124 cm length for red foxes). The compactness of this canid might seem to be a detriment in the Far North, but the arctic fox has a host of special features that allow it to survive and thrive in the Arctic. First, its winter fur is such good insulation that it doesn't start shivering until temperatures fall to around -70°C (-94°F).[88] That fur is twice as long as the

summer fur. About 70% of the coat of an arctic fox is fine underfur; in red foxes only about 20% is underfur. Ears, legs, and muzzle are short, reducing heat loss. The pads of the feet have fur on them, another adaptation to reduce heat transfer to the cold snow and ice. As is the case for gulls, ptarmigan, caribou, and wolves, arctic foxes have countercurrent heat exchangers in their legs that prevent heat loss and also prevent icing of the paws. Finally, arctic foxes develop a subcutaneous fat layer for insulation and energy storage.

The arctic fox is the only canid that goes through a change in coat color during the molt. The winter white is shed early in April and replaced with a short coat of brown fur over most of the body, with yellowish-white on the belly. The reversal of coat color back to white begins in September and is completed by November. Actually, there are two color variants of arctic foxes. The "standard" white fox occurs in continental habitats of arctic Alaska, Canada and Eurasia. The blue phase is found mostly on islands in the North Atlantic, the Aleutians, and in southwest Alaska. In winter, the blue phase is a steel colored bluish-gray; in summer the coat color is darker than that of the standard arctic fox. Blue foxes are, undoubtedly, better camouflaged in coastal and island habitats, where the climate-moderating influence of the oceans and the tides produce habitat less covered with snow than in the extreme Arctic.

In areas where lemming populations fluctuate, arctic foxes prey on them and exhibit ups and downs in population size. However, fox populations are more stable than one might expect. During population lows adult foxes conceive smaller litters, resorb some of these fetuses, and bear fewer young. The young experience much higher mortality rates than either the adults or young born in years of lemming abundance. Food shortages in lean years are partially offset by switching to alternate prey when available.

Brown and collared lemmings are major food resources in the summer months but are much more difficult to obtain in the winter because of windblown and crusted snow. In winter foxes rely in part on carrion and in part on caches of food left from the summer months. On St. Lawrence Island, foxes prey on seabirds only in summer because the birds leave the island in the fall. But bird remains appear in the scats of winter foxes; the foxes are digging up old caches.[89]

Caching behavior is flexible in arctic foxes and depends on the abundance and spatial distribution of prey. If foxes are capturing lemmings that are dispersed across the habitat, they are likely to hide a few individuals at scattered sites on the landscape. In other words, they are scatter hoarding. If they are capturing lots of prey in a concentrated area, such as in seabird colonies, they exhibit larder hoarding, burying numbers of prey in a single cache. A very large larder cache found in the Aleutians contained the following: 107 least auklets, 18 crested auklets, 7 fork-tailed storm petrels, 3 tufted puffins and a horned puffin.[90]

Arctic foxes on islands prey on marine organisms in summer. On St. Lawrence they eat tunicates, small crabs, and sponges. On an island off west Greenland, arctic foxes go fishing in tidepools at low tide and catch gunnels, sculpins, and lumpsuckers.[91]

An important food resource in winter is carrion including whales, caribou, muskoxen, and seals. Newborn seals are occasionally captured by foxes while the seals are in their subnivean birth dens. Arctic foxes often follow polar bears and clean up their kills if given the opportunity. Although normally solitary in winter, groups of arctic foxes may congregate on a large marine mammal. Winter wanderings take arctic foxes far from their denning territories. Individuals may cover hundreds of kilometers and a few have traveled over 1600 km (1000 miles) in a winter.[92]

Arctic foxes have the largest litters among the entire order Carnivora. An average litter is about seven pups, but up to 25 pups may be born to a single female. Litter size is highly variable and appears to be a product of immediate food resources just before and during pregnancy and, perhaps more fundamentally, also a product of the unpredictability of food.

How do we know how many pups are in a litter? Obviously, a starving graduate student can be sent out to actually count the individual pups. However, direct observation has several drawbacks. You would have to see all the pups out of the den simultaneously to be confident that your count was accurate. Pups first emerge from the den from 3-4 weeks after birth. However, some pups may have died before emergence. An alternative method is to collect the carcasses of trapped females and examine their reproductive tracts. On the inside wall of the uterus are tiny scars where the placentas were attached during pregnancy. A count of the scars yields the number of fetuses that were implanted in the uterus. The scar count, at times, is higher than the actual number of live births; occasionally an implanted fetus is resorbed during pregnancy. Therefore, average and maximum litter sizes will always be a little uncertain because the methods used to estimate them are imperfect.

Dens are typically located in soil along riverbanks or small hills. The dens usually have a south-facing aspect, catching the sun's radiant energy. Even with a thawed active layer of soil, excavation of dens is a labor-intensive activity. It is no surprise that dens may be reused and embellished for generations. On average, each den has 12 entrances but some may have 60.[88] Gestation (time from fertilization to birth) is 63 days. Weaning occurs after six weeks and juveniles begin to hunt at about three months.[93] While the pups are confined to the den and its surroundings, both parents provide food. Adults are rarely at the den at the same time, so interactions between them are rare. Pups play with each other but rarely fight; unlike wolves, arctic foxes are not pack animals and don't require a dominant, or alpha, individual to lead them.[94] However, observations on captive arctic foxes showed development of a dominance hierarchy. Dominant individuals would have an advantage in the dead of winter when several individuals might show up at the same carcass.[95] Cases of cannibalism of pups have been reported, but the dead pups weren't killed by either their parents or their siblings.[96]

Populations of arctic foxes in northern Alaska and arctic Canada are relatively healthy and have been, up to now, little impacted by humans. Elsewhere, this species hasn't fared as well. In Iceland, arctic foxes are considered vermin and every effort, so far unsuccessful, has been made to totally eradicate them. In northern Russia and Scandinavia, trapping has reduced arctic fox numbers, and populations in Scandinavia haven't rebounded after a moratorium on hunting and trapping. Red foxes are expanding their geographic range in both the Old and New Worlds. Studies of red and arctic foxes held in enclosures and observations in the field indicate that red foxes dominate arctic foxes.[97] Therefore, when they come in contact with arctic foxes, red foxes displace their smaller cousins. One of the potential outcomes of global warming is the reduction in range and, perhaps, the eventual extinction of the arctic fox.

Arctic ground squirrel

The arctic ground squirrel or parka squirrel, *Spermophilus undulatus*, is the most northerly of ground squirrels in North America and eastern Asia. As I discussed earlier, it may be the only mammal species to tolerate body temperatures below 0°C (32°F). In North America this species occurs from the western shore of Hudson Bay to the Beaufort, Chukchi and Bering Sea coasts. It is missing from the high Canadian arctic islands but is present on St. Lawrence and Kodiak Islands in Alaska.

The parka squirrel is a species of arctic and alpine tundra. However, there are several oddities about its distribution in central Alaska. First, a population occupying disturbed boreal forest habitats in the Yukon River basin in east-central Alaska has a high (15-20%) incidence of **melanism**. That is, about a fifth of these squirrels are black. Melanism in these squirrels was probably selected evolutionarily as they spread into burned forest habitat: predators are more likely to see and capture the normal brown-colored ground squirrels when they occur on a dark or black background.[98] The second odd aspect of this particular subspecies is that it does not occur in the alpine Uplands adjacent to its habitat in the Yukon flats.

Presumably, the 80-85% of the population that is the normal brown coloration would do well in typical alpine tundra. Their absence in the Tanana Uplands, between the Yukon and Tanana Rivers, is a complete mystery.

The annual cycle of above-ground activity begins when territorial males emerge from their hibernation burrows in early spring. Emergence occurs early in May on the Arctic Coastal Plain, near Barrow, and in mid- to late April in the Alaska Range. Males come out earlier than the females in order to establish their territories and defend them against other males. Since the landscape is still mostly snow-covered, these animals are weeks away from seeing any fresh vegetation. They subsist on food cached the previous summer. These caches were once thought to serve as food during the winter. Squirrels were thought to arouse occasionally to eat, defecate, and stretch. In reality, arctic ground squirrels do not eat or defecate during hibernation, and only the males cache food.

The functions of male territories are several. First, the male has almost exclusive reproductive access to all the females whose territories overlap his. Second, he is able to protect his own offspring by serving as a lookout for potential predators. Third, he can protect them from other male ground squirrels. Observations and experiments in which males are removed from their territories have shown that a replacement male moving into undefended territory kills all the young squirrels there. The biological significance is that the new male is killing off his potential competitors for the territory and killing young he did not father. Infanticide favors survival of the new male and improves the

chances that he will pass his new territory on to one of his own sons.

Burrowing behavior produces five distinct kinds of structures. The **boundary pit** is a shallow pit dug by the victorious male in a territorial battle. This pit is a marker establishing a territorial limit or boundary. A **duck hole** is a shallow tunnel occupied by ground squirrels as a temporary shelter. A **refugee burrow** is occupied by an animal without a territory in marginal habitat. All three of these structures are very simple and shallow and, therefore, don't provide as much protection from predators as the more elaborate territorial burrows. These latter burrows may be either **single burrows** (with a single occupant) or **double burrows** (double occupancy). Single burrows may have from 20 to 50 openings to the surface. Thus, a weasel entering one opening isn't assured of capturing the occupant before she/he escapes out another opening.

Females emerge from their dens about three weeks after the males, and both sexes begin feeding on new vegetation as soon as it becomes available. Through May, males are scampering all over, maintaining their territorial boundaries while most females are pregnant. It is no surprise that, by June, males have lost 24% of their emergent body weight and females have gained 4%. Females give birth in June after a 25-day gestation period. Litters average about 8 blind, naked young. These young are first seen above-ground after about 42 days. Along the Chukchi seacoast, the above-ground feeding part of the year (May to September) results in an average weight gain of 31%. Most, if not all, of this weight gain is lost during hibernation. The functional significance of ground squirrel hibernation is a huge energy savings. The squirrel would lose more weight if it remained metabolically active all winter.

Arctic ground squirrels rely primarily on a variety of herbaceous plants for their sustenance. Over 40 species of herbs and shrubs contribute, including milk vetch, bistort, blueberries, and low-bush cranberries, but lichens and evergreens are avoided. Early in the summer, mosses, shrub leaves, and animal matter are important. In mid- to late summer, new shoots, seeds, and horsetails make up about 80% of the diet.

Even though these rodents are considered herbivores, they are known to kill and consume several mammal species. Newborn snowshoe hares fall prey to ground squirrels in habitats where both species occur.[99] Ground squirrels in Northwest Territories occasionally eat collared lemmings. Both hares and lemmings are victims of active predation: ground squirrels actually dig lemmings out of their burrows.[100] Both collared lemmings and snowshoe hares exhibit significant population cycles and ground squirrels are simply taking advantage of an occasionally abundant, high-protein food resource.

Unlike its two prey species, the arctic ground squirrel exhibits relatively stable populations in most of its range. The stability is due, in part, to the fixed number of good burrow sites available within suitable habitat. Dominant and, therefore, successful individuals are able to hold on to territories. Less experienced individuals, including most juvenile males, are driven out of the territories of their elders (or betters) and must try to survive in marginal habitat. These dispersants form a refugee population, and almost all are lost each year to predators (inadequate burrows) and winter kill (insufficient fat reserves to survive hibernation).[101]

A Few Tundra Birds

Snowy owl

The snowy owl, *Nyctea scandiaca*, (see Figure 5.4) is a bird of the open arctic tundra in the breeding season. It is found on the western Aleutians, the western Alaska (wet tundra) coast, Seward Peninsula, throughout the Arctic Coastal Plain to Hudson Bay, the High Canadian Arctic, northern Greenland and Iceland. In Eurasia it occurs from Fennoscandia eastward to the Chukotsk Peninsula opposite Alaska's Seward Peninsula. In winter snowy owls may remain within their breeding range or disperse far southward. They have been seen, on very rare occasions, as far south as southeastern Texas, the Gulf States, Georgia, and Bermuda, but more commonly occur in the northern tier of the United States.

As I mentioned above, lemming cycles have a significant influence on their predators. The years of major incursions of snowy owls into southern Canada and northern states of the U.S.A. coincide with severe population lows among lemmings. Several notable examples occurred in the winters of 1945-46 (across the entire continent) and 1966-67 (confined to the Pacific Northwest).

Lemmings constitute the primary prey over much of the snowy owl's range in the North American Arctic. When lemmings are not abundant, Alaskan snowy owls feed on voles, arctic ground squirrels, ducks, ptarmigan, gulls, and young geese. During irruptions into southern Canada and the northern U.S., these owls prey upon pheasants, quail, grouse, waterfowl and domestic poultry as well as small mammals. In other words, snowy owls are adaptable. Prey animals are captured in three different ways. Primarily, owls perch on a high point and "still-hunt." That is, they spot prey from afar and then go after it. Second, they hop or walk on the ground or snow, looking or listening for prey. Third, snowy owls occasionally hunt by coursing, flying low over the ground looking for prey.

Reproductive success is affected by lemming abundance. During lemming lows, snowy owls on the North Slope of Alaska lay 4-5 eggs; during highs they may lay 11-12. Snowy owl males deliver food to their mates and offspring. Each offspring consumes about 1500 lemmings from hatching to complete independence.[102] That requires a lot of successful hunting by, first, the father and, then, by both parents. No wonder lemming population size is so important to these owls.

Nests are established early in May on sites that have some elevation over the surroundings: raised ground polygons, hillocks or, where available, boulders. Egg laying begins between May 10 and 22 and is completed by early June. Intervals between successive eggs laid are 2-5 days, averaging 42 hours. A clutch varies considerably, ranging from 4 to 15 eggs over the owl's entire geographic range. Incubation lasts about 32 days. Young begin to leave the nest 14-28 days after hatching, staying within the boundaries of the parents' territory. Young cannot fly until about 30 days after hatching and don't fly well until 50 days old.[103]

As fall begins, adults may depart for more southerly locations. Young of the year often stay on the breeding grounds into winter if lemmings are abundant. Eventually, all age classes move southward, with the largest age category, adult females, occupying areas the farthest north. Members of the smallest size-age category, immature males, occupy the most southerly areas. This outcome appears to be the result of dominance hierarchy; the females push the smaller birds farther south.[104]

Golden eagle

Dale Guthrie and I were lying on a limestone pinnacle in the White Mountains, north of Fairbanks. As we scanned the slopes for sheep, we saw a golden eagle soaring along the ridge top. The three of us were intimately connected at that moment; we were all looking for a Dall sheep to make the wrong move. Of course, Dale and I were looking for rams and the eagle was looking for lambs.

Alaskan golden eagles lead a hard life compared to their relatives in the temperate zone— one more feature Alaskan humans and eagles share. In temperate areas, golden eagles are resident birds, occupying the same landscape year round. However, in Alaska, winters are so harsh that these mighty birds pick up and fly south, sometimes thousands of miles and for up to five months or more. Alaskan golden eagles really are snowbirds.

Golden eagles, *Aquila chrysaetos*, nest in high, mountainous habitats, that is, alpine tundra. Ongoing studies in Denali National Park have provided a lot of information about golden eagles. Reproduction was monitored from 1988 to 1997, all the way through a snowshoe hare ten-year cycle. During the ten-year study the eagles' egg-laying rates, mean brood size and overall productivity varied and were significantly correlated with variation in abundance of snowshoe hares and willow ptarmigan. Production of fledglings during hare highs is seven times what it is at a hare population low. Both hares and ptarmigan are relied on early in the nesting season, the very time when birds are completing their clutches. Laying rates (percentage of nests containing eggs) vary from 33% during the hare low to 90% during the high. However, the number of adults does not fluctuate significantly.[105]

Juvenile golden eagles have been radio-tagged and followed by satellite. Birds hatched in Denali National Park fly south and overwinter over a huge area from northern Mexico to southern Canada. This isn't too surprising. More interesting, perhaps, is that in their first spring migration back to the north, they bypass their natal stomping grounds in the Alaska Range and continue on to the North Slope. By summering on the North Slope, young birds avoid competition with breeding adults, some of which may be their own parents. Also, there is a strong seasonal pulse of food on the North Slope with the birth of caribou calves, emergence of juvenile ground squirrels from their burrows, and the hatching of chicks of a variety of waterfowl and shorebird species.

Winter and summer are both characterized by the movement of juvenile birds. That is, birds don't find a good spot and stay there. Rather, they move a few to hundreds of kilometers a day. Juveniles do not necessarily return to the same locations in their second and third years, either summer or winter.

Birds fledge in late July or early August and remain with their parents until late September or early October. They are on their own from the moment of departure.

Let's return to our golden eagle looking for lambs. Eagles aren't a significant factor in Dall sheep mortality. In response to the presence of eagles, ewes stand over their lambs, making a successful attack on a lamb pretty unlikely. Even though golden eagles are not significant predators on Dall sheep lambs, the bones of Dall sheep juveniles do occasionally show up in the bone piles beneath nests and in the pellets regurgitated by golden eagles.[61]

Over its entire range in North America, golden eagles have been documented to prey on 52 species of mammals, 48 birds, 5 reptiles and 2 fish species.[106] Lagomorphs are important everywhere, including snowshoe hares in the Far North and two species of jackrabbits and the desert cottontail in the lower 48. Ground squirrels and marmots are also significant, both in Alaska and elsewhere.

One controversial aspect of golden eagle feeding is the extent to which they kill domestic lambs. Predation on domestic stock varies considerably but seems to be at its highest levels when hares, including jackrabbits, are at population lows, when alternate prey is hibernating, and when ranchers exhibit poor management practices.[107]

Other than starvation in the first winter, how do eagles meet their doom? One would think that eagles are so formidable that they would be immune from attack by other aerial predators, but that is not the case. Unfledged chicks are susceptible to predation. A group of seven ravens were observed mobbing a golden eagle nest, driving the parent off, and then killing and carrying off the chicks. A cooperative effort by a team of predators can, at times, overpower the most powerful.

Ptarmigan

Ptarmigan, along with grouse, are species of the subfamily Tetraoninae within the family of pheasant-like birds, the Phasianidae. The grouse subfamily is the most northern of the pheasant-like birds and the three ptarmigan species found in Alaska are probably the very best of the grouse at tolerating arctic conditions. All three go through an autumn molt to a white plumage that includes feathers down the legs and onto the toes. The white plumage is, undoubtedly, a camouflage in snow-covered habitats. The feathers on the toes serve two functions. They help insulate the toes, thereby reducing heat loss and saving the bird energy. and feathered toes have a larger surface and, act as snowshoes, facilitating walking on top of the snow.

An important part of their adaptation to arctic and alpine conditions is burrowing. At dusk, ptarmigan seek out snow deep enough and soft enough to allow burrowing. Some birds land on the snow surface and then dig their way through the surface. Others simply fly toward the surface, fold their wings and plunge through the surface. Once under the surface, the bird moves horizontally several body lengths. Often the entrance hole fills in or the tunnel collapses, leaving the bird completely enclosed. The ptarmigan warms its own surroundings to near the bottom of its thermoneutral zone, the range of temperatures where it does not have to shiver. Digging through snow is aided by claws that grow longer in winter.

Fat storage is also important. Rock ptarmigan at Svalbard, Norway are an extreme example; by November, fat accounts for 30% of their body mass. That amount of fat meets only 30% of their total metabolic requirement for winter so they must continue feeding.[108] Although metabolic requirements are higher than in summer, necessitating a considerable food intake, the buds and twigs that make up most of their winter foods are high in fiber and low in protein and metabolizable carbohydrates.

Ptarmigan are visual feeders, and day lengths are very short during the coldest months. Thus, birds in winter have to eat a lot fast. One early February day I went ptarmigan hunting and got eight willow ptarmigan. Two birds collected in the morning had food in their crops weighing less than 1% of their body weights. The other six birds were collected at dusk and their crops averaged 13% of their body weights. There is a seasonal cycle in crop weights in willow ptarmigan from northern Alaska: highest in January, lowest in June and July when forage quality is high.[109]

Two ptarmigan species, willow and rock ptarmigan, are found all the way around the world at high latitudes. That is, they are **holarctic** (entire arctic) or **circumpolar** (around the pole) in distribution. All the other 14 grouse species are confined to either North America or Eurasia.

Willow ptarmigan—The willow ptarmigan, *Lagopus lagopus*, is the largest and most numerous of North America's ptarmigan. It occurs on arctic tundra and alpine habitat in summer, occupying moist tundra with low shrubs of willow and dwarf birch. Populations often exhibit a winter movement to lower elevations (interior Alaska, Alaska Range) or to lower latitudes (barren grounds in Canada, Russia). This southward dispersal may, occasionally, result in willow ptarmigan appearing in the northern tier of the lower 48 states. In Eurasia, the willow ptarmigan occupies a far larger geographic area than the rock ptarmigan. Populations occur in Ireland, Scotland, and England and are more broadly distributed in the Scandinavian countries than the rock ptarmigan. In Scotland, this species is referred to as the red grouse; in Europe it is the willow grouse.

In Alaska, fall altitudinal movements result in dispersal of birds a few to a hundred kilometers or more away from breeding habitat. Willow ptarmigan that breed north of the Brooks Range fly south of the range and occupy winter habitat in the Koyukuk River valley. In the Tanana Uplands, north of Fairbanks, some birds move downslope a short distance into willow thickets while other birds fly down into the boreal forest, occupying valleys along the Chatanika, Chena and Tanana Rivers. These movements tend to segregate the sexes. Males, especially adults, don't move very far from breeding habitat; females may travel considerable distances. One of the factors driving these movements undoubtedly is the crusting of snow on windswept tundra. Birds have a difficult to impossible time trying to burrow through heavily crusted snow to roost for the evening.

Willow ptarmigan are easily confused with rock ptarmigan in the field. Willows have a larger and higher bill than rocks and it is grayish at the base compared to the all-black bill of rocks. This difference persists year-round. In winter, when both species are all white except for the black tail feathers, all male and some female rock ptarmigan have a black line running from the bill through the eye and beyond.

In the spring on the breeding grounds, male willow ptarmigan have chestnut brown plumage on the neck and head (Figure 8.8a); the rest of the body is still winter white. Females have already molted to a mottled reddish-brown plumage that makes them blend in well with their surroundings. In contrast, rock ptarmigan on the breeding grounds in spring are still almost entirely white while females have molted to a brownish-black pattern that provides them with camouflage.

The plumage of red grouse in Scotland, a subspecies of willow ptarmigan, differs from that of Alaskan birds in several ways. The wing feathers of red grouse are brown throughout the year; they never turn white. The feathers on the body don't molt to completely white either. Males, year-round, tend to look like Alaska males do when on the breeding grounds. Clearly, the lack of consistent and persistent snow cover in Scotland is acting as a selective pressure on the basic willow ptarmigan pattern.

At what point will it be appropriate to call the red grouse a separate, recognizable species? Not yet. Scottish birds are, undoubtedly, capable of producing fully fertile offspring if mated to non-Scottish willow ptarmigan. When they cannot or, because of newly evolved behavioral differences, will not produce offspring, they will have evolved into a separate species.

In early spring willow ptarmigan move back to their breeding habitat on the tundra. Adult males attempt to establish and defend breeding territories. A territorial male displays by standing on an exposed rock or in the top of a spruce tree above tree line. While displaying, males call in a characteristic posture, leaning forward with a bend in the neck. A similar neck configuration is adopted by males during song flights. Once a male establishes his territory he occasionally patrols the boundaries with a **walking-in-line** display with the male from the adjacent territory. The parallel sets of tracks in the snow, 0.5-2.0 m apart, mark the boundary line. A territorial male will chase an intruding male from his territory. If the intruder flies away, the territorial male often gives chase, crossing several adjacent territories in the process. Each successive territorial male takes up the chase.

Females arrive on the breeding grounds about two weeks after the males. They are attracted to males with large territories, that display vigorously and that have large eye combs. Courtship by the male involves song flights and, on the ground, tail fan and wing droop displays. Some additional displays described for willow ptarmigan include a rapid-stamping display and a head-wagging display.[111] If the male makes all the right moves, copulation follows. Willow ptarmigan are unique among grouse in that males maintain a pair bond with the female throughout the reproductive season and until his brood of young are independent.

Clutch size varies from year to year and at different geographic locations. First clutches range from 4 to 14 eggs. Several instances of larger numbers of eggs in a single nest have been recorded, but these are likely the result of a female laying some of her eggs in another female's nest. This phenomenon is called **brood parasitism** and saves the sneaky female the energy of incubating and feeding some of her own chicks. The incubation period lasts 21-23 days, during which the female centers the eggs under her **brood patch**, a featherless area on her underside that warms the eggs.

After less than 24 hours of tapping by the chicks, they emerge from the shell with a complete covering of cryptic, downy feathers. Eyes are already open and wing primary feathers are present as quills tipped with down. In good weather, chicks are thermally independent of parents by the 10th day. However, in inclement weather they are brooded at least through the third week. Chicks can fly by 10-12 days of age; wings reach adult length in 60 days.

Both willow and rock ptarmigan exhibit pronounced population cycles over much of their ranges. The period between population peaks is 8-11 years in Newfoundland and Northwest Territories, 4-8 years in Scotland and 3-4 years in Norway.[111] There is some evidence that willow ptarmigan populations cycle roughly in synchrony with those of snowshoe hares. Thus, predators unable to find hares during their population declines may switch to alternative prey, ptarmigan. In Norway, lemmings are the principal small mammals undergoing population fluctuations; they exhibit 3-4 year cycles. So, predation might drive the cycle.

A second idea, first articulated from studies of red grouse in Scotland, is that ptarmigan change their territorial spacing behavior through the cycle. At high population densities, males are thought to be more aggressive and establish larger territories. The result is that a high proportion of birds fail to establish territories, are forced into marginal habitat, and, therefore, are exposed to higher mortality due to starvation and predation. The driving force of the cycle, in this case, is the bird's behavior, not predation. A third possibility is that variation in chick production during the breeding season causes the cycles. The potential causes for this variation might be weather cycles, cyclic availability in food resources, or endogenous cycles in the birds themselves.[111]

Willow ptarmigan eat a variety of foods. Summer foods include the fruits of blueberries, cranberries and crowberries, horsetail tips and the leaves of willows and blueberries. Insects and other terrestrial invertebrates are important, especially to young of the year. Insects are higher in protein content than plant material and, thus, would benefit rapidly growing, young birds. In winter, the buds and twigs of willows make up 80% of the diet; most of the remainder consists of dwarf birch buds and catkins. In Newfoundland, the buds and twigs of cranberry, blueberry, birch and alder are also eaten. The switch to higher quality forage in spring is accompanied by a reduction in the size of the ceca and small intestine. Recall, the ceca are an adaptation for digesting fiber found in many herbivorous birds and mammals.

Rock ptarmigan—The rock ptarmigan, *Lagopus mutus,* is even better adapted to the Arctic than the willow ptarmigan. In North America, rock ptarmigan can be found on all the islands of the Canadian High Arctic whereas the willow is missing on many of those islands. Rock ptarmigan are found on Greenland, Iceland and Spitsbergen, where willow ptarmigan are absent. Relict populations of rock ptarmigan exist in the Pyrenees and the Alps. The ptarmigan my son, Andy, and his family see in the mountains of central Honshu, Japan, are rock ptarmigan.

Habitats frequented by rock ptarmigan are higher, rockier and drier than those of willow ptarmigan. When not actively feeding, flocks typically hunker down out of the wind in skree slopes and boulder fields on tops of domes in interior Alaska. In summer and early fall in the Alaska Range, rock ptarmigan are found upslope from willow ptarmigan but lower than white-tailed ptarmigan.

Rock ptarmigan, as do the other two species, go through a series of three molts from spring to autumn. The camouflage plumage of late spring through early fall differs somewhat from the rusty, reddish-brown of willows. Rock ptarmigan tend to be yellow-black in Alaska's interior, although there is considerable color variation across the 26 subspecies recognized worldwide. In breeding season males are entirely white except for the black tail feathers and red eye comb (Figure 8.8b); females have already molted to a camouflage plumage.

Winter habitat is, in interior Alaska, close to breeding habitat. Rock ptarmigan move downslope to shrubby areas at timberline, where they find their principal winter food, dwarf birch. Buds and catkins of this species make up from 80% to 100% of the winter diet, with much of the remainder consisting of willow buds and twigs.[112] Rock ptarmigan feed mainly from the ground, whereas willow ptarmigan can often be seen feeding in the tops of willows in winter. In late winter, snow may be so crusted as to preclude feeding. Inuits report that rock ptarmigan follow caribou and muskoxen in winter and early spring, feeding where these large mammals have broken through the crust.

Late spring through early fall, rock ptarmigan enjoy a greater variety of foods including lowbush cranberries, crowberries, bog blueberries, the buds and twigs of arctic willow, arctic poppy seed capsules, *Dryas* leaves, saxifrage buds, buttercup flowers and heather buds.[113,114] Chicks eat berries and caterpillars to a greater extent than do adults.

Rock ptarmigan chicks, upon hatching, remain in the nest until their feathers are dry. Then they make brief forays of up to 1 m away from the nest, then return to be brooded. They grow rapidly, doubling body weight every week for the first five weeks. Alaskan rock ptarmigan chicks are better able to maintain body temperature than are willow ptarmigan of similar ages.[115] This fact could be due to larger hatching weights or the faster growth rates exhibited by the rock ptarmigan. The critical comparisons, yet to be done, are (a) between Alaskan rock and Alaskan willow ptarmigan chicks and (b) between Alaskan and Norwegian rock ptarmigan chicks.

Predators of rock ptarmigan are numerous. Adults fall prey to golden eagles, gyrfalcons, peregrine falcons, snowy owls, arctic foxes and red foxes. Eggs and chicks are taken by arctic ground squirrels, ravens, short-tailed weasels, gulls and long-tailed jaegers.[114]

White-tailed ptarmigan—The white-tailed ptarmigan, *Lagopus leucurus*, is entirely North American; it can be found the farthest south of the ptarmigans. It occurs from the Kenai Peninsula and the central Alaska Range through much of the Yukon, Northwest Territories and British Columbia southward into the Cascades of Washington and the Rocky Mountains from Montana to New Mexico. Vancouver Island, B.C., supports a population of white-tailed ptarmigan. This species has been introduced into the Wallawa Mountains of Oregon, the Sierra Navadas in California and the Uinta

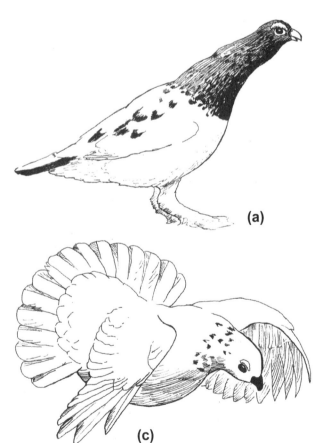

Figure 8.8: Male ptarmigan exhibiting spring-time breeding plumage and inflated combs over their eyes. a) willow ptarmigan in a calling posture. Head and neck covered with reddish-brown feathers; b) rock ptarmigan beginning a courtship display. All white except for tail feathers; c) white-tailed ptarmigan exhibiting strutting behavior. All white except for a few dark feathers around neck. During courtship and breeding the females of all three species are mottled and camouflaged. Redrawn from Johnsgard (1983).

Mountains in Utah and reintroduced into the Pecos Wilderness of New Mexico. Distribution through the Rockies is sporadic; white-tailed ptarmigan are missing from some areas to which they are suited.

As the name suggests, this is the only ptarmigan or grouse species, worldwide, with white tail feathers in winter. The white-tailed ptarmigan is the smallest of North American grouse species and the most limited in its North American distribution. Where this species occurs with willow and rock ptarmigan, it occupies habitats with highest elevation, including rocky skree slopes and boulder fields near glaciers and snowfields.[116]

The male courtship display or strut is similar to that exhibited by male willow ptarmigan, with tail fanned and wings drooping, but the white-tailed male holds its head lower to the ground. Males in breeding season can be distinguished from willows and rocks by the indistinct "necklace" of dark feathers around the neck of an, otherwise, white bird (Figure 8.8c). Females, as in the other two species, are ahead of males in the molt during breeding season and appear camouflaged.

At hatching, chicks begin to grow rapidly and can fly after 10 to12 days. Wing primary feathers grow at 5-6 mm per day. The plumage of the hatchling is continuously replaced for the first 16 weeks, transitioning from down to winter plumage. By mid-October to early November the birds are completely white. The other two ptarmigans are on approximately the same molting timetable.

What happens when snow comes late to the tundra? Since molting is keyed by changes in day length, a ptarmigan population may have molted to white while the tundra is still brown.

These birds are more susceptible to predation than normally. Lack of snow, year after year, would eventually lead to a population that retained its summer camouflage plumage. Such is the case with the Scottish red grouse variant of willow ptarmigan, mentioned above.

In Alaska, this species feeds on the catkins of alder and dwarf birch, the leaves of willows and mountain avens and the buds of willow and dwarf birch. Crowberries are also a part of the diet.[117] When white-tailed ptarmigan co-occur with the other two species, they select different foods and, thus, avoid competition.[113]

Tundra and trumpeter swan

Most falls, my wife and I, sometimes accompanied by my younger son, fly out west of Iliamna Lake for a week of camping and caribou hunting. One of the most enjoyable aspects of the trip is looking down from the plane and seeing the pairs of swans on the tundra lakes. If we schedule our trip in early September, we often see groups of four or five swans, clear evidence that some adults successfully raised a brood of young. We always see swans flying gracefully low over the tundra, moving from pond to pond, presumably to feed.

Actually, there are two swan species in Alaska: the tundra swan, *Olor columbianus*, and the trumpeter swan, *Olor buccinator*. Both breed in Alaska. The trumpeter swan, near extinction in the 1930s, made a spectacular comeback in the late 20th century. Alaskan trumpeters breed in the forested areas of interior and south-central Alaska and number over 13,000 birds.[118] This represents about 80% of the world's trumpeters. The trumpeter is our largest waterfowl species, with males and females averaging about 12.7 kg (28 lb) and 10.0 kg (22 lb), respectively. Adults are all-white, their bills are black, wedge-shaped and appear to merge with the eye. Trumpeters have huge eggs, sometimes 13 cm (5 inches) long. Trumpeters build nest sites in marshes by pulling vegetation and piling it into a mound. The mound is 0.3-0.6 m (1-2 ft) above water level, 2-4 m (6-12 ft) in diameter and surrounded by a moat. The female lays 2-7 eggs that she alone incubates. Her mate sticks around to defend the nest.

Tundra swans are smaller, males and females averaging 7.2 kg (16 lb) and 6.3 kg (13.8 lb), respectively. Adults are usually all white but, unlike trumpeter swans, have bills with convex upper surface. The black bill often has a yellow spot near the eye; the eye appears to be separate from the bill.

Tundra swans nest near tundra ponds or lakes, usually in coastal delta areas. In western Alaska, the highest population densities are found in areas of low relief, wet meadows and shallow lakes with emergent vegetation. On the North Slope, birds prefer larger lakes but also use polygon ponds near a larger body of water. Tundra swans build nests similar to those of trumpeters. Unlike trumpeters, both sexes participate in incubation. During the incubation first one adult, then the other begins molting, which leaves them temporarily flightless. Eggs are incubated for 31-35 days. The young, or **cygnets,** spend 11-15 weeks before fledging. Young of the year are able to fly about three weeks earlier than young trumpeter swans, allowing tundra swans to successfully raise a brood in a shorter breeding season.

In summer tundra swans feed on a variety of marsh plants, including horsetail, pondweed, sedge, water milfoil, pond lily, *Nostoc* alga and bulrush. Their long necks make it easy to feed up to 1 m below the surface simply by dabbling. Cygnets are fed a high-protein diet of invertebrates for the first several weeks and then gradually switch to the vegetarian diet of their parents. Several observations have been made of parents presenting food directly to a cygnet. In addition, parents use their feet to paddle submerged food to the surface; their chicks follow closely behind and feed on this surface material. If the parent ceases paddling up submerged food, the cygnet may peck the parent on the rump[119] as if saying, "hey, where's my food?" On the wintering grounds, swans feed on waste grains, agricultural crops and some aquatic vegetation.

I mentioned the eastern and western populations of tundra swans in Chapter 2. All swans migrate long distances in the fall to reach wintering habitat. Swans that breed on Alaska's Arctic Coastal Plain, part of the eastern population, fly to the Chesapeake Bay area. These birds tend to depart on favorable winds and travel both day and night to reach widely spaced staging areas. On the return migration in the spring, birds travel relatively short distances and occupy more staging areas. Wintertime is stressful on swans with adult birds losing about 15% to 19% of their body weight. Spring staging areas are probably critical for picking up energy reserves that will be needed for breeding. Western population swans, breeding in western and south-central Alaska, fly to wintering areas in southern Alberta, Utah, Nevada and coastal locales in Washington, Oregon, and California.[119]

Jaegers

Jaegers are gull-like, predatory birds that breed at high latitudes and migrate south for the winter. Three species occupy tundra nesting sites in summertime Alaska and a fourth may also be seen occasionally. European birders refer to the jaeger species as skuas and, indeed, the primarily Southern Hemisphere skuas are closely related to Northern Hemisphere jaegers. The three species that regularly breed in Alaska are: pomarine jaeger (pomarine skua), parasitic jaeger (arctic skua), and long-tailed jaeger (long-tailed skua). The occasional visitor is the skua, *Catharacta skua*, referred to by European birders as the great skua.

When viewed in flight or while on the ground, jaegers look like gulls. In fact, they are related to gulls. According to some biologists, jaegers and skuas constitute a subfamily within the Laridae (gulls, terns, kittiwakes and jaegers). In another scheme, jaegers and skuas are placed in their own family, the Stercocorariidae, closely related to the Laridae.

The flight muscles and flight feathers of jaegers are stronger than those of gulls and allow them to fly faster and be more maneuverable than gulls. Their feet are webbed like gull feet but, unlike gulls, their toes have claws. The lower leg (tarsus) of jaegers has hard scutes like raptors and unlike the softer, fleshier skin on gull legs. The bills of jaegers are more strongly hooked than those of gulls. The central pair of tail feathers of jaegers protrude from the back of the tail to some extent whereas those of gulls do not. Finally, jaegers have **supraorbital salt glands** and gulls don't. These glands, positioned over the eye, can secrete a highly concentrated salt solution, allowing these birds to drink seawater. No wonder jaegers and skuas can spend months at sea in their nonbreeding seasons.

Because of their physical characteristics, flight capabilities, and feeding habits, jaegers are often referred to as sea falcons. Their close relatives, terns and gulls, are also predatory but not to the extreme exhibited by the jaegers. All jaegers, to some extent, harass other birds in flight in order to make them either drop or regurgitate their food. Once the victim releases the food item, the jaeger dives for it. This food stealing is another example of kleptoparasitism, similar in principle to pikas' theft of their neighbor's hay piles. The parasitic jaeger is the most adept at and dependent on kleptoparasitism for its nutrition. Under some circumstances the harassment turns into a predatory attack in which the victim bird is forced down to the surface and killed. In addition, small fish and invertebrates are killed and eaten at sea. On or near land, during breeding season, jaegers rely on rodents, young birds and scavenging to meet their nutritional requirements.

Jaegers exhibit three different plumages. Summertime finds adults in their **definitive alternate plumage**. This corresponds to breeding plumage, and each species exhibits its own distinctive configuration of central tail feathers (central retrices). In each species there are light, dark, and intermediate morphs of this plumage. During Northern Hemisphere winter, when birds are absent from Alaska, adults adopt a **basic plumage** featuring barring of dorsal and ventral surfaces and loss of the distinctive central retrices. The **juvenal plumage** of immature birds differs from the other two plumages and also occurs in light, intermediate and dark morphs. Identification of jaeger species in basic and juvenal plumages is extremely difficult.[120]

Long-tailed jaeger—Many years ago, I walked off the Denali Highway into the mountains looking for caribou. On a high ridge I watched a kestrel hovering, waiting for a vole to show itself. At first, I thought it was a kestrel. After watching a while I realized that the bird looked a lot like a gull and it had very long tail feathers; it wasn't a kestrel. I had seen my first long-tailed jaeger. This is the only jaeger that hovers in the air, waiting for prey.

The long-tailed, *Stercorarius longicaudus*, is the smallest and most abundant of the jaegers and is the most widely distributed in North America. Long-tailed jaegers breed farther north than the other two, occupying nesting habitats on the north and east coasts of Greenland and all the High Canadian Arctic islands. Nests of long-tailed jaegers are found in passes, valleys and foothills of the Brooks Range but not on the Arctic Coastal Plain. Birds also breed in the mountains of central Alaska, that is, the Alaska Range and Tanana Uplands. It was one of these Alaska Range birds that I mistook for a kestrel. In addition, summer breeders are found in the western Alaska Yukon-Kuskokwim delta and in the Kodiak Island group.

Although the long-tailed jaeger is fairly dependent on lemmings for its breeding success, it does not exhibit large fluctuations in population size. In other words, these jaegers are able to switch to other prey to at least maintain adult populations. In years of high lemming density a maximum of two eggs are produced per clutch, and these eggs are somewhat larger than eggs laid in years of intermediate lemming popula-

tion density. Usually no eggs are laid during lemming population lows.[121]

Typically, two eggs are laid two days apart and, should predators get them, there is always only a single replacement egg. Eggs are greenish to olive brown with a few dark brown spots or wavy lines. Incubation begins with the first egg so chicks hatch separately and there is a sizable (20-50%) difference in chick sizes. Both sexes incubate their eggs, but the female has the larger role. Both adults have incubation patches where the feathers are missing. The egg is held between one foot and the patch on that side. Of course, the bare skin of the patch warms the egg better than if it were held against the feathers. Adults may brood hatchlings for a day to a week after they hatch. In northern Alaska, young begin flying by the end of July or early August. From hatching to fledging takes about 50 days in years of high rodent density and a few days longer at lower prey densities.

In the High Arctic, long-tailed jaegers feed almost exclusively on collared lemmings. In addition to the hovering mentioned above, birds also watch from high points for rodents. Lemmings are often pursued on foot. Hunting success on lemmings is about 27% of strikes, one kill per 102 min or 3.5 lemmings per day. Intact lemmings are too large for jaeger chicks; parents dismember the rodents and feed bits to their young.

Other prey includes voles, small fish, midges, juvenile birds and insects. Fledgling snow buntings and Lapland longspurs are pursued in the air, forced to the ground, and killed. Young sandpipers are sometimes caught in flight. Other birds in the diet of long-tailed jaegers include king eider, red knot, black-bellied plover, sanderling, ruddy turnstone, lesser yellowlegs and ptarmigan.[121] Insects in the diet include flies, beetles, ants, earwigs, mayflies, and moths, especially caterpillars.

Pomarine jaeger—The pomarine jaeger, *Stercorarius pomarinus*, is the largest of the three species frequenting Alaska's tundra. This jaeger is distinguished from the other two by its heavier build, broader wings, and relatively larger head and bill. The central tail feathers are twisted and shorter than those of the long-tailed jaeger.

It is also, of the three, the species most closely tied to lemmings for successful reproduction. As I mentioned above, lemming cycles tend to produce high population densities every third or fourth year; those population highs are essential for breeding success in pomarine jaegers. When lemmings are absent over large areas, pomarine jaegers leave the Arctic in early to mid-summer.

Pomarine jaegers have the most restricted breeding distribution in Alaska and elsewhere in North America. They don't breed as Far North as the long-tailed or as far south as either of the other two species. Their breeding habitat is low-lying, wet tundra. In Alaska, pomarine jaegers breed on the Yukon River delta, around Barrow, Bethel, Hooper Bay, Cape Lisburne, Wainwright, and much of the Arctic Coastal Plain. On the Asian side of Bering Strait, birds breed on the northern Chukotsk Peninsula, Wrangel Island, and numerous points to the westward. Experts on jaegers describe breeding in this species as erratic. There are numerous breeders in years when lemming populations are high, but few to none when lemmings are low or absent. For example on Bathurst Island there were many breeding birds in 1969 and 1971 (lemming highs) but none in 1970, 1972, or 1973

when lemmings were low. Where no lemmings are ever present, such as in eastern Greenland, pomarine jaegers don't breed at all.[122]

Northward migration in the spring is typically along coasts; there is no clear evidence that this species regularly flies continental routes to arctic North America. Instead, the Bering Sea (Pacific) and Davis Strait (Atlantic) are the gateways or flyways to the Arctic. In western North America, St. Lawrence Island is passed in mid-May.[123] Birds are near Barrow by late May and continue to arrive and roost until mid-June. In a good breeding year, birds return westward and then head southward beginning in August. In years characterized by low population densities of lemmings, initial arrival in the Far North is delayed until the first week in June, fewer birds show up, and they turn around and fly westward shortly thereafter. This poses an interesting question: how do pomarine jaegers anticipate poor lemming years? Do they have biological clocks with alarms programmed to go off every three years? We just don't know.

Brown lemmings are, in the North American Arctic, the single most important food. Pomarine jaeger nesting and breeding occurs in several places with high concentrations of other rodents: tundra vole in northern Alaska; collared lemming on Bathurst Island. Lemming availability is highest in early June as snows melt, exposing these rodents to predation. Due to their reproductive output, lemmings increase again in mid-July as jaegers begin to feed young. Nesting densities can be as high as 9-10/ km², perhaps ten times the breeding density of long-tailed jaegers.

How many lemmings do pomarine jaegers eat? The 24-day development from new hatchling to fledged bird requires about 200 collared lemmings, and an additional 170 are needed to make it through the rest of the summer. Adults eat about 340 collared lemmings of about 50 g each. Brown lemmings, at 150 g each, are easier to subsist on; jaegers could, perhaps, spend less time and be more efficient foraging for these larger prey. Pomarine jaegers account for about 60% of all predation on brown lemmings, about 75 lemmings per hectare.[124]

Pomerine jaegers hunt (fly) closer to the ground than long-tailed jaegers, about 3-10 m (10-33 feet), and hover less. After the ground thaws, pomarines actively dig up lemmings, a behavior not practiced by the other two jaegers. In addition to lemmings, these predators take the eggs of Lapland longspurs, short-eared owls, snow geese, black brant and the chicks of shorebirds and ducks. Apparently, they are capable of killing adult phalaropes and other shorebirds.

In Alaska these birds also feed on arctic cod in the north and capelin in the south. They usually take fish and fish waste from the water's surface but can dive from the surface or while in flight. They can swim underwater and pursue prey. Kleptoparasitism is relied on far less by this species than by the parasitic jaeger. To the extent that food is pirated from other birds, it is mainly accomplished by attacking birds that have just surfaced.

Winter habitat is productive tropical and subtropical waters. Birds are commonly seen in the Caribbean, including the Lesser Antilles, north coast of South America and off Florida. Our Alaskan birds probably winter along the Pacific coast from California to Peru.[122]

Parasitic jaeger—As the common name suggests, the parasitic jaeger, *Stercorarius parasiticus*, is the most accomplished of jaegers at kleptoparasitism (Figure 8.9). In the northeast Atlantic, pirating food from other birds is the primary means of food acquisition. However, in the North American Arctic, kleptoparasitism is uncommon, with only an occasional report of this jaeger pestering gulls, loons, or terns. No one has studied parasitic jaegers breeding near seabird colonies in the Aleutians or Bering Sea. I would guess that seabird colonies offer jaegers more opportunities for pirating food than tundra habitats and that kleptoparasitism would, therefore, be more common in the Aleutians. In the Atlantic a variety of seabirds are attacked, including common and thick-billed murres, black-legged kittiwakes, black guillemots, arctic terns, and puffins. In addition to pirating from adults, parasitic jaegers prey on seabird chicks. One final point: parasites often have their own parasites. A study on the lower St. Lawrence River in Canada found that parasitic jaegers hunting birds lost most of their prey to larger

Figure 8.9: Parasitic jaeger pursuing a common tern. The tern will probably drop the food and the jaeger will retrieve it. The jaeger will often kill the other bird, especially if it is much smaller.

herring gulls. Single birds lost 75% of their prey; birds hunting in pairs lost only 42%.

In the Far North parasitic jaegers rely on birds as prey and, sometimes, on rodents. This jaeger is least tied to rodents for breeding success. Adult birds that fall prey to these birds include plovers, sandpipers, phalaropes, willow ptarmigan, common eider and other ducks, snow buntings, Lapland longspurs, horned lark, yellow wagtail and savannah sparrow. The eggs and chicks of a variety of birds are also taken. Predation on adult birds is often accomplished in flight by grasping with the beak or striking with the wings. The prey is usually forced out of the air and then killed.

Cooperative hunting was mentioned above. One obvious advantage is reduction of losses to other kleptoparasites. The other potential advantage is more effective hunting. Pairs often leave their chicks for a time to hunt together. Shorebirds and small perching birds are often hunted by pairs of jaegers. One individual chases the prey near the ground; the other flies 6-10 m above to prevent escape by flying upward. Sometimes the prey is seized in mid-air; sometimes it lands and is caught on the ground. Predation on eggs is also often a cooperative venture. Incubating gulls and loons are driven off their nests and their eggs taken. The nests of snow geese are occasionally pilfered in the same way, although the geese put up a stout defense.

Mammalian prey in northern Alaska include brown lemming, collared lemming, arctic ground squirrel, ermine, tundra vole, and arctic shrew. When voles are hunted, the jaeger often hops along the ground with wings spread, herding voles until they can be seized. The diet of birds and mammals is occasionally supplemented with insects and, when handy to the nest, tundra berries. Because of its ability to take birds for food, the parasitic jaeger is more independent of lemming cycles for its reproductive success.

Breeding in Alaska occurs along the Arctic Coastal Plain and inland to the foothills of the Brooks Range. Breeding populations also occur on the Bering Sea coast, Alaska Peninsula, Aleutians, Kodiak Island and the south-central coastline near Yakutat and Glacier Bay. In the Far North, birds first arrive in foothills and passes of the Brooks Range in the last week of May and in Barrow the first or second week in June.[126] Since parasitic jaegers aren't observed migrating along the Bering coast and since earliest arrivals are inland, birds are probably migrating north overland. This contrasts with the migration patterns of the other two jaegers. In southwest Alaska birds are on breeding territories by the middle of May.

Egg laying in the Brooks Range foothills occurs around May 29-June 10 with hatching from June 25 to July 7. Near Barrow, the corresponding dates are June 14-19 and June 25-July 17, respectively. This gives an incubation period of about 26.5 days. Incubation begins with the laying of the first egg; the second egg is usually laid 2-2.5 days later. Therefore, chicks hatch about 2-2.5 days apart. Young birds fly by the last week in July or first week in August, that is, 27-30 days after hatching. Clutch size is usually two eggs but first-time breeders typically have only a single egg.

Mortality in the first year is about 28% in Scotland and probably 10-20% per year thereafter.[127] What actually kills these birds? Arctic foxes and gulls take a toll on both eggs and chicks. Inclement weather also is a significant factor. Since both parents are absent from their chicks about 50% of the time in northern Alaska as compared to less than 5% for long-tailed jaegers, predation on chicks may be higher than is the case for the other two jaegers.

Snow bunting

I described the migration of snow buntings in Chapter 2. Males arrive on the breeding grounds four to six weeks ahead of the females. These birds initially roost in groups in protected areas in rocky habitat but, shortly, begin to establish territories. A suitable territory is one that has cavities or deep crevices in broken rock or cliffs. These cavities are the potential nesting sites to which females will be attracted. Optimal habitat consists of rock and boulder patches near areas of vegetated tundra that thaw early in the spring. Poor habitat is open tundra with few or no rocks; in such areas population densities of snow buntings are low. Good breeding territories in some areas are at a premium and males arrive as early as possible to compete for these limited sites.

Once a territorial male has courted and won a female, the pair begins a search for a nest site. Nests are placed in narrow cracks between rocks, averaging 27 cm (10 inches) from the cavity entrance. The nest itself is thick and made primarily of mosses and dry grasses. The nest is lined with fine grass, bird feathers and fur for better insulation against the cold. The feathers of buntings, rock ptarmigan, jaegers, gulls, and snowy owls and the fur of arctic fox, lemmings, hare, muskoxen, and caribou have been found in snow bunting nests.

The day the nest is completed the female begins to lay eggs. A clutch of 5-6 eggs is laid, and each egg is about 9% of the body weight of the female. Incubation of the eggs doesn't begin until the clutch is complete or almost complete, and hatching is not entirely synchronous. Only the female incubates the eggs, but her mate brings her food. Why do males bring food to their mates? In Lapland longspurs, which nest in more open tundra habitats, males do not feed their females during incubation. Apparently, female buntings need the extra energy because of the very cold microclimate of the nesting cavity itself. These birds lay their eggs where the sun never shines and where ground temperatures are much colder than out in the open.[127]

What, then, is the advantage of nesting in one of the coldest microhabitats on the tundra? Undoubtedly, snow buntings suffer lower rates of nest predation than do birds that nest out in the open.[128] In spite of being tucked away and hidden, nests are still discovered and eggs and chicks are still lost to predators. The principal predator in the High Canadian Arctic is the arctic fox, but the short-tailed weasel is also important. Eggs are also taken by lemmings (*Dicrostonyx* and *Lemmus*) and arctic ground squirrels. Adults fall prey to gyrfalcons, peregrine falcons, long-tailed jaegers and snowy owls.[129] Nest predation is higher in years following a lemming population high. This is one more example of predators switching to alternative prey when their principal food resource becomes scarce.

Feeding by snow buntings is almost always conducted on the ground. In most seasons these birds concentrate on vegetation recently exposed by melting. Birds walk or hop along the ground pecking at food. Sometimes a bird will jump on a plant to knock its seeds to the ground; sometimes it will step on the plant to bend it within range of its beak. In the Far North, important food items are grass seeds, crowberry, bog blueberry, bistort, and poppy. The diets of nestlings consist almost entirely of animal matter. Prey groups include cranefly adults and larvae, midges, spiders, butterflies, mosquitoes, and beetles. Several studies suggest that adult snow buntings are not very selective about the invertebrates they bring to the nest; they simply take what is out there. In other words, the proportions of invertebrate prey are about the same as the potential prey abundance in the locale. Again, the significance of a seed-eating bird feeding its offspring insects and spiders is to provide them with enough protein to accomplish the rapid growth in body tissues required to complete this early development.

Newly hatched chicks are altricial, with their eyes closed. Development is rapid, with hatching weight doubling by day 2 and increasing tenfold, to about 30 g, by day 10. So, by the tenth day, chicks have attained about 80% of the adult weight and are almost ready to leave the nest cavity. By the eleventh or twelfth day the young birds can fly.

Here are some other interesting facts about snow buntings. Birds roost each evening. In winter, they roost in slight depressions in the snow and during snowstorms may allow themselves to be covered by the snow. At temperatures below -7°C, they roost on the lee sides of snowdrifts; at severe temperatures (-35°C) they burrow into the snow much as do ptarmigan. In the high arctic summer when there is no nighttime, snow buntings still spend 2-5 hours roosting in what would be night at lower latitudes.[129] Average date of first arrival in spring in Fairbanks is March 18.

REFERENCES

1 Geist, V. 1991. Bones of contention revisited: did antlers enlarge with sexual selection as a consequence of neonatal security strategies? Applied Animal Behaviour Science 29: 453-469.

2 Fancy, S. G. and White, R.G. 1985. Energy expenditures by caribou while cratering in snow. Journal of Wildlife Management 49: 987-993.

3 Cameron, R. D. 1994. Reproductive pauses by female caribou. Journal of Mammalogy 75: 10-13.

4 Cameron, R. D., Smith, W.T., Fancy, S.G., Gerhart, K.L. and White, R.G.. 1993. Calving success of female caribou in relation to body weight. Canadian Journal of Zoology 71: 480-486.

5 Hemming, J.E. 1994. Caribou. Alaska Department of Fish and Game Wildlife Notebook Series, 2 pp.

6 Russell, D. E., Fancy, S.G., Whitten, K.R. and White, R.G. 1991. Overwinter survival of orphan caribou, *Rangifer tarandus*, calves. Canadian Field-Naturalist 105: 103-105.

7 Gasaway, W.C., Stephenson, R.O., Davis, J.L., Shepherd, P.E.K. and Burris, O.E. 1983. Interrelationships of wolves, prey, and man in interior Alaska. Wildlife Monographs 84: 1-50.

8 Dale, B.W., Adams, L.G. and Bowyer, R.T. 1994. Functional response of wolves preying on barren-ground caribou in a multiple-prey ecosystem. Journal of Animal Ecology 63: 644-652.

9   Skogland, T. 1986. Density dependent food limitation and maximal production in wild reindeer herds. Journal of Wildlife Management 50: 314-319.

10   Syroechkovskii, E.E. 1995. Wild reindeer. Smithsonian Institution Libraries, Washington D.C.

11   Morschel, F.M. 1996. Effects of weather and parasitic insects on summer ecology of caribou of the Delta herd. MS Thesis, University of Alaska Fairbanks, 80 pp.

12   Kuropat, P. J. 1984. Foraging behavior of caribou on a calving ground in northwestern Alaska. MS Thesis, University of Alaska Fairbanks, 95 pp.

13   Klein, D. R. 1982. Fire, lichens and caribou. Journal of Range Management 35: 390-395.

14   Klein, D. R. and Vlasova, T.J. 1992. Lichens, a unique forage resource threatened by air pollution. Rangifer 12(1): 21-27.

15   Klein, D.R. 1991. Caribou in the changing north. Applied Animal Behaviour Science 29: 279-291.

16   Dau, J.R. and Cameron, R.D. 1986. Effects of a road system on caribou distribution during calving. Rangifer Special Issue No. 1: 95-101.

17   Whitten, K.R. and Cameron, R.D. 1985. Distribution of caribou calving in relation to the Prudhoe Bay Oilfield. In: A.M. Martell and D.E. Russell, editors, Caribou and Human Activity, Proceedings of the first North American Caribou Workshop, Whitehorse, Y.T., Canada, 1983. Canadian Wildlife Service Special Publication, Ottawa, pp. 35-39.

18   Mead, J. I. 1987. Quaternary records of pika, Ochotona, in North America. Boreas 16: 165-171.

19   Orr, R.T. 1977. The little-known pika. Macmillan, New York, 144 pp.

20   Meany, C. A. 1987. Cheek-gland odors in pikas (Ochotona princeps): discrimination of individual and sex differences. Journal of Mammalogy 68: 391-395.

21   Conner, D. A. 1985. The function of the pika short call in individual recognition. Zeitschrift fur Tierphyschology 67: 131-143.

22   Broadbooks, H. E. 1965. Ecology and distribution of the pikas of Washington and Alaska. American Midland Naturalist 73: 299-335.

23   Conner, D. A. 1984. The role of an acoustic display in territorial maintenance in the pika. Canadian Journal of Zoology 62: 1906-1909.

24   Huntly, N. J. 1987. Influence of refuging consumers (pikas: Ochotona princeps) on subalpine meadow vegetation. Ecology 68: 274-283.

25   del Moral, R. 1984. The impact of the Olympic marmot on subalpine vegetation structure. American Journal of Botany 71: 1228-1236.

26   Holmes, W. G. 1991. Predator risk affects foraging behaviour of pikas: observational and experimental evidence. Animal Behavior 42: 111-119.

27   Huntly, N. J., Smith, A.T. and Ivins, B.L. 1986. Foraging behavior of the pika (Ochotona princeps), with comparisons of grazing versus haying. Journal of Mammalogy 67: 139-148.

28 McKechnie, A. M., Smith, A.T. and Peacock, M.M. 1994. Kleptoparasitism in pikas (*Ochotona princeps*): theft of hay. Journal of Mammalogy 75: 488-491.

29 Gessaman, J. A. and Goliszek, A.G. 1989. Marmot scats supplement hay pile vegetation as food energy for pikas. Great Basin Naturalist 49: 466-468.

30 Rausch, R. L. 1962. Notes on the collared pika, *Ochotona collaris* (Nelson), in Alaska. Murrelet 42: 22-24.

31 Southwick, C. H., Golian, S.C., Whitworth, M.R., Halfpenny, J.C. and Brown, R. 1986. Population density and fluctuations of pikas (*Ochotona princeps*) in Colorado. Journal of Mammalogy 67: 149-153.

32 Brandt, C. A. 1989. Mate choice and reproductive success of pikas. Animal Behavior 37: 118-132.

33 Petterson, J. R. 1992. Yellow-bellied marmot, *Marmota flaviventris*, predation on pikas, *Ochotona princeps*. Canadian Field-Naturalist 106: 130-131.

34 Chitty, D. 1996. Do lemmings commit suicide: beautiful hypotheses and ugly facts. Oxford University Press, 268 pp.

35 Reid, D.G. and Krebs, C.J. 1996. Limitations to collared lemming population growth in winter. Canadian Journal of Zoology 74: 1284-1291.

36 Engstrom, M.D. 1999. Collared lemmings, pp. 658-659 In: D.E. Wilson and S. Ruff, editors, The Smithsonian book of North American mammals. Smithsonian Institution Press, Washington, 750 pp.

37 Fedorov, V.B. and Styenseth, N.C. 2002. Multiple glacial refugia in the North American Arctic: inference from phylogeography of the collared lemming (*Dicrostonyx groenlandicus*) Proceedings of the Royal Society of London, Series B: 269: 2071-2077.

38 Maier, H.A. 1991. Influence of photoperiod, temperature and winter acclimatization on Alaskan collared lemming (*Dicrostonyx groenlandicus rubricatus*) thermoregulation, growth and reproduction. MS Thesis, University of Alaska Fairbanks, 67 pp.

39 Sage, B. 1986. The Arctic and its wildlife. Facts on File Publications, New York and Oxford, 190 pp.

40 Batzli, G.O. and Lesieutre, C. 1995. Community organization of arvicoline rodents in northern Alaska. Oikos 72: 88-98.

41 Bergman, C.M. and Krebs, C.J. 1993. Diet overlap of collared lemmings and tundra voles at Pierce Point, Northwest Territories. Canadian Journal of Zoology 71: 1703-1709.

42 Anthony, R.M., Barten, N.L. and Seiser, P.E. 2000. Foods of arctic foxes (*Alopex lagopus*) during winter and spring in western Alaska. Journal of Mammalogy 81: 820-828.

43 Fay , F.H. and Rausch, R.L. 1992. Dynamics of the arctic fox population on St. Lawrence Island, Bering Sea. Arctic 45: 393-397.

44 Borowski, Z. 1998. Influence of weasel (*Mustela nivalis* Linnaeus, 1766) odour on spatial behaviour of root voles (*Microtus oeconomus* Pallas, 1776). Canadian Journal of Zoology 76: 1799-1804.

45 Magoun, A.J. 1985. Population characteristics, ecology, and management of wolverines in northwestern Alaska. PhD Thesis, University of Alaska Fairbanks, 197 pp.

46 Gardner, C.L. 1985. The ecology of wolverines in south-central Alaska. MS Thesis, University of Alaska Fairbanks, 82 pp.

47 Hoefs, M. and Konig, R. 1984. Reliability of aging old Dall sheep ewes by the horn annulus technique. Journal of Wildlife Man agement 48: 980-982.

48 Picard, K., Thomas, D.W., Festa-Bianchet, M. and Lanthier, C. 1994. Bovid horns: an important site for heat loss during winter? Journal of Mammalogy 75: 710-713.

49 Geist, V. 1971. Mountain sheep: a study in behavior and evolution. University of Chicago Press, Chicago, 383 pp.

50 Guthrie, R.D. 1972. Fannin's color variation of the Dall sheep, Ovis dalli, in the Mentasta Mountains of eastern Alaska. Canadian Field-Natruralist 86:288-289.

51 Hoefs, M. and Beyer, M. 1983. Demographic characteristics of an unhunted Dall sheep (*Ovis dalli dalli*) population in southwest Yukon, Canada. Canadian Journal of Zoology 61: 1346-1357.

52 Nichols, L. 1978. Dall's sheep. pp.173-189, In: J.L. Schmidt and D.L. Gilbert, editors, Big game of North America: ecology and management. Stackpole Press, Harrisburg, Pennsylvania, 494 pp.

53 Klein, D.R. 1973. The impact of oil development in the northern environment. Petrolio e ambiente 109-121.

54 Stephenson, R.O., Grangaard, D.V. and Burch, J. 1991. Lynx, *Felis lynx*, predation on red foxes, *Vulpes vulpes*, caribou, *Rangifer tarandus*, and Dall sheep, *Ovis dalli*, in Alaska. Canadian Field-Naturalist 105: 255-262.

55 Hoefs, M. Hoefs, H. and Burles, D. 1986. Observations on Dall sheep, *Ovis dalli dalli*-gray wolf, *Canis lupus pambasileus*, interactions in the Kluane Lake area, Yukon. Canadian Field-Naturalist 100: 78-84.

56 Clarkson, P.L. and Liepins, I.S. 1993. Grizzly bear, *Ursus arctos*, predation on muskox, *Ovibos moschatus*, calves near the Horton River, Northwest Territories. Canadian Field-Naturalist 107: 100-102.

57 Miller, F.L. and Gunn, A. 1985. Muskox defense formations in response to helicopters in the Canadian High Arctic. pp. 123-126 In: D.R. Klein, R.G. White and S. Keller, editors, Proceedings of the first international muskox symposium, University of Alaska, Fairbanks, 218 pp.

58 Tener, J.S. 1965. Muskoxen in Canada: a biological and taxonomic review. Queen's Printer, Ottawa, 166 pp.

59 Robus, M.A. 1985. Summer food habits of muskoxen in northeastern Alaska. pp.81-85, In: D.R. Klein, R.G. White and S. Keller, editors, Proceedings of the first international muskox symposium, University of Alaska, Fairbanks, 218 pp.

60 Ihl, C. 1999. Comparative habitat and diet selection of muskoxen and reindeer on the Seward Peninsula, western Alaska. MS Thesis, University of Alaska, Fairbanks, 81 pp.

61 Murie, A. 1981. The grizzlies of Mt. McKinley. U.S. National Fark Fauna Series No. 14, 251 pp.

62 Barash, D.P. 1981. Mate guarding and gallivanting by male hoary marmots (*Marmota caligata*). Behavioral Ecology and Sociobiology 9: 187-193.

63 Holmes, W.G. 1984. The ecological basis of monogamy in Alaskan hoary marmots. pp. 250-274 In: J.O. Murie and G.R. Michener, editors The biology of ground-dwelling squirrels. University of Nebraska Press, Lincoln, 459 pp.

64 Taulman, J.F. 1977. Vocalizations of the hoary marmot, *Marmota caligata*. Journal of Mammalogy 58: 681-683.

65 Barash, D.P. 1975. Marmot alarm-calling and the question of altrustic behavior. American Midland-Naturalist 94: 468-470.

66 Hansen, R.M. 1975. Foods of the hoary marmot on Kenai Peninsula, Alaska. American Midland-Naturalist 94: 349-353.

67 Holmes, W.G. 1984. Predation risk and foraging behavior of the hoary marmot in Alaska. Behavioral Ecology and Sociobiology 15: 293-301.

68 Taulman, J.F. 1990. Observations on scent marking in hoary marmots, *Marmota caligata*. Canadian Field-Naturalist 104: 479-482.

69 Armitage, K.B. 1999. Evolution of sociality in marmots. Journal of Mammalogy 80: 1-10.

70 Mainini, B., Neuhaus, P. and Ingold, P. 1993. Behaviour of marmots *Marmota marmota* under the influence of different hiking activities. Biological Conservation 64: 161-164.

71 O'Conner, J. 1967. The art of hunting big game in North america. Outdoor Life Books, NY, 404 pp.

72 Mech, D.L. 1970. The wolf: the ecology and behaviour of an endangered species. The Natural History Press, New York, 384 pp.

73 Mech, L.D., Adams, L.G., Meier, T.J., Burch, J.W. and Dale, B.W. 1998. The wolves of Denali.University of Minnesota Press, Minneapolis, 227 pp.

74 Peterson, R.O., Thomas, N.J., Thurber, J.M., Vucetich, J.A. and Waite, T.A. 1998. Population limitation and the wolves of Isle Royale, 1987-1995. Journal of Mammalogy 79: 828-841.

75 Murie, A. 1944. The wolves of Mt. McKinley. U.S. National Park Fauna Series No. 5, 238 pp.

76 Ballard, W.B., Whitman, J.S. and Gardner, C.L. 1987. Ecology of an exploited wolf population in south-central Alaska. Wildlife Monographs 98: 1-54.

77 Ballard, W.B., Ayres, L.A., Krausman, P.R., Reed, D.J. and Fancy, S.G. 1997. Ecology of wolves in relation to a migratory caribou herd in northwest Alaska. Wildlife Monographs 135: 1-47.

78 Dale, B.W., Adams, L.G. and Bowyer, R.T. 1994. Functional response of wolves preying on barren-ground caribou in a multiple-prey ecosystem. Journal of Animal Ecology 63: 644-652.

79 Kelsall, J.P. 1968. The migratory barren ground caribou of Canada. Queen's Printer, Ottawa, 340 pp.

80 Gray, D.R. 1970. The killing of a bull muskox by a single wolf. Arctic 23: 197-199.

81 Joslin, P.W.B. 1966. Summer activities of two timber wolf (*Canis lupus*) packs in Algonquin Park. MS Thesis, University of Toronto, 99 pp.

82 Thurber, J.M., Peterson, R.O., Woolington, J.D. and Vucetich, J.A. 1992. Coyote coexistence with wolves on the Kenai Peninsula, Alaska. Canadian Journal of Zoology 70: 2494-2498.

83 Theberge, J.B. and Wedeles, C.H.R. 1989. Prey selection and habitat partitioning in sympatric coyote and red fox populations, southwest Yukon. Canadian Journal of Zoology 67: 1285-1290.

84 Todd, A.W., Keith, L.B. and Fischer, C.A. 1981. Population ecology of coyotes during a fluctuation of snowshoe hares. Journal of Wildlife Management 45: 629-640.

85 Voigt, D.R. and Earle, B.D. 1983. Avoidance of coyotes by red fox families. Journal of Wildlife Management 47: 852-857.

86 Dekker, D. 1983. Denning and foraging habits of red foxes, *Vulpes vulpes*, and their interaction with coyotes, *Canis latrans*, in central Alberta 1972-1981. Canadian Field-Naturalist 97: 303-306.

87 Henry, J.D. 1996. Living on the edge: foxes. NorthWord Press, Minocqua,WI, 143 pp.

88 Anderson 1999. Arctic fox/ *Alopex lagopus*, pp. 146-148, In: D.E. Wilson and S. Ruff, editors, The Smithsonian book of North American mammals. Smithsonian Institution Press, Washington, 750 pp.

89 Fay, F.H. and Stephenson, R.O. 1989. Annual, seasonal, and habitat-related variation in feeding habits of the arctic fox (*Alopex lagopus*) on St. Lawrence Island, Bering Sea. Canadian Journal of Zoology 67: 1986-1994.

90 Murie, O.J. 1959. Fauna and flora of the Aleutian Islands and Alaska Peninsula. North American Fauna No. 61.

91 Nielsen, S.M. 1991. Fishing arctic foxes *Alopex lagopus* on a rocky island in west Greenland. Polar Research 9: 211-213.

92 Underwood, L.S. 1983. Outfoxing the arctic cold. Natural History 12/83: 38-46.

93 Stephenson, R.O. 1994. Arctic fox. Alaska Department of Fish and Game Wildlife Notebook Series, 2 pp.

94 Garrott, R.A., Eberhardt, L.E. and Hanson, W.C. 1984. Arctic fox denning behavior in northern Alaska. Canadian Journal of Zoology 62: 1636-1640.

95 Wakely, L.G. and Mallory, F.F. 1988. Hierarchical development, agonistic behaviours, and growth rates in captive arctic fox. Canadian Journal of Zoology 66: 1672-1678.

96 Sklepkovych, B.O. 1989. Kannibalism hos fjallraver, *Alopex lagopus*, I de svenska lapplandsfjallen. Fauna och flora 84: 145-150.

97 Schamel, D. and Tracy, D.M. 1986. Encounters between arctic foxes, *Alopex lagopus*, and red foxes, *Vulpes vulpes*. Canadian Field-Naturalist 100: 562-563.

98 Guthrie, R.D. 1967. Fire melanism among mammals. The American Midland Naturalist 77: 227-230.

99 O'Donoghue, M. 1994. Early survival of juvenile snowshoe hares. Ecology 75: 1582-1592.

100 Boonstra, R., Krebs, C.J. and Kanter, M. 1990. Arctic ground squirrel predation on

collared lemmings. Canadian Journal of Zoology 68: 757-760.

101 Carl, E.A. 1971. Population control in arctic ground squirrels. Ecology 52:395-413.

102 Watson, A. 1957. The behavior, breeding and food ecology of the snowy owl, *Nyctea scandiaca*. Ibis 99: 419-462.

103 Johnsgard, P.A. 1988. North American owls: biology and natural history. Smithsonian Institution Press, Washington and London, 295 pp.

104 Kerlinger, M.R. and Lein, M.R. 1986. Differences in winter range among age-sex classes of snowy owls (*Nyctea scandiaca*) in North America. Ornis Scandia 17: 1-7.

105 McIntyre, C.L. and Adams, L.G. 1999. Reproductive characteristics of migratory golden eagles in Denali National Park, Alaska. Condor 101: 115-123.

106 Olendorff, R.R. 1975. Golden eagle country. Knopf, New York, 202 pp.

107 Matchett, M.R. and O'Gara, B.W. 1987. Controlling golden eagle sheep predation. Journal of Raptor Research 21: 85-94.

108 Stokkan, K.A. and Blix, A.S. 1986. Survival strategies 9in the Svalbard rock ptarmigan. Proceedings of the 19th Ornithological Congress 14: 2500-2506.

109 Irving, L., West, G.C. and Peyton, L.J. 1967. Winter feeding program of Alaska willow ptarmigan shown by crop contents. The Condor 69: 69-77.

110 Hannon, S.J., Eason, P.K. and Martin, K. 1998. Willow ptarmigan (*Lagopus lagopus*). The birds of North America No. 369, Academy of Natural Saciences, Philadelphia, PA and American Ornithological Union, Washington D.C.

111 Bergerud, A.T., Mossop, D.H. and Myrberget, S. 1985. A critique of the mechanics of annual changes in ptarmigan numbers. Canadian Journal of Zoology 63: 2240-2248.

112 Moss, R. 1974. Winter diets, gut lengths and interspecific competition in Alaskan ptarmigan. Auk 91: 737-746.

113 Weeden, R.B. 1969. Foods of rock and willow ptarmigan in central Alaska with comments on interspecific competition. Auk 83: 587-596.

114 Holder, K. and Montgomerie, R. 1993. Rock ptarmigan, *Lagopus mutus*. The birds of North America No. 51, Academy of Natural Saciences, Philadelphia, PA and American Ornithological Union, Washington D.C.

115 Pederson, H.C. and Steen, J.B. 1979. Behavioural thermoregulation in willow ptarmigan chicks *Lagopus lagopus*. Ornis Scandinavica 10: 17-21.

116 Weeden, R.B. 1994. Ptarmigan. Wildlife Notebook Series. Alaska Department of Fish and Game.

117 Weeden, R.B. 1967. Seasonal and geographic variation in the foods of adult white-tailed ptarmigan. The Condor 69: 303-309.

118 Rosenberg, D. and Rothe, T. 1994. Swans. Alaska Department of Fish and Game Wildlife Notebook Series, Juneau, 2 pp.

119 Limpert, R.J. and Earnst, S.L. 1994. Tundra swan. The birds of North America No. 89, Academy of Natural Saciences, Philadelphia, PA and American Ornithological Union, Washington D.C.

120 Olsen, K.M. and Larsson, H. 1997. Skuas and jaegers: a guide to the skuas and jaegers of the world. Pica Press, East Sussex. 190 pp.

121 Wiley, R.H. and Lee, D.S. 1998. Long-tailed jaeger. The birds of North America No. 365, Academy of Natural Saciences, Philadelphia, PA and American Ornithological Union, Washington D.C.

122 Wiley, R.H. and Lee, D.S. 2000. Pomarine jaeger. The birds of North America No. 483, Academy of Natural Saciences, Philadelphia, PA and American Ornithological Union, Washington D.C.

123 Fay, F.H. and Cade, T.J. 1959. An ecological analysis of the avifauna of St. Lawrence Island, Alaska. University of California Publications in Zoology 63:73-150.

124 Maher, W.J. 1970. The pomarine jaeger as a brown lemming predator in northern Alaska. Wilson Bulletin 82: 130-157.

125 Maher, W.J. 1974. Ecology of pomarine, parasitic and long-tailed jaegers in northern Alaska. Pacific Coast Avifauna 37.

126 Wiley, R.H. and Lee, D.S. 1999. Parasitic jaeger. The birds of North America No. 445, Academy of Natural Saciences, Philadelphia, PA and American Ornithological Union, Washington D.C.

127 Lyon, B.E. and Montgomerie, R. D. 1987. Ecological correlates of incubation feeding: a comparative study of high arctic finches. Ecology 68: 713-722.

128 Lyon, B. and Montgomerie, R. 1995. Snow bunting/McKay's bunting. The Birds of North America No. 198-199. Academy of Natural Saciences, Philadelphia, PA and American Ornithological Union, Washington D.C.

129 Parmelee, D.F. 1968. *Plectrophenax nivalis nivalis* (Linnaeus): Snow bunting. pp. 1652-1675 In: O.L. Austin Jr., editor, Life histories of North American cardinals, grosbeaks, buntings, towhees, finches, sparrows, and allies. U.S. National Museum Bulletin No. 237.

9.

THE WATERY WORLD OF ALASKA
AND SOME FISHES THAT LIVE THERE

A summer visitor to the great land might or might not notice peculiarities or differences in the freshwater environment of Alaska. Certainly the annual cycles of life in lakes and streams are somewhat more severe than in upstate New York or in Minnesota and considerably more difficult for life than in Georgia or Florida. A chief factor is the presence of ice, its duration, and the effects it produces. The length of winters, the severity of air temperatures, and the lack of a thick, insulating snow cover often combine to produce very thick river and lake ice. In many streams of interior and arctic Alaska, streams freeze to the bottom, eliminating fish habitat. Even when liquid water remains under the ice, its suitability for fish may be compromised by **hypoxia** (low oxygen) or **anoxia** (absence of oxygen).

Glaciation and glacially produced sediments also affect freshwater fishes in Alaska. First, glaciers occupy watersheds that could provide fish habitat were the glaciers not there. Second, glaciers, by abrading and scouring the underlying bedrock, produce fine sediments (glacial flour) that flow down glacial streams and make them turbid and, therefore, less desirable as fish habitat. Third, glacial episodes in Alaska were more arid than the present in the interior of Alaska and the Yukon Territory. Certainly, some of our present-day streams, ponds, and lakes did not exist at the height of the cold, arid glacial maxima.

Keep in mind that most of interior and western Alaska plus an extensive land area north of the Brooks Range were ice-free during glacial episodes. In addition, the Bering Land Bridge was also ice-free during glacial advances. This land connection to Asia resulted from the drop in sea level due to the volumes of ice locked up in glaciers worldwide.

The fish and invertebrate faunas of interior and northern Alaska are impoverished in comparison to those at lower latitudes. The physical rigors of the environment have constrained many species that exist further south. Also, many species that could live in Alaska and, perhaps, did live in Alaska before the Pleistocene, may not have been able to disperse back into the Far North. For example, only one of the sixty species of suckers of North America and only one of the 230 native minnow species of North America occur in Alaska. None of the 141 native species of perches occur in Alaska. The freshwater fish fauna numbers about 42 species.

Finally, a visitor to Alaska might notice the importance of salmon to the freshwaters of this land of the midnight sun. Arguably, salmon have greater significance to the human and natural economy of this state than in any other state of the U.S.A. or province of Canada.

RIVERS AND STREAMS

Hydrology

The stream systems of Alaska fall into three major groups: interior, northern (arctic), and southern coastal. In climate, these three are influenced by continental, arctic and maritime conditions, respectively. Probably as much as 75% of the landmass of Alaska falls under the influence of continental conditions. Much of this landmass is home to Alaska's boreal forests. Interior streams begin to discharge in April as meltwater from winter snow enters drainages. Discharge peaks during and shortly after breakup and may peak again due to late summer rainfall. Discharge slows at freezeup, typically dropping to very low levels under the winter ice.

In contrast, glacially fed streams, such as are found in the Alaska Range, show a somewhat simpler pattern, with discharge peaking in July and August when summer sun maximizes glacial melt. Typically, glacial stream discharge falls to zero in the winter; no melt occurs and streams freeze to the bottom.[1]

Water Temperature

Streams in interior and northern Alaska include creeks with a more or less closed canopy of riparian vegetation, more open canopy streams, and tundra beaded streams. Temperature data from two interior Alaska (subarctic) and one Alaska North Slope (arctic) streams show mean annual temperatures of 1.1 -2.9^{0}C, maximum temperatures of 5.8 -21.4^{0}C and maximum daily fluctuations of 4.1 -11.6^{0}C.[2] Surprisingly, the tundra stream had the highest values for all three.

Extent of shading by streamside vegetation is important and is influenced by timber harvest, road construction, fires, mining and beavers. Another critical factor is presence or absence of permafrost underlying streams. Temperature extremes and daily changes may limit or kill different life stages of fish.

Sources of Organic Production

Organic material to serve as the food base for streams can come from the stream itself or from the surrounding landscape. Within-stream primary producers are primarily **benthic** (attached to the bottom of the stream) algae. Generally, the biomass of stream algae is low. But because of the long day length in summer, reproductive rates are high and overall productivity is comparable to that in lower-latitude streams.[3] Emergent vegetation in streams contributes to productivity, especially in sloughs and quiet backwaters.

Organic material of terrestrial origin, including leaf litter, constitutes another input. Leaf litter input may be low compared to that in temperate streams but can be very important in streams with limited in-stream primary production.

Another source of organic carbon is the peat deposits that are exposed and erode out of many stream channels in the interior and arctic hydrologic regions. This peat is incompletely decomposed plant material, originally produced in the Pleistocene, that wasn't completely decomposed due to low soil temperatures. One of the obvious effects of global warming will be increasing decomposition rates of these "fossil" peats. The contribution of anadromous salmon to the productivity of streams and lakes is addressed below.

Stream Insects

As is true of the fish fauna, the invertebrate fauna of streams in Alaska is impoverished. Aquatic insects of interior Alaska streams consist of representatives of only four orders: Diptera (flies and mosquitoes), Trichoptera (caddisflies), Ephemeroptera, (mayflies) and Plecoptera (stoneflies). In the arctic region, one additional insect order is represented, the Coleoptera (beetles). Three insect orders typically found in temperate streams are, apparently, completely absent from the interior and arctic hydrologic regions: Hemiptera (true bugs), Neuroptera, (lacewings) and Megaloptera (dobsonflies).[1]

There are five feeding categories of aquatic insects: predators, shredders, scrapers, collector-filterers, and collector-gatherers. In terms of relative abundance (numbers of individuals), collector-gatherers appear to dominate streams in the arctic and interior regions, probably due

to the dominance of the Chironomidae (midges: Diptera) in the fauna.

Seasonal changes in food resources may result in a progression or succession in insect feeding types. For example, in an Alaskan forest stream, shredders are unimportant numerically in the summer. They increase after autumn leaf fall and dominate the insect fauna by early winter.[4] Similarly, within the caddisflies, scrapers increase in abundance in midsummer, when benthic algal production is highest, but shredders exhibit greatest numbers in the fall, when leaves are falling into streams.[5]

Nutrient and Energy Transfer from Aquatic Habitats

Fish provide an energy source to surrounding habitats, including the riparian zone, wetlands, forests, and tundra. Every time a predator captures and eats a fish and moves away from the river, it carries some of the fish's energy and nutrients with it. In short, fish feed the surrounding countryside to a significant extent. The influence of fish on these systems depends on how many fish are eaten and/or transported off the river or lake.

The most obvious examples of energy transfer away from the waters are those involving bears, mink, otters, gulls, ravens, and eagles feeding on salmon. Waterfowl feed on stream invertebrates yet may transfer the energy obtained to locations away from the rivers or lakes. Similarly, water ouzels feed on stream invertebrates and kingfishers prey on small fishes in the rivers. A permanent energy transfer might occur if any of these fish predators takes up permanent residency away from the river. Or the predator may die away from the river and its body be eaten by another predator or scavenger. Without the input from spawning salmon, virtually all Alaskan rivers would be significantly impoverished in terms of energy.[6] The surrounding terrestrial habitats would also be depleted of nutrients.

Finally, dead salmon carcasses wash downstream and often end up on stream banks, where they are vulnerable to fly larvae. These maggots consume the fish, grow, metamorphose to the adult form, and fly away. These adult flies enter terrestrial (nonaquatic) food webs when eaten by dragonflies, swallows, or other terrestrial fly predators.

Peat deposits are, in places, quite extensive and quite thick in the Far North. Peat is the accumulated organic material in soil that hasn't been decomposed by fungi and bacteria. Peat consists mainly of pieces of dead plant organic matter. These pieces are **particulate organic matter**. Peat also contains dissolved organic chemicals: **dissolved organic matter**.

As rivers and streams flow through and erode peat deposits, some of the material is carried away.[7] The dissolved organic chemicals are directly available for absorption by stream bacteria, but the particulate matter has to be decomposed before its carbon (energy) can be used. Peat particles become covered with a coating of decomposing bacteria. These bacteria incorporate peat carbon into their own cells.

Detritus-feeding stream invertebrates are really after the bacterial coating, not the actual dead plant material. As these bacteria are harvested and digested by stream invertebrates, their carbon is incorporated into invertebrate bodies. Therefore, stream productivity is increased by the addition of peat derived from plants that may have lived thousands of years ago. If the landscape of the Far North continues to warm due to climate change, we might expect peat decomposition to accelerate and the peat contribution to stream productivity to increase.

LAKES

The lakes of Alaska vary tremendously in size from the giants such as Iliamna Lake and Becharof Lake down to small bog ponds that may, in dry years, nearly disappear. There are many other physical and chemical differences among lakes of interior and northern Alaska. In spite of these differences, virtually all of them share one feature: they freeze over in winter.

One way of thinking about lakes relates to their productivity. At one extreme are lakes having high levels of dissolved nutrients, including phosphate and nitrate. These nutrients fuel plant productivity. Plants and plantlike organisms that occur in lakes include **emergent** (rooted underwater but emerging above the water) vegetation along the shores, **benthic** (bottom-dwelling) algae and small, drifting plantlike organisms called **phytoplankton**. The high plant production, in turn, typically leads to large populations of plant-consuming invertebrates. The invertebrates are food for fish and, therefore, fish production can be high. These lakes are **eutrophic lakes**. At the other extreme are relatively barren lakes with low nutrient concentrations and low plant, invertebrate and fish production. Such lakes are **oligotrophic lakes**.

Contrary to what one might expect, eutrophic lakes do not always maintain healthy fish populations. The Goldstream Valley, north of Fairbanks, has a number of shallow, eutrophic thaw lakes that don't maintain permanent fish populations. These lakes are often connected to Goldstream Creek during springtime breakup or flooding. In spring a variety of fishes disperse into the lakes. As water levels fall in late spring and summer the lakes are isolated. Lake temperatures can reach 25°C (77°F) during the summer, fueling both plant productivity and bacterial decomposition. As fall approaches, oxygen may be used up by plant and bacterial respiration, leaving none for the fish. If fish do survive through the fall, they may be faced with anoxia under the ice or with a lake that freezes to the bottom. Either of these insults will kill most fish in a lake.

Another "problem" is **hypereutrophication**. This happens when humans put too many nutrients into a lake. Plant nutrients are found in agricultural fertilizers, human sewage, and municipal wastewater. Inadequately treated wastewater can trigger runaway plant production and, eventually, massive fish kills. This situation is familiar to residents of the lower 48 states but is unknown in Alaska, right? Wrong. Small, remote villages sometimes don't have a central collecting system, much less the capability to adequately treat municipal wastewater. In the past, remote villages were periodically relocated. If there were waste or eutrophication problems, they were simply left behind. However, most villages in bush Alaska now have permanent schools, making it unlikely that the village will simply move to a new location if pollution problems get too bad.

I will mention one final twist in the lake eutrophication story. Sockeye salmon rely on lakes as nursery habitat. Most sockeye salmon lakes are toward the oligotrophic end of the spectrum. Some Canadian scientists tried an experiment in which they dumped fertilizer in Great Central Lake on Vancouver Island to see if salmon production would improve. After fertilization the lake's plankton productivity increased, and the following year, salmon returns also increased.[8] The take-home messages are (1) sockeye salmon productivity of lakes can be improved and (2) dumping tons of fertilizer in remote lakes is really expensive.

Lakes in interior Alaska exhibit annual cycles of temperature, ice, nutrient concentrations and stability of the water column. Smith Lake, a small (72,000 m² surface area), shallow (mean depth 1.8 m) boreal forest lake near Fairbanks, has been studied repeatedly because it is on the campus of the University of Alaska.[9] Temperature and ice cycles are probably the most obvious features of interior lakes.

The ice-free period on Smith Lake begins in the last week of May after severe winters and two to three weeks earlier following mild winters. Ice formation in the fall occurs by late September or early October. After ice-melt, surface warming can be as rapid as 4-5°C per day, with maximum summer temperatures reaching 23-26°C (73-79°F). At a water depth of 2 m, the annual range of surface sediment temperatures is 15°C.

Dissolved oxygen varies seasonally, from mid- to late-winter lows (oxygen undetectable) to moderate values in the ice-free months. At ice-melt, oxygen concentrations increase rapidly due to plant photosynthesis and to atmospheric input. Inorganic nutrients (phosphate and ammonium) are high in winter, decrease rapidly at ice-melt due to photosynthetic activity, and remain low through the ice-free months.

One source of energy available to lakes and ponds in Alaska is solar energy, a portion of which is captured and locked into chemical energy by primary producers in the lakes. These primary producers consist of phytoplankton, benthic algae, and emergent vegetation (vascular plants).

Additional energy inputs are made in the form of detritus washed into lakes by runoff (inlet streams) and blown by winds from the lake surroundings or even further away. Much of this detritus consists of leaves of deciduous trees and probably is most significant in the fall. If the lake receives spawning runs of fishes, it gets additional energy and nutrient inputs. These inputs are in the form of fish eggs and milt spawned into the lake or inlet stream and in the form of the carcasses of fish that die after spawning.

An occasional, large input of detritus can occur. For example, one spring I observed a dead moose submerged in Lower Tangle Lake. The moose was beginning to disintegrate, adding organic matter and inorganic nutrients to the lake.

The water column of a lake is stable during the winter. That is, there is little vertical movement. Typically the lake is ice-covered, effectively preventing winds from mixing the water. Further, the column is thermally stratified with low-density surface waters near freezing and denser, warmer (1- 4°C) water near the bottom.

Instability occurs in the spring after the ice melts. Then winds can push the lake surface, pile it up on one end of the lake and cause **down-welling**, a vertical movement of surface water to greater depth. The opposite shore of the lake will exhibit the reverse process, **upwelling**, to replace surface water blown by the wind.

As the lake surface heats during the summer, it typically becomes thermally stratified. Above a temperature of 4°C, water decreases in density with increasing temperature. Therefore, warm water layers on top of cool water. This stratification can be eliminated by winds across the lake.

At the onset of autumn the lake surface water becomes cooler and more dense than underlying layers and, therefore, sinks. This is another instance of instability in the water column of the lake. These vertical movements can be important in terms of lake production. Summer phytoplankton production in the surface layers results in nutrient depletion. However, wind-induced upwelling brings additional nutrients up to the surface layers, thereby stimulating further production.

TURBIDITY: POTENTIAL EFFECTS ON FRESHWATER SYSTEMS

Turbidity is the scattering of light in water by inorganic and organic particles. High turbidities typically correlate with high levels of inorganic, predominately sediment, particles. Some fresh-waters may be naturally turbid. For example, glacial streams and rivers receive fine suspended sediments, glacial silt, in runoff. On the other hand, some streams, rivers and lakes that would, otherwise, be clear systems have been made turbid by human activities such as placer mining, timber harvest and road construction.

One problem with increased turbidity is a decrease in light penetration into lakes. Since light is necessary for photosynthetic production, turbidity reduces the **euphotic volume**, the volume of a lake that actually produces plant material. Naturally clear Alaskan lakes have active primary production down to 16 m (52 feet) depth while production in a glacially turbid lake is limited to the upper 1 m (3.2 ft).[10] In the Northwest Territories, turbid lakes have decreased primary production, decreased plant diversity and changes in plant species composition in comparison to clear lakes.[11]

Zooplankton consists of the small, drifting animals of lakes (and oceans) that feed upon phytoplankton (microscopic, drifting plants) and, in turn, are eaten by larger animals including fish. Zooplankton is also affected by turbidity. Turbid lakes have zooplankton densities as low as 5 % of those found in clear Alaskan lakes. Turbid lakes in Alaska appear to be devoid of cladocerans, a favorite crustacean food group for juvenile salmon; 20 clear lakes examined in Alaska all had cladocerans.[10]

Studies of effects of turbidity on lake fish production at high latitudes seem to have focused almost solely on sockeye salmon young. Though not relevant to much of interior and northern Alaska because of their lack of sockeye, these studies suggest that turbidity affects lake populations of other fish species. Sockeye production in southwest Alaska is correlated with euphotic volume rather than surface area. Thus, there appears to be a clear link from light penetration to primary and secondary production to fish production.[10,12]

In Alaskan streams light penetration[13] and plant production[14] are both reduced by turbidity. Abundance of large invertebrates is reduced in mined, compared to unmined, streams in Alaska, primarily due to turbidity.[15]

Feeding by Arctic grayling in turbid streams is reduced,[16] presumably by decreasing the dis-

tance at which fish can detect food organisms.[17] Arctic grayling avoid turbid streams if possible but may be forced to traverse them during their annual fall downstream migration.[18] Young (age-0) grayling exhibit skin abrasion and gill problems when exposed to turbid waters.[19]

Finally, there is a large literature indicating that sedimentation (siltation) has a devastating effect on reproduction of salmon-like fishes and other species primarily by reducing the porosity of the spawning gravels. Embryos incubating within the gravels are smothered because oxygenated flow cannot penetrate a fine sediment layer.

Several human activities related to fish are also influenced by turbidity. First, sport fishing activity is curtailed in turbid waters.[20] Second, aerial surveys of salmon on the spawning grounds have been obstructed by sediment discharge into Alaskan streams.[10]

FISH LIFE CYCLES, AND SEASONAL HABITATS

A variety of life histories are exhibited by the fishes of Alaska. As an example, slimy sculpins probably live out their entire lives within the confines of a limited stretch of stream or river, moving perhaps several miles in a lifetime. In contrast, the salmon species occupy the open ocean of the north Pacific as maturing juveniles and adults but start life as embryos down in the gravels of freshwater streams and lake margins. Fishes that mature in the ocean but run upriver to spawn in freshwater habitats are referred to as **anadromous** fishes. Chum (dog) and chinook (king) salmon are anadromous fishes. The habit of moving, entirely within freshwaters, upstream and downstream seasonally or for reproduction is referred to as diadromy. Arctic grayling are **diadromous**. **Catadromous** fishes mature in fresh water but move to the oceans to spawn. Freshwater eels in the genus *Anguilla* are catadromous fishes.

The major problems faced by fishes in winter at high latitudes are ice, low temperature, and restricted food supplies, dissolved oxygen and physical space.[21] Ice formation forces fish into unfrozen stretches of rivers or into lakes, causing them to concentrate in the remaining (liquid) habitat. If trapped in ice, most fish freeze and are killed. Deep holes in rivers may exhibit hypoxia or, in extreme circumstances, anoxia. Hypoxia reduces fish metabolic capabilities; anoxia usually kills fish.

Availability of food for planktivores (feeders on small, drifting organisms) is greatly reduced. Availability of fish for predators of fish may be good where fish concentrate to overwinter. Normal behaviors such as territoriality in arctic grayling may be relaxed in areas of high concentration. Indeed, grayling of most size classes in the population all coexist in the same pools in winter.

Among lake and pond habitats, several types are not suitable as overwintering habitat. Lakes of volcanic or thermokarst origin may be either inaccessible to fishes or too shallow. Lakes of glacial origin are usually suitable for overwintering primarily because of their size and depth. Oxygen depletion sufficient to trigger winterkill of fishes doesn't occur in lakes with average depths of 5 m or greater.[22] In Alaska, species overwintering in deep lakes include lake trout, burbot, northern pike, chinook salmon, arctic grayling, and slimy sculpin.

Beaver ponds also serve as overwintering habitat for fishes if they are sufficiently deep so as not to freeze to the bottom. Dolly Varden char occupy beaver ponds in the upper reaches of the Copper River drainage.[23] Similarly, in Southeast Alaska, beaver ponds increase the overwinter habitat for coho salmon.[24] We don't know enough about overwinter habitat in interior Alaska.

Most streams and rivers serve as overwintering habitat for fish. Exceptions are streams draining lowlands with very low discharge in winter. These streams typically freeze to the bottom. Large glacial rivers are important winter habitat even though they may have a thick ice cover. Under-ice flows are primarily groundwater and are clear. Larger fishes (whitefish, pike) congregate in deep holes; smaller fish (sculpins, young-of-the-year salmon) may occupy rock-cobble and sunken-log habitats.[21] Dissolved oxygen falls steadily over the winter and may also fall as one progresses downriver.

Clearwater streams, due to their low volumes, are less important for fish in winter. Winter habitat in upper reaches is probably limited to springs or areas of groundwater discharge. Such areas support arctic char, Dolly Varden, burbot, arctic grayling, and slimy sculpin.

Summer in Alaska is the season of liquid water. This is such an obvious statement but is significant nevertheless. Springtime breakup and runoff result in rises in river levels. Some fishes, such as the arctic grayling, move upstream during high water and occupy some of the highest reaches in a stream system. These shallow riffles and pools are good habitat for drift-feeding fish but are uninhabitable in the dead of winter.

Local flooding in spring also allows fish to disperse into lakes and ponds that, in the fall, may be completely disconnected from streams.

These lakes may be suitable for life in the summer but not in the winter. If a connection from a stream to a shallow pond persists into the fall, fish will often leave the pond to avoid freezing. Otherwise, they become trapped and may die.

ALASKAN FISHES

The Salmons

The Pacific salmons, genus *Oncorhynchus*, tend to dominate our thinking about fish in Alaska. They are a huge resource of importance to commercial fishers, but also to personal use, subsistence and sport fishing as well. There are eight species of Pacific salmon although, in Alaska, we typically hear about only five of them.

Two salmon not found in Alaska are the cherry salmon, *Oncorhynchus masou*, and the amago salmon, *Oncorhynchus rhodurus*. The amago salmon is restricted to the Japanese islands of Honshu, Shikoku and Kyushu. The masu or cherry salmon occurs in the freshwaters of Japan and the Far East, including the east coast of Korea north to the Sea of Okhotsk and the Kamchatka Peninsula. The fish is called *sakuramasu* in Japan, meaning cherry trout. This common name derives from the fact that cherry trout move into Japanese rivers during the time of cherry blossoms, March to May.[25]

The rainbow trout, *Oncorhynchus mykiss,* is now classified as a salmon based on its genetic relatedness to the other Pacific salmon species. Rainbows exhibit both resident and sea-run forms. The sea-run fish are known as steelheads and are anadromous, like the other salmons. Both rainbows and steelheads are discussed below. The other five salmon species that occur

in Alaska are: chinook (king), *O. tshawytscha;* coho (silver), *O. kisutch;* chum (dog), *O. keta;* sockeye (red), *O. nerka;* and pink (humpback), *O. gorbuscha.*

Anadromy—Before describing details of individual salmon life histories, we should think about the anadromous life style. Recall, anadromy is the habit of returning from the sea as an adult to spawn in freshwater. Put simply, why go to all the trouble to migrate down to the ocean, sometimes thousands of kilometers, when you could just stay at home? Or, conversely, why return from the ocean at all? One of the answers can be gleaned from comparing landlocked sockeye salmon, referred to as kokanee, with normal sockeyes. Mature, spawning-condition kokanee are much smaller, averaging about 35 cm (14 inches) in length compared to 65 cm (26 inches) for sea-run sockeye. So sea-run fish grow much larger. The same is true of stream-resident rainbow trout and sea-run steelheads from the same river; the steelheads attain a much larger size.

Size matters. Body size relates directly to the number of eggs a female can produce and the amount of milt a male can produce. Reproductive success is enhanced with larger body size. What accounts for the larger body size of sea-run fish? It has to be the availability of food out there in the ocean. Not only do anadromous salmonids grow larger (and faster), but much larger populations can be supported. Thus, spawning runs in anadromous salmon streams are much larger than they would be if the fish were forced to subsist on within-stream food sources.

The other question about anadromy (Why return to the river at all?) can be answered based on experiments on salinity tolerance of developing embryos and newly mobile salmon fingerlings. None of the salmon embryos can tolerate seawater. When fingerlings of the five Pacific salmon species are exposed to full-strength seawater, all five species show an increase in internal salt concentrations. Pink and chum fingerlings eventually get the salt levels under control, but the other three species die of osmotic shock. Rainbow/steelhead fingerlings aren't able to tolerate seawater either. The limitation preventing salmon from becoming entirely marine is the inability of early life stages to deal effectively with full strength seawater. Interestingly, the two that are best at handling seawater, pinks and chums, are the two species that proceed directly to estuaries after wiggling up out of their gravel nests.

Life history—All Pacific salmon plus steelheads spend most of their juvenile and adult lives out in the Pacific Ocean and/or Bering Sea. While at sea, fish feed on the (usually) rich supplies of plankton and forage fishes. The geographic area covered in the Gulf of Alaska by populations of these salmons is quite extensive. Figure 9.1 shows the overall distribution of chum salmon that represent Alaskan, Asian and other North American stocks. Obviously, there is considerable overlap of stocks in the open ocean. The other salmon species show much the same pattern of ocean distribution. This fact ultimately led to an international ban on high seas salmon fisheries. How could you tell whether the fish in the net belonged to (were hatched in streams of) Japan, Russia, Canada or the U.S.? Yet, catching large numbers of these fish might selectively affect stocks in one or another of the countries contributing these fish. Meaningful regulation of high seas catches of salmon is impossible.

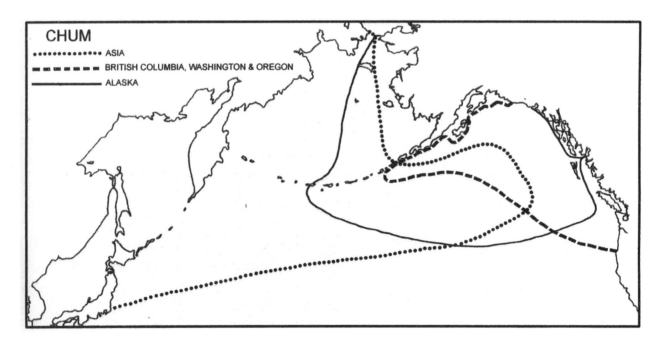

Figure 9.1: Chum salmon ocean distribution. Fish originating in Asian streams disperse most widely (dotted line). Alaskan fish overlap Asian fish over much of their oceanic range (solid line). Fish originating in British Columbia, Washington and Oregon have a more eastern distribution but still overlap the other two stocks (dashed line).

Over the course of a year, several salmon species may occupy the same geographical area. In fact, several species may occupy the same area simultaneously. These different species have somewhat different requirements for living even if they co-occur. For example, there may be differences in the depth distributions of sockeyes and chums even if they occupy the same body of water. In addition, the salmons have been shown to select somewhat different assortments of food organisms out in the open ocean. Sockeyes take mainly zooplankton, pinks take fish in addition, and steelhead take fish and squid.[26] Conversely, the different species may be separated geographically by temperature preferences. For example, wintertime salmon distributions in the Pacific correspond to temperature ranges of 1.5 to 6°C for sockeyes, 1.5 to 10°C for chums, 3.5 to 8.5°C for pinks and 5.5 to 9°C for cohos.[27] Preferred temperature ranges are higher in summer.

At an appropriate time in the late spring or summer, maturing salmon begin to move toward the coastline. This prespawning migration is probably triggered by day length and/or sea surface temperatures. The direction of migration differs depending on the river of origin and must be programmed into the genes of the population; Copper River (Alaska) salmon move northward, Columbia River (Washington) salmon move generally eastward. How can a salmon tell north from east?

Several possibilities exist. First, many fish species can navigate by sun-compass orientation. That is, they can detect north based on the plane of polarized sunlight. Second, salmon and other fishes have been shown to be able to detect and orient to the earth's magnetic fields.

Either or both methods might be used. Once the fish approach the coastline, they move along the coast until they detect chemical cues or odors emanating from their river of origin. Salmon with their nostrils damaged experimentally or plugged with petroleum jelly cannot successfully find their home rivers or streams.

If the school has only a short distance to run upstream, fish may mill around in the bay or estuary until they take on their breeding colors and ripen their gonads. If the journey is to be a long one, the fish begin their upstream swim immediately and retain their silvery, sea-run appearance. Gonads are matured on the way up river in these latter fish. The result is that no matter how far upriver the fish move, they arrive on the spawning grounds ready to breed.

By the time salmon reach the spawning grounds, they have fully adopted breeding coloration, males have added extra teeth, powerfully hooked jaws (the **kype**), and a hump on their backs (Figure 9.2a). These male characteristics are important in establishing dominance and, therefore, access to females on the spawning grounds. Gonads are fully mature in both sexes. Spawning habitat is gravel bottom of a size that can be excavated by the females. Each female digs a shallow depression, the nest or **redd**, by fanning her tail. While she digs, a dominant male guards and chases away any other males that try to intrude. She and her mate spawn into the depression and she moves upstream to dig another nest. Digging the second nest effectively buries the first nest. Spawning continues until fertilized eggs have been deposited in a succession of several nests and the female has shed all her eggs. **Fecundity** (total number of eggs) in salmon is related to body size, ranging from 800-2,000 in pinks

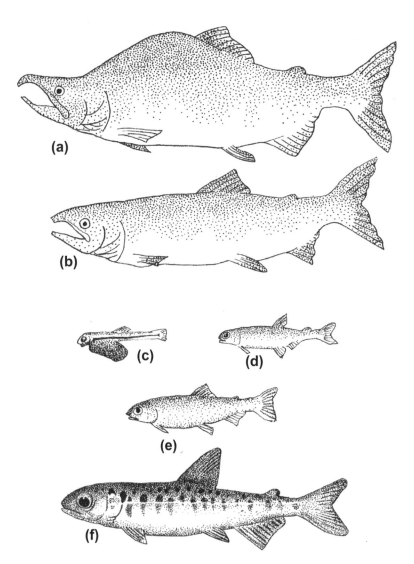

Figure 9.2: Stages in the life of the pink salmon. Spawning males (a) have strongly hooked jaws and a pronounced hump. Spawning females (b) have a slight hooking but no hump. A soon-to-emerge fry (c) still has part of its yolk sac attached. Fingerling fry (d,e) are miniature versions of the adults and are the only salmonid fingerlings with no dark, vertical bars or parr marks. A chinook salmon fingerling (f), with parr marks, is shown for comparison.

(smallest salmon) and 2,600-8,500 in chinooks (largest salmon). The female will stay by her nests and defend them from other females. After hours or days, her physiological reserves of energy are exhausted. Males may last a little longer and attempt to spawn with additional females before they also die. All post-spawning Pacific salmon (steelheads are the exception) die after a single spawning season.

The number of fish running up river is referred to as the **escapement**. It is important to allow enough fish to escape capture by commer-cial, subsistence, personal use and sport fisheries and capture by predators to insure continuation of the run. Does that mean that the larger the escapement, the larger the number of fish produced? Not necessarily. In any stream or lake there is only a finite amount of suitable spawning habitat. Salmon that reach the spawning grounds early in the run use the preferred sites. However, later spawners often use these very same sites, digging up the nests of embryos of the earlier spawners. This tendency or competition is more intense the larger the escapement.

Once the eggs (embryos) are in the gravel, their survival depends on percolation of oxygenated water through the interstices of the gravel. The **porosity** of the gravels is compromised by addition of fine-grained sediments from any source, including natural sedimentation, volcanic ash fallout, placer mining, road building or logging practices. I'd like to stress that these human activities, if carried out within appropriate guidelines, don't have to pose a threat to developing salmon. A natural cause of mortality of salmon eggs is unusually cold weather and/or low water levels in the winter, either of which can cause freezing of the stream to the bottom. Freezing kills the developing embryos.

Salmon eggs are large, averaging about 4 to 9 mm (roughly a sixth to a third of an inch). The yolk material of these eggs is sufficient to fuel development to a fry stage of about 3-5 cm in length. Typically, fry wiggle up through the gravel and become mobile with a bit of the yolk sac remaining. These young fish are called **alevins** (Figure 9.2c). The embryonic development time varies depending on temperature; higher temperatures lead to faster embryonic development rates. Populations of salmon at different latitudes have different spawning times, typically later in the fall at lower latitudes. High-latitude salmon spawn earlier, on average, because embryonic development takes longer at the temperatures the embryos actually experience in the gravel. Thus, the fingerlings emerge the following spring at an appropriate time to feed, grow or move down to the ocean.

All salmon fry are resident in fresh water for at least a short time. With a single exception, all salmonid fry develop dark vertical bars, called **parr marks**, on the body (Figure 9.2f). These parr marks camouflage the fish in submerged vegetation. Only pink salmon fry lack the parr marks. Young salmon with parr marks are often called **parr**. After varying periods in freshwater, parr go through a transformation process that adapts them to marine conditions. This process is often called the **parr-smolt transformation**. Changes include loss of the parr marks and replacement with a completely silvery coloration, reversal of the chloride-secreting cells of their gills, olfactory imprinting and a big surge in thyroxine hormone levels in the blood.

The silvery color will serve them well in the pelagic zone of the oceans. The chloride-secreting cells allow salmon to maintain osmotic balance in a salty environment rather than the very dilute freshwater environment they are leaving. **Olfactory imprinting** is a process, not completely understood, in which the salmon imbed the memory of the exact chemical, olfactory cues of their home streams into their brains. The silver, marine-adapted juveniles are called **smolts** and one often hears reports on smolt **outmigrations** from rivers. **Estuaries**, areas where rivers run into the sea, are the first stop for these smolts. Residence time in estuaries may range from several days to a month or more. It isn't clear if these juveniles move offshore into the open ocean in schools or as individuals.

One final aspect of salmon biology needs to be mentioned. Salmon "enhancement" programs have been instituted by Japan, Canada, Russia and various states in America. With few exceptions, these efforts could be viewed as salmon ranching in which fish are raised to the smolt or outmigrant stage and then released to the wild. These programs are designed to offset the loss (to development or pollution) of wild spawning habitat and serve to smooth out the natural fluctuations in wild salmon returns. In the early 1990s, these hatchery releases around the north Pacific rim amounted to 6-10 billion "extra" salmon. Aside from questions of spread of hatchery diseases to wild stocks, genetic inferiority of hatchery fish compared to wild stocks and cost/benefit analyses, there is the issue of competition for food resources out in the ocean.

The question, simply put, is this: is there a carrying capacity for Pacific salmon in the Pacific Ocean? If there is, are we at or below carrying capacity? Recent oceanographic studies have focused on what has been called "regime shifts." Basically, the north Pacific goes through (roughly) ten-year cycles of atmospheric and oceanic conditions that cause changes in plankton and fish production.[28,29] Carrying capacity for salmon probably fluctuates based, in part, on these regime shifts.

Two possible signs of reaching or exceeding carrying capacity for salmon would be either a decrease in returning salmon numbers or a decrease in returning salmon sizes. A review of size trends in Pacific salmon showed that 45 of 47 salmon stocks (including all five species) from Asia and North America exhibited decreasing body size since 1975.[30] We, collectively, need to rethink the old myth of the inexhaustible oceans.

Pink salmon—Pinks are the smallest of the Pacific salmon, averaging about 1.8 kg (4 pounds) but the most abundant salmon species in the North Pacific Ocean. Among salmon, these are the nearest thing to a completely marine species. Some populations of pinks in Prince William Sound (Alaska) actually spawn in portions of the intertidal zone through which freshwater percolates. Fingerlings are silver right from the start; no parr-smolt transformation is necessary. Alaskan pinks spawn in relatively short coastal streams, usually only several miles from the ocean. In western Alaska drainages, spawning migrations may amount to as much as 160 km (100 miles). In all these populations the juveniles have a short run to the sea and they move directly downstream to the ocean.

Although deposition of eggs in a gravel nest, the redd, protects the developing embryos from many predators, there is still some nest predation. Several species of sculpins (coastrange, reticulate) actually burrow into the gravel and consume some of the eggs. Leeches have been shown in hatcheries to attach to alevins and become engorged with blood. The alevin invariably dies. One would expect leeches to perform similarly in natural nest sites.

Embryonic development in pinks and other salmon is affected by temperature. Generally, higher temperatures mean faster development. This relationship accounts, in part, for the differences in timing of spawning runs from different parts of the latitudinal range of salmon. One could imagine, however, that pink salmon embryos deposited in the gravels of one tributary stream might experience different intra-gravel temperatures than those of another tributary stream depending on the sources of groundwater discharge and on the amount of solar heating available to the stream.

Individual spawning stocks have probably evolved slightly different temperature-development relationships to fine-tune the emergence time. There is nothing to be gained by emergence and downstream migration in the absence of food for the fish to eat.

Fry at emergence are about 28-35 mm (1.1-1.4 inches) in length. They begin their downstream migration and immediately begin to fall prey to a variety of predators. Among fish predators, sculpins and the smolts of coho salmon may be the most significant. Dolly Varden char, in spite of their reputation as predators of salmon fry, have a low incidence of pink fry in their stomachs. Other fishes known to take pink fry include cutthroat trout, steelhead trout, herring, northern pike and walleye pollock. Other predators include caddisfly larvae, arctic terns, water ouzels and American mergansers.

One last point on predation: the proportion of a fry population lost to predators appears to be inversely related to the size of the fry population. In other words, there is safety in numbers. In addition, synchrony of outmigration will reduce the proportion of fry lost. These are cases of predator swamping, in which there may simply be too many salmon fry for the predators to eat.

While at sea, pink salmon fall prey to several shark species including the salmon shark, a warm-bodied, high-speed cruiser. Large Pacific halibut occasionally take pinks. Fifteen marine mammal species in the north Pacific prey on salmon; those documented to feed on pinks include the harbor seal, northern fur seal, Pacific whitesided dolphin and humpback whale.

Pink salmon differ from other salmons in another respect. Virtually all pinks have a two-year life cycle. Individuals deposited in the gravel as embryos in the fall move downstream to the ocean the next spring, and return to freshwater to spawn the following fall. So an embryo formed in, say, 2002, an even year, will return to spawn in the year 2004, another even year. A single stream, then, can support an **even-year run** and an **odd-year run**. These runs are genetically isolated, discrete runs. Even- and odd-year runs may differ considerably in both the size of the return (number of fish) and in the average size of the fish returning. Generally, large runs are characterized by small fish and *vice versa*.

If the genetic isolation between even- and odd-year runs in a stream were total, we could consider the two runs as representing separate species. Two factors work to make the isolation less than complete and, therefore, allow genetic mixing among spawning runs. First, there is an occasional three-year old pink salmon. Such a salmon might have started as an even-year fish but will spawn with the odd-year run. Second, pink salmon exhibit a less than perfect fidelity to their natal streams. This means that a pink salmon destined to spawn, say, in Tonsina Creek near Seward might, instead, end up spawning in Fourth of July Creek, across Resurrection Bay. These mistakes in homing are probably due to defects in the salmon's ability to correctly discriminate the unique combination of odors of its stream of origin.

Both these factors, three-year-old fish and occasional straying, operated in the Great Lakes after the accidental introduction of pink salmon into Thunder Bay, Ontario (Lake Superior) in the spring of 1956. An odd-year run into Thunder Bay was established by 1959, but, within several years, additional odd-year runs were established in streams of northern Minnesota. By 1969, spawning runs were established along the eastern shore of Lake Superior and at two locations in Lake Huron, almost 300 km from the original point of introduction. In 1976, even-year spawning runs started on the upper peninsula of Michigan and in Ontario (Lake Superior), evidence that at least a few three-year-olds had been produced. By 1979, pink salmon spawning runs had been established in all of the Great Lakes.[31]

Of all the Pacific salmon, pinks show the greatest degree of **dimorphism** (different body forms in the two sexes) on the spawning grounds. Males develop a huge hump on their backs, hence the common name "humpback" or "humpy." The hump is composed of additional cartilage and fat added during the transformation to breeding condition. The hump is used in lateral displays to intimidate other males in much the same way as the ruff (shoulder hair) on a wolf is used in dominance-hierarchy interactions.

The heads of males elongate and widen, primarily due to the addition of cartilage between and around the frontal bones of the skull. The anterior part of the skull elongates by an additional two-thirds and widens by one-third. In addition, the bones tend to elongate too, especially the premaxillary (upper jaw) and dentary (lower jaw) bones. The growth of bone and cartilage and the separation of the upper jaw bones, premaxillary and maxillary, tends to make the jaws curve or hook. The hooked jaws of spawning males are called kypes.

The geographic range of pink salmon spawning streams is very broad. The southern limits for sustained spawning stocks are the Sacramento River on the eastern Pacific side and, on the Asian side, southern Hokkaido and the Korean Peninsula. In Asia, pinks occupy rivers all along the Sea of Okhotsk, Kamchatka Peninsula and the Gulf of Anadyr.[32] To the north and west, pinks become less abundant. Pinks spawn as far west as the Lena River in Siberia. On the American side, pinks occur in small numbers in streams north of the Bering Strait including

Kotzebue Sound, to well east of Point Barrow. Occasional strays reach as far east as the Mackenzie River on the Beaufort Sea.

Sockeye salmon—Sockeyes are the salmon most closely tied to lakes. All sockeye juveniles spend at least some time in lakes. The lake systems of southwest Alaska, Kodiak Island and the Copper River basin all support runs of sockeyes. In fact, the Bristol Bay (southwest) runs are the largest in the North Pacific, accounting for over 50% of the North American sockeyes.[33]

Spawning habitats for sockeyes include inlet streams to lakes and, often, the shallow, gravelly lakeshore itself. Iliamna Lake, west of Anchorage, is the largest sockeye-producing lake in the world. In Iliamna Lake, island beaches may account for up to 30% of the total spawning run.

These island beaches consist of large gravels with very little fine material. The gravel can be excavated easily by the females, but the interstices are large enough to allow coastrange sculpins and slimy sculpins to move through the gravel and, potentially, prey on the embryos. Stomachs of these sculpins were examined during salmon runs and the larger sculpins were found to eat salmon eggs. The bigger the sculpin, the more eggs were eaten.[34] Sculpins migrate into the spawning gravels of these islands just before the salmon arrive, ready for a free meal. While the sockeyes spawn, sculpins burrow into the nests and try to find eggs they can swallow. Freshly spawned eggs are easier because they are smaller. A process of water-hardening causes the embryos to swell and also toughens the egg membranes. These island-spawning stocks in Iliamna apparently have evolved a partial defense against egg predation; they have the largest egg diameters of any known sockeye stock. Many of these eggs are more than a mouthful.

As sockeye fingerlings emerge from their nests in the gravel, they move downstream into their nursery lake. The lake provides food in the form of insects and zooplankton such as copepods and cladocerans. The young salmon feed and grow. When fry first enter the lakes in early summer, daylight is continuous and young fish stay at shallow depths (less than 10 m), close to shore and near the bottom. This is the **littoral zone** in the lake. By midsummer, fry have extended their depth range during the day to 20 m (66 feet) and disperse into the water column, the **limnetic zone**, during the short night.[35] Sockeye fry exhibit vertical migrations in some lakes, as do some of their zooplankton prey.

At some threshold size, the young are fit for beginning the process of going to sea. Of course, timing is everything. The complex physiological adjustments of the parr-smolt transformation are coordinated with or driven by photoperiod. Increasing day length is necessary for successful completion of this process. So a sockeye reaching appropriate size in the fall or winter will have to wait until the following spring to begin the transformation process.

Over their whole range, sockeyes exhibit quite a bit of variability in length of stay in freshwater. In some lake systems, some juveniles spend only part of one summer before migrating. In others fish may spend up to two full summers. Why the variability? Some lakes are simply more productive than others because they have higher algal and plant production, leading to higher production of sockeye food. Even within a single lake there is variation in length of stay. Some sockeye juveniles are more aggressive and get more than their share of the food available. These fish grow faster and reach threshold size for outmigration earlier than other members of their cohort.

For sockeyes, the availability of spawning habitat is a limiting factor for production, but so also is the size and/or productivity of the lake. Lake **carrying capacity** amounts to the number of sockeye juveniles that can be supported. General productivity (algae > zooplankton > sockeyes) is a factor, but so is the actual size of the lake: generally, the bigger the lake, the bigger the population of juvenile sockeyes. An even better indicator than lake surface is the euphotic volume.

The Alaska Department of Fish and Game has experimented at enhancing sockeye returns to Alaskan lakes by adding fertilizer to lakes. The rationale is to stimulate primary production (algal and plant production) and, thereby, promote the production of more sockeye food organisms. To date, there has been some success in enhancing the size of natural runs by lake fertilization. If you are ever boating on an Alaskan lake and see someone dumping 100 pound bags of Miracle Grow in the lake, you will know why.

Actual outmigration is synchronized in a river so that all the juveniles that are going to leave freshwater do it at about the same time. This results in a huge pulse of small fish moving out into the estuary in a short period of time. The predators of small sockeye, and other salmon species, show up in the estuary to take advantage of an abundant food supply. These predators include sea-run Dolly Varden char, beluga whales and benthic fishes such as the staghorn sculpin. Back in territorial days, Dolly Varden were considered such a threat to sockeyes in the Wood River system, southwest Alaska, that the U.S. Bureau of Commercial Fisheries placed a bounty on them. You had to turn in the tail to receive your money.

While at sea, Alaskan juvenile and adult sockeyes are dispersed broadly through the Bering Sea and north Pacific Ocean. They, like other salmon species, overlap in ocean distribution with stocks from Asia and Canada. Recall that distribution of salmon at sea is, generally, influenced by sea surface temperature. Cold temperatures cause the fish to move south in the winter; warming in the spring causes them to move back northward. Sockeyes are mainly found near the sea surface. Japanese longline fisheries for sockeye were very successful setting longlines no deeper than 2 m and gillnets no deeper than 8 m.[33] Though they are concentrated at shallower depths, sockeyes are found down to 61 m (200 feet).[36] Sockeyes move closer to the surface at night.

Upstream migration of adults is probably synchronized primarily by photoperiod cues. Fish enter a river system over a period of weeks with the stocks that are to move the farthest upstream entering the river first. Based on Fraser River (British Columbia) studies, swimming speeds range from about 50 km (31 miles) per day in the really long-range migrators to about 35 km (22 miles) per day in fish that have a much shorter distance to swim. Fish bound for a specific spawning stream, that is, an identifiable spawning population, may be spread out in arrival times by as much as a week or two.

Swimming upstream is an energetically demanding process. Sockeyes (and all other salmon species) take advantage of eddies and slow water (near shore and near the bottom) in their migration. Since prehistoric times, dipnetters for salmon have taken advantage of this information and centered their fishing on these areas of fish congregation. These are the traditional and customary sites of subsistence fishing for salmon. Dip-netting has been largely replaced by fish wheels on the Yukon, but the fish wheels are placed strategically to take advantage of this aspect of salmon biology. The migration process, coupled with final preparation of the gonads for spawning, depletes most of the fat and protein reserves in these fish. Fat content may drop from 15% to less than 2% and protein reserves are also depleted.

One puzzle about sockeye salmon is their absence in the lakes of the upper Yukon River, in the Yukon Territory and northern British Columbia. One would expect these lakes to be suitable nursery habitat for sockeye juveniles. Perhaps the distance to be traveled is simply too great for this species to accomplish. In Alaska, the nursery lake most distant from the sea is Chauekuktuli Lake in the Tikchik River system in southwestern Alaska. This lake is 257 km (160 miles) from the sea. However, in British Columbia, there are nursery lakes in the Fraser River system that are 1000 km (620 miles) upstream.[33]

Finally, the other common name for sockeyes (red salmon) has led to confusion about the freshwater distribution of this species in Alaska. In spawning coloration, sockeyes are red-bodied with greenish heads and bear no spots on either the body or tail fin. Coho salmon take on a somewhat similar coloration but have lots of black spots on the back and upper lobe of the tail fin. Chinooks can, on the spawning grounds, show a very deep red coloration with dark spots on both lobes of the tail fin. While counting fish at the Chena River flood control dam in North Pole, Alaska, a friend had to repeatedly explain to visitors that a red-colored salmon crossing under the dam was not a red (sockeye) salmon.

Chum salmon—Chums are often called dog salmon because of one of the major uses of these salmon by Athabascans in Alaska. Before the advent of snowmachines, Alaskan natives traveled primarily by dog team. Maintaining enough dogs to provide transportation was as essential and common then as maintaining the family car is now for most Americans. Chum salmon were the fuel for the dogs as well as for the humans. In the interior, chum salmon runs were and are extremely important in maintaining the subsistence life style of Athabascans. Chinook and coho also contribute, but neither pinks nor sockeyes occur in interior Alaska.

In terms of maximum distances covered in upstream migration, chum salmon are on a par with chinooks. Stocks of both species move up the Yukon River all the way to streams near Whitehorse and Teslin in British Columbia some 3200 river km (2000 miles) from the mouth of the Yukon. Bear in mind that these fish may have covered an even greater distance in the ocean before ever arriving at the mouth of the river. As is the case with chinook salmon, chums in the Yukon have the highest fat content of all chums in Alaska.

Chum salmon fingerlings begin their downstream outmigration as soon as they exit the gravel. You can imagine that it takes some time to negotiate the great distances these fish must traverse if they originate on the upper Yukon or

Tanana Rivers. The journey takes many days. The little fish orient to light and current in such a way as to position themselves in fast current at night and slow (or no) current during the daylight hours. Chum fingerlings have to pass through a lot of river miles laden with predators including northern pike, sheefish and even grayling. These predators orient to prey primarily by vision so chums tend to hide during the day and move at night.

Once the juvenile chums reach the estuary, they share the nearshore habitat with juvenile pink salmon that are about the same size. Do they divide up the potentially available food or fight over the same foods? In Prince William Sound, chum salmon young tend to feed mainly on small calanoid copepods that swim up in the water. Juvenile pinks select prey closer to the bottom, primarily harpacticoid copepods. Harpacticoids crawl over the surface of the bottom or, occasionally, swim an inch or two off the bottom for a brief time. So the juveniles of these salmon species seem to effectively partition the available resources and don't appear to directly compete with each other.[32]

At sea, chums occupy northeast Pacific waters at least as far south as 45°N. Chum diets during their last summer at sea consists of the following: in May and June euphausiids (krill) are the main food; from June-July pteropods (pelagic snails) dominate, and in August fish make up over half their prey.

How mobile are chum salmon out at sea? Mature individuals make vertical excursions, swimming down to depths as great as 100 meters at times but remain above the **thermocline**. That is, they stay in the upper, warm, well-mixed surface waters. Fish return to the upper

5 meters 2-8 times per hour. Most fish stay in the upper 20 meters. Chums are, on average, shallower during flooding tide stage and swim a little faster than during ebbing tides. Maximum swimming speeds measured in the ocean are just under 10 miles per hour.[37]

Chum salmon have the widest natural geographic range of all the Pacific salmon species. On the North American side of the Pacific, chums occurred as far south as the San Lorenzo River near Monterey, California, but fish are now seen in northern California only on rare occasions. Columbia River stocks have been radically reduced by hydroelectric dams on the Columbia and Snake Rivers. Even though fish ladders have been installed to aid the upstream migration of spawners, the dams are still a significant barrier. Downstream migrants, the fry, are typically sucked through the turbines and killed.

On the Asian side, chums spawn in the freshwaters of the Korean Peninsula, the waters of the Japanese islands of Kyushu, Honshu and Hokkaido. In the north, chums spawn in rivers of the Russian Arctic as far west as the Lena River. In the eastern Arctic, chums occasionally spawn in the Mackenzie River and its tributaries. The farthest north commercial chum fisheries are in the Kotzebue Sound (Kobuk and Noatak Rivers).

Coho salmon—Cohos run up both coastal and interior Alaska rivers. In the interior, spawners move up the Tanana River at least as far as Delta Junction. In the Yukon, cohos reach Eagle and may move across the border into Canadian waters. The Porcupine River, a tributary of the Yukon in extreme northeastern Alaska, maintains runs of cohos that also cross upstream into Canada.

Cohos are cultured in hatcheries to enhance natural runs and also to establish separate hatchery stocks. Coho salmon stocks, as well as chinook, occasionally produce diminutive males on the spawning grounds. These males, called **jacks**, are reproductively mature but much smaller than typical males. Jacks return after only one year at sea. One would think that such a small male on the spawning grounds would have absolutely no chance of successfully competing with a large male. Apparently, large, dominant males don't recognize jacks as males. The small males hang around the periphery of a female territory until she is ready to spawn with the territorial male. When both large fish are in the redd and begin to spawn, the jack sneaks in quickly and releases his milt too. So, if successful, his sperm are competing directly with those of the dominant male. Thus, even these jacks have some measure of spawning success if they can slip past the territorial male. I should stress that the proportion of jack males in natural populations is very low.

Hatchery studies in British Columbia have shed light on the production of jack cohos. The Canadians found that there is a positive correlation of smolt body weight and the yield of jacks that return. In other words, the bigger the smolts, the larger the jack and the more jacks in the returning population. Also, increasing the jack production reduced the production of normal adults. Finally, larger smolts led to larger adults but not more adults. Therefore, hatchery programs designed to maximize the value of the returning spawners should attempt to reduce the production of jack males. This amounts to release of moderately sized smolts rather than large ones;

their release should be pretty late in the outmigration season (early June in Vancouver).[38]

Chinook salmon—chinook or king salmon are the largest of the Pacific salmons, averaging 7-9 kg (15- 20 pounds) in Cook Inlet. The largest officially recorded chinook came from the Petersburg area and weighed 57.3 kg (126 pounds).[39] Chinooks run up streams in North America from Ventura, California to Point Hope, Alaska. On the Asian side, chinooks reach Hokkaido, in Japan, and the Anadyr River of northern Chukotsk Peninsula.[39] In North America, chinooks are divided into a thousand or more individual spawning populations, each of which consists of no more than a few tens of thousands. Most of these populations average less than 1,000 fish each.[40] Occasionally, a few fish stray into the Beaufort Sea; chinooks have been seen as far east as the Coppermine River, Northwest Territories.

Chinook populations have been separated into two behavioral types, a "stream-type" and an "ocean-type." The stream-type occurs in Asian and Alaskan populations, and in headwater stream populations at lower latitudes in North America. These fish typically spend one or more years in freshwater before migrating to sea. Once at sea, they make extensive excursions offshore into the Gulf of Alaska. At maturity, stream-type fish return to freshwater in the spring or summer, several months before they actually spawn. In contrast, ocean-type chinooks outmigrate in their first year, spend their saltwater existence near shore in coastal waters and return to freshwater only a few days to a week before spawning in the fall. Young of the year chinooks nearing time to outmigrate (ocean-type) are about 70 mm (2.75 inches);

1-year olds (stream-type) from a variety of rivers average 94 mm (3.75 inches).[40] There are even larger outmigrating juveniles, however. It appears that some Yukon River chinook stay in the river 2-3 years.

A few estimates have been made of the survival, in freshwater, of chinook from spawning to fry and/or smolt stages. Unfortunately, none of those studies were done in Alaska. Mortality may range as high as 80-90 %. The most critical times appear to be (1) at egg deposition, (2) during flood events when nests are eroded or covered with silt, and (3) low-water events that dry the nests.

As is characteristic of other salmon species, chinook smolts spend a brief time in estuaries completing their adaptation to seawater and feeding. The main foods of ocean-type smolts in the Fraser River estuary are chironomid (midge) larvae and pupae and, secondarily, benthic amphipods (beachhoppers), mysids (opossum shrimps) and cladocerans (water fleas).[41] Larger smolts (typically stream-type) occupy deeper channels in the estuary and feed heavily on chum salmon smolts plus the invertebrates mentioned above.

There is quite a long list of foods of chinook at sea. Fish prey dominate the diets of chinooks in the ocean; anchovy and rockfishes predominate in coastal waters south of Washington, and herring and sand lance are the major items north of Washington. Invertebrate prey organisms consist mainly of euphausiids (krill) and squid. Most feeding studies rely on fish caught in nearshore, commercial fisheries and, thus, may not tell us the whole story.

All salmon have salmon-colored flesh, right? Wrong. In southeastern Alaska, about 30% of chinook salmon have white flesh. There are very few white-fleshed fish from populations north or south of this area. This raises the question: what is the function of pink-colored flesh? The pink or salmon color is, chemically, carotenoids. Carotenoids are a common set of pigments in crustacea and undoubtedly enter the salmon body in the diet. There are genetically-controlled mechanisms for mobilizing and depositing these pigments in the flesh and also in the eggs of salmon and also chars.

What is the point, evolutionarily, of messing with carotenoids? It turns out that deposition of carotenoids in flesh and in eggs is linked; a salmon can't do one without doing the other. It is thought that heavily pigmented salmon eggs are better able to respire at low oxygen concentrations such as might occur at high stream temperatures or at low water percolation rates in winter. Populations of chinook with white flesh and nonpigmented eggs are only found in short coastal streams or in the lower reaches of larger rivers of the area, habitats in which non-pigmented eggs (embryos) would be less likely to experience low oxygen availability.[42]

This pigmentation problem probably goes back to the reestablishment of salmon spawning runs in southeast Alaska and British Columbia after the last ice age. Founder populations of chinook in these recently deglaciated drainages of southeast consisted (as they almost always do) of a few stray fish that couldn't or wouldn't find their natal streams. Small founder populations can be skewed, genetically, because there are so few fish. If one of only a few spawners had a genetic defect so that it couldn't store pigment in egg (or flesh), most of its offspring would probably have had the same trait. Some

ingenious marketing person came up with the idea of calling these fish "ivory kings."

Dolly Varden char

The Dolly Varden char gets its common name from the novel "Barnaby Rudge" by Charles Dickens. A female character, Dolly Varden, is always brightly arrayed with colorful gingham dresses. The Dolly Varden, *Salvelinus malma*, fish is similarly adorned with bright colors during spawning season. Dolly Varden and other chars are members of the trout/salmon family (the Salmonidae), along with trout, grayling, Atlantic and Pacific salmons. All the chars, including the brook trout, Arctic char, lake trout and Dolly Varden, are placed in the genus *Salvelinus*. One of the distinguishing features of the chars is the presence on the body of light-colored spots on a darker background. Typical trouts (in the genera *Salmo* and *Oncorhynchus*) including brown and cutthroat trouts, Atlantic and Pacific salmons all, to the extent they have spots, have dark spots on a lighter background.

Populations of Dolly Varden are widespread in Alaska including the North Slope, Aleutians, southwestern and southeastern Alaska. On the Asian side of Bering Strait, this fish ranges from the Chukhotsk Peninsula through the Kamchatka Peninsula and southward to Japan and Korea. Somewhere in southern British Columbia, the Dolly Varden is replaced by a close relative, the bull trout, *Salvelinus confluentus*. The closest living relative, however, is the Arctic char, *Salvelinus alpinus*. The arctic char is distributed all the way around the Arctic including Greenland, Iceland, arctic Canada, Alaska, all across Eurasia to Scotland and Ireland. It also co-occurs with Dolly Varden along the east Asian coast down to Japan. Why did evolution work to provide two almost indistinguishable char species whose geographic ranges almost completely overlap in Alaska and the Far East? We don't know the answer, but it seems likely that during one of the Pleistocene glacial events a population of Arctic char was isolated south of the Bering Land Bridge. This isolated population was undoubtedly exposed to a different set of selective pressures than its nearest relatives north of the land bridge. Natural selection acted on this set of pressures and altered the population enough to make it recognizably different. Presumably, that altered population, Dolly Vardens, dispersed at the end of the glaciation.

Alaskan Dolly Vardens exhibit two different life histories, often in the same stream or drainage. Some fish are stream residents. That is, they spend their entire lives in freshwaters, and presumably in the very same stream. Other fish are anadromous. A comparison of body size and reproductive potential of these two forms from the same river again highlights the advantage of anadromy over stream residency. In southeast Alaska, stream-resident, mature females average 17 grams (6 ounces) in weight and bear about 66 eggs each. Anadromous females average 635 grams (11.25 pounds; over 30 times larger) and 1888 eggs (almost 30 times more) each. The feeding habits and potential food resources differ in these two groups, too. Stream residents feed on fingerlings of pink and chum salmon in late spring and, in late summer switch to salmon eggs. Sea-run fish feed primarily on herring, sand lance and capelin, abundant forage fishes in southeastern Alaska.[43]

Populations on the North Slope of Alaska also exhibit both anadromous and resident life histories. Resident females are small, have a fecundity range of 42-346 eggs, with egg diameters of 2.8-4.0 mm (0.11-0.16 inches). Anadromous females have a fecundity range of 1500-7000 eggs with larger (3.5-6.0 mm) eggs. Resident fish eat insects while anadromous fish eat amphipods, mysids and fish, including arctic cod, sculpins and outmigrating salmon smolts.[44]

What could be the advantage of staying in the stream? Anadromous Dollys spend their first 3-4 years in freshwater before undergoing the parr-smolt transformation and outmigration. They spend another six years reaching maturity. Therefore, most anadromous adults are 7-9 year olds at first spawning. In the Sagavinirtok River, about 5% of the adults spawn in consecutive years; the other 95% are alternate year (or less frequent) spawners. Very few of these fish reach 10 years. Thus, very few fish spawn more than twice, and many may die after a single spawning run. In contrast, resident fish mature as 3-4 year olds, just as the anadromous fish are outmigrating. These resident fish spawn annually but live to be about only seven years old.[44] Resident fishes avoid the dangers and benefits of going to sea, spawn relatively few eggs but spawn three to four times. These multiple strategies are a hedge against the possibility of disastrous conditions befalling either the resident fish in the stream or the sea-run fish at sea.

Embryonic development in the spawning gravels of the North Slope requires seven to eight months. Conversely, the open-water feeding season in these streams is only two to three months long. No wonder resident fish grow so slowly.

Lake trout

To the fanatic sport fisherperson, the lake trout is misnamed. It really should be called the lake char. Lake trout can be distinguished from arctic char and/or Dolly Varden by the presence of white (rarely yellow) spots as opposed to the red, pink, orange or yellow spots on the other two. Also, lake trout have a deeply forked tail; the other two don't. The largest lake trout ever caught (that everyone can agree on) was a 46.4 kg (102 lb) fish netted in Lake Athabasca in 1961. The fish was over 125 cm (49 in) long. The largest taken by an angler came from Lake Bennett, Yukon Territory, and weighed 39.5 kg (87 pounds). Maximum age measured on a lake trout was 62 years; the fish was caught in the Northwest Territories. Generally, lake trout from high latitudes and colder waters live longer and grow more slowly than those from lower latitudes and warmer waters.

Lake trout are confined in their distribution to northern North America and, more specifically, to areas that experienced the Pleistocene glaciations. Previously glaciated areas that don't have lake trout are the extreme southern limits of the continental ice sheets, such as Nebraska, Iowa, Indiana and South Dakota. Also, the lowlands of the Hudson's Bay and James Bay, northern Canada are missing lake trout. In Alaska, lake trout are found in lakes of the Brooks Range, alpine lakes on the north (but not south) side of the Alaska Range, lakes on the north side of the Alaska Peninsula and other lakes draining into Bristol Bay. The lake trout's apparent inability to successfully tolerate lowland lakes may account for the fact that lake trout didn't disperse across the Bering Land Bridge to Asia at the heights of the Pleistocene glacial episodes.

Lake trout are primarily residents of deep-water lakes, and one wonders how they dispersed throughout most of the previously ice-covered landscape to their current locations. First, in the northern part of their range, lake trout, *Salvelinus namaycush*, do frequent clear rivers and, presumably, have used rivers as routes of dispersal in the past. A second means of dispersal that undoubtedly worked during the melt-back of the glaciers was occupation of large lakes that formed at the melting face of the glaciers. These **periglacial lakes** followed the receding glaciers, changing their sizes and boundaries as the glaciers melted. The lakes were often large enough and deep enough to cut across entire watersheds and allow fishes to move from one river system to the next. Lake trout probably occupied these periglacial lakes. Many of the lakes in Alaska and northern Canada are the remnants of glacial melt-back and could have been populated by lake trout before their isolation from connections with a larger, periglacial lake or a nearby river.

The lake trout has a reputation as a predator of other fishes, including grayling, ciscoes, round whitefish, sticklebacks, longnose suckers, slimy sculpin and even other lake trout. Indeed, large lake trout in many areas feed almost exclusively on other fishes.[45] Some years ago some friends and I were fishing from canoes in Landlocked Tangle Lake, in the Alaska Range. I landed a nice lake trout, about 16 inches long. Being an ever curious biologist, I examined the stomach and its contents as I prepared the fish for the frying pan. Instead of fish in the stomach, I found snails.

In the absence of fish prey, lake trout concentrate on the types of prey that are available. Small (10 cm; 4 in) lake trout in arctic lakes feed on plankton using vision as their main sense.[46] This form of planktivory differs from a non-selective filtration of the water column as the fish swims. Rather, the fish selects individual prey and secures them, one by one. In some lakes with little or no access to fish and with very little in the way of bottom-dwelling invertebrates, lake trout are almost totally dependent on plankton. These fish have low growth rates, mature late in life and don't live as long as they do elsewhere, presumably because they burn up too much metabolic energy pursuing lots of individual, small prey.[47,48]

In Toolik Lake, on the Arctic Coastal Plain, lake trout occur with grayling and round whitefish. As we might expect, these fish fall prey to lake trout. But, surprisingly, the single most important prey item is the snail, *Lymnaea,* occurring in 70% of the fish. The fish select relatively large snails (more energy intake per item consumed). Does the lake trout have an effect on prey populations? Yes. In nearby, trout-less lakes, adult *Lymnaea* are significantly larger and more abundant than in Toolik Lake.[49] The lake trout also affects the competition between *Lymnaea* and the other snail, *Valvata,* by effectively eliminating the larger snail (*Lymnaea*) from the bare sediment habitat in the lake.[50] This leaves the smaller *Valvata* free to occupy and feed in the bare sediment. Thus, the lake trout affects the benthic community structure and composition by its selective feeding.

In these same arctic lakes, lake trout often occur together with slimy sculpins. When lake trout are present, the sculpins tend to stay in the shallow, rocky habitat instead of deeper, bare sediment habitat. Since the sculpin's main food, midge larvae, are much more common in the bare sediment, the lake trout are limiting the sculpin's access to food and, thereby, limiting their growth. So, when they occur together, slimy sculpins grow more slowly and are less common.[51]

Spawning occurs in the fall. In Alaska, this means late August to mid- September. At the southern part of lake trout distribution, spawning may be delayed until early December. Boulders and rubble in lakes is the typical spawning habitat. Pairs or small groups release eggs and milt, and the fertilized eggs fall into the cracks or spaces between boulders. Lake trout, therefore, differ from the salmon species in that they neither dig a nest nor bury the embryos. Time to hatching depends primarily on water temperature; the colder the water, the longer it takes to complete embryonic development.

Hatching can occur as late as June in some high-latitude lakes. Hatching in May or June does not necessarily mean that these larval fish are late. Cold temperatures also dictate the timing of production of the organisms that will serve as food for lake trout larvae. As often as not, larvae are in the water, ready to feed as food organisms become available. At lower latitudes, lake trout probably spawn every fall. In the Far North, there is evidence that spawning typically occurs every other year or, possibly, every third year.[39] Maximum age in Alaska is 38 years.[48]

In Alaska, lake trout are part of the Alaska Department of Fish and Game stocking program. For example, in 1999, ADF&G planned to stock 4,000 catchable fish in Harding Lake, east of Fairbanks, and 15,000 fish in landlocked lakes of south-central Alaska (south of the Alaska

Range). Elsewhere, lake trout have been introduced to California, Nevada, Colorado, Oregon, Idaho, Utah, Wyoming, Massachusetts, Connecticut, Argentina, Peru, Bolivia, Finland, Sweden, Switzerland, France and New Zealand.[52]

Arctic grayling

The arctic grayling, *Thymalus arcticus*, is one of the most attractive members of the trout/salmon family (Salmonidae). Its long, tall, colorful dorsal fin sets it apart from its cousins. The dorsal fin has 17-25 fin rays (supports) compared to a range of 8-16 for all the other Alaskan salmonids. The fin itself is often as tall as the body depth of the fish, edged in purple and covered with spots of red to orange and/or purple to green (Figure 9.3). Males have larger fins than females. If you lay the dorsal fin flat on the body and it extends back to the little adipose fin behind it, you have a male. The dorsal fin of females doesn't quite reach the adipose fin.

Grayling have dark backs of blue-gray or purple-blue and lighter sides and bellies. There is a scattering of small black spots above the

pectoral fins that become less distinct as the fish grows and matures.

Size and age at sexual maturity vary considerably over the grayling's geographic range, as do growth rates. Lengths at age for interior Alaska grayling are: age 1, 14.8 cm (6 inches); age 2, 19.2 cm (7.5 inches); age 3, 22.8 cm (9 inches); age 4, 26.5 cm (10.5 inches); age 5, 30.4 cm (12 inches). Generally, Alaskan populations grow more slowly and probably mature later than populations at lower latitudes. In most Alaskan streams and lakes, 12-14 inch grayling are very large, respectable fish. The current North American record is a fish from the Katseyedie River, Northwest Territories. It weighed 2.7 kg (5 lb 15 oz) and measured 75.7 cm (just under 30 inches).

The arctic grayling's geographic range is quite large, extending from the western shore of Hudson's Bay, Canada, across Alaska and into central Asia, where it is replaced by the European grayling. The southern extremes of its range are northern Mongolia and the upper Yalu River (China) in Asia and the headwaters of the Missouri River (Montana) in North America. Northern Michigan stocks of grayling

Figure 9.3: Arctic grayling. The long dorsal fin is its most unique feature.

became extinct early in the 20th century. The geographically isolated populations in Michigan and Montana are/were relict populations left behind by the retreating ice sheets at the end of the last ice age. The grayling has been introduced into southeast Alaska, Kodiak Island and into numerous lakes and streams in Canada.[45]

My friend, Dale Guthrie, and I had just packed our Dall sheep off an interior Alaska mountain. We were at least 12 hours ahead of our scheduled pick-up time. It was a warm, sunny August evening; why not spend some time fishing for grayling? We had had the forethought to pack two collapsible fishing rods in the airplane that had dropped us off, and had left them on the gravel bar where we were to be retrieved. We started fishing the pool just opposite the landing strip, and Dale immediately caught a grayling about 14 inches long—nice fish. I cast and immediately caught a 13-inch grayling. On successive casts we caught successively smaller grayling. At this point, we decided to move downstream to see if different pools would produce the same pattern of catches. The next five pools and the fish we caught from them revealed that, invariably, the first fish from a pool to take the spinner was the biggest fish we caught from that pool. And, invariably, the second fish caught was the second largest.

In other words, these grayling seemed to have a dominance hierarchy in each pool with the dominant (largest) fish occupying the most favored position for capturing food (lure, in this case) drifting downstream. As we removed the dominant fish, the next fish in the hierarchy moved into the position previously occupied by the largest fish. A solitary grayling in a pool will pick the position that will yield the best return

in food energy for the energy expended in swimming.[53] It is maximizing net energy intake. If there are more than one fish, the dominant fish takes the best position and the rest of the fish take less desirable feeding positions based on their ranks in the hierarchy. Experiments in which the dominant fish in a pool was removed showed that all the remaining fish moved up a step in the hierarchy.[54]

In the fishing experiment we conducted on that wilderness stream, we were lucky. It was a remote river that hardly ever experienced fishing pressure. A similar fishing experiment on a stream that saw heavy fishing pressure would probably come out differently. Older, wiser fish on the Chena River, near Fairbanks, might not be quite so cooperative.

Dale and I were observing grayling distribution on just a very short reach of the river. Would we have caught bigger fish elsewhere on this same river? Summertime sampling on several interior Alaska rivers shows that, over distances of 180 km (110 miles) on the Goodpaster and shorter distances on tributaries of Birch Creek, grayling get larger as you go upstream. This trend is the opposite of that seen in most other fishes. The largest fish tend to occupy headwaters; juvenile fish occupy the lower reaches. Why do the big fish go so far upstream? One possibility is that the upper reaches are the most favorable grayling habitat, and the big, dominant fish simply push out the more subordinate fish. Another possibility is that small fish require or prefer quiet waters typical of the lower reaches of Alaskan rivers and don't even try to occupy the headwaters. When large fish are removed from the headwaters smaller fish move in.[55] Thus, it appears that size-related dominance is important in determining the size distribution of grayling in a river, at least during the summertime when feeding is so critical.

As summer turns to fall, the headwaters and upper reaches of streams and rivers cool and eventually freeze. Generally these are shallow waters that freeze to the bottom in the absence of the influence of a hot spring or significant groundwater input. Thus, stream-dwelling arctic grayling over most of Alaska move downstream during the fall, seeking suitable habitat in which to survive the long winter. "Suitable" means unfrozen. Typical overwintering habitat consists of deep holes in streams, lakes or the channels of major rivers such as the Yukon or Tanana Rivers. Wintertime is a season of low activity due to very low water temperatures and low food availability. Water flow under the ice is very slow, and these fish don't have to swim hard to maintain position; they probably look pretty lethargic under the ice. Presumably, the large, aggressive fish of the summer relax their dominating behaviors and become much more gregarious under the ice in the winter, when they are packed together a lot tighter.

Springtime brings the thawing of ice and snow all along the course of Alaskan streams and rivers. Breakup is a time when river ice goes downstream with a rush. Mature grayling begin their upstream, spawning migration during or immediately after breakup (typically in April) and, in some systems, may swim as much as 160 km (100 miles) to reach their spawning grounds. Spawning can occur from mid-May to June.[39]

Males establish territories in the spawning streams and defend them by making lateral displays in which the large dorsal fin (and, sometimes the pelvic fins too) is erected. Smaller males are often chased when they encroach too closely. The dorsal fin is also used by the male in courtship displays. If everything goes right, the male grasps the female by curving its dorsal fin over the body of the female and by wrapping its tail over the female's tail. The grasp is made more secure by the presence of small fleshy bumps (tubercles) on the posterior ends of the spawning fish.[56] These tubercles constitute a non-skid surface much like the palms of work gloves that have a pattern of rubber bumps. This is the moment for release of the eggs and milt. Fertilized eggs fall to the bottom of the stream and are adhesive. Swimming movements of the spawning pair stir up sediment that may cover the fertilized eggs. Unlike Pacific salmon, Arctic grayling don't dig a well-defined nest.

The number of eggs released by each female is size-dependent, averaging 4,000-7,000 per fish. Very large females may produce up to 16,000 eggs. Embryonic development to hatching varies from 11 to 21 days, depending on water temperature. Larval grayling begin feeding on the third day even though the yolk sac isn't completely absorbed until the eighth day.

Survival of embryos and newly hatched larvae depends, at least in part, on stream flow. High rates of stream flow, such as would be produced by the melt of higher than usual snow levels, are potentially devastating to these young grayling. First, the embryos may be dislodged from the bottom and tumbled downstream.[57] Second, newly hatched larvae are weak swimmers and could be flushed downstream into unfavorable habitat including high-water pools that will dry up in early summer.

Growth rates of these young of the year vary widely across Alaska depending mainly on the overall level of plant productivity. An experiment was conducted in which the Kuparuk River (North Slope) was fertilized by addition of soluble phosphorus. Presumably, the added phosphorus increased plant (primary) productivity that, in turn, added to the food available to young grayling. The result was that grayling attained body sizes 1.4 to 1.9 times bigger in the first year than fish in a control stream that wasn't fertilized.[58]

Let's go back to grayling feeding behavior. In streams, grayling feed largely on drifting organisms that have been dislodged from the bottom or have fallen into the water. Individual fish maintain position in the flowing stream and let the water bring the food to them. Grayling detect prey visually, scanning about 60° to each side of their body axis in front of them. This is their **search volume**. How effective are they in detecting prey? That depends on size of prey, size of fish, light intensity, water velocity and the amount of debris suspended in the water.[59] Debris is probably always present in streams. But higher than normal water flows following unusual snowmelt or intense rainstorms can increase debris levels dramatically. These conditions probably result in less feeding and, perhaps, to slowing or to a complete stop in growth.

Lake populations of grayling have somewhat different feeding behaviors. First, the suspended prey (zooplankton) are not necessarily being moved by a current. Grayling, rather than swimming continuously to maintain a fixed position in the stream, must move about to find slowly moving prey. Locomotion consists of alternating bursts of swimming with coasting. The coasting period is when grayling search for

prey. Prey can be detected in the forward 220° of the visual field in lakes, producing a larger search volume than in streams.[60] Small grayling in lakes eat plankton, but large individuals tend to feed on bottom-dwelling animals or on emergent insects. Not all zooplankton organisms are selected by grayling. A large, red-pigmented copepod, *Diaptomus pribilofensis*, is not eaten by grayling, apparently because it is almost always successful in avoiding the grayling's attack.[61]

Are grayling much affected by human activity? In Alaska's interior, the arctic grayling is the most popular target of anglers. Grayling populations in streams and rivers accessible to Fairbanks and its surrounding road system have been, in the past, hit hard by fishing pressure. These problems have been dealt with using catch-and-release and minimum size restrictions. Remember that arctic grayling are slow-growing fish that don't mature sexually until about age 6-9 years. Other human activities that can affect grayling include air pollution, road building, logging, mining, and even commercial and residential property development.

Arctic grayling and lake trout from remote lakes in the Brooks Range have been tested and found to contain organochlorine compounds such as pesticides and PCBs. Local sources for such pollutants are extremely unlikely; these chemicals are undoubtedly being blown in from other parts of the globe. The most abundant organochlorine compound in both muscle and liver of grayling is p,p'-DDE, a degradation product of DDT. Ten different PCBs have been identified from grayling, eleven from lake trout. If I were to catch a fish of either species in Alaska I would not hesitate to cook and eat it; total concentrations of organochlorines were under 10ng/g of flesh and total PCBs were under 2 ng/g.[62]

Such long-range atmospheric transport also has been documented for radioactive isotopes of elements produced in the testing of nuclear weapons. Several that have been deposited at high latitudes from such tests include ^{131}I and [90]Sr. Other trace elements and heavy metals are also moved by atmospheric aerosols.[63] This means that metal concentrations in lakes and streams may result from multiple sources, not just mining activity.

Mining would seem to be the most obvious human activity in terms of potential to negatively impact grayling. Placer mining for gold in Alaska involves sluicing, that is, washing stripped ground over a sorting box to collect the gold. In many cases, the washed material is released into a settling pond where sediment settles to the bottom of the pond. This process can greatly reduce or eliminate problems relating to addition of solids to the stream itself. Even if most solids are removed, the effluent water, typically, has higher heavy metal concentrations than upstream of the mining operation. For example, on Birch Creek, in interior Alaska, mining in the early 1980s was associated with elevated iron, arsenic, zinc and copper.[64] These heavy metals may present problems to the fish depending on the concentrations and the particular array of metals.

In many mining situations a considerable amount of solid material is added to the stream in the sluicing process. That material includes inorganic sediment and organic debris. As we saw earlier, added debris reduces the search volume in grayling feeding. An experiment on potential effects of mining-induced turbidity on grayling was conducted in the mid-1980s. Young of the year sac fry, the larvae still having a yolk sac, and two-year-old juveniles were caged and placed in two streams. One was an unmined tributary of Birch Creek; the other, a similar sized, mined branch of Birch Creek. Exposure to turbidity in this case was associated with reduced fat reserves and higher mortality in sac fry. Juveniles caged in the turbid stream exhibited reduced food intake, increased mucus production and pathological changes in gill tissue, probably due to abrasion by sediment particles. The riffles in the turbid stream had a lower density of insect prey.[65]

In the wild, grayling probably choose to avoid high turbidity and would respond by moving downstream until they find a clearwater tributary. Such movements really amount to a loss of habitat (or an overcrowding of remaining habitat) for grayling when intense feeding and growth are normally occurring. If high turbidity occurs during or shortly after spawning, the eggs or developing embryos could be covered with sediment, smothered and killed.

Surprisingly, some forms of development may in some cases enhance wildlife habitat. An example is the use of gravel extraction pits on the North Slope as overwintering habitat for grayling. The problem is that small tundra streams on the North Slope typically have no overwintering habitat because they freeze to the bottom. The gravel pits, however, are much deeper and can provide a winter haven for grayling.[66]

Alaska blackfish

The geographic distribution of the Alaska blackfish is an excellent example of the effects of the last great ice age in the Far North. Presently, blackfish, *Dallia pectoralis*, are found on the mainland in western and interior Alaska and the Arctic Coastal Plain east to the Colville River. In addition, blackfish occur on St. Lawrence, Nunivak and St. Matthews Islands in the Bering Sea and on the Chukotsk Peninsula, northeastern Siberia. At the heights of the Pleistocene glaciations, sea level was considerably lower than at present and Alaska was directly connected to Asia by a broad lowland, the Bering Land Bridge. The Alaska blackfish thrived in this Beringian glacial refuge. The lowland was punctuated by a few highlands that, as the ice sheets melted, became isolated as islands in the Bering Sea. Populations of blackfish were isolated on these islands and on the Siberian side of the expanding sea.

Alaska blackfish (Figure 9.4) typically inhabit lowland streams and ponds characterized by slow-moving or stagnant water. However, they also occur in faster-moving streams and rivers and larger lakes if there is an abundance of aquatic vegetation. These fish exhibit an annual cycle of movement, common among Alaskan fishes, involving downstream migration in the fall and early winter followed by upstream migration around breakup in the spring. All but a few young of the year blackfish vacate tundra ponds in the winter.

Several features of blackfish biology account for their ability to survive in stagnant waters with very low oxygen content. First, blackfish are sluggish, lie-in-wait predators of aquatic insects that hang motionless most of the time. Movement and maneuvering is usually accomplished by undulations of the large pectoral fins while holding the body rigid. In other words, these fish have a very low metabolic demand for oxygen.

Second, blackfish breathe air. They have a standard set of gills for aquatic respiration but, when needed, gulp bubbles of air at the pond's surface. The bubble is held in a part of the esophagus that is very well supplied with blood vessels. Oxygen is absorbed from the bubble and carbon dioxide is diffused into the bubble.[67] After a time, the fish belches and, if necessary, swallows another bubble. If you chop or drill a hole through the ice of a pond containing

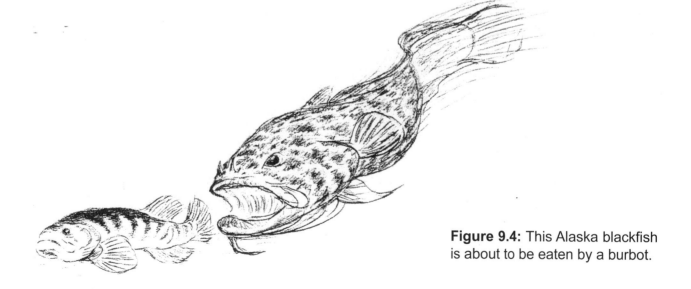

Figure 9.4: This Alaska blackfish is about to be eaten by a burbot.

blackfish, they congregate in the hole as if they were trying to escape the pond. Actually, they are coming up for air. In the summer, I used to catch blackfish in Goldstream valley using weighted minnow traps. I fished the traps in stagnant pools off Goldstream Creek itself. When I checked the traps daily, the fish came up healthy and vigorous. Once I delayed and waited an extra day to check the traps. The blackfish in the traps were dead, presumably, because they couldn't gulp air.

Perhaps the most fascinating and controversial aspect of blackfish natural history is their ability to withstand cold. Natives in western Alaska have known of the blackfish's special qualities for centuries; western culture's exposure to these fish began with the Harriman Expedition to Alaska in 1884. One of the expedition scientists observed dogs eating "frozen" blackfish that thawed in their stomachs, causing the dogs to vomit up the fish alive. In the early 1950s a scientist "proved" that blackfish cannot tolerate freezing by dipping them in liquid nitrogen at -90°. Very few, if any, creatures on this planet could survive such an artificial treatment although, as we saw in Chapter 2, many plants and animals can survive freezing.

Blackfish were traditionally caught in willow fish traps. The willow has been replaced with hardware cloth. Before the advent of snowmachines, blackfish were caught in large quantities for dog food as well as for human consumption. As dog mushing has declined in bush Alaska, the use of blackfish has shifted primarily to use as human food.

Sheefish

The sheefish, *Stenodus leucichthys*, (Figure 9.5) is a large predatory whitefish found over much of northern Eurasia, Alaska and Canada as far east as the Anderson River, just to the east of the Mackenzie River. The common name derives from an Athabascan name, *shees*, for this fish in the Great Slave Lake area. The other common name applied to this species in North America is inconnu. French Canadian members of the Richardson expedition in the 1820s were unfamiliar with this fish from their travels further south. So they called it *poisson inconnu*, unknown fish.

I have heard sheefish described as the tarpon of the Far North. I can't say if that amounts to a bit of hyperbole from an overzealous sportfishing guide or not. However, this species has one of most restricted ranges of any sport fish in North America. The rarity of sheefish should add to its sport fish appeal. Sheefish reach maximum sizes in North America of about 150 cm

Figure 9.5: Sheefish, or inconnu. This large-mouthed fish preys primarily on other fish. It is the largest whitefish species in North America.

(60 inches) in length and 28 kg (63 pounds). As young fish, sheefish feed primarily on invertebrates. Older fish are mainly **piscivorous** (fish-eating), feeding voraciously on least cisco, chinook salmon fingerlings, smelt, lampreys, char, blackfish, suckers and chubs.

The sheefish of northwestern Alaska support a subsistence fishery for native villages near Kotzebue Sound and along the Kobuk and Selawik Rivers. These fish are anadromous, spending a significant portion of fall and winter in estuaries. Upstream migration begins in some rivers as soon as breakup occurs with fish arriving on the spawning streams as early as July. In the Selawik area spawning grounds are about 200 km (124 miles) upriver; spawning occurs as much as 670 km (415 miles) up the Kobuk River. In the Yukon River drainage, spawning habitats in the clearwater tributaries (Charley River, Fortymile River) are upwards of 1900 km (1180 miles) from the sea.[68]

For decades there had been nagging doubts about the upper Yukon River sheefish. Do they really go all the way out to the sea and migrate all the way back to spawning sites? Or, instead, do some of these fish simply stay in the Yukon River over the winter and avoid the long migration? The sheefish in the headwaters of the Yukon such as Teslin Lake were thought to be permanent residents, not anadromous fish. To answer these questions, **otoliths** (ear bones) of sheefish were collected along the Yukon River in the vicinity of Circle and Eagle, Alaska, and additional fish from Yukon Territory. The mineral composition of the otoliths was examined with a technique called the electron microprobe. The vast majority of material in otoliths is calcium, but strontium is deposited when a fish spends time in salt water. The strontium is absorbed by the gills directly from the water and can't be absorbed from food.

Analysis of the ear bones shows that spawners from the Yukon all the way up to Eagle had the strontium "marine signature" in their otoliths.[69] Fish from Teslin Lake did not. In addition, the largest of the Teslin Lake adults were about the same size as the smallest spawners from further downriver. The anadromous Yukon River spawners ranged from 7-28 years old, and each had been to sea at least once. These fish probably spawn every third or fourth year. Sheefish do, indeed, migrate very long distances on the Yukon to spend time in the sea, but the headwaters are simply too far. A separate population of this species may be resident in the Minto Lakes of interior Alaska. These Minto Lakes fish spawn in the Tolovana and Chatanika Rivers and are thought to overwinter in the Yukon.

By its current geographic distribution, we can assume that the sheefish is an arctic-subarctic species, adapted to at least limited excursions at sea. Yet, at least the eastern two-thirds of northern Canada are excluded for the sheefish's range. Why? Apparently, the sheefish is still expanding its range since the disappearance of the last of the Pleistocene ice sheets. Its ability, or inability, to handle full seawater salinities may be acting as a brake on the dispersal of this species into suitable but, as yet, unoccupied habitat.

Northern pike

The northern pike, *Esox lucius*, is an important game fish sought after by sport fishers in most of the areas in which it occurs in North America. In Alaska, many of the lakes of the interior provide excellent pike fishing and are beginning to receive considerable fishing pressure. The Minto Lakes area west of Fairbanks has supported a subsistence fishery (from the village of Minto) for generations. Potential conflicts between subsistence and sport fishing in the Minto Lakes can, in part, be avoided by separating the fisheries in time and place by fishery regulations.[70] Many other rural communities in Alaska also fish for pike, primarily in the winter with gillnets set through the ice. Nets are set in the larger rivers where the fish congregate in the winter. Pike support commercial fisheries in both the U.S.A. and Canada with most of Canada's product being shipped to the U.S.

The largest pike caught in North America was 133 cm (4 feet 4 inches) long and weighed 22.3 kg (49 pounds). Larger pike have been caught in Europe. A 34 kg (69 pound) pike was caught in a lake south of Leningrad, Russia in 1930.

Northern pike have a circumpolar distribution in freshwater, extending from Scandinavia, to eastern Siberia and Alaska to Labrador. Its southern extreme in distribution occurs in Nebraska and Missouri in North America and, in Eurasia, in England, Ireland, northern Italy, the Dead and Caspian Seas. Pike are missing in the Canadian High Arctic and Keewatin (west of Hudson Bay) probably because they have not gotten there yet. In addition, pike have been introduced widely in North America as a sport fish.

Deep waters of lakes or major rivers are the preferred habitats in winter because these waters do not completely freeze. In springtime, after breakup, pike move to shallower waters. This could be an inshore movement to lake margins and/or upstream to marsh areas for spawning. Spawning is temperature-cued at 6-9°C (43-48°F).

Adult pike feed almost entirely on fish but, occasionally, take waterfowl (Figure 9.6), small rodents and, rarely, insects. In Alaska, important foods include whitefishes, small pike, blackfish, burbot, suckers and dragonfly nymphs. Stunting of pike has been reported in small lakes in Wisconsin; lack of suitable fish prey causes reduced growth rates.[71] There are undoubtedly examples of stunting of pike in Alaskan lakes as well.

One of the prey fishes in Alaska is the lake chub, the only minnow species occurring in the state. Minnows are interesting as potential prey because they produce alarm substances. These substances are secreted or released from the skin

Figure 9.6: Northern pike pushing aside lily pads to engulf a duckling. Pike eat fish, muskrats, water shrews and other aquatic life.

when a minnow is injured or killed by a predator. Detection of this chemical in the water elicits an escape response in other minnows. Thus, one individual may sacrifice itself and help save some of its relatives. The pike itself also gives off chemical cues that, to a naive minnow, produce no reaction. But minnows quickly associate the pike odor with the alarm substance and are soon able to exhibit the escape response without actually smelling the minnow alarm substance. It gets even more interesting. The alarm substance is apparently resistant to digestion and comes out the back end of the pike with the feces. Minnows exhibit the escape response when they sense the feces of pike that have eaten minnows recently. Not to be outdone, pike have either learned or evolved innate behavior in which they move out of their typical hunting habitat to defecate. In so doing, they give off fewer cues to potential prey.

Two forms of pike occur at high latitude in North America. One form, found in the Yukon River drainages and Bering Sea drainages, has a high vertebral count. A form with lower vertebral count is found in the Mackenzie River drainage system and points south. The first of these forms survived the Pleistocene in the Beringian refuge; the latter survived and dispersed from the Mississippi River refuge.

Burbot

Most burbot, *Lota lota*, harvested in Alaska are caught in the winter with set lines. The process involves augering or chopping a hole through the ice, setting your baited hook (attached to a pole) on the bottom of the river and waiting 24 hours. In the dead of winter, it is helpful to plug the hole with moss or clods of snow so that it doesn't freeze solid. According to my friend Tony Hillis, the way to catch a big burbot is to use a big bait. Burbot get pretty large in Alaska; the record for the state is 34 kg (75 pounds) and 152 cm (5 feet) in length. This fish was caught before the turn of the 20th century.

Winter habitat consists of deep lakes and deeper water in major rivers such as the Tanana and Yukon. Spawning occurs in December and January and involves writhing masses of individuals, perhaps 2 feet in diameter, moving over the bottom. Fertilized embryos move downriver and hatch under the ice. Large females have lots of eggs; one 6.1-pound female had 1.36 million eggs.

Growth of the young is rapid for cold-water fish. Young of the year may reach 3-8 inches in length by the end of the first summer. Small fish eat drift and benthic invertebrate. By the time fish reach lengths of 500 mm (20 inches), they have switched almost entirely to a diet of fish (Figure 9.4).

The burbot is the only freshwater cod of North America. Over its range on this continent, it is called by many names, some of them not very complimentary. Those names include lush, ling, loche, lawyer, methy, maria, eelpout and poor man's lobster. Burbot are distributed in freshwaters of Eurasia and North America southward to about 40°N. The species is absent from the Kamchatka Peninsula, western Norway, Scotland and Ireland and the Canadian High Arctic. Because burbot can tolerate brackish water, they occur in the Gulf of Bothnia, the upper end of the Baltic Sea.

Lakes and streams are intimately tied to forests and tundra

This chapter has explored some of the connections between streams, rivers, lakes and their finny inhabitants. The fishes relate to each other as predators, prey, and, perhaps, competitors. They have a significant influence on the terrestrial plants and animals of Alaska's boreal forests and tundra habitats as food of bears, mink, foxes, kingfishers and eagles. They, by virtue of falling prey to those animals, end up fertilizing the forest and tundra through those animals' feces.

The streams and lakes themselves affect soil temperature patterns and, therefore, vegetation patterns of terrestrial systems. As mentioned previously, the meandering of rivers and streams produce gravel bars and sandbars, the bare ground for plants to invade in the process of ecological succession. In the next chapter we will focus on several aquatic mammals with important ties to and influences on Alaska's terrestrial world. Also included is a brief overview of waterfowl and other birds that subsist on aquatic systems.

REFERENCES

1 Reynolds, J. B. 1997. Ecology of overwintering fishes in Alaskan freshwaters. pp. 281-302, In: A.M. Milner and M.W. Oswood, editors, Freshwaters of Alaska: ecological syntheses. Springer-Verlag, New York and Berlin.

2 Mathias, J.A. and Barica, J. 1980. Factors controlling oxygen depletion in ice-covered lakes. Canadian Journal of Fisheries and Aquatic Sciences 37: 185-194.

3 Gregory, L.S. 1988. Population characteristics of Dolly Varden in the Tiekel River, Alaska. M.S. Thesis, University of Alaska Fairbanks.

4 Bryant, M. D. 1984. The role of beaver dams as coho salmon habitat in southeast Alaska streams. pp. 183-192 In: J. M. Walton, and D. B. Houston editors, Proceedings of the Olympic Wild Fish Conference, Port Angeles, Washington.

5 Irons, III, J. G. and Oswood, M.W. 1992. Seasonal temperature patterns in an arctic and two subarctic Alaskan (U.S.A.) headwater streams. Hydrobiologia 237: 147-157.

6 Oswood, M. W., Irons, J. G., III and Milner, A. M. 1995. River and stream ecosystems of Alaska. pp. 9-32 In: C. E.Cushing, K. W. Cummins and G. W. Minshall editors. Ecosystems of the world 22: River and stream ecosystems. Elsevier Amsterdam.

7 LaPerriere, J. D., Van Nieuenhuyse, E. E. and Anderson, P. R. 1989. Benthic algal biomass and productivity in high subarctic streams, Alaska. Hydrobiologia 172: 63-75.

8 Cowan, C.A. and Oswood, M.W. 1984. Spatial and seasonal associations of benthic macroinvertebates and detritus in an Alaskan subarctic stream. Polar Biology 3: 211-215.

9 Irons III, J. G. 1988. Life history patterns and trophic ecology of Trichoptera in two Alaskan (U.S.A.) subarctic streams. Canadian Journal of Zoology 66: 1258-1265.

10 Kline, T. C. Jr., Goering, J. J. and Piorkowski, R. J.. 1997. The effect of salmon carcasses on Alaskan freshwaters. pp. 179-204, In: A.M. Milner and M.W. Oswood, editors, Freshwaters of Alaska: ecological syntheses. Springer-Verlag, New York and Berlin.

11 Peterson, B.J., Hobbie, J.E. and Corliss, T.L. 1986. Carbon flow in a tundra stream ecosystem. Canadian Journal of Fisheries and Aquatic Science 43: 1259-1270.

12 LeBrasseur, R.J., McAllister, C.D., Barraclough, W.E., Kennedy, O.D., Manzer, J., Robinson, D. and Stephens, K. 1978. Enhancement of sockeye salmon (Oncorhynchus nerka) by lake fertilization in Great Central Lake: summary report. Journal of the Fisheries Research Board of Canada 35: 1580-1596.

13 Alexander, V. and Gu, B. 1997. The limnology of Smith Lake. pp. 131-153, In: A.M. Milner and M.W. Oswood, editors, Freshwaters of Alaska: ecological syntheses. Springer-Verlag, New York and Berlin.

14 Lloyd, D. S., Koenings, J. P. and LaPerriere, J. D. 1987. Effects of turbidity in fresh waters of Alaska. North American Journal of Fisheries Management 7: 18-33.

15 McCart, P. J., Cross, P. M., Green, R., Mayhood, D. W., Tsui, P.T.P. and Green, R.H. 1980. Effects of siltation on the ecology of Ya-Ya Lake, N.W.T. Department of Indian Affairs and Northern Development, Northern Affairs Program, Environmental Studies 13, Ottawa, Canada.

16 Ruggles, C.P. 1965. Juvenile sockeye studies in Owikeno Lake, British Columbia. Canadian Fish Culturist 36: 3-21.

17 Van Nieuenhuyse, E.E. 1983. The effects of placer mining on the primary productivity of interior Alaska streams. Master's thesis, University of Alaska, Fairbanks.

18 Van Nieuenhuyse, E.E. and LaPerriere, J.D. 1986. Effects of placer gold mining on primary production in subarctic streams of Alaska. Water Resources Bulletin 22: 91-99.

19 Wagener, S.M. and LaPerriere, J.D. 1985. Effects of placer mining on the invertebrate communities of interior Alaska streams. Freshwater Invertebrate Biology 4: 208-214.

20 Simmons, R.C. 1984. Effects of placer mining sedimentation on arctic grayling in interior Alaska. Master's thesis. University of Alaska, Fairbanks.

21 Schmidt, D. and O'Brien, W.J. 1982. Planktivorous feeding ecology of Arctic grayling (Thymallus arcticus). Canadian Journal of Fisheries and Aquatic Sciences 39: 475-482.

22 LaPerriere, J. D. and Reynolds, J. B. 1997. Gold placer mining and stream ecosystems of interior Alaska. pp. 265-280, In: A.M. Milner and M.W. Oswood, editors, Freshwaters of Alaska: ecological syntheses. Springer-Verlag, New York and Berlin.

23 McLeay, D. J., Knox, A. J., Malick, J. B., Birtwell, I. K., Hartman, G. and Ennis,

G. L. 1983. Effects on Arctic grayling (*Thymallus arcticus*) of short-term exposure to Yukon placer mining sediments: Laboratory and field studies. Canadian Technical Report of Fisheries and Aquatic Sciences No. 1171. Fisheries and Oceans, Ottawa, Canada.

24 Miller, P. 1981. Fisheries resources of streams along the park road and in Kantishna Hills, Denali National Park and Preserve. Unpublished manuscript, U.S. Department of the Interior, National Park Service, Anchorage, Alaska.

25 Kato, F. 1991. Life histories of masu and amago salmon (*Oncorhynchus masou* and *Oncorhynchus rhodurus*). pp.447-520, In: C. Groot, and L. Margolis, Pacific salmon life histories. UBC Press, Vancouver.

26 LeBrasseur, R.J. 1966. Stomach contents of salmon and steelhead trout in the northeastern Pacific Ocean. Journal of the Fisheries Research Board of Canada 23:85-100.

27 Birman, I.B.1960. New information on the marine period of life and the marine fishery of Pacific salmon, pp. 151-164 In: Trudy Soveshchaniia po biologicheskim osnovam okeanicheskovo rybolovostva, 1958.

28 Mantua, N.J., Hare, S.R., Zhang,Y., Wallace, J.M. and Francis, R.C. 1997. A Pacific interdecadal climate oscillation with impacts on salmon production. Bulletin of the American Meterological Society 78: 1069-1079.

29 Cooney, R.T. and Brodeur, R.D. 1998. Carrying capacity and north Pacific salmon production: stock-enhancement implications. Bulletin of Marine Science 62: 443-464.

30 Bigler, B.S., Welch, D.W. and Helle, J.H. 1996. A review of size trends among Pacific salmon (*Oncorhynchus* spp.). Canadian Journal of Fisheries and Aquatic Sciences 53: 455-465.

31 Kwain, W. and Lawrie, A.H. 1981. Pink salmon in the Great Lakes. Fisheries 6:2-6.

32 Heard, W.R. 1991. Life history of pink salmon (*Oncorhynchus gorbuscha*). pp. 119-230, In: C. Groot, and L. Margolis, Pacific salmon life histories. UBC Press, Vancouver. 564 pp.

33 Burgner, R.L. 1991. Life history of sockeye salmon (*Oncorhynchus nerka*). pp.1-117, In: C. Groot, and L. Margolis, Pacific salmon life histories. UBC Press, Vancouver. 564 pp.

34 Foote, C.J. and Brown, G.S. 1998. Ecological relationship between freshwater sculpins (genus *Cottus*) and beach-spawning sockeye salmon (*Oncorhynchus nerka*) in Iliamna Lake, Alaska. Canadian Journal of Fisheries and Aquatic Sciences 55: 1524-1533.

35 Pella, J.J. 1968. Distribution and growth of sockeye salmon fry in Lake Aleknagik, Alaska, during the summer of 1962, pp. 45-111 In: R.L. Burgner, editor, Further studies of Alaska sockeye salmon. University of Washington Publications in Fisheries New Series No. 3.

36 Manzer, J.I. 1964. Preliminary observation on the vertical distribution of Pacific salmon (genus *Oncorhynchus*) in the Gulf of Alaska. Journal of the Fisheries Research Board of Canada 21: 891-903.

37 Ichihara, T. and Nakamura, A. 1982. Vertical movement of mature chum salmon

contributing to the improvement of set net structure on the Hokkaido coast. Proceedings of the North Pacific Aquaculture Symposium, 1982. pp. 39-49, Alaska Sea Grant Program, University of Alaska.

38 Bilton, H.T. 1978. Returns of adult coho salmon in relation to mean size and time at release of juveniles. Canadian Fisheries Marine Service Technical Report No. 832, 73 pp.

39 Morrow, J. E. 1980. The freshwater fishes of Alaska. Anchorage, Alaska Northwest Publishing Co.

40 Healey, M.C. 1991. Life history of chinook salmon (*Oncorhynchus tshawytscha*). pp. 311-393, In: C. Groot, and L. Margolis, Pacific salmon life histories. UBC Press, Vancouver. 564 pp.

41 Levy, D.A. and Northcote, T.G. 1981. The distribution and abundance of juvenile salmon in marsh habitats of the Fraser River estuary. Westwater Research Center University of British Columbia Technical Report 25: 117 pp.

42 Hard, J.J. and Wertheimer, A.C. 1989. Geographic variation in the occurrence of red- and white-fleshed chinook salmon in western North America. Canadian Journal of Fisheries and Aquatic Science 46: 1107-1113.

43 Blackett, R. F. 1973. Fecundity of resident and anadromous dolly varden (*Salvelinus malma*) in southeastern Alaska. Journal of the Fisheries Research Board Canada 30: 543-548.

44 Craig, P.C. 1989. An introduction to anadromous fishes in the Alaskan arctic.

Biological Papers University of Alaska 24: 27-54.

45 Scott, W. B. and Crossman, E. J. 1973. Freshwater fishes of Canada. Fisheries Research Board of Canada Bulletin 184, Ottawa, Environment Canada.

46 Kettle, D. and O'Brien, W. J. 1978. Vulnerability of arctic zooplankton species to predation by small lake trout (*Salvelinus namaycush*). Journal of the Fisheries Research Board of Canada 35: 1495-1500.

47 Konkle, B. R. and Sprules, W. G. 1986. Planktivory by stunted lake trout in an Ontario lake. Transactions of the American Fisheries Society 115: 515-521.

48 Burr, J. M. 1997. Growth, density and biomass of lake trout in arctic and subarctic Alaska. Pages 109-118 in J. Reynolds, editor. Fish ecology in Arctic North America. American Fisheries Society Symposium 19, Bethesda, Maryland.

49 Merrick, G. W., Hershey, A. E. and McDonald, M. E. 1992. Salmonid diet and the size, distribution, and density of benthic invertebrates in an arctic lake. Hydrobiologia 240: 225-233.

50 Merrick, G. W., Hershey, A. E. and McDonald, M. E. 1991. Lake trout (*Salvelinus namaycush*) control of snail density and size distribution in an arctic lake. Canadian Journal of Fisheries and Aquatic Sciences 48: 498-502.

51 Hanson, K. L., Hershey, A. E. and McDonald, M. E. 1992. A comparison of slimy sculpin (*Cottus cognatus*) populations in arctic lakes with and without piscivorous predators. Hydrobiologia 240: 189-201.

52 Martin, N.V. and Olver, C.H. 1980. The lake charr, *Salvelinus namaycush*. pp. 205-277, In: E.K. Balon, editor, Charrs, salmonid fishes of the genus *Salvelinus*. Junk Publishers, The Hague.

53 Hughes, N. F. and Dill, L. M. 1990. Position choice by drift-feeding salmonids: model and test for Arctic grayling (*Thymallus arcticus*) in subarctic mountain streams, interior Alaska. Canadian Journal of Fisheries and Aquatic Science 47: 2039-2048.

54 Hughes, N. F. 1992. Ranking of feeding positions by drift-feeding arctic grayling (*Thymallus arcticus*) in dominance hierarchies. Canadian Journal of Fisheries and Aquatic Science 49: 1994-1998.

55 Hughes, N. F. and Reynolds, J.B.1994. Why do Arctic grayling (*Thymallus arcticus*) get bigger as you go upstream? . Canadian Journal of Fisheries and Aquatic Science 51: 2154-2163.

56 Kratt, L. F. and Smith, R. J. F. 1978. Breeding tubercles occur on male and female Arctic grayling (*Thymallus arcticus*). Copeia 1978 (1): 185-188.

57 Clark, R. A. 1992. Influence of stream flows and stock size on recruitment of Arctic grayling (*Thymallus arcticus*) in the Chena River, Alaska. Canadian Journal of Fisheries and Aquatic Science 49: 1027-1034.

58 Deegan, L. A. and Peterson, B. J. 1992. Whole-river fertilization stimulates fish production in an Arctic tundra river. Canadian Journal of Fisheries and Aquatic Science 49: 1890-1901.

59 O' Brien, W. J. and Showalter, J. J. 1993. Effects of current velocity and suspended debris on the drift feeding of Arctic grayling. Transactions of the American Fisheries Society 122: 609-615.

60 Evans, B.I. and O'Brien, W.J. 1988. A re-analysis of the search cycle of a planktivorous salmonid. Canadian Journal of Fisheries and Aquatic Sciences 45: 187-192.

61 Schmidt, D. and O'Brien, W.J. 1982. Planktivorous feeding ecology of Arctic grayling (*Thymallus arcticus*). Canadian Journal of Fisheries and Aquatic Sciences. 39: 475-482.

62 Wilson, R., Allen-Gil, S., Griffin, D. and Landers, D. 1995. Organochlorine contaminants in fish from an Arctic lake in Alaska, USA. The Science of the Total Environment 160/161: 511-519.

63 Barrie, L. A , Gregor, D., Hargrave, B., Lake, R. Muir, D. Shearer, R., Tracey, B. and Bidlemann, T. 1992. Arctic contaminants: sources, occurrence and pathways. Science of the Total Environment 122: 1-74.

64 LaPerriere, J. D., Wagener, S. M. and Bjerklie 1985. Gold-mining effects on heavy metals in streams, Circle Quadrangle, Alaska. Water Resources Bulletin 21: 245-252.

65 Reynolds, J. B., Simmons, R. C. and Burkholder, A. R. 1989. Effects of placer mining discharge on health and food of Arctic grayling. Water Resources Bulletin 25: 625-635.

66 Hemming, C. 1997. Experimental introduction of Arctic grayling to a rehabilitated gravel extraction site, North Slope, Alaska. American Fisheries Society Symposium 19: 208-213.

67 Crawford, R.H. 1974. Structure of an air-breathing organ and the swim bladder in the Alaska blackfish, *Dallia pectoralis* Bean. Canadian Journal of Zoology 52: 1221-1225.

68 Alt, K. T. 1969. Taxonomy and ecology of the inconnu, *Stenodus leucichthys nelma*, in Alaska. Biological Papers of the University of Alaska 12: 1-61.

69 Brown, R.J. 2000. Migratory patterns of Yukon River inconnu as determined with otolith microchemistry and radio telemetry. MS Thesis, University of Alaska Fairbanks, 80 pp.

70 Andrews, E.F. 1989. A low-profile subsistence fishery: pike fishing in Minto Flats, Alaska. Arctic 42: 357-361.

71 Margenau, T.L., Rasmussen, P.W. and Kampa, J.M. 1998. Factors affecting growth of northern pike in small northern Wisconsin lakes. North American Journal of Fisheries Management 18: 625-639.

10.
WEBBED FEET, FLAT TAILS AND FEATHERS: AQUATIC MAMMALS AND WATERFOWL

What is an aquatic mammal?

What constitutes an aquatic mammal? Across the mammal spectrum we find species that never get into water and those that never get out of water. The permanently aquatic members of the Mammalia are confined to the oceans and very large rivers. Examples are the baleen and toothed whales, including porpoises. We might add seals and sea lions, the pinnipeds, but these emerge onto land or ice flows to give birth to pups and to rest. Among the mammals of Alaska's boreal forests we could count the beaver, muskrat, land otter, mink and water shrew. The water shrew and mink were discussed in a previous chapter; here I will treat beavers and muskrats.

In terms of fine-tuning for permanent residence in a watery medium, whales and pinnipeds have a variety of morphological and physiological adaptations. These include streamlining, insulation, ability to slow the heart and restrict circulation to non-critical parts of the body. These last two features combined with superior breath-holding allow whales and seals to dive to great depths and/or for long periods of time. Certainly, muskrats and beavers aren't in the same league as marine mammals, but let's see what they have going for them.

Beaver

The sound of the tail-slap was so loud, so close and so unexpected that I almost shouted. I was bowhunting along the Goldstream Valley, near Fairbanks, in mid-September, straining my senses listening for the slightest footfall or vocalization of a moose. I hadn't realized I'd gotten so close to a meander of Goldstream Creek. After getting my heart rate back down to nearly normal, I began to daydream about the beaver's now-extinct larger cousin from Alaska's Pleistocene. *Casteroides* was a giant weighing up to 500 pounds, five feet in body length, with a skull a foot long (Figure 10.1). This is about the size of a large interior Alaska black bear. I imagined

Figure 10.1: Comparison of the modern American beaver with the extinct, giant beaver. Giant beavers were as large as modern-day black bears, reached 1.5 meters in length and, perhaps, 225 kilograms.

the tail-slap would have sounded like an artillery piece going off. Of course, no one is sure that *Casteroides* exhibited the tail-slap behavior or was even aquatic.

The tail is a remarkable adaptation for the modern-day beaver, *Castor canadensis*, the largest of North American rodents. On large, adult beavers, the tail may be 12 inches or longer and eight inches wide. When swimming, the tail can be sculled both vertically and horizontally. It also serves as a rudder for steering and diving. When on land, the tail is used as a prop, allowing the beaver to stand on its hind legs while cutting the larger trees in its domain. A beaver also can use the tail to gain leverage to move heavy objects.

Tail-slaps are used as warning signals to other members of the colony. Typically, the perpetra-tor may dive immediately after the slap, then resurface to keep an eye or nose on the animal or odor it detected. The response of the other members of the colony depends on their location. Beavers in deep water don't exhibit much of a response. Those in shallow water move deeper and beavers on land immediately scamper for the water. Adults do most of the slapping while young kits rarely do the tail-slap.

The tail is covered with an outer coating of epidermis patterned in the form of scales. Without fur, the tail is subjected to, at times, icy cold water. Thus, there is the potential for a tremendous heat loss through the naked tail. But, instead of maintaining a warm tail (requiring lots of blood and lots of heat lost from that warm blood), beavers allow their tails to cool to near water temperature. The trick is to run the blood supply through a countercurrent system of blood vessels that serve as a heat exchanger. This circulatory system adaptation is very similar to that described earlier for gull feet and caribou legs. Like muskrats, beavers have evolved nerves and muscles that keep on working at temperatures near freezing. By the way, the fatty tail of beaver is a real delicacy in many Alaskan communities.

Locomotion on land is usually accomplished on all fours, but when the beaver is carrying branches, stones or mud with its front paws, it will walk upright on its hind legs. In the water the larger hind legs provide most of the propulsion. The hind feet are fully webbed; the front feet are only partially webbed. While swimming the beaver holds its front legs close to the body.

Beavers exhibit several other adaptations that suit them to their life in the water. First, while underwater, beaver nostrils and ears close completely, each having a little flap or valve. Second, during a dive beavers exhibit several physiological adjustments common to other diving mammals. These adjustments include a shunting of blood away from the extremities, an effective measure for heat conservation. Slowing of the heart rate, bradycardia, is also useful in divers. The heart does not need to pump as much blood since less blood is actually coming back to the heart. Also, slowing blood return slows the return of lactic acid to the heart and aorta. Lactic acid and carbon dioxide are the byproducts of metabolism that act as signals to stimulate breathing. But during an underwater excursion the beaver should not be breathing. Therefore, the stimulus to breathe is delayed and the beaver can hold its breath longer than if its circulation were normal.

When a beaver finally does breathe, it is much more efficient in taking up oxygen and ridding carbon dioxide than is a human. Beavers under the ice often expel air, forming a gas bubble under the ice. The bubble will exchange gases with oxygenated water, absorbing oxygen and releasing carbon dioxide. The beaver can (and does) come back and re-breathe this trapped air.

Aside from humans, the beaver is perhaps the mammal that most significantly modifies its environment. It makes its impact by constructing dams, burrows and lodges and also by its logging activities. Dams are built to stabilize or regulate water level. A beaver begins dam construction by pushing up a ridge of gravel that stretches across the bottom of the stream. Sticks are pushed into and around the gravel. Additional sticks are added to form a lattice that retains grasses, mud and more sticks. The dam is built evenly across the stream rather than one section at a time. Once construction is completed, the proud owner immediately begins maintenance activity; humans and beavers are remarkably alike in this aspect. In times of high water, beavers may gnaw a breach in the dam to lower water level.

As the water accumulates and deepens behind a dam, the surroundings are flooded. The beaver has built an impoundment that isolates its lodge from all but the most tenacious terrestrial predators. It also brings its food supply closer to the water. Actually the reverse. It brings the water closer to the food supply and, thereby, increases the safety with which it can harvest its food.

Lodge building occurs in late summer and early fall. Sticks are piled on the bottom of the pond, eventually making a mound that emerges from the pond. The builder then excavates the entrances from below and chews away the interior chamber. There are usually several sections or chambers in the lodge, one at water level, the feeding platform, and another higher up, the sleeping chamber. The outside cracks are chinked with mud except for the top foot or two. This upper, more open part is important for air circulation within the lodge. A colony (extended family unit, typically, four to eight individuals) may have several lodges within its home range and one or two bank burrows as well. Colony density ranges from 0.4 to 16 per square kilometer with dams ranging from two to 16 per kilometer of stream.[1]

Bank burrows or dens are dug with an underwater entrance. These burrows are, in some cases, up to 9 m (30 feet) long. There may be multiple chambers and, typically, sticks are piled on top. Dens are useful as escape refuges during the open water season and as sources of air to breathe during the winter. Dens, instead of lodges, are built along larger rivers or in areas with few trees. Beavers without lodges are often called bank beavers.

Beavers, by their presence and activities, change the riparian (streamside) habitat and biological community. Obviously, they cut trees and shrubs for food and building materials. Since deciduous trees, primarily quaking aspen, are preferred, they are often completely removed, leaving alder, and black spruce to dominate the streamside flora. In the north, beavers cut as much as a metric ton (2200 pounds) of trees per year within 100 meters of their home pond. This change or succession alters the amount of sunlight reaching the stream/pond and changes the amount and kinds of plant detritus falling into the water. Typically, beaver ponds have higher summertime temperatures than nearby stream riffles, stimulating aquatic productivity and fish growth.[2] Beaver impoundments alter the stream invertebrate fauna to a pond fauna in which the mass of animals is much greater than the original stream fauna. In southeastern Alaska these ponds are a favored habitat for sockeye and coho salmon young of the year.[3] The ponds provide habitat even during periods of low runoff when streams without beavers could not support young coho salmon.[4,5] In the interior, beaver ponds provide habitat for Alaska blackfish, arctic grayling and other fishes.

Sometimes, or maybe inevitably, aspen and poplar stands that beavers prefer are thinned or removed within a portion or throughout the entire home range of a beaver colony. Maintenance of several lodges is, undoubtedly, necessary to take full advantage of shifting availability of preferred foods within the home range.

When preferred and other foods are exhausted, beavers abandon the home range. I have seen several extinct beaver ponds and lodges while flying over the tundra west of Lake Iliamna. The remnants of lodges are simply grassy mounds in the middle of tundra ponds. There may be no trees within miles of these old ponds. Undoubtedly, climatic change played a role in these local extinctions. Interglacial episodes with more luxuriant tree growth favored proliferation of beaver habitat and allowed the widespread dispersal of beavers into deglaciated terrain. Presently, trees simply haven't dispersed sufficiently to repopulate these areas with either trees or beavers.

These observations are consistent with the idea that vegetative succession in a beaver stream is a cyclic phenomenon: beaver ponds age, are abandoned, degenerate and a stream reforms. A competing idea is that the formation of ponds, bogs and forested wetlands associated with beaver activities may persist for centuries.[1] The geographic distribution of beavers in Alaska, especially the North Slope and the Brooks Range, is, over the long run, a dynamic affair influenced by local topography, climate and the activities of beavers.

As everyone knows, beavers use their front teeth, the incisors, for cutting trees and stripping bark. There are four incisors; the uppers are about 2.5 cm (1 inch) long and the lowers about 4.5 cm (1 3/4 inches). Beavers exhibit an overbite with upper teeth projecting outside the lowers. The front surfaces are covered with a bright orange enamel layer. Behind this hard enamel is a softer dentine layer that wears to form a beveled surface like the point of a chisel. Chewing through trees causes a lot of wear and, consequently, beaver incisors grow continuously through life.

Occasionally, a beaver may find it necessary to chew through a tree or strip bark off a limb underwater. Beaver lips are specially adapted to seal the mouth behind the incisors so chewing underwater does not fill the beaver's mouth with water. The bark, one of the beaver's chief foods, is peeled from the tree by using the teeth as a lathe chisel. Smaller pieces are held in the forelegs, rotated and stripped of bark, a technique that very much resembles a human eating corn on the cob. Once stripped, the bark is chewed by the beaver's set of 16 molars.

Tree felling is accomplished in several ways. Small trees are chewed through from one side while the beaver stands on all fours. Larger trees, greater than 15 cm (6 inch) diameter, require the beaver to work its way around the tree. These larger trees are cut higher off the ground because the beaver typically stands on its hind legs, bracing with its tail while cutting. No matter what the size of tree, the beaver removes large chunks with each bite. A typical piece would be 2.5 x 2.5 x 10 cm (1x 1 x 4 inches). If a tree hangs up in other trees, the beaver gives up. There is a misconception that beavers can control the direction a tree falls. They cannot and, once in a while, a hiker finds a beaver skeleton underneath a felled tree.

Like humans, beavers put up food for use in the winter. Food caching begins in late summer and intensifies in fall. Brush is dragged into the pond and towed near the lodge entrance. One end of the branch or sapling is pushed into the mud on the bottom of the pond. At ice-up, food storage stops. If an insufficient supply was laid in, beavers may come out in winter and cut down more trees. The stumps of these winter-cut trees may be 0.9- 1.5 m (3-5 feet) tall, depending on snow depth at the time of cutting.

In summer, aquatic vegetation is eaten in addition to the bark of preferred tree and shrub species. Smooth-barked trees are preferred to those with rough bark and small trees are more fully used than larger trees. Studies in Wyoming compared the proportion of poplar actually used by beavers. For 5 cm (2 inch) diameter poplar, 88% was used; for 10 cm (4 inch) trees only 34% was used. This isn't surprising if we take into account the proportionally greater surface area of bark on a smaller tree.

Beaver family life begins with breeding in March in Alaska. Females first breed at 1.5 or 2.5 years old. Gestation lasts 100-110 days with young being born in June. The newborn kits are precocial, that is, fully furred, eyes open, teeth well developed and weigh about one pound. A litter is usually 2-4 kits but sometimes as many as eight are born. They stay in the lodge for the first two months, being watched by either their mother or an older sibling. Mother's milk is supplemented at 2-3 weeks with leafy material and at one month by solid food (bark). Kits are completely weaned by 6-8 weeks. Weight gain is rapid: by one month kits weigh 1.8 kg (4 pounds), by four months, 4.5 kg (10 pounds) and by one year, 11.4 kg (25 pounds).

Beaver kits are very buoyant, riding high in the water and occasionally falling prey to hawks and eagles. Mothers will swim with kits on their backs, sometimes submerging and resurfacing under the kit. Young of the year stay with the parents for the first two winters, learning the skills they will need to contribute to the colony and/or survive on their own. Other predators in their first year include pike, mink and river otters.

Beavers have anal scent glands, or castor glands, near the base of the tail. These glands produce a secretion that waterproofs the fur. The secretion is applied to the fur in a combing behavior using, primarily, the hind feet. The claw on the second toe of the hind foot is split, a special adaptation that aids the combing.

The glands also serve in scent-marking. A beaver will squeeze a little musk onto the mud, make it into a mud pie and leave it in a prominent place. Repeated visits and remarkings by the same individual and/or other members of its colony establish the site as a scent mound or sign heap. The mound is a place where family members groom their fur and, perhaps, advertise for mates. In addition, the scent mound marks the boundary of the colony's territory. When a beaver encounters the scent of a strange beaver, it hisses, charges the scent and piles mud and sticks on the scent mound. It is no wonder that trappers use the musk gland secretions of beavers to attract other beavers to their traps.

In the second year, juvenile beavers leave their natal territories. It isn't clear if the adults kick them out or if they just leave on their own. The juvenile seeks out unoccupied habitat or a nearby colony with a vacancy, or a member of the opposite sex without a mate. The dispersal movement from the home colony can be extensive. One Alaskan beaver traveled over 320 km (200 miles) before settling down.

These dispersal movements carry beavers far from familiar habitat and, often, have them traversing country far from water. Susceptibility to predation is much higher for these dispersing beavers and they may be picked off by owls, bears, lynx, wolverines and, especially, wolves. Studies of wolf diets in the upper midwest indicate that, in addition to white-tailed deer, beaver is one of the staples in their diet. Wolves in Denali National Park also prey on beaver.

My wife and I probably observed one of these dispersal events one spring day near Fairbanks. I was driving my pickup into town and had to swerve around a beaver in the middle of Chena Pump Road. I continued into town. Marsha, in the next vehicle, also swerved but turned around and went back to pick up what she thought was a roadkill. The beaver scurried off the road and down the embankment of the Tanana River, probably dispersing from the oxbow lake system nearby.

Tularemia is one of the diseases known to affect beavers in Alaska. This is the same disease affecting muskrats and snowshoe hares in the Far North. Tularemia disease is transmitted by tick bite, deerfly bite and is also water-borne.

The fur of beavers consists of long, coarse guard hairs over a dense, short underfur. The fur is waterproof and serves as an excellent insulator, especially in concert with the subcutaneous fat layer each healthy beaver wears. Beavers have been trapped for their fur in North America for thousands of years. The prehistoric population of beavers in North America has been estimated at between 60 and 120 million; beavers were probably more abundant than bison. Since the influx of western Europeans, the numbers of beavers has been drastically reduced by both trapping and by habitat destruction. From a population low around the turn of the 20th century, beaver populations have markedly increased.

In Alaska, beaver populations statewide are healthy, but there are certainly human impacts on beavers. Population density of beavers in the northern Bristol Bay area reflects the pattern of trapping near villages. Close to villages, beavers are scarce; farther away, beavers are more abundant.[6]

Muskrat

I was driving down the Parks Highway, west of Fairbanks one morning in early May. There were still patches of snow on the north sides of trees and down in the gullies. The road runs along a ridge top through the Bonanza Creek Experimental Forest about 780 m (2500 feet) above the floodplains of the Tanana River and Goldstream Creek. A muskrat crossed the road in front of me and I was so surprised that I braked to a stop and watched it amble off the road and

over the snow berm alongside the road. That muskrat was at least a mile from the nearest habitable marsh or pond.

Dispersal movements can carry muskrats far from their home pond or marsh. Paul Errington once followed an Iowa muskrat 2.55 km (1.6 miles) overland, a distance the rat accomplished in half a day.[7] One would suppose that a muskrat on land would be clumsy and that supposition is born out by observation. The hind legs look too long and the gait is almost comical. On land, muskrats are more vulnerable to predators, including mink, foxes, raptorial birds, wolves and lynx.

Why risk the dangers of overland travel, especially far from a body of water? Suitable habitat characteristics such as burrow sites and food may become restricted or limiting at high muskrat population densities. Whatever the specific reason for a "walkabout," a muskrat must feel much more at home in the water.

As an aquatic rodent, the muskrat, *Ondatra zibethicus*, is a great success. It has a dense underfur and long, coarse, shiny guard hairs. The fur traps a layer of air near the skin, providing an excellent insulation. Muskrats swim mainly by paddling the hind feet alternately with most of the power deriving from flexion at the ankle joint. The tail is virtually naked and laterally flattened. When swimming at the surface, the tail is trailed straight behind; underwater, the tail is actively undulated to aid in locomotion (see Figure 4.9).

The tail itself is a marvel of adaptation to cold. The fats in the tail are very unsaturated in comparison to those deeper in the body.[8] The unsaturation allows the tail to be flexible and achieve fluid motion even when it is near freezing temperatures. The circulation in the tail includes a counter current heat exchanger (see chapter 2) that allows the tail to cool but prevents it from freezing under most circumstances. Finally, the motor nerves in the tail are well adapted to conduct nerve impulses at temperatures near freezing. At similar temperatures, human hand nerves sometimes do not conduct and the muscles may be too cold to respond.

Underwater, muskrats share some common traits with other diving mammals. During a dive the heart rate slows, blood flow is reduced to the skeletal muscles while being maintained to heart, brain and, in the case of pregnant females, to the uterus. Heart rate is relatively insensitive to high carbon dioxide concentrations in the blood. In a laboratory setting, unrestrained dives (periods of submergence) average 21 sec in duration with a range of 2 to 69 sec.[9] While submerged, muskrat metabolic rates increase to about three times their resting metabolic rate in the thermoneutral zone. Oxygen stores in lungs, blood and myoglobin are adequate for about 48 sec underwater. Therefore, most underwater excursions by muskrats are within their aerobic metabolic limits. Repeated, forced dives exhaust their aerobic capacity and cause them to incur an oxygen debt. If pressed to the extreme, muskrats will eventually refuse to submerge even when provoked by humans.

In spite of their insulation and elevated metabolism, muskrats cool significantly while submerged. Upon emergence, a muskrat spends additional energy to rewarm and to groom itself to maintain its insulative layer. In the burrow or den in the winter, muskrats are able to survive pretty rigorous conditions. Within muskrat lodges, air temperatures may fall into the 0°C to -10°C (32°F to 14°F) range in the Far North.

Muskrats relax their territoriality in the winter and as many as six individuals may occupy the same lodge. In groups of four, muskrats are able to reduce their metabolic rates about 12% in these lodges, primarily by huddling.[10] The inside walls of the lodge often ice up and, at least partially, are sealed from the outside air. This causes an increase in the levels of the carbon dioxide (CO_2) in burrows to as high as 6-8%. Oxygen concentrations fall as low as 14% (normal air has 0.03% CO_2 and 20% O_2). Muskrats tolerate this elevated CO_2 without any effect on their total metabolism but do increase their depth of breathing (tidal volume).[11] These wintertime carbon dioxide concentrations would kill human beings.

Although herbivores, muskrats are known to eat crayfish, freshwater clams and fish. One study found that muskrats completely denuded nearshore areas of clams. Areas further from shore maintained clam populations presumably because of the muskrat's reluctance to get too far away from the safety of burrow or lodge. Among their plant foods, cattails are important wherever they occur. The roots and rhizomes of cattails are a submerged source of energy-rich carbohydrates. Other plants in the diet of muskrats are emergent vegetation such as duckweed and aquatic horsetails.

On the Mackenzie River Delta, Northwest Territories, in summer, muskrats feed primarily on emergent horsetails, high in proteins and minerals. In fall and winter, submerged roots and rhizomes are the main foods. To optimize their feeding on these resources, muskrats shift their preferred habitats and their lodgings in a seasonal pattern. In spring and summer, burrows are located close to shallow water where the horsetails grow. In the fall and winter, burrows and lodges are close to deeper water sites where submerged vegetation is accessible.[12] Body fat, and therefore condition, is high in spring and low in the fall. During winter, muskrats deal with the rigors of the Arctic but gain weight and put on fat. In the spring, these rodents are engaged in the metabolically demanding activities of breeding, fighting, defense of territory and, in females, milk production for their newborns.

If you are after some nice, fat muskrats for the stewpot, you don't want to wait too late in the spring. Similarly, if you are after prime hides with long fur and few scars, you need to trap them before they molt and before they engage in fighting. Individuals are sometimes seen with bite wounds penetrating the abdominal cavity. Also, if you are intending to sew a muskrat parka you will need at least 68 prime hides, and a lot of patience.

BIRDS AND AQUATIC HABITATS

Many bird species in Alaska depend on aquatic systems for their survival. These include ducks, geese, swans, gulls, kittiwakes, murres, puffins, kingfishers, loons and dippers. Some species nest very close to the water; some use water as escape terrain. Some birds use bodies of water as feeding habitat. Let's look at birds foraging in or near the water. I'll mention birds from coastal and marine habitats of Alaska because some of these birds reach interior and northern Alaska and/or are well known examples of the point I'm discussing.

First, several species forage very near streams or lakes. The five swallow species of Alaska are often seen performing aerobatics over streams and lakes as they forage on mosquitoes, mayflies and other aerial insects with aquatic life stages. Swallow foraging over water becomes more intense during periods of adult insect emergence, or "hatches."

A few birds feed to some extent on aquatic vegetation in Alaska. In the autumn, black brant, *Branta bernicla*, congregate in staging areas such as Izembek Lagoon, southeastern Bering Sea, where they ingest large quantities of eelgrass. A host of minute invertebrates grow on the grass blades and they also provide nutrition to the brant.

Several groups of birds feed at the surface of the water. Dabbling ducks like mallards, *Anas platyrhynchos*, and pintails, *Anas acuta*, turn "bottoms up" to filter the surface layers of pond or stream for aquatic invertebrates. Kittiwakes and gulls **patter** (hover) just above the sea or lake surface and pick organisms off the surface, occasionally landing to rest or forage on concentrations of prey. Belted kingfishers, *Ceryle alcyon*, patter or **surface plunge** for small fish. Surface plunging is simply diving headlong into the water without penetrating more than about a body length. Red-necked phalaropes, *Phalaropus lobatus*, employ a technique called **spinning** to help feed at the surface. The bird spins, swims in a tight circle, creating an upward-directed movement of water that brings potential food organisms to the surface.[13]

Some birds "up the ante" energetically in seeking aquatic or marine prey. These are the **pursuit divers**. A leisurely form of pursuit diving is practiced by diving ducks like scaup and bufflehead. These birds swim down to the bottom of the pond and filter bottom invertebrates. The four loon species found in Alaska are pursuit divers seeking and capturing fish underwater

(Figure 10.2). Both diving ducks and loons are foot-propelled pursuit divers.

The other pursuit divers are wing-propelled. These birds literally fly through the water chasing fish and crustaceans. The puffins and murres are in this category. Puffins are quite dexterous underwater, often managing to capture four or five sand lances in a single dive. In breeding season a male tufted puffin will proudly display his catch to a prospective mate.

As one might imagine, these two modes of pursuit diving have led to different sorts of specializations. First, both types of birds are sleek with relatively short body feathers. Underwater, these birds leave a trail of bubbles of air,

squeezed out of the plumage as the bird swims downward into increasing hydrostatic pressure. Foot-propelled divers have their legs positioned far back on the body, similar to the propeller on the back of a boat. Wings can remain fairly large since they aren't flapped underwater.

Conversely, wing-propelled divers have reduced, streamlined wings that generate less drag underwater (Figure 10.3). These wings are inefficient for flying through air, and it is no accident that murres and puffins are reluctant to fly off the sea and only do so clumsily. Legs and feet aren't set as far back on the body as they are in loons.

As is the case elsewhere in the natural world, specialists are targeted by other specialists. Gulls and kittiwakes that are successful in foraging are harassed by parasitic jaegers. If the gull drops its catch, the jaeger usually gets it. Puffins with their inefficient aerial flight are often outflown, outmaneuvered and captured by large, predatory gulls.

The muddy and sandy tidal flats of beaches all along the Alaska coastlines are visited by migratory shorebirds. These birds include the phalaropes, plovers and sandpipers. The lengths and

Figure 10.2: Loon pursuing fish underwater. Wings are held close to body and propulsion is provided by the webbed feet.

Figure 10.3: Thick-billed murre pursuing a herring underwater. The bird is literally flying underwater.

configurations of shorebird bills are adaptations for feeding on specific beach invertebrates at specific depths below the sand or mud surface.

Aquatic systems in boreal forest and tundra

I'd like to summarize or reiterate points made above and in earlier chapters about the many interactions of aquatic systems and species with the boreal forest. First, rivers and streams are means of erosion or deposition. Erosion often removes plant communities along riverbanks. Deposition provides the starting conditions for ecological or plant succession.

Second, there is a dynamic interaction between forest and stream in terms of food webs and the resulting energy transfer. Salmon and other fish nourish a variety of forest animals including bears, mink, otters, kingfishers, gulls and ravens. The wastes of these animals fertilize parts of the forest. On the other hand, leaf litter and other forest detritus, as it is decomposed in the river, fuels aquatic food webs involving shredding and filtering invertebrates and the animals that feed on them.

Ponds and lakes are the residences of some "forest" creatures such as beavers and muskrats. Ponds and their margins provide the nesting sites of others such as loons, trumpeter swans, sandhill cranes, grebes and a variety of ducks. Lakes and streams are the habitations for the aquatic life stages of many of the "terrestrial" insects that make up the fauna of Alaska's boreal forests. These insects include mosquitoes, dragonflies, mayflies, caddisflies and midges.

Finally, recall that due to the heat capacity of water, lakes and rivers affect the soils surrounding them. Heat transfer from river to riverbank allows for a permafrost-free zone along rivers. That zone is reflected in the vegetation of riverbanks. Similarly, lakes transfer heat to their surroundings. This transfer is one of the factors influencing the expansion of thaw lakes and the succession of plant communities surrounding lakes.

Many of the relationships between aquatic systems and the boreal forest also apply to tundra systems. Streams erode tundra, deposit sediments and, therefore, reset the timer on plant succession. To the extent that migratory fish reach tundra streams, they transfer nutrients and energy to the nearby tundra. As is true of forest ponds, tundra ponds provide nesting habitat for birds such as loons, tundra swans, and many waterfowl species.

REFERENCES

1 Naiman, R. J., Johnston, C. A. and Kelley, J. C. 1988. Alterations of North American streams by beaver. Bioscience 38 (11): 753- 762.

2 Alexander, M. D. 1998. Effects of beaver (*Castor canadensis*) impoundments on stream temperature and fish community species composition and growth in selected tributaries of Miramichi River, New Brunswick. Canadian Technical Report, Fisheries and Aquatic Science, 44 pp.

3 Murphy, M. L. and Milner, A. M . 1997. Alaska timber harvest and fish habitat, pp. 229-264, In: A.M. Milner and M.W. Oswood, editors, Freshwaters of Alaska: ecological syntheses. Springer-Verlag, New York and Berlin.

4 Bryant, M. D. 1984. The role of beaver dams as coho salmon habitat in southeast Alaska streams. pp. 183-192 In: J. M. Walton and D. B. Houston, editors, Proceedings of the Olympic Wild Fish Conference, Port Angeles, Washington.

5 Leidholt-Bruner, K., Hibbs, D. E. and McComb, W. C. 1992. Beaver dam locations and their effects on distribution and abundance of coho salmon fry in two coastal Oregon streams. Northwest Science 66 (4): 218-223.

6 Taylor, K.P. 1983. Factors influencing beaver management in rural Alaska, northern Bristol Bay. Proceedings of the third Theriological Congress, Helsinki: pp. 127-128.

7 Errington, P.L. 1963. Muskrat populations. Iowa State University Press, Ames, 665 pp.

8   Kakela, R. and Hyvarinen, H. 1996. Site-specific fatty acid composition in adipose tissues of several northern aquatic and terrestrial mammals. Comparative Biochemistry and Physiology 115B: 501-514.

9   MacArthur, R.A. and Krause, R.E. 1989. Energy requirements of freely diving muskrats (*Ondatra zibethicus*). Canadian Journal of Zoology 67: 2194-2200.

10   Bazin, R.C. and MacArthur, R.A. 1992. Thermal benefits of huddling in the muskrat (*Ondatra zibethicus*). Journal of Mammology 73: 559-564.

11   MacArthur, R.A. 1984. Microenvironment gas concentrations and tolerance to hypercapnia in the muskrat *Ondatra zibethicus*. Physiological Zoology 57: 85-98.

12   Jelinski, D.E. 1989. Seasonal differences in habitat use and fat reserves in an arctic muskrat population. Canadian Journal of Zoology 67: 305-313.

13   Rubega, M.A., Schamel, D. and Tracy, D.M. 2000. Red-necked phalarope. The birds of North America, No. 538, Academy of Natural Sciences, Philadelphia, PA and American Ornithological Union, Washington, D.C.

11.
THE FUTURE OF INTERIOR AND NORTHERN ALASKA

What is in store for Alaska in the future? From the perspective of the last million years or even of the last 50 years, we can be certain that there will be change, perhaps profound change. In this chapter I will reiterate some points I made in previous chapters about current trends that are likely to continue into the future such as human-induced land disturbance caused by resource development and population expansion. In addition, aquatic systems will be influenced by human activities such as mineral extraction, forestry practices, and electric power generation.

Perhaps as significant or even more significant is the suite of effects tied to climate change. Whatever those effects might turn out to be, they will, from a scientific point of view, be neither good nor bad. Science doesn't make value judgments. If, for example, permafrost soils on a hillside thaw and the soil begins to erode, the erosion is neither good nor bad from a scientific perspective. The erosion may be viewed as

a "bad" thing but only in some political, economic, cultural, or esthetic framework.

The second point to be made about climate change is that, with or without human activity, the climate will change. Bill McKibben, in his book *The End of Nature*, talked about increasing atmospheric greenhouse gas concentrations and our tendency to assume that humans "control" this aspect of our natural world.[1] We, collectively, bear a great deal of responsibility for those gases, but it is, perhaps, the height of arrogance to assume that we truly control them. To assume thus is, as McKibben argues, equivalent to assuming that nature is dead and humans are completely in the driver's seat.

Expanding Human Populations

The increase in human population has and will continue to have impacts on the living systems of Alaska. The population of Alaska is slowly increasing, and as that population increases, it occupies an ever larger physical space. But modern humans, with their Western industrial society, don't merely stand on the landscape, they modify it. Tracts of land are converted to tracts of homes, malls, and industrial parks. For most wild plant and animal species, these tracts are no longer habitat.

Humans require domestic water supplies and generate solid, liquid and gaseous wastes. Therefore, there are competing uses for water (human versus wildlife) and issues related to solid waste disposal and water and air quality. Alteration of air and water quality can have direct, negative effects on living organisms.

The living landscape of Alaska, including the people, is being directly affected by human population expansion elsewhere on the globe. What are some of these human-induced activities and effects? Resources are required to produce the material goods consumed by humankind. This demand leads to mineral (metals, hydrocarbons) extraction in Alaska. Power generation involves, primarily, burning fossil fuels that generate lots of carbon dioxide, a greenhouse gas, and particulate matter that produces a haze in the Arctic. I will have more to say on greenhouse gases and global warming below. I will discuss several aspects or spinoffs of human population expansion both in Alaska and elsewhere: habitat destruction/reduction, water, pollution, and exploitation of living resources.

Habitat destruction/reduction—In Alaska, as elsewhere, conversion of forest or tundra to residential, commercial, industrial, or agricultural land usually eliminates the fauna and flora existing on that habitat. Warehouses surrounded by asphalt pavement simply do not support willows, moose, spruce grouse, and

other boreal forest life as well as the unmodified forest. Similarly, drainage of wetlands reduces their ability to support aquatic vegetation, fish, and nesting waterfowl.

Habitat alteration or destruction elsewhere may also affect Alaskan species directly. Recall the discussion of migratory birds that winter in Central America and South America but spend the summers breeding in Alaska. Depletion of tropical forests is leading to reduction in numbers of many migratory birds in Alaska and elsewhere in North America. For example, violet-green swallows spend wintertime in Central America; cliff swallows overwinter in Brazil and Argentina. Therefore, the continued survival of swallows depends on events in Alaska, Central America, South America and points in between.

Sandhill cranes destined to summer in Alaska all funnel through a very small area on the Platte River in south-central Nebraska each spring. Alteration or destruction of that Platte River habitat would have negative impacts on cranes in Alaska. Tundra swans of northern Alaska rely on winter habitats in Chesapeake Bay and North Carolina; birds that summer elsewhere in Alaska fly to the western United States for the winter. Therefore, swans need intact habitat in a variety of locations including intermediate, staging locations.

Water—Population increases elsewhere may, ultimately, affect water availability in Alaska. I'll mention two ideas that were proposed but, due to economics and politics, probably will not be built any time soon (if ever).

The American Southwest, with its rapidly growing human population has an almost inexhaustible demand for water. Many schemes have been put forward to secure added water supplies. Probably the most ambitious of these, to date, was the North American Water and Power Alliance. In the early 1960s, an engineering firm in Pasadena California, the Ralph M. Parsons Corporation, put the plan together. The U.S. Army Corps of Engineers completed the feasibility studies and was ready to start the project.

One of the first phases was to be the Rampart Dam, a reservoir and hydroelectric project, on the Yukon River. It would have been 530 feet high and 4700 feet long and would have created a lake as big as Lake Erie, 10,800 square miles. It would have drowned the entire Yukon Flats. Wildlife losses would have included 1.5 million ducks, 12,500 geese, and thousands of cranes, swans, and moose. The salmon runs above Rampart would, most likely, have been wiped out, some 250,000 fish a year. A sustainable fur yield of 40,000 pelts would have been lost, according to the U.S. Fish and Wildlife Service. The plan repeatedly talked about using the "excess" water of the Yukon River, among others. At completion, the alliance would have dammed the Yukon, Tanana, Copper, Taku, Skeena, Stikine, Bella Coola, and Fraser rivers, pumped the water into the Rocky Mountain trench (and drowned the city of Prince George, British Columbia, among others), and redistributed the water as far south as northern Mexico.[2]

The North American Water and Power Alliance makes former Governor Walter Hickel's plan to build a seafloor water pipeline from Alaska to southern California look pretty simple. In Hickel's plan, the fresh water from an Alaskan river, possibly the Copper or Stikine, would be put in a pipeline to northern California. The water would have entered the California water distribution system via Lake Shasta. It was proposed that the pipeline be laid on the seafloor, a distance of over 2200 kilometers (1350 miles). The engineering problems would have been significant since fresh water is buoyant in comparison to seawater. Some means of holding the pipeline on the seafloor would have been necessary. Repairing leaks in a pipeline on the bottom of the ocean would also have been challenging.

A feature common to both these schemes is the assumption that Alaska doesn't need or use the water. In both cases, the natural flow of river water would be radically reduced, seawater would encroach into the river mouths, migratory fish stocks would be at great risk and some terrestrial habitat would be inundated behind impoundments. Both projects probably would have been tied to hydroelectric dams.

The typical outcome of large hydroelectric dams is that, even with fish ladders, the numbers of returning salmon that make it to the spawning grounds are significantly reduced. In addition, the turbines through which the outlet water passes generate so much turbulence that outmigrating salmon fry that pass through them (and most do) are, quite literally, torn to pieces.

Two of the "successes" of the environmental movement in North America have been the virtual elimination of nuclear power from the United States and the halting of hydroelectric dam projects on the nation's "wild" rivers. Certainly both dams and nuclear power plants have their political "down" sides. However, the alternative to these sources of electric power generation has been, primarily, power plants using fossil fuels such as coal, oil and natural gas. I will return to the burning of fossil fuels below.

Mineral Extraction—Mineral extraction includes oil field development, placer and hard rock mining, gravel mining and the networks of roads required by these activities. The future of interior and northern Alaska, undoubtedly, will involve more roads and more mineral extraction. What are the likely changes to the landscape or impacts on the landscape from these developments?

The impacts of oil fields on the Arctic Coastal Plain involve direct and indirect effects. Direct effects include roads and gravel pads for buildings. Both roads and pads occupy space that was formerly tundra. In the Prudhoe Bay oil field, an area of about 500 km², 21 km² (4 %) was covered by gravel in the first 15 years of development.[3]

Several indirect effects result from the placement of roads and gravel pads. First, these structures are thick and elevated above the tundra. They may block the natural drainage of the landscape and often result in flooding. Flooded ground added an additional 14 km² of impacted land within the first 15 years at Prudhoe.[3]

Second, gravel, road dust, and the accumulating water absorb sunlight energy (heat) more effectively than tundra vegetation. Vegetation itself has an insulative effect on tundra. Thus, removal of the vegetation allows the ground to warm. The resulting warming causes melting of permafrost, leading to land subsidence (thermokarst). Thermokarst develops slowly and may have its effects such as thaw pits and road disruption many years after the initial development activities.

Construction on the thaw-lake plains of the North Slope is preferentially located on well-drained sites in what is typically a wetland mosaic. These sites are the ones favored by waterfowl and shorebirds for nesting and foraging. The other

major habitat in the Prudhoe Bay field consists of floodplains and terraces. Because they are better drained, these areas are favored both by large mammals as movement corridors and by humans for road construction.

I mentioned in an earlier chapter that caribou are affected by gravel roads in the Prudhoe field. Pregnant cows tend to avoid crossing these roads; calving areas are being reduced by the proliferation of gravel roads on the Arctic Coastal Plain. At some point in the future, this habitat reduction might become significant to caribou populations.

These impacts relate to the nationwide dialog about opening part of the Arctic National Wildlife Refuge to oil and gas exploration. Boosters of exploration argue that only 2000 acres of the refuge will be affected, that is covered with gravel. However, additional acreage will exhibit the indirect effects mentioned above: flooding and thermokarst land subsidence. Also, the 2000 acres will not be in a single, well-contained parcel, isolated from the rest of the refuge. Rather, it will probably consist of an expansive network of roads and widely spaced drilling pads. We can argue about just how large a footprint ANWR oil exploration will leave but it will certainly be bigger than 2000 acres.

Gravel mining is another form of mineral extraction. Certainly, gravel will be used in oil exploration and development but also will be necessary for residential and commercial construction. Removal of associated vegetation along river channels in order to get to the gravel, of course, reduces the extent of riparian habitat. But, as I pointed out in the previous chapter, the resulting deep pits in river channels can provide additional overwintering habitat for fishes that, otherwise, might not be able to survive in the river.

Placer mining will likely continue or increase in the future. Many negative impacts on aquatic habitats can be avoided if mining companies adhere to state and federal clean water regulations. Otherwise, there is a very real potential to add toxic metals and particulate matter to streams. However, since placer mining involves moving large quantities of stream gravels and other sediments, riparian vegetation, with its impacts on streams, is removed. Revegetation, either fostered by human efforts or a more natural plant succession, will eventually return streamside systems to approximately their original condition.

Pollution—To pollute is to contaminate with human waste. What constitutes waste? Anything that is a byproduct of human activity that is left in the environment could be considered pollution. Such pollutants end up in the air, water and on the landscape. One form of pollution that is visible every winter in Fairbanks is thermal pollution. The power plant in downtown Fairbanks uses Chena River water as a coolant. The water is warmed by waste heat and then returned to the Chena. Stretches of the river several kilometers downstream never freeze, even in the coldest winters. Mallards, mergansers and other ducks are able to overwinter along the Chena now whereas they couldn't survive without the power plant. The frozen Chena is not available as a transportation corridor as it was in the 19th and early 20th centuries. You will have to decide if this thermal pollution is a good or a bad thing. Certainly, it isn't a natural thing on the Chena although there are several natural hot springs in the interior that might

support small populations of overwintering waterfowl. The Alaska Department of Fish and Game is looking into the possibility of using the heated water for a fish hatchery in Fairbanks. Additional power plants along interior and northern Alaska rivers could mean more waste heat in rivers.

Streams and rivers are likely to receive additional impacts from increased levels of human activity. Those impacts will probably include heavy metal pollution, increased turbidity and sewage input. Metals and acids resulting from mining activity may be released to streams from leaking ponds or, in rare cases, directly from mine tailings.

Turbidity is due to the addition of particulate matter to streams and rivers. Particulate matter can include fine-grained sediments, organic matter from peat or detrital material from forests. These materials can (but don't always) result from road-building, mining, timber harvest or recreational activities. If you look in the Tanana and Yukon rivers in the summer, you will notice a high level of turbidity. Both rivers carry a tremendous silt load accumulated from glacially fed streams that enter them. Are they, therefore, polluted? No, not necessarily.

Glaciers produced the silt by grinding bedrock to powder, a natural process. Any additional silt resulting from human activity could be classified as pollution. Certainly the fish species that inhabit the Tanana River in summer or migrate up the Yukon are, for a time, able to tolerate a high suspended sediment load. However, as I described in an earlier chapter, many streams in interior and northern Alaska are clearwater streams. Increased turbidity in these streams may make them uninhabitable for most of their resident fishes. Grayling abandon turbid streams because the sediment clogs their gills, reduces their food supplies, and cripples their ability to see the food organisms that might still be in the stream. Siltation destroys salmon, grayling, char and trout spawning habitat by smothering the eggs residing on or beneath the gravel.

Increased sewage contamination of rivers, streams and lakes is a potential outcome of increased human population and activity in Alaska. The most obvious problem with sewage contamination, aside from the antibiotics, hormones, heavy metals and toxic organic chemicals in human sewage, is organic enrichment. Most freshwater lakes and streams in Alaska have relatively low levels of nitrogen and phosphorus nutrients. Natural fertilizers derive from decaying detritus and remineralization by soil and stream bacteria. In many streams the primary source of detritus is dead, rotting adult salmon. The problem is that too much fertilizer is a "bad" thing in the sense that too many algae are able to grow, crowd the water and, certainly in still waters, use up all the oxygen needed by fish and aquatic invertebrates.

Again, from a scientific point of view, mass die-offs of fish in streams and lakes are neither good nor bad. If you enjoy fishing or hate the stench of rotting fish, mass die-offs could be bad. In these latter cases you are probably using aesthetic, economic or cultural frameworks to decide that die-offs are bad.

Air pollution is, at times, a significant problem in interior and northern Alaska. In Fairbanks on a still, cold winter day, air quality can get pretty bad. On such days the exhausts from automobiles and smoke from power plants and residential heating systems produce ice fog con-sisting of frozen water vapor, soot, unburned hydrocarbons, carbon dioxide and carbon monoxide. Persons with breathing difficulties often have trouble in ice fog. The carbon monoxide levels, on rare occasions, exceed clean air standards as determined by the Environmental Protection Agency. In addition, the fog gets thick enough to constitute a hazard to drivers and pedestrians. As the populations of Fairbanks and some interior villages increase, the ice fog problem may worsen.

On a grander scale, air quality in Alaska is influenced by power generation and industrial activity around the world. The airshed north of the Alaska Range receives considerable input of aerosols and air-borne pollutants of human origin from distant sources. Episodes of arctic haze at Barrow in the 1970s apparently emanated from central Eurasia.[4] A particularly dense haze event in April 1986, originated in central Europe ten days previously.[5] In that event, the concentration of particles reached 70,000 per cm^3 and sulfur dioxide reached 15 parts per billion. Therefore, at times, air quality at Point Barrow has been less than pristine in spite of their remoteness. Air-borne sampling in the troposphere has shown that the highest concentrations of black carbon and sulfur are at intermediate altitudes, not at ground level.[6]

Surprisingly, there was a recent trend to reduced arctic haze on the North Slope. Records from 1976 to 1993 show a maximum haze level in 1982 followed by a significant decline.[7] Similarly, the haze enshrouding Denali (Mt. McKinley) through the 1980s cleared considerably in the 1990s, a result of reduced industrial activity following the breakup of the Soviet Union and reduced emissions in North America and

Europe.[8] In spite of recent declines, arctic haze in northern Alaska will likely intensify in the near future as economically underdeveloped countries race to increase industrial production. But, at least for the present, we have some good news on environmental quality in Alaska.

Of course, dust and other air-borne particulates eventually settle out of the atmosphere or are washed out during precipitation. Local dust from roads through interior and northern Alaska settle nearby and affects the pattern of vegetation. In both acidic and non-acidic tundra, road dust reduces the amount of vegetation near the roads.[9] Acidic tundra appears to be more sensitive; the dominant moss in acidic tundra, *Sphagnum*, is almost completely eliminated alongside tundra roads. The filamentous lichen *Usnea* that hangs from interior Alaska trees is reduced or eliminated along roads subjected to heavy exhaust from automobiles. Increasing the number of roads, paved or unpaved, will increase the effects on nearby vegetation.

Particulate matter can include radionuclides, generated by nuclear accidents, atmospheric nuclear testing and released by the burning of fossil fuels. These particles are distributed widely at high latitude. When they reach the tundra, they are often incorporated into lichens that, in turn, pass these elements along to caribou and, ultimately to the predators of caribou (including humans). An increase in release of radionuclides, either accidental or from atmospheric testing, could lead to increased levels of radionuclides in high latitude humans with the resultant increase in potential for cancers and other diseases triggered by ionizing radiation.

Exploitation of Living Resources—A variety of living resources are exploited either commercially, during subsistence activities, or for recreation. These activities include logging, fishing, hunting, trapping and berry picking. An important question relating to these activities is: do rates of exploitation equal or exceed rates of renewal?

Logging in interior Alaska is focused on Native lands and in the Tanana State Forest. Timber from these lands yield house logs, saw timber and firewood. In addition, there are designated areas for personal firewood cutting. In order to sustain a timber industry, harvest rates per year for white spruce should not exceed about 1/200th of the available acreage since succession from open fields to pure white spruce stands requires about 200 years. If birch and aspen were the target species, a shorter time span would apply since mature birch and aspen require less time, perhaps 100 years. Therefore, clear-cutting all the mature spruce in the interior over a ten-year period would result in at least a 100 year hiatus before additional harvest of mature spruce would be practical.

Hunting and trapping are both dependent, to an extent, on timber harvest. Recall I discussed the natural succession of animal species that parallels the succession of plant communities. For instance, the dominant grouse species in boreal forests changes from sharp-tailed to ruffed to spruce grouse as plant communities progress from open meadows to mixed deciduous-conifer forests to mature spruce forests. Moose and snowshoe hare have better forage early in succession than in mature spruce forests. If you are a moose hunter, earlier successional stages are great. If you are trapping marten, a mosaic of early, mid- and late successional stages is great because mosaics with lots of edges produce lots of marten. If you are a scientist, successional stages are interesting but neither good nor bad.

Sport, commercial and subsistence harvest of fish and wildlife are potentially competing uses of renewable resources. In Alaska and elsewhere there has been a lot of controversy over which of these three uses should have the highest priority, especially in the event that the resources are threatened or become severely limited. The arguments get especially troublesome when there are cultural and/or racial overtones. For instance, on the Yukon River, does subsistence use by villagers automatically trump commercial harvest by Native fishers downstream who are living in a cash (rather than subsistence) economy? In the context of this chapter, increasing human population in Alaska will increase the pressure on fish and wildlife stocks. We may reach a point at which rural populations are simply too great to allow a purely subsistence life style. Additional pressure from urban and nonresident hunters and fishers will further complicate these issues.

Greenhouse Effect

Most Alaskans are familiar with greenhouses. The frost-free period in Alaska in which to grow crops and ornamentals outdoors is short. Greenhouses allow us to get a jump on nature by germinating seeds and producing seedlings before they could survive outside. A greenhouse works like this: sunlight shines through the glass and warms the soil, plants and tables. Part of the sunlight energy is reradiated from the soil and plants as long-wavelength, infrared radiation. The greenhouse glass absorbs part of this infrared radiation and radiates it again. Part of the infrared or heat radiation is sent out into

space and part is sent back into the greenhouse. Thus, the effect of the greenhouse is to maintain a space at a temperature higher than expected.

The earth's atmosphere acts very similarly to the greenhouse glass. There are atmospheric constituents that absorb and reradiate the heat coming up from the earth's surface. Greenhouse gases have functioned over hundreds of millions of years to make the earth's surface habitable by living organisms. In other words, without the greenhouse effect there probably would be little life on this planet. Without this effect the average temperature of the earth's surface would be about -20°C (-4°F); actual mean temperature, averaged over all latitudes and throughout the year, is 15°C (59°F) instead.

The gases—Which gases are greenhouse gases? The important atmospheric gases are water vapor, carbon dioxide, methane, nitrous oxide, ozone in the troposphere and several human-made chlorofluorocarbons (CFCs). Of these, water vapor is highly variable in the atmosphere, ranging from less than 1% to as much as 3% by volume. The two major CFCs are CFC-11 (trichlorofluoromethane) and CFC-12 (dichlorodifluoromethane). As of the early 1990s, CFC-11 amounted to 0.2 parts per billion by volume (ppb) and CFC-12 was 0.4 ppb. Carbon dioxide, in 1988, was at 350 parts per million by volume (ppm), methane was 1.8 ppm and nitrous oxide was at 0.30 ppm. By 2001, the values for atmospheric gases were: 372 ppm, 1.84 ppm and 0.32 ppm for carbon dioxide, methane and nitrous oxide, respectively.[10]

Sources—Let's look at the sources of these greenhouse gases. Carbon dioxide is the product of any chemical reaction in which hydrocarbons are oxidized. These reactions include the burning of coal, natural gas, oil and wood. They also include the metabolic reactions in living organisms by which carbohydrates, lipids and proteins are oxidized to produce useable energy. These reactions are respiration. Decomposition of dead organic matter by fungi and microorganisms is also respiration and also releases carbon dioxide. The processes of burning fossil fuels and biomass burning/deforestation, worldwide, add 5 petagrams and 2 petagrams of carbon, respectively, to the atmosphere annually (1 petagram [Pg]= 1 x 10^{15} g). The oceans absorb 2 Pg of carbon per year, the terrestrial biosphere absorbs 2 Pg, leaving a balance of 3 Pg added to the atmosphere each year.

Methane is produced in several ways. Burning of biomass (trees, grasses, dead animals) produces some methane, especially when combustion is incomplete. Burning produces between 10 and 100 Tg (1 Tg = 10^{12} g) per year. **Methanogenic** bacteria produce methane in wetlands (ca. 150 Tg/year), rice paddies (ca. 100 Tg/year) and in the digestive tracts of cattle, sheep and other fermenting mammals (100-150 Tg/year). Other sources include termites tundra and the oceans. An important source of methane, especially in the north, is lake sediments. In the atmosphere, methane is destroyed by hydroxyl radical.

Nitrous oxide is produced in soils and the oceans by bacteria. Nitrifying bacteria convert ammonium to nitrate under aerobic conditions, liberating nitrous oxide in the process. Denitrifying bacteria reverse the above process under anaerobic conditions. There are additional sources of nitrous oxide, as yet incompletely understood. The net result of all the sources and sinks is an increase in atmospheric nitrous oxide of about 3 Tg per year.

Chlorofluorocarbons are synthesized in chemical factories and have many commercial and industrial applications. In the past, CFC-11 and CFC-12 were used in closed-cell foams, aerosol propellants, open-cell foams and refrigeration and air conditioning. Cessation of use of CFCs, as agreed to in the Montreal Protocol of 1987, will lead to a gradual reduction in their concentrations in the atmosphere because CFCs are slowly destroyed in the stratosphere by **photolysis**, dissociation of the CFC molecule by solar radiation. In a second mechanism, CFCs chemically react with atomic oxygen and are oxidized. The products of these chemical reactions have the effect of chemically destroying ozone molecules in the upper atmosphere. Ozone, itself, is a weak greenhouse gas, but its more important function in the stratosphere is to absorb incoming ultraviolet radiation.

Ozone depletion: an ancillary problem— The problem with ozone depletion at high latitudes is separate and distinct from climatic warming but is obviously a part of changing conditions on our planet that influence living creatures. Among humans, the health problems associated with ozone depletion and the increased levels of UV radiation exposure include skin cancers, premature aging of the skin, cataracts and other eye damage, and suppression of the immune system. To date, ozone depletion in the northern hemisphere has not reached the intensity of that over Antarctica, but it is progressing in that direction. A northern hemisphere ozone hole the size of the current ozone depletion area in the south would expose 700 million people to damaging levels of UV radiation. Arctic and alpine plants and animals would also be affected.

Terrestrial animals with eyes similar to human eyes would be expected to experience the same sorts of UV-related, visual problems that humans do. There is already evidence that domestic sheep in southern South America, under the seasonal ozone hole, have higher occurrences of cataracts than do sheep elsewhere. UV-related disorders of the skin of non-humans may not be much of a problem since fur, feathers and, for naked animals, highly pigmented epidermis protect from UV radiation.

We might expect that creatures living in shallow waters could be liable to UV damage. One of the hypotheses about worldwide reductions in amphibian populations suggests that increased UV radiation may be a causative agent. Studies of marine phytoplankton in the Southern Ocean show that these primary producers are susceptible to UV damage while very near the sea surface. However, turbulence and vertical mixing would periodically carry these organisms down below the depth of UV penetration into seawater. Again, the ultraviolet radiation problem is separate and distinct from potential problems associated with climate warming.

Extrapolations—How high will the concentrations of greenhouse gases go? Extrapolations have been made using several different scenarios, and there is always uncertainty about what will happen in the future. One uncertainty revolves around how long these greenhouse gases remain in the atmosphere. It is unclear what the atmospheric lifetime for carbon dioxide is because of the complex pathways involved in the **biogeochemical carbon cycle**, that is, where it comes from and where it goes.

But, for argument's sake we could assume that rates of increase of the major greenhouse gases will remain about the same through the year 2100. That would mean carbon dioxide would reach 818 ppm, methane would climb to 9.91 ppm and nitrous oxide levels would be at 1432 ppb. In comparison to levels of 1985, carbon dioxide would more than double; methane would be 4.5 times higher and nitrous oxide would be 3.7 times higher.[10]

How realistic such predictions are depends on a combination of political, economic, technological and biological factors. Enactment of worldwide treaties for the reduction of greenhouse gases would have some effect. So would a shift to alternative means of power generation that don't rely on burning of carbon-based fuels. Certainly, as climate warms, there will be feedback mechanisms that may accelerate release of carbon dioxide to the atmosphere, producing a **positive feedback loop** that will be hard to control. I mention the effect of climate warming on peat deposits below.

Global Climate Change

We established in the first chapter that climate in Alaska has changed dramatically and repeatedly in the last 20,000 years. On a geologic time scale, the earth seems to be in a series of oscillations with an overall downward temperature trend. In other words, we seem to be slipping down into the next glacial episode. At least, that was the apparent trend until the last 100 years. We need to assess the recent climate trends relevant to Alaska, project those trends into the near future based on climate models currently in use, and then think about how these recent and projected changes are affecting and will affect Alaska and its living systems.

Alaska's climate—What can we say about the recent climate history of Alaska? First, in the last 100 years observed temperatures have gone up significantly. This trend has been especially notable in the interior, where average temperatures are 4°F (2°C) higher now than in the 1950s. Winters in the interior are, on average, 7°F (4°C) warmer.[11] Precipitation over most of the state has trended upward as well, increasing 30% between 1968 and 1990.[12]

There are other signs of warming. Most glaciers in Alaska have been in retreat for much of the twentieth century, melting faster than they accumulate new snow and ice. Columbia Glacier, a tidewater glacier in Prince William Sound, has retreated 12 km (7.4 miles) in the last 20 years. A survey of 67 glaciers in Alaska from the mid-1950s to the mid-1990s and a follow-up survey in 2000-2001 showed a general thinning of glaciers in the region. In the earlier period (1950s-1990s), average glacier thinning was 0.52 m per year; the most recent data (1990s-2001) show a thinning rate of 1.8 m per year. These thinning rates applied to all glaciers in Alaska leads to estimates of annual losses in ice volumes. For the earlier period the loss amounted to about 52 km³ per year (water equivalent); for the last decade the figure was 96 km³ per year.[13] These latest results yield a much higher contribution of Alaska's glaciers to sea level increase and, in fact, Alaska's glaciers account for half the entire world's glacial contribution to sea level rise[14] and about 9% of the total increase in sea level.[13]

The amount of sea ice in the polar ice cap is in serious decline. Generally, sea ice is present for six months of the year along the Bering Sea coast (western Alaska) and for ten months along the coasts of the Chukchi (northwest coast) and Beaufort Seas (northern coast). In spite of a large amount of inter-annual variability, there have been significant reductions in Arctic sea ice cover over the last several decades.[15,16] There is evidence that the ice pack is thinning as well. The result of melting of glaciers and sea ice worldwide is a measurable increase in sea level verified as early as 1993.[17]

Are humans responsible for this warming? Oceanographers have established that climate in the Gulf of Alaska and Bering Sea fluctuates on a roughly ten-year cycle.[18,19] This variability affects interior and northern Alaska both directly and indirectly. However, the recent trends mentioned above transcend interdecadal cycles in ocean regimes. According to one recent review, about half of the high-latitude warming over the last 30 years is attributable to natural patterns of climate variability and the other half is consistent with climate change models predicting the effects of human activity.[11] The burning of fossil fuels and the resulting greenhouse effect are therefore major drivers of global climate change.

Permafrost—Permafrost is also being affected by warming. Recall that discontinuous permafrost (from 3-100 m thick) is found in much of interior Alaska, and continuous permafrost (up to 670 m thick) underlies almost the entire area north of the Brooks Range. Soils in Alaska, warming for over 100 years, are currently being affected in areas of discontinuous permafrost such as is found in the interior. In the interior, permafrost soils are at or above -2°C (28°F) and appear to have warmed 0.5-1.5°C in less than a decade.[20,21] Therefore, some of these permafrost soils are now thawing. Warming, peaty soils are sources of additional atmospheric carbon dioxide.

Moisture and growing seasons—On a broader scale, mean annual snow cover of the northern hemisphere decreased 10% from 1972 to 1992.[22] Growing seasons at mid- to high latitudes in the northern hemisphere have increased by 7-14 days over a similar time period.[23]

Climate predictions for Alaska (see next section) indicate that, in the near future, the actual moisture available for boreal forest and tundra vegetation in interior and northern Alaska will be less than what is available today. Bog species may be affected more than other plants. This could be especially true of vegetation that is adapted to polygonal ground underlain by permafrost that is melting. Once the ice is gone, water may percolate downward and reduce soil moisture.

Climate models—What do the experts predict for the near future in Alaska? First, all climate models predict that warming will be most extreme at very high latitudes as opposed to the tropics. The reason has to do with ice and snow reflecting incoming radiation. Since warming will lead to less ice and shorter snow seasons, less radiation will be reflected. Instead, the solar radiation will actually hit the earth's surface and warm it, adding to the warming trend.

Two of the climate models being used to predict Alaska's near future: the Hadley model and the Canadian model. Both models predict warming to be lowest in southeast Alaska and greatest in the northwest. Expect an additional warming by the year 2030 of 1.1-2.8°C (Canadian model) or 0.8-2.2°C (Hadley model). By 2100, it will be 4-10°C (Canadian) or 3-6.5°C

(Hadley) warmer than in the year 2001. Both climate models predict increases in annual precipitation over most of Alaska, 20-25% in the northwest and north but perhaps 10% less in southeast Alaska. Combining these two features means that soil moisture will actually decrease over most if not all the interior and northern Alaska. The Hadley model projects a small area of increased soil moisture centered east of Fairbanks along the Alaska-Yukon border.[11]

Boreal forests—What are the probable outcomes of these projected changes? First, perhaps as much as the top 9 m (30 feet) of discontinuous permafrost will thaw during the 21st century. This will lead to landslides and ground subsidence with effects on forests and tundra habitats.

Second, forests will be stressed in several ways. They will continue to experience outbreaks of insect pests such as the spruce bark beetle that previously was limited by cold. The wet, heavy snows of warmer winters will intensify breakage and blow-downs of trees, further increasing forest vulnerability to insect damage. With less soil moisture, white spruce growth rates will probably be reduced, and it will take longer to replace cut or burned spruce with mature spruce. The increased frequency and intensity of wild fires observed in recent years due to warmer summers will probably continue.

Another effect is that long-distance, migratory species will arrive earlier in the spring. The spring of 2004 produced a new record for earliest arrival of Canada geese in Fairbanks, just the latest datum in a trend. This same phenomenon is occurring all across the north. Other attributes of the trend include earlier reproduction in birds, earlier springtime flowering and earlier plant shoot elongation.[24]

Tundra systems—Warming eventually will cause the replacement of alpine and arctic tundra habitat with boreal forest or some new plant assemblages that don't occur now. Indeed, the upward trend of forest vegetation has already been documented in the European Alps by comparing historical vegetation records with recent surveys.[25] In some locations in the Alps, vegetation is moving up at rates of 4 m (13 feet) per decade. The animals that depend on alpine and arctic tundra for their livelihood, such as caribou, marmots, muskoxen, pikas, and nesting migrant birds, will be affected. The northward dispersal of plant and animal species will continue and/or accelerate. Based on syntheses from all over the world, this shift poleward amounts to about 6.1 km (3.8 miles) per decade.[26] Some species, such as the lodgepole pine, could be beneficial to humans because of its commercial value. Others such as arthropod pests (ticks and other insect vectors of human and animal diseases) will have negative effects on human commerce.

The increase in shrubs across northern Alaska, Canada, Scandinavia and Russia is additional evidence that warming is affecting tundra systems. Aside from the impact of changing plant species composition, the presence of shrubs is likely to produce a positive feedback loop leading to further warming. In the absence of tall shrubs, reflectivity of solar radiation (**albedo**) is high. The stems and branches of shrubs projecting above snow level absorb solar radiation and decrease albedo. One estimate of the effect of these shrubs suggests that they increase absorbed solar radiation by 69-75% during the snow-cover period.[27]

Bering, Chukchi and Beaufort Seas—One of the major effects of climate change relates to sea ice in northern waters. Sea ice serves several functions: habitat for marine mammals and invertebrates, wind and wave damper, water column stabilizer and contributor to primary production. In all the climate scenarios and in actual fact, sea ice is retreating northward as climate warms.

All the primary production processes will go on even if the pack ice is farther north in the future. However, the depth of water will dictate that much of current day production will be lost. Today, the ice edge blooms and under-ice algae both occur over relatively shallow water. In both cases, organisms now settle onto a bottom that is lit by sunlight and within the diving range of walruses and seals. In other words, these plant-like creatures can continue to perform photosynthesis and contribute to food webs near the shore. Once the pack ice retreats off the continental shelf, the ice-edge and under-ice production will fall into water too deep for these organisms to continue their production and their production will be lost to the nearshore marine habitat.[28]

One possible result is that there will be insufficient benthic invertebrates and fishes to fuel walruses, seals and seabirds at anywhere near their current population levels. Finally, the nearshore, coastal environment in the ice-free season is home to many species of freshwater and anadromous fishes. Grayling, arctic char, whitefish and arctic cisco all ply these waters relying on nearshore primary productivity. These populations could also be reduced as a result of the retreat of pack ice farther offshore.

Coasts and estuaries—Melting of sea ice will expose more of the northern coast to storm surge and inundation. Human habitation along the coast in places such as Point Barrow, Barter Island, Shishmareff and Nome may become more difficult. Increased sea level will encroach on estuarine habitat, moving it inland from its present locations. I am guessing that this inland transgression of estuaries will be slow enough for the seagrasses, algae and invertebrates to keep pace. If not, outmigrating salmon fingerlings that rely on estuaries for food and habitat may be negatively affected.

Marine mammals—Marine mammals that depend on sea ice for haul-outs, denning habitat and for transportation will be negatively impacted. These mammals include polar bear, walrus, ringed seal and bearded seal. Polar bears use ice flows for resting, denning, hunting and transportation. Their principal prey, seals, use the pack ice for haul-outs and for denning sites. Indeed, polar bears hunt seals in their lairs on the sea ice. Retraction of sea ice northward, far offshore from Alaska in the summer, will place these prey and predators far from land. Traditionally, few bears are seen on the multi-year pack ice in the polar basin. The waters are simply too unproductive for seals to live there and, hence, the bears do not find enough prey. Females typically den in snow caves on land and, occasionally, on pack ice. They mate in spring, move onto land through summer and begin fetal development in fall. Females eat nothing for five months, from denning in October through giving birth in February. Therefore, climate change, if it prevents females from accessing pack ice, may leave females ashore on land for many months longer than usual, prolonging their fasting period and, possibly, adversely affecting their reproduction and survival. Females that den on pack ice would also be affected. Den sites are typically in old ice with pressure ridges that cause snow to accumulate in lee areas. These snowdrifts are easily dug. New pack ice, because of its topography, has few suitable den sites. Polar bears are already being impacted. Populations are declining as is average bear size.

Seabirds—Seabirds that rely on today's coastal productivity for forage to feed their young of the year may suffer reproductive failures in the near future. Indeed, a significant population decline has been documented in black guillemots nesting on Cooper Island, off the Beaufort Sea coast west of Barrow.[29] Black guillemots reached a population high at that location in 1982. Parents forage close to the island for fish and invertebrates associated with the arctic pack ice edge. Since the pack ice has receded far to the north in recent summers, the ice edge fauna is not as accessible as it was previously.

Acceptable changes—There has been a certain amount of glib confidence that human ingenuity or the self-regulating natural systems of the earth will rescue us from any really radical changes in the earth systems we are familiar with and upon which we rely. A critical issue facing humanity is that of deciding what are acceptable changes and to whom they are acceptable.

Several examples come to mind. If, for the supposed economic benefit of all mankind, we continue to burn fossil fuels to drive our industries, we will surely drive up average global temperatures and experience a continuing rise in sea level. In the process, tundra habitats will contract and the organisms such as caribou, muskoxen and the peoples who rely on these organisms will be put at risk. Similarly, people occupying coral atolls across the Pacific Ocean may lose their homes, their islands and their entire way of life. Indeed, many people around the globe living in coastal areas will be impacted in some negative way: their homes may be inundated, their beachfront property may be eroded, their taxes may go up to help pay for retaining walls and other accommodations to rising sea level.

Previews of Coming Attractions

In summary, what can we expect in the way of changes in the flora and fauna of interior and northern Alaska? The climate models predict a large-scale loss of tundra habitats as they are replaced by boreal forest. Tree line will, undoubtedly, creep upslope into alpine tundra. Within the tundra itself large shrubs will probably dominate much more area than is currently the case. Animal species occupying tundra habitats, either seasonally or year-round, will be affected by vegetation changes. Humans that rely on tundra plants and animals will, in turn, be affected.

Therefore, the geographic distributions of northern tree species are predicted to change significantly. Lodgepole pine has been dispersing northward since the end of the last glaciation. Currently, its northwestward distributional limit is in the Yukon, northwest of Whitehorse. Its range expansion will continue and include east-central Alaska, perhaps, before the end of this century. It already occurs as an introduced ornamental and has been planted in old burns in the interior and south-central Alaska.

Paper birch distribution will retract along its current southern boundaries and, according to the Canadian model, will largely disappear from the upper midwestern and northeastern United States. Both climate models predict a retraction of birch in interior Alaska as the species recedes northward through the Brooks Range to the coast of the Beaufort Sea.

Douglas fir, a tree of the Rocky Mountains and coastal forests, currently has its northward distributional limit in southeast Alaska. By 2099, according to both climate models, this tree will be established in south-central Alaska, the Alaska Peninsula and the Bering Sea coast as Far North as the Seward Peninsula. The Canadian model predicts that Douglas fir will be present along the Beaufort Sea coast into Arctic Canada by the start of the twenty-second century. Climate suitability is one thing. Personally, it is hard for me to imagine that the actual dispersal of seeds and establishment of viable trees will have occurred on the North Slope of Alaska by the end of this century. However, stranger things have undoubtedly happened in earth history.

Recent warm winters have coincided with major outbreaks of forest insect pests. Spruce bark beetle infestations have killed thousands of hectares of white spruce on the Kenai Peninsula since 1991. It is reasonable to expect these infestations to continue, spread northward and intensify.

In interior Alaska, spruce budworm outbreaks are taking a toll on white spruce. The caterpillar of this moth feeds on buds in May and June, then attacks new needles. The branch tips on most of the white spruce around our house were completely naked this spring, a result of last summer's budworm activity.

Spruce budworm outbreaks intensify after warm winters; we can expect an increase in budworm depredations in the near future. Ultimately, white spruce distribution in interior Alaska may be significantly retracted due to pests and reduced soil moisture.

In 1997 and 1998 Alaska experienced a major outbreak of larch sawflies. The epidemic resulted in the loss of 75% of the larch trees in the state. The sawfly outbreak was linked to recent warming in Alaska.

In 2004, the quaking aspen forests in the interior suffered a third successive year of a major infestation of aspen leaf miners. This pest is a small moth species that lays its eggs on aspen leaves. The eggs produce minute caterpillars, about 5 mm long, that burrow inside the aspen leaf. Their tunneling destroys photosynthetic cells, leaves a maze of tunnels, and causes the foliage to appear silver instead of green from a distance. Outbreaks of leaf miners are thought to be related to climate warming. All these pests of Alaskan trees may, collectively, have a significant impact on the geographic extent of forest, the competition between tree species and, ultimately, the species composition in the boreal forest.

Circumstantial evidence suggests that the winter tick, an external parasite associated with mule deer and moose, has dispersed as far west as Kluane Lake, Yukon. This tick appears to be moving northward. It is not clear if this dispersal is merely a slow process that started at the end of the Pleistocene or, instead, is related to very recent climate trends. For whatever reason, this species is apparently on its way to Alaska.

On the other hand, mule deer are expanding their range in the Far North. Sightings of mule deer west of Whitehorse, Yukon, are becoming common. There are occasional reports of mule deer tracks in extreme eastern Alaska. What now amounts to a few strays perhaps will in a hundred years lead to a resident population.

REFERENCES

1 McKibben, B. 1989. The end of nature. Random House, New York. 226 pp.

2 Reisner, M. 1986. Cadillac desert: the American west and its disappearing water. Viking Press, New York, 582 pp.

3 Walker, D.A., Webber, P.J., Binnian, E.F., Everett, K.R., Lederer, N.D., Nordstrand, E.A. and Walker, M.D. 1987. Cumulative impacts of oil fields on northern Alaskan landscapes. Science 238: 757-761.

4 Shaw, G.E. 1982. Evidence for a central Eurasian source area of Arctic haze in Alaska. Nature 299: 815-818.

5 Bridgman, H.A., Schnell, R.C., Kahl, J.D., Herbert, G.A. and Joranger, E. 1989. A major haze event near Point Barrow, Alaska: analysis of probable source regions and transport pathways. Atmospheric Environment 23: 2537-2549.

6 Hansen, A.D.A. and Rosen, H. 1984. Vertical distribution of particulate carbon, sulfur and bromine in the Arctic haze and comparison with ground-level measurements at Barrow, Alaska. Geophysical Research Letters 11: 381-384.

7 Bodhaine, B.A. and Dutton, E.G. 1993. A long-term decrease in Arctic haze at Barrow, Alaska. Geophysical Research Letters 20: 947-950.

8 Wilcox, W.J. II. 2001. The origin and composition of aerosols in the Alaskan airshed. MS Thesis, University of Alaska Fairbanks, 182 pp.

9 Auerbach, N.A., Walker, M.D. and Walker, D.A. 1997. Effects of roadside disturbance on substrate and vegetation properties in arctic tundra. Ecological Applications 7: 218-235.

10 Levine, J.S. 1992. Global climate change, pp. 1-25, In: P. Firth and S.G. Fisher, editors, Global climate change and freshwater ecosystems. Springer-Verlag, New York and Berlin.

11 Weller, G., Lynch, A., Ostercamp. T. and Wendler, G. 1998. Climate trends and scenarios In: G.A. Weller and P.A. Anderson, editors, Implications of global change in Alaska and the Bering Sea region, Proceedings of a workshop, June 3-6, 1997, University of Alaska Fairbanks.

12 Parson, E.A., Carter, L., Anderson, P. Wang, B. and Weller, G. 2001. Alaska pp.283-314 In: National Assessment Synthesis Team: Climate change impacts on the United States: the potential consequences of climate variability and change. Report for the U.S. Global Change Research Program. Cambridge University Press, Cambridge, UK, 620 pp.

13 Arendt, A.A., Echelmeyer, K.A., Harrison, W.D., Lingle, C.S. and Valentine, V.B. 2002. Rapid wastage of Alaska glaciers and their contribution to rising sea level. Science 297: 382-386.

14 Meier, M.F. and Dyurgerov, M.B. 2002. How Alaska affects the world. Science 297: 350-351.

15 Maslanik, J.A., Serreze, M.C. and Barry, R.G. 1996. Recent decreases in Arctic summer ice cover and linkages to atmospheric circulation anomalies. Geophysical Research Letters 23: 1677-1680.

16 Maslanik, J.A., Serreze, M.C. and Agnew, T. 1999. On the record reduction in 1998

Western Arctic sea-ice cover. Geophysical Research Letters 26: 1905-1908.

17 Meier, M.F. 1993. Ice, climate and sea level: Do we know what is happening? pp. 141-160 In: W.R. Peltier, editor, Ice in the climate system. NATO ASI Series Vol. 112. Springer-Verlag, Berlin.

18 Royer, T.C. 1982. Coastal freshwater discharge in the northeast Pacific. Journal of Geophysical Research 87: 2017-2021.

19 Francis, R.C., Hare, S.R., Hollowed, A.B. and Wooster, W.S. 1998. Effects of inter-decadal climate variability on the oceanic ecosystems of the northeast Pacific. Fisheries Oceanography 7: 1-21.

20 Ostercamp, T.E. Esch, D.C. and Romanovsky, V.E. 1998. Permafrost (Chapter 10) In: G.A. Weller and P.A. Anderson, editors, Implications of global change in Alaska and the Bering Sea region, Proceedings of a workshop, June 3-6, 1997, University of Alaska Fairbanks.

21 Ostercamp, T.E. and Romanovsky, V.E. 1999. Evidence for warming and thawing of discontinuous permafrost in Alaska. Permafrost and Periglacial Processes 10: 17-37.

22 Groisman, P.Y. and Easterling, D.A. 1994. Variability and trends of precipitation and snowfall over the United States and Canada. Journal of Climate 7: 184-205.

23 Mynini, R.B., Keeling, C.D., Tucker, C.J., Asrar, G. and Nemani, R.R. 1997. Increased plant growth in the northern high latitudes from 1981 to 1991. Nature 386: 698-702.

24 Walther, G.-R., Post, E., Convey, P., Menzel, A. and Parmesan, C. 2002. Ecological responses to recent climate change. Nature 416: 389-395.

25 Grabherr, G., Gottfried, M. and Pauli, H. 1994. Climatic effects on mountain plants. Nature 369: 448.

26 Parmesan, C. and Yohe, G. 2003. A globally coherent fingerprint of climate change impacts across natural systems. Nature 421: 37-42.

27 Sturm, M., Douglas, T., Racine, C., and Liston, G. 2005. Changing snow and shrub conditions affect albedo with global implications. Journal of Geophysical Research 110, No. G1.

28 Alexander, V. 1992. Arctic marine ecosystems, pp. 221-232 IN: R.L. Peters and T.E. Lovejoy, editors, Global warming and biological diversity. Yale University Press, New Haven.

29 Divoky, G. 1998. Factors affecting growth of a black guillemot populastion in northern Alaska. PhD Thesis, University of Alaska Fairbanks, 144 pp.

ADDITIONAL PERTINENT REFERENCES

Chapin, F.S. III, Shaver, G.R., Giblin, A.E., Nadelhoffer, K.J. and Laundre, J.A. 1995. Responses of arctic tundra to experimental and observed changes in climate. Ecology 76: 694-711.

Crawford, R.M.M., Chapman, H.M., Abbott, R.J. and Balfour, J. 1993. Potential impact of climatic warming on arctic vegetation. Flora 188: 367-381.

Karl, T.R. and Trenberth, K.E. 2003. Modern global climate change. Science 302: 1719-1723.

Karoly, D.J., Braganza, K., Stott, P.A., Arblaster, J.M., Meehl, G.A., Broccoli, A.J. and Dixon, K.W. 2003. Detection of human influence on North American climate. Science 302: 1200-1203.

King, D.A. 2004. Climate change science: adapt, mitigate or ignore? Science 303: 176-177.

Klein, D.R., Murray, D.F., Armstrong, R.H. and Anderson, B. A. 1998. Regional trends of biological resources-Alaska. pp. 707-745, In: M.J. Mac, P.A. Opler, C.E. Puckett Haecker and P.D. Doran, editors, Status and trends of the nation's biological resources. Volume 2. U.S. Dept. of the Interior, U.S. Geological Survey, Reston, Virginia, 964 pp.

Krummel, E.M., Macdonald, R.W., Kimpe, L.E., Gregory-Eaves, I., Demers, M.J., Smol, J.P., Finney, B. and Blais, J.M. 2003. Delivery of pollutants by spawning salmon. Nature 425: 255-256.

Whitfield, J. 2003. Too hot to handle. Nature 425: 338-339.

Wookey, P.A., Parsons, A.N., Welker, J.M., Potter, J.A., Callaghan, T.V., Lee, J.A. and Press, M.C. 1993. Comparative responses of phenology and reproductive development to simulated environmental change in sub-arctic and high arctic plants. Oikos 67: 490-502.

Index

snowshoe hares, 34, 36, 54, 69
        (Fig. 3.1), 75, 91, 95–96,
        127, 371. *See also hares*
    craters, 132
    digestive tract, 131 (Fig. 4.4)–
        132
    disease, 357
    habitat, 130, 182
    litter / leverets (newborns),
        134, 135
    pellets, 131 (Fig. 4.4)–132
    population, and cycles /
        fluctuations, 133 (Fig.
        4.5)–134, 139, 145, 239,
        249, 280, 285, 286, 290
    as prey, 133–134, 136, 139,
        144, 151, 153, 163, 190,
        256, 262, 279, 285, 287
soapberry, 269
sockeye salmon, 313, 315, 317,
        319, 324–327, 354. *See
        also salmon*
sodium. *See mineral licks*
soils, 361
    erosion and deposition, 361,
        365
    permafrost, 375–376
    tundra 211–213, 221, 222
solar energy (lakes), 314
solar radiation, 377
Solecki, Ralph, 101
solifluction lobe, xviii (Fig. 0.5)
songbirds, 54, 150, 194
Soricinae, 167
sorrel, mountain, 233
Sousa, Marsha, 199
south-facing slopes, plants, 72,
        77, 96, 213, 230
sparrow, 139, 299
spiders, 202
sponges, 282
spruce, xx, 14, 22, 40, 48, 56, 57,
        69 (Fig. 3.1), 71, 72, 82,
        84, 86, 121, 148. *See also
        black spruce; white spruce*
    cones, 77 (Fig. 3.4), 82
    fungi attacking, , 75–77, 80, 81
    needles, 179, 180, 197
    rodents in forests of, 164
    rust attacking, 81
    seed dispersal, 69

    wind effect on, 213
spruce bark beetle, 376, 379
spruce budworm, 206 (Fig. 6.4),
        207, 379–380
squid, 319, 329
squirrels, 170, 265. *See also
        ground squirrel; northern
        flying squirrel, red squirrel*
    burrows, 61
    Douglas, 143
    flying, 56, 81 (Fig. 3.6), 108,
        148
    parka, 29, 283
    tree, 143
Stack, J.W., 148
stadial. *See glacier(s)*
Stephenson, Bob, 136
steppes and steppe habitat, 14,
        15, 23, 27, 28, 30, 236
    bison, 22–25, 28, 29–30
    grass-dominated, 183
    mammals, 31
    mammoth, 18–19, 29, 30
    saigas, 28
    vegetation, 30
sticklebacks, 332
St. Matthews Island, 339
Steese Highway, xviii, xx, xxi
Stercocorairiidae family, 295
St. Lawrence Island, 282, 297,
        339
stoat, 150. *See weasel*
streams, 312, 336, 344, 361, 362,
        369
    braided and beaded, 9
    Clearwater, 316
    frozen, xxiii
    glacially fed, 310
    insects, 311
    invertebrates, 311, 312
    riparian habitat, 354
    systems of Alaska, 310
    turbidity, 338
strutting, 180
succession, plant / vegetative, 74,
        81, 170, 354, 362, 371–
        372. *See also trees*
    glacial epoch soils and, 212
    post-fire, 164, 181, 246
    on interior floodplains, 91
    on north-facing slopes, 73, 89

    on south-facing slopes
        (Uplands), 72
    on tundra, 223–224, 236
suckers, 310, 332, 341, 342
sun tracking, 216 (Fig. 7.1)–217,
        226
supercooling, 49, 50, 51, 61
surface plunging, 359
Susitna River basin, 256
swallows, 38, 43–44, 192, 194,
        198, 205, 206, 312, 366
swamping, predator, 39, 119, 192
swans
    in aquatic habitats, 359
    cygnets, 294
    migration, 294
    trumpeter, 43, 194, 293–294
    tundra, 40, 41, 43, 293–294,
        362, 366
sweet pea, wild, 102–103, 132,
        160, 222, 264
symbiotic associations, 105
sympatric associations, 191

T

taiga, 165. *See also boreal forest*
tail
    beaver, 352–353, 356
    furred versus naked, 59–60
    mastodon, 22
    muskrat, 357–358
    woolly mammoth, 20
Talkeetna Mountains,   dinosaur
        fossils, 2
tamarack xxi, 67, 71 (Fig. 3.2), 72,
        76, 78, 81, 83–84, 183
    cones, 77 (Fig. 3.4)
Tanana River
    bears along, 126, 269
    caribou along, 245
    floodplain and bluffs, 8, 68, 72,
        357
    grayling, 336
    ptarmigan along, 289
    salmon and other fish, 327,
        328, 343, 369
    vegetation along, 83, 84, 96,
        103, 108
Tanana State Forest, 371

Index of Scientific Names

A

Achillea, 100, 101
    borealis, 100
    lanulosa, 100
    millefolium, 100, 101
Aconitum
    delphinifolium, 234
    maximum, 233
Adelges lariciatus, 83
Aedes, 198, 199
    communis, 200
Aegolius funereus, 190
Aeshna caerulea, 203
Agrilis anxius, 90
Alamosaurus, 8
Alectoria, 147
Albertosaurus, 4, 5
Alces alces, 115
    A. a. americanum, 116
    A. a. andersoni, 116
    A. a. gigas, 116
    A. a. shirasi, 116
Alectrosaurus, 4, 5
Alnus
    fruticosa, 90
    sinuata, 91
    tenuifolia, 91
Alopex lagopus, 281
Amanita muscaria, 144
Anas
    acuta, 359
    platyrhynchos, 359
Anchiceratops, 4
Andromeda polifolia, 76
Anemone
    drummondii, 234
    multifida, 234
    narcissiflora, 234
    parviflora, 234
    richardsonii, 234

Anguilla, 316
Anopheles, 199, 200
    earlei, 199
Antennaria, 216
Aquia chrysaetos, 286
Arctodus, 15, 16, Fig 1.7, 17, Fig. 1.8, 18
    simus, 15
Arctoparmalia centrifuga, 110
Arctostaphylos, 232
    alpina, 125, 232
    rubra, 233
    uva-ursi, 80, 125, 232
Armillaria, 81, 83, 89, 100
Arnica, 218
    alpina, 235
    frigida, 235
    lessingii, 235
Artemisia
    alaskana, 96
    frigida, 96
    krushiana, 96
Asio flammeus, 191
Aster sibericus, 236
Astragalus, 267
    alpinus, 102
    americanus, 102
    umbellatus, 102

B

Bacillus, 101
Betula
    glandulosa, 90
    kenaica, 89
    nana, 90, 218
    neoalaskana, 89
    papyrifera, 89
Bison
    antiquus, 23
    bison, 23, 29, 30, 158

    latifrons, 23, 24
    occidentalis, 23, 24
    priscus, 22, 23, 24, 29
Boletus elegans, 76
Bonasa umbellus, 180
Brachiosaurus, 2
Branta bernicla, 359
Brucella
    abortus, 124
    suis, 124
Bubo virginianus, 187

C

Calamagrostis canadensis, 72
Calypso bulbosa, 76
Camelops hesternus, 27
Campanula
    aurita, 232
    lasiocarpa, 231
    paniculata, 231
    rotundifolia, 231
    uniflora, 231
Camponotus herculeanus, 206, 207
Canachites canadensis, 179
Canis
    latrans, 279
    lupus, 271
Cardimine bellidifolia, 214
Carex, 218
    aquitilus, 215
    bigelowi, 224, 226
Cassiope stelleriana, 76
Castor canadensis, 352
Casteroides, 351, 352
Catharacta skua, 295
Cephenemyia trompe, 246
Cervus elaphus, 29
Ceryle alcyon, 359

ABOUT THE AUTHOR

Ron was born in Marshall, Texas. The next eight years Ron's family lived in 14 different places. His wife Marsha is amazed he is nearly normal after all that. His plan to be a chemistry major was side-tracked by a calculus professor who, when asked questions by her students, responded that the answer should be "intuitively obvious." Ron decided to switch to biology. Following undergraduate school at Occidental College, Ron went to Miami, Florida for his post-graduate work.

This decision resulted in a rewarding, intriguing career. Upon completion of a PhD at the University of Miami, Ron took a faculty position at the University of Alaska in Fairbanks (UAF). In 1968 he headed up the highway in a '68 Bronco and remained at UAF for 31 years involved in teaching and research.

Those years were filled with swimming in Aialik Bay, beach seining in Izembek Lagoon, sample collections on bucking boats in the Chukchi Sea, sabbaticals, research work at the UAF Seward Marine Center and collaboration with other scientists resulting in some 44 scientific publications. Ron's favorite experiences were the interactions with his students, many of whom have become lasting friends. He taught 18 different classes including Natural History of Alaska. His lifelong love of the outdoors, hunting, camping, hiking and observing animals added a personal touch to the lectures heard by thousands of students.

After 39 Alaska winters, Ron and Marsha are now blessed to spend summers in Fairbanks and warmer winters in the Texas Hill Country. The best of both worlds is watching moose, fox, grouse and ptarmigan in the north plus exotic critters (Russian boar, sika, fallow and axis deer and black-buck antelope) munching the grass in their Texas front yard.